A CLASSIFIED CATALOGUE OF

The Negro Collection

IN THE
COLLIS P. HUNTINGTON LIBRARY
HAMPTON INSTITUTE

Compiled by
Mentor A. Howe and Roscoe E. Lewis

Hampton Institute, Hampton, Virginia
1940

Republished 1971
Negro History Press – P. O. Box 5129 – Detroit, Michigan 48236

Library of Congress Catalog Card Number: 70-129188
Standard Book Number 403-00486-1

This edition is printed on a high-quality,
acid-free paper that meets specification
requirements for fine book paper referred
to as "300-year" paper

INTRODUCTION

I am delighted to write this new introduction for "A Classified Catalogue of the Negro Collection in the Collis P. Huntington Library." I am happy mainly because most Americans are finally beginning to recognize both the existence and contributions of the Black man to the total development of the United States. It is quite apparent that for many years a deliberate, systematic, and designed attempt has been made to keep this information from ever becoming available to the general public. This fact can best be illustrated by looking at any printed material used for educational purposes up to and including the present time. I am positive that the present day crisis is a direct result of this attempted cover-up.

This bibliography covers the holdings of this collection up to 1940. Most of this material is now out of print. The collection is made up of manuscripts, documents, clippings, periodicals, pamphlets and other forms of printed materials by and about the Black man. It is exceptionally strong on Civil War and Reconstruction history. The newspaper clipping collection is unusually strong on slavery, reconstruction, lynching and other race problems. The collection is also reasonably strong on African history. Efforts are constantly being made to strengthen this area of the collection.

The collection has grown tremendously since the preparation of this bibliography. Arrangements are underway at the present time to up-date it. There are in excess of 14,000 book volumes and 1,300 documents in this collection.

Scholars from throughout the world have made extensive use of material in this collection for years. Over the past several years, our students have increased their use of this material by 700 percent. This trend is expected to continue for some time.

All of the members of the library staff are proud of this collection. We are proud mainly because we have much primary source material that will be used to write the true history of America.

Hillis D. Davis
Director of the Library

FOREWORD

The classification of the material on the Negro in the Collis P. Huntington Library began as a necessary stage in the preparation of "The Negro in Virginia," a book written by the Virginia Writers' Project and sponsored by Hampton Institute. The many requests that have been made for source materials on various aspects of Negro life have revealed the urgent need for a catalogue of this valuable collection.

We have tried to include all printed items pertaining to the Negro in the collection. Entries are arranged alphabetically within specific subject classification. Although desirable, the repetition of entries under more than a single subject heading has been impossible because of space limitations. In the use of this catalogue, therefore, it should be kept in mind that the subject content of numerous items is not limited to the classification heading. Thus, item number 4159, 'The Negro in Virginia,' is listed under the single classification of "Histories, Historical, Sociological, and other studies relating to the Negro," although it would have been appropriate to include it under (I) Histories and Historical Studies of Slavery, (III) Slave Insurrections in the United States, (IV) The Free Negro, (VII) Religious Aspects of Slavery, (XXIX) The Civil War and Slavery, (XLII) Negro Health, Housing and Social Conditions, etc.

In both the catalogue and the index, all references are to item numbers, rather than to page numbers. The major reference in the index is to authors, although much subject material has been indexed. The index also includes cross references.

We have attempted to include all printed references to the Negro in the Hampton Institute collection. In classifying the items in this collection we have consulted standard bibliographical works and in addition the following, relating to particular subjects:

Bartlett, J. R.   The literature of the rebellion...with works on
                   American slavery

Brown, S. A.   The Negro in American fiction

DuBois, W. E. B. A select bibliography of the Negro American

Hubbard, G. H.	A classified catalogue of the collection of anti-slavery propaganda in the Oberlin College Library
May, S. J.	Catalogue of anti-slavery publications in America
Turner, L. D.	Anti-slavery sentiment in American literature prior to 1865
Work, M. N.	A bibliography of the Negro in Africa and America

The compilers believe that the catalogue will be useful not only to Hampton Institute students and faculty but also to all others who are interested in source materials by and about the Negro in Africa and America.

Mentor A. Howe

Roscoe E. Lewis

Compilers

CONTENTS

PART ONE

The Negro in Africa

PART TWO

The Negro in the United States

Part One

THE NEGRO IN AFRICA

I. Discovery, geography, and history of Africa, early expeditions and explorations, autobiographies and biographies of explorers prior to 1900.

ANDERSSON, KARL JOAN. Lake Ngami; or, Explorations and discoveries during four years' wanderings in the wilds of South Western Africa. New York, Harper bros. 1856. 521p.   1

ANDERSSON, KARL JOAN. The Okavango river: . . . travel, exploration, adventure. New York. Harper bros. 1861. xviii, 414p.   2

BACKHOUSE, JAMES. A narrative of a visit to the Mauritius and South Africa. London, Hamilton, Adams & co. 1846. 648p., lvi.   3

BAKER, SIR SAMUEL WHITE. The Albert N'yanza, great basin of the Nile, and explorations of the Nile sources. New ed. Philadelphia, J.B. Lippincott co. 1870. xxvii, 499p.   4

BAKER, SIR SAMUEL WHITE. In the heart of Africa. Condensed by E.J.W. from "The Nile tributaries of Abyssinia," and "The Albert N'yanza," New York, Funk & Wagnalls. 1884. vii, 286p.   5

BAKER, SIR SAMUEL WHITE. The Nile tributaries of Abyssinia, and the sword hunters of Hamram Arabs. 4th ed. Philadelphia, J.B. Lippincott co., 1868. xlx. 413p. 6

BARNARD, LADY ANNE. South Africa a century ago; letters written from the Cape of Good Hope (1797-1801). Edited with a memoir and notes by W.H. Wilkins. London, Smith, Elder & co. New York, Dodd, Mead & co., 1901. x, 316p.   7

BARROW, SIR JOHN. Travels into the interior of Southern Africa, in which are described the character and condition of the Dutch colonists of the Cape of Good Hope, and of the several tribes of natives beyond its limits . . . also a typographical and statistical sketch of the Cape colony, etc. 2d ed. rev. & enl. New York, J. Conrad & co. 1802. 386p.   8

BARTH, HEINRICH. Travels and discoveries in North and Central Africa: a journal of an expedition under the auspices of H.B.M's government, 1849-1855. New York, D. Appleton & co. 1857. 5 v., Harper & bros. 1857. 3v.   9

BARTLETT, W. H. The Nile boat; or, glimpses of the land of Egypt. 5th ed. New York. Charles Scribner & co. n.d. 229p.   10

BELL, MRS. N. M. Heroes of North African discovery. London. M. Ward & co. 1877. 388p.   11

BELZONI, GIOVANNI. Adventures . . . in Egypt and Nubia, with an account of his discoveries in the Pyramids, among the ruins of cities, and in the ancient tombs. New York, Charles S. Francis. 1843. 190p.   12

BRADLEY, MRS. ELIZA. An authentic narrative of the shipwreck and sufferings of the wife of Capt. James Bradley, of Liverpool, commander of the ship Sally, which was wrecked on the coast of Barbary, in June 1818, written by herself . . . Boston, Geo. Clarke, 1821. 108p.   13

BROWN, WILLIAM HARVEY. On the South African frontier; the adventures and observations of an American in Mashonaland and Matabeleland. London, S. Low, Marston & co.; New York, Charles Scribner's sons. 1899. xxii, 430p. 14

BRUCE, JAMES. Travels to discover the source of the Nile, 1768-1773. 2d ed. Edinburgh, Archibald Constable & co. 1805. 8v. 15

BURCKHARDT, JOHN LEWIS. Some account of the travels. . . in Egypt and Nubia. 2d ed. London, John Murray; for the assn. for promoting the discovery of the interior parts of Africa. 1822. 498p. 16

BURTON, RICHARD FRANCIS. Abeokuta and the Camarooms mountains; an exploration. London, Tinsley bros. 1863. 2v. 17

EῡRTON, RICHARD FRANCIS. The lake regions of Central Africa, a picture of exploration. London, Longman, Green, Longman & Roberts. 1860. 2v. New York, Harper & bros. 1860. 572p. 18

CAILLIE, RENE. Travels through Central Africa to Timbuctoo; and across the great desert to Morocco, 1824-1828. London, H. Colburn & R. Bentley. 1830. 2v. 19

CAMERON, VERNEY LOVETT. Across Africa. New York. Harper & bros. 1877. xvi, 15-508p. 20

CAMPBELL, ROBERT. A pilgrimage to my motherland. An account of an journey among the Egbas and Yorubas of Central Africa, 1859-60. New York, Thomas Hamilton; Philadelphia, the auth. 1861. 145p. 21

CHAILLE-LONG, CHARLES. Central Africa, naked truths of naked people. An account of expeditions to the Lake Victoria Nyanza and the Makraka Niam-Niam, west of Bahr-el-Abiad. New York. Harper & bros. 1877. xv, 330p. 22

CHANLER, WILLIAM ASTOR. Through jungle and desert; travels in Eastern Africa. New York, London, Macmillan & co. 1896. 4p., 519p. 23

CHAPMAN, JAMES. Travels in the interior of South Africa; comprising fifteen years' hunting and trading; with journeys across the continent from Natal to Walvisch bay, and visits to Lake Ngami and the Victoria Falls. London, Bell & Daldy. 1868. 2v. 24

CLAPPERTON, HUGH. Journal of a second expedition into the interior of Africa from the Bight of Benin to Soccatoo . . . the journal of Richard Lander from Kano to the sea-coast . . . Philadelphia, Carey, Lea & Carey. 1829. 422p. 25

COOLEY, WILLIAM DESBOROUGH. The Negroland of the Arabs examined and explained; or, an inquiry into the early history and geography of Central Africa. London, J. Arrowsmith. 1841. xvi, 143p. 26

CROW, CAPTAIN HUGH. Memoirs of the late Captain Hugh Crow, of Liverpool; comprising a narrative of his life, together with descriptive sketches of the western coast of Africa; particularly of Bonny; the manners and customs of the inhabitants, the productions of the soil, and the trade of the country. To which are added, Anecdotes and observations illustrative of the Negro character. London, Longmans, Rees, Orme, Brown, and Green. 1830. 316p. 27

CURTIS, GEORGE WILLIAM. Nile

notes of a Howadji. New York, Harper & bros. 1856. 362p.   28

DE MAY, R. Narrative of the suffering and adventures of Henderick Portenger . . . wrecked on the shores of Abyssinia, in the Red Sea. London, Sir Richard Phillips & co. 1819. 27p.   29

DENHAM, DIXON. Narrative of travels and discoveries in Northern and Central Africa, (1822-1824) . . . across the Great Desert to the tenth degree of northern latitude, and from Kouka in Bornou, to Sackatoo, the capital of the Felatah empire, Boston, Cummings, Hilliard & co. 1826. lxiv, 255p. Philadelphia, Carey & Lea. 1826. iv, 216p. 2d ed. London, John Murray. 1828. 255p. 3d ed. 1828. 2v.   30

DRUMMOND, HENRY. Tropical Africa. New York, Scribner & Welford. London, Hodder & Stoughton. 1888. xiv, 228p.   31

DU CHAILLU, PAUL. Explorations and adventures in equatorial Africa; with accounts of the manners and customs of the people, and of the chase of the gorilla, the crocodile, leopard, elephant, hippopotamus, and other animals. New York, Harper & bros. 1861. xxii, 531p. 32

DU CHAILLU, PAUL. A journey to Ashangoland; and further penetration into equatorial Africa. New York, Harper & bros. 1874. xxiv, 501p.   33

DUMAN, ALEXANDERE, pere. Impressions of travel in Egypt and Arabia Petraea. Transl. from the French by "a lady of New York." New York, John S. Taylor, 1839. 318p.   34

DUPUIS, JOSEPH. Journal of a residence in Ashantee . . . notes and researches relative to the Gold Coast, and the interior of Western Africa; chiefly collected from Arab mms. and information communicated by the Moslems of Guinea . . . an account of the origin and causes of the present war. London, Henry Colburn. 1824. 399p.   35

ELLIS, ALFRED B. A history of the Gold Coast of West Africa. London, Chapman & Hall. 1893. xi, 400p. 36

ELLIS, WILLIAM. Three visits to Madagascar (1853-1856), including a journey to the capital; the natural history of the country and the present civilization of the people. New York. Harper & bros. 1859. 514p.   37

ELTON, JAMES F. Travels and researches among the lakes and mountains of Eastern and Central Africa. Ed. & comp. by H.B. Cotterill. London, John Murray. 1879. xxii, 417p.   38

FIELD, HENRY M. The barbary coast. 3d ed. New York, Charles Scribner's sons. 1899. 258p.   39

FLEMING, REV. FRANCIS. Southern Africa; a geography and natural history of the country, colonies, and inhabitants . . . notices of their origins, manners, habits, customs, traditions, superstitions, religious usages, languages, past and present conditions, manufacturers, weapons, etc. London, Arthur Hall, Virtue & co. 1856. 487p.   40

GEDDIE, JOHN. The lake regions of central Africa. A record of modern discovery. London, T. Nelson & sons. 1881. 275p.   41

GOLBERRY, SILVESTER M. X. Travels in Africa (1785-1787) . . . authentic observations and discoveries together with plans, views,

3

etc. Transl. from the French by W. Mudford. London, M. Jones. 1803. 2v. 42

GOODRICH, S. G. Lights and shadows of African history. Boston, Geo. C. Rand. 1852. 336p. 43

GOODRICH, S. G. A history of Africa. Louisville, Ky. The auth. 1850. 216p. 44

GRAY, WILLIAM. Travels in western Africa (1818-1821), from the river Gambia . . . to the river Niger. London, John Murray. 1825. xv, 413p. 45

GREELY, A. W. Men of achievement: explorers and travelors. New York, Charles Scribner's sons. 1893. 373p. 46

HANNO. The Periplus of Hanno; a voyage of discovery down the west African coast, by a Carthaginian admiral of the fifth century, B.C. The Greek text, with a translation, by W. H. Schoff . . . with explanatory passages. Philadelphia, Commercial museum. 1912. 31p.47

HAWKS, FRANCIS L. The monuments of Egypt, or Egypt a witness for the Bible. 2d ed. rev. & enl. New York, Geo. P. Putnam sons. 1850. 298p. 48

HEAD, MAJOR F. B. The life of Bruce, the African travellor. London, John Murray. 1830. 535p. 49

HOLMES, PRESCOTT. The story of exploration and adventure in Africa. Philadelphia, Henry Altemus. 1896. 264p. 50

HOLUB, EMIL. Seven years in South Africa: travels, researches, and hunting adventures, between the diamond-fields and the Zambesi (1872-79). Transl. from the Dutch by Ellen Frewer . . . 2d ed. London,

S. Low, Marston, Searle & Rivington. 1881. 2v. 51

HORNE, C. SILVESTOR. David Livingston. London, Macmillan & co. 1912. 248p. 52

JACKSON, JAMES G. An account of Timbuctoo and Hausa, in the interior of Africa, by El Hayo Abd Salam Shaboeny, with notes critical and explanatory, . . . letters descriptive of travels through west and south Barbary and across the mountains of Atlas, fragments, notes and anecdotes, specimens of the Arabic epistolary style, London, Longman, Hurst. Rees, Orme and Brown. 1820. xx, 527p. 53

JAMESON, PROFESSOR, WILSON, JAMES, AND MURRAY, HUGH. Narrative of discovery and adventure in Africa, geology, minerology, and zoology. New York, J.&J. Harper. 1831. 359p. 2d ed. rev. & enl. Edinburgh, Oliver & Boyd. 1832. 503p. 54

JOANNES, LEO AFRICANUS. de Africao. Descriptione pars altera. Lugd Batar apud Elzevir 1⁰. 1632. 2v. 800p. 55

JOHNSTON, SIR HARRY. The river Congo, from its mouth to Bolobo; with a general description of the natural history and anthropology of its western basin. London, Sampson, Low, Marston Searle & Rivington. 1884. 470p. 56

JOHNSTON, JAMES. Reality versus romance in South Central Africa; an account of a journey across the continent . . . New York, Chicago, Fleming H. Revell co. 1893. 353p. 57

JOHNSON, KEITH. Africa. 3d ed. rev.

& corr. London, Edward Stanford. 1884. 616p.   58

JONES, CHARLES H. Africa; the history of exploration and adventure as given in the leading authorities from Herodotus to Livingstone. New York, Henry Holt & co. 1875. x, 496p.   59

JONES, CHARLES H. Negroland; or light thrown upon the dark continent. New York, Hurst & co. 1881. viii, 488p.   60

JONVEAUX, EMILE. Two years in East Africa: adventures in Abyssinia and Nubia, with a journey to the sources of the Nile. London, T. Nelson & sons. 1875. xii, 407p.   61

KAY, STEPHEN. Travels and researches in Caffraria: describing the character, customs, and moral condition of the tribes inhabiting that portion of Southern Africa . . . New York, B. Waugh & T. Mason. 1834. ix, 428p.   62

KELTIE, JOHN S. The story of Emin's rescue as told in Stanley's letters. New York, Harper & bros. 1890. 176p.   63

KERR, WALTER M. The far interior: a narrative of travel and adventure from the Cape of Good Hope across the Zambesi to the lake regions of Central Africa. Boston, Houghton, Mifflin & co. 1886. 2v.   64

KINGSLEY, MARY H. Travels in West Africa, Congo Francais, Corisco, and Cameroons. London, New York, Macmillan co. 1897. xvi, 473p.   65

LACERDA, DR. FRANCISCO J.M. Journey to Cazembe in 1798. Transl. from the Portuguese and annotated by Captain R.F. Burton. Also journey of the Pombeiros across Africa from Angola to Tettle on the Zambeze, transl. by B.A.

Beadle; and a resume of the journey of Monteiro and Gamitto by C.T. Beke. London, John Murray. 1873. 271p.   66

LAING, ALEXANDER G. Travels in the Timannee, Kooranko, and Soolima countries in western Africa. London, John Murray. 1825. x, 465p.   67

LAIRD, MACGREGOR, AND OLDFIELD, R.A.K. Narrative of an expedition into the interior of Africa by the river Niger in the steam-vessels Quorra and Alburkah (1832-34). London, Richard Bentley. 1837. 2v.   68

LANDER, RICHARD L. AND JOHN. Journal of an expedition to explore the cause and termination of the Niger, with a narrative of a voyage down that river to its termination. London, John Murray. 1832. 3v. New York, Harper & bros. 1832. 2v.   69

LATROBE, CHRISTIAN I. Journal of a visit to South Africa in 1815 & 1816. London, L.B. Seeley. 1818. vii, 406p.   70

LICHTENSTEIN, HINRICH. Travels in Southern Africa in the years 1803-1806. Tr. from the German by Anne Plumptie. London, Henry Colburn. 1812. 383p.   71

LIVINGSTONE, DAVID. The last journals of David Livingstone, in Central Africa, 1865 to his death, continued by a narrative of his last moments and sufferings obtained from his faithful servants Chuma and Susi, by Horace Waller. New York, Harper & bros. 1875. 541p.   72

LIVINGSTONE, DAVID and CHARLES. Narrative of an expedition to the Zambesi and its tributaries; and of the discovery of the lakes Shirwa and Nyassa.

1858-64. New York, Harper & bros, 1866. 638p.   73

LUCCA, GAUDENTIO di. Adventures; being the substance of his examination before the Fathers of the inquisition at Bologna . . . giving an account of an unknown country in the deserts of Africa . . . Baltimore, Bonsal & co. 1800. 234p.   74

LYON, CAPTAIN G. F. A narrative of travels in Northern Africa (1818-20). London, John Murray, 1821. 383p.   75

MINUTOLI, BARONESS VON. Recollections of Egypt. London, Treuttel & Wartz, Trenttel, Jun. & Richter, 1827. 279p.   76

MOISTER, W. Africa: past and present, a concise account of the country, its history, geography, explorations, climates, productions, resources, population, etc. New York, American tract society. 1881. iv, 387p.   77

MOLLIEN, GASPARD THEODORE COMTE DE. Travels in the interior of Africa, to the sources of the Senegal and Gambia; performed by the command of the French government, in the year 1818. ed. by T.E. Bowdich. London, H. Colburn & co. 1820. xi, 378p.   78

MONTEIRO, JOACHIM J. Angola and the river Congo. New York, MacMillan co. 1876. xii, 354p. 79

MOORE, FRANCIS. Travels into the inland parts of Africa: a description of the several nations for the space of six hundred miles up the River Gambia; their trade, habits, customs, language, manners, religion and government; the power, disposition and characters of some Negro princes; with a particular account of Job Ben Solomon . . . to which is added, Capt. Stibb's

voyage up the Gambia in the year 1723 . . . with an accurate map of that river taken on the spot . . . Also extracts from the Nubian's geography, Leo the African, and other authors ancient and modern, concerning the Niger, Nile, or Gambia, and observations thereon. London, D. Henry and R. Cave, 1736. 315p.   80

MORELL, JOHN REYNELL. Algeria: the topography and history, political, racial, and natural of French Africa. London, Nathaniel Cooke. 1854. viii, 490p.   81

MORTIMER, MRS. M. Africa and America described with anecdotes. New York, Robert Carter & bros. 1854. 323p.   82

MURRAY, JOHN. A handbook for travellers in lower and upper Egypt . . . London, John Murray. 1891. 8th ed. rev. 568p.   83

PARK, MUNGO. The journal of a mission to the interior of Africa in the year 1805, together with other documents, official and private, relating to the same mission to which is prefixed an account of the life of the author. Philadelphia, Edward Earle, 1815. 302p.   84

PARK, MUNGO. The life and travels of Mungo Park. Also, an account of the progress of African discovery. Edinburgh, W.&R. Chambers. 1850. 88p.   85

PARK, MUNGO. The life and travels of Mungo Park; with an account of his death from the journal of Isaaco, the substance of later discoveries relative to his lamented fate, and the termination of the Niger. New York, Harper & bros. 1840. xii, 248p.   86

PARK, MUNGO. Travels in the interior districts of Africa performed under the direction and

6

patronage of the African Association, in the years, 1795, 1796, and 1797, with an appendix containing geographical illustrations of Africa by Major Reunell. 2d ed. enl. 1813. vii. 261p. 87

PARKE, THOMAS HEAGLE. My personal experiences in equatorial Africa. New York, C. Scribner's sons. 1891. xxvi, 526p. 88

PEEL, CAPTAIN W. A ride through the Nubian Desert. London, Longman, Brown, Green, & Longmans. 1852. 135p. 89

PIMBLETT, W. True stories from African history; from the first Egyptian dynasty to the present day. New York, E.P. Dutton & co., n.d. 316p. 90

RANKIN, F. HARRISON. The white man's grave, a visit to Sierra Leone in 1834. London, Richard Bentley. 1836. 2v. 91

RAPELJE, GEORGE. A narrative of excursions, voyages, and travels, performed at different periods in America, Europe, Asia, and Africa. New York, The auth. 1834. 5-416p. 92

RAVENSTEIN, E. G., ed. The strange adventures of Andrew Batte II of Leigh, in Angola and the adjoining regions. (Reprinted from Purch as "His Pilgrimes . . .") and a concise history of Kongo and Angola. London, Hakluyt Society. 1901. xx, 210p. 93

RAWLINSON, GEORGE. History of ancient Egypt. Boston, S.E. Cassino. 1882. 2v. 94

READE, WINWOOD. The martyrdom of man. New York, A.K. Butts & co. 1874. 543p. 95

READING, JOSEPH HANKINSON. The Ogome band; a narrative of African travel. Philadelphia,

Reading & co. 1890. xv, 278p. 96

RILEY, JAMES. An authentic narrative of the loss of the American brig Commerce, wrecked on the western coast of Africa, in August, 1815, with an account of the sufferings of her surviving officers and crew, who were enslaved by the wandering Arabs on the great African desert, or Zahahrah. New York, The auth. 1817. 554p. xvi. 97

RILEY, W.WILLSHIRE. Sequel to Riley's Narrative . . . from the period of his return to his native land . . . until his death. Columbus, Ohio. The auth. 1851. 448p. 98

RITCHIE, J. EWING. The pictorial edition of the life and discoveries of David Livingstone. London, James Sangster & co., n.d. 2v. 99

ROBBINS, ARCHIBALD. A journal, comprising an account of the loss of the Brig Commerce, upon the western coast of Africa. Aug. 28, 1815 with the manners, customs, and habits of the wandering Arabs. Hartford, Silas Andrews & son. 1851. 275p. 100

ROBERTS, JOHN S. The life and explorations of David Livingstone, including extracts from Dr. Livingstone's lost journal. Augusta, Maine. E.C. Allen & co. 1875. 384p. 101

ROMER, JONATHAN. Kaloolah, or journeyings to the Djebel Kumri: an autobiography; edited by W.S. Mayo. 2d ed. New York, George P. Putnam. 1849. 514p. 102

RUSSELL, MICHAEL.History and present condition of the Barbary states; comprehending a view of their civil institutions, antiquities, arts, religion, literature, commerce, agriculture, and natural productions. New York, Harper & bros. 1846. 343p. 103

SAINT-JOHN, JAMES AUGUSTUS. The lives of celebrated travellers. New York, Harper & bros. 1839. 3v. 104

SCHEINFURTH, GEORG ANGUST. The heart of Africa. Three years' travels and adventures in the unexplored regions of Central Africa, from 1868 to 1871. New York, Harper & bros. 1874. 2v. 105

SHOBERL, FREDERIC ed. Africa: containing a description of the manners and customs with some historical particulars of the Moors of the Zahara, and of the Negro nations between the rivers Senegal and Gambia. London, R. Ackerman. 1821. 3v. (World in miniature series) 106

SELOUS, FREDERICK COURTENEY. Travel and adventure in Southeast Africa; being the narrative of the last eleven years spent by the author on the Zambesi and its tributaries; with an account of the colonization of Mashuma land the progress of the gold industry in that country. London, Rowland Ward & co., 1893. xviii. 503p. 107

SMITH, C. S. Glimpses of Africa; west and southwest coast. Nashville, Tennessee, Publishing House A.M.E. Church, 1895. 288p. 108

SMITH, J. Trade and travels in the gulph of Guinea, western Africa, with an account of the manners, habits, customs, and religion of the inhabitants. London, Simpkin, Marshall & co. 1851. 225p. 109

SMITH, WILLIAM. A voyage to new Guinea: describing the customs, manners, soil, climate, habits, buildings, education . . . habitations, diversions, marriages, and whatever else is memorable among the inhabitants. Likewise, an account of their animals, minerals, etc. With great variety of entertaining incidents, worthy of observation, that happened during the author's travels in that large country. London, John Nourse. 1744. iv, 276p. 110

SNELGRAVE, WILLIAM. Nouvelle relation de quelques parties de la Guinee. (In Prevost, Antoine F. Histoire generale des voyages. La Haye. 1747-80. t.4 (1747) pp. 548-611). English translation. London. 1734. 111

SPEKE, JOHN HANNING. Journal of the source of the Nile. 2d ed. New York, Harper & bros. 1868. 590p. 112

STANLEY, SIR HENRY MORTON. The autobiography of Sir Henry Morton Stanley. Ed. by his wife, Dorothy Stanley. Boston and New York, Houghton, Mifflin co. 1909. xvii, 551p. 113

STANLEY, SIR HENRY MORTON. How I found Livingstone: travels, adventures, and discoveries in Central Africa, including an account of four months' residence with Dr. Livingstone. 2d ed. New York, Charles Scribner's sons. 1899. 736p. 114

STANLEY, SIR HENRY MORTON. In darkest Africa or the quest, rescue, and retreat of Emin, governor of Equatoria. New York, Charles Scribner's sons. 1890. 2v. 115

STANLEY, SIR HENRY MORTON. Through the dark continent: or, The sources of the Nile around the great lakes of equatorial Africa and down to the Livingstone River to the Atlantic ocean. New York, Harper & bros. 1879. 2v. 116

STEEDMAN, ANDREW. Wanderings and adventures in the interior of southern Africa. London, Longman & co. 1835. 2v.　　　117

STEPHENS, J. L. Incidents of travel in Egypt, Arabia Petraea and the Holy Land. New York, Harper & bros. 1837. 2v.　　　118

TAYLOR, BAYARD. A journey to Central Africa or, life and landscapes from Egypt to the Negro kingdoms of the White Nile. 10th ed. New York, G.P. Putnam & son. 1854. 522p.　　　119

TAYLOR, BAYARD. Lake regions of Central Africa. New York, G.P. Putnam & son. 1875. 397p.　　120

THOMAS, CHARLES W. Adventures and observations on the west coast of Africa, and its islands . . . accounts of places, peoples, customs, trade, missionary operations, etc. New York, Derby & Jackson. 1860. 479p.　　121

THOMPSON, GEORGE. The Palm land; or, west Africa. 3d ed. Cincinnati, The auth. 1859. 456p.　　122

THOMPSON, JOSEPH. Through Masai Land: a journey of exploration among the snow clad volcanic mountains and strange tribes of eastern equatorial Africa; being the narrative of the Royal Geographical society's expedition to Mount Kenia and Lake Victoria Nyanza, 1833-84. Boston, Houghton, Mifflin & co. 1885. 583p.　　123

THOMPSON, JOSEPH. To the Central African lakes and back: the narrative of the Royal Geographical society's East Central African expedition, 1878-80. 2d ed. Boston, Houghton, Mifflin & co. 1881. 2v.　　　124

TISSOT, V. AND AMERO. C. Au Pays Des Negres Peupladeset Passages D'Afrique Paris, Didot et Cit, 1889. 234p.　　　125

VEDDER, HEINRICH. South West Africa in early times . . . transl. and ed. by Cyril G. Hall. London, Oxford University Press. 1938. xv, 525p.　　　126

WANTERS, ALPHONSE JULES. Stanley's Emin Pasha expedition. Philadelphia, J.B. Lippincott. 1890. 378p.　　　127

WILKINSON, SIR GARDNER. A popular account of the ancient Egyptians. London, John Murray. 1854. 2v.　　　128

WILSON, JAMES. Narrative of discovery and adventure in Africa. New York, Harper & bros. 1868. 359p.　　　129

WILSON, JOHN LEIGHTON. Western Africa: its history, condition and prospects. New York, Harper & bros. 1856. 527p.　　　130

WOODSON, CARTER GODWIN. The African background outlined, or handbook for study of the Negro. Washington, Association for the study of Negro life and history. 1936. viii, 428p.　　　131

WORSFOLD, WILLIAM BASIL. A history of South Africa. 2d ed. London, J.M. Dent & co. 1900. viii, 199p.　　　132

II.　Adventure, description, and observation of travelers in Africa since 1900.

AKELEY, CARL AND MARY L. Adventures in the African jungle. New York, Dodd, Mead & co. 1930. xvi, 275p.　　　133

AKELEY, CARL ETHAN. In brightest Africa. Garden City, New York, Doubleday, Page and co. 1923. xvii, 267p.   134

AKELEY, DELIA J. Jungle portraits. New York, The Macmillan co. 1930. 251p.   135

AKELEY, MRS. MARY L. Carl Akeley's Africa; the account of the Akeley-Eastman-Pomeroy African Hall expedition of the American museum of natural history. New York, Dodd, Mead & co. 1929. xix, 321p.   136

BALLS, W. LAWRENCE. Egypt of the Egyptians. New York, Charles Scribner's sons. 1916. 266p.   137

BARNES, JAMES. Through Central Africa from coast to coast. New York, Appleton. 1915. 18, 283p.   138

BARROWS, HARLAN H. AND EDITH PUTNAM PARKER AND MARGARET TERRELL PARKER. Geography, southern lands. New York, Newark, etc., Silner, Burdett & co. 1934. vii, 296p.   139

BELL, ARCHIE. The spell of Egypt. Boston, The Page co. 1916. 366p.   140

BLYDEN, EDWARD WILMOT. West Africa before Europe, and other addresses, delivered in England in 1901 and 1903. London, C.M. Phillips, 1905. iv, 158p.   141

BODLEY, R.V.C. Algeria from within Indianpolis, Bobbs-Merrill. 1927. 308p.   142

BOYCE, WILLIAM D. Illustrated Africa, north, tropical, south. Chicago and New York, Rand McNally & co. 1925. 686p.   143

BRADLEY, MARY HASTINGS. Caravans and cannibals. New York, London, D. Appleton & co. 1926. 320p.   144

BUCHAN, JOHN. Prester John. London and New York, Thomas Nelson & sons. 1910. 376p.   145

CAMPBELL, DUGOLA. Wanderings in Central Africa, the experiences and adventures of a lifetime in pioneering and exploration. London, Seeley, Service & co. 1929. 2, 13-284p.   146

CARNEY, MABEL. African letters . . . Privately printed. 1927. 28p.   147

CARPENTER, FRANK GEORGE. Africa. New York, Cincinnati, etc., American book co. 1929. 397p. 148

CHAMBERLAIN, JAMES FRANKLIN AND ARTHUR HENRY . . . Africa, a supplementary geography. New York, Macmillan co. 1914. vii, 210p. 149

CUDAHY, JOHN. African horizons. New York, Duffield & co. 1930. 159p.   150

CURTIS, CHARLES P. and RICHARD C. Hunting in Africa east and west. Boston, New York, Houghton, Mifflin co. 1925. 281p.   151

DEAN, HARRY. The Pedro Gorino: the adventures of a Negro sea-captain in Africa and on the seven seas in his attempts to found an Ethiopian empire; an autobiographical narrative . . . with the assistance of Sterling North. Boston, New York, Houghton, Mifflin co. 1929. xvi, 262p.   152

DONNITHORNE, FRED A. Wonderful Africa; being the 7,000 miles travel in South and Central Africa. London, Hutchison & co. New York, Frederick A. Stokes co. 1925. xi, 13-302p.   153

DOUGLAS, ROBERT DICK, DAVID R. MARTIN, AND DOUGLAS L. OLIVER. Three Boy Scouts in Africa, on safari with Martin Johnson. New York, G.P. Putnam's sons. 1928. 215p.   154

DRAYSON, ALFRED WILKS. Sporting scenes amongst the Kaffirs of South Africa. London, G. Routledge & co. 1858. xiv, 327p. 155

DU CHAILLU, PAUL BELLONI. In African forest and jungle. New York, C. Scribner's sons. 1903. rev. ed. 1929. xii, 193p. 156

DUGMORE, ARTHUR RADCLYFFE. Camera adventures in the African wilds; being an account of a four months' expedition in British East Africa . . . New York, Doubleday, Page & co. 1910. xix, 233p. 157

DUGMORE, ARTHUR RADCLYFFE. The vast Sudan. New York, Frederick A. Stokes. 1924. 312p. 158

EASTMAN, GEORGE. Chronicles of an African trip. Rochester, New York. The Auth. 1927. 87p. 159

EDWARDS, AMELIA B. A thousand miles up the Nile. New York, Lovell, Coryell & co. n.d. 468p. 160

EGERTON, F. CLEMENT . . . African majesty; a record of refuge at the court of the kind of Bangangte in the French Cameroons. London, G. Routledge & sons. 1938. xx, 348p. 161

FITZGERALD, WALTER. Africa, a social, economic and political geography of its major regions. New York, Dutton. 1933. xv, 462p. 162

FLANDRAU, GRACE. Then I saw the Congo. New York, Harcourt, Brace & co. 1929. 308p. 163

FORBES, EDGAR ALLEN. The land of the white helmet, lights and shadows across Africa. New York, Chicago, Fleming H. Revell co. 1910. 365p. 164

FORREST, A. S. AND BENSUSAN, S.L. Morocco. London, A&C Black. 1904. 231p. 165

FRASER, SIR JOHN FOSTER. The land of veiled women, some wanderings in Algeria, Tunisia and Morocco. London, New York, Cassell & co. 1911. xviii, 288p. 166

FULLER, ROBERT HART. South Africa at home. London, G. Newnes. 1908. xiii, 235p. 167

FURLONG, CHARLES WELLINGTON. The gateway to the Sahara, observations and experiences in Tripoli. New York, Charles Scribner's sons. 1909. 306p. 168

GIBBONS, ALFRED ST. HILL. Africa from south to north through Marotseland. London and New York, J. Lane. 1904. 2v. 169

GIDE, ANDRE P. . . . Le retour du Tchad, suite du voyage au Congo, carnets de route. Paris, Gallimard. 1928. 7-252p. 170

GIDE, ANDRE P. Travels in the Congo. Translated from the French by Dorothy Bussy. New York, Alfred A. Knopf. 1929. 375p. 171

GREEN, LAWRENCE G. Secret Africa. London, S. Paul & co. 1936. 287p. 172

GREENE, GRAHAM. Journey without maps. Garden City, New York, Doubleday, Doran & co. 1936. 310p. 173

GRIFFITH, FRANCIS L. Egypt exploration fund. London, Egypt exploration fund, 1900. 64pp. 174

GROGAN, EWART S. AND ARTHUR H. SHARP. From the cape to Cairo; the first traverse of Africa from south to north. New and rev. ed. London, Hurst and Blackett. 1902. xvi, 402p. 175

HAHN, EMILY. Congo solo, misadventures two degrees north. Indianapolis, Bobbs-Merrill. 1933. 315p. 176

HALL, ARTHUR V. "Table Mountain," pictures with pen,

brush, and camera. Cape Town, Juba & co. n.d. 27p. 177

HAYWOOD, AUSTIN. Sport and service in Africa; a record of big game shooting, campaigning and adventure . . . Philadelphia, J.B. Lippincott co. 1926. xiii-xvi, 17-285p. 178

HOEFLER, PAUL L. Africa speaks; a story of adventure . . . the first trans-African journey by motor-truck . . . through central equatorial Africa. Philadelphia, Chicago, The John Winston co. 1931. xii, 469p. 179

HORN, ALFRED A. pseud. (ETHELREDA LEWIS). Trader Horn; being the life and works of . . . an "old visitor . . . the works written by himself at the age of seventy-three . . . New York, The Literary Guild of America. 1927. viii, 302p. 180

HOYNINGEN-HUENE, GEORGE. African mirage, the record of a journey. New York, Charles Scribner's sons and London, B.T. Batsford. 1938. 114p. 181

HUXLEY, JULIAN S. Africa view. New York, London, Harper & bros. 1931. viii, 478p. 182

JOHNSON, FRANK E. Here and there in Northern Africa. From the National Geographic Magazine, Jan. 1914. Washington, The National Geographic Society. 1914. 132p. 183

JOHNSON, MARTIN. Camera trails in Africa. New York, Grossett & Dunlap. 1924. 342p. 184

JOHNSON, MARTIN. Congorilla; adventures with pygmies and gorillas in Africa. New York, Brewer, Warren & Putnam. 1931. xi, 281p. 185

JOHNSON, MARTIN. Over African jungles . . . the record of a glorious

adventure . . . by airplane . . . New York, Harcourt, Brace & co. 1935. x, 263p. 186

JOHNSON, MARTIN. Safari, a saga of the African blue. New York, London, G.P. Putnam's sons. 1928. 294p. 197

JOHNSTON, SIR HARRY. The Nile quest, a record of the exploration of the Nile and its basin. New York, Frederick A. Stokes co. 1903. 341p. 188

JOHNSTON, SIR HARRY. The opening up of Africa. New York, Henry Holt & co.; London, Williams & Norgate. 1910. 255p. 189

KHUN dePROROK, BYRON. Mysterious Sahara, the land of gold, of sand, and of ruin. Chicago. The Reilly & Lee co. 1929. xx, 348p. 190

KIRKLAND, CAROLINE. Some African highways, a journey of two American women to Uganda and the Transvaal. Boston, Dana Estes & co. 1908. 345p. 191

KUMM, HERMANN K. The Sudan, a short compendium of facts and figures about the land of darkness. London, Marshall bros. 1907. xv, 224p. 192

LANNING, JOHN F. My trip to South Africa. Richmond, Va., Williams print co. 1905. 112p. 193

LEGENDRE, SIDNEY J. Okovango, desert river. New York, J. Messner. 1939. vi, 9-300p. 194

LEYS, NORMAN. Kenya. London, Leonard & Virginia Woolf. 1925. 13, 409p.. 2nd ed. 195

LITTLE, JAMES S. South Africa, a sketch book of men, manners and facts. London, W. Swan Sonnenschem & co. 1884. 2v. 196

LOUISE, H.H. PRINCESS MARIE. Letters from the Gold Coast; a

tour. London, Methuen & co. 1926. 240p. 197

LOW, SIDNEY. Egypt in transition. New York, The Macmillan co. 1914. 316p. 198

LOYSON, EMILIE J. To Jerusalem through the lands of Islam . . . Chicago, the open court publishing co. 1905. viii, 325p. 199

LUDWIG, EMIL. The Nile; the life-story of a river. (transl. from the German by Mary H. Lindsay) New York, Viking Press, 1937. xvi, 619p. 200

MACKENZIE, JEAN K. African clearings. Boston, New York, Houghton, Mifflin co. 1924. x, 270p. 201

MACKENZIE, JEAN K. Black sheep: adventures in west Africa. Boston, New York, Houghton, Mifflin co. 1916. 314p. 202

MACQUEEN, PETER. In wildest Africa, the record of a hunting and exploration trip through Uganda, Victoria Nyanza, etc . . . and a description of the various native tribes. Boston, L.C. Page & co. 1909. v-xiii, 402p. 203

MARGOLIOUTH, D. S. Cairo, Jerusalem, and Damascus. New York, Dodd, Mead & co. 1907. 473p. 204

MAUGHAM, R. C. F. Portuguese East Africa, the history, scenery, and great game of Manica and Sofala. New York. E.P. Dutton & co. 1906. xii, 340p. 205

MC LAURIN, HAMISH. What about North Africa? Travel in Morocco, Algeria, and Tunisia. New York, London, C. Scribner's sons. 1927. xiv, 362p. 206

MEAKIN, BUDGETT. The land of the Moors. London, Swan, Sonnenschein & co. 1901. New York, The Macmillan co. 1901. 464p. 207

MILLER, JANET. Jungles preferred. Boston, New York, Houghton, Mifflin co. 1931. 321p. 208

NASSAU, ROBERT H. My Ogowe, being a narrative of daily incidents during sixteen years in equatorial Africa. New York, The Neale publishing co. 1914. 705p. 209

NESBITT, FRANCES E. Algeria and Tunis, painted and described. London, A.&C. Black. 1906. 229p. 210

NEUMANN, OSKAR. From the Somali coast through Southern Ethiopia to the Sudan. Smithsonian Institute. Annual Report, 1903. p. 775-792. Washington, The Institute, 1904. (Reprinted from the Geographical Journal. Oct. 1902. v. 20) 211

O'NEIL, OWEN R. Adventures in Swaziland, the story of a South African Boer. New York, The Century co. 1921. 381p. 212

OSSENDOWSKI, FERDINAND. The fire of desert folk. The account of a journey through Morocco. (English text by Lewis Stanton Palen) New York, E.P. Dutton & co. 1926. 354p. 213

PATTERSON, JOHN H. In the grip of the Nyika; further adventures in British East Africa. London, Macmillan & co. 1909. xiv, 389p. 214

PHILLIPS, PHILLIP L. (comp.) A list of geographical atlases in the Library of Congress. Washington, Government printing office. 1909-14. 3v. 215

POWELL, EDWARD A. The map that is half unrolled, equatorial Africa from the Indian Ocean to the Atlantic. New York and London, Century co. 1925. xv, 355p. 216

POWELL, EDWARD A. In Barbary, Tunisia, Algeria, Morocco, and the

13

Sahara. New York, London, The Century co. 1926. 483p. 217

POWERS, H. H. Egypt. New York, The Macmillan co. 1924. 327p. 218

REID, C. L. An amateur in Africa. New York. The Adelphi co. 1925. 218p. 219

ROSENTHAL, ERIC. Stars and stripes in Africa; history of American achievements in Africa by explorers; account of Africans who played part in American affairs. London, George Routledge & sons. 1938. 306p. 220

SAVORY, ISABEL. In the tail of the peacock. New York, James Pott & co.; London, Hutchinson & co. 1903. 352p. 221

SCHILLINGS, CARL G. Flashlights in the jungle, a record of hunting adventures and of studies in wild life in equatorial East Africa. New York, Doubleday, Page & co. 1906. xxx, 782p. 222

SCHWEITZER, ALBERT. From my African notebook. (transl. from the German by Mrs. C.E.B. Russell). New York, Henry Holt & co. 1939. 144p. 223

SEABROOK, WILLIAM B. Air adventure. Paris-Sahara-Timbuctoo. New York, Harcourt, Brace & co. 1933. 211p. 224

SELOUS, FREDERICK C. A hunter's wanderings in Africa; being a narrative of nine years spent amongst the game of the far interior of South Africa. London, Macmillan & co. 1920. 504p. 225

SHEEAN, VINCENT. An American among the Riffi. London, New York, The Century co. 1926. 345p. 226

SHOEMAKER, MICHAEL M. Islam lands: Nubia, the Sudan, Tunisia and Algeria. New York, London, G.P. Putnam's sons. 1910. iii-xii, 251p. 227

SOUTH AFRICAN RAILWAYS AND HARBOURS. Travel in South Africa 2d ed. Pretoria, The Government printer. 1924. xxi, 324p. 228

STIGAND, CHAUNCY H. The land of Zinj, being an account of British East Africa, its ancient history and present inhabitants. London Constable & co. 1913. xii, 351p. 229

WHARTON, EDITH. In Morocco. New York, Charles Scribner's sons. 1920. 289p. 230

WHITE, STEWART E. The land of footprints. Garden City, New York, Doubleday, Page & co. 1912. x, 440p. 231

WILLIAMS, JOSEPH J. Hebrewisms of West Africa, from Nile to Niger with the Jews. New York. L. Mac Veagh, 1930. 451p. 232

WOLLASTON, ALEXANDER F. From Ruwenzori to the Congo; a naturalists journey across Africa. London. J. Murray. 1908. xxv. 315p. 233

III. African races and peoples, general descriptions of customs and laws. Biographies of Africans.

AZIKIWE, NNAMDI. Renascent Africa. Accra, Gold Coast, West Africa. The auth. 1937. 313p. 234

BAKER, RICHARD ST. B. Men of the trees; in the mahogany forests of Kenya and Nigeria. New York, I.. Macveagh; Toronto. Longmans, Green & co. 1931. xv. 19-283p. 235

BAIRD, JAMES B. Children of Africa.

New York, Fleming H. Revell co. n.d. 95p. 236

BARROWS, DAVID P. Berbers and blacks; impressions of Morocco, Timbuktu, and the Western Sudan. New York, The Century co. 1927. 251p. 237

BASDEN, G. T. Among the Ibos of Nigeria, an account of the curious. and interesting habits, customs and beliefs of a little known African people . . . Philadelphia, J. B. Lippincott co. 1921. xii, 315p. 238

BATES, ORIC. The eastern Libyans, an essay. London, Macmillan & co. 1914. xxii, 298p. 239

BLYDEN, EDWARD W. The people of Africa; a series of papers. New York, Randolph 1871. v, 157p. 240

BROWN, J. T. Among the Bantu nomads. A record of forty years spent among the Bechuana, a numerous and famous branch of the central south African Bantu, with the first full description of their ancient customs, manners, and beliefs. Philadelphia, J.B. Lippincott co. 1926. 272p. 241

CAMPBELL, DUGALD. In the heart of Bantuland; a record of twenty-nine years' pioneering in central Africa among the Bantu peoples, with a description of their habits, customs, secret societies and languages. Philadelphia, J.B. Lippincott co. 1922. 313p. 242

CASALIS, EUGENE. Les Bassoutos; ou, vingt-trois annees de sejour et d'observations au sud de l'Afrique. Paris, Meyrueis et cie. 1859. xvi, 371p. 243

CENDRARS, BLAISE. The African saga; translated from l'Anthologie Negre by Margery Bianco. New York, Payson & Clarke. 1927. 378p. 244

CLARIDGE, G. C. Wild bush tribes of tropical Africa; an account of adventure and travel amongst pagan people in tropical Africa, with a description of their manners of life, customs, heathenism, rites, and ceremonies, secret societies, sport and warfare, collected during a sojourn of twelve years. London, Seeley, Service & co. 1922. 314p. 245

COLVILE, ZELIE. Round the black man's garden. Edinburgh, London, William Blackwood & sons. 1893. xv, 344p. 246

CONDENHOVE, HANS. My African neighbors, man, bird, and beast in Nyasaland. Boston, Little, Brown & co. 1925. xi, 245p. 247

DAWSON, W. H. South Africa; people, places and problems. London, New York, Longmans, Green & co. 1925. xi, 448p. 248

DELAFOSSE, MAURICE. Les noirs de l'Afrique avec 4 cartes. Paris, Payot et cie. 1922. 160p. Amer. ed. The Negroes of Africa: history and culture, transl. from the French by F. Fligelman. Washington, The Associated publishers. 1931. xxxiii, 313p. 249

DENNETT, RICHARD E. Seven years among the Fjort; being an English trader's experiences in the Congo district. London, S. Low, Marston, Searle & Rivington, 1887. xvi, 240p. 250

DOKE, CLEMENT M. The lambas of Northern Rhodesia: a study of their customs and beliefs. London, George G. Harrap & co. 1931. 407p. 251

DOWD, JEROME. Negro races; a sociological study. v. I. West Africans. New York, Macmillan co. 1907. xxiii, 493p. 252

DOWD, JEROME. Negro races; a sociological study. v. II. East

Africans and South Africans. New York, Neale publishing co. 1931. 310p. 253

DRIBERG, JACK H. The Lango, a Nilotic tribe of Uganda. London, T. Fisher Unwin, 1923. 468p. 254

DUGMORE, ARTHUR R. African jungle life. London, Macmillan & co. 1928. viii, 246p. 255

DUNCAN, DAVID (comp.) African races. New York, Appleton & co. 1875. 47p. (in Herbert Spencer's Descriptive Sociology, No. 4). 256

EARTHY, E. DORA. Valenge women; the social and economic life of the Valenge women of Portuguese East Africa. An ethnographic study. London, Oxford Press. 1933. 245p. 257

EGERTON, F. C. C. African majesty, a record of refuge at the court of the King of Bangangte in the French Cameroons. London, George Routledge & sons. 1938. xx, 348p. 258

EICHER, LILIAN. The customs of mankind. London, W. Heinemann. 1924. xvii, 753p. 259

FIFE, C. W. Savage life in the black Sudan. Philadelphia, J. B. Lippincott co. 1927. 284p. 260

FINCK, HENRY T. Specimens of African love, (In his primitive love and love stories 1899). p.354-415. 261

GOLLOCK, G. A. Daughters of Africa. London, New York, Longmans, Green & co. 1932. 175p. 262

GOLLOCK, G. A. Lives of eminent Africans. New York and London, Longmans, Green & co. 1928. 152p. 263

GOLLOCK, G. A. Sons of Africa. New York, missionary education movement. (Friendship press). 1928. 264

GORER, GEOFFREY. Africa dances; a book about West African Negroes. London, Faber & Faber. 1935. xv, 363p. 265

GRANT, CYRIL F. Studies in North Africa. New York, E.P. Dutton & co. 1923. xi, 304p. 266

HESSE-WARTEGG, ERNEST. Tunis, the land and the people. London, Chalto & Windus. 1899. 302p. 267

HILLEGAS, HOWARD C. Oom Paul's people. New York, D. Appleton & co. 1899. 308p. 268

HOLLOWAY, J. E. American Negroes and South African Bantu. Pretoria, South Africa. The Carnegie visitor's grants committee. 1932. 26p. 269

JAMES, F. L. The wild tribes of the Soudan, an account of travel and sport chiefly in the Base country. New York, Dodd, Mead & co. 1883. 280p. 270

JENNER, ALICE. Stories from South African history. London, New York, Longmans, Green & co. 1927. ix, 179p. 271

KAGWA, SIR APOLO. The customs of the Baganda. Transl. by Ernest B. Kalibala. Ed. by M.M. Edel. New York, Columbia university press. 1934. 199p. 272

KAHN, MORTON C. Djuka, the Bush Negroes of Dutch Guiana. New York, Viking press. 1931. xx, 233p. 273

LANE, EDWARD WILLIAM. An account of the manners and customs of the modern Egyptians, written in Egypt during the years 1833-35. London, Ward, Lock & co. 1842. 552p. 274

LOWIE, ROBERT H. Primitive society. New York, Boni & Liveright. 1925. 463p. 275

MACKENZIE, JEAN K. African clearings. Boston and New York, Houghton, Mifflin co. 1924. 270p. 276

MASSAM, J. A. The cliff dwellers of Kenya; an account of a people, driven by raids, famine and drought to take refuge on the inaccessible ledges of precipitous mountains, with a description of their ways of living, social system, manners, and customs, religion, magic and superstitions. Philadelphia, J.B. Lippincott co. 1927. 268p.　277

MIGEOD, FREDERICK W. A view of Sierra Leone. New York, Brentano's. 1927. xi, 351p.　278

MILLIGAN, ROBERT H. The jungle folk of Africa. New York, Chicago, F.H. Revell co. 1908. 9-380p.　279

MILLIN, SARAH G. The South Africans. New York, Boni & Liveright. 1927. 287p.　280

NYABONGO, AKIKI K. The story of an African chief. New York, Scribner's sons. 1935. 312p.　281

ORDE-BROWNE, GRANVILLE ST. JOHN. The vanishing tribes of Kenya; a description of the manners and customs of the primitive and interesting tribes dwelling on the vast southern slopes of Mount Kenya, and their fast disappearing native methods of life. Philadelphia, J. B. Lippincott co. 1925. 284p.　282

OSSENDOWSKI, FERDINAND. Slaves of the sun. New York, E.P. Dutton & co. 1928. 489p.　283

PATTERSON, JOHN H. The man-eaters of Tsavo and other East African adventures. London, Macmillan & co. 1910. xx, 338p.　284

PURVIS, JOHN B. Through Uganda to Mount Elgon. New York, American Tract Society. 1909. 371p.　285

QUATREFAGES de BREAU, ARMAND. The pygmies. Transl. from the French by Frederick Starr. London, Macmillan & co.

New York, D. Appleton co. 1895. xiv, 255p.　286

RATTRAY, ROBERT S. Ashanti law and constitution. London, Oxford university press. 1929. 420p.　287

SANCHO, IGNATIUS. The life of Ignatius Sancho, an African. London. J. Nichols & co. 1782. 2v.　288

SCHAPERA, ISAAC. The Khoisan peoples of South Africa; Bushmen and Hottentots. London, George Routledge & sons. 1930. 430p. 289

SEABROOK, WILLIAM B. Jungle ways. New York, Harcourt, Brace & co. 1931. 3-308p.　290

SELIGMAN, CHARLES G. Races of Africa. London, T. Butterworth. 1930. 256p.　291

SHOOTER, JOSEPH. The Kafirs of Natal and the Zulu country. London, E. Stanford. 1857. iii, 403p.　292

STANLEY, SIR HENRY M. My dark companions and their stories. London, 1893. 335p. Also N.Y. ed. 1893.　293

STANLEY, SIR HENRY M. My Kalulu, prince, king and slave; a story of Central Africa. New York, 1874. xiv, 432p.　294

THACKERAY, LANCE. The people of Egypt (paintings) Intro. by Gordon Home. London, Adam & Charles Black. 1910.　295

THEAL, GEORGE M. The yellow and dark-skinned people of Africa south of the Zambesi; a description of the Bushmen, the Hottentots, and particularly the Bantu . . . and numerous folklore tales of these different people. London, S. Sonnenschein & co. 1910.　296

TORDAY, EMILE. On the trail of the Bushongo; an account of a remarkable and hitherto unknown African people; their origin, art, high social

17

and political organization and culture, derived from the author's personal experience amonst them. London, Seeley, Service & co. 1925. 286p.   297

TREMEARNE, ARTHUR J.N. The tailed head-hunters of Nigeria; an account of an official's seven years' experiences in the northern Nigerian pagan belt, and a description of the manners, habits, and customs of the native tribes. Philadelphia, J.B. Lippincott co.; London, Sealey, Service & co. 1912. xvi, 341p.   298

WALKER, F. Africa and her peoples. London, Edinburgh House press. 1924. 144p.   299

WARD, HERBERT AND D. D. BIDWELL. Five years with the Congo cannibals. New York, Robert Bonner's sons. 1890. 308p.   300

WARD, HERBERT. A voice from the Congo, comprising stories, anecdotes, and descriptive notes. New York, Charles Scribner's sons. 1910. viii, 330p.   301

WAUGH, EVELYN. They were still dancing. New York, Farrar & Rinehart. 1932. 3-317p.   302

WEEKS, JOHN H. Among the primitive Bakongo; a record of thirty years' close intercourse with the Bankongo and other tribes of equatorial Africa, with a description of their habits customs, and religious beliefs. London, Seeley, Service & co. 1914. 318p.   303

WERNER, ALICE. The natives of British Central Africa. London, Archibald Constable & co. 1906. 303p.   304

WESTERMANN, DIEDRICH. The African today. London, The International Institute of African languages and cultures. 1934. xv, 343p.   305

WOODSON, CARTER G. African heroes and heroines. Washington, The associated publishers. 1939. 249p.   306

WYNDHAM, RICHARD. The gentle savage, a sudanese journey in the province of Bahr-el-ghazal . . . New York, William Morrow & co. 1936. 287p.   307

IV.   African arts, culture, and languages, reports of anthropological, archeological, and ethnological investigations, and other scientific studies.

ABBOTT, WILLIAM LOUIS. Ethnological collections in the United States. National museum from Kilima-Njaro, East Africa. (In U.S. National Museum, annual report, 1891.) Washington, 1892. pp. 381-428.   308

BALFOUR, H. The origin of West African crossbows. Repository Smithsonian Inst. 1910. pp. 635-650; v. 1. Tabl. Washington, 1911.   309

BARTLETT, E. ASHMEAD. The passing of the Shereefian empire. New York, Dodd, Mead & co.; Edinburgh, London, William Blackwood & sons. 1910. 532p.   310

BARTH, HEINRICH. Collection of vocabularies of Central-African languages, etc. German and English. Gotha, J. Perthes, 1862-66. 3 parts. Library has pts. 2-3.   311

BATES, ORIC. The Eastern Libyans;

an essay. London, Macmillan co. 1914. 298p. 312

BATES, ORIC. (ed.) et al. Harvard African studies I. 292p. 1917. Harvard African studies II. 373p. 1918. Harvard African studies III. E. A. Hooten & others, ed. 374p. 1922. Cambridge, Mass. African Department, Peabody Museum, Harvard University. 313

BELL, CLIFE. Negro sculpture. (Reprinted from living age for September 25, 1920. pp. 786-89). 314

BELL, CLIFE. Since Cezanne. New York, Harcourt, Brace & co. 1922. 230p. 315

BRYK, FELIX. Dark rapture, the sexlife of the African Negro. Transl. by Dr. Arthur J. Norton. New York, Walden publication. 1939. xvi, 167p. 316

BUCKMAN, ETHEL CLARK. Culture of the African Negro. 138p. M.S. in educ. Thesis, Boston university, 1930. 317

BURKITT, M. C. South Africa's past in stone and paint. Cambridge university press. 1928. 183p. 318

CULIN, STEWART (ROBERT STEWART). Mancala, the national game of Africa. (In the U.S. National Museum. Annual report, 1894. Washington. 1896. pp. 595-607). 319

CUNNINGHAM, JAMES FREDERICK. Uganda and its people; notes on the protectorate of Uganda, especially the anthropology and ethnology of its indigenous races. London. Hutchinson & co. 1905. xxix. 370p. 320

DRIBERG, J. H. At home with the savage. New York, William Morrow. 1932. 267p. 321

EINSTEIN, CARL. Negerplastik. Leipzig, Verlag der Weissen Bucher, 1915. 115p. 322

ELLIS, GEORGE W. Negro culture in West Africa; a social study of the Negro group of Vai-speaking people, with its own invented alphabet and written language . . . fifty folklore stories, and one hundred and fourteen proverbs . . . New York, Neale publishing co. 1914. 290p. 323

ERSKINE, MRS. STEWART. Vanished cities of Northern Africa. Boston, New York, Houghton, Mifflin co. 1927. 284p. 324

FRAZER, SIR JAMES G. (comp.) Anthologia anthropologica. The native races of Africa and Madagascar . . . arranged and edited from the mss. by Robert Angus Downie. London, P. Lund, Humphries & co. 1938. xii, 578p. 325

FROBENIUS, LEO. African genesis. New York, Stackpole. 1937. 236p. 326

FROBENIUS, LEO. Kulturgeschichte Afrikas; Prolegomena zu einer historichen gestaltlehre. Zurich., PhaidonVerlag. 1933. 3-652p. 327

FROBENIUS, LEO. The origin of African civilizations. Washington, Annual report Smithsonian Institute. 1898. 328

FROBENIUS, LEO. Das unbekannte afrika, aufhellung der schicksale eines erdteils. Munchen: C.H. Beckische Verlag, 1923. 184p. 329

GUILLAUME, PAUL AND MUNRO, THOMAS. Primitive Negro sculpture. New York, Harcourt, Brace & co. 1926. 134p. 330

HAMBLY, W.D. Tribal dancing and social development. London, H.F. & G. Witherby. 1926. 292p. 331

HARDY, GEORGES. L'art Negre l'art animiste des noirs d'afrique. Paris,

19

Henri Laurens. 1927. 166p. 332

HERSKOVITS, MELVILLE J. Dahomey, an ancient west African kingdom. New York, J.J. Augustin. 1938. 2v. 333

HOFFMAN, MALVINA. Heads and tales. New York, C. Scribner's sons. 1936. xx. 416p. 334

JOHNSON, JAMES WELDON. Native African races and culture. Charlottesville, Virginia. 1927. 26p. (John P. Slater Fund, occasional papers, no. 25.) 335

KHUN de PROROK, BYRON. Digging for lost African gods; the record of five years archaeological excavation in North Africa. New York, London, G.P. Putnam's sons. 1926. xv, 369p. 336

KINGSLEY, MARY HENRIETTA. West African studies. London and New York, Macmillan co. 1899. xxvii, 639p. 337

KJERSMEIER, CARL. Centres de style de la sculpture Negre africaine. Paris, Albert Morance; Copenhague, Fischers Forlag. 1938. 4v. 338

LEAKEY, L. S. B. Stone age Africa, an outline of prehistory in Africa. London, Humphrey Milford, 1936. xii, 218p. 339

MALINOWSKI, BRONISLAW. Crime and custom in savage society. New York, Harcourt, Brace & co. 1926. xii, 132p. 340

MEEK, CHARLES K. The northern tribes of Nigeria; an ethnographical account of the northern provinces of Nigeria, together with a report on the 1921 decennial census. Oxford, Clarendon press. 1925. 2v. 341

MEINHOF, CARL. An introduction to the study of African languages. Transl. from the German by Alice Werner. London, J.M. Dent & sons:

New York, E.P. Dutton & co. 1915. 169p. 342

NAVILLE, EDOUARD HENRI. The origin of Egyptian civilization. Washington, Annual report Smithsonian Institute. 1907. pp. 549-64. 343

PHILIP, JOHN. Researches in South Africa; illustrating the civil, moral, and religious condition of the native tribes; including journals of the author's travels in the interior; together with detailed accounts of the progress of the Christian mission, exhibiting the influence of Christianity in promoting civilization. London, J. Duncan. 1828. 2v. 344

RATTRAY, ROBERT S. (comp.). Religion and art in Ashanti. Oxford university press, 1927. xviii, 414p. 345

RIVERS, FOX P. Antique works of art from Benin. London, privately printed. 1900. 100p. 346

ROSCOE, JOHN. The Bakitara or Banyoro. The first part of the report of the Mackie Ethnological expedition to Central Africa. Cambridge, England, university press. 1923. xiii, 205p. 347

ROSCOE, JOHN. The soul of Central Africa; a general account of the Mackie Ethnological Expedition. London, Cassell & co. 1922. 327p. 348

SADLER, MICHAEL. (ed.) Arts of West Africa (excluding music). Oxford university press. 1935. 129p. 349

SCHAPERA, ISAAC. (ed.) The Bantu speaking tribes of South Africa; an ethnographical survey. London, George Routledge & sons. 1937. xv, 453p. 350

SCHWEINFURTH, GEORG AUGUST. Artes africanae.

20

Abbildungen und beschreibungen von erzeugnissen des kunstfleisses central afrikanischer volker. London, S. Low, Marston, Low & Searle. 1875. x, 42, xxiv. 351

SMITH, EDWIN W. The golden stool, some aspects of the conflict of cultures in modern Africa. Garden City, New York, Doubleday Doran & co. 1928. 328p. 352

STARR, FREDERICK. A bibliography of Congo languages. Chicago, university of Chicago press. 1908. 97p. (Department of anthropology, bul. v.). 353

STOW, GEORGE W. (copier). Rock-paintings in South Africa from parts of the Eastern province and Orange Free State. London, Methuen & co. 1930. 354

SWEENY, JAMES J. African Negro art. New York, Museum of modern art. 1935. 58p. plates. 355

WERNER, ALICE. The language-families of Africa. 2d ed. London, Kegan Paul, Trench, Trubner & co. 1925. 151p. 356

WESTERMANN, DIEDRICH. The Shilluk people, their language and folklore. Philadelphia, Board of foreign missions of the United Presbyterian Church. 1912. lxiii 312p. 357

WEULE, DR. KARL. Native life in East Africa; the results of an ethnological research expedition. Transl. from the German by Alice Werner. New York, D. Appleton & co. 1909. 431p. 358

YOUNG, S. Primitive Negro sculpture (Bloudiau African collection) Reprinted from the "New Republic" Feb. 23. 1937. 359

V. African folklore, mythology, and religious beliefs.

ASHLEY-MONTAGU M. F. Coming into being among the Australian Aborigines, a study of the procreative beliefs of the native tribes of Australia. New York, E. P. Dutton & co. 1938. xxxv, 362p.360

BARKER, WILLIAM H. AND SINCLAIR, CECILIA. (colls.) West African folk-tales. London, G. G. Harrap & co. 1917. 183p. 361

BAUDIN, R. P. Fetichism and fetich worshippers. Transl. from the French by McMahon. New York, Cincinnati, and St. Louis, Benziger bros. 1885. 127p. 362

BLEEK, WILHEIM H. I. A brief account of Bushman folk-lore and other texts. London. 1911. 21p.363

BLYDEN, EDWARD W. Christianity, Islam and the Negro race. 2d ed. London, W.B. Whittingham & co. 1888. xv, 432p. 364

BURLIN, MRS. NATALIE C. Songs and tales from the dark continent. Recorded from the singing and the sayings of C. Kamba Simango, Ndau tribe, Portuguese East Africa, and Madikane Cele, Zulu tribe, Natal, Zululand, South Africa. New York, G. Schirmer. 1920. 170p.365

CARY, JOYCE. The African witch. New York, W. Morrow & co. 1936. 3-416p. 366

CENDRARS, BLAISE (comp.) The African saga. Transl. from the French (l'Anthologie Negre) by Margery Bianco. New York, Payson & Clarke, 1927. 378p. 367

CHATELAIN, HELI. Folk-tales of Angola. Fifty tales, with Ki-mbundu text, literal English translation, introduction, and notes. Boston and New York, Published for American Folklore

Society. Houghton, Mifflin co.; London, D. Nutt; Leipzig, K.F. Koehler. 1894. xii, 315p.　　368

CHAUVET, STEPHEN. Musique Negre. Paris, societie d'editions geographiques, maritimes et coloniales, 1929. 242p.　　369

CRONISE, FLORENCE M. AND WARD, HENRY W. Cunnie rabbit, Mr. spider and other beef. West African folk-tales. London, S. Sonnenschein & co. 1903. 330p. 2d ed. New York, E.P. Dutton co. 1905. 330p.　　370

DENNETT, RICHARD E. Folklore of the Fjort. London, S. Low, Marston & co. 1898. 116p.　　371

DENNETT, RICHARD E. Nigerian studies; or, the religious and political system of the Yoruba. London, Macmillan co. 1910. xiii, 235p.　　372

DURKHEIM, EMILE. The elementary forms of the religious life; a study in religious sociology. Transl. from the French by J.W. Swain. London, Allen & Urwin. 1915.　　373

EINSTEIN, KARL. Afrikanische legenden. Berlin, Rowohlt. 1925. 280p.　　374

FELL, J. R. Folk tales of the Batonga and other sayings. London, Holborn publishing house. 1923. 247p.　　375

FISHER, R. B. Twilight tales of the black Baganda. London, Marshall bros. 1911. 198p.　　376

FLETCHER, ROLAND S. Hausa sayings and folklore with a vocabulary of new words. London, New York, Oxford university press. 1912. 173p.　　377

FRAZER, JAMES G. The golden bough. A study in magic and religion. 3d ed. London, Macmillan & co. 1913-15. 12v.　　378

HOFFMAN, CARL VON. Jungle gods. ed. by Eugene Lohrke. New York, Henry Holt & co. 1929. 286p.　　379

HORNBOSTEL, ERIC M. VON. African Negro music. (Reprinted from "Africa" London, Jan. 1928. v. 1, no. 1)　　380

HUFFMAN, RAY. Nuer customs and folklore. London, International institute of African languages and cultures. 1931. xi, 108p.　　381

JONES, A. M. African drumming. A study in the combination of rhythms in African music. Johannesburg, university of Witwatersrand press. 1930. 16p. (Reprinted from Bantu studies, v. 8, no. 1. Mar. 1934).　　382

KIRBY, PERCIVAL R. The musical instruments of the native races of South Africa. London, Oxford university press. 1934. 72p.　　383

LLOYD, L. C.(ed.) Specimens of Bush folklore. Collected by W.H.I. Bleek and L.C. Lloyd. London, George Allen & co. 1911. 468p.　　384

MACKENZIE, D. R. The spirit-ridden Konde, a record of the interesting but speedily vanishing customs and ideas . . . amongst these shy inhabitants of the lake Nyasa region, from witch-doctors, diviners, hunters, fishers, and every native source. Philadelphia, J.B. Lippincott co. 1925. xii, 318p. 385

MELLAND, FRANK H. In witch-bound Africa, an account of the primitive Kaonde tribe and their beliefs. London, Seeley, Service & co. 1923.　　386

MYTHS OF THE ZULUS. n.d. n.p.387

NASSAU, ROBERT H. Bantu folk tales; where animals talk. Boston. Four seas co. 1919.　　388

NASSAU, ROBERT H. Fetichism in West Africa; forty years observance of native customs and superstitions.

22

New York, Charles Scribner's sons. 1904. 405p.   389

OESTERLEY, W. O. E. The sacred dance. London, Cambridge university press. 1923. 234p.   390

PASTOR, W. Music of primitive peoples and the beginnings of European music. Reprinted by the Smithsonian Institute. Washington. 1912. 21p.   391

PULESTON, FRED. African drums. New York, Farrar & Rivehart co. 1930. 318p.   392

SCHWEITZER, ALBERT. African notebook. Transl. from the German by Mrs. C.E.B. Russell. New York, Henry Holt & co. 1939. 144p.   393

TALBOT, PERCY A. In the shadow of the bush. New York, George H. Doran co.; London, William Heineman. 1912. 480p.   394

TALBOT, PERCY A. Life in southern Nigeria, the magic beliefs and customs of the Ibibio tribe. London, Macmillan & co. 1923. xvi, 356p.   395

TAYLOR, SAMUEL COLERIDGE. African romances. Words by Paul Laurence Dunbar; set to music by Samuel Coleridge Taylor. (op. 17. Augener's ed. no. 8817) London, Angener & co. 1897. 21p.   396

TUCKER, A. N. Tribal music and dancing in the southern Sudan, at social and ceremonial gatherings. London, William Reeves. 1932. 57p.   397

UNKULUNKULU; or, the traditions of creation as existing among the Amazulu and other tribes of South Africa. n.p. n.d. 408p.   398

WERNER, ALICE. Myths and legends of the Bantu. London, George G. Harrup & co. 1933. 335p.   399

WILKINSON, JAMES J. G. The African and the true Christian religion has magna charta. A study in the writings of Emanuel Swedenborg. London, James Speirs. 1892. x, 245p.   400

WILLOUGHBY, WILLIAM C. The soul of the Bantu; a sympathetic study of the magico-religious practices and beliefs of the Bantu tribes of Africa. 1st ed. New York, Doubleday, Doran & co. 1928. 476p.   401

WOODSON, CARTER G. African myths together with proverbs; a supplementary reader composed of folk tales from various parts of Africa, adapted to the use of children in the public schools. Washington, Associated publishers. 1928. 184p.   402

VI. Fiction by Africans or with African characters.

BAPTIST, R. HERNEKIN. Wild deer. New York, Day. 1934. 347p.   403

BELL, WILLIAM C. (ed.) African bridge builders. New York, Friendship press. 1936. xiii, 168p.   404

BELOT, ADOLPHE. Article 47, a romance. Transl. from the French by James Furbish. Philadelphia, J.B. Lippincott & co. 1873. 161p.   405

BOOTHBY, GUY NEWELL. Dr. Nikola's experiment. New York, D. Appleton & co. 1899. 308p.   406

BOOTHBY, GUY NEWELL. Pharos, the Egyptian. A romance. New York, D. Appleton & co. 1899. 328p.   407

BUCHAN, JOHN. Prester John. Boston, Houghton, Mifflin. 1910.. 272p.   408

CARTER, THOMAS L. Out of Africa.

A book of short stories. New York and Washington, Neale publishing co. 1911. 288p.　　　　　409

CHISWELL, ARCHDEACON. The slave prince. A story founded on fact. New York, Paris, Chicago, London and Washington, Brentano's. 1890. 376p.　　410

DARLOW, DAVID J. Khama, a poem. South Africa, Fort Hare, Alice, C.P. 1923. 15p.　　　　　411

DAWSON, ALEC J. African nights entertainment. New York, Dodd, Mead and co. 1900. 346p.　　412

DU CHAILLU, PAUL. Stories of the gorilla country. New York, Harper & bros. 1871. 292p.　　413

DUMAS, ALEXANDER. Louise Goillard; or, the secret practitioner. Tr. from the french. 1st Am. ed. New York, Burgess, Stringer & co. 1846. 40p.　　　　　414

ELLIS, GEORGE W. The leopard's claw; a thrilling story of love and adventure from a European castle through the West African jungle, disclosing a deep insight into the quality and spiritual influence of African social institutions and conditions, and revealing a profound psychic interpretation of African inner life, all clustered about the mysterious function and significance of the leopard's claw. New York, International auths. 1917. 172p.　　　　　415

FLAUBERT, GUSTAVE. Salammbo. Paris , C.et M. Levy Freres. 1866. 474p.　　　　　416

GRANT, JOHN C. The Ethiopian; a narrative of the society of human leopards. New York, Black Hawk press. 1935. 287p.　　417

HAGGARD, H. RIDER. Child of storm. London. Cassell & co. 1913. xvi, 248p.　　　　　418

HAGGARD, H. RIDER. King Solomon's mines. London, Cassell & co. 1885. 320p.　　　419

HAINES, ELWOOD. L. Poems of the African trail. Milwaukee, Wisconsin, Morehouse publishing co.; and London, A.R. Mowbray & co. 1928. ix, 62p.　　　420

HAIGH, RICHMOND. Ethiopian saga. New York, Henry Holt & co. 1919. v, 209p.　　　　　421

HALE, MRS. SARAH J. Liberia; or Mr. Payton's experiments. n.p. n.d.　　　　　422

HELSER, ALBERT D. African stories. New York, Chicago, Flaming H. Dovell. 1930. 223p.　　423

HUGO, VICTOR M. The slave-king. Philadelphia, The library of romance, v. 6, Carey, Lea & Blanchard. 1833. 259p.　　424

LANCASTER, WILLIAM J. R. (pseud. COLLINGWOOD, HARRY.) The Congo rovers; a story of the slave squadron. New York, Scribner & W. Welford. 1903. 352p.　　425

LEAVITT, A. J. AND EAGAN, H.W. A trip to Paris: an Ethiopian sketch; together with eight other dramas relating to the African. New York, London, Samuel French. n.d.　　　　　426

LEE, MRS. SARAH R. African Crusoes: or, the adventures of Carlos and Antonio. Boston, Lee & Shepard, publishers. n.d. 454p. 427

MACKENZIE, JEAN K. Talking woman. London, Sheldon press. 1936. (Little books for Africa. no. 50).　　　　　428

MANNERS-SUTTON. Black god; a story of the Congo. London, Longmans, Green & co. 1934. 299p.　　　　　429

MARAN, RENE. Batouala; veritable roman negre. Paris, Albin Michel. 1921. 189p.　　　430

MARRYAT, FREDERICK. The mission: or, scenes in Africa; Written for young people. New York and Philadelphia, D. Appleton & co. 1851. 2v.   431

MEYERBEER, GIACOMO. L'Africana, opera in cinque atti . . . Milano, Ricordi. n.d. 54p.   432

MILLIN, MARS. SARAH G. God's stepchildren. New York, Boni & Liveright. 1924. 319p.   433

MOFOLO, THOMAS. Chaka, an historical romance, translated from the original Seonto by F.H. Dutton. London, published for the International Institute of African languages and cultures by Oxford university press. 1931. xv, 198p.
434

MORAND, PAUL. Black magic. Transl. from the French by Hamish Miles. New York, The Viking press. 1929. 218p.   435

OVERS, W. H. Stories of African life. New York, E.S. Gorham. 1924. 436

PHILIPS, FRANCIS C. A question of color. New York, Frederick A. Stokes co. 1895. 147p.   437

PLOMER, WILLIAM C. F. Turbott wolf. New York, Harcourt, Brace & co. 1926. 244p.   438

POWYS, LLEYLYN. Black laughter. New York, Harcourt, Brace & co. 1924. x, 216p.   439

SCHREINER, OLIVE (pseud. RALPH IRON). The story of an African

farm; a novel. London, Hutchinson & co. 1896. 346p.   440

SCHREINER, OLIVE Trooper Peter Halket of Mashonaland. Boston, Roberts bros. 1897. 133p.   441

SCHUYLER, GEORGE S. Slaves today; a story of Liberia. New York, Brewer, Warren & Putnam. 1931. 290p.   442

SHAW, GEORGE B. Back to Methuselah; a meta-biological pentateuch. New York, Brentano's. 1921. ci, 300p.   443

SHEPARD, R. H. W. Literature for the South African Bantu. A comparative study of Negro achievement. Pretoria, S. A., Carnegie Corporation Visitors' Grant. 1936. 80p.   444

SOUTHON, ARTHUR E. A yellow Napoleon; a romance of West Africa. London, Hodder & Stoughton, 1923.   445

THARAUD, JEROME AND THARAUD, JEAN. Long walk of Samba Diouf. Transl. from the French by Willis Steell. New York, Duffield & co. 1924. 201p.   446

WILLSON, BECKLES (pseud.) HENRY BECKLES. Harold; an experiment. New York, London, Globe publishing co. 1891. 230p.
447

YOUNG, FRANCIS B. They seek a country. New York, Reynal & co. 1937. 602p.   448

VII. African independent governments.

1. Abyssinia (Ethiopia)

BAUM, JAMES E. Savage Abyssinia, New York, H. J. Sears & co. 1927. xxi, 336p.   449

BEARDSLEY, GRACE H. The Negro in Greek and Roman civilization. A study of the Ethiopian type.

Baltimore, John Hopkins press; London, Oxford university press. 1929. (The Johns Hopkins University studies in archeology, no. 4). 143p.   450

BENT, JAMES T. The sacred city of

25

the Ethiopians, being a record of travel and research in Abyssinia in 1893 . . . London, New York, Longmans, Green & co. 1893. xv, 309p. 451

BORTON, ELIZABETH. Our little Ethiopian cousin, children of the Queen of Sheba. Boston, L.C. Page & co. 1935, 134p. 452

CARTER, BOAKE. Black shirt, black skin. Harrisburg, Pa. Telegraph press. 1935. 178p. 453

CHRISTY, DAVID. Ethiopia: her gloom and glory, as illustrated in the history of the slave trade and slavery, the rise of the Republic of Liberia and the progress of African missions. Cincinnati. Rickey, Mallory & Webb. 1857. iv, 255p. 454

COON, CARLETON S. Measuring Etheopia and flight into Arabia. Boston, Little, Brown & co. 1935. ix, 3-333p. 455

FARAGO, LADISLAS. Abyssinia on the eve. New York, G.P. Putnam's sons. 1935. x, 286p. 456

FORBES, MRS. ROSITA. From Red Sea to Blue Nile; Abyssinian adventure. New York, The Macaulay co. 1925. 386p. 457

FORD, JAMES W. AND HARRY GANNES. War in Africa, Italian fascism prepares to enslave Ethiopia. New York, Workers library publishers. 1935. 31p. 458

GLEICHEN, ALBERT E. W. With the mission to Menelik, 1897. London, Arnold. 1889. xi, 363p. 459

GOBAT, SAMUEL. Journal of a three years' residence in Abyssinia, in furtherance of the objects of the church missionary society. To which is prefixed a brief history of the church of Abyssinia . . . 2d ed. New York, M.W. Dodd, 1850. 480p. 460

HAHN, EMILY. Congo solo, misadventures two degrees north. Indianapolis, Bobbs-Merrill co. 1933. 315p.

HAHN, EMILY. With naked foot. Indianapolis, Bobbs-Merrill. 1934. 302p. 462

HAIGH, RICHMOND. An Ethiopian saga. New York, H. Holt & co. 1919. x, 207p. 463

HARMSWORTH, GEOFFREY. Abyssinian adventure. London, Hutchinson & co. 1935. xvii, 306p. 464

HARRIS, WILLIAM C. The highlands of Ethiopia . . . 1st ed. New York, J. Winchester. 1843. 332p. (From the first London edition). 465

HAYFORD, CASELY (i.e. JOSEPH EPHRAIM). Ethiopia unbound: studies in race emancipation. London, Phillips. 1911. 216p. 466

HOTTEN, JOHN C. (ed.) Abbyssinia and its people; or, life in the land of Prester John. London, J.C. Hotten. 1868. vi, 384p. 467

HOUGH, WALTER. The Hoffman Philip Abyssinia ethnological collection. (In U.S. National Museum. proceedings. Washington, 1911. v. 40, pp. 265-267). 468

HUBBARD, WYNANT DAVIS. Fiasco in Ethiopia; the story of a so-called war by a reporter on the grounds. New York, London, Harper & bros. 1936. 391p. 469

LUDOLF, HIOB. (i.e. JOB LUDOLPHUS). A new history of Ethiopia. Being a full and accurate description of the kingdom of Abessinia, vulgarly, though erroneously called the empire of Prester John. In four books . . . made English, by J. P., gent. London, Samuel Smith. 1682. 398p. 470

MACCALLUM, ELIZABETH P.

Rivalries in Ethiopia. Boston, New York, World peace foundation. 3, 5-64p. (World affairs pamphlet no. 12).   471

MACCREAGH, G. The last of free Africa; the account of an expedition into Abyssinia. New York, Century. 1928.   472

MACLEAN, ROBINSON. John Hoy of Ethiopia (HAILE SELASSIE I). New York, Farrar & Rinehart. 1936. 264p.   473

NESBITT, LUDOVICO M. . . .Hell-hole of creation; the exploration of Abyssinian Danakil. New York, A.A. Knopf. 1934. v-x, 3-382p. viii.   474

PARKYNS, MANSFIELD. Life in Abyssinia: being notes collected during three years' residence and travels in that country. 2d ed. London, John Murray. 1868. 446p.   475

POWELL, EDWARD A. Beyond the utmost purple rim; Abyssinia, Somaliland, Kenya Colony, Zanzibar, the Comoros, Madagascar. New York and London, Century co. 1925. xx, 431p.   476

REY, CHARLES F. Unconquered Abyssinia as it is today; an account of a little known country, its peoples and their customs, considered from social, economic and geographic points of view, its resources and possibilities, and its extraordinary history as a hitherto unconquered nation. Philadelphia, J.B. Lippincott co.; London, Seeley, Service & co. 1924. 312p.   477

ROYAL INSTITUTE OF INTER-NATIONAL AFFAIRS. Abyssinia and Italy. New York, Oxford university press. 1935. 48p.   478

SALT, HENRY. A voyage to Abyssinia, and travels into the interior of that country, executed under the orders of the British government, in the years 1809 and 1810; in which are included, an account of the Portuguese settlements on the east coast of Africa, visited in the course of the voyage; a concise narrative of late events in Arabia Felix; and some particulars respecting the aboriginal African tribes, extending from Mosambique to the borders of Egypt; together with vocabularies of their respective languages. London, F.C. & J. Rivington, 1814. xi, 506p.   479

SKINNER, ROBERT P. Abyssinia of today, an account of the first mission sent by the American Government to the court of the King of Kings (1903-04). London, E. Arnold; New York, Longmans, Green & co. 1906. xvi, 227p.   480

STEER, GEORGE. Caesar in Abyssinia. Boston, Little, Brown & co. 1937. 411p.   481

THOMAS, NORMAN M. War; no glory, no profit, no need. New York, Frederick A. Stokes co. 1935. xii, 234p.   482

WORK, ERNEST. Ethiopia, a pawn in European diplomacy. New Concord, O., The auth. 1935. xii, 354p.   483

WYLDE, AUGUSTUS B. Modern Abyssinia. London, Methuen & co. 1900. 506p. (Methuen's colonial library).   484

VII. African independent governments.
2. Liberia.

CRUMMELL, ALEXANDER. The English language in Liberia. An address . . . at Cape Palmas, July 26, 1860. New York, Bunce & co. 1861. 32p.   485

CRUMMELL, ALEXANDER. The future of Africa; being addresses, sermons, etc. delivered in the republic of Liberia. New York, Charles Scribner's sons. 1862. 354p.   486

DE LA RUE, SIDNEY. The land of the pepper bird, Liberia. New York, Putnam's. 1930. 330p.   487

GREENE, GRAHAM. Journey without maps. Garden City, New York, Doubleday, Doran & co. 1936. 3-310p.   488

HARVARD AFRICAN EXPEDITION, 1926-27. . . . The African republic of Liberia and the Belgian Congo. Richard P. Strong, ed. Cambridge, Mass., Harvard university press. 1930. 2v.   489

HUGHSON, SHIRLEY C. The green wall of mystery; venture and adventure in the hinterland of West Africa. New York, Holy Cross press. 1928. 222p.   490

JOHNSON, EDWARD A. A school history of the Negro race in America . . . also a short sketch of Liberia. New York, Isaac Goldman, print. 1911. 400p.   491

JOHNSTON, SIR HARRY H. Geography, resources and inhabitants of Liberia. Washington, Smithsonian Institute. 1905. 17p.
                                                       492

JOHNSTON, SIR HARRY H. Liberia, with an appendix on Liberian flora by Dr. Otto Stapf. New York, Dodd, Mead & co. 1906. 2v.   493

JONES, H. H. Twenty-five years in Liberia and how Africa must be redeemed. Hampton Institute, Virginia. 1927. 15p.   494

KNIGHT, MRS. HELEN. The new republic, written for the Massachusetts Sabbath school society and approved by the committee of publication. Boston, The society. 1850. 252p.   495

LIBERIA. United States representatives to Liberia, 1871-1901, with biographies. (In national cyclopedia of American biography, index vol., p. 69).   496

LIBERIA BULLETINS. Nos. 1-34; November 1892-February 1909. Issued by the American colonization society. Washington, 1892-1909. 34v.   497

LIBERIA COLLEGE. Souvenir program of the seventy-fifth anniversary of the diamond jubilee celebration of Liberia college 1862-1937, held in the auditorium and on the grounds of the college, Monrovia, January 23 and 28, 1938. Monrovia, Scott & sons. 1938. 42p.   498

LUGENBEEL, J. W. Sketches of Liberia: comprising a brief account of the geography, climate, productions and diseases of the Republic of Liberia. Washington, 1850. 43p.   499

MAUGHAM, REGINALD C.F. The Republic of Liberia, being a general description of the Negro republic, with its history, commerce, agriculture, flora, fauna, and present methods of administration. London, George Allen & Unwin. New York, Charles Scribner's sons. 1920.   500

MCALLISTER, AGNES. A lone

woman in Africa; six years on te Kroo coast. New York, Hunt & Eaton; Cincinnati, Cranston & Curts. 1896. 295p.   501

MILLS, LADY DOROTHY R.M. (WALPOLE). Through Liberia. London, Duckworth. 1926. 240p.   502

ROBERTS, J. J. The republic of Liberia; an address delivered . . . Jan. 19, 1869. Washington. 1869. 20p. (In Blyden, E. W. Negro in ancient history. 1869).   503

SILBEY, J. L. Liberia — old and new; a study of its social and economic background with possibilities of development. New York, Doubleday, Doran & co. 1928.   504

STARR, FREDERICK. Liberia: description, history, problems. Chicago, 1913. xiv, 277p.   505

STEWART, T. MCCANTS. Liberia: the Americo-African republic. Being some impressions of the climate, resources, and people, resulting from personal observations and experiences in West Africa. New York, Edward O. Jenkin's sons. 1886. 107p.   506

TRUSTEES OF DONATIONS FOR EDUCATION IN LIBERIA. Annual report . . . 1st, 1851. Boston, T.R. Marvin, 1851. 32p.   507

TURNER, WALTER L. Under the skin in Africa. A complete outline of the history of the republic of Liberia. Monrovia. The auth. 1928. 152p.   508

WILKESON, SAMUEL. A concise history of the commencement, progress and present condition of the American colonies in Liberia. Washington, The Madisonian office. 1839. 88p.   509

WILLIAMS, GEORGE W. History of the Negro race in America . . . and an account of the Negro governments of Sierra Leone and Liberia. Popular ed. New York, London, G.P. Putnam's sons. 1882. 2v.   510

YOUNG, JAMES C. Liberia rediscovered. New York, Doubleday Doran & co., inc. 1934. 212p.   511

VII. African race relations

BARROWS, DAVID P. Berbers and blacks; impressions of Morocco, Timbuktu and the western Sudan. New York and London, Century co. 1927. xvi, 251p.   512

BEER, GEORGE L. African questions at the Paris peace conference with papers on Egypt, Mesopotania and the colonial settlement. New York. Macmillan co. 1923. xliv, 628p. 513

BIGELOW, POULTREY. White man's Africa. New York, London, Harper & bros. 1898. xvi, 271p.   514

BLYDEN, EDWARD W. The African problem and the method of its solution. The annual discourse delivered at the seventy-third anniversary of the American colonization society in Washington, D. C., January 19, 1890. Washington, Gibson bros. 1890. 24p.   515

BRYCE, JAMES. Impressions of South Africa. 3rd ed. rev. . . . with the Transvaal conventions of 1881 and 1884. London, Macmillan & co. 1899. lxiii, 499p.   516

BRYCE, JAMES. The relations of the advanced and the backward races of mankind. Oxford, Clarendon press. 1902. 46p.   517

BUELL, RAYMOND L. The native problem in Africa. New York, Macmillan co. 1928. 2v.   518

CRIPPS, ARTHUR S. An Africa for

Africans: a plea on behalf of territorial segregation areas and of their freedom in a South African colony. London, Longmans, Green & co. 1927. xvi, 203p. 519

CRUMMELL, ALEXANDER. The future of Africa; being addresses, sermons, etc. delivered in the republic of Liberia. Springfield, Mass. auth. 1891. 466p. 2d ed. New York, Charles Scribner's sons. 1862. 372p. 520

DAWSON, WILLIAM H. South Africa: people, places and problems. London and New York, Longmans, Green & co. 1925. xi, 448p. 521

EVANS, MAURICE S. Black and white in South East Africa, a study in sociology. London, Longmans, Green & co. 1911. xviii, 341p. 522

FERRIS, WILLIAM H. The African abroad, or, his evolution in western civilization, tracing his development under Caucasian milieu. New Haven, Tuttle, Morehouse co. 1913. 2v. 523

GREGORY, JOHN W. Menace of colour; a study of the difficulties due to the association of white and coloured races; with an account of measures proposed for their solution, and special reference to white colonization in the tropics. 2d ed. Philadelphia, J.B. Lippincott co. 1925. 264p. 524

HAILEY, WILLIAM M. An African survey a study of problems arising in Africa south of the Sahara. London, New York, Committee of the African research survey, The Royal institute of international affairs, Oxford university press. 1938. xxviii, 1837p. 525

HUNTER, MONICA. Reaction to conquest: effects of contact with Europeans on the Pondo of South Africa. London, Oxford press. 1936. 582p. 526

MAC CRONE, I. D. Race attitudes in South Africa; historical, experimental and psychological studies. London, Oxford university press. 1938. 328p. 527

MILLIN, MRS. SARAH G. The south Africans. New York, Boni and Liveright, 1927. vii, 287p. 528

NIELSON, PETER. The black man's place in South Africa. Cape Town, J.C. Juta & co. 1922. 149p. 529

NIELSON, PETER. The colour bar. Cape Town, J. C. Juta & co. 148p. 530

NORDEN, HERMANN. White and black in East Africa; a record of travel and observation in two African crown colonies. London, H.F. & G. Witherby. 1924. 304p. 531

OLDHAM, JOHN H. Christianity and the race problem. London, Student Christian movement. 1924. xx, 280p. 532

OLDHAM, JOSEPH H. White and black in Africa; a critical examination of the Rhodes lectures of general Smuts. London, New York, Longmans, Green & co. 1930. vi, 73p. 533

OLIVIER, SIR SIDNEY H. The anatomy of African misery. London, Hogarth press. 1927. 234p. 534

OLIVIER, SIR SIDNEY H. White capital and coloured labour. London, Independent labour party. 1906. 175p. (Socialist library, no. 4). 535

PHILLIPS, RAY E. The Bantu are coming, phases of South Africa's race problem. New York, Richard R. Smith. 1930. 238p. 536

PICKSTONE, H. E. V. A reply to Lord Selborne's questions, showing the urgent need of a national native constructive policy, and ideas on which it might be based. Cape Town. Cape Times. 1909. 23p. 537

READ, HOLLIS. The Negro problem solved; or, Africa as she was, as she is, and as she shall be. New York, auth. 1864. 418p. 538

SINGER, CAROLINE, AND BALDRIDGE, CYRUS LEROY. White Africans and black. New York, W.W. Norton & co. 1929. 120p. 539

SMITH, EDWIN W. The golden stool; some aspects of the conflict of cultures in modern Africa. New York, Doubleday, Doran & co. 1928. 328p. 540

THURNWOLD, RICHARD C. Black and white in East Africa; the fabric of a new civilization. London, Routledge. 1935. 419p. 541

TILLINGHAST, JOSEPH A. The Negro in Africa and America. New York, Macmillan co. 1902. vi, 231p. 542

UNION OF SOUTH AFRICA. Report of the commission appointed to enquire into assults on women. Cape Town, Cape Times. 1913. 41p. 543

WILLOUGHBY, WILLIAM C. Race problems in the new Africa. A study of the relation of Bantu Africa which are under British control. Oxford, Clarendon press. 1923. 296p. 544

ZIERVOGEL, C. Brown South Africa. Cape Town, Maskew Miller. n.d. 96p. 545

IX. European nations and African colonization.

BARKER, J. ELLIS. German designs in Africa. (Reprinted from the "19th century and after," Aug., 1911. pp. 201-214). New York, L. Scott publishing co. 1911. 546

BARNS, THOMAS A. An African Eldorado, the Belgium Congo. London, Methuen & co. 1926. xv, 229p. 547

BARTHOLOMEW, J. G. A literary and historical atlas of Africa and Australia, etc. A gazetteer of towns and places in Africa and Australia. London, J.M. Dent & sons. 1913. xi, 218p. 548

BEAVER, CAPTAIN PHILIP. African memoranda: relative to an attempt to establish a British settlement on the island of Bulama on the western coast of Africa in 1792 with a brief notice of the neighboring tribes, soil, productions, etc. and some observations on the facility of colonizing that part of Africa, with a view to cultivation and the introduction of letters and religion to its inhabitants, but more particularly as the means of gradually abolishing African slavery. London, C.&R. Baldwin. 1805. 500p. 549

BEER, GEORGE L. African questions at the Paris peace conference . . . New York, The Macmillan co. 1923. xliv, 628p. 550

BELGIUM COMMISSION OF ENQUIRY. The Congo: a report of the commission of enquiry appointed by the Congo free state government. New York, London, G.P. Putnam's sons. 1906. 171, (72)p. 551

BIGELOW, POULTREY. White man's Africa; New York, London, Harper & bros. 1900. 271p. 552

BLAKE, JOHN W. European beginnings in West Africa,

1454-1578. A survey of the first century of white enterprise in West Africa, with special emphasis upon the rivalry of the great powers. London, New York, The Royal Empire Society. 1937. viii, 212p.
553

BRYCE, JAMES. Impressions of South Africa. New York, The Century co. 1897. 499p.
554

CARDINALL, A. W. In Ashanti and beyond, the record of a resident magistrate's many years in tropical Africa . . . Philadelphia, J.B. Lippincott co. 1927. 288p.
555

COLVIN, IAN D. Romance of Empire, South Africa. London, T.C. and E.J. Jack. n.d. xii, 328p.
556

THE CONGO: A report of the Belgium commission of enquiry appointed by the Congo Free State government. New York and London, G.P. Putnam's sons. 1906. 171p.
557

COUPLAND, REGINALD. East Africa and its invaders from early times to the death of Seyyid Said in 1856. Oxford, Caarendon press. 1938. vi, 2, 584p.
558

DAVIS, RICHARD H. With both armies in South Africa. New York, Charles Scribner's sons. 1900. 237p.
559

DE WET, CHRISTIAAN R. Three years' war New York, Charles Scribner's sons. 1903. 448p.
560

DILKE, CHARLES W. Greater Britain. A record of travel in English-speaking countries during 1866-7. Philadelphia, J.P. Lippincott & co. 1869. 2v.
561

DOYLE, ARTHUR C. The crime of the Congo. New York, Doubleday, Page & co. 1909. 128p.
562

DOYLE, A. CONAN. The war in South Africa, its course and conduct. New

York, McClure, Phillips & co. 1902. 140p.
563

DRAKE-BROCKMAN, RALPH E. British Somaliland. London, Hurst and Blackett, 1912. 334p.
564

DRIBERG, JACK H. Map of Luga district eastern province of Uganda. (In "The Lango, a Nilotic tribe. 1923. p. 354 fold.").
565

FITZPATRICK, J. P. The Transvaal from within. 9th impr. London, William Heinemann. 1900. 364p.
566

FRANK, LOUIS. Recent developments in the Belgium Congo. London, F.J. Parsons. 1924. 16p. (Reprinted from the Journ. of the Royal Soc. of Arts.)
567

FROUDE, JAMES A. Oceana, or England and her colonies. New ed. London, Longmans, Green & co. 1886. 341p.
568

FULLER, ROBERT H. South Africa at home. London, Geo. Newns. n.d. 236p.
569

GIBBONS, HERBERT A. The new map of Africa (1900-1916); a history of European colonial expansion and colonial diplomacy. New York, The Century co. 1916. xiv, 503p.
570

GODDARD, THOMAS N. The handbook of Sierre Leone. London, G. Richards. 1925. xvi, 335p.
571

GREEN, JAMES. Causes of the War in South Africa. 2d ed. Worcester, Mass., The auth. 1900. 28p.
572

GUGGISBERG, SIR FREDERICK G. The Gold Coast. A review of events of 1920-1926 and the prospects of 1927-1928. Accra. Govt. print. works. 1926. 347p.
573

HAGGARD, H. RIDER. A history of the Transvaal. New York. New Amsterdam book co. 1900. xxv, 244p.
574

HARRIS, NORMAN D. Europe and

Africa, being a revised edition of Intervention and Colonization in Africa. Boston, New York, Houghton, Mifflin co. 1927. xviii, 479p. 575

HARRIS, LAWRENCE. With Mulai Hafid at Foz, behind the scenes in Morocco. Boston, Richard Badger. 1910. 270p. 576

HERTSLET, SIR EDWARD. The map of Africa by treaty. v. 1. Abyssinia to Great Britain., nos. 1 to 102. Colonies, maps. London, Harrison & sons. 1894. 2v. 577

JARDINE, DOUGLAS. The mad mullah of Somaliland. London, Herbert Jenkins. 1923. x, 336p. 578

JOHNSON, KATHRYN M. Stealing a nation; a brief story of how Swaziland, a South African kingdom, came under British rule — without consent of the people. Chicago, Pyramid publ. co. 1939. 50p. 579

JOHNSTON, SIR HARRY H. The opening up of Africa. New York, Henry Holt & co. 1911. viii. 255p. (Home university library, no. 18) 580

JOHNSTON, SIR HARRY H. The Uganda protectorate; an attempt to give some description of the physical geography, botany, zoology. anthropology, languages and history of the territories under British protection in east central Africa . . . 2d ed. New York, Dodd, Mead & co. 1904. 2v. 581

KELTIE, JOHN S. The partition of Africa. 2d ed. London. E. Stanford. 1895. xv, 564p. 582

LARRYMORE, MRS. CONSTANCE (BELCHER). A resident's wife in Nigeria. 2d ed. rev. London, G. Routledge & sons; New York, E.P. Dutton & co. 1911. 299p. 583

LATIMER, MRS. ELIZABETH (WORMELEY). Europe in Africa in the nineteenth centry. Chicago, A.C. McClurg & co. 1895. 451p. 584

LUGARD, SIR FREDERICK J. D. The dual mandate in British tropical Africa. 3d ed. Edinburgh, London, William Blackwood & sons. 1926. 643p. 585

MACKENZIE, W. DOUGLASS. South Africa, its history, heroes and wars. Chicago. Thompson & Hood. 1899. 663p. 586

MARTIN R. MONTGOMERY. The British colonial library comprising a popular and authentic description of all the colonies of the British Empire. v. x, British possessions in the Indian Ocean. London, Henry G. Bohn. 1844. 358p. 587

MEARS, JOHN WILLIAM. The story of Madagascar. Philadelphia. Presbyterian board of publication. 1873. 313p. 588

MICHELL, SIR LEWIS. The life of the Rt. Hon. Cecil Jon Rhodes, 1853-1902. London, E. Arnold. 1910. 2v. 589

MIDDLETON, LAMAR. The rape of Africa. New York, H. Smith & R. Haas. 1936. 331p. 590

MOFFAT, J. S. The black man and the war. (Vigilance papers, no. 8). Cape Town, South African vigilance committee. 1900. 11p. 591

MOREL, EDMUND D. The Congo slave state. a protest against the new African slavery; and an appeal to the public of Great Britain, of the United States, and of the continent of Europe. Liverpool, J. Richardson & sons. 1903. 112p. 592

MOREL, EDMUND D. King Leopold's rule in Africa. New York. Funk & Wagnalls. 1905. 466p. 593

MOREL, EDMUND D. The treatment of women and children in the

Congo state, 1895-1904. An appeal to the women of the British Empire, and of the United States of America. Liverpool, J. Richardson & sons. 1904. 46p.   594

POWELL, EDWARD A. The last frontier; the white man's war for civilization in Africa. New York, C. Scribner's sons. 1912. xv, 291p.595

QUARTERLY REVIEW. No. 386, April, 1901. London, John Murray. The settlement of South Africa. pp. 544-583.   596

RIDPATH, JOHN C. AND EDWARD S. ELLIS. The story of South Africa, an account of the historical transformation of the dark continent by the European powers . . Cincinnati, Jones bros. publ. co. 1899. 640p.   597

RUDIN, HARRY R. Germans in the Cameroons, 1884-1914. A case study in modern imperialism. New Haven, Yale university press. 1938. 456p.   598

SCHAPERA, ISAAC (ed.). Western civilization and the natives of South Africa; studies in culture contact. London, George Routledge & sons. 1934. 312p.   599

SIERRA LEONE. COMPANY. Substance of the report delivered by the court of directors of the Sierra Leone company to the general court of proprietors, on March 27, 1794. London, J. Phillips. 1795. 175p.   600

SLATER, SIR RANSFORD. Address . . . the opening of the 1928-29 session of the legislative council of the gold coast. Accra, Gov. print. office. 1928. 107p.   601

SLOANE, W. M. Greater France in Africa. 1924. xvi, 293p.   602

SMUTS, JAN C. Africa and some world problems, including the Rhodes memorial lectures . . .

Oxford, The Clarendon press. 1930. 5, 3-184p.   603

SNOW, ALPHEUS H. The question of aborigines in the law and practice of nations. Including a collection, authorities and documents. Washington, Gov. print. office. 1921.   604

SOCIETE BELGE D'ETUDES COLONIALES (de la). Vingtieme annee; nos. 9-10, Sept., Oct. 1913. Bruxelles, Hayez. 1913. pp. 667-775.   605

SOLANKE, LADIPO. United West Africa (or Africa) at the bar of the family of nations. London, West African students' union of great Britain and Ireland. 1927. 68p. 606

SOUTH AFRICAN NATIVE AFFAIRS COMMISSION. Report . . . with annexures, nos. 1-9. 1903-1905. Cape Town, Cape Times, 1905. 98-(29)p.   607

SOUTH AFRICAN NATIVE AFFAIRS COMMISSION. Report . . . 1912. Cape Town, Cape Times. 1913. 116p.   608

STANLEY, SIR HENRY M. The Congo and the founding of its free state: a story of work and exploration. New York, Harper & bros. 1885. 2v.   609

STARR, FREDERICK. The truth about the Congo; the Chicago Tribune articles. Chicago, Forbes & co. 1907. viii, 129p.   610

STEEVENS, G. W. With Kitchener to Khartum. New York, Dodd; Mead & co. 1900. 326p.   611

TRANSVAAL INDIGENCY COMMISSION. Report . . . 1906-08. Prentoria. Gov. print. office. 1908. 230p.   612

THORNHILL, J. B. Adventures in Africa, under the British, Belgian and Portuguese flags. New York, Dutton. 1915. 9, 330p.   613

34

TWAIN, MARK. King Leopold's soliloquy. A defense of his Congo rule. Boston, P. R. Warren co. 1905. 40p. 614

VEDDER, HEINRICH. South West Africa in early times, being the story of South West Africa up to the date of Maharero's death in 1890. (Transl. from the German by Cyril G. Hall) London, Humphrey Milford, 1938. 525p. 615

WACK, HENRY W. The story of the Congo free state: social, political, and economic aspects of the Belgium system of government in Central Africa. New York, London, G.P. Putnam's sons. 1905. 634p. 616

WORSFOLD, W. BASIL. A history of South Africa. London, J.M. Dent & co. 1900. 199p. 617

WORSFOLD, W. BASIL. The redemption of Egypt. London, George Allen. 1899. 333p. 618

WORSFOLD, W. BASIL. South Africa, a study in colonial administration and development . . . London, Methuen & co. 1895. xii, 256p. 619

WORSFOLD, W. BASIL. The union of South Africa, with chapters on Rhodesia and the native territories of the high commission. Boston, Little, Brown & co. 1913. ix, 529p. 620

ZACHARIAH, O. Travel in South Africa. Johannesburg, South African railways & harbours. 1927. 331p. 3rd ed. 621

ZIMMERMANN, EMIL. The German empire of Central Africa as the basis of a new German world-policy. Transl. from the German by Edwyn Bevan. New York, George H. Doran. 1918. xlii, 63p. 622

X. Native African labor (including modern slavery).

ANTI-IMPERIALIST. Slavery and polygamy reestablished . . . by authority of William McKinley . . . in his effort to deprive the people of the Philippine Islands of their liberty. V. I, no. 5; September 15, 1899. Brookline, Mass., Edward Atkinson. 1899. 16p. 623

ANTI-SLAVERY AND ABORIGINES PROTECTION SOCIETY. Annual report . . . London, The Society. Collection has: 1910; 1911. 624

ANTI-SLAVERY AND ABORIGINES PROTECTION SOCIETY. The anti-slavery reporter and Aborigines' friend . . . London, Anti-slavery and Aborigines protection society. 1910. Collection has: series V, v. 1-27 (1911-1937). 625

BAKER, SIR SAMUEL W. Ismailia: a narrative of the expedition to Central Africa for the suppression of the slave trade, organized by Ismail, khedive of Egypt. New York, Harper & bros. 1875. 542p. 626

BERLIOUX, ETIENNE F. The slave trade in Africa in 1872. Principally carried on for the supply of Turkey, Egypt, Persia, and Zanzibar. Transl. from the French by Joseph Cooper. London, Edward Marsh. 1872. 64p. 627

BRITISH AND FOREIGN ANTI-SLAVERY SOCIETY. Annual report . . . 1901, 1905, 1907. London, The society. 1902. 1906. 1908. 628

35

BRITISH AND FOREIGN ANTI-SLAVERY SOCIETY. Anti-slavery reporter . . . London, British and foreign anti-slavery society. 1841. Collection has: series 4, v. 19-30. (1899-1909). 629

BRITISH AND FOREIGN ANTI-SLAVERY SOCIETY. Scandals at Cairo in connection with slavery. Cairo. The society. 1885. 12p. 630

CAMERON, VERNEY L. Across Africa. New York, Harper bros. 1877. 508p. 631

CHATELAIN, HELI. Africa's internal slave-trade and practical plan for its extinction. New York, Philafrican liberators league. 1896. 16p. 632

COOPER, JOSEPH. The lost continent; or, slavery and the slave-trade in Africa, 1875. With observations on the Asiatic slave-trade, carried on under the name of the labour traffic and some other subjects. London, Longmans, Green & co. 1875. 130p. 633

DARLEY, HENRY A. Slaves and irony: a record of adventure and exploration in the unknown Sudan, and among the Abyssinian slave-raiders. London, H. F. & G. Witherby. 1926. xvii, 219p. 634

DAVIS, J. MERLE (ed.). Modern industry and the African; an enquiry into the effect of the copper mines of Central Africa upon native society and the work of Christian missions . . . Dept. of social and industrial research, International missionary council. London. Macmillan & co. 1933. xviii, 425p. 635

HARRIS, JOHN H. Africa: slave or free? New York, E.P. Dutton & co. 1920. xxi, 261p. 636

HARRIS, JOHN H. Dawn in darkest Africa. New York, E.P. Dutton & co. 1912. xxxvi, 308p. 637

HARRIS, JOHN H. Domestic slavery in Southern Nigeria, being a report to the committee of the anti-slavery and Aborigines protection society . . . London, The society. 1911. 16p. 638

HARRIS, JOHN H. Present conditions in the Congo; being the report of the anti-slavery and Aborigines protection society. Section VI. London, Denison house. 1911. 10p. 639

HARRIS, JOHN H. Portuguese slavery: Britain's dilemma. London, Methuen & co. 1913. 127p. 640

LADD, DURANT F. Trade and shipping in West Africa . . . a report for the U.S. Shipping Board. Washington, Gov. print. office. 1920. 641

LAUIGERIE, CARDINAL. Slavery in Africa. A speech made in London, July 31, 1888. Boston, Cashman, Keating & Co. 1888. 20p. 642

LEAGUE OF NATIONS. Permanent mandates commission. Memorandum by Mr. Grineshaw on slavery and labour (in annexes to the minutes of the third session, 1923). pp. 262-75. 643

MACNAMARA, T. J. La main-d'oeuvre aux colonies: documents officials sur le contrat de travail et le louage d'ouvrage aux colonies. Paris, Institut colonial international. 1896-98. 3v. 644

MOORE, ERNST D. Ivory, scourge of Africa. New York, London, Harper & bros. 1931. xviii, 256p. 645

MOREL, EDMUND D. The Congo slave state. A protest against the new African slavery; and an appeal to the public of Great Britain, of the United States, and of the continent of Europe. Liverpool, J. Richardson & sons. 1903. 112p. 646

MOREL, EDMUND D. Red rubber; the story of the rubber slave-trade flourishing on the Congo in the year of grace, 1906. New York, Nassau print. 1906. 213p.   647

MOREL, EDMUND D. The treatment of women and children in the Congo state, 1895-1904. An appeal to the women of the United States of America, with comments by Robert E. Park. Boston, Congo reform assn. 1904. 30p.   648

NEVINSON, HENRY W. A modern slavery. London, New York, Harper & bros. 1906. 215p.   649

NOBLE, FREDERIC P. The African slave-trade of 1890. p. 81-104 (Our day: a record and review of current reform. v. VII, no. 38. Feb. 1891.).   650

OLIVER, LORD. The anatomy of African misery. London, Leonard & Virginia Woolf. 1927. 233p.   651

OLIVIER, SIR SIDNEY H. White capital and coloured labor. London, Independent labour party. 1900. vi, 175p.   652

PORTUGUESE DELEGATION TO THE VI ASSEMBLY OF THE LEAGUE OF NATIONS. Some observations on professor Ross's report. Submitted for the information of the temporary slavery commission of the league of nations. Geneva, Imprimerie du journal. 1925. 40p.   653

ROSS, EDWARD A. Report on employment of native labor in Portuguese Africa. New York, Abbott press. 1925. 61p.   654

STANLEY, SIR HENRY M. Slavery and the slave trade in Africa. New York, Harper & bros. 1893. 86p.   655

SWANN, ALFRED J. Fighting the slave-hunters in Central Africa. A record of twenty-six years of travel and adventure . . . Philadelphia, J.B. Lippincott co. 1910. xxvi, 359p.   656

UNITED STATES SENATE. 58th Congress, 2d session. Document no. 282. Memorial concerning conditions in the independent state of the Kongo. April 19, 1904. Washington, Gov. print. Office. 1904. 136p.   657·

XI. Progress in education, health, and schools in Africa.

BESOLOW, THOMAS E. From the darkness of Africa to the light of America, the story of an African prince. Boston, F. Wood. 1891. ix, 160p.   658

BLYDEN, EDWARD W. Philip and the eunuch; or, the instruments and methods of Africa's evengelization. A discourse. Cambridge, Mass., John Wilson & son. 1883. 30p. 659

BOWEN, T. J. Central Africa, adventures and missionary labors in several countries in the interior of Africa, from 1849 to 1856. Charleston, Southern Baptist publ. society. 1857. xii, 359p.   660

BUCHANAN, REV. CLAUDIUS. The star in the east. A sermon . . . preached . . . for the benefit of the society for missions to Africa and the east. February 26, 1809. Republ. for the Connecticut bible society. Hartford, By the society. 1809. 24p.   661

CAMPBELL, JOHN. Travels in South Africa: undertaken at the request of the missionary society, Andover, Flagg & Gould, 1816. xv, 398p. 662

CLAVER, PETER. Peter Claver: a sketch of his life and labors in behalf of the African slave. Boston, Lee & Shepard. 1868. 117p.   663

CRAWFORD, DANIEL. Thinking black; 22 years without a break in the long grass of Central Africa. London, Morgan & Scott. 1912. xvi, 485p.   664

CROWTHER, SAMUEL A. Journals of the Rev. James Frederick Schon and Mr. Samuel Crowther, who . . . accompanied the expedition up the Niger, in 1841, in behalf of the church missionary society. London, Hatchard & son. 1842. 393p.   665

CUMMINS, GEORGE D. Life of Mrs. Virginia Hale Hoffman late of the Protestant Episcopal mission to Western Africa. 2d ed. Philadelphia, Lindsay & Blakiston. 1859. 256p.   666

DALY, J. FAIRLEY. Livingstonia (missions of the United Free Church of Scotland). Edinburgh, Morrison & Gibb. 1903. 95p.   667

DRAPER, CHARLOTTE. A free-will offering for the benefit of Africa. The Island of Corsica, in Western Africa, January 25, 1860 . . . Baltimore, The Presbyterian female of color's enterprising society. 96p. n.d.   668

EDDY, A. D. The wife of Jacob Hodges, an African Negro. Philadelphia, Sunday-school union. 1842. 94p.   669

FOX, GEORGE T. (Rev.) A memoir of the Rev. C. Colden Hoffman, missionary to Cape Palmas, West Africa. London, Seeley, Jackson & Halliday. 1868. 365p.   670

FRASER, DONALD. African idylls; portraits and impressions of life on a Central African mission station. London, Seeley, Service & co. 1923. 229p.   671

FRASER, DONALD. The new Africa. London, Church missionary society, 1927. 202p.   672

FRASER, DONALD. The future of Africa. Edinburgh, Foreign mission committee. Church of Scotland. 1922. 175p.   673

FREEMAN, FREDERICK. Africa's redemp. — the salvation of our country. New York, The auth. 1852. 383p.   674

GALTON, FRANCIS. Memories of my life. New York, The auth. 1909. 339p.   675

GEORGES, NORBERT. The life of blessed Martin De Porres, saintly American Negro. (adapted from the French) New York, The Torch. 1936. 63p.   676

GRIFFIN, EDWARD D. A plea for Africa; a sermon preached October 26, 1817, in the city of New York, before the synod of New York and New Jersey. New York, Gould. 1817. 76p.   677

GROUT, REV. LEWIS. Zulu-land or, life among the Zulu-kafirs of Natal and Zulu-land, South Africa. Philadelphia, Presbyterian publ. comm. 1864. 351p.   678

HANCE, GERTRUDE R. The Zulu yesterday and today; twenty-nine years in South Africa. New York, Chicago, Fleming H. Revell & co. 1916. 274p.   679

HARTFORD-BATTERSBY, CHARLES F. Pilkington of Uganda. New York, Fleming H. Revell co. 1899. 321p.   680

HARRIS, JOHN H. Dawn in darkest Africa. New York, E. P. Dutton & co. 1912. 308p.   681

HARRISON, MRS. ALEXINA M. The story of the life of Mackay. New York, A.C. Armstrong & son. 1900. 323p.   682

HARRISON, MRS. ALEXINA M. A.M. MacKay, pioneer missionary of the church missionary society to

38

Uganda. New York, A.C. Armstrong & son. 1890. 488p. 683

HEARD, WILLIAM H. The bright side of African life. Philadelphia, A.M.E. publ. house. 1898. 184p. 684

HERBERT, LADY. The life of blessed Martin De Porres, a Negro saint. (Transl. from the Italian). New York, Catholic publ. society. 1889. 110p. 685

HOLMES, JOHN. Historical sketches of the missions of the united brethern . . . among the heathen . . . Dublin, R. Napper. 1818. 551p. 686

HORNE, REV. MELVILLE. Sermon . . . before the society for missions to Africa and the east St. Andrew by the wardrobe and St. Anne, Blackfriars. June 4, 1811. London, 1811. Boston, reprinted by Samuel T. Armstrong. 1811. 28p. 687

IRELAND, WILLIAM. Historical sketch of the Zulu mission in South Africa . . . as also of the Gaboon mission in Western Africa. Boston, American board of commissioners for foreign missions. 32p. 688

HOUGHTON, LOUISE S. David Livingstone: one who followed Christ. Philadelphia, Presbyterian board of publ. 1882. 332p. 689

JACK, JAMES W. Daybreak in Livingstonia; the story of the Livingstonia mission, British Central Africa. New York, Chicago, Fleming H. Revell & co. 1900. 371p. 690

JAPP, ALEXANDER H. Master missionaries, chapters in pioneer effort throughout the world. New York, Robert Carter & bros. 1881. 398p. 691

KRAPF, J. LEWIS i.e. JOHAN LUDWIG. Travels, researches, and missionary labours, during an eighteen years' residence in Eastern Africa; together with journeys to Jagga, Usambara, Ukambani, Shoa, Abessinia and Khartum; and a coasting voyage from Mombaz to Cape Delgado. London, Trubner & co. 1860. 566p. 692

KNOSPLER, MARIE C. Our African diamond. The life and undertakings of Paul Nyecka Revere. Watsontown, Pa., George M. Zettlemoyer, printer. 1926. 15p. 693

LATROBE, CHRISTIAN I. Journal of a visit to South Africa, in 1815 and 1816. With some account of the missionary settlements of the united brethren near the Cape of Good Hope. London, L. B. Seeley. 1818. vii, 406p. 694

LAMBERT, J. C. The romance of missionary heroism. London, Seeley & co. 1908. 695

LIVINGSTONE, DAVID. Missionary travels and researches in South Africa; including a sketch of sixteen years' residence in the interior of Africa, and a journey from the Cape of Good Hope to Loanda, on the west coast; thence across the continent, down the river Zambesi, to the eastern ocean. New York, Harper bros. 1858. 732p. (Under title: Missionary travels and researches in South Africa, etc.). Philadelphia, J. W. Bradley. 1859. xiv, 440p. 696

LONDON MISSIONARY SOCIETY. Scenes and services in South Africa. The story of Robert Moffat's half-century of missionary labours. London, John Snow & co. 1876. 255p. 697

MACKENZIE, JOHN. Day-dawn in dark places: a story of wanderings and work in Bechwana land. London, Paris, New York. Cassell & co. 1883. 278p. 698

MACKENZIE, JEAN K. African adventures. West Medford, Mass., The central committee on the united study of foreign missions. 1917. 119p. 699

MACKENZIE, JEAN K. An African trail. West Medford, Mass., Central committee on united study of foreign missions. 1917. 222p. 700

MILUM, REV. JOHN. Thomas Birch Freeman, missionary pioneer to Ashanti, Dahomey and Egba. New York, Fleming A. Revell co. n.d. 160p. 701

MISSIONARY MUSEUM; or, an account of missionary enterprises in conversations between a mother and her children. First series. India and America. New Haven. Jeramy L. Cross. 1831. 2v. 702

MOFFATT, ROBERT. Rivers of water in a dry place; an account of the introduction of Christianity into South Africa and of . . . missionary labours. London, Religious tract society. n.d. 252p. 703

MYERS, JOHN B. The Congo for Christ. The story of the Congo mission. 2d ed. New York, Fleming H. Revell & co. 1895. 163p. 704

NASSAU, ROBERT H. Crowned in palmland. A story of African mission life. Philadelphia, J. P. Lippincott & co. 1874. 390p. 705

NAYLOR, WILSON S. Daybreak in the dark continent. rev. ed. New York, Missionary education movement. 1912. xiv, 313p. 706

NOBLE, FREDERIC P. The redemption of Africa; a story of civilization. Chicago, New York, Fleming H. Revell & co. 1899. 2v. 707

PAGE, JESSE. Bishop Patterson, the martyr of Melanesia. New York, Fleming H. Revell co. n.d. 160p. 708

PAGE, JESSE. Samuel Crowther. The slave boy who became bishop of the Niger. London, S.W. Partridge & co. 1888. 709

PARSONS, ELLEN C. Christian liberator, an outline study of Africa. London, New York, Macmillan co. 1905. viii, 309p. 710

PARSONS, ELLEN C. A life for Africa: Rev. Adolphus Clemens Good, American missionary in equatorial West Africa. New York, Fleming H. Revell co. 1900. 316p. 711

PHILIP, REV. JOHN. Researches in South Africa; illustrating civil, moral and religious condition of native tribes: including journals of the author's travels in the interior; together with detailed accounts of the progress of the Christian missions, exhibiting the influence of Christianity in promoting civilization. London, James Duncan, 1828. 2v. 712

PITMAN, EMMA R. Central Africa, Japan, and Fiji: a story of missionary enterprise, trials and triumphs. New York, American tract society. n.d. 296p. 713

READE, T. C. Sketch of the life of Samuel Morris (Prince Kaboo). Upland, Ind., Taylor University. n.d. 19p. 714

REVERE, PAUL NYECKA. The story of my life, an autobiography. Krutown, Liberia. n.d. 19p. 715

ROBSON, WILLIAM. James Chalmers, missionary and explorer of Rarotonga and New Guinea. Chicago, Fleming H. Revell co. n.d. 176p. 716

ROWLEY, HENRY. The story of the universities' mission to Central Africa, from its commencement under Bishop Mackenzie, to its withdrawal from the Zambesi.

London, Saunders, Otley & co. 1866. xii, 493p.   717

SCOTT, MRS. ANNA M. Day dawn in Africa; or, progress of the Protestant Episcopal mission at Cape Palmas, West Africa. New York, Protestant society for . . . evangelical knowledge. 1858. 314p.   718

SHEPPARD, WILLIAM H. Pioneers in Congo. Louisville, Ky. Pentecostal publ. co. n.d. 157p.   719

SMITH, EDWIN W. Aggroy of Africa, a study in black and white. New York, Doubleday, Doran & co. 1929. 292p.   720

SMITH, EDWIN E. The secret of the African. London, Student Christian movement press. 1929. 142p.   721

STEWART, JAMES. Dawn in the dark continent; or, Africa and its missions. (The Duff Missionary Lectures for 1902) Edinburg and London: Oliphant, Anderson & Ferrier. 1903. 400p.   722

STUBBEFIELD, SAMUEL B. (Bah Guey, pseud.) Out of Africa . . . story of my youth . . . of conditions there, and of my coming to the United States . . . Hampton Institute, Va. The auth. 1931. 29p.   723

TAYLOR, WILLIAM. The flaming torch in darkest Africa. Introduction by Henry M. Stanley. New York, Eaton & Mains. 1898. 675p.   724

TRACY, JOSEPH. History of the American board of commissioners for foreign missions. 2d ed. rev. enl. New York, M.W. Dodd. 1842. 452p.   725

TUCKER, CHARLOTTE. Abbeokuta; or, sunrise within the tropics: an outline of the origin and progress of the Yoruba mission. 3d ed. London, J. Nisbet & co. 1853. vi, 278p.   726

TYLER, REV. JOSIAH. Forty years among the Zulus. Boston, Congregational Sunday-school & publ. society. 1891. 300p.   727

VERNER, SAMUEL P. Pioneering in Central Africa. Richmond, Va. Presbyterian committee of publications. 1903. ix. 500p.   728

WALKER, F. DEAUVILLE. Thomas Birch Freeman, the son of an African. London, Student Christian movement. 221p.   729

WALLER, HORACE. The last journals of David Livingstone in Central Africa . . . a narrative of his last moments and sufferings. New York, Harper & bros. 1872. 541p.   730

WHITON, SAMUEL J. Glimpses of West Africa, with sketches of missionary labor. Boston, American tract society. 1866. 208p.   731

WILKINSON, JAMES J. G. The African and the true Christian religion, his magna charta. London, J. Speirs. 1892. x, 245p.   732

XII. African missions and missionaries.

AFRICAN EDUCATION COMMISSION. Education in Africa. A study of West, South, and equatorial Africa by the African education commission, under the auspices of the Phelps-Stokes fund and foreign mission societies of North America and Europe. Report prepared by Thomas Jesse Jones. New York, Phelps-Stokes fund. 1922. 323p.   733

AFRICAN EDUCATION COMMISSION. Education in East Africa; a study of East, Central and

41

South Africa by the second African education commission under the auspices of the Phelps-Stokes fund, in cooperation with the International education board. Report prepared by Thomas Jesse Jones. New York, Phelps-Stokes fund. London, Edinburgh house press, 1925. 416p.   734

BULL, OSWIN B. Training Africans for trades; a report on a visit to the United States of America and Canada under the auspices of the Carnegie corporation visitors' grants committee. 1935. 75p.   735

CAPE OF GOOD HOPE DEPARTMENT OF PUBLIC EDUCATION. Report of the superintendent-general of education. 1909-1911. Cape Town, Cape Times. 1910-1913.   736

CLOUGH, ETHLYN T. (ed.) Africa: an account of past and contemporary conditions and progress. Detroit, Bayview reading club. 1911. 237p.   737

COLQUHOUN, MRS. ETHEL M. (COOKSON). The real Rhodesia. London, Hutchinson & co. 1924. xvi. 311p.   738

HUSS, BERNARD. People's banks or use and value of cooperative credit for African natives. (Reprinted from ''Umteteli'') Mariannhill, Natal. 1928. 124p.   739

GRIFFIN, EDWARD D. A plea for Africa; a sermon preached October 26, 1817, in the First Presbyterian Church in the city of New York, before the synod of New York and New Jersey . . . at the African school established by the synod. New York, Gould. 1817. 76p.   740

LORAM, C. T. An address . . . before the Phelps-Stokes fund, in New York, October 25, 1926, on the needs of Africa. New York. 1926. 14p.   741

LORAM, C. T. The education of the South African native. London, New York, Longmans, Green & co. 1917. xx, 340p.   742

MEAD, MARGARET. Growing up in New Guinea; a comparative study of primitive education. New York, William Morrow & co. 1930. x, 372p.   743

MORRILL, MADGE H. Fighting Africa's black magic. The fight of E. G. Marcus, M.D. against disease and superstition in East Africa. Mountain View, California, Pacific press publ. assn. 1938. 155p.   744

PARKE, THOMAS H. My personal experiences in equatorial Africa as a medical officer of the Emin Pasha relief expedition. New York, Charles Scribner. 1891. 526p.   745

SINGH, SAINT N. Messages of uplift for India; being essays, descriptive, educational and critical. Boston, the Arena, Madras, Gauesh & co. n.d. 328p.   746

SOUTH AFRICAN NATIVE RACES COMMITTEE. The South African natives; their progress and present condition . . . a supplement to "The natives of South Africa; their economic and social condition." New York, E.P. Dutton & co. 1909. xii, 247p.   747.

STOKES, REV. ANSON P. Report . . . on education, native welfare, and race relations in East and South Africa. New York, Board of Trustees of the Carnegie corporation of New York. 1934. African report series, 7. 59p.   748

WESTERMANN, DIEDRICH. The African today. London, The International Institute of African languages and cultures by the Oxford university press. 1934. xv, 343p.   749

AMERICAN BOARD OF FOREIGN MISSIONS. The missionary herald . . . v. xxi, no. 1. January 1825. 398p.   750

BOWEN, J. W. E. (ed.) Addresses and proceedings of the congress on Africa, held under the auspices of the Stewart Missionary Foundation for Africa of Gammon Theological Seminary in connection with the cotton states and international exposition. Atlanta, The seminary. 1896. 242p.   751

CONGO PROTESTANT COUNCIL. Congo mission news . . . Leopoldville, Congo Belge, Afrique. 1912. Quarterly. Collection has: nos. 101-108 (Jan. 1938-Oct. 1939).   752

DIFFENDORFER, R. E. (ed.) The world service of the Methodist Episcopal Church. Chicago, M. E. Church, council of boards of benevolence, committee on conservation and advance. 1923. 704p.   753

FOREIGN MISSIONS CONFERENCE OF NORTH AMERICA. The Christian occupation of Africa: the proceedings of a conference of mission boards engaged in work in the continent of Africa, held in New York city, November 20, 21, and 22, 1917, together with the findings of the conference. Issued by the Committee of Conference. 1917. 185p.   754

HAND BOOKS ON THE MISSIONS OF THE EPISCOPAL CHURCH. No. iv, Liberia. New York, National council of Protestant episcopal churches. 1924. 127p.   755

INTERNATIONAL AFRICAN SERVICE BUREAU. International African opinion. London, International African service bureau. v. 1, no. 1. (July, 1938).   756

INTERNATIONAL INSTITUTE OF AFRICAN LANGUAGES AND CULTURES. Africa . . . London, International Institute of African languages and cultures. 1928, quarterly. Collection has: v. 11-13 (1938-1940).   757

THE INTERNATIONAL REVIEW OF MISSIONS. v. xiv, no. 56. Oct., 1925. International missionary bibliography. London, International review of missions. 1925. 158p.   758

THE INTERNATIONAL REVIEW OF MISSIONS. v. xv, no. 59. July, 1926. Special double African number. London, International review of missions. 1926. 300p. 759

LEWIN, EVANS (comp.). Subject catalogue of the library of the royal empire society (formerly royal colonial institute.) London, The society. 1930-37. 4 v.   760

LIVINGSTONIA COMMITTEE. The Livingstonia Mission (British Central Africa). Report for 1898-99, twenty-third year. v. 23. Edinburg, Lorimer and Gillies. 1899. 74p. (V. 24-Report for 24th year, 1899-1900.) (V. 25-Report for 25th year, 1900-01).   761

THE LIVINGSTONIA NEWS . . . Livingstonia, Mission press. 1908. Collection has: v. 2, nos. 2-3 (Feb., April, 1909); v. 4, no. 2. (April, 1911); v. 5, no. 3 (June, 1912); v. 6, no. 4. (Aug. 1913); v. 9, no. 3 (Dec. 1916); v. 10, nos. 1-2 (Feb., April, 1917); v. 10 (Jan. 1918-June 1919), v. 11, (Jan., March 1924); (April-June, 1924); July-Sept. 1924); (Oct., Dec., 1924).   762

SMITH, EDWIN W. The Christian mission in Africa; a study based on the work of the international conference at Le Zoute, Belgium, September 14-21, 1926. London, International missionary council; Edinburgh, New York. 1926. 200p. 763

SOUTH AFRICA MISSIONARY ADVOCATE. Cleveland and Transvaal. Central mission press quarterly. Collection has: v. 19, no. 3 (No. 1938). 764

SOUTH AFRICAN HEALTH SOCIETY. Magazine . . . Victoria hospital. Lovedale, S. A., The Society quarterly. Collection has: nos. 80-87 (1938-1940). 765

SOUTH AFRICAN OUTLOOK. Lovedale, C. P. Lovedale press monthly. Collection has: vols. 68-69 (Sept. 1938, Oct. 1939). 766

STEWART MISSIONARY FOUNDATION FOR AFRICA. Addresses and proceedings of the congress on Africa held under the auspices of the Stewart Missionary Foundation for Africa of Gammon Theological Seminary in connection with the Cotton States and the International Exposition, Dec. 13-15, 1895. Ed. by J. W. E. Bowen. Atlanta, Gammon Theological Seminary. 1896. 242p. 767

STRONG, WILLIAM E. The story of the American board; an account of the first hundred years of the American board of commissioners for foreign missions. Boston, New York, Pilgrim press. 1910. xv, 523p. 768

UNITED FREE CHURCH OF SCOTLAND. Annual report of the Livingstonia mission of the United Free Church of Scotland (British Central Africa) for the year 1905. Glasgow, Maclure, MacDonald & co. 1906. 134p. 769

VOICE OF ETHIOPIA. New York, voice of Ethiopia, inc. weekly. Collection has: vols. 2-4 (1938-1940). 770

WEST AFRICAN PILOT. Lagos, Nigeria, Zik's press. ltd. (A daily newspaper). Collection has: complete files for 1938, 1939. 771

XIV. African slavery and the slave trade within Africa.

BAKER, SIR SAMUEL W. Ismailia, a narrative of the expedition to Central Africa for the suppression of the slave trade organized by Ismail, Khedive of Egypt. New York, Harper & bros. 1875. 542p. 772

BENEZET, ANTHONY. A short account of that part of Africa, inhabited by Negroes; with respect to the fertility of the country; the good disposition of many of the natives and the manner by which the slave trade is carried on. Extracted from several authors in order to show the iniquity of that trade, and the falsity of the arguments usually advanced in its vindication. With a quotation from George Wallis's system of laws, etc., and a large extract from a pamphlet, lately published in London, on the subject of the slave trade. Philadelphia. 1762. 56p. 773

BENEZET, ANTHONY. Some historical account of Guinea, its situation, produce, and the general disposition of its inhabitants with an inquiry into the rise and progress of the slave trade, its nature and lamentable effects. etc. Philadelphia. 1771; London. 1772. 198p.   774

BERLIOUX, ETIENNE F. The slave-trade in Africa in 1872. Principally carried on for the supply of Turkey, Egypt, Persia, and Zanzibar. By Etienne Felix Berlioux, professor of history in the Lyceum of Lyons. From the French. With a preface by Joseph Cooper. London, Edward Marsh. 1872. 64p.   775

CLARKSON, THOMAS. Essay on the slavery and commerce of the human species, particularly the African. In three parts. Transl. from a Latin dissertation written in 1785. Philadelphia, Nathaniel Wiley. 1804. 259p.   776

EDWARDS, JONATHAN. The injustice and impolicy of the slave trade, and of the slavery of Africans: illustrated in a sermon preached before the Connecticut society for the promotion of freedom, and for the relief of persons unlawfully holden in bondage, at New Haven, September 15, 1791, 2d ed. Boston, Wells & Lilly. 1822. 40p. 3d ed. New

Haven, New Anti-slavery society. Whitmore and Buckinham. 1833. 32p.   777

FALCONBRIDGE, ALEXANDER. An account of the slave trade on the coast of Africa. London, J. Phillips. 1788. 55p.   778

JOHNSTON, SIR HENRY H. The history of a slave. London, Kegan Paul, Trench & co. 1899. 168p. 779

KMANYO, THE LIFE OF AN AFRICAN SLAVE MERCHANT. Philadelphia, American sunday school union. 1850. 90p.   780

LUNN, ARNOLD. A saint in the slave trade, Peter Claver, 1581-1654. New York, Sheed & Ward. 1935. 256p.   781

QUESNE, J. S. (coll.). Narrative of thirty-four years slavery and travels in Africa, by P. J. Dumont. London, Sir Richard Phillips & co. 1819. 42p.   782

TRACY, JOSEPH. A historical examination of the state of society in Western Africa, as formed by paganism and Mohammedanism, slavery, the slave trade and piracy, and of the remedial influence of colonization and missions. 2d ed. Boston, T. R. Marvin. 1845. 40p.
783

XV. The Negro in the West Indies, Latin America, and South America.

BRYCE, JAMES. South America: observations and impressions. n.d. cor. rev. New York, Macmillan co. 1914. xxiv, 611p.   784

CALIXTE, DEMOSTHENES. Haiti, cavalry of a soldier. New York, W. Malliet & co. 1939. xv, 125p. 785

CLARK, B. C. A plea for Hayti, with a glance at her relations with France, England, and U. S. Boston, Eastburn's press. 1853. 50p.   786

COCHRAN, HAMILTON. These are the Virgin Islands. New York,

Prentice Hall. 1937. 236p.   787

CRAIGE, JOHN H. Cannibal cousins. New York, Minton, Balch & co. 1934. 304p. A personal history of Haiti; a narrative of adventure with the U. S. Army of occupation. 788

FABENS, JOSEPH W. Resources of Santo Domingo . . . a paper read before the American Geographical & Statistical Society. New York. 1862; Wash., The Society. 1869. 22p.   789

FORD, JOSEPH C. AND FINLAY,

A.A.C. Handbook of Jamaica for 1906, comprising historical, statistical and general information concerning the island. London, Edward Stanford; Kingston, gov. print. office. 1906. 582, xp. 790

FORREST, A. S. AND HENDERSON, JOHN. The West Indies. London, Adam & Charles Black. 1905. 271p. 791

GLAS, GEORGE. The history of the discovery and conquest of the Canary Islands: transl. from a Spanish manuscript, lately found in the island of Palm with an enquiry into the origin of the ancient inhabitants; to which is added a description of the Canary Islands, including the modern history of the inhabitants and an account of their manners, customs, trade, etc. London, R. & J. Dodsley. 1764. 368p. 792

HARTZELL, CHARLES (comp.). Register of Porto Rico for 1903. San Juan, L. E. Tuzo & co. 1903. 256p. 793

HERSKOVITS, MELVILLE J. Life in a Haitian Valley. New York, Knopf. 1937. 370p. 794

HERSKOVITS, MELVILLE J. Rebel destiny; among the bush Negroes of Dutch Guiana. New York, London, McGraw-Hill. 1934. 366p. 795

HERSKOVITS, MELVILLE J. Suriname folklore . . . with transcriptions of Suriname songs. New York, Columbia university press. 1936. xx, 766, xxviip. 796

HORNE, SAMUEL G. Letters on the proposed annexation of Santo Domingo, in answer to certain charges in the newspapers. Boston, Wright & Potter, print. 1871. 32p. 797

JAMES, C. L. R. The black jacobins, Toussaint Louverture and the San Domingo revolution. New York, Dial press. xvi, 328p. 798

KELLEY, WILLIAM D. (Penna.) Speech . . . on the recognition of Hayti and Liberia. Delivered in the House of representatives, June 3, 1862. Washington, Scammel & co. 1862. 8p. 799

KELLEY, WILLIAM D. Speech . . . on Dominica. Delivered in the House of representatives, January 27, 1871. Washington, F. & J. Rives & Geo. A. Bailey. 1871. 14p. 800

KING, REV. DAVID. The state and prospects of Jamaica: with appended remarks on its advantages for the cure of pulmonary diseases, and suggestions to invalids and others going to that colony. London, Johnstone & Hunter. 1850. 235p. 801

LINDO, ABRAHAM. Dr. Underhill's testimony on the wrongs of the Negro in Jamaica examined in a letter to the editor of "The Times." London, Effingham Wilson. 1866. 32p. 802

LIVINGSTONE, W. P. Black Jamaica, a study in evolution. London, Sampson Low, Marston, & co. 1899. 329p. 803

NILES, BLAIR. Black Haiti, a biography of America's eldest daughter. New York, London, G.P. Putnam's sons. 1926. 325p. 804

POLITICAL CONSTITUTION OF THE DOMINICAN REPUBLIC. Transl. from the official edition. New York, 1885. 45p. 805

PRICHARD, HESKETH. Where black rules white. A journey across the about Hayti. New York, Charles Scribner's sons. 1900. 288p. 806

RAMOS, ARTHUR. The Negro in Brazil. Washington, The associated publ. 1939. xx, 203p. 807

ROSARIO, JOSE C. y CARRION,

JUSTINA. Problemas sociales. El Negro: Haiti-Estados Unidos-Puerto Rico. San Juan, P. R.: Negociado de materiales. 1940. 174p. Bulletin of the University of Porto Rico. 808

SAINT-JOHN, SIR SPENSER. Hayti, or the black republic. London, Smith, Elder & co. 1884. 343p. 809

SEWELL, WILLIAM G. The ordeal of free labor in the British West Indies. New York, Harper & bros. 1861. 325p. 810

SPINNER, ALICE. Study in color, . . . London, T. Fisher Unwin. 1894. 214p. 811

STARK, JAMES H. Jamaica guide: containing a description of everything relating to Jamaica . . . Boston, The auth. London, S. Low, Marston & co.; Jamaica, Ashton W. Gardiner. 1902. 207p. 812

STATISTICS OF CITIES. Labor conditions in Cuba. (Bulletin 42, U.S. dept. of Labor, Sept. 1902) Birth and death rates by color. Washington, Gov. print. off. 1902. 185p. 813

SUAREZ, BERNARDO R. (Dr.) The color question in the two Americas. Transl. from the Spanish by John Crosby Gordon. New York, Hunt publ. co. 1922. 111p. 814

TROLLOPE, ANTHONY. The West Indies and the Spanish main. New York, Harper & bros. 1860. 385p. 815

U. S. CONGRESS, 41st, 3d SESSION. Senate documents, no. 34. Message of the president of the United States issued to the commander of our naval squadron in the waters of the island of San Domingo since the commencement of late negotiations. Washington, Gov. print. off. 1871. 38p. 816

VANDERCOOK, JOHN W. Dark islands. New York, London, Harper & bro. 1937. 367p. 817

VANDERCOOK, JOHN W. "Tom-tom." New York, Harper & bros. 1926. 258p. 818

VERRILL, ALPHEUS H. Porto Rico; past and present and San Domingo of today. New York, Dodd, Mead & co. 1914. 358p. 819

WALKER, H. DE R. The West Indies and the empire. A study and travel in the winter of 1900-1901. London, T. Fisher Unwin. 1901. 253p. 820

THE NEGRO IN AMERICA

Section One

The slave trade, slavery, colonization, the slavery controversy, the Civil War and slavery, freedmen and contrabands.

I. Histories and historical studies of slavery.

AIKEN, JOHN F. The history of liberty; a paper read before the New York historical society, Feb. 6, 1866. New York, A.S. Barnes & co. 1876. 163p.   821

ARTHUR, T. S. AND CARPENTER, W.H. The history of Virginia from its earliest settlement to the present time. Philadelphia, J.B. Lippincott co. 1865. 332p.   822

BALLAGH, JAMES C. White servitude in the colony of Virginia. Baltimore, Johns Hopkins press. 1895. 99p.   823

BALLAGH, JAMES C. History of slavery in Virginia. Baltimore, Johns Hopkins press. 1902. viii, 160p.. (Johns Hopkins University studies, extra vol. xiv.).   824

BANCROFT, GEORGE. History of the United States of America. New York. D. Appleton & co. 1883. 6 v. (V. 1, Negro slaves, slavery.)   825

BANCROFT, HURBERT H. History of Central America, 1501-1887. New York, Bancroft co. 1887. 3 v.   826

BASSETT. JOHN SPENCER. Slavery and servitude in the colony of North Carolina. Baltimore, Johns Hopkins press. 1896. 86p. (Johns Hopkins University studies series 14, no. 4-5.)   827

BASSETT. JOHN SPENCER. Slavery in the state of North Carolina. Baltimore, Johns Hopkins press.

1899. 111p. (Johns Hopkins University studies, series 17, no. 7-8.)   828

BASSETT, JOHN SPENCER. The southern plantation overseer as revealed in his letters. Northampton, Mass., Smith College. 1925. vii, 280p.   829

BEASLEY, DELILAH L. The Negro trail blazers of California; a compilation of records from the California archives in the Bancroft library at the University of California . . . and from the diaries, old papers and conversations of old pioneers in the state of California . . . . Los Angeles, Times print. & bind. house. 1919. 323p.   830

BEAUMONT, GUSTAVE DE. Marie, ou l'esclavage au Etats-Unis. Tableau de moeurs americaines. Paris, Charles Gosselin. 1835. 2 v.   831

BEVERLY, ROBERT. The history and present state of Virginia in four parts. 2d ed. London, R. Parker. 1722.   832

BLAIR, WILLIAM. An inquiry into the state of slavery amongst the Romans, from earliest period, till the establishment of the Lombards in Italy, Edinburgh, Thos. Clark. 1833. 301p.   833

BLAKE, WILLIAM O. comp. The history of slavery and the slave trade, ancient and modern. The forms of slavery that prevailed in ancient nations particularly in Greece and Rome. The African slave trade and the political history of slavery in the United States. Compiled from authentic materials . . . Columbus, Ohio.. H. Miller. 1857. 866p.   834

BOURNE, EDWARD G. Spain in America, 1450-1580. New York, London, Harper bros. 1904. v. 3.
                                    835

BRACKETT, JEFFREY R. The Negro in Maryland; a study of the institution of slavery. Baltimore, Johns Hopkins press. 1889. (Johns Hopkins University studies, extra v. vi.   836

BROWN, WILLIAM H. An historical sketch of the early movement in Illinois for the legalization of slavery, read at the annual meeting of the Chicago historical society, Dec. 5, 1864. Chicago, Goodman & Donnelley. 1865. 44p.   837

BRUCE, PHILIP A. The economic history of Virginia in the seventeenth century. New York, Macmillan co. 1896. 2 v.   838

BRUCE, PHILIP A. Institutional history of Virginia in the seventeenth century; an inquiry into the religious, moral, educational, legal, military, and political condition of the people based upon original and contemporaneous records. New York, 1910. 2 v.   839

CAMPBELL, CHARLES. History of the colony and ancient dominion of Virginia. Philadelphia, J. P. L. Lippincott & co. 1860. 765p.   840

CAREY, JOHN L. Slavery in Maryland briefly considered. Baltimore, John Murphy. 1845. 51p.   841

COBB, THOMAS R. R. An historical sketch of slavery, from the earliest periods. Philadelphia, T. & J. W. Johnson & co. Savannah, W. Thorne Willia. 1858. 302p.   842

CONVERSE, J. K. The history of slavery & means of elevating the African race. A discourse . . . delivered at Montpelier, Vt. Oct. 15, 1840. 24p.   843

COOKE, JOHN E. Virginia – A history of the people with a supplementary chapter by William Garrott Brown. Boston & New York, Houghton, Mifflin co. 1903. 535p.   844

COOLEY, HENRY S. A study of slavery in New Jersey. Baltimore, Johns Hopkins press. 1896. 60p. (Johns Hopkins studies, series 14, no. 9-10).   845

COPLEY, ESTHER. A history of slavery & its abolition. 2d ed. enl. London, Houlston & Stoneman. 1839. 648p.   846

FLANDERS, RALPH B. Plantation slavery in Georgia. Chapel Hill: The University of North Carolina press. 1933. x, 326p.   847

FLIPPEN, PERCY S. The Royal Government in Virginia, 1624-1775. New York, Longmans, Green & co. 1919. 393p. biblio. (Studies in history, economics & public law, Columbia University. vol. lxxxiv no. 1).   848

GAINES, FRANCIS P. The southern plantation; a study in the development & the accuracy of a tradition. New York, Columbia University press, 1924. viii, 243p.   849

GEORGE, JAMES Z. The political history of slavery in the United States. . . New York. Neal publishing co. 1915. 342p.   850

GUROWSKI, ADAM. Slavery in history. New York, A. B. Burdick. 1860. 260p.   851

HELPS, SIR ARTHUR. The conquerors of the new world and their bondsmen; being a narrative of the principal events which led to Negro slavery in the West Indies and America. London. Wm. Pickering. 1848. 1849. 2v.   852

HELPS, SIR ARUTHUR. The Spanish conquest in America and its relation to the history of slavery and to the government of colonies. London. New York. J. Lane. 1900-1904. 4 v.   853

HENRY, HOWELL M. The police control of the slave in South Carolina. Emory, Va. 1914. 216p.   854

HILLER, OLIVER P. A chapter on slavery: presenting a sketch of its origin and history, with the reasons for its permission, and the probable manner of its removal. London. Hodson & son. New York, Mason bros. Boston, Otis Clapp. 1860. 175p.   855

HODGE, F. W. and LEWIS, T. H. (eds.) Spanish explorers in the southern United States, 1528-1543. New York. 1907.   856

HOWE, HENRY. Historical collections of Virginia; containing a collection of the most interesting facts, traditions, biographical sketches, anecdotes, etc. relative to its history and antiquities, together with geographical and statistical descriptive sketch of the District of Columbia. Charleston, S.C., Babcock & co., 1845. 528p.   857

JEFFERSON, THOMAS. Notes on the State of Virginia 2d Am. ed. Philadelphia, Mathew Carey, 1794. 336p.   858

JOHNSTON, WILLIAM D. Slavery in Rhode Island, 1775-1776. Providence. Rhode Island historical society. 1894. 164p.

JOHNSTON, SIR HARRY H. Negro in the new world. New York, Macmillan co. 1910. xxix, 500p.   860

KINGSBURY, SUSAN M. (ed.) Records of the Virginia company of London, 1619-1624. Washington. Govt. print. office. 1906-33-35. 4 v.   861

LA RONCIERE, CHARLES G.M.B. de. Negres et negriers. 7th ed. Paris. Editions des protiques. 1933. 265p. front pl.   862

LASCELLES, E. C. P. Granville Sharp & the freedom of slaves in England. New York. London. Oxford University press. 1928. 151p.   863

LAUBER, ALMON W. Indian slavery in colonial times within the present limits of the United States. New York, Columbia University press. 1913. 352p.   864

LOWERY, WOODBURY. The Spanish settlements within the present limits of the United States. London. New York. G. P. Putnam's   865

MC CRADY, EDWARD. Slavery in the province of South Carolina, 1670-1770. (In American historical association, annual report ... 1895. Washington. 1896.   866

MC DOUGLE, IVAN E. Slavery in Kentucky, 1792-1865. (Reprinted from the Journal of Negro History, v. 3. no. 3, July, 1918.) Lancaster, Pa., New Era print. co. 125p.   867

MIELZINER, M. Slavery among the ancient Hebrews: from Biblical and Talmudic sources. Tr. from the German by Francis Lieber. n.d., n.p. 206p.   868

MOORE, GEORGE H. Notes on the history of slavery in Massachusetts. New York. D. Appleton & co. 1866. 256p.   869

MOORE, GEORGE H. Additional notes on the history of slavery in

Massachusetts. (From the Historical magazine, Dec. 1866.) Mr. Moore's reply to his Boston critics. New York, New York historical society. 1867. 15p.   870

NEWMAN, FRANCES W. Anglo-Saxon abolition of Negro slavery. London, Kegan, Paul, Trench & co. 1889. 136p.   871

NORTHRUP, ANSEL J. Slavery in New York. A historical sketch. Albany, University of the state of New York. 1900. 313p. (State library bulletin, history no. 4.) 872

NUNEZ CABEZA DE VACA, ALVAR. The journey . . . from Florida to the Pacific, 1528-1536; tr. from his own narrative by Fannie Bandelior, together with the report of Father Marcos of Nizza and a letter from the viceroy Mondoza; ed. with introd. by A.F. Bandelier. New York, A.S. Barnes & co. 1922. xxii, 231p.   873

PALFREY, JOHN G. A chapter of American history. Five years' progress of the slave power; a series of papers. (Reprinted from the Boston "Commonwealth" for July, August & September, 1851.) Boston, Benj. B. Mussey & co. 1852. 84pp.   874

PARSONS, THEOPHILUS. Slavery, its origin, influence, and destiny. 2d ed. Boston, Wm Carter & bro. 1863. 36p.   875

PATTERSON, CALEB P. The Negro in Tennessee, 1790-1865. Austin, Tex. University of Texas, bull. no. 2205. 1922. 213p.   876

PHILLIPS, ULRICH B. The origin and growth of the southern black belt. (Reprinted from the American historical review. v. 1, no. 4, July, 1906. pp. 798-816.   877

PHILLIPS, ULRICH B. American Negro slavery; a survey of the supply, employment and control of Negro labor as determined by the plantation regime. New York, London, D. Appleton. 1918. xi, 529p.   878

PICKETT, ALBERT J. The history of Alabama and incidentally of Georgia and Mississippi, from the earliest period. Atlanta, T.J. Doonan. 1900. 650p.   879

PRESCOTT, WILLIAM H. History of the conquest of Mexico, with a preliminary view of the ancient Mexican civilization and the life of the conqueror, Hernando Cortes. New York, Harper & bros. 1843. 3 v.   880

PRICE, THOMAS. Slavery in America: with notices of the present state of slavery and the slave trade throughout the world. London, G. Wightman. 1837. 320p.   881

SAWYER, GEORGE S. Southern institutes: or, An inquiry into the origin and early prevalence of slavery and the slave trade: with an analysis of the laws, history, and government of the institution in the principle nations, ancient and modern, from the earliest ages down to the present time. With notes and comments in defence of the Southern institutions. Philadelphia, J.B. Lippincott & co. 1858. 393p.   882

SHERMAN, HENRY. Slavery in the United States of America; its national recognition and relations from the establishment of the confederacy to the present time. A word to the North and South 2d ed. Hartford, Hurlburt & Pond. 1858. 187p.   883

SMITH, CAPTAIN JOHN. A true relation of Virginia, with introductory notes by Charles Deane. Boston, Wiggin & Lunt.

1866. xlvii, 88p. 884

STEINER, BERNARD C. History of slavery in Connecticut. Baltimore, Johns Hopkins press. 1893. 82p.. (Johns Hopkins University, series 11, no, ix) 885

STEPHENSON, WENDELL H. Isaac Franklin, slave trader and planter of the old South; with plantation records. University, La., State University press. 1938. xi, 368p. 886

TAYLOR, C. B. A universal history of the United States of America, embracing the whole period from the earliest discoveries to the present time. New York, Ezra Strong. 1835. 540p. 887

THOMPSON, GEORGE. Lectures on British India, delivered in Manchester, Oct., 1839. With a preface by William Lloyd Garrison. Pawtucket, R. I., Wm & Robert Adams. 1840. 206p. 888

THORNTON, THOMAS C. An inquiry into the history of slavery; its introduction into the United States causes of its continuance; and remarks upon the abolition tracts of William E. Channing. Washington, William M. Morrison. 1841. 345p. 889

TREXLER, HARRISON A. Slavery in Missouri, 1804-1865. Baltimore, John Hopkins University studies, series 32, no. ii) 890

TURNER, EDWARD R. Slavery in Pennsylvania. Lord Baltimore press. 1911. 88p. 891

TURNER, EDWARD R. The Negro in Pennsylvania, slavery-servitude-freedom, 1639-1861. Washington, American Historical association. 1911. 314p. 892

WADE, DEBORAH B. L. The Burman slave girl; also, narratives of the first Burman inquirer, and of the first converted Burman. Letters of christian Burmans, description of a Burman school and Mr. Judson's visit to the Burman emperor. Boston, James Loring. n.d. 108p. 893

WASHBURN, EMORY. Slavery as it once prevailed in Massachusetts; a lecture for the Massachusetts historical society, Jan. 22, 1869. Boston, John Wilson & son. 1869. 35p. 894

WERTENBAKER, THOMAS J. The planters of colonial Virginia. Princeton. Princeton University press. London, Oxford University press. 1922. 260p. 895

WESTON, GEORGE M. The progress of slavery in the United States. Washington, The auth. 1857. 301p. 896

WHITBY, WILLIAM. American slavery; a sketch. London, Richard Davies. 1864. 210p. 897

WILSON, HENRY. History of the rise and fall of the slave power in America. Boston, James Osgood & co. 1872. 3v. 2d ed. Boston, New York, Houghton, Mifflin co. 1877. 3 v. 898

WINSOR, JUSTIN (ed.) Narrative and critical history of America. Boston, New York., Houghton, Mifflin co. 1884-1889. 8 v. (v. 2, Spanish settlements). 899

YONGE, SAMUEL H. The site of old "Jamestowne" 1607-1698. A brief historical and topographical sketch of the first American metropolis. Richmond. author. 1907. 151p. 900

II. African and Domestic Slave Trade.

AFRICAN SLAVE TRADE. Facts and observations relating to the participation of American citizens. Philadelphia. Religious society of friends. 1841. 36p.   901

AMERICAN ANTI-SLAVERY SOCIETY (Executive Committee). Slavery and the internal slave trade in the United States of North America. Being replies to questions transmitted by the committee of the British and foreign anti-slavery society for the abolition of slavery and the slave trade throughout the world. Presented to the general anti-slavery convention held in London, June, 1840. London, Thomas Ward & co. 1841. viii, 280p.   902

ANDREWS, ETHAN A. Slavery and the domestic slave-trade in the United States. Boston, Light & Stearns. 1836. xii, 201p.   903

BANDINEL, J. Some account of the trade in slaves. London, Longmans, Green & co. 1842.   904

BENJAMIN, JUDAH P. Intercepted instructions . . . The African slave trade. The secret purpose of the insurgents to revive it. Philadelphia, C. Sherman & co. Print. 1863. 24p.   905

BRIDGE, HORATIO. Journal of an African Cruiser . . . Edited by Nathaniel Hawthorne. New York, Geo. P. Putnam & co. 1853. 179p.   906

BUXTON, THOMAS F. The slave trade and remedy; prospectus of the society for the extinction of the slave trade and for the civilization of Africa. Instituted June, 1839. London, John Murphy. xv, 240p.; Philadelphia, Merrihew & Thompson. 1839. 188p.   907

CAREY, HENRY C. The slave trade, domestic and foreign; why it exists, and how it may be extinguished. Phila., H. C. Baird. 1862. 426p. 908

CLARKE, RICHARD F. (ed.) Cardinal La Vigerie and the African slave trade. London, Longmans, Green & co. 1889. 379p.   909

COLLINS, WINFIELD H. The domestic slave trade of the southern states. New York, Broadway pub. co. 1904. 154p.
                                                          910

COLOMB, (CAPTAIN) Slave-catching in the Indian Ocean. A record of naval experiences. London, Longmans, Green & co. 1873. 503p.   911

DANA, JAMES. The African slave trade. A discourse delivered in the city of New Haven, Sept. 9, 1790, before the Connecticut society for the promotion of freedmen . . . New Haven, T. & S. Green. 1791. 33p.   912

DICKY SAM (pseud.) Liverpool and slavery: an historical account of the Liverpool-African Slave Trade. Containing – the ships' names, masters, owners – where bound tons numbers of slaves on each ship, and time of sailing for the year 1799. Complete list of ships which left the Port of Liverpool for Africa from 1709 to 1807 . . . an interesting plate of the famous slave ship The "Brookes" of Liverpool . . . her living cargo packed for the voyage. Together with numerous anecdotes. Life of Hugh Crow, the Liverpool slave captain, etc. Liverpool, Bowker & son, 1884. 137p.   913

DONNAN, ELIZABETH (ed.) Documents illustrative of the

history of the slave trade to America . . . Washington, Carnegie Institution of Washington. 1930-35. 4 v. refs. (publication 409, papers of the department of historical research). 914

DOW, GEORGE F. Slave ships and slaving. Salem, Mass. Marine research society. 1927. 349p.. (publication no. 15 of the Marine research society). 915

DUBOIS, WILLIAM E. The enforcement of the slave trade laws. (In the American historical association. Annual report . . . 1891. Washington. 1892. 916

DUBOIS, WILLIAM E. The suppression of the African slave trade to the United States of America, 1638-1870. New York, London and Bombay, Longmans Green & co. 1896. 335p. (v. 1, no. 1, Harvard historical series). 917

EDWARDS, JONATHAN. The injustice and impolicy of the slave trade, and of the slavery of the Africans; illustrated in a sermon preached before the Connecticut society for the promotion of freedom, and for the relief of persons unlawfully holden in bondage, at their annual meeting in New Haven. New Haven anti-slavery society. 1833. 32p. 918

ENGLAND, BISHOP. Letters . . . to the Hon. John Forsyth on the subject of domestic slavery to which are prefixed copies, in Latin and English, of the Pope's Apostolic letter, concerning the African slave trade, with some introductory remarks, etc. Baltimore, John Murphy. 1844. 156p. 919

FISHER, RUTH A. (coll.) Extracts from the records of the African companies. Washington.

Association for the study of Negro life and history. n.d. 108p. 920

FRIENDS SOCIETY IN LONDON. Case of the Vigilante, a ship employed in the slave trade; with some reflections on that traffic. London, Harvey Darton & co. 1826. 13p. 921

FRIENDS, (SOCIETY OF) IN PENNSYLVANIA, NEW JERSEY, ETC. Present state of the African slave trade. Philadelphia, The society. 1824. 69p. 922

FRIENDS SOCIETY OF PHILADELPHIA. An exposition of the African slave trade, from the year 1840 to 1850, inclusive. Prepared from official documents and published by direction of the representatives of the religious society of friends in Pennsylvania, New Jersey & Delaware. Philadelphia, Friend's bookstore. 1851. 160p. 923

GORDON, GEORGE W. The record of . . . the slave trade at Rio de Janeiro, Seizure of slave vessels, conviction of slave dealers. Boston, National American Party, 1856. 15p. 924

HILL, PASCOE G. Fifty days on board a slave vessel in the Mozambique Channel, April & May, 1842. New York, New World Press. 29p. 925

JERVEY, THEODORE D. The slave trade; slavery and color. Columbia, S. C. State co. 1925. vi, 344p. 926

MATSON, HENRY J. Remarks on the slave trade and African Squadron. London, James Ridgway. 1848. 94p. 927

MAYER, BRANTZ. Captain Canot, or twenty years of an African slaver. Being an account of his career and adventures on the coast, in the interior, on shipboard, and in the

West Indies. Written out of and edited from the captain's journals, memoranda and conversations. New York, D. Appleton & co. 1854. 448p.   928

MORSE, JEDIDIAH. A discourse, delivered at the African meetinghouse, Boston, July 14, 1808, in grateful celebration of the abolition of the African slave-trade by the governments of the United States, Great Britain & Denmark. Boston, Lincoln & Edmonds. 1808. 25p.   929

NEWTON, JOHN. Thoughts upon the African Slave Trade. London, J. Buckland. 1788. 41p.   930

OWEN, NICHOLAS. Journal of a slave-dealer on the coasts of Africa and America from the year 1746 to the year 1757. Edited by Eveline Martin. Boston & New York, Houghton & Mifflin. 1930. 120p.
                                                          931

PALFREY, JOHN G. The inter-state slave trade. New York. American anti-slavery society. n.d. 8p.   932

ROYAL AFRICAN COMPANY. A true state of the present difference between the Royal African Company, and the separate traders: Written by a true lover of his country, and humbly submitted to the wise consideration of both houses of Parliament. London. 1710. map. 40p.   933

SHEPPARD, MOSES. African slave trade in Jamaica and a comparative treatment of slaves, read before the Maryland Historical Society, Oct. 1854. Baltimore, Maryland Hist. Society, 1854. 14p.   934

SIERRA LEONE COMPANY. Substance of the report delivered by the court of directors of the Sierra Leone company to the general court of Proprietors, the 27th March, 1794. London, James Phillips. 1794. 175p.   935

SNELGRAVE, CAPTAIN WILLIAM. A new account of some parts of Guinea and the slave trade; containing 1) The history of the late conquest of the kingdom of Whidaw by the king of Dahome. The author's journey to the conqueror's camp; where he saw several captives sacrificed, etc. 2) The manner how Negroes become slaves. The numbers of them yearly exported from Guinea to America. The lawfulness of that trade. The mutinies among them on board the ships where the author has been, etc. 3) A relation of the author's being taken by pirates, the many dangers he underwent. London, James, John, & Paul Knapton. 1734. 288p.   936

SOMERVILLE, THOMAS. A discourse on our obligation to Thanksgiving for the prospect of the abolition of the African slave-trade, with a prayer. Kelso, England, J. Palmer, print. 1792. 49p.   937

SPEARS, JOHN R. The American slave-trade. An account of its origin, growth and suppression. New York, Charles Scribner's sons. 1900. 232p.   938

SWAN, JAMES. A dissuasion to Great Britain and the colonies from the slave-trade to Africa, showing the injustice thereof, etc. rev. & abr. Boston, J. Greenleaf. 1773. 41p.
                                                          939

TAUSSIG, CHARLES W. Rum, romance and rebellion. New York. Minton, Balch & co. 1928. 289pp. illus.   940

TORREY, JESSE. American slave trade; or, an account of the manner in which slave dealers take free

56

people from some of the United States of America and carry them away and sell them as slaves in other of the states; and of the horrible cruelties practised in the carrying on of this most infamous traffic: with reflections on the project for forming a colony of American blacks in Africa, and certain documents respecting that project. London, J. M. Corbett. 1822. 119p.   941

U. S. CONGRESS. (Senate documents, no. 93, 1822.) Message from the President of the United States, transmitting . . . a report of the attorney general, relative to the introduction of slaves into the United States, contrary to existing laws. Washington, Gales & Seaton. 1822. 93p.   942

U. S. CONGRESS. Report of the committee on the suppression of the slave trade. April 12, 1822. Washington. 1822. 92p.   943

U. S. CONGRESS. (House of Representatives Document no. 16, 19th Congress, 1st session). Slave trade. message from the President of the United States, communicating correspondence with Great Britain in relation to the convention for suppressing the slave trade. December 27, 1825. Washington. Gales & Seaton. 1825. 11p.   944

U. S. DEPARTMENT OF STATE. Documents . . . papers in relation to the convention between the United States and Great Britain, for the suppression of the slave trade, communicated, with the President's message, to Congress, on December 7, 1824. Washington. 1825. 56p.   945

WILSON, JOHN L. The Foreign slave-trade, can it be revived without violating the most sacred principles of honor, humanity, and religion? (From the Southern Presbyterian Review). 1859. 22p.   946

ZOOK, GEORGE F. The company of royal adventurers trading into Africa. Lancaster, Pa., New Era print. co. 1919. 105p. (Reprinted from the Journal of Negro History, v. 4, no. 2, April, 1919).   947

III. Slave insurrections in the United States.

AMERICAN NEGRO MONOGRAPHS. The confession, trial and execution of Nat Turner, the Negro insurgent, also a list of persons killed . . . (v. 1, no. 1, 1910). Washington, American Negro Monograph co. 1910. 15p.   948

CARROL, JOSEPH C. Slave insurrections in the United States, 1800-1865. Boston, Chapman & Grimes. 1939. 229p. refs. biblio.   949

COFFIN. JOSHUA. An account of some of the principal slave insurrections, and others which have occurred, or been attempted, in the United States and elsewhere during two centuries. With various remarks. Collected from various sources. New York. American anti-slavery society. 1860. 36p. 950

CORPORATION OF CHARLESTON, S. C. An account of the late intended insurrection among a portion of the blacks of this city. Published by the authority of the corporation of Charleston. 2d ed. Charleston, S. C. 1822. 48p.   951

HIGGINSON, THOMAS W. Travellers

and outlaws; episodes in American history. Boston. Lee and Shepard. New York, C.T. Dillingham. 1899. 340p.   952

HORSEMANDEN, DANIEL. A journal of the proceedings in the detection of the conspiracy formed by some white people in conjunction with Negro and other slaves for the burning of the city of New York in America and murdering the inhabitants . . . containing a narrative of the trials, etc. Some additional evidence, and lists of persons committed. New York, Recorder of the city of New York. 1745. London, John Clarke. 1747. 433p.   953

HORSEMANDEN, DANIEL. The New York conspiracy; or, A history of the Negro plot, with the journal of the proceedings against the conspirators at New York in the years 1741-42. 2d ed. New York, Southwick & Pelsue. 1810. 388p.
954

JAMES, CYRIL. A history of Negro revolt. London. Fact, monographs, no. 18. 1938. 97p.   955

JERVEY, THEODORE D. Robert Y. Hayne and his times. New York.

Macmillan & co. 1909. xix, 555p. (Denmark Versey, bk. 1, ch. 12).
956

(TURNER, NAT) The confession, trial and execution of Nat Turner, the Negro insurrectionist; also, a list of persons murdered in the insurrection in Southampton county, Virginia, on the 21st and 22nd of August, 1831, with introductory remarks by Thomas R. Gray. Petersburg, Va. J.B. Ege. 1881. 23p.   957

(TURNER, NAT). Confession of Nat Turner, leader of the Negro insurrection in Southampton county, Virginia, made to Thomas R. Gray. Richmond. 1832. 23p.
958

VICTOR, ORVILLE J. History of American conspiracies: a record of treason, insurrection, rebellion, etc. in the United States from 1760 to 1860. New York. James D. Torrey. n. d. 579p.   959

WHIPPLE, CHARLES K. The non-resistance principle: with particular application to the help of slaves by abolitionists. Boston, R.F. Wallcut. 1860. 24p.   960

IV. The Free Negro.

ALLEN, RICHARD. Life, experience and gospel labors, with an address to the people of color in the United States. Philadelphia, Lee & Yeecum. 1887. 69p.   961

CONVENTION FOR THE IMPROVEMENT OF THE FREE PEOPLE OF COLOR IN THESE UNITED STATES. Minutes and proceedings of the third annual convention . . . held in Philadelphia, June 3-13, 1833. New York, The Convention. 1833. 40p.   962

CROMWELL, JOHN W. The early Negro convention movement. Washington, Academy. 1904. 23p.
963

CRUMMELL, ALEXANDER. The relations and duties of free colored men in America to Africa. A letter to Charles B. Dunbar. Hartford. Case, Lockwood & co. 1861. 54p.
964

DANIELS, JOHN. In freedom's birthplace: a study of Boston Negroes. Boston. New York,

Houghton, Mifflin co. 1914. xii, 495p. 965

DELANY, MARTIN R. The condition, elevation, emigration, and destiny of the colored people of the United States, politically considered. Philadelphia. author. 1852. 215p. 966

DODGE, DAVID. Free Negroes of North Carolina. 1886. 30p. 967

DOUGLASS, WILLIAM. Sermons preached in the African protestant episcopal church of St. Thomas, Philadelphia. King & Baird. 1854. 251p. 968

EASTON, HOSEA. A treatise on the intellectual character, and civil and political condition of the colored people of the United States; and the prejudice exercised towards them: with a sermon the the duty of the church to them. Boston, Isaac Knapp. 1837. 54p. 969

FITCH, JAMES D. Report of the resident physician of the colored home of the city of New York, from January, 1849 to January, 1850. New York, Vinten. 1850. 12p. 970

FRAZIER, E. FRANKLIN. The free Negro family; a study of family origins before the Civil War. Nashville. Fisk University press. 1932. 75p. 971

FREEDOM'S GIFT; or, Sentiments of the Free. Hartford, S. S. Cowles. 1840. 108p. 972

HAMILTON, WILLIAM. Address to the fourth annual convention of the free people of color of the United States. Delivered at the opening of their session in the city of New York, June 2, 1834. New York, S. W. Benedict & co. 1834. 8p. 973

HAWKINS, WILLIAM G. "Lunsford Lane;" another helper from North Carolina. Boston, Crosby & Nichols. 1863. xii, 305p. 974

HERSHAW, LAFAYETTE M. Status of the free- Negro prior to 1860. Washington, American Negro academy. 1915. (Papers of the Academy) 975

THE HISTORY OF PRINCE LEE BOO . . . The life of Paul Cuffee, a man of color; also, some account of John Sackhouse, the Esquimeaux. Dublin. C. Crookes, 1820. 180p. 976

HURD, JOHN C. Topics of jurisprudence connected with freedmen; inquiry into the conditions of the Negro in the United States. By an American. 1839. 977

LANE, LUNSFORD. The narrative of Lunsford Lane, formerly of Raleigh, N. C., embracing an account of his early life, the redemption by purchase of himself and family from slavery, and his banishment from the place of his birth for the crime of wearing a colored skin. 3d. ed. Boston, Hewes & Watson. 1845. iv, 54p. 978

MINUTES AND PROCEEDINGS of the third annual convention for the improvement of the free people of color in these United States. Held by adjournments in the city of Philadelphia, in 1833. New York. 1833. 344p. 979

PENNINGTON, JAMES W. C. A textbook of the origin and history of the colored people. Hartford, L. Skinner. 1841. 96p. 980

PENNSYLVANIA SOCIETY FOR PROMOTING THE ABOLITION OF SLAVERY, ETC. The present state and condition of the free people of color in the city of Philadelphia and adjoining districts, as exhibited by the report of a committee of the Pennsylvania society for promoting the abolition of slavery, read Jan. 5, 1838.

Philadelphia. Merrihew & Gunn for the society. 1838. 48p. Centennial anniversary ed. Philadelphia. Grant, Faires & Rodgers. 1857. 82p.   981

PICKENS, WILLIAM. Status of the free Negro from 1860 to 1870. Washington. American Negro academy. 1915. (Papers of the Academy).   982

REGISTER OF TRADES of the Colored People in the city of Philadelphia and districts. Philadelphia, Merrihew & Gunn. 1838. 8p.   983

RUSSELL, JOHN H. The free Negro in Virginia, 1619-1865. Baltimore. Johns Hopkins press. 1913. viii, 194p.   984

UNITED STATES CONGRESS. (House of representatives, 27th Congress, 3d session. Report no. 80.) Free colored seamen-majority and minority reports, January 20, 1843. 56p.   985

WALKER, DAVID Walker's appeal, in four articles; together with a preamble, to the colored citizens of the world, but in particular, and very expressly, to those of the United States of America, written in Boston, state of Massachusetts, September 28, 1829. 3d ed. notes. cor. etc. Boston, D. Walker. 88p. (Slavery pamphlets, v. 52. no. 1).   986

WOODSON, CARTER G. Free Negro heads of families in the United States in 1830, together with a brief treatment of the free Negro. Washington, Assn. for the study of Negro life and history. 1925. lviii. 296p.   987

WOODSON, CARTER G. (comp.) Free Negro owners of slaves in the United States in 1830, together with absentee ownership of slaves in the United States in 1830. Washington, Assn. for the study of Negro life and history. 1924. viii, 78p.   988

WOODSON, CARTER G. The mind of the Negro as reflected in letters during the crisis, 1800-1860. Washington. Associated pub. 1926. xxii, 672p.   989

WRIGHT, JAMES M. The free Negro in Maryland, 1634-1860. New York. Longmans, Green & co. 1921. 362p.   990

V. Colonization.

THE AFRICAN REPOSITORY . . . Published by the American colonization society. v. 1-67, 68, no. 1. (March, 1825-January, 1892). Washington. 1826-1892. Collection has complete set. v. 1-25 have title: African repository and colonial journal; superseded by Liberia. Ed. by R. R. Gurley and others.   991

AN AMERICAN (pseud.) An inquiry into the condition and prospects of the African race in the United States and the means of bettering its fortunes . . . Philadelphia. Haswell, Barrington & Haswell. 1839. 214p.   992

AMERICAN COLONIZATION SOCIETY. Memorial of the semi-centennial anniversary of the American colonization society, at Washington, January 15, 1867, with documents concerning Liberia. Washington, The society, 1867. viii 9. 191p.   993

AMERICAN COLONIZATION SOCIETY. Constitution. government and digest of the laws of Liberia. Washington, by the Society, 1825. 11p.   994

AMERICAN COLONIZATION SOCIETY. Annual report . . . 1st-93d, 1818-1910. Washington, the society. 1818-1910. Titles and imprints vary slightly. Collection has: v. 1-2, 1818-19; v. 5, 1822; v. 6-8, 1823-25; v. 10-17, 1827-34; v. 24-25, 1841-42; v. 29, 1846; v. 34-37, 1851-54; v. 40, 1857; v. 48-49, 1865-66; v. 51-53, 1868-70; v. 55-57, 1872-74.   995

AMERICAN COLONIZATION SOCIETY. Address of the managers . . . to the people of the United States. Washington, The society. 1832. 16p.   996

AMERICAN SOCIETY FOR COLONIZING. The Free People of Color of the United States. Address . . . read at a special meeting . . . City of Washington, Nov. 21, 1818. Washington, The society. 1818. 56p.   997

AMERICAN SOCIETY FOR COLONIZING. Annual report . . . 1st to 17th (1818-34) Washington. D. Rapine. 1818-1834.   998

ARMISTEAD, WILSON. Calumny refuted, by facts from Liberia. Presented to the Boston anti-slavery bazaar, U. S. London, Charles Gilpin. New York, William Harned. 1848. 46p.   999

BALDWIN, EBENEZER. Observations on the physical, intellectual, and moral qualities of our colored population: With remarks on the subject of Emancipation and Colonization. New Haven, L. H. Young. 1834. 48p.   1000

BRECKINRIDGE, ROBERT J. An address . . . before the Colonization Society of Kentucky. Frankfort, Ky., A. G. Hodges 1831. 24p. 1001

BROWN, ISAAC V. A. Biography of

the Rev. Robert Finley with an account of his agency as author of the American Colonization Society; also a sketch of the slave trade . . . 2d. ed. enl. Philadelphia, John W. Moore, 1857. 336p.   1002

CAREY, MATHEW. Letters on the colonization society with a view of its probable results . . . 3d ed. enl. imp. Philadelphia. Young. 1832. 32p. 7th ed. Philadelphia. author. 1833. 32p. 13th ed. Philadelphia. author. 32p.   1003

CLAY, HENRY. An address before the American Colonization Society, Dec. 17, 1829. Lexington, Ky. The society. 1829. 26p.   1004

COATES, BENJAMIN. Cotton cultivation in Africa. Suggestions on the importance of the cultivation of cotton in Africa, in reference to the abolition of slavery in the United States, through the organization of an African Civilization Society. Philadelphia, Sherman & Son. 1858. 52p.   1005

COLONIZATION SOCIETY OF THE CITY OF NEW YORK. Fifth annual report . . . with the Constitution of the Society. New York. The society, 1837. 47p. 1006

COLONIZATION SOCIETY OF THE STATE OF CONNECTICUT. Annual report of the board of managers . . . 1830. New Haven, The society. 1830. 28p.   1007

COLONIZATION SOCIETY (NEW YORK STATE). Annual report of the board of managers . . . 1892. Upon the present needs of Liberia. O. F. Cook, secretary. New York, The society. 1892. 27p.   1008

COLTON, CALVIN. Colonization and abolition contrasted. Philadelphia, Herman Hooker. n.d. 16p.   1009

CRUMMELL, ALEXANDER. The future of Africa: being addresses,

61

sermons, etc. . . delivered in the republic of Liberia. New York, Charles Scribner, 1862. 354p. 1010

DANA, DANIEL. Discourse to the New Hampshire auxiliary colonization society. Concord, The society. 1825. 24p. 1011

DEWEES, JACOB. The great future of America and Africa; an essay showing our whole duty to the black man, consistent with our own safety and glory. Philadelphia, The author. 1854. 236p. 1012

EVERETT, EDWARD. Address . . . at the anniversary of the American colonization society, Jan. 18, 1853. Washington, The Society. 1853. 11p. 1013

FOOTE, ANDREW H. Africa and the American flag. New York. London, D. Appleton & co. 1854. 390. 1014

FOWLER, WILLIAM C. Discourse before the Vermont colonization society, Oct. 17, 1834. Middlebury, The society. 1834. 32p. 1015

FREEMAN, F. Africa's redemption the salvation of our country. New York, D. Fanshaw. 1852. 383p. 1016

GURLEY, RALPH R. Address at the annual meeting of the Pennsylvania Colonization Society. Nov. 11, 1839. Philadelphia, The society. 1839. 40p. 1017

GURLEY, RALPH R. Letter to the Hon. Henry Clay, president of the American colonization society, and Sir Thomas Fowell Buxton, chairman of the General committee of the African civilization society, on the colonization and civilization of Africa. With other documents on the same subject. London, Wiley & Putnam. 1841. 66p. 1018

GURLEY, RALPH R. Life of Jehudi Ashmun, late colonial agent in Liberia. 2d ed. New York.

Robinson & Franklin, 1839. 554p. 1019

GURLEY, RALPH R. Mission to England, in behalf of the American colonization society. Washington. W. W. Morrison. 1841. xii, 264p. 1020

HALE, SARAH J. (Buell) Liberia: or, Mr. Peyton's experiments. New York. Harper & bros. 1853. 304p. 1021

HARPER, ROBERT G. A letter . . . to Elias R. Caldwell, Esq. secretary of the American Society for Colonizing The Free People of Colour, in the United States, with their own consent. Baltimore, The society. 1818. 32p. 1022

HOUGH, JOHN. Sermon delivered before the Vermont colonization society, Montpelier, Oct. 18, 1826. Montpelier. The society. 1826. 20p. 1023

INJUSTICE AND IMPOLICY OF THE SLAVE TRADE, and of the slavery of the Africans; illustrated in a sermon preached before the Connecticut society for the promotion of freedom, and for the relief of persons unlawfully holden in bondage, by Jonathan Edwards. New Haven, T. & S. Green. 1791. 37p. 1024

JUNKIN, GEORGE. The integrity of our national union vs. abolitionism: an argument from the Bible, in proof of the position that believing masters ought to be honored and obeyed by their own servants, and tolerated in, not excommuniated from the church of God: being part of a speech delivered before the Synod of Cincinnati, on the subject of slavery, Sept. 19 and 20, 1843. Cincinnati, R. P. Donogh. 1843. 79p. 1025

KNIGHT, MRS. H. C. The new

republic. Written for the Massachusetts sabbath school society, and approved by the committee of publication. Boston, The society. 1850. 252p.   1026

LATROBE, JOHN H. B. Address . . . on the Christian civilization of Africa. Delivered before the American colonization society, January 16, 1877. Washington, American Colonization Society. 1877. 10p.   1027

LATROBE, JOHN H. B. African colonization; an address delivered . . . at the anniversary meeting of the Massachusetts colonization society held in Boston, May 25, 1853. Baltimore, John D. Toy, 1853. 26p.   1028

LATROBE, JOHN H. Colonization and abolition. An address delivered at the anniversary meeting of the New York colonization society, held in New York, May 13th, 1852. Baltimore, John D. Toy, 1852. 46p.   1029

LATROBE, JOHN H. Colonization. A notice of Victor Hugo's views of slavery in the United States in a letter . . . to Thomas Suffern, Baltimore, John D. Toy. 1851. 48p.   1030

MASSACHUSETTS COLONIZATION SOCIETY. Annual report . . . 1844-1868. Collection has: 7th, 18th, 19th, 20th; 1848, 1860, 1861, 1862. Boston, T. R. Marvin. 1848. 1860-62.   1031

MCGILL, ALEXANDER T. The hand of God with the black race. A discourse delivered before the Pennsylvania colonization society. Philadelphia. William E. Geddes. 1862. 19p.   1032

MEMORIAL of two hundred and fifty-nine members of the New York and Liberia emigration and agricultural association, for an appropriation . . . New York. Authority of the legislature, Jan. 29, 1852. 3p.   1033

MITCHELL, JAMES. Letter on the relation of white and African races in the United States, showing the necessity of the colonization of the latter. Addressed to the president of the United States. Washington. Govt. print. office. 1862. 28p. 1034

NEW HAMPSHIRE AUXILIARY COLONIZATION SOCIETY. Fifth annual report of the managers . . . June 4, 1829. Concord, N. H. The society, 1829. 19p.   1035

NEW HAMPSHIRE AUXILIARY COLONIZATION SOCIETY. Report of the Board of Managers. June 4, 1835. Concord, N. H. The society. 1835. 24p.   1036

NEW YORK (STATE) COLONIZATION SOCIETY. Annual report . . . 1832-1896. Collection has: 5th, 7th, 9th; 1837, 1839, 1841. New York. imprints vary. 1837-39-41.   1037

NEW YORK (STATE) COLONIZATION SOCIETY. African colonization. Proceedings, on the formation of the New York state colonization society; together with an address to the public. Albany. Webster & Skinners, 1829. 24p.   1038

NEW YORK (STATE) COLONIZATION SOCIETY. African colonization. Proceedings of the New York state colonization society on its first anniversary; together with an address to the public. Albany, Webster & Skinners, printers, 1830. 24p. 1039

NEW YORK (STATE) COLONIZATION SOCIETY. Statement . . . as to its differences with the American Colonization

Society. March, 1870. New York, The society. 1870. 29p. 1040

NEW YORK (STATE) COLONIZATION SOCIETY. A few facts and figures for the friends of Africa. New York, The New York State Colonization Society. 1850. 24p. 1041

NEW YORK (STATE) COLONIZATION SOCIETY. Memorial . . . to the honorable the legislature of the state of New York. 9p. N.Y. State senate documents, no. 333, March 24, 1830. Albany. 1042

NEW YORK (STATE) COLONIZATION SOCIETY. Report of the committee on charitable societies on the memorial of the colonization society. 4p. (State of New York, Assembly reports, No. 71, February 18, 1851). 1043

ORCUTT, JOHN. African colonization, an address . . . before the American Colonization Society, Jan. 19, 1875. New York, The society. 1875. 22p. 1044

PEARL, CYRIL (pseud.) A citizen of New England. Remarks of African colonization and the abolition of slavery. In two parts. Windsor, Vt., Richards & Tracy. 1833. 47p. 1045

POLLOCK, A. D. Africa and her children and her prospect; a discourse in behalf of African colonization. Richmond, Peter D. Bernard. 1840. 19p. 1046

REESE, DAVID M. Letters to the Hon. William Jay; being a reply to his "Inquiry into the American colonization and anti-slavery societies." New York, Leavitt, Lord & co. 1835. 120p. 1047

REVIEW OF PAMPHLETS on slavery and colonization. (First published in the Quarterly Christian Spectator, March, 1833 Separate 2d ed. New Haven. A. H. Maltby. Boston, Pierce & Parker. 1833. 24p. 1048

RICE, NATHAN L. Lectures on Slavery with an appendix containing a discussion with Rev. Mr. Wolcott. Chicago, Church, Goodman, Cushing. 1860. 100p. 1049

ROBERTS, JOSEPH J. The Republic of Liberia. An address delivered at the fifty-second anniversary meeting of the American colonization society, held in Washington, D. C. January 19, 1869. Washington, American Colonization Society, 1869. 20p. 1050

SPRING, GARDINER. Memoirs of the Rev. Samuel J. Mills, late missionary to the southwestern section of the U.S., and agent of the American Colonization Society, deputed to explore the coast of Africa. New York, N. Y. Evangelical Missionary Society. 1820. 247p. 1051

THORNTON, JOHN W. The first records of Anglo-American Colonization: Their history. Boston, Gould & Lincoln, 1859. 12p. 1052

TRACY, JOSEPH. Natural equality. A sermon delivered before the Vermont colonization society, Montpelier, Oct. 17, 1833. Windsor, Vt., The society. 1833. 24p. 1053

TORREY, JESSE. JR. A portraiture of domestic slavery in the United States; with reflections on the possibility of restoring the moral rights of the slave, without impairing the legal rights of the possessor; and a project of a colonial asylum for free persons of colour; including memoirs of facts on the interior traffic in slaves and on kidnapping . . . 2d ed. Ballston Spa. Pa. The author. 1818. 108p.

1054

TYSON, JOB R. A discourse delivered before the Young men's colonization society of Pennsylvania, Oct. 24, 1834, in Philadelphia. With a notice of the proceedings of the society, and of their first expedition of coloured emigrants to found a colony at Bassa Cove, Philadelphia, The society. 1834. 63p.   1055

U . S . H O U S E O F REPRESENTATIVES Naval Committee Report . . . on establishing a line of mail steamships to the western coast of Africa, and thence via the Mediterranean to London, with an appendix added by the Amer. colonization society. Washington, Gideon & co. 1850. 79p.   1056

VERMONT COLONIZATION SOCIETY. Annual report . . . collection has: 17th, 19th, 23d, 26th; 1836, 1838, 1842, 1845. Imprints vary.   1057

A VIEW OF EXERTIONS lately made for the purpose of colonizing the free people of colour, in the United States, in Africa, or elsewhere. Washington, J. Elliott. 1817. 22p.

1058

WILKERSON, SAMUEL. A concise history of the commencement, progress and present condition of the American colonies in Liberia. Washington, American colonization society. 1839. 88p.   1059

VI. Anti-colonization.

BIRNEY, JAMES G. Letter on colonization, addressed to the Rev. Thornton J. Mills, corresponding secretary of the Kentucky colonization society. New York. American anti-slavery society. 1838. 46p.   1060

BRITISH opinions of the American colonization society. Boston. Garrison & Knapp. 1833. 36p. 1061

BROWN, THOMAS C. Examination of Mr. Thomas C. Brown, a free colored citizen of South Carolina, as to the actual state of things in Liberia in the years 1833 and 1834. New York. Anti-slavery society reporter supplement. 1834. 32p.

1062

CLERICUS pseud.) The real character and tendency of the American colonization society. Liverpool. 1833. 19p.   1063

THE COLONIZATION scheme considered . . . in its rejection by the colored people . . . in its tendency to uphold caste . . . putting an end to the African slave trade . . . Newark. 1840. 26p. 1064

GARRISON, WILLIAM L. The Maryland scheme of expatriation examined. By a friend of liberty. Boston. Garrison & Knapp. 1834. 20p.   1065

GARRISON, WILLIAM L. Thoughts on African colonization: or, an impartial exhibition of the doctorines, principles, and purposes of the American colonization society. Together with the resolutions, addresses, and remonstrances of the free people of color. Boston. Garrison & Knapp. 1832. iv, 160. 76p.   1066

JAY, WILLIAM. An inquiry into the character . . . of American colonization, and American anti-slavery societies. Boston, Crocker & Brewster. 1835. 206p. 1067

NOURSE, JAMES. Views on colonization. Philadelphia, Merrihew & Gunn. 1837. 52p. 1068

PHILLIPS, WENDELL. Review of Webster's speech on slavery. Boston. American anti-slavery society. 1850. 44p. 1069

RESOLUTIONS and remonstrances of the people of color against colonization on the coast of Africa. Philadelphia. 1818. 8p. 1070

STEBBINS, GILES B. Facts and opinions touching the real origin, character, and influence of the American colonization society; views of Wilborforce, Clarkson and others, and opinions of the free people of the United States. . . Boston. John P. Jewett & co. 1853. viii, (5)-224p. 1071

STUART, CHARLES. Supplement to the emancipation. A letter to Thomas Clarkson by James Cropper and Prejudice vincible . . . in relation to the American colonization society. Liverpool. The author. 1832. 24p.. 2d ed. New York. 1833. 15p. 1072

THOMPSON, GEORGE. Discussion on American slavery, between George Thompson and Rev. Robert J. Breckinridge. . . in Glasgow, Scotland, June 13-17, 1836. Boston, Isaac Knapp. 1836. 187p. 1073

VII. Religious Aspects of Slavery.
  1. The Bible and Slavery
    a. Anti-slavery
    b. Pro-slavery
  2. Religious Instruction of Slaves.
  3. The Churches and Slavery.

a. Anti-slavery.

BARNES, ALBERT. An inquiry into the Scriptural views of slavery. Philadelphia, Perkins & Purves. Boston, B. Perkins & co. 1846. 384p. 2d ed. Philadelphia, Parry & Macmillan. 1846. 384p., 3d ed. Philadelphia, Parry & Macmillan. 1857. 384p. 1074

BIBLICUS (pseud). The Bible view of slavery reconsidered. A letter to the Right Rev. Bishop Hopkins. 2nd ed. rev. & enl. Philadelphia. Henry B. Ashmead, print. 1863. 15p. 1075

BOURNE, GEORGE (pseud.) A citizen of Virginia. A condensed anti-slavery Bible argument; by a citizen of Virginia . . . New York. S. W. Benedict. 1845. 91p. 1076

BOURNE, GEORGE (pseud.) Pictures of slavery in the United States of America. Boston. Isaac Knapp. Middleton, Conn. Edwin Hunt. 1834. 227p. 1077

BOURNE, GEORGE (pseud.) A Presbyter of The Church in Philadelphia. Review of Bishop Hopkins' Bible View of slavery. 15p. n.d. 1078

BRISBANE, WILLIAM H. Slaveholding examined in the light of the Holy Bible. Philadelphia. U. S. job print. office. 1847. 205p. 1079

CHEEVER, GEORGE B. The fire and hammer of God's word against the sin of slavery. Speech . . . at the anniversary of the American abolition society. May, 1858. New York. American abolition society. 1858. 16p.   1080

CHEEVER, GEORGE B. God against slavery; and the freedom and duty of the pulpit to rebuke it, as a sin against God. New York, Joseph H. Ladd. 1857. 272p.. 2d ed. Cincinnati. American reform tract & book society. 1859. 272p.   1081

CHEEVER, GEORGE B. The guilt of slavery and the crime of slaveholding, demonstrated from the Hebrew and Greek scriptures. Boston, John P. Jewett & co. 1860. viii, xx, 472p.   1082

DUNCAN, JAMES. A treatise on slavery, in which is shown forth the evils of slaveholding both from the light of nature and divine revelation, Vevay, Ind. Register office. 1824. 136p. Reprint ed. Cincinnati. Ohio anti-slavery society. 1840. 136p.   1083

ELLIOTT, CHARLES. Sinfulness of American slavery; proved from its evil sources; its injustice; its wrong; its contrariety to many Scriptural commands, prohibitions, and principles, and to the Christian spirit; and from its evil effects; together with observations on emancipation. and the duties of American citizens in regard to slavery. Ed. by B. F. Tofft. Cincinnati. L. Swormstedt & J. H. Power. 1851. 2v.   1084

FITZGERALD, W. P. N. Scriptural view of slavery and abolition. 2d ed. New York, The author. 1839. 24p.   1085

FULLER, RICHARD and WAYLAND, FRANCIS. Domestic slavery considered as a Scriptural institution; in a correspondence between the Rev. Richard Fuller, of Beaufort, S. C. and the Rev. Francis Wayland, of Providence, R. I. 5th ed. rev. corr. New York, Lewis Colby & co. Boston, Gould, Kendall and Lincoln. 1845. viii, 254p.   1086

GANSE, HERVEY D. Bible slaveholding not sinful; a reply to "Slaveholding not sinful, by Samuel B. How." New York, R. & R. Brinkerhoff. 1856. 85p.   1087

HAGUE, WILLIAM. Christianity and slavery; a review of the correspondence between Richard Fuller . . . and Francis Wayland . . . on domestic slavery, considered as a Scriptural institution. Boston, Gould, Kendall & Lincoln. 1847. 54p.   1088

JAY, WILLIAM. An examination of the Mosaic laws of servitude. New York. M. W. Dodd. 1854. 56p.1089

LEE, LUTHER. Slavery examined in the light of the Bible. Syracuse, Wesleyan Methodist book room. 1855. 185p.   1090

LIBERTY OR SLAVERY the great national question; three prize essays on American slavery. Boston, Congregational board. 1857. 138p.
                    1091

LUNDY, JOHN P. Review of Bishop Hopkins', Bible view of slavery. By a presbyter of the church. 15p.
                    1092

MCKEEN, SILAS. A Scriptural argument in favor of withdrawing fellowship from churches and ecclesiastical bodies tolerating slaveholding among them. New York, American & Foreign anti-slavery society. 1848. 37p.
                    1093

NEW TESTAMENT against slavery. n.p. n.d. 71p.   1094

THE NUTSHELL. The system of American slavery "Tested By

Scripture," being "A Short Method" with preslavery D. D.'s, whether Doctors of Divinity, or of Democracy embracing axioms of social, civil, and political economy, as divinely impressed upon the human conscience and set forth in divine revelation. In two lectures. By a layman of the Protestant Episcopal church in the Diocese of Connecticut. To which are added brief extracts, "Teachings of Patriots and Statesmen," etc., etc., also an outline compend of the African Slave Trade. New York, The author. 1862. 72p.   1095

PAXTON, JOHN D. Letters on slavery; addressed to the Cumberland congregation, Virginia, Lexington, Ky. A. T. Skillman. 1833. 207p.   1096

SMITH, GOLDWIN. Does the Bible sanction slavery? Cambridge, Sever & Francis. 1863. 107p.   1097

SOCIETY for the Diffusion of Political Knowledge. No. 8. Bible Vien of Slavery. n. p., n. d. 16p.   1098

STROUD, GEORGE M. Southern slavery and the Christian religion, Philadelphia, 1863.   1099

SUNDERLAND, L. The testimony of God against slavery; or, A collection of passages from the Bible, which show the sin of holding property in man, with notes. Boston, Webster & Southard. 1835. 104p.   1100

THOMPSON, JOSEPH P. Christianity and emancipation; or, The teachings and the influence of the Bible against slavery. New York. Anson D. F. Randolph. 1863. 86p.   1101

THOMPSON, JOSEPH P. Teachings of the New Testament on slavery. New York, J. H. Ladd. 1856. 52p.   1102

TOWNSEND, LUCY. To the law, and to the testimony or questions on slavery answered by the scriptures . . . London, Hamilton, Adams & co. 1832. 24p.   1103

TYLER, EDWARD R. Slaveholding a malum in so, or invariably sinful. 2d ed. Hartford, Case, Tiffany & co. 1839. 48p.   1104

UNITED PRESBYTERIAN BOARD OF PUBLICATION. The Bible against slavery; or, An inquiry into the genius of the Mosaic system, and the teachings of the Old Testament on the subject of human rights. Pittsburg, United presbyterian board of pub. 1864. 154p.   1105

VAIL, STEPHEN M. The Bible against slavery, with replies to the "Bible view of slavery," by John H. Hopkins, bishop of Vermont; and to a "northern presbyter's second letter to ministers of the Gospel," by Nathan Lord . . . and to "X," of the New Hampshire patriot. Concord. Fogg, Hadley & co. 1864. 63p.   1106

VIEWS OF AMERICAN SLAVERY taken a century ago . . . Philadelphia. Association of Friends for the diffusion of religious and useful knowledge. 1858. 1388p.   1107

WELD, THEODORE DWIGHT. The Bible against slavery; or, An inquiry into the genius of the mosaic system, and the teachings of the Old Testament on the subject of human rights. Pittsburgh. United Presbyterian board of pub. 1864. xiii, 154p. (Enl. from anti-slavery examiner, no. 4.)   1108

WESLEY, JOHN. Slavery — a sin against God (25)-45p. Thoughts on slavery . . . written and (originally) published in 1774. Reprinted by

Joseph Cruikshank, Philadelphia.
1774. 84p.   1109

b. Pro-slavery

ARMSTRONG, GEORGE D. The Christian Doctrine of slavery. New York, Charles Scribner. 1857. 148p.   1110

EWART, DAVID. A scriptural view of the moral relations of African slavery. 1849, rev. & amend. in 1859. Charleston, S. C. The author. 12p.   1111

HOLCOMBE, WILLIAM H. Suggestions as to the Spiritual philosophy of African slavery, addressed to the members and friends of the church of the New Jerusalem. New York, Mason bros. 1861.   1861

HOPKINS, JOHN H. (bishop of Vermont) Bible view of slavery, n.p. n.d. 16p.   1113

HOPKINS, JOHN H. Letter . . . on the Bible view of slavery. New York, W. K. Kost. 1861. 12p.   1114

HOWE, SAMUEL B. Slaveholding not sinful. Slavery the punishment of man's sin, its remedy, the Gospel of Christ. An argument before the General Synod of the Reformed Protestant church, Dutch. 1856. 136p.   1115

JONES, JOHN R. Slavery sanctioned by the Bible. The first part of a general treatise on the slavery question. A tract for northern Christians. Philadelphia, J. B. Lippincott & co. 1861. 34p.   1116

LORD, NATHAN. A letter of inquiry to the ministers of the gospel of all denominations, on slavery, by a northern presbyter. Boston, Fetridge & co. 1854. 32p. 2d ed. Boston, Little, Brown & co. 1854. 32p.   1117

MCCAINE, ALEXANDER. Slavery defended from scripture, against the attacks of the abolitionists. A speech delivered before the General conference of the Methodist protestant church. Baltimore, 1842. Baltimore, W. Woody. 1842. 28p.   1118

PRIEST, JOSIAH, AND BROWN, W. S. Bible defence of slavery; or, The origin, history, and fortunes of the Negro race, as deduced from history both sacred and profane, their natural relations-moral, mental, and physical — to the other races of mankind, compared and illustrated, their future destiny predicted, etc. To which is added a plan of national colonization, adequate to the entire removal of the Free Blacks and all that may hereafter become free in a manner harmonizing with the peace and well-being of both races. 6th ed. stereotyped. Glasgow, Ky., W. S. Brown. 1851. 569p. Louisville, Wm. Bush. 1851. 569p.   1119

PRIEST, JOSIAH AND BROWN, W. S. Slavery, as it relates to the Negro, or African race, examined in the light of circumstances, history and the holy scriptures with an account of the origin of the black man's color, causes of his state of servitude and traces of his character as well in ancient as in modern times; with scriptures on abolitionism. Albany, C. Van Benthuysen and co. 1843. 340p.   1120

RAPHALL, MORRIS J. Bible View of slavery. A discourse. New York,

69

publ. by author. 1861. 41p.   1121
ROSS. FREDERICK A. Slavery ordained of God . . . Philadelphia, J. B. Lippincott & co. 1857. 186p.   1122
SLOAN. JAMES A. The great question answered; or is slavery a sin in itself. Answered according to the teaching of the scriptures. Memphis, Hutton, Gallaway & co. 1857. 294p.   1123

STRINGFELLOW, REV. THORNTON. Slavery; its origin, nature, and history considered in the light of bible teaching, moral justice, and political wisdom. New York, John F. Trow. 1851. 56p.   1124
STRINGFELLOW, REV. THORNTON. Scriptural and statistical views in favor of slavery. 4th ed. with additions. Richmond, Va., J. W. Randolph, 1856. 149p.   1125
STRINGFELLOW, REV. THORNTON. A brief examination of Scripture testimony on the institution of slavery, in an essay,

first published in the Religious herald. . . with remarks on a review of the essay. Richmond. Religious herald. 1841. 40p. New ed. Washington. Congressional Globe Office. 1850. 32p.   1126
THOUGHTS ON SLAVERY. Lowell, Daniel Bixby and co. 1848. 70p.   1127
WHEAT, MARVIN T. The progress and intelligence of Americans; collateral proof of slavery, from the first to the eleventh chapter of Genesis, as founded on organic law; and from the fact of Christ being a Caucasian, owing to his peculiar parentage; progress of slavery south and southwest; with free labor advancing, through the acquisition of territory; advantages enumerated and explained. Louisville. 1862. 615p.   1128
WILSON, JOSEPH R. Mutual relation of masters and slaves as taught in the Bible. A discourse preached in the First Presbyterian church, Augusta, Ga. Jan. 6, 1861. Augusta, Ga., Chronicle & sentinel press. 1861. 21p.   1129

2. Religious Instructions of Slaves.

THE ENORMITY of the slave trade; and the moral and spiritual elevation of the colored race. Speeches of Wilberforce, and other documents and records. New York, American tract society. 1846. 144p.   1130
GLENNIE, ALEXANDER. Sermons preached on plantations to congregations of Negroes. Charleston, S. C. author. 1844. 164p.   1131
HARRISON, W. P. The Gospel among the slaves . . . of the southern states. Compiled from original

sources. Nashville. Pub. house of M. E. Church, South. 1893. 394p..   1132
INCORPORATED society for the conversion and religious instruction and education of Negro slaves in the British West Indian islands. Some account of the society . . . incorporated by royal charter, 1794. London, Gilbert. 1823. 13p.   1133
JERNEGAN, MARCUS W. Slavery and conversion in the American colonies. New York, Macmillan co. 1916. 23p. (Reprinted from the

American historical review, v. xxi, no. 3, April, 1916). 1134

NISBET, RICHARD. The capacity of Negroes for religious and moral improvement considered; with cursory hints, to proprietors and to government, for the immediate melioration of the condition of slaves in the sugar colonies; to which are subjoined short and practical discourses to Negroes, on the plain and obvious principles of religion and morality. London, J. Phillips. 1789. xii, 207p. 1135

PLUMER, WILLIAM S. Thoughts on the religious instruction of Negroes of this country. Savannah, E. J. Purse. 1848. 28p. 1136

RAMSEY, JAMES. An essay on the treatment and conversion of African slaves in the British sugar colonies. London, J. Phillips. 1784. xx, 298p. 1137

RICHMOND, LEIGH. Annals of the poor; containing the dairy man's daughter, the Negro servant, and the young cottager. . . New ed. enl. Philadelphia, Wm. Stavely. 1830. 226p. 1138

SEWARD, WILLIAM. Journal of a voyage from Savannah to Philadelphia and from Philadelphia to England. London, 1740. 1139

THORNWELL, JAMES H. The rights and duties of masters; a sermon preached at the dedication of a church erected at Charleston, S. C. for the benefit and instruction of the colored population. Charleston. Walker & James. 1850. iv, 51p. 1140

WEEKS, STEPHEN B. Religious development in the province of North Carolina. Baltimore. Johns Hopkins press. 1892. 128p. 1141

3. The Churches and Slavery.

AN AMERICAN citizen (pseud). The ethics of American slavery, being a vindication of the word of God and a pure Christianity in all ages, from complicity with involuntary servitude: and a demonstration that American slavery is a crime in substance and concomitants. New York. Ross & Tousey. 181. 146p. 1142

BAIRD, R. Christianity in the United States of America; with remarks on the subject of slavery . . . London, Partridge & Oakey, 1851. 72p. 1143

BARNES, ALBERT. The church and slavery. 3d thousand. Philadelphia. Parry & Macmillan. 1856. 204p. 1144

BERRY, PHILIP. Review of the Bishop of Oxford's counsel to the American clergy with reference to the Institution of slavery. Washington, William M. Morrison, 1848. 26p. 1145

BIRNEY, JAMES G. The American churches, the bulwarks of American slavery. By an American. 2d American ed. rev. Newburyport. Chas. Whipple. 1842. 44p. 3d. ed. enl. 1842. 48p. 1146

BIRNEY, JAMES G. Second letter to the ministers and elders of the Presbyterian church in Kentucky. Mercer County, Ky. n.p. 1834. 16p. 1147

BOURNE, GEORGE (pseud., Presbyter) An address to the Presbyterian Church, enforcing the duty of excluding all slaveholders from the "communion of saints." New York, 1833. 16p. 1148

BOURNE, GEORGE (pseud.,

Presbyter). Man stealing denounced by the Presbyterian and Methodist churches. Boston, Garrison & Knapp. 1834. 19p.   1149

BRISBANE, WILLIAM H. A speech delivered April 30, 1844, before the Baptist home mission society, on the question of the propriety of recognizing slaveholding ministers as proper missionaries of the gospel. 7p.   1150

BUSH, GEORGE. New church miscellanies; or, essays . . . republished from the New church repository. New York, W. George. 1855. Boston. O. Clapp. 372p. Aphorisms on slavery and abolition, p. 165-238.   1151

CASWALL, HENRY. The American church and the American union. London, Saunders, Otley & co. 1861. x; 311p.   1152

CHEEVER, GEORGE B. The sin of slavery, the guilt of the church, and the duty of the ministry. An address delivered before the Abolition Society at New York, 1858. (Tracts for thinking men and women. no. 1). Boston, John P. Jewett and co., Cleveland, Henry P.B. Jewett, 1858. 23p.   1153

CHEEVER, HENRY T. A tract for the times, on the question. Is it right to withhold fellowship churches or from individuals that tolerate or practice slavery? New York. John A. Gray. 1859. 23p.   1154

CLARKSON, THOMAS. A letter to the clergy of various denominations and to the slaveholding planters in the southern parts of the United States . . . London, Johnson & Barrett, 1841. 64p.   1155

CONGREGATIONALIST DIRECTOR (pseud). The tables turned. A letter to the Congregational Association of New York. . . "The relation of the American Tract Society" to the subject of slavery. Boston, Crocker & Brewster, n.d. 44p.   1156

CONVENTION OF CONGREGATIONAL ministers of Massachusetts. Report of the committee on slavery, presented May 30, 1849. Boston, T. R. Marvin. 1849. 92p.   1157

CONVENTION OF MINISTERS . . . on slavery, held at Worcester, Dec. 5 and 6, 1837. Proceedings . . . Worcester, 1838. 22p.   1158

DEAN, HENRY C. Letter to Gov. Wright of Indiana, upon the connexion of the Methodist Episcopal church with the subject of slavery. n.p., n.d. iii, 13p.   1159

DE CHARMS, RICHARD. Some views of freedom and slavery in the light of the new Jerusalem. Philadelphia, The author. 1851. 108p.   1160

FOSTER, STEPHEN S. The brotherhood of thieves; or, A true picture of the American church and clergy. A letter to Nathaniel Barney of Nantucket. New London. Wm. Bolles. 1843. 64p.   1161

FREE CHURCHMAN (Pseud). The free church and her accusers in the matter of American slavery. Edinburgh; John Johnstone, 1846. 35p.   1162

FRIENDS, ASSOCIATION OF, for advocating the cause of the slave, and improving the condition of the free people of color. Extracts from writings of friends on the subject of slavery. Philadelphia, The Association. 1839. 24p.   1163

THE FRIENDS' LIBRARY: Comprising journals, doctrinal treatises, and other writings of members of the religious society of friends. Edited by Wm. Evans and Thomas Evans. Philadelphia, the editors. Library has: Vol. III, 1839, containing memoirs of Edward Chester and others; Vol. VI, 1842, containing life of Thos. Chalkley, journal of John Churchman, etc. 1164

FRIENDS OF NEW ENGLAND. Yearly meeting . . . An appeal to the professors of Christianity, in the Southern states and elsewhere, on the subject of slavery. Providence. Knoles & Vose. 1842. 24p. 1165

FRIENDS, RELIGIOUS SOCIETY OF. Address of the yearly meeting . . . to the professors of Christianity in the United States. New York, The society. 1852. 10p. 1166

FRIENDS, RELIGIOUS SOCIETY OF. The appeal of . . . friends of Pennsylvania, New Jersey, Delaware, etc. to their fellow-citizens of the United States on behalf of the coloured races, Philadelphia. Friends' book store. 1858. 48p. 1167

FRIENDS, RELIGIOUS SOCIETY OF. Testimony . . . against slavery. Boston. Representatives of the New England yearly meeting. 1847. Boston, The society. 12p. 1168

FRIENDS, RELIGIOUS SOCIETY OF. Appeal . . . on behalf of the coloured races. Philadelphia. The society. 1859. 48p. 1169

FRIENDS, YEARLY MEETING OF. Address to the Quarterly monthly, and preparative meetings . . . by the committee . . . to have charge of the subject of slavery. Philadelphia. The committee. 1839. 12p.s. 1170

GENERAL ASSOCIATION OF MASSACHUSETTS. Report . . . of the committee of correspondence with Southern ecclesiastical bodies on slavery; to the General association of Massachusetts. Salem, John P. Jewett & co. 1844. 23p. 1171

GOODELL, WILLIAM. Come - outerism. . The duty of secession from a corrupt church. Boston, The author. 1845. 38p. 1172

GOODWIN, DANIEL R. Southern slavery in its present aspects; containing a reply to a late work of the Bishop of Vermont on slavery. Philadelphia, J.B. Lippincott & co. 1864. 343p. 1173

GREVILLE, ROBERT K. Slavery and the slave trade in the United States of America; and the extent to which the American churches are involved in their support. Edinburgh, W. Oliphant & sons. 1845. 24p. 1174

HARRIS, WILLIAM L. The constitutional powers of the General conference, with a special application to the subject of slaveholding. Cincinnati. Methodist book concern. 1860. 156p. 1175

HOLCOMBE, WILLIAM H. Suggestions as to the spiritual philosophy of African slavery, addressed to the members and friends of the church of the New Jerusalem. New York, Mason bros. 1861. 24p. 1176

HOSMER, WILLIAM. Slavery and the church. Auburn, N. Y. Wm. J. Moses. 1853. 200p. 1177

LEO XIII. Letter . . . to the bishop Brazil on the church and slavery. Baltimore, St. Joseph's Seminary for colored missions. 1888. 16p. 1178

LEWIS, REV. GEORGE. Slavery and slave holders in the United States of America, being excerpts from "Impressions of America and the American churches." Edinburgh, W.P. Kennedy, 1846. 52p. 1179

LONG, JOHN D. Pictures of slavery in church and state, including personal reminiscences, biographical sketches, anecdotes, etc. . . with an appendix, containing the views of John Wesley and Richard Watson on slavery. Philadelphia, author. 1857. 418p.   1180

MATTISON, HIRAM. The impending crisis of 1860, or, the present connection of the Methodist Episcopal church with slavery, and our duty in regard to it. New York, Mason brothers, 1859. 136p.   1181

"THE NEGRO PEW" being an inquiry concerning the propriety of distinctions in the House of God on account of color. Boston, Isaac Knapp. 1837. 108p.   1182

PATTON, WILLIAM W. The unanimous remonstrance of the Fourth Congregational Church, Hartford, Conn. against the policy of the American tract society on the subject of slavery. Hartford, Silas Andrus & son. 1855. 34p.   1183

PENNSYLVANIA PROTESTANT EPISCOPAL CHURCH. Christianity versus treason and slavery. Religion rebuking sedition. Philadelphia. n.d. 16p.   1184

PILLSBURY, PARKER. The church as it is, or the forlorn hope of slavery. Boston, A. Forbes. 1847. 96p. 2d ed. Rev. and imp. Boston. Bela Marsh. 1847. 90p.   1185

PRINCETON REVIEW. Essays theological and miscellaneous . . . 2d series. New York, Wiley & Putnam. 1847.   1186

REMSBURG, JOHN E. Piety and the slave trade. The record of Methodism. New York, Truth seeker tracts, no. 1. 17p.   1187

SAWYER, LEICESTER A. A dissertation on servitude: embracing an examination of the scripture doctrines on the subject, and an inquiry into the character and relations of slavery. New Haven, Durrie & Pock, 1837. 108p.   1188

STROUD, GEORGE M. Southern slavery and the christian religion communication . . . to the editor of North American and U.S. Gazette. n.p., n.d. 4p.   1189

THOMAS, THOMAS E. Correspondence . . . mainly relating to the anti-slavery conflict in Ohio, especially in the Presbyterian church. Dayton. 1809. 137p. 1190

VERMONTER, A (pseud.) Review of a "Letter from the Right Rev. John H. Hopkins, Bishop of Vermont on the Bible view of slavery." Burlington, Free Press, 1861. 28p.   1191

WEEKS, STEPHEN B. Southern Quakers and slavery; a study in institutional history. Baltimore, The Johns Hopkins Press. 1896. 400p. (Johns Hopkins University Studies in Political Science; extra vol. xv.)   1192

WHIPPLE, CHARLES K. Relation of the American board of commissioners for foreign missions to slavery. Boston, R. F. Wallcut. 1861. 247p.   1193

VIII. Economic Aspects of Slavery.

ATKINSON, EDWARD (pseud.) A cotton manufacturer. Cheap cotton by free labor. 2d ed. Boston, A. Williams & co. 1861. 54p.   1194

CAREY, HENRY C. (ed.) The North and the South. New York, Tribune office. 1854. 48p. (Reprinted form the New York Tribune). 1195

CAREY, HENRY C. (ed.) The Slave question. p. 401-411. The plough, the loom, and the anvil. vol. 1, no. vii. January, 1849. 1196

CHASE, HENRY & SANBORN, CHARLES W. The North and the South; a statistical view of the condition of the free slave states . . . compiled from official documents. Cleveland, P. B. Jewett, 1856. 191p. 1197

COLWELL, STEPHEN. The five cotton states and New York, or, Remarks upon the social and economical aspects of the southern political crisis. Jan. 1861. 64p. 1198

ESTIMATES OF THE VALUE OF SLAVES, Documents. 1815. (Reprinted from the American Historical Review, vol. xix, no. 4, July, 1914. p. 813-838.) 1199

FRIENDS, RELIGIOUS SOCIETY OF. Address . . . on the propriety of abstaining from the use of the produce of slave labour. Philadelphia, The society. 1838. 11p. 1200

GALLATIN, ALBERT. Letter from the Secretary of the treasury to the chairman of the committee of ways and means . . . to make the valuations of lands and dwelling houses, and the enumeration of slaves in the State of South Carolina. Dec. 10, 1804. 11p. 1201

HAMMOND, MATHEW B. Cotton industry, an essay in American economic history. American economic assn. (publ. no. 1). 1897. 1202

HARDY, JOHN. Letter to a New Jersey farmer. New York, Young Men's Fremont and Dayton Central Union. 1856. 4p. 1203

HARRISON, JESSE BURTON (pseud. A virginian). Review of the slave question, extracted from the American Quarterly Review, December, 1832; based on the speech of Thomas Marshall, of Fauquier; showing that slavery is the essential hindrance to the prosperity of the slave-holding states; with particular reference to Virginia, though applicable to other states where slavery exists. Richmond. T.W. White, 1833. 48p. 1204

HELPER, HINTON R. Compendium of the impending crisis of the South. New York, A. B. Burdick, 1860. 214p. 1205

HELPER, HINTON R. The impending crisis of the South; how to meet it. New York, A. B. Burdick. 1859. 420p. enl. ed. New York, A. B. Burdick. 1860. 438p. 1206

HICKS, ELIAS. Observations on the slavery of the Africans and their descendents, and on the use of the produce of their labour. Recommended to the serious perusal, and impartial consideration of the citizens of the United States of America, and others concerned. 2d ed. New York, Chapman. 1839. 32p. 1207

HILLIER, RICHARD. A vindication of the address to the people of Great Britain, on the use of West India produce, with some observations and facts relative to the situation of slaves. 2nd ed. . London, M. Gurney, L. Wayland, T. Knott, 1791. 24p. 1208

HODGSON, ADAM. A letter to M. Jean — Baptiste Say, on the comparative expense of free and slave labour. 2nd ed. Liverpool, Hatchard & son. 1823. 58p. New York Reprinted for the

Manumission Society, 1823. 50p. 14p. 1209

JACKSON, WILLIAM. Views of slavery, in its effects on the wealth, population, and character of nations. Philadelphia, Junior anti-slavery society. 1838. 12p. 1210

KEITT, LAWRENCE M. (S.C) Speech. . . on slavery, and the resources of the South, delivered in the House of Representatives, January 15, 1857. Washington, Congressional Globe. 1857. 14p. 1211

LIEBER, FRANCIS. Plantations for slave labor. The death of Yeomanry. n.d., n.p. 8p. 1212

MARRIOTT, CHARLES. Address . . . to the members of religious society of friends, on the duty of declining the use of the products of slave labour. New York, Isaac T. Hopper. 1835. 18p. 1213

A MARYLANDER, (pseud.) Slavery, its institution and origin. Its status under the law and under the gospel. Its agricultural, commercial and financial, aspects. Baltimore, J.P. Des Forges, n.d. 8p. 1214

MELISH, JOHN. Letter . . . to James Monroe, esq. President of the United States, on the state of the country with a plan for improving the condition of society. Philadelphia, J. Melish. 1820. 32p. 1215

NOTES ON "Southern wealth and Northern profits." Philadelphia, C. Sherman & son. 1861. 31p. 1216

REED, HENRY. Southern slavery and its relations to northern industry; a lecture delivered at Cincinnati, Jan. 24, 1862. Cincinnati, Enquirer press. 1862. 36p. 1217

SANFORD, H. S. Free cotton and free cotton states (from the Albany Evening Journal). Derby, Conn. 1860. n.p. 4p. 1218

TAYLOR, JAMES W. Alleghania; A geographical and statistical memoir, exhibiting the strength of the Union, and the weakness of slavery, etc. St. Paul, Minn., James Davenport, 1862. 24p. 1219

U. S. HOUSE OF REPRE-SENTATIVES. 19th Congress. 1st Session. H. R. documents Number 104. Letter from the Secretary of War, transmitting information . . . in relation to the execution of the law of March 3, 1825, for the relief of Nimrod Farrow and Richard Harris. Feb. 24, 1826. Washington. Gales & Seaton. 61p. 1220

WESTON, GEORGE M. The poor whites of the south. Washington, Buell & Blanchard. 1856. 7p. 1221

IX. Traveler's Observations on Slavery.

ABBOTT, JOHN S. C. South and North; or, Impressions received during a trip to Cuba and the South. New York, Abbey & Abbott. 1860. 352p. 1222

ALEXANDER, J. E. Transatlantic sketches, comprising visits to the most interesting scenes in North and South America and the West Indies, with notes on Negro slavery and Canadian emigration. London, Richard Bentley, 1833. 2v. 1223

BAXTER, W. E. American and the Americans. London, Geo. Rutledge & co. 244pp. 1855. 1224

BREMER, FREDRIKA. The homes of

the new world; impressions of America. tr. from the Swedish by Mary Howlitt. New York, Harper & bros. 1853. 2v.   1225

BUCKINGHAM, JAMES S. The slave states of America. London, Fisher, son, & co. Paris. 1842. 2v.   1226

CHEVALIER, MICHAEL. Society, manners and politics in the United States; being a series of letters on North America. Tr. from the 3d. Paris ed. Boston, Weeks, Jordan & co. 1839. 467p.   1227

CHILD, MRS. LYDIA M. Letters from New York (Second series) New York, Boston, C. S. Francis & co. 1845. 287p.   1228

COLTON, CALVIN (pseud., An American Gentleman) A voice from America to England. London, Henry Colburn, 1834. 321p.   1229

DIXON, JAMES. Personal narrative of a tour through a part of the United States and Canada with notices of the history and institutions of Methodism in America. New York, Lane and Scott, 1850. 560p.   1230

FEATHERSTONEHAUGH, G. W. Excursion through the slave states from Washington on the Potomac to the frontier of Mexico; with sketches of popular manners and geological notices. First Am. ed. New York, Harper & bros. 1844. 168p. refs. Second ed. London. John Murray. 1844. 2v.   1231

FELTON, MRS. A narrative of two year's city and country residence in the United States. Boston, The author. 1843. 136p.   1232

FOSTER, WILLIAM. Way-side glimpses, North & South. New York, publ. by author. 1859. 250p.
                                                    1233

GODLEY, JOHN R. Letters from America, vol. II. London, John Murray. 1844. 243p.   1234

GUROWSKI, ADAM G. de. Diary from November 18, 1862 to October 18, 1863. New York, Carleton, 1864. 2v.   1235

KAPP, FRIEDRICH VON. Geschichte der sklaverei in den vereinington Staaten von Amerika. New York, Drud und Berlag von L. Haufer, 516p.   1236

KEMBLE, FRANCES ANN. Journal of residence on a Georgian plantation in 1839-1839. . .New York, Harper & bros. 1863. 337p.
                                                    1237

KIRKE, EDMUND (pseud.) James Roberts Gilmore. Among the pines, or, South in secession times. 34th thousand. New York, G. P. Putnam. 1862. 310p.   1238

KIRKE, EDMUND (pseud.) My southern friends. New York, Carleton, 1863. 308p.   1239

LYELL, CHARLES. A second visit to the United States of North America. New York, Harper & bros. 1855. 2v.   1240

MACKAY, CHARLES. Life and Liberty in America, or, sketches of a tour in the U. S. and Canada in 1857-8. London, Smith, Elder & co., 2 vols. New York, Harper & bros. 1859. 413p.   1241

MACRAE, DAVID. The Americans at home, Pen and ink sketches of American men, manners, and institutions. Glasgow, Horn & Connell, 1855. 488p.   1242

MALLARD, R. Q. Plantation life before emancipation. Richmond, Va., Whittet & Shepperson, 1892. 237p.   1243

MARTINEAU, HARRIET. Society in America. New York, Saunders and Otley, 1837. 2v.   1244

MARTINEAU, HARRIET. Retrospect of Western travel. New York, Charles Lorman, 1838. 2v.   1245

MARRYAT, CAPTAIN. A diary in America with remarks on its institutions. Philadelphia, Carey & Hart, 1839. 2 vols. 1246

MORDECAI, SAMUEL. Virginia, especially Richmond, in bygone days. 2d ed. Richmond, West & Johnston. 1860. 359p. 1247

MURRAY, AMELIA M. Letters from the United States, Cuba and Canada. New York, G. P. Putnam & co. 1856. 402p. 1248

MURRAY, CHARLES A. Travels in North America during the years 1834, 1835, and 1836, including a summer residence with the Pawnee tribe of Indians . . . New York, Harper and bros. 1839. 2v. 1249

A NORTHERN MAN (pseud.) The planter, or thirteen years in the South. Philadelphia, H. Hooker, 1853. 275p. 1250

OLMSTED, FREDERICK LAW. A Journey in the Seaboard Slave States in the years 1853-1854 with remarks on their economy. New York, Mason bros. 1863. 723p. New York and London, G. P. Putnam's sons, 1904. 2v. 1251

OLMSTED, FREDERICK L. A journey in the back country. New York, Mason bros., 1860. 492p. 1252

OLMSTED, FREDERICK L. The Cotton Kingdom, a traveller's observations in cotton and slavery in the American slave state, based upon three former volumes of journeys and investigations. New York, Mason bros. London, Sampson, Low, son & co. 1861. 2v. 1253

PARSONS, CHARLES G. Inside view of slavery, or, A tour among the planters . . . with an introductory note by Mrs. H. B. Stowe. 4th thousand. Boston, John P. Jewett &

co. Cleveland, Jewett, Proctor & Worthington. 1855. 318p. 1254

PIERRE, J. H. G. A Parisian Pastor's glance at America. Boston, Gould & Lincoln, 1854. 132p. 1255

REID, H. Sketches in North America, with some accounts of Congress and of the slavery question. London, Longman, Green, Longman & Roberts, 1861. 320p. 1256

ROBSON, W. Why I have not gone to the South. (letter written by an English traveler.) New York, American Anti-slavery society. 1858(?) 4p. 1257

RUSSELL, ROBERT. North America, its agriculture and climate. Edinburgh. Adam & Charles Black. 1857. 390p. 1258

RUSSELL, WILLIAM H. My diary north and south. New York, Harper & bros. 225p. Boston, T. O. H. P. Burnham, 1863. 602p. 1259

RUSSELL, WILLIAM H. Pictures of southern life, social, political, and military. New York, Jas. G. Gregory, 1861. 143p. 1260

STIRLING, JAMES. Letters from the slave states. London, John W. Parker & son, 1857. 374p. 1261

STUART, JAMES. Three years in North America. New York, J. & J. Harper, 1833. 2v. 1262

STURGE, JOSEPH. A visit to the United States in 1841. London, Hamilton, Adams & co., 1842. xciii, 192p. 1263

THOMASON, A. Men and things in America; being the experience of a year's residence in the United States, in a series of letters . . . London, William Smith, 1838. 296p. 1264

TOWER, PHILO. Slavery unmasked. Being a truthful narrative of a three years' residence and journeying in eleven southern states; to which is added the invasion of Kansas, including the last chapter of her wrongs. Rochester, E. Darrow & bro. 1856. 432p.   1265

VAIL, EUGENE A. Response a Quelques imputations contre les Etats-Unis, enoncees dans des ecrits et journaux re cens. Paris, Delaunay, 1837. 36p.   1266

WORTLEY, EMMELINE S. Travels in the United States, etc. during 1849 & 1850. Paris, A. & W. Galignani & co. 1851. 236p.   1267

YATES, EDWARD. A letter to the women of England, on slavery in the southern states of America; considered especially in reference to the condition of the female slaves. Most of the facts from observation . . . while traveling in the South. New York, Calvin Blanchard, 1863. 68p.   1268

X. Slave Narratives.

ANDERSON, JOHN. The story of the life of John Anderson, the fugitive slave. Ed. by Harper Twelve-trees. London, W. Tweedlie. 1863. xv. 182p.   1269

BALL, CHARLES. Fifty years in chains, or the life of an American slave. New York, H. Dayton, 1859. 430p.   1270

BALL, CHARLES. Slavery in the United States, A narrative of the Life & Adventures of . . . a black man. Lewiston, Pa., John W. Shugert, 1836. 400p.   1271

BIBB, HENRY. Narrative of the adventures of . . . an american slave, written by himself. New York, The author. 1849. 204p.   1272

BROWN, JOHN. Slave life in Georgia, a narrative of the life, sufferings, and escape of John Brown, a fugitive slave, now in England. Ed. by L. A. Chamerovzow. London, W. M. Watts. 250p.   1273

BROWN, JOSEPHINE. Biography of an American bondman, (William Wells Brown) by his daughter. Boston. R. F. Wallcut. 1856. 104p.   1274

BROWN, WILLIAM W. The black man, his antecedents, his genius, and his achievements. Rev. enl. ed. New York, Thos. Hamilton. 1863. 812p.   1275

BROWN, WILLIAM W. Narrative of William Wells Brown, a fugitive slave, written by himself. Boston, Anti-slavery office. 1847. 110p. 2d. ed. enl. 1848. 144p.   1276

CHARLTON, DIMMOCK. Narrative of a British subject. Taken from the Brig "Peacock" by the U. S. sloop "Hornet" . . . and retained forty-five years in bondage. 1858. 15p.   1277

CHILD, MRS. LYDIA M. F. The Freedmen's book. Boston, Ticknor & Fields. 1865. vi, 277p.   1278

CLARK, LEWIS G. Narrative of the sufferings of Lewis Clarke, during a capivity of more than twenty-five years, among the Algerines of Kentucky, one of the so-called Christian states of North America. Dictated by himself. Boston, David H. Ela. 1845. 108p.   1279

CLARK, LEWIS G and MILTON. Narrative of the sufferings of Lewis and Milton Clark, sons of a soldier of the revolution, during a captivity of more than twenty years among the slaveholders of Kentucky, one of the so-called Christian states of North America, dictated by themselves. Boston, Bela Marsh. 1846. 144p. 1280

DAVIS, NOAH. A narrative of the life . . . of a colored man, written by himself, at the age of fifty-four. Baltimore, The author. 1859. 86p. 1281

DOUGLASS, FREDERICK. Narrative of the life of Frederick Douglass, an American slave, written by himself. Boston, Anti-slavery office. 1845. xvi, 125p. 1282

DOUGLASS, FREDERICK. My bondage and my freedom. New York & Auburn, Miller, Orton & Mulligan, 464p. 1855. 1283

DREW, BENJAMIN. The Refugee, or the narratives of fugitive slaves in Canada, related by themselves, with an account of the history and condition of the colored population of upper Canada. A North-side view of slavery. Boston, John P. Jewett & co. 1856. 387p. 1284

ELIOT, WILLIAM G. The story of Archer Alexander from slavery to freedom. Boston, The author. 1885. 123p. 1285

ELDRIDGE, ELLEANOR. Memoirs . . . Providence, B. T. Albro. 1841, 127p. 1286

ELDRIDGE, ELLEANOR. Elleanor's second book. Providence, B. T. Albro. 1843. 128p. 1287

EQUIANO, OLAUDAH. The interesting narrative of the life of Olaudah Equiano, or Gustavus Vassa, the African. Written by himself. New ed. cor. Leeds, Eng. J. Nichols. 1814. 236p. Rev. enl. ed. Boston. Isaac Knapp. 1837. 294p. 1288

GILBERT, OLIVE. Narrative of Sojourner Truth, a northern slave, emancipated from bodily servitude by the state of New York, in 1828. Boston, author. 1850. 144p. 1289

GRIFFITHS, MATTIE. Autobiography of a female slave. New York, Redfield. 1857. 401p. 1290

HALE, EDWARD E. (ed.) James Freeman Clarke: autobiography, diary and correspondence. Boston. New York, Houghton, Mifflin & co., 1891. 430p. 1291

HARRISON, C. W. Silvia Du Bois . . . a biography of the slave who whipt her Mistres and gand her freedom. Ringos, N. J. The author. 1883. 124p. 1292

HAYDEN, WILLIAM. Narrative containing a faithful account of his travels for a number of years, whilst a slave in the south. Cincinnati, Ohio, publ. by author. 1846. 156p. 1293

HENSON, JOSIAH. An autobiography of the Rev. Josiah Henson from 1789 to 1876. Edited by John Lobb. Mrs. H. B. Stowe's "Uncle Tom." London, Christian Age. 1877. 227p. 1294

HENSON, JOSIAH. Father Henson's story of his own life. Introduction by Mrs. H. B. Stowe. Boston, John P. Jewett & co. 1858. xii. 212p. 1295

HENSON, JOSIAH. The life of Josiah Henson, formerly a slave, now an inhabitant of Canada. Boston, Arthur D. Phelps, 1849. 76p. 1296

HUGHES, LOUIS. Thirty years a slave. From bondage to freedom. The institution of slavery as seen on the plantation and in the home of the planter. Autobiography of Louis Hughes. Milwaukee. Southside print. co. 1896. 210p. 1297

JACOBS, HARRIET B. Incidents in the life of a slave girl, written by herself, ed. by L. Maria Child.

Boston, publ. by author. 1861. 306p. 1298

JONES, THOMAS H. The experience of Thomas H. Jones, who was a slave for forty years, written by a friend as given to him by brother Jones. Worcester, Henry J. Howland, 1849. 48p. 2d ed. Boston. Bazin & Chandler. 1862. 48p. 1299

KECKLEY, ELIZABETH. Behind the scenes, or, thirty years a slave, and four years in the White House. New York, G. W. Carleton & co., 1868. 371p. 1300

LOGUEN, JEREMIAH W. As a slave and as a freeman; a narrative of real life. Syracuse, J. G. K. Truair & co., 1859. 444p. 1301

MARS, JAMES. Life of . . . a slave born and sold in Connecticut. Written by himself. Hartford, Case, Lockwood & co., 1868. 38p. 1302

MATHEWS, REV. E. Autobiography of the "Father Dicksom," of Mrs. Stowe's "Dred," etc. London, Houlston & Wright; Bristol, Thomas Mathews, 1866. New York, Amer. Baptist Free Mission Soc. 444p. 1303

MEADE, BISHOP. Sketches of Old Virginia Family Servants. Philadelphia. The author, 1847. 126p. 1304

MOTT, ALEXANDER (comp.) Narratives of colored Americans. New York, Lindley Murray Estate, 1875. 276p. 1305

NEILSON, PETER. The life and adventures of Zamba, an African Negro King, and his experiences in slavery in South Carolina. Written by himself. London. Smith, Elder & co. 1847. xx, 258p. 1306

NORTHUP. SOLOMN. Twelve years a slave, the narrative of a free colored man. kidnapped in Washington City

in 1841, sold into slavery, and after a twelve years' bondage, reclaimed by state authority from a cotton plantation in Louisiana. Auburn, N. Y. Derby & Miller, London, Sampson, Low, son & co., 1853. 360p. eng. revised Philadelphia, Jno. E. Potter & co., 1870. 336p. 1307

PETERSON, D. H. The looking-glass being a true . . . narrative of the life . . . of the Rev. D. H. Peterson. 1854. 63p. 1308

PICKARD, MRS. KATE E. R. The kidnapped and the randsomed. Being the personal recollections of Peter Hill and his wife "Vina" after forty years of slavery . . . Syracuse, W. T. Hamilton. 1856. 409p. 1309

PIERSON, MRS. EMILY C. Janie Parker, the fugitive . . . Hartford, Brockett, Fuller & co. 1851. 64p. 1310

PLATT, SMITH H. REV. Martyrs, and the fugitive, or, a narrative of the captivity, sufferings, and death of an African family, and the slavery and escape of their son. New York. Daniel Fanshaw, 1859. 95p. 1311

RANDOLPH, PETER. From slave cabin to the pulpit; the autobiography of Rev. Peter Randolph, the southern question illustrated and sketches of slave life. Boston. J. H. Earle. 1893. 220p. 1312

RELIGIOUS TRACTS. An authentic account of the conversion and experience of a Negro. Northampton, Mass., Thomas M. Pomroy. 1806. 16p. 1313

SMITH, JAMES L. Autobiography: including also reminiscences of slave life, recollections of the war, education of freedmen, causes of the exodus. Norwich, Conn., Bulletin co. 1881. xiii, 150p. 1314

SMITH, VENTURE. A narrative of the life and adventures of Venture, a native of Africa. Related by himself. rev. by H. M. Selden. Middletown, Conn., H. M. Selden. 1897. 41p. 1315

STEWARD, AUSTIN. Twenty-two years a slave, and forty years a freeman . . . Rochester, N. Y., Allings & Cory. 1859. 3d ed. 1861. 13-360p. 1316

STOWE, MRS. HARRIETT E. (BEECHER). A key to Uncle Tom's cabin; presenting the original facts and documents upon which the story is founded, together with corroborative statements verifying the truth of the work. Boston, J. P. Jewett co.; Cleveland, Jewett, Proctor & Worthington; London, Low & co. 1853. 262p. 2d ed. Boston, J. P. Jewett co. 1854. 508p. 1317

STRAYER, JACOB. My life in the South. enl. ed. Salem, Mass., The auth. 1890. 83p. 1318

THOMPSON, JOHN. The life of . . . a fugitive slave; containing his history of 25 years in bondage, and his providential escape, written by himself. Worcester, The auth. 1856. 146p. 1319

TILMON, LEVIN. A brief miscellaneous narrative of the more early part of the life of L. Tilmon, written by himself. Jersey City, The auth. 1853. 97p. 1320

TOLMAN, GEORGE. John Jack, the slave, and Daniel Bliss, the tory. Read before the Concord antiquarian society. Concord, N. H., The society. n.d. 21p. 1321

TRUTH, SOJOURNER. Narrative of Sojourner Truth, a northern slave, emancipated from bodily servitude by the state of New York in 1828. Boston, The auth. 1850. 144p. 1322

WARD, SAMUEL R. Autobiography of a fugitive Negro: His anti-slavery labours in the United States, Canada and England. London, John Snow. 1855. 412p. 1323

WATSON, HENRY. Narrative of Henry Watson, a fugitive slave. 3d ed. Boston, Bela Marsh. 1850. 48p. 1324

WILLIAMS, JAMES. Narrative of James Williams, an American, who was for several years a driver on a cotton plantation in Alabama . . . New York, American anti-slavery society. 1838. 108p. 1325

WILLIAMSON, PASSMORE. Narrative of the facts in the case of Passmoro Williamson. Philadelphia, Pennsylvania, anti-slavery society. 1855. 24p. 1326

XI. Histories of the abolition movement in the United States.

ANDREWS, CHARLES C. The history of the New York African free-schools . . . also a brief account of the successful labors of the New York manu-mission society, with an appendix. New York. Printed by Mahlon Day. 1830. 148p. 1327

CARPENTER, S. B. Logic of history. Five hundred political texts being concentrated extracts of abolitionism. 2d ed. Madison, Wis., The auth. 1864. 351p. 1328

CHAPMAN, MRS. MARIE (WESTON). Right and wrong in Massachusetts . . . Boston, Dow & Jackson. 1839. 177p. 1329

CLARKE, JAMES F. Anti-slavery days; a sketch of the struggle which ended in the abolition of slavery in the United States. New York, R. Worthington. 2d ed. New York. John W. Lovell. 1883. 224p.   1330

DANVERS HISTORICAL SOCIETY. Old anti-slavery days. Proceedings of the commemorative meeting, held by the Danvers historical society, April 26, 1893. With introduction, letters and sketches. Danvers, Mass., Danvers mirror print. 1893. 151p.   1331

DOUGLASS, FREDERICK. The nature, character, and history of the anti-slavery movement; a lecture delivered before the Rochester Ladies' Anti-slavery Association. Glasgow, G. Gallie. 1855. 32p.   1332

ESTLIN, J. B. A brief notice of American slavery and the abolition movement. 2d ed. rev. London, The Leeds anti-slavery association. 54p.   1333

GOODELL, WILLIAM. Slavery and anti-slavery; a history of the great struggle in both hemispheres; with a view of the slavery question in the United States. New York, William Harned. 1852. x, 604p.   1334

LOCKE, MARY STOUGHTON. Anti-slavery in America from the introduction of African slaves to the prohibition of the slave trade, 1619-1808. Boston, Ginn & co. 1901. 255p.   1335

MARTIN, ASA EARL. The anti-slavery movement in Kentucky prior to 1850. Louisville, Standard print. co. 1918. 165p.   1336

MASSACHUSETTS ABOLITION SOCIETY. The true history of the late division in the anti-slavery societies; being part of the second annual report of the executive committee of the Massachusetts abolition society. Boston, David H. Fla. 1841. 45p.   1337

MASSACHUSETTS PEACE SOCIETY. A catalogue of the officers and members of the Massachusetts peace society, including thirteen branches or auxiliaries, March 1, 1820. Cambridge, Hilliard & Metcalf. 1820. 15p.   1338

OBERLIN COLLEGE. A classified catalogue of the collection of anti-slavery propaganda in the Oberlin college library. Comp. by Geraldine Hopkins Hubbard. Oberlin, Ohio. 1932. Bull. v. II, no. 3. x, 84p.   1339

SIXTY YEARS AGAINST SLAVERY. A brief record of the work and aims of the British and foreign anti-slavery society, 1839-1899. London, British anti-slavery society. 1900. 15p.1340

TURNER, LORENZO D. Anti-slavery sentiment in American literature prior to 1865. Washington, Assn. for the study of Negro life and history. 1929. 188p.   1341

WEBB, RICHARD D. The national anti-slavery societies in England and the United States. Dublin, Charles Hedgelong. 1852. 56p.   1342

WILLEY, AUSTIN. The history of the anti-slavery cause in state and nation. Portland, Me., Brown Thurston & Hoyt, Fogg & Donham. 1886. 503p.   1343

XII. Anti-slavery societies.

1. Reports, proceedings, constitutions, platforms, addresses, etc.
2. Series publications, newspapers and periodicals.

1. Reports, proceedings, constitutions, platforms, addresses, etc.

AMERICAN ABOLITION SOCIETY. The constitution against slavery. The constitution of the American abolition society. Principles and measures of the convention of "Radical political abolitionists," New York, The society. 1856. 8p. 1344

AMERICAN ANTI-SLAVERY SOCIETY. Address . . . to the anti-slavery Christians of the United States. New York, American anti-slavery society. 1852. 16p. 1345

AMERICAN ANTI-SLAVERY SOCIETY. Annual report. 1st-4th. (1834-1837). 21st (1853). 23d (1855). 27th (1860). 28th (1861). New York, American anti-slavery society, etc. 1834-61. Titles and imprints vary slightly. No annual reports issued 1840-41. 1346

AMERICAN ANTI-SLAVERY SOCIETY. African servitude: when, why, and by whom instituted. By whom, and how long shall it be maintained? New York, Davies & Kent. 1860. 54p. 1347

AMERICAN ANTI-SLAVERY SOCIETY. Commemoration of the Fiftieth anniversary of the organization. Philadelphia, Thos. S. Dando & co. 1884. 65p. 1348

AMERICAN ANTI-SLAVERY SOCIETY. Declaration of sentiments and constitution, together with those parts of the constitution of the United States which are supposed to have any relation to slavery. New York, American anti-slavery society. 1835. 16p. 2d ed. Philadelphia, Pennsylvania anti-slavery society. 1861. 22p. 1349

AMERICAN ANTI-SLAVERY SOCIETY. Declaration of sentiments . . . adopted at the formation of the said society, in Philadelphia, Dec. 4, 1833. Philadelphia. 1833. 2p. (tract, 1). Tract no. 2, reissue. Philadelphia. 8p. 1350

AMERICAN ANTI-SLAVERY SOCIETY. Letter to Louis Kossuth, concerning freedom and slavery in the United States, in behalf of the American anti-slavery society. Boston, R. F. Wallcut. 1852. 112p. 1351

AMERICAN ANTI-SLAVERY SOCIETY. Platform of the Society and its auxiliaries. New York, American anti-slavery society. Collection has: 1853; 1855; 1860. 1352

AMERICAN ANTI-SLAVERY SOCIETY. Proceedings at its second decade, held in the city of Philadelphia, Dec. 3, 4, 5, 1853. New York, American anti-slavery society. 1854. 176p. 1353

AMERICAN ANTI-SLAVERY SOCIETY. Report of the twenty-fourth national anti-slavery festival. Boston, The society. 1858. 32p. 1354

AMERICAN ANTI-SLAVERY SOCIETY. Thirty-fifth national

subscription anniversary. New York. 1860. 3p.   1355

AMERICAN AND FOREIGN ANTI-SLAVERY SOCIETY. An address to the anti-slavery Christians of the United States. New York, J. A. Gray. 1852. 17p.   1356

AMERICAN AND FOREIGN ANTI-SLAVERY SOCIETY. Annual report . . . 9th, 10th, 12th, 13th. (1849-1850, 1852-1853). New York, American and foreign anti-slavery society. 1849-50. 1852-53. Titles and imprints vary slightly.   1357

AMERICAN AND FOREIGN ANTI-SLAVERY SOCIETY. The fugitive slave bill: its history and unconstitutionality, with all account of the seizure and enslavement of James Hamlet and his subsequent restoration to liberty. New York, William Harned. 1850. 36p.   1358

AMERICAN AND FOREIGN ANTI-SLAVERY SOCIETY. Liberty almanac. New York, American and foreign anti-slavery society. 1847-51. 40p. ea. Collection has: 1847, 1848, 1849, 1851.   1359

AMERICAN BOARD OF COMMISSIONERS FOR FOREIGN MISSIONS. Report of the committee on anti-slavery memorials. September. 1845. With a historical statement of the previous proceedings. Boston, T. R. Marvin. 1845. 32p.   1360

AMERICAN CONVENTION FOR PROMOTING THE ABOLITION OF SLAVERY AND IMPROVING THE CONDITION OF THE AFRICAN RACE. Minutes of proceedings of conventions . . . of abolition societies established in different parts of the United States.

(Twenty-seven conventions held. 1794-1837). Collection has: Philadelphia meetings, 1794, 1795, 1797, 1798. Baltimore meetings, 1826, 1828. Philadelphia, Baltimore, The convention. 1794-95. 1797-98. 1826. 1828.   1361

AMERICAN CONVENTION FOR PROMOTING THE ABOLITION OF SLAVERY AND IMPROVING THE CONDITION OF THE AFRICAN RACE. Address of a convention of delegates from abolition societies established in different parts of the United States to the citizens of the United States. January 1, 1794. Philadelphia, The convention. 1794. 7p.   1362

AMERICAN TRACT SOCIETY. The suppressed tract! and the rejected tract! (Scriptual duties of masters . . .) New York, The society. 1858. 76p.   1363

AMERICAN UNION FOR THE RELIEF AND IMPROVEMENT OF THE COLORED RACE. Exposition of the objects and plans. Boston, Light & Horton. 1835. 23p. (Society formed in Boston on Jan. 14, 1835.)   1364

ANTI-SLAVERY CONVENTION OF AMERICAN WOMEN. 1st. New York, 1837. An appeal to the women of the nominally free states, issued by an anti-slavery convention of American women . . . 9th-12th of May, 1837. New York, William S. Dorr. 1837. 32p. 2d ed. Boston, I. Knapp. 1838. 70p.   1365

ANTI-SLAVERY CONVENTION OF AMERICAN WOMEN. 2d. Philadelphia. 1838. Address to the senators and representatives of the free states, in the Congress of the United States. Philadelphia. Merrihew & Gunn. 1838. 11p. 1366

ANTI-SLAVERY CONVENTION OF

AMERICAN WOMEN. 3d. Philadelphia, 1839. Address to the society of friends on the subject of slavery by Mary Lewis, president. Philadelphia, The convention. 1839. 10p.   1367

ANTI-SLAVERY CONVENTION OF AMERICAN WOMEN. Address to the free colored people of the United States. Philadelphia, Merrihew & Gunn. 1838. 14p. 1368

ANTI-SLAVERY CONVENTION OF AMERICAN WOMEN. Proceedings . . . May 9th-12th, 1837. New York, Wm. S. Dorr. 1837. 23p.1369

ANTI-SLAVERY CONVENTION OF AMERICAN WOMEN. Proceedings. May 15th-18th, 1838. Philadelphia, Merrihew & Gunn. 1838. 18p. 1370

ANTI-SLAVERY MEETING held in Stacy hall, Boston, on the twentieth anniversary of the mob of Oct. 21, 1835. Proceedings . . . Wm. Lloyd Garrison, main speaker. Boston, R. F. Wallcut. 1855. 24p. Title page: The Boston mob of "gentlemen of property and standing."   1371

ANTI-SLAVERY SOCIETY OF WEST BROOKFIELD. An exposition of difficulties in West Brookfield connected with anti-slavery operations; together with a reply to some statements in a pamphlet put forth by "Moses Chase, pastor of the church," purporting to be a "statement of facts in the case of Deacon Henshaw." West Brookfield, Mass., The society. 1844. 59p.   1372

BOSTON, FEMALE ANTI-SLAVERY SOCIETY. Annual report. 1st-3d (1835-1837). 6th (1840). Boston, Isaac Knapp for the society. 1835-42. Title varies. 2d report, 1836, (2d ed.) Boston, I. Knapp. 1836.   1373

CHURCH ANTI-SLAVERY SOCIETY

OF THE UNITED STATES. Proceedings of the convention at Worcester, Mass., March 1, 1859. New York, John F. Trow. 1859. 31p.   1374

DUNLOP, JOHN. American anti-slavery conventions: a series of extracts illustrative of the proceedings and principles of the "library party" in the United States with the bearing of the anti-slavery cause on missions. Edinburgh, William Oliphant & sons. 1846. 47p.   1375

HOLDEN ANTI-SLAVERY SOCIETY. Report of the Holden slave case, tried at the January term of the court of common pleas. County of Worcester, 1839. Worcester, The society. 1839. 32p.   1376

MANUMISSION SOCIETY OF NORTH CAROLINA. An address to the people of North Carolina on the evils of slavery. By the friends of liberty and equality . . . Greensborough, N. C., William Swaim. 1830. 68p.   1377

MASSACHUSETTS ANTI-SLAVERY SOCIETY. An address to the abolitionists of Massachusetts, on the subject of political action, by the board of managers of the Massachusetts anti-slavery society. n.d. n.p. 20p.   1378

MASSACHUSETTS ANTI-SLAVERY SOCIETY. Annual report. 4th-15th (1836-1847). Boston, T. Knapp. 1836-1847.   1379

NEW ENGLAND ANTI-SLAVERY SOCIETY. Address to the people of the United States, by a committee of the New England anti-slavery convention, held in Boston May 27-29, 1834. Boston Garrison & Knapp. 1834. 16p.   1380

NEW ENGLAND ANTI-SLAVERY SOCIETY. Annual report to the

board of managers . . . 1st (1833). Boston, New England anti-slavery society. 1833. 54p.   1381

NEW ENGLAND ANTI-SLAVERY SOCIETY. Constitution, with an address to the public. Boston, Garrison & Knapp. 1832. 16p. 1382

NEW ENGLAND ANTI-SLAVERY CONVENTION, BOSTON. Proceedings . . . 1st (1834); 3d (1836); 4th (1837). Boston, Isaac Knapp. 1834-37. Imprint varies slightly.   1383

NEW YORK ANTI-SLAVERY SOCIETY. Address of the New York city anti-slavery society to the people of the city of New York. New York, West & Trow. 1833. 46p. (p. 45, constitution of the society).   1384

NEW YORK SOCIETY FOR THE PROMOTION OF EDUCATION AMONG COLORED CHILDREN. An act to incorporate the New York society for the promotion of education among colored children. Albany, New York state assembly. 1847. 8p.   1385

PENNSYLVANIA ANTI-SLAVERY SOCIETY. Address . . . to the coloured people of the state of Pennsylvania. Philadelphia, Merrihew & Gunn. 1837. 7p. 1386

PENNSYLVANIA ANTI-SLAVERY SOCIETY. Annual . . . proceedings . . . 12th, 14th, 21st, 1849, 1851, 1858. Philadelphia, anti-slavery office. 1849. 1851. 1858.   1387

PENNSYLVANIA SOCIETY FOR PROMOTING THE ABOLITION OF SLAVERY, for the relief of free Negroes unlawfully held in bondage, and for improving the condition of the African race. Centennial anniversary. Philadelphia, Grant, Faires & Rodgers. 1876. 82p.   1388

PENNSYLVANIA SOCIETY FOR PROMOTING THE ABOLITION OF SLAVERY. Address from the Pennsylvania society for promoting the abolition of slavery, for the relief of free Negroes unlawfully held in bondage, and for improving the condition of the African race; on the origin, purposes and utility of their institution. Philadelphia, Hall & Atkinson for the society. 1819. 6p.   1389

PENNSYLVANIA SOCIETY FOR PROMOTING THE ABOLITION OF SLAVERY. Constitution and act of incorporation of the Pennsylvania society for promoting the abolition of slavery and for the relief of free Negroes unlawfully held in bondage, and for improving the condition of the African race. Philadelphia, The society. 1820. 31p.   1390

PHILADELPHIA ANTI-SLAVERY SOCIETY. Address . . . to their fellow citizens. Philadelphia, Board of managers, The society. 1835. 24p.   1391

REESE, DAVID M. A brief review of the "first annual report of the American anti-slavery society, with the speeches delivered at the anniversary meeting, May 6, 1834," addressed to the people of the United States. New York, Howe & Bates. 1834. 45p.   1392

STARKSBOROUGH AND LINCOLN ANTI-SLAVERY SOCIETY. Address . . . to the public, Nov. 8, 1824. Middlebury, Conn., The society. 1835. 36p.   1393

2. Series publications, newspapers and periodicals.

AMERICAN ANTI-SLAVERY
ALMANAC . . . 1836-1840;
1842-1844; 1847. Ed. by N.
Southard, L. M. Child, etc. 48p. ea.
Boston, Webster & Southard, etc.
1835-1846. 1836-40 numbered v.
1, nos. 1-5; 1842 numbered v. 2,
no. 1.   1394

ANTI-SLAVERY EXAMINER . . .
New York. American anti-slavery
society. 1846-1845. 14
monographs. Collection has:

no. 2. Grimke, A. E. Appeal to
        the Christian women of
        the South. Rev. cor. 3d ed.
        1836. 36p.

no. 3. Smith, Gerrit. Letter . . .
        Rev. James Smylie of the
        state of Mississippi. 1837.
        66p.

no. 4. Weld, T. D. The Bible
        against slavery. 1837. 74p.

no. 5. Weld, T. D. Power of
        congress over the District
        of Columbia. 1838. 55p.

no. 6. Weld, T. D. The Bible
        against slavery. 3d ed. rev.
        1838. 64p.

no. 6a. Williams, James. Narrative
        of . . . an American slave.
        (Extracts from a longer
        narrative). "Drawn up by
        John G. Whittier." 1838.
        8p.

no. 7. Thome, James, and
        Kimball, Horace.
        Emancipation in the West
        Indies. 1838. 128p.

no. 7a. Green, Beriah. The chattel
        principle . . . 1839. 71p.

no. 8. Correspondence between
        Hon. F. H. Elmore. . . and
        J. G. Birney. 1838. 68p.

no. 9. Smith, Gerrit. Letter to

Hon. Henry Clay. 1839.
54p.

no. 10. Weld, T. D. American
        slavery as it is. 1839.
        224p.

no. 11. Phillips, Wendell. The
        constitution a pro-slavery
        compact. 1845. 131p.
                                   1395

ANTI-SLAVERY RECORD . . . v. 1-3.
(Jan. 1835—Dec. 1837). Published
monthly. New York, American
. anti-slavery society. 1835-1837.
Collection has: v. 1, nos. 1-12. 1396

ANTI SLAVERY TRACTS. New
York. American anti-slavery
society. 1855-56. 20 pamphlets.
Collection has:

no. 1. Bowditch, W. I. The
        United States constitution.
        1855. 12p.

no. 2. Bowditch, W. I. White
        slavery in the United
        States. 1855. 8p.

no. 3. Frothingham, O. B.
        Colonization. 1855. 8p.

no. 4. Higginson, T. W. Does
        slavery christianize the
        Negro? 1855. 8p.

no. 5. Palfrey, J. G. The
        interstate slave-trade.
        1855. 8p.

no. 6. Hildreth, R. The "ruin" of
        Jamaica. 1855. 12p.

no. 7. Foster, S. S. Revolution
        the only remedy for
        slavery. 1855. 20p.

no. 8. Follen, Mrs. E. L. To
        mothers in the free states.
        1856. 4p.

no. 9. Barker, Mrs. L. J.
        Influence of slavery upon
        the white population.
        1855. 12p.

no. 10. Burleigh, C. C. Slavery and the North. 1855. 12p.

no. 11. Hodges, C. E. Disunion our wisdom and our duty. 1855. 12p.

no. 12. Follen, Mrs. E. L. Where is thy brother? 1855. 8p. (Poems)

no. 13. Stowe, Mrs. H. B. The two alters. 1855. 12p.

no. 14. Chapman, Mrs. M. W. "How I can help to abolish slavery." 1855. 12p.

no. 15. Cabot, S. C. What have we, as individuals to do with slavery? 1855. 7p.

no. 16. Hartford, Conn. Fourth congregational church. The unanimous remonstrance . . . on the subject of slavery. 1855. 36p.

no. 17. Beecher, C. The God of the Bible against slavery. 1855. 7p.

no. 18. May, S. Jr. The fugitive slave law and its victims. 1856. 48p.

no. 19. Whipple, C. K. Relations of anti-slavery to religion. 1856. 20p.

no. 20. Higginston, T. W. A ride through Kansas. 1856. 24p.   1397

ANTI SLAVERY TRACTS, NEW SERIES. New York. American anti-slavery society. 1860-61. 16 pamphlets. Collection has:

no. 1. Child, Mrs. Lydia M. F. Correspondence . . . (with) Gov. Wise and Mrs. Mason of Virginia. 1860. 28p.

no. 2. Garrison, Wm. L. (com.) Letters on American slavery from Victor Hugo, de Toqueville, de Girardiu, Carnot, Passy, Mazzini,

Humboldt, O. Lafayette, etc. 1860. 24p.

no. 3. Coffin, Joshua. An account of some of the principal slave insurrections. 1860. 36p.

no. 4. Garrison, Wm. L. The new "reign of terror" in the slaveholding states. 1860. 144p.

no. 5. O'Donnell, Daniel . . . American slavery. 1860. 48p.

no. 6. Child, Mrs. Lydia M. F. The right way the safe way . . . 1860. 95p.

no. 7. Brown, John. Testimonies. 1860. 16p.

no. 8. Phillips, Wendell. The philosophy of the abolition movement. 1860. 48p.

no. 9. Child, Mrs. Lydia M. F. The duty of disobedience to the fugitive slave act. 1860. 36p.s,

no. 10. Garrison, Wm. L. The ''infidelity'' of abolitionism. 1860. 12p.

no. 11. Hossack, John. Speech. 1860. 12p.

no. 12. Child, Mrs. Lydia M. F. The patriarchical institution. 1860. 55p.

no. 13. Phillips, Wendell. No slave-hunting in the Old Bay State. 1860. 23p.

no. 14. Garrison, Wm. L. A. fresh catalogue of southern outrages. 1860. 72p.

no. 15. May, Samuel. The fugitive slave law . . . rev. ed. 1861. 168p.

no. 16. Channing, W. E. Tribute . . . to the . . . abolitionists. 1861.   1398

THE EMANCIPATOR (complete). Ed.

89

and pub. by Elihu R. Embree. Jonesborough, Tenn. 1820. (A reprint of The Emancipator, to which is added a biographical sketch of the author and publisher and two hitherto unpublished anti-slavery memorials bearing the signature of Elihu Embree). Nashville, B. H. Murphy. 1932. 112p.   1399

FREDERICK DOUGLASS' PAPER. Rochester, N. Y., Published weekly. Collection has: v. v, no. 25. June 10, 1852.   1400

FRIENDS' REVIEW. A weekly religious, literary and miscellaneous journal. Edited by Samuel Rhoads. Philadelphia, Merrihew & Thompson. 1847-1865. Collection has: v. xi, 1858; v. xii, 1859; v. xv, 1862; v. xviii & xix, 1865.   1401

THE LIBERATOR. Published weekly. Boston, Edited by William Lloyd Garrison. Robert F. Wallcut, general agent. 1831-1865. 35v. Collection has: v. 32, no. 27; v. 33, no. 41; v. 34, nos. 2, 38, 44; v. 35, nos. 34, 36, 37.   1402

PLEA FOR THE SLAVE. New York. American anti-slavery society. 1838-40. Published quarterly. Collection has: v. 1, no. 1. v. 1, no. 3.   1403

QUARTERLY ANTI SLAVERY MAGAZINE . . . v. 1-2 (October, 1835–July, 1837). Ed. by Elizur Wright. New York, American anti-slavery society. 1836-37. 1404

TRACTS. Cincinnati. American reform tract and book society. 1840-1863. Collection has:

no. 4.   Agitation-the doom of slavery. 16p.

no. 5.   Slavery and the Bible. 12p.

no. 19. Thompson, George. Pleas for slavery answered. 24p.

no. 40. Whipple, Chas. K. The family relation, as affected by slavery. 24p.   1405

TRACTS. Philadelphia. Pennsylvania anti-slavery society. Collection has:

no. 4   The political economy of slavery. 1840. 4p.

no. 6   Immediate emancipation safe and profitable. 1840. 4p.   1406

XIII.   General anti-slavery and abolition arguments.

ADAMS, CHARLES F. An oration, delivered before municipal authorities of Fall River, Mass. July 4, 1860. Fall River, Almy & Milne. 1860. 20p.   1407

ADAMS, CHARLES F. What makes slavery a question of national concern? a lecture delivered at New York, Jan. 10, and at Syracuse, Feb. 1, 1855. Boston, Little, Brown & co. 1855. 46p.   1408

ALLEN, GEORGE. Resistance to slavery every man's duty. A report on American slavery read to the Worcester central association, Mar. 2, 1847. Boston, Wm. Crosby & H.

P. Nichols. 1847. 40p.   1409

ALLEN, GEORGE. Report of a declaration of sentiments on slavery. Dec. 5, 1837. Worcester, Howland. 1838. 12p.   1410

THE AMERICAN HOME MISSIONARY SOCIETY and slavery. n.d., n.p. 8p.   1411

AMES, JULIUS RUBENS (ed.). The legion of liberty! and force of truth, containing thoughts, words, and deeds of some prominent apostles, champions and martyrs . . . 2d division. New York, American anti-slavery society. 1842. 207p. 2d ed. New York, American anti-slavery society. 1843. 384p. 3d ed. New York, American anti-slavery society. 1857. 336p. 1412

AMES, JULIUS RUBENS (ed.). The legion of liberty: Remonstrance of free men, states, and presses, to the Texas rebellion, against the laws of nature and nations . . . Albany, N. Y., Patriot office. 1843. 66p. 1413

AMES, JULIUS RUBENS (ed.). "Liberty" . . . the image and superscription on every coin issued by the United States of America . . . proclaim liberty throughout all the land unto all the inhabitants thereof . . . the inscription on the bell in the old Philadelphia statehouse, which was rung July 4, 1776, at the signing of the Declaration of Independence. n.p. 1837. 231p. 1414

ATLEE, EDWIN P. An address to the citizens of Philadelphia on the subject of slavery. Philadelphia. By the auth. 1833. 15p. 1415

AUSTIN, JAMES T. (pseud.) Abolitionist. Extracts from remarks of Dr. Channing's slavery, with comments. By an abolitionist. Boston, John H. Eastburn, 1835. 48p. 2d ed. Boston, Russell, Shattuck co. 1835. 48p. 3d ed. Boston, D. K. Hitchcock. 1836. 55p. 1416

BACON, LEONARD. A plea for Africa: delivered in New Haven, July 4, 1825. New Haven, The auth. 1825. 22p. 1417

BALLOU, ADIN. The superiority of moral over political power. n.d., n.p. (No. 5, Pennsylvania anti-slavery office). 1418

BALLOU, ADIN. The voice of duty. An address delivered at the anti-slavery picnic at Westminister, Mass. July 4. 1843. Hopedale.

Milford, Mass., Community press. 1843. 11p. 1419

BARNES, GILBERT H. AND DUMOND, DWIGHT L. (eds.) Letters of Theodore Dwight Weld, Angelina Grimke Weld, and Sarah Grimke. 1822-1844. New York, London, D. Appleton Century co. 1934. 2v. 1420

BEECHER, CATHERINE E. An essay on slavery and abolition with reference to the duty of American females. Philadelphia, Henry Perkins. 1837. 152p. 1421

BENEZET, ANTHONY. Serious considerations on several important subjects; viz: on war and its inconsistency with the observations on slavery, and remarks on the nature and bad effects of spirituous liquors . . . Philadelphia, Joseph Crukshank. 1778. 48p. 1422

BLANCHARD, JONATHAN. A debate on slavery, held on Oct. 1, 2, 3, and 6, 1845, upon the question: Is slave-holding in itself sinful . . . in Cincinnati, between J. Blanchard and N. L. Rice. 4th thousand. Cincinnati, Wm. H. Moore & co.; New York, Mark H. Newman. 1845. 482p. 1423

BONYNGE, FRANCIS. The future wealth of America: being a glance at the resources of the U. S. and the commercial and agricultural advantages of cultivating tea, coffee, indigo, the date, mango, etc. etc., with a review of the china trade. New York, The auth. 1852. 242p. 1424

BOSTON COURIER. Observations on the Rev. Dr. Gannett's sermon "Relation of the North to slavery." (Republished from the editorial columns, June 28 & 30, and July 6, 1853.) Boston, Redding & co. 1854. 29p. 1425

BOWLES, CHARLES. A sermon on the covenant of grace which God made with Abraham. Oxford, Wm. B. Chapman, print. 1841. 32p. 1426

BRADFORD, GAMALIEL. A letter .. . Boston, James Munroe & co. 1836. 35p. 1427

BRANAGAN, THOMAS. A preliminary essay, on the oppression of the exiled sons of Africa. Philadelphia, 1804. 1428

BRANAGAN, THOMAS. The guardian genius of the federal union; or, patriotic admonitions on the signs of the times, in relation to the evil spirit of party, arising from the roots of all our evils, human slavery. Being the first part of the beauties of philanthropy. New York, American anti-slavery society. 1839. 104p. 2d ed. enl. New York, American anti-slavery society. 1839. 288p. 1429

BROWNLOW, WILLIAM G. AND PRYNE, ABRAHAM. Ought American slavery be perpetuated? A debate . . . held in Philadelphia, Sept. 1858. Philadelphia, J. B. Lippincott & co. 1858. 305p. 2d ed. New York, Carleton; London, Parker, son & co. 1862. xiii, 171p. 1430

BURT JAIRUS. The law of Christian rebuke, a plea for slave-holders; a sermon delivered at Middleton, Conn. before the anti-slavery convention . . . on October 18, 1843. Hartford, N. W. Godrich & co. 1843. 20p. 1431

CHILD, DAVID L. Abolitionist's library . . . no. 1. The despotism of freedom; or, the tyranny and cruelty of American republican slave masters, shown to be the worst in the world; in a speech, delivered at the first anniversary of the New England anti-slavery

society, 1833. Boston, Boston young men's anti-slavery association, for the diffusion of truth. 1833. 72p. 1432

CHILD, MRS. LYDIA M. F. Anti-slavery catechism. 2d ed. Newburyport, Charles Whipple. 1835. 36p. 2d ed. Boston. 1839. 36p. 1433

CHILD, MRS. LYDIA M. F. An appeal in favor of that class of Americans called Africans. Boston, Allen & Ticknor. 1833. 232p. 2d ed. New York, John S. Taylor. 1836. vi, 216p. 1434

CHILD, MRS. LYDIA M. F. The evils of slavery, and the cure of slavery. The first proved by the opinions of Southerners themselves, the last shown by historical evidence. Newburyport, Charles Whipple. 1839. 23p. 1435

CLARK, RUFUS W. A review of Rev. Moses Stuart's pamphlet on slavery, entitled conscience and the consitution. Boston, C. C. P. Moody. 1850. 103p. 1436

CLARKE, JAMES F. Sermon on thanksgiving day . . . Boston, Benj. H. Green. 1843. 25p. 1437

CLARKE, WALTER. A discourse . . . at Canterbury, Conn. Hartford, Elihu Geer. 1844. 21p. 1438

CLAY, CASSIUS M. Letters . . . New York, Greeley & McElrath. 1843. 10p. 1439

CLAY, CASSIUS M. Slavery: the evil — the remedy. Letters to the New York Tribune. New York, The tribune. 1844. 8p. 1440

CLAY, CASSIUS M. The writings . . . including speeches and addresses. Ed. with a memoir by Horace Greeley. New York, Harper & bros. 1848. 535p. 1441

CLEVELAND, CHARLES D. Anti-slavery addresses of 1844 and

1845. By Salmon Portland Chase and Charles Dexter Cleveland. London, S. Low, son & Marston; Philadelphia, J. A. Bancroft & co. 1867. 167p. 1442

A COLLECTION OF VALUABLE DOCUMENTS, being Birney's vindication of abolitionists — protest of the American anti-slavery society — to the people of the United States; or, to such Americans as value their rights. Letter from the executive committee of the New York anti-slavery society, to the executive committee of the Ohio anti-slavery society at Cincinnati. Outrage upon Southern rights. Boston, Isaac Knapp. 1836. 80p. 1443

• CONWAY, MONCURE D. The one path: or, the duties of the North and South. A discourse delivered in Washington, D. C. Jan 26, 1856. Washington, Republican assn. of Washington. 1856. 8p. 1444

CRAPSEY, ALGERNON S. Political crimes and their consequences. n.d., n.p. 27p. 1445

THE CREOLE CASE AND MR. WEBSTER'S DESPATCH; with comments from the New York American. New York, The American. 1842. 39p. 1446

CURTIS, H. Sermon on African slavery preached before the synod of Indiana . . . Madison. Iowa, The synod. 1848. 28p. 1447

DAY, THOMAS. Fragment of an original letter on the slavery of Negroes, written in the year 1776. London. J. Stockdale. 1784; Boston. Reprinted by Garrison & Knapp. 1841. 12p. 1448

DICKINSON, JAMES T. A sermon delivered at Norwich, Conn., July 4. 1834. at the request of the anti-slavery society of Norwich and vicinity. Norwich, The society. 1834. 40p. 1449

DRESSER, AMOS. Jonathan Clark's narrative of . . . and two letters from Tallahassee, relating to the treatment of slaves. New York, American anti-slavery society. 1836. 42p. 1450

DUNLOP, JOHN. American slavery: organic sins; or the iniquity of licensed injustice. Edinburgh, Wm. Oliphant & sons. 1846. 31p. 1451

DWIGHT, THEODORE. An oration . . . before the Connecticut society, for the promotion of freedom and the relief of persons unlawfully holden in bondage. Hartford, Conn., May 8, 1794. 24p. 1452

EDGAR, CORNELIUS H. The curse of Canaan rightly interpreted, and kindred topics. Three lectures delivered at Easton, Pa. in 1862. New York, Baker & Godwin. 1862. 48p. 1453

ELDER, WILLIAM. Periscopics; or, current subjects extemporaneously treated. New York, J.C. Derby; Boston, Phillips, Sampson & co.; Cincinnati, H. W. Derby. 1854. 408p. 1454

FITCH, CHARLES. Slaveholding weighed in the balance of truth and its comparative guilt illustrated. Boston, Isaac Knapp. 1837. 36p. 1455

FOSTER, EDEN B. The rights of the pulpit, and perils of freedom. Two discourses preached in Lowell, Sunday, June 25, 1854. Lowell, Mass., J. J. Judkins. 1854. 72p. 1456

FREEDLEY, EDWIN T. The issue and its consequences. An address. Philadelphia, King & Baird. 1856. 200p. 1457

FURNESS, WILLIAM H. An address delivered before a meeting of the members and friends of the Pennsylvania anti-slavery society December 19, 1849, Philadelphia, Merrihew & Thompson. 1850. 16p. 1458

FURNESS, WILLIAM H. A discourse delivered in the First Congregational Unitarian Church, (Philadelphia) Sunday, July 1, 1860. Philadelphia, C. Sherman & son. 1860. 26p. 1459

FURNESS, WILLIAM H. The right of property in man. A discourse delivered in the First Congregational Unitarian Church (Philadelphia) July 3, 1859. Philadelphia, C. Sherman & son. 1859. 23p. 1460

GARRISON, WILLIAM L. Selections from the writings and speeches . . . Boston, R. F. Wallcut. 1852. 416p. 1461

GARRISON, WILLIAM L. No compromise with slavery; an address delivered in New York, Feb. 14, 1854. New York, American anti-slavery society. 1854. 36p. 1462

GENIN, THOMAS H. Selections from the writings of the late Thomas Hedges Genin. With a biographical sketch. New York, Edward O. Jenkins. 1869. 615p. 1463

GOODLOE, DANIEL R. Slavery in the southern states . . . By a Carolinian. Cambridge, John Bartlett. 1852. 53p. 1464

GRANGER, AMOS P. The consitution against slavery. A speech. New York. 6p. (Abolition documents, no. 2). 1465

GRIMKE, ANGELINA E. Appeal to the Christian women of the South. New York, American anti-slavery society. n.d. 36p. 1466

GRIMKE, ANGELINA E. Letters to Catherine E. Beecher, in reply to essay on slavery and abolitionism, addressed to A. E. Grimke. Boston, Isaac Knapp. 1838. 130p. 1467

GROSVENOR, CYRUS P. Address . . . before the anti-slavery society of Salem and vicinity in Salem, Feb. 24, 1834. Salem, Mass., W. & S. B. Ives. 1834. 48p. 1468

GUROWSKI, ADAM. America and Europe. New York, D. Appleton & co. 1857. 441p. 1469

HAMILTON, JOHN C. The slave power: its heresies and injuries to the American people. A speech . . . Nov. 1864. New York, John A. Gray & Green. 1864. 23p. 1470

HALL, NATHANIEL. The iniquity: a sermon preached in the First Church, Dorchester, Sunday, Dec. 11, 1859. Boston, John Wilson & son. 1859. 37p. 1471

HILDRETH, RICHARD. Despotism in America: or, an inquiry into the nature and results of the slave-holding system in the United States. Boston, Whipple & Damrell. 1840. 186p. 2d ed. Boston, Mass., anti-slavery society. 1840. 186p. 3d ed. enl. Boston, John P. Jewett & co. 1854. 307p.

HOPKINS, SAMUEL. A dialogue concerning the slavery of the Africans, showing it to be the duty and interest of the American colonies to emancipate all the African slaves. With an address to the owners of such slaves. Dedicated to the honorable continental congress. An address to the owners of Negro slaves in the American colonies . . . A discourse upon the slave trade and the slavery of Africans. Delivered before the Providence society for abolishing the slave trade . . . May 17, 1793 . . . Norwich, Judah P. Spooner. 1776. 68p. 1473

HOPKINS, SAMUEL. Timely articles on slavery. Boston, Congregational board of pub. 1854. vi, 624p.　1474

HOWE, M. A. DEWOLFE. Reply to the letter of Bishop Hopkins. . . in the print called "The Age," of Dec. 8, 1863. Philadelphia, King & Baird, print. 1864. 18p.　1475

IRON GRAY (pseud.) The gospel of slavery; primer of freedom. New York, T. W. Strong. 1864. 26p.
1476

JAY, WILLIAM. Address to the non-slaveholders of the South on the social and political evils of slavery. New York, S. W. Benedict & co. 1843. 28p.　1477

JAY, WILLIAM. An examination of the Mosaic laws of servitude. New York, M. W. Dodd, 1854, 56p. 1478

JAY, WILLIAM. A letter to the committee chosen by the American tract society, to inquire into the proceedings of its executive committee in relation to slavery. 1857. 38p.　1479

JAY, WILLIAM. Miscellaneous writings on slavery. Boston, John P. Jewett & co. 1853. v, 670p.　1480

JAY, WILLIAM. Reply . . . to Moses Stuart. 1850. 12p.　1481

JAMES, HORACE. Our duties to the slave. A sermon preached before the original Congregational church and society in Wrentham, Mass., November 28, 1846. Boston, Richardson & Filmer. 1847. 23p.
1482

JONES, CHARLES J. (ed.) Fast day sermons; or, the pulpit on the state of the country. Twelve pro and anti-slavery sermons by outstanding ministers of the North and South. New York, Rudd & Carleton. 1861. 336p.　1483

KEMBLE, MRS. FRANCES A. The views of Judge Woodward and

Bishop on Negro slavery at the South, illustrated from the journal of a residence on a Georgian plantation in the winter and spring of 1838-39. Philadelphia, 1863. 32p.　1484

KINGSBURY, HARMON. The slavery question settled. Man stealing, legitimate servitude, etc. New York, John A. Gray. 1862. 36p.　1485

LAURENS, HENRY. A South Carolina protest against slavery: being a letter from Henry Laurens . . . to his son, Col. John Laurens, dated Charleston, S. C. August 14, 1776. New York, G. P. Putnam. 1861. 34p.　1486

LOUNSBURY, THOMAS. Pro-slavery overthrown; and the true principles of abolitionism declared. 2d ed. Geneva, N. Y., George H. Derby. 1847. 155p.　1487

LYMAN, DARIUS. Leaven for dough-faces: or, Threescore and ten parables touching slavery, by a former resident of the South. Cincinnati, Bangs & co.; Cleveland, L. E. Barnard & co. 1856. 332p.
1488

LYMAN, THEODORE III (ed.) Papers relating to the Garrison mob. Cambridge, Welch, Bigelow, & co. 1870. 73p.　1489

MANN, HORACE. Slavery: letters & speeches. Boston, B. B. Mussey & co. 1854. xii, 564p.　1490

MARSH, LEONARD. A bake-pan for the dough-faces, by one of them. Try it. Burlington, Vt., C. Goodrich. 1854. 64p.　1491

MARTIN MAR Q. (pseud.) A brief review of the first annual report of the American anti-slavery society, by David M. Reese, M. D. of New York. Dissected by Martin Mar Quack, M.D. L.L.D. M. Q. L. H. S. O. S. M. F. M. P. S. etc. of that ilk.

New York. Howe, Bates. 1834. 15p. 1492

MARTINEAU, HARRIET. The martyr age in the United States of America: an article from the London and Westminster Review, for Dec. 1838. New York, S. W. Benedict. 1839. 36p. 1493

MARTINEAU, HARRIET. Views of slavery and emancipation, from "Society in America." New York, Pierce & Reed. 1837. iv, 379p. 1494

MAY, SAMUEL J. The right of colored people to education, vindicated. Letters . . . to Andrew T. Judson, esq. and others in Canterbury, remonstrating with them on their unjust and unjustifiable procedure relative to Miss Crandall and her school for colored females. Brooklyn, Advertiser press. 1833. 24p. 1495

MAYO, AMORY D. Herod, John and Jesus; or, American slavery and its Christian cure. A sermon preached in Albany, N. Y. Albany, Weed, Parsons & co. 1860. 29p. 1496

MCLEOD, ALEXANDER. Negro slavery unjustifiable, a discourse. New York, author. 1802. 42p. 11th ed. with appendix. New York, 1863. 48p. 1497

MECHANICS AND LABORING MEN OF LOUISVILLE. Address to the nonslaveholders of Kentucky, read and adopted at a meeting of the mechanics and laboring men of Louisville, April 10, 1849. Louisville, 1849. 16p. 1498

MEETING OF NEW YORK CITIZENS. Proceedings and report of the committee on the memorial to Congress, appointed by a meeting of New York citizens on Jan. 18, 1861. New York, R. C. Root, Anthony co. 1861. 22p.1499

MICHELET, M. The people. Transl. from the French by G. H. Smith. New York, D. Appleton & co. 1846. 185p. 1500

MORAL, LEGAL AND DOMESTIC CONDITION OF OUR COLORED POPULATION. A discourse delivered at Montpelier, Vt., Oct. 17, 1832. Burlington. 1832. 32p. 1501

MORSE, SAMUEL F. B. An argument on the ethical position of slavery in the social system, and its relation to the politics of the day. (Papers from the society for the diffusion of political knowledge, no. 12, 1863.) New York, The society. 1863. 20p. 1502

MORSE, SIDNEY E. Premium questions on slavery, each admitting of a yes or no answer; addressed to the editors of the New York Independent and the New York Evangelist. New York, Harper bros. 1860. 30p. 1503

THE NORTH AND THE SOUTH. New York, Tribune. 1854. 40p. Inscribed by Wendell Phillips. (Reprinted from the New York Tribune). 1504

NOTES ON "SOUTHERN WEALTH AND NORTHERN PROFITS." Philadelphia, C. Sherman & son. 1861. 31p. 1505

ON THE ABOLITION OF NEGRO SLAVERY. London, Charles Wood. n.d. 85p. 1506

PALFREY, JOHN G. Correspondence between Nathan Appleton and John G. Palfrey intended as a supplement to Mr. Palfrey's pamphlet on the slave power. Boston, Eastburn's press. 1846. 20p. 1507

PALFREY, JOHN G. Papers on the slave power, first published in the "Boston Whig." Boston, Merrill,

Cobb & co. n.d. 91p. 1508

PALFREY, JOHN G. Remarks on the proposed state (Mass.) constitution. By a free soiler from the start. Boston, Crosby, Nichols & co. 1853. 35p. 1509

PARKER, THEODORE. Address . . . delivered before the New York city anti-slavery society, at its first anniversary, held in Broadway Tabernacle, May 12, 1854. New York, American anti-slavery society. 1854. 46p. 1510

PARKER, THEODORE. The function and place of conscience, in relation to the laws of men; a sermon for the times; preached September 22, 1850. Boston, Crosby & Nichols. 1850. 40p. 1511

PARKER, THEODORE. The great battle between slavery and freedom, considered in two speeches delivered before the American anti-slavery society, at New York, May 7, 1856. Boston, Benjamin H. Greene. 1856. 93p. 1512

PARKER, THEODORE. A letter to the people of the United States touching the matter of slavery. Boston, James Munroe & co. 1848. 120p. 1513

PARKER, THEODORE. The present aspect of slavery in America and the immediate duty of the North: a speech delivered in the hall of the State House, before the Massachusetts anti-slavery convention, Jan. 29, 1858. Boston, Bela Marsh. 1858. 44p. 1514

PARKER, THEODORE. A sermon of the dangerous classes in society, preached Jan. 31, 1847. Boston, C. & J. M. Spear. 1847. 48p. 1515

PARKER, THEODORE. A sermon of the dangers which threaten the rights of man in America; preached

July 2, 1854. Boston, Benjamin B. Mussey & co. 1854. 56p. 1516

PARKER, THEODORE. Speeches, addresses and occasional sermons. Boston, Horace B. Fuller. 1871. 3v. 1517

PEABODY, ANDREW P. Position and duties of the North with regard to slavery. (Reprinted from the Christian Examiner, July, 1843). Newburyport, Charles Whipple. 1848. 22p. 1518

PERKINS, GEORGE W. Sermons . . . 2d ed. with additions. New York, Anson D. F. Randolph. 1853. 331p. 1519

PETERSON, HENRY. Address on American slavery. Delivered before the semi-annual meeting of the junior anti-slavery society of Philadelphia, July 4, 1838. Philadelphia, For the society by Merrihew & Gunn. 1838. 28p. 1520

PHELPS, AMOS A. Lectures on slavery and its remedy. Boston, New England anti-slavery society. 1834. 284p. 1521

PHILLIPS, WENDELL. Review of Lysander Spooner's essay on the unconsitutionality of slavery. (Reprinted from the "Anti-slavery Standard," with additions). Boston, Andrews & Prentiss. 1847. 95p. 1522

PHILLIPS, WENDELL. Review of Webster's speech on slavery. Boston, American anti-slavery society. 1850. 344p. 1523

PHILLIPS, WENDELL. Speech . . . at the Worcester disunion convention, Jan. 15, 1857. Boston, American anti-slavery society. 1857. 16p. 1524

PHILLIPS, WENDELL. Speech . . . on the philosophy of the abolition movement. Delivered in Boston, Jan. 27, 1853. 47p. 1525

PHILLIPS, WENDELL. Speeches, lectures, letters. Boston, Lee & Shepard. 1892. 2v.   1526

QUINCY, JOSIAH. The nature and power of the slave states, and the duties of the free states; an address delivered at Quincy, Mass. on June 5, 1856. Boston, Ticknor & Fields. 1856. 32p.   1527

RANKIN, JOHN. Letters on American slavery addressed to Mr. Thomas Rankin, merchant at Middlebrook, Augusta County, Virginia, 2d ed. Newburyport, Mass., Charles Whipple. 1836. 118p.   1528

RAUMER, FREDERICK VON. America and the American people. Transl. from the German by William W. Turner. New York, J. & H. G. Langley. 1844. 501p.   1529

REMARKS ON SLAVERY AND EMANCIPATION. Boston, Hilliard, Gray & co. 1834. 105p.   1530

THE RESPONSIBILITY OF THE NORTH IN RELATION TO SLAVERY. Cambridge, Allen & Farnham. 1856. 15p.   1531

ROSS, ALEXANDER M. Speech . . . delivered Oct. 21, 1864 at the annual meeting of the society for the abolition of human slavery, held in Montreal, Canada. Montreal, John Lovell. 1864. 8pp.   1532

RICE, DAVID. Slavery inconsistent with justice and good policy. Proved in a speech delivered in the convention held at Danville, Kentucky. Augusts, Me., Peter Edes. 1804. 23p. (Reprinted in 1804 by the society of friends).   1533

RUFFNER, HENRY. Address to the people of West Virginia showing that slavery is injurious to the public welfare, and that it may be gradually abolished, without detriment to the rights and interests of slaveholders. Lexington, Va., R. C. Noel. 1847. 40p. (Reprinted by the Green Bookman, Bridgewater, V. Jan. 1933).   1534

RUSH, BENJAMIN. An address to the inhabitants of the British settlements, on slavery of the Negroes in America. To which is added, a vindication of the address, in answer to a pamphlet entitled "slavery not forbidden in scripture . . ." By a Pennsylvanian. 2d ed. Philadelphia, John Dunlap. 1773. 28p.   1535

SAWTELL, E. N. Treasured moments: being a compilation of letters on various topics, written at different times, and in different countries; together with notes, incidents of travel, and reminiscences of men and things. London, Robert K. Burt; Glasgow, David Bryce. 1860. 583p.   1536

SCOTT, O. Address to the general conference of the Methodist Episcopal Church . . .during its session in Cincinnati, Ohio, May 19, 1836 . . . New York, H. R. Piercy, print. 1836. 24p.   1537

SLAVERY IN THE UNITED STATES: its evils, alleviations, and remedies. (Reprinted from the North American review, Oct. 1851). Boston, Charles C. Little & James Brown. 1857. 36p.   1538

SLAVERY AND ITS PROSPECTS IN THE UNITED STATES. Cambridge, Mass., Metcalf & co. 1857. 28p.   1539

SLAVERY OF POVERTY, with a plan for its abolition. New York Society for the abolition of all Slavery. John Windt. 1842. 16p. (New York quarterly pamphleteer, no. 1. May, 1842).   1540

SLAVERY AND THE AMERICAN BOARD OF COMMISSIONERS

FOR FOREIGN MISSIONS. New York, American anti-slavery society. 1859. 24p. 1541

SLOANE, J. R. W. Review of Rev. Henry J. Van Dyke's discourse on "the character and influence of abolitionism." A sermon preached Dec. 23, 1860. New York, William Erving. 1861. 40p. 1542

SMITH, GERRIT. Letter . . . to Hon. Henry Clay. New York, American anti-slavery society. 1839. 54p. 1543

SOLEMN TRUTH. Abolition tract! New York, American anti-slavery society. n.d. 4p. 1544

STANTON, E. CODY. The slave's appeal. Albany, Anti-slavery depository. 1860. 7p. 1545

STEWARD, ALVAN. Writings and speeches . . . on slavery. Ed. by Luther Rawson Marsh. New York, A. B. Burdick. 1860. vii (9), 426p. 1546

STEWART, CHARLES. Immediate emancipation . . . an outline for it and remarks on compensation. (Reprinted from the Eng. quarterly magazine and review, for April, 1832) 2d American ed. Newburyport, Mass., Charles Whipple. 1838. 35p. 1547

STONE, THOMAS T. An address before the Salem female anti-slavery society, December 7, 1851. Salem, William Ives & co. 1852. 27p. 1548

SUMNER, CHARLES. The anti-slavery enterprise: its necessity, practicability, and dignity, with glimpses at the special duties of the North. Address before the people of New York, at the Metropolitan theatre, May 9, 1855. Boston, Ticknor & Fields. 1855. 36p. 1549

SUMNER, CHARLES. White slavery in the Barbary states. A lecture

before the Boston mercantile library association, Feb. 17, 1847. Boston, Wm. Ticknor & co. 1847. 60p.; London, S. Low & co. 1853. 135p. 1550

SUMNER, CHARLES. Works . . . Boston, Lee & Shepard. 1870. 11v. 1551

SUNDERLAND, REV. LaROY. Anti-slavery manual, containing a collection of facts and arguments on American slavery. New York, S. W. Benedict. 1837. 142p. 1552

TAPPAN, LEWIS. Address to the non-slaveholders of the South, on the social and political evils of slavery. New York, American & foreign anti-slavery society. n.d. 58p. 1553

THOMAS, WILLIAM (pseud. DEFENSOR.) The enemies of the constitution discovered; or, an inquiry into the origin and tendency of popular violence. Containing a complete and circumstantial account of the unlawful proceedings at the city of Utica, Oct. 12, 1835; the dispersion of the state anti-slavery convention by the agitators, the destruction of a democratic press, and of the causes which led thereto. Together with a concise treatise on the practice of the court of His Honor Judge Lynch . . . Accompanied with numerous highly interesting documents. New York, Leavitt, Lord & co. Utica; G. Tracy. 1836. 183p. (New York State anti-slavery society). 1554

THOME, JAMES A. Debate at the Lane Seminary, Cincinnati. Speech . . . at the annual meeting of the American anti-slavery society, May 6, 1834. Letter of the Rev. Samuel Cox against the American colonization society. Boston, Garrison & Knapp. 1834. 16p. 1555

THOMPSON, GEORGE. Letters and addresses during his mission in the United States from Oct. 1, 1834, to Nov. 27, 1835. Boston, Isaac Knapp, 1837. xii. 126p. 1556

THOMPSON, GEORGE. The substance of (his) lecture on slavery, delivered in the Wesleyan chapel, Manchester, (Eng.) Manchester, Chronicle office; Boston, reprint. by Isaac Knapp. 1836. 24p. 1557

THOMPSON, GEORGE. Speech . . . delivered at the anti-slavery meeting, Broadmead, Bristol, Sept. 4, 1851. Bristol, "Examiner" office. n.d. 36p. 1558

THOMPSON, GEORGE AND BRECKINRIDGE, ROBERT. Discussion on American slavery . . . A debate held at Glasgow, Scotland, on the 13, 14, 15, 16, and 17 of June, 1836. 2d American ed. with notes by William Lloyd Garrison. Boston, Isaac Knapp. 1836. 23p. 1559

TUCKER, GEORGE. Political economy for the people. Philadelphia, C. Sherman & son. 1859. 238p. 1560

WAKEFIELD, DAVID G. England and America. A comparison of the social and political state of both nations. New York, Harper & bros. 1834. 376p. 1561

WALKER, JONATHAN. A brief view of American chattelized humanity, its supports. Boston, The auth. 1846. 36p. 2d ed. Boston. J. Walker. 1847. 36p. 1562

WEBSTER, DANIEL . . . On slavery. Extracts from some of his speeches; together with his great compromise speech, of March 7, 1850, and the Boston memorial, on the subject of slavery. To which is added the Constitution of the United States.

Boston, Carter & bros. 1861. 60p. 1563

WELD, THEODORE D. American slavery as it is: testimony of a thousand witnesses. New York, American anti-slavery society. 1839. 224p. 1564

WELD, THEODORE D. The suppressed book about slavery. (Prepared for publication in 1857.) New York, Carleton. 1864. 432p. 1565

WHIPPLE, CHARLES K. The family relation, as affected by slavery. Premium tract, no. 40. Cincinnati, American reform tract & book society. 1858. 24p. 1556

WHIPPLE, CHARLES K. The non-resistance principle; with particular application to the help of slaves by abolitionists. Boston, R. F. Wallcut. 1860. 24p. 1567

WIKOFF, HENRY. A letter to Viscount Palmerston, K. G., Prime minister of England, on American slavery. New York, Ross & Tousey. 1861. 84p. 1568

WOOLMAN, JOHN. Journal, with an introduction by John G. Whittier. Boston, Houghton, Mifflin. 1882. 315p. 1569

WRIGHT, ELIZUR (ed.) Perforations in the "latter-day pamphlets" by one of the "Eighteen millions of Bores." No. I Universal, suffrage, capital punishment-slavery. Boston, Phillips, Sampson & co. 1850. 48p. 1570

WRIGHT, HENRY C. The dissolution of the American union, demanded by justice and humanity, as the incurable enemy of liberty. Addressed to the abolitionists of Great Britain and Ireland. Glasgow, Glasgow emancipation society. 1845. 46p. 1571

WRIGHT, HENRY C. The Natick

resolution; or, resistance to slaveholders the right and duty of Southern slaves and Northern freemen. Boston, The auth. 1859. 36p.
1572

YATES, EDWARD. A letter to the women of England on slavery in the southern states of America; especially considered in reference to the condition of the female slaves. New York, Clavin Blanchard. 1863. 68p.
1573

XIV. Anti-slavery fiction.

ADAMS, FRANCIS C. Manuel Pereira: or, the sovereign rule of South Carolina. With views of southern laws, life and hospitality. Washington, Buell & Blanchard. 1853. 302p.
1574

ADAMS, FRANCIS C. Our world: or, the slaveholder's daughter. New York, Miller, Orton & Mulligan. 1855. 597p.
1575

ASHTON, WARREN T. (pseud. Adams, William T.) Hatchie, the guardian slave; or, the heiress of Bellevue. A tale of the Mississippi and the southwest. Boston, B. B. Mussey & co. 1853. 313p.
1576

BRACKENRIDGE, HUGH H. Modern chivalry, or the adventures of Captain Farrago and Teague O'Regan. 2d ed. Philadelphia, Carey & Hart. 1846. 189p.
1577

BROWN, WILLIAM W. Clotel; or, the president's daughter; a narrative of slave life in the United States, with a sketch of the author's life. London, Partridge & Oakey. 1853. viii, 245p.
1578

CABIN BOY'S STORY: a semi-nautical romance, founded on fact. New York, Garrett & co. 1854. 438p.   ·
1579

CHAPMAN, MARIA W. Pinda: a true tale . . . New York, American anti-slavery society. 1840. 23p.
1580

CHILD, MRS. LYDIA M. Fact and fiction. A collection of stories. New York, C. S. Francis & co. 1846. 282p.
1581

GILMORE, JAMES R. (pseud. Kirke, Edmund.) Among the pines; or, South in secession time. New York, G. P. Putnam. 1862. 310p.
1582

HALL, BAYARD R. Frank Freeman's barber shop. A tale. New York, Charles Scribner. 1852. 343p.
1583

HILDRETH, RICHARD. Archy Moore, the white slave; or, Memoirs of a fugitive. New York, Miller, Orton & co. 1855. 408p.
1584

HILDRETH, RICHARD. The slave; or, Memoirs of Archy Moore. Boston, John H. Eastburn. 1836. 163p.
1585

HILDREITH, RICHARD. The white slave; or, Memoirs of a fugitive. Boston, Tappan & Whittemore. 1852. 408p.
1586

HOPKINS, SAMUEL. Youth of the old dominion. Boston, John P. Jewett & co. New York, Sheldon, Blakeman & co. 1856. 473p.
1587

JAMES, GEORGE P. Old Dominion; or, the Southampton massacre. A novel. New York, Harper & bros. 1855. 152p.
1588

LIVERMORE, ELIZABETH D. Zoe; or, the quadroon's triumph. Cincinnati, Truman & Spofford. 1855. 2v.
1589

MARTINEAU, HARRIET. The hour

and the man. New York, 1840. 2d
ed. New York. 1873.   1590
MCDOUGALL, FRANCES H.
Shahmah in pursuit of freedom; or,
the branded hand. Tr. from the
original Showiah, and ed. by an
American citizen. New York,
Thatcher & Hutchinson. 1858.
599p.   1591
M'KEEHAN, HATTIA. Liberty or
death; or, Heaven's infraction of
fugitive slave law . . . Cincinnati,
author. 1858. 104p.   1592
MORE, HANNAH. Shepard of Salis-
burg plain, and other tales. New
York, H. W. Derby. 1861. 489p.
                               1593
PEARSON, MRS. EMILY C. Cousin
Franck's household; or, scenes in
the Old Dominion. By
"Pocahontas." Boston, Upham,
Ford & Olmstead. 1852. vii, 259p.
                               1594
PEARSON, MRS. EMILY C. Ruth's
sacrifice; or, life on the Rappahan-
nock. Boston, Charles H. Pearson.
1863. 259p.   1595
PEARSON, MRS. EMILY
CATHERINE. Jamie Parker, the
fugitive. Hartford, Brockett, Fuller
& co. 1851. 192p.   1596
PIKE, MARY H. (pseud. Sydney A.
Story, Jr.) Caste: a story of republi-
can equality. Boston, Phillips,
Sampson & co. New York, J.C.
Derby. 1855. 540p.   1597
PIKE, MARY H. Ida May; a story of
things actual and possible. Boston,
Phillips, Sampson & co. New York,
J. C. Derby. 1854. 478p.   1598
PLANTER'S VICTIM: or, incidents of
American slavery. Philadelphia, Wm.
White Smith. 1855. 365p.   1599

REDPATH, JAMES. The roving
editor; or, talks with slaves in the
southern states . . . New York, A.

B. Burdick. 1859. xvi, 349p.   1600
SCHOOLCRAFT, MRS. MARY H.
The black gauntlet: a tale of plan-
tation life in South Carolina. Philadelphia, J. B. Lippincott & co.
1860. 569p.   1601
STOWE, HARRIETT B. Dred, a tale
of the great dismal swamp. Boston,
Phillips, Sampson & co. 1856. 2v.;
Boston, New York, Houghton,
Mifflin & co. 1896. 491p.   1602
STOWE, HARRIET B. Key to Uncle
Tom's cabin; presenting the original
facts and documents upon which
the story is founded together with
corroborative statements verifying
the truth of the work. Boston, J. P.
Jewett & co. London, S. Low & co.
1853. 262p.   1603
STOWE, HARRIET B. The story of
"Uncle Tom's cabin." Boston, Old
South work dir. 1897. 28p.
(Written in 1878 as an introduction
to new ed. of "Uncle Tom's
cabin.")   1604
STOWE, HARRIET B. Uncle Tom's
cabin; or, life among the lowly.
Boston, J. P. Jewett & co.; Cleveland, Jewett, Procter & Worthington. 1851. 322p.; London, Clarke
& co. 1852. 380p.; London, H. G.
Bohn. 1852. 483p.; Paris, Aux
bureaux du magasin pittoresque.
1853. 563p.   1605
STOWE, HARRIET B. Uncle Sam's
emancipation; earthly care, a
heavenly discipline; and other
sketches . . . with a sketch of Mrs.
Stowe's family. Philadelphia, Willis
P. Hazard. 1853. 124p.   1606
DE L'ESCLAVAGE AUX
ETATS-UNIS a l'occasion de la
case de L'oncle Tom. (Extrait de
la Revue Suisse, 1853). 21p.
                               1607

ADAMS, JOHN CALVIN (ed.). Our day. A gift for the times. Boston, B. B. Mussey & co. 1848. 288p.　1608

BARLOW, JOEL. Columbiad, (8th book, liberty - all hail, no. 3.) New York, 1861.　1609

BIRKETT, M. A poem on the African slave trade. 2d ed. Dublin, J. Jones. 1792. 25p.　1610

BRANAGAN, THOMAS. Avenia: a tragical poem, on the oppression of the human species, and infringement on the rights of man. In six books with notes explanatory and miscellaneous written in imitation of Homer's Illiad. Philadelphia, S. Engles, printer. 1805. 358p.　1611

BROWN, WILLIAM W. (comp.). The anti-slavery harp; a collection of songs for anti-slavery meetings, Boston. Bela Marsh. 1848. 48p.
　1612

BROWN, WILLIAM W. (comp.). The escape; or a leap for freedom. A drama in five acts. Boston, R. F. Wallcut, 1858. 52p.　1613

BURKE, JOHN (pseud. Sennoia Rubek.) The burden of the South, in verse, or poems on slavery, grave, humorous, didactic, and satirical. New York, Everardus Warner. 1864. 96p.　1614

BURLEIGH, WILLIAM H. Poems . . . Philadelphia, J. M. M'Kim; Pittsburg, Ingram & M'Candless, New York, Wiley & Putnam. 1841. 248p.　1615

CHANDLER, ELIZABETH M. The poetical works . . . Philadelphia, Lemuel Howell. 1836. 120p.　1616

CHILD, MRS. LYDIA M. (ed.) The oasis. Boston, Benj. C. Bacon. 1834. xvl, 276p. (An anthology of anti-slavery poems, articles, biographies, and interesting inci-

dents connected with the abolition of slavery.)　1617

CLARK, GEORGE W. (comp.) The liberty minstrel. 6th ed. New York, The auth. 1844. iv, 215p.　1618

CLARK, GEORGE W. (comp.) The harp of freedom. New York, Miller, Orton & Mulligan. 1856. 335p.
　1619

DAY, THOMAS. The dying Negro, a poem. n.d. cor. enl. London, W. Flexney. 1773. 24p.　1620

GARRISON, WILLIAM L. Sonnets and other poems. Boston, Oliver Johnson. 1843. 96p.　1621

GRIFFITHS, JULIA (ed.). Voices of freedom. Stories by H. B. Stowe, G. F. Adams, Theodore Parker et al . . . with facsimiles of their signatures, etc. New York, Worthington co. 1853. 309p.　1622

HATFIELD, EDWIN F. (comp.) Freedom's lyre: or, Psalms, hymns, and sacred songs for the slave and his friends. New York, S. W. Benedict. 1840. 265p.　1623

HOLMES, DANIEL. Dialogue on slavery, and miscellaneous subjects . . . Dayton, Ohio, Gazatte book & job rooms. 1854. 29p.　1624

KEEFER, JUSTUS. Slavery: its sins, moral effects, and certain death. Also, the language of nature compared with divine revelation, in prose and verse, with extracts from eminent authors. Baltimore, J. Keefer. 1864. 120p.　1626

THE LIBERTY BELL. An annual containing selections of poetry and prose by anti-slavery leaders. By friends of freedom . . . Boston, Massachusetts anti-slavery fair. 1839-46; national anti-slavery bazaar. 1847-58. 15v. Edited annually by Marie W. Chapman from 1839-1858, except for the years 1840, 1850, 1854, 1855, 1857; these years by Foxton, Thompson, Barton, Cones, Bowring, Dall, et al. 1626

THE LIBERTY BELL. EXTRACTS .. . Follen, Eliza Lee. Pious trust. (From the German of Korner). William Lloyd Garrison. The course of emancipation. 1627

THE LIBERTY BELL. EXCERPTS .. . Chapman, Marie Weston. The British India society. Phillips, Wendell. Extract from a letter, read before the Glasgow emancipation society. 1628

LOWELL, JAMES R. Poetical works . . . household ed. (containing anti-slavery poems). Boston, New York, Houghton, Mifflin & co. 1895. 515p. 1629

MONTGOMERY, JAMES. The abolition of the slave trade, a poem in four parts. London, R. Bowyer. 1814. 53p. 1630

MOTT, MRS. ABIGAIL F. (comp.). Biographical sketches and interesting anecdotes of persons of color, to which is added a selection of pieces of poetry. New York, Mahlon Day. 1826 and 1837. 192p. Rev. & enl. ed. New York, L. Murray estate. 1839 and 1850. 408p. 1631

PRATT, SMAUEL J. Humanity, or the rights of nature. A poem in two books. London, T. Cadell. 1788. 114p. 1632

OPIE, AMELIA. The Negro boy's tale, a poem addressed to children. London, Harvey & Darton, S. Wilkin. 1824. 16p. 1633

STAR OF EMANCIPATION. Boston, Fair of the Massachusetts female

emancipation society. 1841. 108p. 1634

STANFIELD, JAMES F. The Guinea voyage, a poem, in three books. To which are added observations on a voyage to the coast of Africa, in a series of letters to Thomas Clarkson. Edinburgh. 1807. 77p. 1635

STOWE, MRS. HARRIETT B. (pseud. Aunt Mary). Peep into Uncle Tom's cabin . . . with an address from Mrs. H. B. Stowe to the children of England and America. London, Sampson Low & son. Boston, J. P. Jewett & co. 1853. 421p. 1636

STOWE, MRS. HARRIETT˙ B. The Christian slave. A drama founded on a portion of Uncle Tom's cabin. Boston, Phillips, Sampson & co. 1855. 67p. 1637

STOWE, HARRIETT B. Religious poems. Boston, Ticknor and Fields. 1867. 107p. 1638

THOMPSON, GEORGE. The prison bar: or poems on various subjects . . . Hartford, William H. Burleigh. 1848. 215p. 1639

TRAGEDY OF ERRORS . . . Boston, Ticknor and Fields. 1861. 249p. 1640

TRAGEDY OF SUCCESS . . . Boston, Ticknor and Fields. 1862. 191p. 1641

WEAVER, EMILY (comp.) Dialogues and scenes, from the writings of Harriett Beecher Stowe. Boston, Houghton, Mifflin & co. n.d. 96p. 1642

THE WEST INDIES. A poem in four parts. Written in honour of the abolition of the African slave trade by the British legislature, in 1807. London. 1807. 126p. 1643

WHITTIER, JOHN G. Poems written during the progress of the abolition question in the United States, between the years 1830 and 1838.

Boston, Isaac Knapp. 1857. 103p.
1644
WHITTIER, JOHN G. A Sabbath scene. Boston, J. P. Jewett, Procter & Worthington. London, S. Low, son & co. 1854. 29p. 1645
WHITTIER, JOHN G. Voices of freedom. . . 4th ed. Philadelphia, T. S. Cavander. 1846. 192p. 1646
YOUTH'S POETICAL INSTRUCTOR. A selection from modern poets, British and American. Part 2. Belfast, Me., Alexander Mayne. 1851. 144p. 1647

XVI. Autobiographies, biographies, journals, memoirs, collected works, etc. of anti-slavery leaders and others connected with the abolition movement.

ARMISTEAD, WILSON. Anthony Benezet. From the original memoir: revised with additions. London, A. W. Bennett; Philadelphia, Lippincott & co. 1859. 144p. 1648

AUSTIN, GEORGE L. The life and times of Wendell Phillips. Boston, B. B. Russell & co. 1884. 431p. new ed. Boston, Lee & Shepard. 1888. 431p. 1649

BARROWS, JOHN H. Henry Ward Beecher, the Shakespeare of the pulpit. New York, Funk & Wagnalls co. 1893. 541p. 1650

BARTOL, C. A. A discourse preached in the West church on Theodore Parker. Boston, Crosby, Nichols, Lee & co. 1860. 28p. 1651

BASSETT, JOHN S. Anti-slavery leaders of North Carolina. Baltimore, John Hopkins press. 1898. 74p. (Johns Hopkins studies, series 16, no. 6) 1652

BEECHER, CHARLES (ed.). Autobiography, correspondence, etc. of Lyman Beecher. New York, Harper & bros. 1864. 2v. 1653

BIRNEY, CATHERINE H. The Grimke sisters, Sarah and Angelina Grimke. The first American advocates of abolition and women's rights. Boston, Lee and Shepard. 1885. 319p. 1654

BRADFORD, SARAH E. Harriet, the Moses of her people. New York, The auth. 1886. 149p. 1655

BRADFORD, SARAH E. Scenes in the life of Harriet Tubman. Auburn, N. Y., W. I. Moses. 1869. 132p. 1656

BRAITHWAITE, JOSEPH B. (ed.). Memoirs of Joseph John Gurney with selections from his journal correspondence. Philadelphia, J. B. Lippincott & co. 1856. 608p. 1657

BROWNE, ALBERT G. Sketch of the official life of John A. Andrew, as governor of Massachusetts. New York, Hurd & Houghton. 1868. 211p. 1658

BROWN, DAVID P. Eulogium upon William Wilberforce; with a brief incidental review of the subject of colonization; delivered in Philadelphia, March 10, 1834. Philadelphia, The abolition society. 1834. 40p. 1659

BUXTON, CHARLES. Memoirs of Sir Thomas Fowell Buxton, baronet, with selections from his correspondence. Philadelphia, Henry Longstreth. 1849. 510p. 1660

CHANDLER, PELEG W. Memoir of governor John Andrew, with personal reminiscences. Boston, Roberts bros. 1880. 298p. 1661

CHADWICK, JOHN W. (ed.). A life for liberty. Anti-slavery and other letters of Sallie Holley. 2d ed. New York; London, G. P. Putnam's sons. 1899. 292p. 1662

CHANNING, WILLIAM H. The life of William Ellery Channing. Boston, American unitarian assn. 1880. 719p. 1663

CHANNING, WILLIAM H. ed. Memoir of William Ellery Channing with extracts from his correspondence and manuscripts. Boston, Wm. Crosby & H. P. Nichols; London, John Chapman. 1848. 3v. 1664

CHILD, LYDIA M. Isaac T. Hooper: a true life . . . Boston, J. P. Jewett & co. 1853. xvi, 493p. 1665

CHILD, LYDIA M. Letters . . . Boston. New York, Houghton, Mifflin co. 1882. 280p. 1666

CHOATE, RUFUS. A discourse delivered at Dartmouth College, July 27, 1853, commemorative of Daniel Webster. Boston, Jas. Munroe & co. 1853. 88p. 1667

CHOATE, JOSEPH H., WASHINGTON, BOOKER T. and others. Addresses in memory of Carl Schurz delivered at New York, November 21, 1906. (New York committee of the Carl Schurz memorial). 1906. 44p. 1668

COFFIN, LEVI. Reminiscences of an abolitionist; thrilling incidents, heroic actions, and wonderful escapes of fugitive slaves in connection with the anti-slavery underground railroad related by its president. London, Dyer bros. n.d. 207p.; Cincinnati, Western tract society. 1876. 712p. 1669

COLTON, CALVIN. The life, correspondence, and speeches of Henry Clay. New York. A. S. Barnes & co. 1857. 6v. 1670

CONGDON, CHARLES T. Reminiscences of a journalist. Boston,

Jas. R. Osgood & co. 1880. 393p. 1671

CONWAY, MONCURE D. Autobiography, memories and experiences. Boston; New York, Houghton, Mifflin & co. 1904, 2v. 1672

COUPLAND, R. Wilberforce; a narrative. Oxford, Clarendon press. 1923. 528p. 1673

CROW, ROBERT. Reminiscences. n.p. n.d. 32p. 1674

CURTI, MERLE. The learned blacksmith, the letters and journals of Elihu Buritt. New York, Wilson-Erickson. 1937. 241p. 1675

CURTIS, CLARA K. Fighters for freedom. Rochester. Privately printed. 1933. 168p. 1676

DAWES, ANNA L. Charles Sumner. New York, Dodd, Mead & co. 1892. 330p. (Makers of America series) 1677

DAVIS, WILLIAM F. Saint indefatigable; a sketch of the life of Amarancy Paine Searle. Boston, D. Lathrop & co. 1883. 97p. 1678

EARLE, THOMAS. The life, travels and opinions of Benjamin Lundy including journeys to Texas and Mexico; with a sketch of contemporary events, and a notice of the revolution in Hayti. Compiled under the direction of his children. Philadelphia, Wm. D. Parrish. 1847. 316p. 1679

EIMES, JAMES. Thomas Clarkson; being a contribution towards the history of the abolition of the slave trade and slavery. London, Blackader & co. 1854. 320p. 1680

EVERETT, EDWARD. An eulogy on the life and character of John Quincy Adams, delivered at the request of the legislature of Massachusetts in Faneuil Hall, April 15, 1848. Boston, Dutton &

Wentworth. 1848. 71p. 1681

FAUSET, ARTHUR H. Sojourner Truth: God's faithful pilgrim. Chapel Hill, University of North Carolina press. 1938. 187p. 1682

FIELDS, ANNIE (ed.). Life and letters of Harriet Beecher Stowe. Boston, New York, Houghton, Mifflin & co. 1897. 406p. 1683

FOOTE, MRS. JULIA A. A brand plucked from the fire; an autobiographical sketch. Cleveland, The auth. 1886. 124p. 1684

FRIENDS, RELIGIOUS SOCIETY OF. Biographical sketches and anecdotes of members . . . Philadelphia, Tract association of friends. 1870. 427p. 1685

FROTHINGHAM, OCTAVIUS B. Gerrit Smith. A biography. New York, G. P. Putnam's sons. 1878. 381p. 2d ed. New York, G. P. Putnam's sons. 1879. 381p. 1686

FROTHINGHAM, PAUL R. William Ellery Channing, his messages from the spirit. Boston, New York, Houghton, Mifflin co.. 1903. 52p. 1687

GARRISON, WILLIAM L. Tributes to William Lloyd Garrison at the funeral services. Boston, Houghton, Osgood & co. 1879. 56p. 1688

GARRISON, WENDELL P. AND FRANCIS J. William Lloyd Garrison, 1805-1879. The story of his life told by his children. New York, Century co. 1885. 4v. 1689

GREGORY, JAMES M. Frederick Douglass, the orator. Springfield, Mass., The auth. 1893. 215p. 1690

GREEN, BERIAH. The martyr. A discourse in commemoration of the martyrdom of the Rev. Elijah P. Lovejoy. New York, American anti-slavery society. 1838. 18p. 1691

GREEN, BERIAH. Sketches of the life and writings of James Gillespie Birney . . . Utica, N. Y., Jackson & Chaplin. 1844. 119p. 1692

GRIGGS, EARL L. Thomas Clarkson, the friend of slaves. London, Geo. Allen & Unwin. 1936. 210p. 1693

GRIMKE, ARCHIBALD H. William Lloyd Garrison, the abolitionist. New York, Funk & Wagnalls. 1891. 405p. (American reformer series) 1694

GRIMKE, ARCHIBALD H. Charles Sumner. The scholar in politics. New York & London, Funk & Wagnalls co. 1892. 415p. (The American reformer series) 1695

HALLOWELL, ANNA D. James and Lucretia Mott. Life and letters. Boston, Houghton, Mifflin & co. 1884. 566p. 1696

HALSEY, LUTHER (comp.). Memoirs of John Frederick Oberlin, compiled from authentic sources, chiefly French and German. Translations by compiler. New York. Robert Carter & bros. 1857. 246p. 1697

HARSHA, DAVID A. The life of Charles Sumner. New York, H. Dayton, publ. 1860. 329p. 1698

HARVEY, PETER. Reminiscences and anecdotes of Daniel Webster. Boston, Little, Brown & co. 1880. 480p. 1699

HILLARD, GEORGE S. Life, letters, and journals of George Ticknor. 2d ed. London, Sampson Low, Marston, Searle, & Rivington. 1876. 2v. 1700

HOLLAND, FREDERIC M. Frederick Douglass: the colored orator. rev. ed. New York, Funk & Wagnalls co. 1895. 431p. 1701

HUME, JOHN F. The abolitionists together with personal memories of the struggle for human rights, 1830-1864. New York, London, G.

P. Putnam's sons. 1905. 224p. 1702

JAMIESON, ANNIE S. William King, friend and champion of slaves. Toronto. Missions of evangelism. 1925. 209p.   1703

JAY, WILLIAM. Autobiography . . . with reminiscences of some distinguished contemporaries, selections from his correspondence, and literary remains. Ed. by George Redford and John A. James. New York, Robert Carter & bros. 1855. 2v.   1704

JOHNSON, OLIVER. William Lloyd Garrison and his times; or, sketches of the anti-slavery movement in America . . . with an introduction by John Greenleaf Whittier. Boston, Russell & co. 1880. 432p. Rev. enl. ed. Boston, Houghton, Mifflin & co. 1881. 490p. new ed. Boston, Houghton, Mifflin co. 1885. 490p.   1705

KENNEDY, WILLIAM S. John G. Whittier, the poet of freedom. New York, London, Funk & Wagnalls. 1892. 330p. (American reformers series)   1706

KIRBY, GEORGIANA B. Years of experience. An autobiographical narrative. New York, London, G. P. Putnam's sons. 1887. 315p.   1707

KNIGHT, MRS. HELEN C. Hannah More; life in hall and cottage. New York, American tract society. 1862. 282p.   1708

KNOX, THOMAS W. Life and work of Henry Ward Beecher . . . from the cradle to the grave. Kansas City, Mo., Hartford pub. co. 1887. 544p. 1709

LESTER, CHARLES E. Life and public services of Charles Sumner. New York, United States pub. co. 1874. 596p.   1710

LEWIS, JOHN W. The life, labors, and travels of Elder Charles Bowles, of the free will baptist denomination; together with an essay on the character and condition of the African race by the same, also, an essay on the fugitive law in the U. S. Congress of 1859 by Arthur Gearing. Watertown, Conn., Ingalls & Stowell's press. n.d. 288p.   1711

LOVEJOY, JOSEPH C. Memoir of Rev. Charles T. Torrey who died in the penitentiary of Maryland, where he was confined for showing mercy to the poor . . . Boston, J. P. Jewett & co. 1847. 364p.   1712

LOVEJOY, JOSEPH C. AND OWEN. Memoir of the Rev. Elijah P. Lovejoy who was murdered in the defence of the liberty of the press, at Alton, Ill., November 7, 1837; with introduction by John Quincy Adams. New York, John S. Taylor. 1838. 382p.   1713

MAY, SAMUEL J. Some recollections of our anti-slavery conflict. Boston, Fields, Osgood & co. 1869. 408p. 1714

MCCRAY, FLORINE T. The life-work of the author of Uncle Tom's cabin. New York, London, Funk & Wagnalls. 1889. 440p.   1715

MILLIGAN, HAROLD V. Stephen Collins Foster. A biography of America's folk-song composer. New York, G. Schirmer. 1920. 116p. 1716

MARTINEAU, HARRIET. Autobiography, edited by Maria W. Chapman. Boston, James R. Osgood & co. 1877. 2v.   1717

MARTYN, CARLOS. Wendell Phillips, the agitator: with three of the orator's masterpieces . . . rev. ed. New York, London, Funk and Wagnalls. 1890. 600p. (Am. reformers series)   1718

NASON, ELIAS AND RUSSELL, THOMAS. The life and public

services of Henry Wilson. Boston, B. B. Russell & co. 1876. 452p. 1719

NASON, ELIAS. The life and times of Charles Sumner. Boston, B. B. Russell. 1874. 355p. 1720

PAINE, THOMAS. Political writings . . . with a brief sketch of the author's life. Middletown, N. J., Geo. H. Evans. 1837. 515p. 1721

PARKER, THEODORE. Speeches, addresses, and occasional sermons. Boston, Horace B. Fuller. 1871. 3v. 1722

PARTON, J. The life of Horace Greeley, editor of the New York Tribune. New York, Mason bros. 1855. 442p. 1723

PHILLIPS, WENDELL. Remarks . . . at the funeral of William Lloyd Garrison. Boston, Lee & Shepard; New York, Charles T. Dillingham. 1884. 16p. 1724

PHILLIPS, WENDELL. Speeches, lectures, letters. 2d series. Boston, Lee & Shepard. 1894. 2v. 1725

PILLSBURY, PARKER. Acts of the anti-slavery apostles. Concord, N. H., Clauge, Wegamn, Schlicht & co. 1883. 503p. 1726

PORTER, A. TOOMER. Led on! Step by step, scenes from clerical, military, educational, and plantation life in the South, 1828-1898. An autobiography. New York, London, G. P. Putnam's sons. 1898. 462p. 1727

POWELL, AARON M. Personal reminiscences of the anti-slavery and other reforms and reformers. New York, Anna Rice Powell. 1899. 279p. 1728

PRENTICE, G. D. Biography of Henry Clay. Lexington, Ky. 1830. 304p. 1729

PRENTISS, GEORGE L. A sermon preached on the occasion of the death of Anson G. Phelps, Dec. 11, 1853, with some extracts from his journal. New York, John A. Gray. 1854. 61p. 1730

PRICE, THOMAS. Memoir of William Wilberforce. Boston, Light & Horton. 1834. 88p. 1731

PRICE, MRS. NANCY. A narrative of my life and travels. Boston, The auth. 1850. 87p. 2d ed. 1853. 1732

QUINCY, EDMUND. Life of Josiah Quincy of Massachusetts. Boston, Fields, Osgood & co. 1869. 560p. 1733

ROOSEVELT, THEODORE. Thomas Hart Benton. Boston, New York, Houghton, Mifflin & co. 1890. 372p. (American statesmen series) 1734

ROOT, DAVID. A memorial of the martyred Lovejoy: in a discourse delivered in Dover, N. H. n.d. n.p. 16p. 1735

ROSS, ALEXANDER M. Recollections and experiences of an abolitionist; from 1855 to 1865. 2d ed. Toronto, Rowsell and Hutchinson. 1876. 203p. 1736

SANBORN, FRANKLIN B. Dr. S. G. Howe, the philanthropist. New York, Funk & Wagnalls. 1891. 370p. 1737

SCHURZ, CARL. Eulogy on Charles Sumner. Boston, Lee & Shepard. 1874. 87p. 1738

SEWARD, WILLIAM H. Autobiography, from 1801 to 1834; with a memoir of his life, and selections from his letters from 1831 to 1846 by Frederick W. Seward. New York, D. Appleton & co. 1877. 822p. 1739

SEWARD, WILLIAM H. Life and public services of John Quincy Adams, sixth president of the United States, with the eulogy. Auburn, N. Y., Derby, Miller & co.

1849. 404p. 1740

SMITH, J. A. Memoir of Nathaniel Colver with lectures, plans of sermons, etc. Boston, George A. Foxcroft, Jr. 1875. 453p. 1741

SPRAGUE, WILLIAM B. Annals of the American pulpit; or commemorative notices of distinguished American clergymen of various denominations from the early settlement of the country to 1855. New York, Carter & bros. 1857. 7v. 1742

STAFFORD, WENDELL P. Wendell Phillips, a centennial oration delivered in Boston, November 28, 1911. New York, National assn. for advancement of colored people, 1912. 1743

STOUGHTON, JOHN. William Wilberforce. New York, A. C. Armstrong & son. 1880. 213p. 1744

STOWE, MRS. HARRIET B. Men of our times; or leading patriots of the day; being narratives of the lives and deeds of statesmen, generals, and orators including biographical sketches and anecdotes of Lincoln, Grant, Garrison and others. Hartford, Hartford publ. co. 1868. 575p. 1745

STUART, CHARLES. A memoir of Granville Sharp, to which is added Sharp's "law of passive obedience" . . . etc. New York, American anti-slavery society. 1836. 156p. 1746

SUMNER, CHARLES. Works . . . Boston, Lee & Shepard. 1875. 15v. 1747

SUMNER, CHARLES. A memorial of Charles Sumner, Massachusetts general court, joint special committee on Sumner memorial. Boston, Massachusetts legislature. 1874. 316p. 1748

TAPPAN, LEWIS. The life of Arthur Tappan. New York, Hurd & Houghton, 1870. 432p. 1749

TAYLOR, ROBERT W. Harriet Tubman, the heroine in ebony. Boston, The auth. 1901. 16p. 1750

TUCKERMAN, BAYARD. William Jay and the constitutional movement for the abolition of slavery. Preface by John Jay. New York, Dodd, Mead & co. 1893. 185p. 1751

U. S. CONGRESS. Obituary addresses on the occasion of the death of Hon. Henry Clay . . . Delivered in the Senate and House of representatives of the U. S. (32d Congress, 1st session) June 30, 1852. Washington, R. Armstrong. 1852. 135p. 1752

VAUX, ROBERTS. Memoirs of the life of Anthony Benezet. Philadelphia, James P. Parke. 1817. 136p. 1753

WARREN, WILLIAM F., NEWHALL, FALES HENRY, AND HAVEN, GILBERT. Parkerism: three discourses delivered on the occasion of the death of Theodore Parker. New York, Carleton & Parker. 1860. 115p. 1754

WEBSTER, DANIEL. A discourse in commemoration of the lives and services of John Adams and Thomas Jefferson. . . Faneuil Hall. Boston, Cummings, Hilliard & co. 1826. 62p. 1755

WEBSTER, DANIEL. Obituary addresses on the death of Daniel Webster delivered in the Congress of the U. S. on the 14th & 15th of Dec., 1852. (32d Congress, 2d session. 1852) Washington, Robert Armstrong. 1853. 86p. 1756

WEBSTER, DANIEL. Speeches and forensic arguments. 8th ed. Boston, Tappan & Dennet. 1844. 2v. 1757

WEBSTER, DANIEL. Works . . . 5th

ed. Boston, Little, Brown & co. 1853. 6v. 18th ed. Boston, Little, Brown & co. 1881. 6v. National ed. (Speeches and writings) Boston, Little, Brown & co. 1903. 18v. 1758

WEBSTER, FLETCHER (ed.). The private correspondence of Daniel Webster. Boston, Little, Brown & co. 1857. 2v.   1759

WEISS, JOHN. Life and correspondence of Theodore Parker. New York, D. Appleton & co. 1864. 2v.   1760

WHIPPLE, EDWIN P. The great speeches and orations of Daniel Webster. Boston, Little, Brown & co. 1879. 707p.   1761

WIGHAM, HANNAH M. A Christian philanthropist of Dublin. A memoir of Richard Allen. London, Hodder & Stoughton. 1886. 256p.   1762

WILBERFORCE, ROBERT I. AND SAMUEL. The life of William Wilberforce. Philadelphia, Henry Perkins. 1839. 544p; rev. enl. Engl. ed. "The correspondence of William Wilberforce." London, John Murray. 1840. 2v.   1763

WINTHROP, ROBERT C. Speeches and addresses. Boston, Little, Brown & co. 1852. 767p.   1764

WOODMAN, JOHN. Works . . . Mount Holly, N. J. 1774. 436p.   1765

WORCESTER, LEONARD. A discourse on the Alton outrage. Peacham, Vermont, Dec. 17, 1837. Concord, N. H., The Caledonia Assn. 1838. 16p.   1766

WRIGHT, ELIZUR. Myron Holley, and what he did for liberty and true religion. Boston, The auth. 1882. 328p.   1767

WYMAN, LILLIE B. AND CRAWFORD, ARTHUR. Elibabeth Buffum Chace, 1806-1899. Her life and its environment. Boston, W. B. Clarke co. 1914. 2v.   1768

XVII. General pro-slavery argument.

ADAMS, NEHEMIAH. A south-side view of slavery: or, three months in the South, in 1854. Boston, T. R. Marvin. 1854. 214p. 4th ed. New York, J. C. Derby. 1855. 222p.   1769

BLAGDEN, G. W. Remarks . . . and a discourse on slavery. Boston, Ticknor, Reed & Fields. 1854. 30p.   1770

BLEDSOE, ALBERT T. An essay on liberty and slavery. Philadelphia, J. B. Lippincott. 1856. 383p.   1771

BROWNLOW, WILLIAM G. The great iron wheel examined; or, its false spokes extracted, and an exhibition of Elder Graves, its builder, in a series of chapters. Nashville. 1856. 331p.   1772

BROWNLOW, WILLIAM G. Speeches . . . with a biographical sketch by Theodore Tilton. New York, E. D. Baker. 1862. 36p.   1773

CHRISTY, DAVID (pseud. AN AMERICAN) Cotton is king: or, the culture of cotton and its relation to agriculture, manufactures, and commerce; and also to the free colored people of the United States, and to those who hold that slavery is in itself sinful. Cincinnati, Moore, Wilstach, Keys & co. 1855. viii, 210p. 2d ed. rev. enl. New York, Derby & Johnson. 1856. 298p.   1774

CLEVELAND, HENRY. Alexander H. Stephens, in public and private. With letters and speeches. Phila-

'delphia, National pub. co. 1866.
833p.   1775

COBB, JOSEPH B. Slavery and the
slave trade in the District of
Columbia, the true issue between
parties in the South, union or
disunion. New York, D. Appleton.
1858. 52p.   1776

COLLINS, ROBERT. Essay on the
treatment and management of
slaves. Written upon the social and
economical aspects of the southern
political crisis. 2d ed. Boston,
Eastburn press. 1861. 64p.   1777

COLWELL, STEPHEN. The South: a
letter from a friend in the North.
With special reference to the effects
of disunion upon slavery. Philadelphia, C. Sherman & son. 1856.
46p.   1778

DEW, THOMAS R. Review of the
debate on the abolition of slavery
in the Virginia legislature of 1831
and 1832, Washington, Duff Green.
1833. 832p. Reprint. pp. 769-832
as v 2, no. 25 of the Political
Register, Washington. Oct. 16,
1833.   1779

DORR, JAMES A. Justice to the
South! An address . . . Oct. 8,
1856. 12p.   1780

ELLIOTT, E. N. (ed.). Cotton is king,
and pro-slavery arguments:
comprising the writings of
Hammond, Christy, Stringfellow,
Hodge, Bledsoe, and Cartwright, on
this important subject. With an
essay on slavery in the light of
international law, by the editor.
Augusta, Ga., Pritchard, Abbott &
Loomis. 1860. xv, 908p.   1781

ESTES, MATTHEW. A defence of
Negro slavery as it exists in the
United States. Montgomery,
"Alabama journal" press. 1846.
260p.   1782

FLETCHER, JOHN. Studies on

slavery, in easy lessons. Compiled
into eight studies, and subdivided
into short lessons for the
convenience of readers. Natchez,
Warner. 1852. 637p.   1783

FROTHINGHAM, O. B. The let-alone
policy. A sermon, June 9, 1861.
New York, The auth. 16p.   1784

FUGITT, JAMES P. Our country and
slavery. Baltimore, The auth. 1861.
36p.   1785

A GENTLEMAN OF BALTIMORE.
(pseud.) A letter . . . to his friend in
the state of New York on the
subject of slavery. Baltimore,
Sherwood & co. 1841. 9p.   1786

GUENEBAULT, J. H. Natural history
of the Negro race, extracted from
the history of mankind, by Dr.
Virey. Charleston, S. C., D. J.
Dowling. 1836. 162p.   1787

HAMMOND, J. H. Letters . . . on
Southern slavery: addressed to
Thomas Clarkson, the English
abolitionist. Charleston, S. C.,
Walker & Burke. 1845. 32p.   1788

HOLCOMBE, WILLIAM H. The
alternative: a separate nationality,
or the Africanization of the South.
New Orleans, Delta job office.
1860. 15p.   1789

HUNDLEY, DANIEL R. Social
relations in our southern states.
New York, Henry B. Price. 1860.
367p.   1790

JACKSON, HENRY R. The Wanderer
case . . . a speech. Appendix with
speech of Daniel Webster at Capon
Springs, Va. June, 1851. Atlanta, E.
Holland. 1852. 83p.   1791

JAGGER, WILLIAM. Information
acquired from the best authorities,
with respect to the institution of
slavery. To the people of Suffolk
county. New York, R. Craighead.
1856. 28p.   1792

LAWS OF RACE AS CONNECTED

112

WITH SLAVERY. . . Philadelphia, Willis P. Hazard. 1860. 70p.　　1793

MACON, NATHANIEL. Letters to Charles O'Connor. The destruction of the union is emancipation. Philadelphia, John Campbell. 1862. 38p.　　1794

MAN, THOMAS. A picture of Woonsocket; or, truth in its nudity; to which are added translations from the best French, Spanish, and Italian writers. Woonsocket, R. I., The auth. 1835. 82p.　　1795

MCTYEIRE, HOLLAND, NIMMONS, ET AL. Duties of masters to servants: three premium essays. Charleston, S. C., Southern Baptist publication society. 1851. 151p.　　1796

NEILL, HENRY. A letter to the editors of the American Presbyterian and Genessee Evangelist. Philadelphia, King & Baird. 1858. 21p.　　1797

O' CONOR, CHARLES. Negro slavery not unjust. Speech . . . at the union meeting at the academy of music, New York City, Dec. 19, 1859. New York, Van Evrie, Horton & co. 1859. 14p.　　1798

PALMER, BENJAMIN M. The South: her peril, and her duty. A discourse delivered in the First Presbyterian church, New Orleans, Nov. 29, 1860. New York, True witness & sentinel. 1860. 16p.　　1799

PAULDING, JAMES K. Slavery in the United States. New York, Harper & bros. 1836. 312p.　　1800

PEARCE, JAMES A. Letter from the Hon. James Alfred Pearce, United States senator from Maryland on the politics of the day. Letter from the Hon. Thomas G. Pratt, United States senator from Maryland to the Whigs of that state. Speech of the Hon. Isaac D. Jones, delivered .

. . at Princes Anne, Md. July 15, 1856 . . . Washington, Standard office. 1856. 16p.　　1801

THE PLANTER, or thirteen years in the South. By a Northern man . . . Philadelphia, H. Hooker. 1853. 275p.　　1802

POLLARD, EDWARD A. Black diamonds gathered in the darkey homes of the South. New York, Pridney & Russell. 1860. 156p.　　1803

QUINN, DAVID. Petition and memorial of David Quinn, asking for the re-establishment of Negro slavery in the United States. Chicago. June 13, 1866. 48p.　1804

RAMSEY, JAMES. Objections to the abolition of the slave trade, with answers to which are prefixed — Strictures on a late publication, entitled "considerations on the emancipation of Negroes, and the abolition of the slave trade," by a West India planter. London, J. Phillips. 1788. 85p.　　1805

RICE, NATHAN L. A debate on slavery, held on Oct. 1, 2, 3, and 6, 1845, upon the question: is slave-holding in itself sinful . . . in Cincinnati, between J. Blanchard and N. L. Rice. 4th thousand. Cincinnati, Wm. H. Moore & co. New York, Mark H. Newman. 1845. 482p.　　1806

ROBINSON, JOHN B. Pictures of slavery and anti-slavery. Advantages of Negro slavery and the benefits of Negro freedom, morally, socially and politically considered. Philadelphia, The auth. 1863. 388p.　1807

ROSS, FREDERICK A., AND COLENSO, JOHN. W. Dr. Ross and Bishop Colenso: or, truth restored in regard to polygamy and slavery. Philadelphia, Henry B. Ashmead. 1857. 82p.　　1808

PRO-SLAVERY ARGUMENT as maintained by the most distinguished writers of the southern states, containing the several essays, on the subject of Chancellor Harper, Gov. Hammond, Dr. Simons and Prof. Dew. Charleston, Walker, Richards & co. 1852. 490p.   1809

SANDS, ALEXANDER H. Recreations of a southern barrister. Philadelphia, J. B. Lippincott & co.; Richmond, A. Morris. 1859. 212p.   1810

SEABURY, SAMUEL. American slavery distinguished from the slavery of English theorists, and justified by the law of nature. New York, Mason bros. 1861. 319p.   1811

SLAVERY INDISPENSABLE to the civilization of Africa. Baltimore, John D. Toy. 1855. 51p.   1812

SMITH, WILLIAM A. Lectures on the philosophy and practice of slavery, as exhibited in the institution of domestic slavery in the United States; with the duties of masters to slaves, edited by Thomas O. Summers. Nashville, Stevenson & Evans. 1856. x, 328p.   1813

THE SOUTH VINDICATED from the treason and fanaticism of the northern abolitionists. Philadelphia, H. Manly. 1836. 314p.   1814

STEARNS, EDWARD J. Notes on Uncle Tom's cabin: being a logical answer to its allegations and inferences against slavery as an institution. With a supplementary note on the key, and an appendix of authorities. Philadelphia, Lippincott, Grambo & co. 1853. 314p.   1815

STILES, JOSEPH C. Modern reform examined; or, the union of the North and South on the subject of slavery. Philadelphia, J. B. Lippincott & co. 1857. 310p. 1816

STILES, JOSEPH C. The national controversy; or, the voice of the fathers upon the state of the country. New York, Rudd & Carleton. 1861. 108p.   1817

STILES, JOSEPH C. Speech . . . on the slavery resolutions delivered in the General Assembly . . . in Detroit, May, 1849. Washington, Jno. T. Towers. 1850. 44p.   1818

STOCKTON, R. F. Letter . . . on the slavery question. Reply to a letter from Daniel Webster. New York, S. W. Benedict, print. 1850. 23p. 1819

STRINGFELLOW, B. F. Information for the people. Two tracts for the times. The one entitled "Negro slavery, no evil;" the other, an answer to the inquiry "Is it expedient to introduce slavery into Kansas?" by D. R. Goodloe, of North Carolina. Boston, Alfred Mudge & son. 1855. 55p.   1820

THAYER, M. RUSSELL. A reply to Mr. Charles Ingersoll's "letter to a friend in a slave state." Philadelphia, C. Sherman & son, print. 1862. 26p.   1821

THORNWELL, JAMES H. The rights and duties of masters. A sermon preached in Charleston, S. C., for the benefit and instruction of the coloured population. Charleston, S. C., Walker & James. 1850. 51p.   1822

THOUGHTS ON SLAVERY. Lowell, Mass., Daniel Bixby & co. 1848. 70p.   1823

TOWNSEND, JOHN. The southern states, their present peril and their certain remedy. Why do they not right themselves? And so fulfill their glorious destiny. Charleston, E. C. Councell. 1850. 31p.   1824

TOWNSEND, JOHN. The South alone

114

should govern the South and African slavery should be controlled by those only who are friendly to it. Charleston, Evans & Cogswell. 1860. 62p. 1825

TYSON, BRYAN. The institution of slavery in the southern states, religiously and morally considered in connection with our sectional troubles. Washington, H. Polkinhorn. 1863. 60p. 1826

VAN DYKE, HENRY J. The character and influence of abolitionism. A sermon preached in the First Presbyterian church of Brooklyn, Dec. 9, 1860. New York, George E. Nesbitt & co. 1860. 31p. 1827

VAN EVRIE, JOHN H. Negroes and Negro "slavery," the first, an inferior race — the latter, its normal condition. Introductory number: causes of popular delusion on the subject. Baltimore, John D. Toy; New York, Day book office. 1853. 32p. 3d ed. New York, Van Evrie, Horton & co. 1863. xvi, 339p. 1828

VAN EVRIE, JOHN H. White supremacy and Negro subordination; or, Negroes a subordinate race, and (so-called) slavery its normal condition . . . 2d ed. New York, Van Evrie, Horton & co. 1867. 339. 60p. 1829

WALSH, ROBERT. An appeal from the judgement of Great Britain, respecting the United States of Africa. Part first, containing an historical outline of their merits and wrongs vs. colonies; and strictures upon the calumnies of the British writers. 2d ed. Philadelphia, Mitchell, Ames & White. 1819. 512p. 1830

WOLFE, SAMUEL M. Helper's impending crisis dissected. New York, J. T. Lloyd. 1860. 223p. 1831

WOODWARD, A. A review of Uncle Tom's cabin; or, an essay on slavery. Cincinnati, Applegate & co. 1853. 216p. 1832

XVIII. Pro-slavery fiction, poetry, etc.

ADAMS, NEHEMIAH. The sable cloud; a southern tale, with northern comments. Boston, Ticknor & Fields. 1861. 279p. 1833

ADVENTURES OF CONGO in search of his master; an American tale. Containing a true account of a shipwreck, and interspersed with anecdotes founded on facts. London, Harris & son. 191p. n.d. 1834

ALLEN, JAMES L. Mrs. Stowe's "Uncle Tom" at home in Kentucky. n.p. n.d. 1835

CHASE, LUCIEN B. English serfdom and American slavery: or, ourselves as others see us. New York, H. Long & bro. 1859. 259p. 1836

CRISWELL, ROBERT. "Uncle Tom's cabin" contrasted with Buckingham Hall, the planter's home, or, a fair view of both sides of the slavery question. New York, D. Fanshaw. 1852. 152p. 1837

DAYTON, H. New England's chattells: or, life in the northern poor-house. New York, The auth. 1858. 484p. 1838

EASTMAN, MRS. MARY H. Aunt Phillis' cabin; or, southern life as it is . . . Philadelphia, Lippincott, Grambo & co. 1852. ii, 280p. 1839

ESTES, MATTHEW. Tit for tat, a reply to Dred. By a lady of New Orleans. New York, Garrett. Dick & Fitzgerald. 1856. 356p. 1840

FITZHUGH, GEORGE. Cannibals all! or, slaves without masters. Richmond, Va., A. Morris. 1857. 379p.   1841

GILMAN, CAROLINE. Recollections of a southern matron. New York, Harper bros. 1838. 272p.   1842

GRAYSON, WILLIAM J. The hireling and the slave, Chicora, and other poems. Charleston, S. C., McCarter & co. 1856. 108p.   1843

HANNIBAL, PROF. JULIUS C., (pseud.) Black diamonds; or, humor, satire and sentiment treated scientifically in a series of burlesque lectures, darkly colored. New York, A. Ranney. 1857. 364p.   1844

RANDOLPH, J. THORNTON. The cabin and parlor: or, slaves and masters. Philadelphia, T. B. Peterson. 1852. 324p.   1845

RUSH, CAROLINE E. The North and the South; or, slavery and its contrasts. A tale of real life. Philadelphia, Crissey & Markley. 1852. 350p.   1846

SARGENT, LUCIUS M. The ballard of the abolition blunderbuss . . .

Boston, The booksellers. 1861. 32p.   1847

SMITH, WILLIAM L. Life at the South; or, "Uncle Tom's cabin" as it is being narratives, scenes, and incidents in the real "life of the lowly." Buffalo, Derby & co. 1852. 519p.   1848

SOUTHWOOD, MARION. Tit for tat, a reply to Dred. New York, 1856. 133p.   1849

TEXAN (pseud.) Yankee slave dealer; or, an abolitionist down South. A tale for the times. Nashville, auth. 1860. 368p.   1850

THOMPSON, WILLIAM T. Slaveholder abroad; or, Billy Buck's visit, with his master, to England. A series of letters from Doctor Pleasant Jones to Major Joseph Jones, of Georgia. Philadelphia, J. B. Lippincott & co. 1860. 512p.
                                 1851

THORPE, THOMAS M. The master's house; a tale of southern life, by Logan. New York, McElrath & co. 1854. 391p.   1852

XIX. Anti-abolitionism, Channingism, etc.

THE ABOLITIONIST ATTACK! Abolitionists against General Pierce. n.d. n.p. 8p.   1853

ANTI-ABOLITION TRACTS, NO. 2. Free Negroism: or results of emancipation in the northern states and the West India islands. New York, Van Evrie, Horton & co. 1862. 32p.   1854

BACON, LEONARD. Slavery discussed in occasional essays, from 1833 to 1846. New York, Baker & Scribner. 1846. 247p.   1855

BARROWS, ELIJAH P. JR. A view of the American slavery question. New

York, John S. Taylor. 1836. 114p.
                                 1856

BEECHER, CATHERINE E. An essay on slavery and abolitionism, with reference to the duty of American females. Addressed to Angelina Emily Grimke. Philadelphia, Henry Perkins; Boston, Perkins & Marvin. 1837. 152p.   1857

BLAIR, MONTGOMERY. Speech . . . on the revolutionary schemes of the ultra abolitionists in defiance of the policy of the president. Delivered at the Unconditional union meeting, Rockville, Md., Oct. 3, 1863. New

York, D. W. Lee. 1863. 20p. 1858

BOSTON COURIER FOR 1858. Radicalism in religion, philosophy, and social life; four papers from the Boston Courier for 1858 . . . Boston, Little, Brown & co. 1858. 79p. 1859

BUSHNELL, HORACE. A discourse on the slavery question, delivered in North church, Hartford, Jan. 10, 1839. . . Hartford, Case, Tiffany & co. 1839. 32p. 1860

CHANNING, WILLIAM E. Emancipation. New York, American anti-slavery society. 1841. 71p. 1861

CHANNING, WILLIAM E. A letter to the abolitionists . . . with comments. Boston, Isaac Knapp. 1837. 32p. (Reprinted from the Liberator, Dec. 22, 1837). 1862

CHANNING, WILLIAM E. Letter . . . to James G. Birney. Cincinnati, The auth. 1836. 14p. 1863

CHANNING, WILLIAM E. Slavery. Boston, James Munroe & co. 1835. 167p.; Edinburgh, Thomas Clarke. 1836. 112p. 1864

CHANNING, WILLIAM E. Works . . . Boston, James Munroe. 1875. 2v. New, rearr. ed. complete. Boston, American Unitarian assn. 1882. 931p. 1865

COLFAX, R. H. Evidences for abolitionists . . . proofs of the natural inferiority of Negroes. New York, T. M. Bleakley. 1833. 33p. 1866

COLTON, CALVIN. Abolition a sedition, by a northern man. Philadelphia, Geo. W. Donohue. 1839. vii, 187p. 1867

COLTON, CALVIN. . . Political ambition, by Junius. New York. Greeley & McElrath. 1844. 16p. (Junius tracts, no. 5) 1868

INFIDELITY AND ABOLITIONISM. An open letter to the friends of religion, morality, and the American union. n.d. n.p. 7p. 1869

LORD, NATHAN. True picture of abolition. Boston, Daily Courier. 1863. 16p. 1870

A SOUTHERNER (pseud.). Fanaticism and its results: or, facts vs. fancies. Baltimore, Joseph Robinson. 1860. 36p. 1871

THOMAS BROTHERS (pseud.). The United States of North America as they are; not as they are generally described: being a cure of radicalism. London, Longman, Orme, Brown, Green & Longmans. 1840. 517p. 1872

TUCKER, NATHANIEL B. Partisan leader, a key to the disunion confederacy. Secretly printed in Washington in 1836 by Duff Green, for circulation in the southern states, but afterwards suppressed. New York, Rpt. by Rudd & Carleton. 1861. 392p. 1873

XX. British and European anti-slavery societies: Reports, letters, memorials, proceedings, and publications.

ANTI-SLAVERY ADVOCATE . . . London, British and foreign anti-slavery society. Ed. by Richard Davis Webb. Collection has: v. 2, no. 9. (1857). v. 2, no. 11 (1857). 1874

ANTI-SLAVERY AND ABOLITION SOCIETIES OF THE UNITED

KINGDOM. The memorial . . . to the right honorable Charles Baron Glenelg, his majesty's principal secretary of state for the colonial department. London, Elizabeth Bagster. n.d. 36p.　　　1875

ANTI-SLAVERY REPORTER . . . A periodical. London, The London society for the mitigation and abolition of slavery in the British dominions. 1827-36. 6v. Collection has: v. 1, nos. 1-6. June-Nov. 1833.　　　1876

BIRMINGHAM ANTI-SLAVERY SOCIETY. Report of the proceedings at the anti-slavery meeting . . . (for) petitioning the House of Commons on the defeat of the act for the abolition of colonial slavery, Monday, Feb. 1, 1836. Birmingham, B. Hudson. 1836. 28p.　　1877

BIRMINGHAM ANTI-SLAVERY SOCIETY. The practical defeat of the abolition act. 2d ed. Birmingham, The society. 1835. 16p.　1878

BRISTOL AND CLIFTON LADIES ANTI-SLAVERY SOCIETY. Special report . . . with a statement of the reasons of its separation from the British and foreign anti-slavery society. London, John Simon. 1852. 68p.　　　1879

BRITISH ANTI-SLAVERY SOCIETY. A second letter from Legion to His Grace the duke of Richmond, etc., chairman of the slavery committee of the House of lords: containing an analysis of the anti-slavery evidence produced before the committee . . . London, S. Bagster. 1833. 152p.　　1880

BRITISH AND FOREIGN ANTI-SLAVERY SOCIETY FOR THE ABOLITION OF SLAVERY and the slave trade troughout the world. Annual report . . . 5th, (1844); 7th (1847); 9th, (1849). London. The

society. 1844. 1847, 1849.　1881

FRIENDS, RELIGIOUS SOCIETY OF. Extracts from the minutes and epistles of the yearly meeting of the religious society of friends, held in London, from its first institution to the present time relating to Christian doctrine, practise, and discipline. Philadelphia, Henry Longstreth. 1862. 260p.　　1882

GLASGOW EMANCIPATION SOCIETY. Third annual report . . . 1837. Britain and America united in the cause of universal freedom. Glasgow, Aird & Russel. 1837. 142p.　　　1883

LADIES' SOCIETY FOR THE RELIEF OF NEGRO SLAVES. Resolutions . . . adopted at a meeting held in Walsall, England, Dec. 8, 1825. Birmingham, R. Peart. 1825. 4p.　　　1884

LEICESTER AUXILIARY ANTI-SLAVERY SOCIETY. An address to the public on the state of slavery in the West Indian islands. By the committee of the society. London, Ellerton & Henderson. 1824. 16p. (Slavery pamphlet v. 6, no. 4).
　　　　　　　　1885

LIVERPOOL SOCIETY FOR THE ABOLITION OF SLAVERY. An address . . . on the safest and most efficacious means of promoting the gradual improvement of the Negro slaves in the British West India islands, preparatory to their becoming free labourers and on the expected consequences of such a change. Liverpool, Jonathan & George Smith. 1824. 18p. (Slavery pamphlet v. 6, no. 7).　1886

LONDON ANTI-SLAVERY SOCIETY. Statements and observations on the working of the laws for the abolition of slavery throughout the British colonies, and on the

118

present state of the Negro population. London, J. Rider. 1836. 68p. 1887

MANCHESTER ANTI-SLAVERY CONFERENCE. Report of the proceedings . . . of the anti-slavery conference and public meeting held at Manchester, England, Aug. 1, 1854, in commemoration of West India emancipation. (Committee of the North of England anti-slavery and India reform league). London, Wm. Tweedle; Manchester, Wm. Bremner. 1854. 40p. 1888

PARIS ANTI-SLAVERY CONFERENCE. Special report of the . . . conference, held in Paris, Aug. 26 and 27, 1867. London, British and foreign anti-slavery society. 1867. 166p. 1889

SOCIETY FOR THE EXTINCTION OF THE SLAVE. Trade and for the civilization of Africa. Proceedings at the first public meeting . . . held at Exeter Hall, June 1, 1840. London, W. Clowes sons. 1840. 73p. 1890

XXI. British and European anti-slavery argument.

ABEL, ANNIE HELOISE, AND KLINGBERG, FRANK JOSEPH (eds.). A side-light on Anglo-American relations, 1839-1858. Furnished by correspondence of Lewis Tappan and others with the British anti-slavery society. Ed. with notes. Washington, Association for the study of Negro life and history. 1927. 407p. 1891

ARMISTEAD, WILSON. A tribute for the Negro; being a vindication of the moral, intellectual, and religious capabilities of the coloured portion of mankind; with particular reference to the African race. Manchester, Wm. Irwin; London, Charles Gilpin; New York, Wm. Harned. 1848. xxxv, 564p. 1892

BABINGTON, CHURCHILL. The influence of Christianity in promoting the abolition of slavery in Europe. Cambridge, J. & J. J. Deighton; London, F. & J. Rivington. 1846. 199p. 1893

BALME, J. M. American states, churches and slavery. London, Liverpool. n.d. 546p. 1894

THE BOW IN THE CLOUD; or, the Negro's memorial. A collection of original contributions, in prose and verse. London, Jackson & Walford. 1834. 408p. 1895

BROUGHAM, LORD HENRY. Immediate emancipation. Speech . . . on slavery and the slave trade. London. 1838. 24p. 1896

BROUGHAM, LORD HENRY. Opinions . . . on politics, theology, law, science, etc. as exhibited in his parliamentary and legal speeches, and miscellaneous writings. London, H. Colburn. 1837. 504p. 1897

BUXTON, THOMAS F. The African slave trade. Philadelphia, J. B. Lippincott co. 1839. 188p. 1898

CAIRNES, JOHN E. Who are the Canters . . . (London ladies emancipation society, tract no. 3). London, The society. n.d. 8p. 1899

CAMPBELL, JAMES R. Address . . . the Congressional union in Scotland to their fellow Christians . . . on the subject of American slavery. New York, American and foreign anti-slavery society. 1840. 12p. 1900

CHAMBERS, WILLIAM. American slavery and colour. London, W. & R. Chambers. 1857. 216p. 1901

CLARKSON, THOMAS. An essay on the slavery and commerce of the human species, particularly the African, tr. from a Latin dissertation . . . 1785, with additions. Philadelphia, Reprinted by Joseph Crukshank. 1786. 155p.   1902

CLARKSON, THOMAS. Thoughts on the necessity of improving the condition of the slaves in the British colonies with a view to their ultimate emancipation; and on the practicability, the safety, and the advantages of the latter measure. 2d ed. cor. London, Richard Taylor. 1823. 57p. New York. 1823. 64p. 3d ed. cor. New York, 1823. 92p. 4th ed. cor. London, The society for the mitigation and gradual abolition of slavery throughout the British dominions. 1824. 57p. (Slavery pamphlet, v. 6, no. 1).   1903

CLARKSON, THOMAS. An essay on the impolicy of the African slave trade, to which is added an oration . . . by J. P. Brisset de Warville. Philadelphia. 1788. 159p.   1904

CLARKSON, THOMAS. The history of the rise, progress, and accomplishment of the abolition of the African slave trade by the British parliament. London, Longman, Hurst, Rees, & Orme. 1808. 2v. From the London ed. Philadelphia, James P. Parke. 1808. 2v. Abridged ed. Augusta, Me., P. A. Brinsmade. 1830. 234p. New York, John S. Taylor. 1836. 3v. n.d. London, John W. Parker. 1839. 615p.   1905

THE COLLIE; his rights and wrongs. Author's ed. New York, Geo. Routledge & sons. 1871. 371p.   1906

CONGREGATIONAL UNION OF SCOTLAND. Remonstrance . . . n.d. 11p. (Anti-slavery tracts, no. 1).   1907

COOPER, THOMAS. Correspondence between George Hibbert and Thomas Cooper, relative to the condition of Negro slaves in Jamaica, extracted from the Morning Chronicle; also a libel on the character of Mr. and Mrs. Cooper, published in 1823, in several of the Jamaica journals; with notes and remarks. London, J. Hatchard & son. 1824. iv, 67p.   1908

A COUNTRY GENTLEMAN'S reasons for voting against Mr. Wilberforce's motion . . . for a bill to prohibit the importation of African Negroes into the colonies. London, 1792. 78p.   1909

CROPPER, JAMES. A letter addressed to the Liverpool society for promoting the abolition of slavery . . . on the injurious effects of high prices of produce, and the beneficial effects of low prices, on the condition of slaves. Liverpool, Hatchard & son. 1823. 32p. (Slavery pamphlet, v. 5, no. 4).   1910

CROPPER, JAMES. Relief for West Indian distress, showing the inefficiency of protecting duties on East India sugar, and pointing out the modes of certain relief. London, Hatchard & son. 1823. 36p. (Slavery pamphlet, v. 5, no. 5).   1911

ENGLAND OPPOSED TO SLAVERY, or some remarks . . . Boston, Benj. H. Greene. 1842. 55p.   1912

FISHER, THOMAS (pseud.) An abolitionist. The Negro's memorial; or, abolitionists catechism. London, auth. 1825. 127p.   1913

THE FRIENDLY REMONSTRANCE of the people of Scotland on the subject of slavery. New York,

American anti-slavery society. 1855. 16p. 1914

GURNEY, JOSEPH J. Speech . . . on the abolition of Negro slavery, delivered in the city of Norwich, Jan. 28, 1824. 15p. (Slavery Pamphlet v. 6, no. 5). 1915

HAGGARD, JOHN. The judgement of the Rt. honourable Lord Stowell, respecting the slavery of the mongrel woman, Grace . . . London, W. Benning. 1827. 49p. 1916

HERALD OF PEACE FOR THE YEAR 1825. v. 4, new series. London, Hamilton, Adams & co. 1825. 256p. 1917

HEYRICK, ELIZABETH C. Immediate, not gradual abolition; or, an inquiry into the shortest, safest, and most effectual means of getting rid of West Indian slavery. Boston, Isaac Knapp. 1838. 35p. 1918

HOVEY, SYLVESTER. Letters from the West Indies: relating especially to the Danish island St. Croix, and to the British islands Antigua, Barbadoes and Jamaica. New York, Gould & Newman. 1838. 4-212p. 1919

IVIMEY, JOSEPH. The utter extinction of slavery an object of scripture prophecy. A lecture . . . delivered at . . . Chelmsford ladies anti-slavery association, April 17, 1832. Dedicated to William Wilberforce. London, J. Messedor. 1832. viii, 74p. 1920

KENRICK, JOHN. Horrors of slavery. In two parts. Part 1: containing observations, facts, and arguments, extracted from the speeches of Wilberforce, Grenville, Pitt, Burke, Fox, Martin, Whithead and other distinguished members of British parliament. Part 2: containing extracts, chiefly American . . .

demonstrating that slavery is impolitic, anti-republican, unchristian, and highly criminal; and proposing measures for its complete abolition through the United States. Cambridge, Hilliard & Metcalf. 1817. 59p. 1921

LETTERS TO A MEMBER OF THE CONGRESS OF THE UNITED STATES OF AMERICA, from an English clergyman; including a republication, with considerable additions, of the tract 'Every man his own property' . . . London, Whittaker, Treacher & Arnot. Birmingham, C. Hammond. 1835. 30p. 1922

THE LONDON MAGAZINE AND MONTHLY CHRONOLOGER. London, T. Astley. 1746. 682p. 1923

MICHAEL, CHARLES D. The slave and his champions, Granville Sharp, Thomas Clarkson, William Wilberforce, and Sir Thomas Fowell Buxton. London, S. W. Partridge & co. n.d. 160p. 1924

ON PROTECTION TO WEST INDIA SUGAR. 2d ed. cor. enl. and containing an answer to a pamphlet, written by Joseph Marryat, entitled "A reply, etc." London, J. M. Richardson & J. Hatchard. 1823. 159p. (Slavery pamphlet v. 5, no. 1). 1925

RAMSEY, JAMES. A reply to the personal invectives and objections contained in two answers, published by certain anonymous persons, to an essay on the treatment and conversion of African slaves, in the British colonies. London, James Phillips. 1785. 107p. 1926

A REVIEW OF SOME OF THE ARGUMENTS WHICH ARE COMMONLY ADVANCED against Parliamentary interference in behalf of the Negro slaves, with a statement of opinions which have been expressed on that subject by many of our most distinguished statesmen, including, Earl Grey, Earl of Liverpool, Lord Grenville, Lords Dudley and Ward, Lord Melville, Mr. Burke, Mr. Pitt, Mr. Fox, Mr. Windham, Mr. Wilberforce, Mr. Canning, etc., etc. London, J. Hatchard & son. 1823. 32p. (Slavery pamphlet v. 6, no. 3). 1927

SCHOELCHER, V. Protestants de Citoyens Francais Negres et mulatres contre des accusations calomnieuses. Paris, De Soye & ce. 1851. 48p. 1928

SEEBER, EDWARD D. Anti-slavery opinion in France during the second half of the eighteenth century. Baltimore, Johns Hopkins press; London, Oxford University press; Paris, Societe d'edition 'les belles lettres.' 1937. 238p. (Johns Hopkins studies, extra v. x). 1929

SHARP, GRANVILLE. The law of passive obedience, or, Christian submission to personal injuries: wherein is shown, that the several texts of scripture, which command the entire submission of servants or slaves to their masters, cannot authorize the latter to exact an involuntary servitude, nor, in the least degree, justify the claims of modern slaveholders. London, E. B. White. 1776. 102p. 1930

SHARP, GRANVILLE. Extract from a representation of the injustice and dangerous tendency of tolerating slavery, or, admitting the least claim of private property in the persons of men in England. American ed. Philadelphia, Joseph Crukshank. 1751. 53p. 1931

SHIRREFF, EMILY. The chivalry of the South. London, Ladies London emancipation society. 1864. 14p. (Tract no. 6). 1932

SLAVERY. From the Hull Rockingham, Jan. 31, 1824. Liverpool, Rushton & Melling. 1824. 8p. (Slavery pamphlet v. 6, no. 6). 1933

SOCIETY OF FRIENDS. The case of our fellow-creatures, the oppressed Africans, respectfully recommended to serious consideration of the legislature of Great Britain by the people called Quakers. London, James Philips. 1784. 259p. 1934

STURGE, JOSEPH. To the abolitionists of the United States, who, by their votes, contributed to place a slaveholder in the Presidential chair. Philadelphia, Committee of the British and foreign anti-slavery society. 1841. 3p. 1935

TRAIN, GEORGE FRANCIS . . . Great speeches in England on slavery and emancipation March 12 & 13, 1862, also, his great speech on the "pardoning of traitors." Philadelphia, T. B. Peterson & bro. 1862. 32p. 1936

TWENTY MILLIONS THROWN AWAY, and slavery perpetuated. By an ex-member of the Jamaica assembly. (Reprinted from the Radical, weekly stamped newspaper). London, J. Morgan; Boston, Isaac Knapp. n.d. 20p. 1937

UNCLE TOM'S CABIN ALMANAC, 1853. Abolitionist mememto. London, John Cassell. 1853. 64p. 1938

UNCLE TOM IN ENGLAND. The London Times on Uncle Tom's cabin. A review from the London Times, Sept. 3, 1852. Rpt. New York, Bruce & bro. 1852. 8p. 1939

WILBERFORCE, WILLIAM. An appeal to the religion, justice and humanity on the inhabitants of the British empire in behalf of the

Negro slaves in the West Indies. London, J. Hatchard & son. 1823. 56p. (Slavery pamphlet v. 5, no. 3).
1940

WILSON, DANIEL. Thoughts on British Colonial slavery, 1827. (From the Amulet, or Christian and literary remembrances, 1828).

London. n.p. 1828. 7p.   1941

WRIGHT, HENRY C. The dissolution of the American union, demanded by justice and humanity, as the incurable enemy of liberty, etc. Glasgow. The Glasgow emancipation society, and hibernian anti-slavery society. 1845. 46p.   1942

XXII. Slavery, insurrection and Emancipation in the West Indies and South America.

AN ABSTRACT of the evidence delivered before a select committee of the House of commons in the years 1790 and 1791 . . . for the abolition of the slave trade. Cincinnati, American reform tract and book society. 1859. 117p.
1943

AN ABSTRACT of the information recently laid on the table of the House of commons . . . Foreign slave trade. London, 1821. 16p.
1944

AN ABSTRACT of the report of the House of lords commission on the condition and treatment of colonial slaves. London, 1854. 57p.   1945

AN ACCOUNT of a shooting excursion. . . the parish of Trelawny on the island of Jamaica, Oct., 1824. London, Harvey & Barton. 1825. 15p.   1946

AMERICAN MUSEUM OR UNIVERSAL MAGAZINE Sept., 1790. v. 8, no. 111. Philadelphia, Carey, Stewart co. 1790. 24p. 1947

ANNUAL REGISTER. Corbett, v. 3. (From Jan. to June, 1803). Reports on the Santo Domingo revolution. London, John Rudd. 1803. 1048p.
1948

BARCLAY, ALEXANDER. A practical view of the present state of slavery in the West Indies: or, An

examination of Mr. James Stephen's "Slavery of the British West India Colonies." Containing more particularly an account of the actual condition of the Negroes in Jamaica: with observations on the decrease of the slave since the abolition of the slave trade, and on the probable effects of legislative emancipation; also: strictures on the Edinburgh Review, and on the pamphlets of Mr. Cooper and Mr. Bickell. 2d ed. London, Smith, Elder & co. 1826. 462p.   1949

BEARD, JOHN R. The life of Toussaint L'Ouverture, the Negro patriot of Hayti: comprising an account of the struggle for liberty in the island, and a sketch of its history to the present period. London, Ingram, Cook & co. 1853. xi, 335p. Rev. enl. and repub. as TOUSSAINT L'OUVERTURE: a biography and autobiography. Boston, James Redpath. 1863. 372p.   1950

BICKELL, R. The West Indies as they are; or a real picture of slavery: but more particularly as it exists in the island of Jamaica. London, J. Hatchard & son. 1822. 256p. 1951

BIGELOW, JOHN. Jamaica in 1850; or, The effects of sixteen years of freedom on a slave colony. New

York, London, George P. Putnam. 1851. 214p. 1952

BIRD, M. B. The black man; or, Haytian independence. Deduced from historical notes. New York, The author. 1869. 461p. 1953

BLEBY, HENRY. Speech . . . on the results of emancipation in the British West India colonies. Boston, R. F. Wallcut. 1858. 36p. 1954

BRIEF HISTORY of the island of Hayti. Boston, Massachusetts sabbath school union. 1831. 68p. 1955

BURNLEY, WILLIAM H. Observations on the present condition of the island of Trinidad. London. 1842. 1956

BUTLER, WEEDEN (transl.) Zimao, the African. Dublin. Gilbert and Hodges. 1800. 104p. 1957

CAMPBELL, JOHN. Negromania . . . Condition of the Negroes in the West Indies before and since emancipation. Philadelphia. Campbell and Power. 1851. 549p. 1958

CARVILL, G and C., et al. Six months in the West Indies in 1825. New York, the authors. 1826. 294p. 1959

CHANNING, WILLIAM E. An address . . . on the anniversary of emancipation in the British West Indies; delivered at Lenox, Aug. 1842. Lenox, Mass. J. G. Stanley. 1842. 38p. Boston ed. Oliver Johnson. 1842. 24p. 1960

CLARK, B. C. A plea for Haiti, with a glance at her relations with France, England and the United States, for the last sixty years. 2d ed. Boston, Eastburn press. 1853. 50p. 1961

CLARK, JOHN, and others. The voice of jubilee: a narrative of the Baptist mission, Jamaica, from its commencement . . . London, John Snow. 1865. xx, 359p. 1962

COCHIN, AUGUSTIN. L'abolition de l'esclavage. Paris, Lecoffre. 1861. 2v. 1963

DALLAS, ROBERT C. The history of the maroons, from their origin to the establishment of their chief tribe at Sierra Leone; including the expedition to Cuba, for the purpose of securing Spanish chasseurs . . . London, Longman and Rees. 1803. 2v. 1964

DEPUTIES OF ST. DOMINGO General Assembly. A particular account of the insurrection in St. Domingo. Tr. from the speech in French made to the National assembly, Aug. 1791 by the deputies from the General assembly of the French part of the island. London, J. Sewell. 1791. 47p. 1965

DUNN, BALLARD S. Brazil, the home for Southerners: or, a practical account of what the author and others, who visited that country . . . saw and did while in that empire. New York, Geo. B. Richardson. 1866. 272p. 1966

EDWARDS, BRYAN. Observations on the disposition, character, manners, and habits of life, of the maroon Negroes of the island of Jamaica; and a detail of the origin, progress, and termination of the late war between those people and the white inhabitants. London. 1801. 57p. 1967

ELLIOTT, C. W. St. Domingo, its Revolution and its hero, Toussaint Louverture. New York, J. A. Dix. 1855. 83p. 1968

EMERSON, RALPH W. An address delivered in Concord, Mass., Aug. 1, 1844, on the anniversary of the emancipation of the Negroes in the British West Indies. Boston, James Munroe. 1844. 34p. 1969

FINLASON, W. F. Justice to a colonial governor; or, some

considerations on the case of Mr. Edward John Eyre: containing the substance of all the documents . . . London, Chapman and Hall. 1868. 176p.   1970

FRANKLIN, JAMES. The present state of Hayti (St. Domingo) with remarks on its agriculture, commerce, laws, religion, finances, and population, etc. London, John Murray. 1827. 411p.   1971

GENERAL RESULTS OF NEGRO APPRENTICESHIP . . . public speeches and dispatches of the governors of various colonies, and of Lord Glenelg, secretary of state for the colonial department. London, For the House of commons. 1838. 24p.   1972

GODWIN, BENJAMIN. Lectures on slavery. From the London ed. with additions to the American ed. Boston. James B. Dow. 1836. 258p.
                                                                 1973

GAUDET, M. An inquiry into the causes of the insurrection of the Negroes in the island of St. Domingo. Read before the national assembly. Feb. 29, 1792. London, J. Johnson. 1792.   1974

GURNEY, JOSEPH J. Familiar letters to Henry Clay of Kentucky, describing a winter in the West Indies. New York, Mahlon Day co. 1840. viii, 282p.   1975

HARGRAVE, FRANCIS. An argument in the case of James Sommersett, a Negro, lately determined by the Court of King's bench: wherein it is attempted to demonstrate the present unlawfulness of domestic slavery in England to which is prefixed a state of the case. London. W. Otridge. 1772. 82p.   1976

HAZARD, SAMUEL. Santo Domingo, past and present; with a glance of

Hayti. New York. Harper bros. 1873. 571p.   1977

HOLLEY, JAMES T. A vindication of the capacity of the Negro race . . . as demonstrated by historical events of the Haytian revolution. New Haven. The auth. 1857. 46p.
                                                                 1978

HOWE, JULIA W. A trip to Cuba. Boston, Ticknor and Fields. 1860. 251p.   1979

HUESTON, SAMUEL. Cuba and the Cubans; comprising a history of the island, its social, political, and domestic condition; also, its relation to England and the United States. New York, G. P. Putnam. 1850. 255p.   1980

HURLBURT, WILLIAM H. Gar-Eden: or, Pictures of Cuba. Boston, J. P. Jewett co. 1854. 235p.   1981

JAMES, CYRIL L. R. The black Jacobins. Toussaint L'Ouverture and the San Domingo revolution. New York, Dial press. n.d. 328p.
                                                                 1982

KIDDER, D. P. and FLETCHER, J. C. Brazil and Brazilians, portrayed in historical and descriptive sketches. Philadelphia, Childs and Peterson. 1857. 630p.   1983

KINGSTON COMMITTEE. The Jamaica movement, for promoting the enforcement of the slave trade treaties, and the suppression of the slave trade . . . London, Charles Gilpin. 1850. 430p.   1984

LEE, MRS. HANNAH F. Memoir of Pierre Toussaint, born a slave in Saint Domingo. Boston, Crosby, Nichols co. 1854. 124p.   1985

LONDON MISSIONARY SOCIETY. Report of the proceedings against the late Rev. J. Smith of Demerara, who was tried under martial law, and condemned to death, on a charge of aiding and assisting in a rebellion of the Negro slaves . . .

London, F. Westley. 1824. vii, 204p.

MACAULAY, ZACHARY. The slave colonies of Great Britain. . . London. 1825.

MADDEN, R. R. A twelve months' residence in the West Indies, during the transition from slavery to apprenticeship . . . Philadelphia. Carey, Lea and Blanchard. 1835. 2v.

MANCINI, JULES. Boliver et l'emancipation des colonies espagnoles des origines a 1815. Paris, Perrin et cie. 1912. 606p.

MANZANO, JUAN F. Poems . . . by a slave in the island of Cuba, recently liberated. Tr. from the Spanish by R. R. Madden. With the history of the early life of the Negro poet, written by himself . . . London, Ward. 1840. 188p

MARTIN, WILLIAM H. A counter appeal, in answer to 'An appeal' from William Wilberforce, designated to prove that the emancipation of the Negroes in West Indies, by a legislative enactment, without consent of the planters, would be a flagrant breach of national honour, hostile to the principles of religion, justice, and humanity and highly injurious to the planter and to the slave. London, C and J. Rivington. 1823. 52p.

MARTINEAU, HARRIET. Illustrations of political economy. No. iv, Demerara, a tale. Boston, Leonard C. Bowles. 1832. 198p.

MATHIESON, WILLIAM L. British slave emancipation, 1838-1849. London, New York. Longmans, Green Co. 1932. xi, 243p.

MOSSELL, CHARLES W. Toussaint L'Ouverture, the hero of St.

Domingo. Soldier, statesman, martyr; or, Hayti's struggle triumph, independence, and achievements. Lockport, N. Y. Ward and Cobb. 1896. 495p.

MURRAY, HENRY A. Lands of slave and the free: or, Cuba, the United States, and Canada. v.1. London. John W. Parker and son. 1855. 452p.

MUSSON, JOHN P. A letter to ministers, suggesting improvements in the trade of the West Indies and Canadas, in which are incidentally considered the merits of the East and West India sugar question, reasons in favor of the independence of Spanish America, and a liberal and practical plan of forwarding slave-emancipation. London. J. M. Richardson. 1825. 109p.

NEGRO SLAVERY; or, A view of some of the more prominent features of that state of society, as it exists in the United States of America and in the West Indies, especially in Jamaica. London, Hatchard son and J. Arch. 1823. 118p. (Slavery pamphlets, v. 5, no. 2)

PALMER, J. L. Statement of facts illustrating the administration of the abolition law, and the sufferings of the Negro apprentices in the · island of Jamaica. London, British anti-slavery society. 1837. 36p.

PHILLIPPO, JAMES M. Jamaica: its past and present state. Philadelphia, James M. Campbell. 1843. 176p.

PINN, COMMANDER BEDFORD. The Negro and Jamaica. Read before the Anthropological society of London, Feb. 1, 1866. London, Trubner co. 1866. 72p.

RAINSFORD, MARCUS. An

historical account of the black empire of Hayti, etc. London, James Cundee. 1805. 467p.   2001

RAYNAL, ABBE. A philosophical and political history of the settlement and trade of the Europeans in the East and West Indies. Rev. enl. ed. Tr. from the French by J. O. Justamond. 2d ed. London, A. Straham, T. Cadell and J and W. Davis. 1798. 6v.   2002

REDPATH, JAMES (ed.) A guide to Hayti. Boston, Haytian bureau of emigration. 1861. 180p.   2003

REPORT OF THE COMMISSION OF INQUIRY to Santo Domingo, with . . . the statements of over seventy witnesses. Washington. Govt. print. office. 1871. 297p.   2004

SALMON, C. S. The Caribbean confederation. A plan for the union of the fifteen British West Indian colonies. . . A true explanation of the Haytian mystery. London, Cassell co. n.d. 175p.   2005

SANBORN, FRANK B. Emancipation in the West Indies. Concord, Mass. 1862. 15p.   2006

SEWELL, WILLIAM G. The ordeal of free labor in the British West Indies. New York, Harper bros. 1861. 325p.   2007

STEPHENS, JAMES. The slavery of the British West India colonies delineated as it exists both in law and practise, and compared with the slavery of other countries, ancient and modern; being a delineation of the state in point of law. London. Joseph Butterworth. 1824. 480p.   2008

STEWART (STUART), CHARLES. The West India question, an outline for immediate emancipation and remarks on compensation . . . London. Simpkin and Marshall. 1832. 44p. 2d ed. New Haven.

Hezekiah Howe and co. 1833. 43p. 2d Amer. ed. Newburyport, Mass. Charles Whipple. 1835. 35p.   2009

STURGE, JOSEPH AND HARVEY, THOMAS. The West Indies in 1837; being the journal of a visit to Antigua, Montserrat, Dominica, St. Lucia, Barbadoes, and Jamaica; undertaken for the purpose of ascertaining the actual condition of the Negro population of those islands. London, Hamilton, Adams and co. 1838. 380p. xcivp.   2010

STEWARD, THEOPHILUS G. Haitian revolution, 1791 to 1804; or, Sidelights on the French revolution. New York, Neale pub. co. 1914. xii, 292p.   2011

SUBSTANCE OF THE DEBATE of the House of commons, on a motion for the mitigation and gradual abolition of slavery throughout the British dominions, May 15, 1823 . . . Containing facts and reasonings illustrative of colonial bondage. London, Society for the mitigation and gradual abolition of slavery throughout the British dominions. 1823. 248p. (Slavery pamphlets, v. 2, no. 2).   2012

THOME, JAMES A. AND KIMBALL, HORACE. Emancipation in the West Indies. A six months' tour in Antigua, Barbadoes, and Jamaica, in the year 1837. New York, American anti-slavery society. 1838. xx, 412p.   2013

TRUMAN, GEORGE; JACKSON, JOHN, AND LONGSTRETH, THOMAS. Narrative of a visit to the West Indies in 1840-1841. Philadelphia, Merrihew & Thompson. 1844. 130p.   2014

U. S. STATE DEPARTMENT. Message from the President of the United States, transmitting a report from the acting secretary of state . . . on traffic carried on in the West Indies, by the sale of Negroes, taken from the United States, by British forces since the present war. Mar. 2, 1815. Washington, Roger C. Weightman. 1815. 8p.   2015

WALSH, R. Notices of Brazil in 1828 and 1829. Boston, Richardson, Lord & Holbrook. 1831. 2v.   2016

WASHINGTON, EMORY. Extinction of villenage and slavery in England; with Sommerset's case. A paper read before the Massachusetts historical society. Boston, J. Wilson & son. 1864. 21p.   2017

A WEST INDIAN (pseud.) A letter to the Lord chancellor on the abolition of slavery. London, B. Fellows. 1833. 16p.   2018

WEST INDIAN EMANCIPATION. Celebration in Leeds, Scotland. (Rpt. from the Leeds Mercury,

Aug. 3, 1861). Leeds, Edward Baines & son. 1p. fold.   2019

WILLIAMS, JAMES. A narrative of events since the first of August, 1834 . . . (by an apprenticed labourer in Jamaica). London, John Haddon. 1837. 23p.   2020

WINN, T. S. Emancipation; or, Practical advice to British slaveholders with suggestions for the general improvement of West India affairs. London, W. P. George, J. Hatchard et al. 1824. 111p. 2021

WURDEMANN, J. G. F. (pseud.) A PHYSICIAN. Notes on Cuba containing an account of the face of the country, its population, resources, and wealth; its institutions, and the manners and customs of its inhabitants. With directions to travellers visiting the land. Boston, James Munroe & co. 1844. 359p.   2022

XXIII. Slavery and the law.

ADAMS, JOHN QUINCY. Argument before the Supreme court of the U. S., in the case of the United States, appellants, vs. Cinque, and others, Africans, captured in the schooner Amistad, by Lieut. Gedney, delivered on Feb. 24, and Mar. 1, 1841. New York, S. W. Benedict. 1841. 135p.   2023

ADDRESS OF THE COMMITTEE appointed by a public meeting . . . at Faneuil hall, Sept. 24, 1846 for the purpose of considering . . . kidnapping from our soil. Boston, White & Potter. 1846. 8p.   2024

AMERICAN AND FOREIGN ANTI-SLAVERY SOCIETY. The fugitive slave bill: its unconstitutionality; with an account of the seizure and enslavement of James Hamlet, and

his subsequent restoration to liberty. New York, William Harned. 1850. 36p.   2025

ARVINE, K. Our duty to the fugitive slave; a discourse. Boston, J. P. Jewett. 1850. 31p.   2026

BALDWIN, ROGER S. Argument . . . before the Supreme court . . . in the case of the United States vs. Cinque, and others, Africans of the Amistad. New York, S. W. Benedict. 1841. 32p.   2027

BARBER, JOHN WARNER (comp.) A history of the Amistad captives; being a circumstantial account of the capture of the Spanish schooner Amistad, by the Africans on board; their voyage and capture near Long Island, N. Y.; with biographical sketches of each of the surviving

Africans also, an account of the trials had on their case, before the District and circuit courts of the United States for the District of Connecticut. New Haven, E. L. & J. W. Barber. 1840. 32p.   2028

BEARSE, AUSTIN. Reminiscences of fugitive slave law days in Boston. Boston, W. Richardson. 1880. 41p.
                                                         2029

BEECHER, CHARLES. A sermon on the fugitive slave law. Newark, J. J. McLivaine. 1851. 22p.   2030

BEECHER, EDWARD. Narrative of riots at Alton: in connection with the death of Rev. Elijah P. Lovejoy. Alton. Ill., George Holton. 1838. 159.   2031

BENTON, THOMAS HART. Historical and legal examination of that part of the decision of the Supreme court of the U. S. in the Dred Scott case, which declares the unconstitutionally of the Missouri compromise act, and the self-extension of constitution to territories, carrying slavery with it. New York. D. Appleton & co. 1857. 193p.   2032

BISHOP, JOEL P. Secession and slavery considered as a question of constitutional law. Boston, A. Williams & co. 1864. 112p.   2033

BORDER RUFFIANCODE IN KANSAS, Chapter 151 . . . Slaves; an act to punish offences against slave property. "Laws of the territory of Kansas." New York, McElrath & Greeley. 1857. 15p.
                                                         2034

BOSTON CITIZENS COMMITTEE. Proceedings of the constitutional meeting at Faneuil hall, Nov. 26, 1850. Boston, Beals & Green. 1850. 46p.   2035

BOSTON SLAVE RIOT and trial of Anthony Burns. Containing the report of the Faneuil hall meeting; the murder of Batchelder; Theodore Parker's lesson for the day; speeches of counsel on both sides . . . detailed account of the embarkation. Boston, Fetridge & co. 1854. 86p.   2036

BOWDITCH, WILLIAM I. The rendition of Anthony Burns. Boston, Robert F. Wallcut. 1854. 40p.   2037

BRADWELL, JAMES B. Validity of slave marriages. Chicago, E. B. Myers & Chandler. 1866. 23p. 2038

BREWSTER, FRANCIS E. Slavery and the constitution, both sides of the question. Philadelphia, The author. 1850. 24p.   2039

BROOKS, ERASTUS. Speech . . . in the U. S. senate, Feb. 7, 8, & 13, 1855. The Lemmon slave case and slavery, etc. 15p.   2040

BROWN, ISAAC. Case of the slave Isaac Brown, an outrage exposed. Philadelphia, The author. 1847. 8p.
                                                         2041

CATTERALL, HELEN TUNNICLIFF (ed.) Judicial cases concerning American slavery and the Negro. With additions by James J. Hayden. Washington, Carnegie institution of Washington. 1937. 5v. (Papers of the division of historical research).
                                                         2042

CLARK, JAMES FREEMAN. The rendition of Anthony Burns. Its causes and consequences. A discourse on Christian politics, delivered in Boston, June 4, 1854. Boston, Crosby, Nichols & co. 1854. 28p.   2043

COBB, THOMAS R. R. An inquiry into the law of Negro slavery in the United States of America. To which is prefixed an historical sketch of slavery. Philadelphia, T. & J. Johnson & co. Savannah, W.

Thorne Williams. 1858. 358p. 2044

COMMISSIONERS OF THE ALMS-HOUSE, vs. Alexander Whistelo, a black man; being a remarkable case of bastardy, tried and adjudged by the mayor, recorder, and several aldermen, of the city of New York, under the act passed 6th March, 1801, for the relief of cities and towns from the maintenance of bastard children. New York, David Longworth. 1808. 56p. 2045

COUNCIL OF THE ANTI-SLAVERY LEAGUE. Slavery at Washington: narrative of the heroic adventures of D. Drayton, an American trader, in "The Pearl," coasting vessel, which was captured by American citizens, near the mouth of the Potomac, having on board seventy-five men, women, and children, endeavouring to escape from slavery in the capital of the American republic; together with the proceedings upon Captain Drayton's trial and conviction. London, Ward & co. 1848. 24p. 2046

CRANDALL, REUBEN. The trial of Reuben Crandall, M. D., charged with publishing seditious libels, by circulating the publications of the American anti-slavery society. Before the Circuit court of the District of Columbia, April, 1836, occupying the court for ten days. New York, H. R. Piercy. 1836. 62p. 2047

DALLAS, A. T. Letter from the Secretary of the treasury transmitting a report on the petition of Gould Hoyt . . . Washington, By order of the U. S. senate. 1815. 10p. 2048

DALLAS, A. T. Letter . . . to the committee on ways and means requesting an appropriation to pay .

. . the judgement recovered by Gould Hoyt . . . Mar. 27, 1816. Washington, 1816. 5p. 2049

DEWEY, D. M. The constitution of the United States, with the acts of Congress relating to slavery. Rochester. The author. 1854. 43p. 2050

DOCUMENT FOR CANVASS containing the fugitive slave law of 1850, etc. n.d. n.p.. 16p. 2051

DORR, JAMES. Objections to . . . the fugitive slave law answered in a letter to Hon. Washington Hunt. New York, The author. 1850. 15p. 2052

ERWING, ELBERT W. R. Legal and historical status of the Dred Scott decision: a history of the case and an examination of the opinion delivered by the Supreme court of the U. S., Mar. 6, 1857. Washington, Cobden pub. co. 1909. 288p. 2053

EXTRACTS From the American slave code. 2d ed. no. 1. Philadelphia, American anti-slavery society. n.d. 35p. 2054

FOOT, SAMUEL A. An examination of the case of Dred Scott vs. Sanford in the Supreme court of the U. S. and a full and fair exposition of the decision of the court and of the opinions of the majority of the judges. Geneva, N. Y., The author. 1857. 19p. 2055

FORD, THOMAS. A history of Illinois from its commencement as a state in 1814 to 1847. Chicago, S. C. Griggs & co. 1854. xviii, 447p. 2056

FORMAN, J. G. The fugitive slave law. A discourse. Boston, Crosby and Nichols. 1850. 36p. 2057

FURNESS, WILLIAM H. Three discourses . . . with reference to the recent execution of the fugitive slave law in Boston and New York. Philadelphia, The author. 1854. 42p. 2058

GIDDINGS, JOSHUA R. (Ohio). The exiles of Florida: or, the crimes committed by our government against the maroons, who fled from South Carolina and other slave states seeking protection under Spanish laws. Columbus, O., Follett, Foster co. 1858. 251p. 2059

G. J. (Reporter). White acre vs. black acre. A case at law. Richmond, Va., W. Randolph. 1856. 251p. 2060

GOOCH, DANIEL W. The Supreme court and Dred Scott: a speech delivered in the House of representatives, May 3, 1860. 8p. 2061

GOODELL, WILLIAM. The American slave code in theory and practice: its distinctive features shown by its statutes, judicial decisions, and illustrative facts . . . New York, American and foreign anti-slavery society. 1853. 431p. 2062

GOODELL, WILLIAM. A view of American constitutional law, in its bearing upon American slavery. Utica, N. Y., Jackson and Chaplin. 1844. 158p. 2063

GOODLOE, DANIEL REEVES. The southern platform: or, Manual of southern sentiment on the subject of slavery. Boston, J. P. Jewett co. 1858. 79p. 2064

GRAY, EDGAR H. Assaults upon freedom . . . a discourse occasioned by the rendition of Anthony Burns. Shelburne Falls, D. B. Gunn. 1854. 22p. 2065

HANCOCK, WILLIAM J. Letter to the Hon. Samuel A. Eliot, Repr. from Boston, in reply to his apology for voting for the fugitive slave bill. Boston, Crosby and Nichols. 1851. 57p. 2066

HENING, WILLIAM W. The new Virginia justice, comprising the office and authority of a justice of the peace, in the commonwealth of Virginia; together with a variety of useful precedents, adapted to the laws now in force; to which is added an appendix containing all the most approved forms in conveyancing, such as deeds of bargain and sale, of lease and release; of trust, mortgages, bills of sale, etc. Also, the duties of a justice of the peace, arising under the laws of the United States. 2d ed. rev. corr. Richmond, Johnson and Warner, 1810. 688p. 2067

HENING, WILLIAM W. AND SHEPHERD, SAMUEL. Hening's and Shepherd's statutes at large; being a collection of all the laws of Virginia from the first session of the legislature in 1619 to the session 1807-08. (First series, v. 1-13, by W. W. Hening; second series, v. 1-3, by S. Shepherd.) Richmond. By act of the legislature. 1808; 1823-36. 16v. 2068

HIGGINSON, THOMAS W. Massachusetts in mourning. A sermon . . . Worcester. J. 4, 1854. Rpt. from Worcester Daily Spy. Boston. James Munroe. 1854. 15p. 2069

HOSMER, WILLIAM. The higher law, in its relations to civil government: with particular reference to slavery and the fugitive slave law. Auburn, N. Y. Derby and Miller. 1852. 204p. 2070

HOWARD, BENJAMIN. A report of the decision of the Supreme Court . . . and the judges thereof, in the case of Dred Scott vs. John F. A. Sandford. D. Appleton and co. 1857. 633p. 2071

HURD, JOHN C. The law of freedom

and bondage. Boston, D. Van Nostrand co. 1858. 2v. 2072

HURD, JOHN C. Topics of jurisprudence connected with conditions of freedom and bondage. New York, D. Van Nostrand. 1856. 113p. 2073

JAY, WILLIAM. A view of the action of the federal government, in behalf of slavery. New York, J. S. Taylor. 1839. 217p. 2d ed. New York, American anti-slavery society. 1839. 240p. 3d. ed. Utica, N. Y. J. C. Jackson. 1844. 112p. 2074

JOHNSON, WILLIAM. Speech . . . before the Franklin circuit court of Kentucky . . . the state of Ohio vs. Forbes and Armitage. 1846. 23p. 2075

KELLEY, W. D., PHILLIPS, WENDELL, AND DOUGLASS, FREDERICK. The equality of all men before the law, claimed and defended. Boston, General Stearns. 1865. 43p. 2076

KEYES, WADE. An essay on the learning of partial, and of future interests of chattels personal. Montgomery, Ala. The author. 1853. 412p. 2077

KIRKLAND, CHARLES P. A letter to the Hon. Benjamin R. Curtis, late judge of the Supreme court of the U. S. in review of his . . . pamphlet "Emancipation Proclamation" of the President. New York, privately issued. 1862. 21p. 2078

KREBS, JOHN M. The American citizen. A discourse on the nature and extent of our religious subjection to the government under which we live: including an inquiry into the scriptual authority of that provision of the constitution of the United States, which requires the surrender of fugitive slaves; delivered in New York city, Dec.

12, 1850. New York, Chas. Scribner. 1851. 40p. 2079

LARNED, EDWIN C. Speech . . . on the fugitive slave law, in reply to Hon. Stephen A. Douglass. Delivered in the city hall, Chicago, Oct. 25, 1850. Chicago, Democrat office. 1850. 16p. 2080

LEGAL REVIEW of the case of Dred Scott as decided by the Supreme court of the United States. Boston, Crosby & Nichols. 1857. 62p. (Rpt. from the Law Reporter, June, 1857). 2081

LONDON CITIZENS. (John Anderson Committee). Report of the great meeting held in London at Exeter hall, July 2, 1861, for the purpose of welcoming John Anderson, the fugitive slave to England. London. 1861. 8p. 2082

LORD, JOHN C. "The higher law" in its application to the fugitive slave bill. A sermon the duties men owe to God and to governments. Delivered at the Central Presbyterian church, Buffalo, on Thanksgiving day, 1851. Buffalo, George H. Derby & co. 1851. 32p. 2083

MANN, HORACE (Mass.) Speech . . . on the fugitive slave law; delivered in the House of representatives, in committee of the whole on the state of the union, Feb. 28, 1851. Washington, Congressional globe office. 1851. 24p. 2084

MASSACHUSETTS (State) DISUNION CONVENTION. Proceedings . . . held at Worcester, Jan. 15, 1857. Boston, 1857. 19p. 2085

MARTINEAU, HARRIET. The manifest destiny of the American union. New York, American anti-slavery society. 1857. 72p. 2086

MELLEN, GEORGE W. F. An argument on the unconstitutionality of slavery, embracing an abstract of the proceedings of the national and state conventions on this subject. Boston, Saxton & Pierce. 1841. 440p. 2087

MEMBER OF THE PHILADELPHIA BAR (pseud.) A history of the trial of Castner Hanway and others, for treason, at Philadelphia, Nov. 1851. With an introduction upon the history of the slave question. Philadelphia, U. Hunt & sons. 1852. 86p. 2088

MOORE, BARTHOLMEW F. AND BIGGS, ASA (Comps.) North Carolina laws and statutes. Revised code of North Carolina, enacted by the General assembly at the session of 1854; together with other acts of a public and general nature, passed at the same sessions; the constitution of the state, the constitution of the United States, etc. Prepared under the acts of the General assembly passed at sessions of 1850 and 1854. Boston, Little, Brown and co. 1855. 728p. 2089

NEW YORK STATE COURT OF APPEALS. Report of the Lemmon slave case: containing points and arguments of counsel on both sides, and opinions of all the judges. New York, Horace Greeley and co. 1860. 146p. 2090

PAINE, LEWIS W. Six years in a Georgia prison, the narrative of imprisonment in Georgia for the crime of aiding the escape of a fellowman from that state after he had fled from slavery. New York, The author. 1852. 187p. 2091

PARKER, JOEL. Personal liberty laws, (statutes of Massachusetts), and slavery in the territories, (cases of Dred Scott). Boston, Wright and Potter. 1861. 97p. 2092

PARKER, THEODORE. The trial of Theodore Parker, for the "misdemeanor" of a speech in Faneuil hall against kidnapping, before the Circuit court of the U. S., at Boston, April 3, 1855. Boston, The author. 1855. 221p. 2093

PARKER, THEODORE. The new crime against humanity. A sermon preached in Boston, June 4, 1854. Boston, Benj. B. Mussey and co. 1854. 76p. 2094

PERKINS, G. W. Prof. Stuart and slave catching. Remarks on Mr. Stuart's book, "Conscience and the constitution" at a meeting in Guilford, Aug. 1, 1850, commemorative of emancipation in the West Indies. West Meriden, Conn. 1850. 28p. 2095

PHILLIPS, WENDELL. Can abolitionists vote or take office under the United States constitution? Cincinnati, Sparhawk and Lytle. 1845. 36p. 2096

PHILLIPS, WENDELL. Argument . . . against the repeal of the personal liberty law, before the committee of the legislature. Jan. 29, 1861. 24p. 2097

PHILLIPS, WENDELL. Speech . . . at the Worcester disunion convention, Jan. 15, 1857. Boston, American anti-slavery society. 1857. 16p. 2098

PHILLIPS, WENDELL. Review of Lysander Spooner's essay on the unconstitutionality of slavery. Boston, Andrew and Prentiss. 1847. 95p. (Rpt. from the Anti-slavery Standard with additions.) 2099

PHILLIPS, WENDELL. (ed.) The constitution, pro-slavery compact: or, Extracts from the Madison papers, etc. 3d ed. enl. New York, American anti-slavery society. 1856. 208p. 2100

PICTURE OF SLAVERY drawn from

the decisions of southern courts. n.d. 16p.   2101

RAND, ASA. The slave-catcher caught in the meshes of eternal law. Cleveland, Smead and Cowles. 1852. 42p.   2102

RANTOUL, ROBERT, Jr. Speech . . . on the fugitive slave law, delivered before the Grand mass convention of the Democratic voters of the 2d congress. district of Massachusetts at Lynn, Apr. 3, 1851. 15p.   2103

REPORT OF THE ARGUMENTS . . . and opinions of the court in the case of Commonwealth vs. Aves. Supreme judicial court of Massachusetts, in the case of the slave child, Med. Boston, I. Knapp. 1836.   2104

ROGERS, EDWARD C. (pseud.) FREEMAN, O. S. Letters on slavery, addressed to the pro-slavery men of America; showing its illegality in all ages and nations; its destructive war upon society and government, morals and religions. Boston, Bela Marsh. 1855. 113p.
2105

SHIPHERD, JACOB R. (comp.) History of the Oberlin-Wellington rescue. View of the jail at Cleveland where the prisoners were confined. Boston, J. P. Jewett and co., New York, Sheldon and co., Cleveland, H. P. Jewett. 1859. 280p.   2106

SLAVERY QUESTION: the Dred Scott decision. To the free voters of Ohio. n.d. 16p.   2107

SPENCER, ICHABOD S. Fugitive slave laws, the religious duty of obedience to law. A sermon . . . at Brooklyn, Nov. 24, 1850. New York, M. W. Dood. 1850. 31p.
2108

SPOONER, LYSANDER. A defence for fugitive slaves, against the acts of Congress of Feb. 12, 1793, and

Sept. 18, 1850. Boston, Bela Marsh. 1845. 289p.   2109

SPOONER, LYSANDER. The unconstitutionality of slavery; including parts first and second. Boston, Bela Marsh. 1845. 281p. 2d ed. Boston, Bela Marsh. 1845. 289p.   2110

STATUTES OF NORTH CAROLINA. Revised statutes of North Carolina . . . 1775-. n.d. n.p. 712-.   2111

STEARNS, OLIVER. The gospel applied to the fugitive slave law, a sermon . . . Higham, Mass., Mar. 2, 1851. Boston, Crosby & Nichols. 1851. 28p.   2112

STEVENS, CHARLES E. Anthony Burns, a history. Boston, John P. Jewett & co. 1856. 295p.   2113

STEWART, ALVAN. A legal argument before the Supreme court of the state of New Jersey, at the May term, 1845, at Trenton, for the deliverance of four thousand persons from bondage. New York, Finch & Weed. 1845. 52p.   2114

STROUD, GEORGE McD. A sketch of the laws relating to slavery in the several states of the U. S. of America. 2d. ed. with some alterations and considerable additions. Philadelphia, H. Longstreth. 1856. 300p.   2115

STUART, MOSES. Conscience and the constitution, with remarks on the recent speech of the Hon. Daniel Webster in the senate of the U.S. on the subject of slavery. Boston, Crocker & Brewster. 1850. 119p.
2116

SUMMER, CHARLES (MASS.) Speech . . . on his motion to repeal the fugitive slave bill, delivered in the U. S. senate, Aug. 26, 1852. Washington, Buell & Blanchard. 1852. 31p.   2117

SUMMER, CHARLES (MASS.). Equality before the law; unconstitutionality of separate colored schools in Mass. Argument . . . before the Supreme court of Mass. in the case of Saeah C. Roberts vs. the city of Boston, Dec. 4, 1849. Washington, F. & J. Rives & Geo. A. Bailey. 1870. 16p.   2118

SUTTON, R. (comp.) The Methodist church property case. Report of the suit of Henry B. Bascom, and others vs. George Lane and others heard before the Hon. Judges Nelson and Betts, in the Circuit court, U. S., for the southern district of New York, May 7, 1851 New York, Lane & Scott. Richmond. Louisville, John Early. 1851. 372p.   2119

SYNDER, WILLIAM L. (comp.) A collection of arguments and speeches before courts and juries New York, Baker, Voorhis & co. 1885. 734p.   2120

THOMAS, BENJAMIN F. A few suggestions upon the personal liberty law and "secession" (socalled). In a letter to a friend Boston, John W. Wilson & son. 1861. 22p.   2121

THOMPSON, GEORGE. Prisons life reflections; or, a narrative of the arrest, trial, conviction, imprisonment, treatment, observation, reflections and deliverance of Work, Burr, and Thompson, who suffered an unjust and cruel imprisonment in Missouri penitentiary, for attempting to aid some slaves to liberty. Hartford . . . Work. 1847. 377p.   2122

THOMSON, M. Abstract of the laws of the District of Columbia. Washington, Wm. M. Morrison & co. 1855. 43p.   2123

TREADWELL, SEYMOUR B. American liberties and American slavery. Morally and politically illustrated. New York, John S, Taylor. Boston, Weeks, Jordan & co. 1838. 466p.   2124

U. S. CONGRESS. Acts passed, 1819-1820. (16th Congress, 1st session) Washington, Davis & Force. 1820. 147p.   2125

U. S. HOUSE OF REPRESENTATIVES. H. R. documents, no. 185 reprint, 26th Congress, 1st session. Containing the correspondence, etc., in relation to the captured Africans taken in the Amistad. New York, Anti-slavery depository. 1840. 48p.   2126

U. S. HOUSE OF REPRESENTATIVES. H. R. Documents, no. 691, 24th Congress, 1st session. Slavery in the District of Columbia, May 18, 1836. Washington. Blair & Rives. 1836. 24p.   2127

U. S. HOUSE OF REPRESENTATIVES. Report no. 471, 36th Congress, 1st session. Wm. Hazard and Wigg — claim for slaves taken by the British in the Revolutionary war. Washington, 1860. 16p.   2128

U. S. SENATE. Senate reports, 1849-50. (31st Congress, 1st session). Proceedings of the U. S. Senate, on the Fugitive slave bill; the abolition of the slave trade in the District of Columbia, — and the imprisonment of free colored seamen in the southern ports; with speeches of Messrs. Davis, Winthrop and others, Aug. 19, 1850. Washington. 1850. 68p.   2129

U. S. SUPREME COURT. The people ex rel. Louis N. Bonaparte, vs. Jonathan Lemmon, appellant. New York. 1853. 13p.   2130

WALKER, JONATHAN. Trial and imprisonment of Jonathan Walker at Pensacola, Fla., for aiding slaves to escape from bondage. With an appendix containing sketch of his life . . . Boston. Anti-slavery office. 1846. 126p. 2d ed. Boston. Anti-slavery office. 1850. 126p. 3d ed. Title cover: The Man with the branded hand . . . Muskegon, Mich., W. M. Hartford. 1879. 29p. 2131

WALSH, ROBERT, Jr. Free remarks on the spirit of the federal constitution, the practice of the federal government, and the obligations of the union, respecting the exclusion of slavery from the territories and new states. Philadelphia. A. Finley. 1819. 116p. 2132

WASHBURN, ISRAEL (Me.). The issues; the Dred Scott decision; the parties. Delivered in the House of Representatives, May 19, 1860. Washington, Congressional republican committee. 1860. 16p. 2133

WASHINGTON, BUSHROD. Reports of cases argued and determined in the Court of Appeals of Virginia. Richmond, Thomas Nicolson. 1798. 2v. 2134

WEISS, JOHN. Reform and repeal; and, legal anarchy. Two sermons . . . preached on June 1854, after the rendition of Anthony Burns. Boston. Crosby, Nichols & co. 1854. 30p. 2135

WHEELER, JACOB D. A practical treatise on the law of slavery. Being a compilation of all the decisions made on that subject, in the several courts of the United States and state courts. With copious notes and references to the statutes and other authorities systematically arranged. New York. Allan Pollock, Jr. New Orleans. Benj. Levy. 1837. 476p. 2136

WHITCOMB, WILLIAM C. A discourse on the recapture of fugitive slaves. Delivered at Stoneham, Mass., Nov. 3, 1850. Boston. The author. 1850. 37p. 2137

WILLIAMSON, PASSMORE. Case of Passmore Williamson; report of the proceedings on the writ of habeas corpus issued by Hon. John K. Kane in the case of the U.S.A. ex rel. John H. Wheeler vs. Passmore Williamson. Philadelphia, Hunt & sons. 1856. 156p. 2138

WILLSON, E. B. The bad Friday: a sermon in the First church, West Roxbury, Mass., June 4, 1854 . . . The Sunday after the return of Anthony Burns to slavery. Boston. John Wilson & son. 1854. 16p. 2139

WILSON, HENRY. The territorial slave code. A speech . . . delivered in the U. S. Senate, Jan. 25, 1860. Washington. 1860. 16p. 2140

XXIV. The Underground Railroad.

BUTLER, M. B. My story of the Civil war and the underground railroad. Huntington, Ind. United brethren pub. 1914. 390p. 2141

DRAYTON, DANIEL. Personal Memoir . . . for four years and four months a prisoner (for charity's sake) in Washington jail. Including a narrative of the voyage and capture of the schooner Pearl. Boston. Bela Marsh. New York. American and foreign anti-slavery society. 1855. 122p. 2142

FAIRBANK, CALVIN. How the way was prepared. Chicago. R. R. Mc Cabe & co. 1890. 207p. 2143

HAVILAND, MRS. LAURA (SMITH). A woman's life work; labors and experiences . . . including thirty year's service on the underground railroad and in the war. Chicago. Cincinnati. Wallice & Stone. 1881. 515p. 2144

HOWE, SAMUEL GRIDLEY. The refugees from slavery in Canada West. Report to the Freedman's inquiry commission. Boston. Wright & Potter. iv. 110p. 2145

JAMIESON, ANNIE STRAITH. William King, friend and champion of slaves. Toronto. Missions of evangelism. 1925. 205p. 2146

MCDOUGALL, MRS. MARION GLEASON. Fugitive slaves (1619-1865). Prepared under the direction of Albert Bushnell Hart. Boston. Ginn & co. 1891. viii. 150p. 2147

MITCHELL, WILLIAM M. The underground railroad. London. William Tweedie. Manchester. William Bremner. Birmingham. Hudson & son. 1860. 172p. 2148

SIEBERT, WILBUR HENRY. The underground railroad from slavery to freedom. New York. Macmillan co. 1899. xxv. 478p. biblio. 2149

SMEDLEY, ROBERT C. History of the underground railroad in Chester and the neighboring counties of Pennsylvania. Lancaster, Pa. The journal. 1833. 407p. 2150

STILL, WILLIAM. Underground railroad records. Rev. ed. With a life of the author. Narrating the hardships, hairbreadth escapes and death struggles of the slaves in their efforts for freedom. Together with sketches of some of the eminent friends of freedom and most liberal aiders and advisers of the road. Philadelphia. The author. 1883. 780p. 2151

XXV. Slavery and the Political Parties.

ADAMS, CHARLES FRANCIS. The Republican party a necessity. Speech . . . in the House of representatives, May 31, 1860. 7p. 2152

THE AGITATION OF SLAVERY; who commenced it? Buchanan and Fillmore compared from the record; or, Is Fillmore an abolitionist? Boston, American patriot office. 1856. 29p. 2153

BALDWIN, JOHN BENISON. Human rights and human races; . . . in reply to James Brooks of New York on the Negro race. Washington, Union Republican congressional committee. n.d. 4p. 2154

BEECHER, LYMAN. The ballot box a remedy for national crimes. A sermon entitled, "The remedy for dueling" . . . applied to the crime of slaveholding. By one of his former parishioners. Boston, Isaac Knapp. 1838. 36p. 2155

BELL, JOHN . . . record. A full explanation of Mr. Bell's course on the slavery question. (Republished by the National executive committee of the "Constitutional Union Party," July 31, 1860. Washington. 1860. 31p. 2156

BIRNEY, JAMES GILLESPIE. James G. Birney and his times. The genesis of the Republican party with some account of abolition movements in the South before 1828. New York, D. Appleton & co. 1889. 443p. 2157

BROOKS, JAMES. Speech . . . two proclamations. Delivered before the Democratic Union association. Sept. 29, 1862. Washington. 1862. 2158

BROOKS, NOAH. Short studies in party politics. New York. Chas. Scribner's sons. 1895. 205p.   2159

BURTON, WARREN. White slavery; a new emancipation cause, presented to the people of the U. S. Worcester, M. D. Phillips, 1839. 199p.   2160

BUSHNELL, HORACE. Politics under God. A discourse delivered in the North congregational church, Hartford, 1844 . . . Hartford. Edwin Hunt. 1844. 23p.   2161

CARTER, LUTHER C. Speech . . . in the House of representatives, Jan. 18, 1860. Discussion of the Helper book and the Republican party. Washington. 1860. 16p.   2162

CASS, LEWIS AND TAYLOR, ZACHARY. Cass and Taylor on the slavery question. Boston, Darnell & Moore. 1848. 23p.   2163

CLUSKEY, M. W. (ed.) The political text-book or encyclopedia; containing everything necessary for the reference of the politicians and statesmen of the United States. Philadelphia, James B. Smith & co. 1860. 808p.   2164

COLTON, CALVIN (pseud., Junius) The test; or, Parties tried by their acts. (Junius tracts, no. 1, Mar., 1843). New York, Greeley & McElrath. 1844. 128p.   2165

CONSTITUTIONAL meetings. Proceedings . . . held in Faneuil hall, Boston, Nov. 26, 1850. Boston. 1850. 46p.   2166

DEMOCRATIC ASSOCIATION. The South in danger. Washington, The association. 1844. 8p.   2167

DEMOCRATIC NATIONAL COMMITTEE. The corruption and extravagance of the Black republican party. (Brookinridge and Lane campaign document, no. 17.)

Washington, The committee. 1860. 12p.   2168

DEMOCRATIC NATIONAL COMMITTEE. The issue fairly presented. The senate bill for the admission of Kansas as a state. Democracy, law, order, and the will of the majority of the whole people of the territory, against Black Republicanism, usurpation, revolution, anarchy, and the will of a meagre minority. Washington, Union office. 1856. 30p.   2169

DEMOCRATIC NATIONAL COMMITTEE. Official proceedings . . . Cincinnati, June 2-6, 1856. Cincinnati. By the Convention. 1856. 78p.   2170

DEMOCRATIC NATIONAL UNION CLUB of Harrisburg. African slavery regarded from an unusual stand-point. Harrisburg, Pa. The union. 1860. 8p.   2171

ELIOT, THOMAS DAWES. The territorial slave policy: The Republican party: What the North has to do with slavery. A speech . . . delivered in the House of representatives, April 25, 1860. Washington, The author. 1860. 8p.   2172

FLETCHER, C. Much in little comprising a history of the charters, governments, and relations of the colonies; the origin and history of political parties and the institution of American slavery. Boston, Hollis & Gunn. 1857. x, 204p.   2173

GANNETT, EZRA STILES. Relation of the North to slavery; a discourse preached in the Federal street meeting house. Boston, June 11, 1854. Boston, Crosby, Nichols & co. 1854. 23p.   2174

GARDINER, OLIVER CROMWELL.

The great issue; or, The three presidential candidates; being a brief historical sketch of the free soil question in the United States, from the Congresses of 1774 and 1787, to the present time. New York, Wm. C. Bryant & co. 1848. 176p. 2175

GREELEY, HORACE. A history of the struggle for slavery extension or restriction in the United States from the Declaration of independence to the present day. Mainly compiled and condensed from the journals of Congress and other official records, and showing the vote by yeas and nays on the most important divisions in either house. New York. Dix, Edwards & co. 1856. 168p. 2176

GREELEY, HORACE AND CLEVELAND, JOHN F. (comps.) A political text-book for 1860; comprising a brief view of presidential nominations and elections; including all the national platforms ever yet adopted; also a history of the struggle respecting slavery in the territories, and of the action of Congress as to the freedom of public lands, with the most notable speeches and letters of Messrs. Lincoln, Douglass, Bell, Cass, Seward, Everett, Breckinridge, H. V. Johnson, etc., touching the questions of the day; and returns of all presidential elections since 1836. New York, The Tribune association. 1860. 248p. 2177

GORDON, GEORGE W. The record. The slave-trade at Rio de Janeiro, seizure of slave vessels — convictions of slave dealers, Personal liberation of slaves. Boston, National American party. 1856. 15p. 2178

HIATT, J. M. The political manual . . .

compiled from official records, with biographical sketches and comments. Indianapolis, Asher & Adams, 1864. 306p. 2179

HOLMES, ARTHUR. Parties and their principles; a manual of political intelligence, exhibiting the origin, growth and character of national parties. New York, D. Appleton & co. 1859. 394p. 2180

INCONSISTENCY ANY HYPOCRISY of Martin Van Buren on the question of slavery. n.d. n.p. 16p. 2181

INGERSOLL, CHARLES JARED. African slavery in America. Philadelphia, The author, 1856. 62p. 2182

INGERSOLL, CHARLES JARED. A letter to a friend in a slave state. Philadelphia. John Campbell. 1862. 66p. Paper ed. Only 49 copies printed. 2183

IS MILLARD FILLMORE an abolitionist? Boston, American patriot office. 1853. 29p. (Reprint of the Agitation of Slavery'). 2184

JAY, JOHN. The rise and fall of the pro-slavery democracy, and the rise and duties of the republican party; an address delivered in Westchester county, N. Y., Nov. 5, 1860. New York, Roe, Lockwood & co. 1861. 45p. 2185

JAY, WILLIAM. Letter . . . to Hon. William Nelson, M. C. on Mr. Webster's speech. New York. Wm. Harned. 1850. 12p. 2186

LINCOLN, ABRAHAM and Douglas, Stephen A. Political debates . . . in the celebrated campaign of 1858, in Illinois . . . Columbus, Follett, Foster & co. 1860. 268p. 2187

MATHEWS, E. The autobiography . . . the 'Father Dickson' of Mrs. Stowe's "Dred": also a description of the influence of the slave-party over the American presidents, and the rise and progress of the anti-slavery reform. London, Heulston & Wright. Bristol. T. Mathews. New York. American free baptist mission society. 1866. 444p. 2188

MASSACHUSETTS STATE DISUNION CONVENTION. Proceedings . . . of the state disunion convention held at Worcester, Mass. Jan. 15, 1857. Boston, the convention. 1857. (60), 19p. 2189

MCKEE, THOMAS HUDSON. The National convention and platforms of all . . . political parties . . . 1789 to 1905. Convention, popular, and electoral vote. Also the political complexion of both houses of Congress at each biennial period. 6th ed. rev. enl. Baltimore, Friedenwald co. 1901. 418p. 2190

MCRAE, JOHN J. (Miss.) Speech . . . the organization of the house; delivered in the House of representatives, December 13 and 14, 1859. Washington, Congressional globe office. 1859. 21p. 2191

NELSON, THOMAS A. (Tenn.) The position of the parties. A speech . . . delivered in the House of representatives, Dec. 6, 1859. Washington, Congressional globe office. 1859. 8p. 2192

PARKER, JOEL. The true issue and duty of the Whigs. An address before the citizens of Cambridge, Oct. 1, 1856. 80p. 2d ed. Boston, James Munroe & co. 1859. 92p. 2193

PEASLEE, CHARLES H. Reply . . . to a letter from Democratic citizens of New Hampshire, and the letter. 1852. 12p. 2194

PEOPLES CLUB OF PHILADELPHIA. Address to the people of the United States . . . in favor of General Simon Cameron for the next presidency of the United States. Philadelphia, The club. 1859. 31p. 2195

PRATT, THOMAS G. and PEARCE, JAMES A. An appeal for the Union! Letters of . . . United States senators to their constituents, the people of Maryland; and a speech of James B. Clay, son of Henry Clay, on the duty of the old-line Whigs in the presidential election. Washington, Union office. 1856. 16p. 2196

QUINCY, JOSIAH. Remarks on the letter of the Hon. Rufus Choate to the "Whig State Committee of Maine," written in answer to a letter of the Hon. John Z. Goodrich. Quincy, Mass. 1856. 7p. 2197

QUINCY, JOSIAH. Speech delivered before the Whig State Convention, in Boston, Aug. 16, 1854. Boston, John Wilson & son. 1854. 8p. 2198

RADICAL POLITICAL ABOLITIONISTS. Principles and measures. Declaration of the convention of Radical political abolitionists, at Syracuse, June 26, 28, 1855. 2p. 2199

REPUBLICAN COMMITTEE OF SEVENTY-SIX. The northern man with southern principles and the southern man with American principles . . . a view of the comparative claims of Gen. William H. Harrison and Martin Van Buren, candidates for the presidency. Washington, Peter Force, 1840. 40p. 2200

REPUBLICAN CONVENTION. Address . . . to the people of the United States. Washington. 1856. 14p. 2201

REPUBLICAN CONVENTION. Official proceedings of the Republican convention convened in

the city of Pittsburgh, Pa. on February 22, 1856. Washington. Republican Assoc. of Washington. 1856. 24p. 2202
REPUBLICAN IMPERIALISM is not American liberty. 1856. 43p. 2203
SCHURZ, CARL. Judge Douglas – a bill of indictment. Speech . . . at Cooper institute, N. Y., Sept. 13, 1860. New York, Republican congressional committee. 1860. 16p. 2204
SEAMAN, L. What miscegenation is! And what we are to expect now that Mr. Lincoln is re-elected. New York. Waller & Willetts. 1864. 8p. 2205
SEDGWICK, C. B. (N.Y.) The Republican party – the result of southern aggression. A speech . . . delivered in the House of representatives, Mar. 26, 1860. Washington, Buell & Blanchard, 1860. 12p. 2206
SEWARD, WILLIAM HENRY. The dangers of extending slavery; (delivered at Albany, N. Y. Oct. 12, 1855); The contest and the crisis . . . (delivered in Buffalo, Oct. 19, 1855). Washington. Republican Assn. 1856. 16p. 2207
SEWARD, WILLIAM HENRY. The irrepressible conflict. A speech . . . at Rochester, Oct. 25, 1858. Albany evening journal. 1850. 15p. (Evening journal tracts, no. 1.) 2208
SEWARD, WILLIAM HENRY. The slave holding class dominant in the Republic. A speech . . . delivered at Detroit, Oct. 2, 1856. Washington, Republican association. 1857. 14p. 2209
SHERMAN, JOHN. The Republican party – its history and policy. Speech . . . at the Cooper Institute, New York, April 13, 1860. New York. 1860. 16p. 2210

SMITH, FRANCIS O. J. Of all political parties in Maine, down to 1856, in opposition to human slavery; speech . . . to the Republican state convention in Portland, July 8, 1856. 14p. 2211
SMITH, THEODORE CLARKE. The American nation; a history. v. 18, Parties and slavery, 1850-1859. New York. London. Harper & bros. 1906. 341p. 2212
SMITH, WILLIAM HENRY. A political history of slavery; being an account of the slavery controversy from the earliest agitations in the eighteenth century to the close of the reconstruction period in America. New York. London. G. P. Putnam's sons. 1903. 2v. 2213
THE "SOUTHERN RIGHTS" and the "Union." Parties in Maryland contrasted. Baltimore, W. M. Innes. 1863. 30p. 2214
STEPHENS, ALEXANDER H. Extract from a speech . . . delivered in the Secession Convention of Georgia, Jan. 1861. Atlanta. 1861. 4p. 2215
TOQUEVILLE, ALEXIS DE. Democracy in America and its political institutions, reviewed and examined. Tr. from the French by Henry Reeves. New York. A. S. Barnes & co. Cincinnati. H. W. Derby co. 1856. 404p. 2d ed. New York. D. Appleton & co. 1899. 2v. 2216
UNION SAFETY COMMITTEE. Report . . . of committee appointed to prepare a plan of operation and rules and by-laws. New York. 1850. 7p. 2217
VALLANDIGHAM, C. L. (Ohio). Speech . . . on the election of speaker. There is a west; for the union forever; outside of the union, for herself. Delivered in the House of representatives, Dec. 15, 1859. (From the appendix to the

Congressional Globe, 1859-60). Washington, L. Towers. 1860. 20p. 2218

VINTON, ALEXANDER H. A sermon . . . preached on Thanksgiving day, November 26, 1863. New York, Geo. F. Nesbitt & co. 1863. 28p. 2219

WALKER, ROBERT JOHN. An appeal for the Union. A letter . . . to Hon. Charles Shaler and others, Democratic committee, Pittsburgh . . . New York, John F. Trow. 1860, 15p. 2220

THE WHIG ALMANAC and politicians' register for 1844. New York, 1844. 72p. 2221

WIDE-AWAKE TRACTS. Collection has: no. 1. What's our duty? 1860. 4p. no. 2. The Union. 1861. 8p. no. 3. The national gag-law. 1861. 6p. Tracts are signed; Republican. 2222

WILSON, HENRY (Mass.) personalities and aggressions of Mr. Butler. Speech . . . in the Senate of the United States. June 13, 1856. Washington, Buell & Blanchard, 1856. 8p. 2223

XXVI. Slavery and politics:

1. Speeches in Congress and in state legislatures, federal and state reports and documents relating to the political controversy over slavery.

2. Materials relating to the general political controversy over slavery.

1. Speeches in Congress and in state legislatures, federal and state reports and documents relating to the political controversy over slavery.

ADAMS, CHARLES FRANCIS (MASS.) Speech . . . in the House of representatives, Jan. 31, 1861. Washington, 1861. 8p. 2224

ALLISON, JOHN (PA.) Speech . . . in the House of representatives, April 1, 1853. Washington, 1856. 8p. 2225

AVERY, WILLIAM T. (TENN.) Speech . . . on our Central American relations and the admission of Kansas into the Union. Washington. 1858. 16p. 2226

BADGER, GEORGE E. (N. C.) Speech . . . on the slavery question in the U. S. Senate, March 18 & 19, 1850. Washington, 1850. 18p. 2227

BELL, JOHN (TENN.) Speech in the U. S. Senate . . . Mar. 3, 1854, on the bill to testablish the Nebraska and Kansas territories and to repeal the Missouri compromise. Washington. Congressional Globe office. 1856. 16p. 2228

BENTON, THOMAS HART. (MO.) Speech . . . on the Texas Annexation Bill in reply to Mr. McDuffie. Delivered in the U. S. Senate. Washington, 1844. 16p. 2229

BINGHAM, JOHN A. (OHIO) Speech in the House . . . Jan. 25, 1858, on the Le Compton conspiracy. Washington, Buell & Blanchard. 1858. 8p. 2230

BINGHAM, JOHN A. Speech in the House, March 6, 1856, on the resolution . . . in the Contested Election Case from the territory of Kansas. Washington, Buell & Blanchard. 1856. 12p.   2231

BIRDSALL, AUSBURN (N.Y.) Speech . . . in the House of representatives, July 24, 1848. On the power of Congress to legislate in regard to the domestic concerns of the people of the territories . . . Washington, Congress Globe office. 1848. 8p.   2232

BISSELL, WILLIAM H. (ILL.) Speech . . . the slave question. In the House of representatives, Feb. 21, 1850. Washington. 1850.   2233

BRIGGS, GEORGE (N.Y.) Remarks . . . in the House of representatives. Jan. 6, 1860. Washington, 1860. 8p.   2234

BROWN, ALBERT G. (MISS.) Speech . . . on the President's Kansas message; delivered in the Senate of the United States, Feb. 3 & 4, 1858. Washington, L. Towers, 1858. 32p.   2235

BUFFINTON, JAMES (MASS.) Position of Massachusetts on the slavery question. A speech . . . in the House of representatives, April 30, 1856. Washington, Buell & Blanchard, 1856. 7p.   2236

BURLINGAME, ANSON (MASS.) Speech . . . in defence of Massachusetts . . . in the U. S. House of representatives, June 21, 1856. Cambridge, Mass., The author. 1856. 33p.   2237

BURNETT, HENRY C. (VA.) Speech on . . . Executive Usurpation . . . in the House of representatives. July 16, 1861. Washington. 1861. 8p.   2238

CALHOUN, JOHN C. (S.C.) Address on the subject of slavery, delivered in the U. S. Senate. Mar. 4, 1850.

Washington. 1850. 31p.   2239

CALHOUN, JOHN C. Speech . . . on the rights of slave ships forced ashore, delivered in the U. S. Senate, Mar. 13, 1840. Washington. 1840. 8p.   2240

CAMPBELL, LEWIS DAVIS (OHIO) Speech . . . on southern aggression, the purposes of the union, and the comparative effects of slavery and freedom; with a facsimile of the signatures to the Articles of the association of the Continental congress. Delivered in the House of representatives, Feb. 19, 1850. Washington, Buell & Blanchard. 1850. 16p.   2241

CARPENTER, DAVIS (N.Y.) Speech . . . in the House of representatives on the Nebraska & Kansas Bill. Washington, Congressional Globe office. 1854. 10p.   2242

CASE, CHARLES (OHIO) Speech . . . in the House of representatives, March 11, 1858. (concerning) The President's Special message. Washington, 1858. 16p.   2243

CASS, LEWIS (MICH.) Speech . . . Kansas — the territories. Delivered in the Senate of the United States, May 13, 1856. Washington. 1856. 24p.   2244

CHANDLER, JOHN A. (VA.) Speech . . . in the House of Delegates of Virginia, on the policy of the State with respect to her slave population. Jan. 17, 1832. Richmond, Thos. White. 1832. 10p.   2245

CHASE, SALMON P. (OHIO) Speech . . . in the U. S. Senate, Feb. 3, 1854, against the repeal of the Missouri prohibition of slavery North of 36° 30'. Washington, Congressional Globe office. 1854. 16p.   2246

CLAY, HENRY (KY.) Free and friendly remarks. Speech . . . in the U. S. Senate . . . New York, Mahlon Day & co. 1839. 24p.   2247

CLAY, HENRY (KY.) Speech . . . on his propositions to compromise on the subject of slavery. Washington, Tower. 1850. 32p. Rev. ed. New York, Strings & Townsend. 1850. 32p. 2248

CLAY, HENRY (KY.) Speech . . . on the subject of abolition petitions. Delivered in the Senate of the United States, Feb. 7, 1839. Washington, Gales & Seaton. 1839. 16p. Boston, Jas. Munroe & co. 1839. 42p. 2249

CLEMENS, BUTLER (VT.) and DAVIS, JEFFERSON (Miss.) Remarks . . . on the Vermont resolutions relating to slavery. Delivered in the Senate of the United States, Jan. 10, 1850. Washington, 1850. 36p. 2250

CLEVELAND, CHAUNCEY F. (CONN.) Speech . . . on the Homestead bill, delivered in the House of representatives, April 1, 1852. 16p. 2251

COLFAX, SCHUYLER (IND.) Speech . . . on the "Laws" of Kansas, in the House of representatives, June 21, 1856. New York, Greeley & McElrath. 1856. 15p. 2252

COLLAMER, JACOB (VT.) Minority report of the Senate committee on territories. Washington, Buell & Blanchard. 1856. 15p. 2253

COLLAMER, JACOB (VT.) Report and speech . . . against the new constitution for Kansas and in favor of a free state constitution. Washington, Buell & Blanchard. 1856. 7p. 2254

COLLAMER, JACOB (VT.) Speech . . . on the affairs of Kansas, delivered in the U. S. Senate, April 3 and 4, 1856. Washington. 1856. 29p. 2255

COLLAMER, JACOB (VT.) Speech . . . on the Kansas question, delivered in the U. S. Senate. Washington. 1858. 20p. 2256

COLLAMER, JACOB (VT.) Speech . . . on slavery in the territories. Delivered in the U.S. Senate, Mar. 8, 1860. Washington. 24p. 2257

CRAGIN, AARON H. (N.H.) Speech . . . on the Kansas question, delivered in the House of representatives, May 24, 1858. Washington. 1858. 8p. 2258

CRISFIELD, JOHN W. (MD.) Speech . . . on slavery and the slave trade in the District of Columbia, delivered in the House of representatives, Feb. 17, 1849. 16p. 2259

CRITTENDEN, JOHN J. (KY.) Speech . . . on the admission of the state of Kansas, in the U. S. Senate, Mar. 17, 1858. Washington, 1858. 16p. 2260

COMMONWEALTH OF MASSACHUSETTS. Massachusetts Senate report no. 56, 1836. Report and resolves on the subject of slavery; being the report of a joint committee, to whom was referred so much of the Governor's message as relates to abolition of slavery, together with documents upon the same subject, communicated to the executive by the several legislatures of Virginia, South Carolina, Georgia, and Alabama, transmitted by his Excellency to the legislature, and hereunto annexed, have considered same, and ask leave, respectfully, to submit the following report. Boston. 1836. 59p. 2261

COMMONWEALTH OF MASSACHUSETTS. Massachusetts Senate report, no. 49, 1850. Resolves of the states of Rhode Island and Virginia on the subject of slavery. Boston. Dutton & Wentworth. 1850. 12p. 2262

CULLOM, WILLIAM (TENN.) Speech . . . on the Kansas-Nebraska bill, in the House of representatives, April

11, 1854. Washington. 1854. 13p.
2263

CURRY, JABEZ LAMAR M. (ALA.)
Speech . . . on the constitutional
rights of the states, in the House of
representatives, Mar. 14, 1860.
Washington. 1860. 8p.   2264

DAVIS, HENRY WINTER (MD.)
Speech . . . on Mr. Corivin's report
in the House of representatives,
Feb. 7, 1861. Washington, L.
Tower. 1861. 16p.   2265

DAVIS, JEFFERSON (MISS.) Speech
. . . on the subject of slavery in the
territories; delivered in the U. S.
Senate, Feb. 14, 1850. Washington.
1850. 32p.   2266

DAVIS, JEFFERSON (MISS.) Reply .
. . to the speech of Senator
Douglas, in the U. S. Senate, May
16 and 17, 1860. Washington.
1860. 16p.   2267

DAVIS, JOHN (MASS.) Speech . . . on
the Compromise bill, delivered in
the Sentate of the U. S. June 28 &
29, 1850. Washington, 1850. 16p.
2268

DIMMICK, MILO M. (PA.) Speech . . .
on the slavery question. In the
House of representatives, June 6,
1850. Washington. 1850.   2269

DIXON, JAMES (MASS.) Speech . . .
on the election in Kansas, delivered
in the U. S. Senate, Feb. 9, 1858.
Washington. 1858. 15p.   2270

DOUGLAS, STEPHEN A. (ILL.)
Letter . . . vindicating his character
and his position on the Nebraska
bill . . . Washington, Sentinel office.
1854. 14p.   2271

DOUGLAS, STEPHEN A. (ILL.)
Speech . . . on Nebraska and
Kansas. Delivered in the U. S.
Senate, Mar. 3, 1854. 30p.   2272

DOUGLAS, STEPHEN A. Speech . . .
against the admission of Kansas
under the Le-Compton

Constitution. In the Senate of the
U. S. March 22, 1858. Washington.
1858. 32p.   2273

DOUGLAS, STEPHEN A. (ILL.).
CHASE, SALMON P. (OHIO) et al
Speeches in the U. S. Senate . . .
together with the history of the
Missouri compromise. New York.
Rodfield. 1854. 119p.   2274

EDMONDS, J. WILEY (MASS.)
Speech . . . on the Nebraska and
Kansas bill, in the House of repre-
sentatives, May 20, 1854.
Washington. 1854. 15p.   2275

EVERETT, EDWARD. (MASS.)
Speech . . . on the Nebraska and
Kansas territorial bill. Delivered in
the Senate of the United States,
Feb. 8, 1854. Washington. 1854.
14p.   2276

FARNSWORTH, JOHN F. (ILL.)
Speech . . . on the admission of
Kansas. Delivered in the House of
representatives, Mar. 20, 1853.
Washington. 1853. 8p.   2277

FAULKNER, CHARLES JAMES
(VA.) Speech . . . on the policy of
the state of Virginia with respect to
her slave population. Delivered in
the Virginia house of delegates, Jan.
20, 1832. Richmond. Thos. W.
White. 1832. 22p.   2278

FENTON, REUBEN E. (N.Y.) Speech
. . . on democratic tests, and the
Nebraska bill, in the House of
representatives, Feb. 15, 1854.
Washington, Towers. 1854. 7p.
2279

FOWLER, ORWIN (MASS.) Speech . .
. on slavery in California and New
Mexico. Delivered in the House of
representatives, Mar. 11, 1850.
Washington. 1850. 15p.   2280

FRENCH, RICHARD (KY.) Speech . .
. on slavery in the territories.
Delivered in the House of representatives, June 29, 1848.

145

Washington. 1848. 9p. 2281

GARTRELL, LUCIUS J. (GA.)
Speech . . . in defence of slavery
and the South. Delivered in the
House of representatives, Jan. 25,
1858. Washington. 1858. 16p.
2282

GIDDINGS, JOSHUA REED (OHIO)
Speech . . . on the payment for
slaves; a bill to pay the heir of
Antonio Pacheo for a slave sent
west of the Mississippi with the
Seminole Indians in 1838.
Delivered in the House of repre-
sentatives, Dec. 28, 1848 and Jan.
6, 1849. Washington, Buell &
Blanchard. 1849. 14p. 2283

GIDDINGS, JOSHUA REED (OHIO).
Speech . . . on his motion to
reconsider the vote upon . . . the
"Bill for the relief of the owners of
slaves lost from on board the
Comet and Encomium." Delivered
in the House of representatives,
Feb. 13, 1843. Washington. 1843.
8p. 2284

GIDDINGS, JOSHUA REED (OHIO).
Speeches in Congress on all
questions touching slavery. Boston,
John P. Jewett & co. Cleveland,
Jewett, Proctor & Worthington.
London. S. Low, son & co. 1853.
511p. 2285

GROVER, MARTIN (N.Y.) Speech . .
. on the Wilmot proviso, delivered
in the House of representatives,
Jan. 7, 1847. Washington. 1847.
8p. 2286

HALE, JOHN P. (N.H.) Speech . . .
upon the slavery resolutions.
Delivered in the House of representatives, June 25, 1846. Boston.
D. H. Ela & co. 1846. 12p. 2287

HALE, JOHN P. (N.H.) Speech . . . on
the wrongs of Kansas. Delivered in
the U. S. Senate, Feb. 12, 1856.
Washington. Republican

association. 1856. 16p. 2288

HALE, JOHN P. (N.H.) Speech . . . on
slavery in the territories. Delivered
in the U. S. Senate, Feb. 14, 1860.
Washington. 1860. 15p. 2289

HAMLIN, HANNIBAL (ME.) Speech..
. . in reply to Governor Hammond,
and in defence of the North and
Northern laborers. Delivered in the
U. S. Senate, Mar. 9 & 10, 1858.
Washington. 1858. 16p. 2290

HAMMOND, JAMES H. (S.C.) Speech
. . . on the admission of Kansas
under the LeCompton Constitution. Delivered in the U.S. Senate,
Mar. 4, 1858. Washington, Lemuel
Towers. 1858. 13p. 2291

HARLAN, JAMES (IOWA) Speech . . .
on admission of Kansas. Delivered
in the U. S. Senate, Mar. 27, 1856.
Washington, Buell & Blanchard.
1856. 14p. 2292

HARLAN, JAMES (IOWA) Speech . . .
shall the territories be Africanized?
Delivered in the U.S. Senate, Jan. 4,
1860. Washington. 1860. 8p. 2293

HICKMAN, JOHN (PA.) Speech . . .
on southern sectionalism. Delivered
in the House of representatives,
May 1, 1860. Washington, L.
Towers. 1860, 8p. 2294

HIESTER, ISAAC E. (PA.) Speech . . .
on the Nebraska and Kansas bill.
Delivered in the House of representatives, April 26, 1854.
Washington, Congressional Globe
office. 1854. 8p. 2295

HOARD, CHARLES B. (N.Y.) A free-
state view of slavery . . . causes of
present agitation – etc. Speech . . .
in the House of representatives,
Mar. 30, 1858. Washington,
Congressional Globe office. 1858.
8p. 2296

HOLMES, ELIAS B. (N.Y.) Speech . .
. on the state of the union.
Delivered in the House of repre-

sentatives, June 7, 1848. Washington, J. & G. S. Gideon. 1848. 15p. 2297

HOWARD, WILLIAM A. (MICH.) Speech . . . on the Le Compton constitution. Delivered in the House of representatives, Mar. 23, 1858. Washington, Congressional Globe office. 1858. 8p. 2298

HUBBARD, JONATHAN H. (N.H.) Speech . . . on the motion not to receive a memorial praying the abolition of slavery in the District of Columbia. Delivered in the Senate of the U.S. March 7, 1836. Washington, Blair & Rives. 1836. 9p. 2299

HUDSON, CHARLES. (MASS.) Speech . . . on the constitutional power of Congress over the territories, and the right of excluding slavery there-from. Delivered in the House or representatives, June 20, 1848. Washington, J. & G. S. Gideon, 1848. 16p. 2300

HUNT, THEODORE G. (LA.) Speech . . . in the House of representatives on the bill to establish the Nebraska and Kansas territories, and to repeal the Missouri compromise, delivered Mar. 23, 1854. Washington, Congressional Globe office. 1854. 8p. 2301

HUNTER, ROBERT M. T. (VA.) Speech . . . on Nebraska and Kansas. Delivered in the U. S. Senate. Feb. 24, 1854. Washington, Sentinel office. 1854. 15p. 2302

INGERSOLL, COLIN M. (CONN.) Speech . . . on the democracy of Connecticut – the slave question. Delivered in the House of representatives, March 31, 1852. Washington, Congressional Globe office. 1852. 6p. 2303

JOHNSON, ANDREW (TENN.) Speech . . . on the constitutionality

and rightfulness of secession. Delivered in the U. S. Senate, Dec. 18 and 19, 1860. Washington, 1860. 23p. 2304

JOHNSON, WILLIAM C. (MD.) Speech . . . on the subject of the rejection of petitions for the abolition of slavery; with supplemental remarks, in reply to certain charges against General Harrison. Delivered in the House of representatives, Jan. 25, 27, 28, 1840. Washington Gales & Seaton. 1840. 63p. 2305

JONES, JAMES C. (TENN.) Speech . . . delivered in the United States Senate, August 9, 1856 . . . on the slavery resolutions. Washington, Rives. 1856. 16p. 2306

JULIAN, GEORGE W. (IND.) Speech . . . on the slavery question . . . delivered in the House of representatives, May 14, 1850. Washington, Congressional Globe office. 1850. 15p. 2307

KING, RUFUS H. (N.Y.) Speeches . . . in the U. S. Senate, and of Messrs. Taylor and Talmadge, in the House of representatives on the bill for authorizing the people of Missouri to form a constitution and state government, and for the admission of the same into the union, in the session of 1818-19. With a report of a committee of the Abolition society of Delaware. Philadelphia. Hall & Atkinson. 1819. 35p. (Papers relative to the restriction of slavery). 2308

LAMAR, L. Q. C. (MISS.) Speech . . . on the slavery question. Delivered in the House of representatives, February 21, 1860. Washington, T. McGill. 1860. 8p. 2309

LEIGH, BENJAMIN W. (VA.) Speech . . . on the question of the reception of certain memorials from citizens of Ohio, praying

147

Congress to abolish slavery within the District of Columbia. Delivered in the U. S. Senate, Jan. 19, 1836. Washington, 1836. 8p.   2310

LOVE, PETER E. (GA.) Speech . . . on the slavery question. Delivered in the House of representatives, March 13, 1860. Washington. 1860. 8p.   2311

LOVEJOY, OWEN (ILL.) Speech . . . on the barbarism of slavery. Delivered in the House of representatives, April 5, 1860. Washington, Buell & Blanchard. 1860. 8p.   2312

LOVEJOY, OWEN (ILL.). Speech . . . human beings, not property. Delivered in the House of representative, Feb. 17, 1858. Washington. 1858. 8p.   2313

MANN, HORACE (MASS.) Speech . . . on the right of Congress to legislate for the territories . . . and its duty to exclude slavery therefrom. Delivered in the House of representatives, June 30, 1848. Washington, Gideon. 1848. 31p. 2d ed. Boston, Wm. B. Fowle. 1848. 31p.   2314

MANN, HORACE (MASS.) Speech . . . on the subject of slavery in the territories and the consequences of the threatened dissolution of the Union. Delivered in the House of representatives, Feb. 15, 1850. Washington, Gideon & co. 1850. 15p.   2315

MANN, HORACE (MASS.) Speech . . . on the institution of slavery. Delivered in the House of representatives, Aug. 17, 1852. Boston, Charles List & co. 1852. 24p. 2316

MARTIN, CHARLES D. (OHIO) Speech . . . on the slavery question. Delivered in the House of representatives, May 19, 1860. Washington, L. Towers. 1860. 16p.   2317

MATTESON, ORSAMUS B. (N.Y.) Speech . . . against the repeal of the Missouri prohibition, north of 36° 30'. Delivered in the House of representatives, April 4, 1854. Washington, Buell & Blanchard. 1854. 16p.   2318

MAYNARD, HORACE (TENN.) Speech . . . on the admission of Kansas — a plea for the Cherokees. Delivered in the House of representatives, April 11, 1860. Washington, L. Towers, 16p. 2319

MCKEAN, JAMES B. (N.Y.) Speech . . . democracy alias slavery. Delivered in the House of representatives, June 6, 1860. Washington, Buell & Blanchard. 1860. 7p.   2320

MCLANAHAN, JAMES X. (PA.) Speech . . . on the slave question. Delivered in the House of representatives. Feb. 19, 1850. Washington, Jno. T. Towers. 1850. 8p.   2321

MEACHAM, JAMES (VT.) Speech . . . on Kansas affairs. Delivered in the House of representatives, April 30, 1856. Washington, Congressional Globe office. 1856. 8p.   2322

MEACHAM, JAMES (VT.) Speech . . . against the Kansas-Nebraska territorial bill, and in favor of maintaining the government faith with the Indian tribes. Delivered in the House of representatives, February 15, 1854. Washington. 1857. 7p.   2323

MINER, CHARLES (PA.) Speech . . . on slavery and the slave trade in the District of Columbia; with notes. Delivered in the House of representatives, Jan. 6 & 7, 1829. Washington. Gales & Seaton. 1829. 24p.   2324

MORRILL, JUSTIN S. (VT.) Speech . . . on the admission of Kansas as a free state into the union. Delivered in the House of representatives,

June 28, 1856. Washington. 1856. 8p. 2325

MORRILL, JUSTIN S. (VT.). Speech . . . on modern democracy, the extension of slavery in our own territory or by the acquisition of foreign territory-wrong, morally, politically and economically. Delivered in the House of representatives, June 6, 1860. Washington, Republican Congressional Committee. 1860. 8p. 2326

MORRISON, GEORGE W. (VT.) Speech . . . on the Kansas-Nebraska bill. Delivered in the House of representative, May 19, 1854. Washington, Congressional Globe office. 1854. 16p. 2327

MURPHY, HENRY C. (N.Y.) Speech . . . on slavery in the territories. Delivered in the House of representatives, May 17, 1848. Washington, Congressional Globe. 1848. 18p. 2328

THE NEBRASKA QUESTION; comprising speeches in the United States Senate by Mr. Douglas, Mr. Chase, Mr. Smith, Mr. Everett, Mr. Wade, Mr. Badger, Mr. Seward, and Mr. Sumner, together with the history of the Missouri Compromise; Daniel Webster's memorial in regard to it — history of the annexation of Texas — organization of Oregon territory — and the compromises of 1850. New York, Redfield. 1854. 119p. 2329

NEW HAMPSHIRE COMMITTEE ON NATIONAL AFFAIRS. Report . . . House joint resolution. Concord. n.d. (New draft, no. 5). 8p. 2330

NIBLACK, WILLIAM E. (IND.) Speech . . . on the admission of Kansas. Delivered in the House of representatives, April 11, 1860. Washington, L. Towers. 1860. 4p. 2331

NICHOLSON, ALFRED O. P. (TENN.) Remarks . . . on the sectional conflict on the subject of slavery. Delivered in the U. S. Senate, Jan. 30, 1860. Washington, Towers. 1860. 24p. 2332

NOELL, JOHN W. (MO.) Speech . . . on the question of slavery in the territories. Delivered in the House of representatives, Dec. 13, 1859. Washington. 1860. 8p. 2333

NORRIS, MORRIS (N.H.) Speech . . . on Kansas and Nebraska. Delivered in the U.S. Senate, Mar. 3, 1854. Washington, Sentinel office. 1854. 16p. 2334

PALFREY, JOHN GORHAM (MASS.) Speech . . . on the political aspect of the slave question. Delivered in the House of representatives. Jan. 26, 1848. Washington, J. & G. S. Gideon. 1848. 16p. 2335

PECK, LUCIUS B. (VT.) Speech . . . on slavery in the territories. Delivered in the House of representatives, Aug. 3, 1848. Washington. 1848. 6p. 2336

PICKENS, FRANCIS W. (S.C.) Speech . . . on the abolition question. Delivered in the House of representatives, Jan. 21, 1836. Rev. & cor. Washington, Gales & Seaton. 1836. 16p. 2337

PINCKNEY, H. L. (S.C.) Remarks . . . on the resolution offered by him relative to the abolition of slavery. Delivered in the House of representatives, Feb. 8, 1836. Washington. Gales. 1836. 2338

POPULAR SOVEREIGNTY in the territories; Judge Douglas in reply to Judge Black. n.d. n.p. 24p. 2339

PRENTISS, SAMUEL (VT.) Remarks . . . in the U. S. Senate on the question of reception of a petition from the Society of friends, praying for the abolition of slavery in the

trade in the District of Columbia, in the House of representatives . . . the intended conclusion of the speech, suppressed by resolution of the House. Dec. 20, 1837. Washington. 1837. 24p.   2356

SLADE, WILLIAM (VT.) Speech . . . on the right of petition; the power of Congress to abolish slavery and the slave trade in the District of Columbia. Delivered in the House of representatives, Jan. 18, 20, 1840. Washington, Gales & Seaton. 1840. 45p.   2357

SMITH, TRUMAN (CONN.) Speech . . . on the Nebraska question. Delivered in the U. S. Senate, Feb. 10 & 11, 1854. Washington, John T. & L. Towers. 1854. 23p.   2358

SMITH, WILLIAM N. H. (N.C.) Speech . . . slavery restriction in conflict with judical authority. House of representatives. May 2, 1860. Washington. 1860. 8p. 2359

SMITH, GERRITT (N.Y.) Speeches . . . in Congress. New York. Mason bros. 1855. 330p.   2360

SPENCER, CHARLES S. (N.Y.) Speech . . . An appeal for freedom, made in the Assembly of the State of New York. Mar. 7, 1859. Albany, Weed, Parsons & co. 1859. 21p.   2361

STANTON, BENJAMIN (OHIO) Speech . . . on the power of Congress to exclude slavery from the territories. Delivered in the House of representatives, April 25, 1856. Washington, Republican Congressional Committee. 1856. 8p.   2362

STEPHENS, ALEXANDER H. (GA.) Speech . . . on Nebraska and Kansas. Delivered in the House of representatives, Feb. 17, 1854. Washington. Sentinel office. 1854. 14p.   2363

STEPHENS, ALEXANDER H. Speech . . . on the report of the Kansas investigating committee in the case of Reeder against Whitfield. Delivered in the House of representatives, July 31, 1856. Washington, Congressional Globe office. 1856. 16p.   2364

STEWART, JAMES A. (MD.) Speech . . . on African slavery. (Powers of the Government of the U. S. – Federal, state and territorial). Delivered in the House of representatives, July 23, 1856. Washington. Congressional Globe office. 1846. 24p.   2365

STOCKTON, ROBERT F. (N.J.) Remarks . . . on the presentation of the resolutions of the legislature of New Jersey upon the Compromise Measures. Delivered in the U. S. Senate, Feb. 12, 1852. Washington, Jno. T. Towers. 1852. 11p.   2366

STUART, CHARLES E. (MICH.) Speech . . . against the admission of Kansas. Delivered in the Senate of the United States, Mar. 22, 1858. Washington, 1858. 16p.   2367

SUMNER, CHARLES (MASS.) Freedom national; slavery sectional. Speech . . . on his motion to repeal the fugitive slave bill. Delivered in the U. S. Senate, Aug. 26, 1852. Washington, Buell & Blanchard. 1852. 31p. Boston, Ticknor, Reed & Fields. 1852. 72p.   2368

SUMNER, CHARLES (MASS.) Speech . . . against repeal of the Missouri prohibition of slavery north of 36° 31'. Delivered in the U.S. Senate, Feb. 21, 1854. Boston, John P. Jewett & co. Cleveland, Jewett, Proctor & Worthington. 1854. 72p.
                                                 2369

SUMNER, CHARLES (MASS.) Speech . . . on his motion to repeal the fugitive slave bill. Delivered in the

U. S. Senate, Feb. 23, 1855. Washington, Buell & Blanchard. 1855. 8p. 2370

SUMNER, CHARLES (MASS.) The crime against Kansas. The apologies for the crime. The true remedy. A speech . . . delivered in the U.S. Senate, May 19 and 20 , 1856. Washington, Buell & Blanchard. 1856. 32p. 2371

SUMNER, CHARLES (MASS.) Usurpation of the Senate. Two speeches. . . on the imprisonment of Thaddeus Hyatt. Delivered in the Senate of the United States, Mar. 12 & June 15, 1860. Washington, Buell & Blanchard. 1860. 8p. 2372

SUMNER, CHARLES (MASS.) The barbarism of slavery. Speech . . . on the bill for the admission of Kansas as a free state. Delivered in the U. S. Senate, June 4, 1860.. Washington, Thaddeus Hyatt. 1860. 31p. Boston, Thayer & Aldridge. 1860. 118p. 2373

TAPPAN, MASON W. (N.H.) Modern "Democracy" the ally of slavery. Speech . . . delivered in the House of representatives, July 22, 1856. Washington, Buell & Blanchard. 1856. 15p. 2374

TAYLOR, JOHN J. (N.Y.) Speech . . . on the Nebraska & Kansas Bill. Delivered in the House of representatives, May 9, 1854. Washington, Congressional Globe office. 1854. 8p. 2375

THAYER, ELI (MASS.) The suicide of slavery. Speech . . . delivered in the House of representatives, Mar. 25, 1858. (Wauseon sentinel supplement). Boston. 1858. 8p. 2376

THOMPKINS, CYDNOR B. (OHIO) Slavery: What it was, what it has done, what it intends to do. Speech . . . in the House of representatives, April 24, 1860. Washington, Republican Congressional Committee. 1860. 8p. 2377

TOOMBS, ROBERT (GA.) Speech . . . on invasion of states. Delivered in the U.S. Senate, Jan. 24, 1860. Washington, G. S. Gideon. 1860. 18p. 2378

UPHAM, CHARLES W. (MASS.) Speech . . . on the compromises of the constitution. Delivered in the House of representatives, 1849. Salem, Mass., 1849. 40p. 2379

UPHAM, CHARLES W. (MASS.) Speech. . . on Nebraska & Kansas. Delivered in the House of representatives, May 10, 1854. Washington. 1854. 7p. 2380

UPHAM, CHARLES W. (MASS.) Speech . . . on the three million bill. Delivered in the U. S. Senate, Mar. 1, 1847. Washington, Congressional Globe office. 1847. 8p. 2381

U. S. CONGRESS. Congressional speeches by political leaders, pro and con, on slavery in the United States. Washington. n.d. 1206p. 2382

U. S. CONGRESS. Message from the President of the United States to the two houses of Congress; read Dec. 27, 1859. Washington, Congressional Globe office. 1859. 15p. 2383

U. S. CONGRESS. Speeches of the 36th congress, 1st session, 1860. Washington. 1861. 2v. 2384

U. S. HOUSE OF REPRE-SENTATIVES. Minority report . . . select committee of fifteen . . . on the Kansas question. 35th congress, 1st session. Washington, Buell and Blanchard. 1858. 16p. 2385

U. S. HOUSE OF REPRE-SENTATIVES. Report of the special committee appointed to investigate the troubles in Kansas;

with the views of the minority of said committee. (H. R. Committee reports, no. 200, 34th Congress, 1st session). Washington, C. Wendell, 1856. 1206p. 2386

U. S. SENATE. Affairs of Kansas in the Senate of the United States. Report of the committee on territories, Mar. 12, 1856. (Senate Committee reports, no. 34, 34th Congress, 1st session). Washington. 1856. 29p. 2387

U. S. SENATE Message of the President of the United States, communicating, in complaisance with the resolution of the Senate, all correspondence of John W. Gerry, late governor of Kansas, not heretofore communicated to Congress, Jan. 7, 1858. (Senate documents, no. 17, 35th Congress, 1st session). Washington. 1858. 192p. 2388

U. S. SENATE. Report of Mr. Calhoun, with Senate Bill no. 122. . . (relating to) "attempts to circulate through the mail, inflammatory appeals, to excite the slaves to insurrection . . ." Feb. 4, 1836. Washington. 1836. 12p. 2389

U. S. SENATE. Resolutions of the Virginia legislature in relation to slavery, Feb. 5, 1849. (Senate miscellaneous reports, no. 48, 30th Congress, 2d session). Washington, Tippen & Streepe. 1849. 2p. 2390

VANCE, ZEBULON B. (N.C.) Speech . . . on the slavery question. Delivered in the House of representatives, March 16, 1860. Washington. L. Towers, 1860. 16p. 2391

VAN WYCH, CHARLES H. (N.Y.) Speech . . . on slave question. True democracy-history vindicated. Delivered in the House of representatives, March 7, 1860. Washington. 1860. 16p. 2392

WADE. BENJAMIN F. (OHIO) Plain truths for the people. Speech . . . in the Senate of the United States. March 13 & 15, 1858. Washington, Buell & Blanchard. 1858. 16p. 2393

WADE, BENJAMIN F. (OHIO). Property in the territories. Speech . . . in the Senate of the United States, Mar. 7, 1860. Washington, Republican executive campaign committee. 1860. 14p. 2394

WALDRON. HENRY (MICH.). Speech . . . on Kansas affairs. Delivered in the House of representatives, April 8, 1856. Washington, Buell & Blanchard. 1856. 8p. 2395

WALLEY, SAMUEL H. (MASS.) Slavery compromises. Speech . . . on the Nebraska & Kansas territorial bill. Delivered in the House of representatives, May 9, 1854. Washington, Congressional Globe office. 1854. 8p. 2396

WALTON, E. P. (VT.) Speech . . . on the bill for the admission of Kansas. Delivered in the House of representatives, Mar. 31, 1858. Washington, Congressional Globe office. 1858. 15p. 2397

WASHBURN, CADWALLADER C. (WIS.) The slavery question. Speech . . . in the U. S. House of representatives, April 26, 1860. Washington, Republican executive congressional committee. 1860. 14p. 2398

WASHBURN, ISRAEL, Jr. (ME.) KANSAS contested election. Speech . . . on the resolution reported by the committee of elections. Delivered in the House of representatives, Mar. 14, 1856. Washington, Buell & Blanchard. 1856. 8p. 2399

WEBSTER, DANIEL (MASS.) Speech . . . upon the subject of slavery. Delivered in the U. S. Senate, Mar.

7, 1850. Boston, Redding & co. 1850. 39p. 2400

WEBSTER, DANIEL (MASS.) Speech . . . on Mr. Clay's resolutions. In the U. S. Senate, Mar. 7, 1850. Washington. 1850. 15p. Boston, Redding & co. 1850. 39p. 2401

WELLS, ALFRED. (N.Y.) The impending crisis. The irrepressible conflict between freedom and slavery. Speech . . . delivered in the House of representatives, April 6, 1860. Washington, Republican executive congressional committee. 1860. 8p. 2402

WILKINSON, MORTON S. (MINN.) Speech . . . on the abolition of slavery in the district of Columbia. Delivered in the Senate of the U. S. Mar. 26, 1862. Washington, Towers. 1862. 16p. 2403

WILSON, HENRY. (MASS.) The state of affairs of Kansas. Speech . . . in the Senate of the United States, Feb. 18, 1856. Washington, Republican association of the District of Columbia. 1856. 15p. 2404

WILSON, HENRY. (MASS.) Aggressions of the slave power. Speech . . . in reply to Hon. Jefferson Davis made in the U. S. Senate, Jan. 26, 1860. Washington, Buell & Blanchard. 1860. 24p. 2405

WILSON, HENRY. (MASS.) The Crittendon compromise — a surrender. Speech . . . on the resolutions of Mr. Crittenden proposing amendments to the Constitution of the U. S. Delivered in the U. S. Senate, Feb. 21, 1861. Washington, Congressional Globe office. 1861. 16p. 2406

YATES, RICHARD (ILL.) Speech . . . on the bill to organize territorial governments in Nebraska & Kansas, and opposing the repeal of the Missouri compromise. Delivered in the House of representatives, Mar. 28, 1854. Washington, Congressional globe office. 1854. 16p. 2407

2. Materials relating to the general political controversy over slavery.

APPLETON, NATHAN and PALFREY, JOHN G. Correspondence, intended as a supplement to Mr. Palfrey's pamphlet on the slave power. Boston, Eastburn. 1846. 20p. 2408

BACON'S GUIDE TO AMERICAN POLITICS; or, A complete view of fundamental principles of the national and state governments, with the respective powers of each . . . London. S. Low, son & co. Bacon & co. 1863. 94p. 2409

BENNERS, ALFRED H. Slavery and its results. Macon, Ga. J. W. Burke co. 1923. 58p. 2410

BENTON, THOMAS HART. Abridgement of the debates of Congress, from 1789 to 1856. From Gales and Seaton's Annals of Congress; from their Register of Debates, by John C. Rives. New York, D. Appleton & co. 1857-61. 17v. 2411

BENTON, THOMAS HART. Thirty years' view; or A history of the American government for 30 years, from 1820 to 1850. By a senator of thirty years. New York, D. Appleton & co. 1854. 2v. 2412

BOSTON COURIER REPORT OF THE UNION meeting in Faneuil hall, Dec. 8, 1859. Speeches of ex-Gov. Lincoln, E. Everrett and C. Cushing; resolutions adopted, letters of ex-president Pierce, Judge Curtis and others. Boston, Clark, Fellows & co. 1858. 32p.　2413

CHANNING, WILLIAM E. A letter to the Hon. Henry Clay, on the annexation of Texas to the United States. Boston, James Munroe & co. 1837. 72p.　2414

CHASE, EZRA B. Teachings of patriots and statesmen: or The "Founders of the Republic" on slavery. Philadelphia. J. W. Bradley. 1860. 495p.　2415

CHILD, DAVID L. Memorial to the twenty-seventh congress from inhabitants of Northampton, Massachusetts. March, 1842. 23p.　2416

A CLERGYMAN (pseud.) Three years on the Kansas border. New York, Orton & Mulligan. 1856. viii, 240p.　2417

COLLIN, JOHN F. Political history of the country, having particular reference to the tariff, slavery, and state sovereignty. Hudson, N. Y., M. Parker Williams, 1884. 4v. 2418

THE CRISIS, NO. I, or Thoughts on slavery occasioned by the Missouri question. New Haven, A. H. Maltby & co. 1820. 14p.　2419

CURRY, JABEZ L. M. The southern states of the American Union considered in their relations to the constitution of the United States and to the resulting union. Richmond, Va. B. F. Johnson pub. co., New York, London, G. P. Putnam's sons. 1894. 248p.　2420

DEWEY, ORVILLE. Discourse on slavery and the annexation of Texas. New York, Charles S. Francis. 1844. 18p.　2421

DODD, WILLIAM E. and MACY, JESSE. The days of the cotton kingdom. Part 1: The cotton kingdom, by William E. Dodd. Part 2: The anti-slavery crusade, by Jesse Macy. New Haven, Yale University press. 1926. vii, 161, ii, 245p.　2422

DONNELL, E. J. Pamphlets: a series of fifteen pamphlets bound in one book. (No. 6; Slavery and "Protection": an historical review and appeal to the workshop and farm.) New York, the author. 1882. 69p. (Read at the request of the New York Free Trade Club). 2423

FARNAM, HENRY W. Chapters in the history of social legislation in the United States to 1860. Ed. by Clive Day. Washington, Carnegie Institution of Washington. 1938. xx, 496p. (Publication no. 488).　2424

FISHER, SIDNEY GEORGE (?) (pseud., "CECIL") Kansas and the constitution. Boston, Damrell & Moore. 1856. 16p. (Also ascribed to Chas. E. Fisher).　2425

FOSTER, EDEN B. The rights of the pulpit and perils of freedom. Two discourses preached in Lowell, June 25, 1854. 72p.　2426

GODWIN, PARKER. Political essays. (From contributions to Putnam's magazine). New York, Dix, Edward & co., 1856. 345p.　2427

GOODLOE, DANIEL R. Is it expedient to introduce slavery into Kansas? A tract for the times. Respectfully inscribed to the people of Kansas. Cincinnati. American reform tract & book society. n.d. 24p.　2428

GRADY, BENJAMIN F. The case of the south against the north; or, historical evidence justifying the southern states of the American union in their long controversy with the northern states . . .

Raleigh, N. C., Edward & Broughton, 1899. 345p. 2429

GRAHAM, SYLVESTER. Letter to the Hon. Daniel Webster on the compromises of the constitution. Northampton, Mass. Hopkins, Bridgeman & co. 1850. 19p. 2430

GREELEY, HORACE. Recollections of a busy life; including reminiscences of American politics and politicians, from the opening of the Missouri contest to the downfall of slavery. New York. Ford & co. 1868. xv, 624p. 2431

HART, ALBERT B. Slavery and abolition. 1831-1841. New York, London, Harper & bros. 1906. xv. 360p. 2432

HART, ALBERT B. and CHANNING, EDWARD. (eds.) American history leaflets, colonial & constitutional. New York, Parker P. Simmons. 1906-12. 36 leaflets. (The following nos. treat of slavery). No. 10, Gov. McDuffie's message on the slavery question. No. 11, Jefferson's proposed instructions to Va. delegates, 1774 . . . No. 12, Ordinances of secession and other documents. No. 17, Documents relating to the Kansas-Nebraska act. No. 18, Lincoln's inaugural and first message to Congress. No. 23, Extracts from the Dred Scott decision. No. 26, Extracts from Lincoln's state papers. No. 30, Constitutional doctrines of Webster, Hayne, and Calhoun. No. 35. Report of the Hartford convention. 2433

HAVEN, GILBERT. National sermons. Sermons, speeches and letters on slavery and its war; from the passage of the Fugitive slave bill to the election of President Grant. Boston, Lee & Shepard. 1869. xii, 656p. 2434

HILLIARD, HENRY W. Speeches and addresses . . . New York, Harper & bros. 1855. 497p. 2435

HOWE, DANIEL W. Political history of secession, to the beginning of the American civil war. New York, London, G. P. Putnam's sons. 1914. xxx, 649. 2436

HUMPHREY, HERMAN. The Missouri Compromise; an address delivered before the citizens of Pittsfield, Mass. Feb. 26, 1854. Pittsfield, Reed, Hull & Peirson. 1854. 32p. 2437

INGLE, EDWARD. Southern side lights; a picture of social and economic life in the south a generation before the war. New York, Thos. Y. Crowell & co. 1896. 373p. 2438

JAY, WILLIAM; A reply to Webster in a letter . . . to Hon. Wm. Nelson . . . Boston, Crosby & Nichols. 1850. 12p. 2439

JAY, WILLIAM. A review of the causes and consequences of the Mexican War. Boston, Benj. B. Mussey & co. Philadelphia, Uriah Hunt & co. New York, M. W. Dodd. 1849. 333p. 2440

JOHNSTON, ALEXANDER. Representative American orations to illustrate American political history. New York, G. P. Putnam's sons. 1884. 3v. 2441

JOHNSON, S. M. The Dual Revolutions: Anti-slavery and Pro slavery. Baltimore, The author. 1863. 48p. 2442

KENNEDY, JOHN P. The border states, their power and duty in the present disordered condition of the country. 1860. 46p. 2443

LEARNED, JOSEPH D. A view of the policy of permitting slaves in the states west of the Mississippi; being a letter to a member of Congress.

Baltimore, Joseph Robinson. 1820. 46p.   2444

LLOYD, ARTHUR Y. The slavery controversy, 1831-1860. Chapel Hill, University of North Carolina press. 1939. 337p.   2445

LONGSTREET, AUGUSTUS B. A voice from the South; comprising letters from Georgia to Massachusetts, and to the southern states. With an appendix containing an article from the Charleston Mercury on the Wilmot proviso, together with the fourth article of the constitution, the law of Congress . . . the resolutions of ten of the free states, the resolutions of Virginia, Georgia, and Alabama, and Mr. Calhoun's resolutions in the senate of the United States. Baltimore, Western continent press. 1847. 72p.   2446

LUNDY, BENJAMIN. The war in Texas; a review of facts and circumstances, showing that this contest is a crusade against Mexico, set on foot and supported by slaveholders, land speculators, etc., in order to re-establish, extend, and perpetuate the system of slavery and the slave trade. 2d ed. rev. enl. By a citizen of the United States, Philadelphia, Merrihew & Gunn. 1837. 64p. 2447

MANN, HORACE. Letters on the extension of slavery into California and New Mexico; and on the duty of Congress to provide the trial by jury for alleged fugitive slaves. Washington, Buell & Blanchard. 1850. 332p. notes.   2448

MOODY, LORING. Facts for people, showing the relations of the United States government to slavery, embracing a history of the Mexican war, its origin and objects compiled from official and other authentic documents. Boston. Anti-slavery office, 1847. 142p.   2449

MURDOCK, WILLIAM D. C. Address . . . on the free-soil question. Georgetown. J. F. & J. A. Crow. 1848. 43p.   2450

NELSON, JEREMIAH. Discourse on the proposed repeal of the Missouri Compromise. April 6, 1854, at Leicester, Mass. Worcester, Mass., Edward R. Fiske. 1854. 14p. 2451

PARKER, THEODORE. The Nebraska question. Some thoughts on the new assault upon freedom in America, and the general state of the country in relation thereto, . . . a discourse preached in Boston, February 12, 1854. Boston, Benj. B. Mussey & co. 1854. 72p.   2452

PEABODY, SELIM H. (comp.) American patriotism: speeches, letters, and other papers which illustrate the foundation, the development, the preservation of the United States of America. New York, John B. Alden, 1881. 674p.   2453

PHILLIPS, STEPHEN C. An address on the annexation of Texas, and the aspect of slavery in the United States. Delivered in Boston, Nov., 1845. Boston, Wm. Crosby & H. P. Nichols. 1845. 56p.   2454

PHILLIPS, WILLIAM. The conquest of Kansas by Missouri and her allies. Boston, Phillips, Sampson & co. 1856. x, 414p.   2455

PORTER, WILLIAM D. State sovereignty and the doctrine of coercion . . . together with a letter from Hon. J. K. Paulding. The right to secede by "States." (Association Tract, no. 2, 1860.) Charleston, S. C. Evans & Cogswell. 1860. 36p.   2456

REMARKS addressed to the citizens of Illinois, on the proposed introduction of slavery. n.d. n.p. 14p.   2457

ROPES, MRS. H. A. C. Six months in Kansas. By a lady. 4th thousand. Boston, John P. Jewett & co. Cleveland, Jewett, Proctor & Worthington. New York, Sheldon, Blakeman & co. 1856. 231p.   2458

SAVAGE, WILLIAM S. The controversy over the distribution of abolition literature, 1830-1860. Washington, Assn. for the study of Negro life & history, 1938. xv, 141p.   2459

SEDGWICK, THEODORE. Thoughts on the proposed annexation of Texas to the United States. New York, The author. 1844. 55p.   2460

SPRING, LEVERETT W. Kansas, the prelude to the war for the Union. Boston, Houghton, Mifflin co. 1885. 334p.   2461

STETSON, CALEB. A discourse on the state of the country. Delivered in the First church in Medford, Mass. April 7, 1842. Boston, James Munroe & co. 1842. 25p.   2462

STUART, ALEXANDER H. H. A narrative of the leading incidents of the organization of the first popular movement in Virginia in 1865 to re-establish peaceful relations between northern and southern states, and of the subsequent efforts of the committee of nine in 1869, to secure restoration of Virginia to the Union. Richmond, Va., the author. 1887. 72p.   2463

THAYER, ELI. A history of the Kansas crusade, its friends and its foes. New York, Harper & bros. 1889. xx, 294p.   2464

THORNWELL, JAMES H. The state of the country. (Republished from The Southern Presbyterian Review.) New York, D. Appleton & co. 1861. 30p. Columbia, S. C.

Southern Guardian, 1861. 32p.
                    2465

TILDEN, SAMUEL. The three secession movements in the United States. Boston, John Wilson & son. 1876. 40p.   2466

WALMSLEY, JAMES E. Documents — The change of secession sentiment in Virginia in 1861. (Reprinted from the American Historical Review, vol. xxi, no. 1, p. 82-101. Oct. 1925).   2467

WASHBURNE, ELIHU B. Sketch of Edward Coles, second governor of Illinois, and of the slavery struggle of 1823-24. Chicago, Jansen, McClurg & co. 1882. 253p.   2468

WEBSTER, DANIEL. A memorial to the Congress of the United States, on the subject of restraining the increase of slavery in the new states to be admitted into the Union. Prepared in pursuance of a vote of the inhabitants of Boston and its vicinity, assembled at the State house, Dec. 3, 1819. Boston, Sewell & Phelps. 1819. 22p.   2469

WELLS, JOHN G. Illustrated national hand-book embracing numerous invaluable documents connected with the political history of America. New ed. New York. The author. 1857. 162p.   2470

WHITFIELD, THEODORE M. Slavery agitation in Virginia, 1829-1832. Baltimore, Johns Hopkins press. London, Oxford University press. 1930. 162p. refs. (Johns Hopkins studies, extra v. new series, no. 10).
                    2471

WILLARD, JOSEPH. Letter to an English friend on the rebellion in the United States, and on British policy. Boston, Ticknor & Fields. 1862. 28p.   2472

CONCESSIONS AND COMPROMISES: A solution to the fugitive slave controversy. Philadelphia, C. Sherman & son. 1860. 14p.   2474

COUTO, JOSE FERRER de. Enough of war! The question of slavery conclusively and satisfactorily solved, as regards humanity at large and the permanent interests of present owners. New York, S. Hallet. 1863. 312p.   2475

COX, SAMUEL S. (OHIO) Speech . . . Conciliation and nationality! Delivered in the House of representatives, Jan. 14, 1861. Washington. 1861.   2476

HALL, MARSHALL. The two-fold slavery of the United States; with a project for self-emancipation. London, Adam Scott. 1854. 159p.
                                          2477

NOTT, SAMUEL. The present crisis; with a reply and appeal to European advisors, from the sixth edition of "Slavery and the Remedy." Boston, Crocker & Brewster. 1860. 43p.   2478

NOTT, SAMUEL. Slavery, and the remedy; or, principles and suggestions for a remedial code. 5th ed. with a review of the Supreme court decision in the case of Dred Scott. New York, D. Appleton & co. 1855. 137p.   2479

NOTT, SAMUEL. The necessities and wisdom of 1861. A supplement to the sixth edition of "Slavery and the Remedy." Boston, Crocker & Brewster. 1861. 12p.   2480

PARRISH, JOHN. Remarks on slavery of the black people; addressed to the citizens of the United States . . . and also to such individuals as hold them in bondage. Philadelphia. The author. 1806. 66p.   2481

PEISSNER, ELIAS. The American question in its national aspects. (Reply to Helper's "Compendium") New York, The author. 1861. 164p.   2482

PHELPS, AMOS A. Lectures on slavery and its remedy. Boston, New England anti-slavery society. 1834. 284p.   2483

RICE, NATHAN L. Ten letters on the subject of slavery; addressed to the delegates from the Congregational association to the last General assembly of the Presbyterian church, St. Louis, Mo. St. Louis, Keith, Woods & co. 1855. 47p. 2d ed. St. Louis, Keith, Woods & co. 1856. 78p.   2484

YELLOTT, COLEMAN. Compromise measures passed by Congress in Sept. 1850. Speech . . . before a meeting of the citizens of York county, Pennsylvania. Jan. 7, 1851. York, 1851. 8p.   2485

XXVIII. The Harper's Ferry Invasion.

ANDERSON, OSBORNE P. A voice from Harper's Ferry. A narrative of events at Harper's Ferry; with incidents prior and subsequent to its capture by Captain Brown and his men. By . . . one of the number. Boston, The author. 1861. 72p.
                                          2486

ANDREW, JOHN A. Speeches, at Hingham and Boston, together with his testimony before the Harper's Ferry committee of the Senate, in relation to John Brown. Also the Republican platform and other matters. Published by order of the Republican state (Mass.)

committee. 1860. 16p. 2487

AVEY, ELIJAH. The capture and execution of John Brown: a tale of martyrdom. Chicago, The author. 1906. 152p. 2488

BROWN, GEORGE W. The truth at last. History corrected. Reminiscences of old John Brown. Thrilling incidents of border life in Kansas . . . and full details of the Pottawotomie massacre. Rockford, Ill., A. E. Smith, 1879. 82p. 2489

BROWN, JOHN. Scrap book: containing clippings from various newspapers concerning the Harper's Ferry affair, 1859; the lesson of St. Domingo, by Elizur Wright, and free labor in British Guiana. (anon.) 1859. 178p. 2490

CHAMBERLAIN, JOSEPH E. John Brown. Boston, Small, Maynard & co., 1899. 138p. (The Beacon Biographies-Eminent Americans) 2491

CHANNING, WILLIAM E. The burial of John Brown. A poem. Boston, 1859. 8p. 2492

DOUGLASS, FREDERICK. John Brown. An address at the 14th anniversary of Storer College. May 30, 1881. 16p. 2493

DREW, THOMAS. The John Brown invasion; An authentic history of the Harper's Ferry Tragedy with full details of the capture, trial, and execution of the invaders, and of all the incidents connected therewith. Boston, James Campbell. 1860. 112p. 2494

DUBOIS, W. E. B. John Brown. Philadelphia. Geo. W. Jacobs & co., 1909. 406p. (American Crisis Biographies) 2495

EHRLICH, LEONARD. God's angry man. New York, Simon & Schuster. 1932. 8, 3-400p. 2496

HALL, NATHANIEL. The iniquity, and The man, the deed, the event.

Two sermons. Boston. J. Wilson. 1859. 37p. 2497

HARPERS FERRY, with sketches of its founder. Martinsburg, W. Va., Josephus, Junior. 1872. 126p. 2498

HINTON, RICHARD J. John Brown and his men, with some account of the roads they traveled to reach Harper's Ferry. London, New York, Funk & Wagnalls co. 1894. 784p. (American reformer series). 2499

HOLST, HERMANN V. John Brown. Tr. from the German by Frank P. Stearns. Boston, Cupples & Hurd. 1889. 232p. 2500

KARSNER, DAVID. John Brown, terrible "Saint". New York, Dodd, Mead co. 1934. 340p. 2501

LEECH, SAMUEL V. The raid of John Brown at Harper's Ferry as I saw it. Washington, The author. 1909. 24p. 2502

THE LIFE, TRIAL AND EXECUTION OF CAPTAIN JOHN BROWN, known as "old Brown of Ossawatomie," with a full account of the attempted insurrection at Harper's Ferry, compiled from official and authentic sources. Including Cooke's confession, and all the incidents of the execution. New York, Robert M. DeWitt. 1859. vii, 108p. 2503

MAYO, AMORY D. Herod, John and Jesus; or, American slavery and its Christian cure. A sermon preached in Division street church, Albany, N. Y. Albany, Weed, Parsons & co. 1860. 29p. 2504

MILLER, SEAVER A. John Brown's grave. (Reprinted from The press, Nov. 13, 1898.) pp. 42-46. 2505

MOORE, SYDENHAM (ALA.) Speech . . . on the resolution concerning John Brown . . . delivered in the House of representatives, December 8, 1859. Washington, T. McGill. 1859. 8p. 2506

PARKER, THEODORE. John Brown's expedition, reviewed in a letter . . . to Francis Jackson. Boston, The Fraternity. 1860. 19p. 2507

REDPATH, JAMES. The public life of Capt. John Brown, with an autobiography of his childhood and youth. Boston, Thayer & Eldridge, 1860. 408p. 41st ed. Sandusky, Kinney bros. 1872. 407p. 2508

ROE, ALFRED S. John Brown: a retrospect. Worcester, Franklin P. Rice. 1885. 25p. 2509

SANBORN, F. B. (ed.) The life and letters of John Brown, liberator of Kansas, and martyr of Virginia, Boston. Roberts bros. 1885. 645p. 2510

SWAYZE, MRS. J. C. Ossawattomie Brown; . . . a drama in three acts as performed at the Bowery Theatre. New York, Samuel French. 1859. 27p. 2511

U. S. SENATE. (Senate reports, 36th Congress, 1st session). Report of the Harper's Ferry invasion; being the report of the Select committee . . . appointed to inquire into the invasion and seizure of public property at Harper's Ferry. Washington, Govt. print. office. 1860. 255p. 2512

VILLARD, OSWALD G. John Brown-1800-1859. A biography fifty years after . . . Boston, New York, Houghton, Mifflin co. 1910. 738p. 2513

WADE, BENJAMIN F. (OHIO) Invasion of Harper's Ferry. Speech . . . in the United States Senate, Dec. 14, 1859. Washington, Buell & Blanchard. 1859. 8p. 2514

WARREN, ROBERT P. John Brown, the making of a martyr. New York, Payson & Clarke. 1929. 474p. 2515

WHEELOCK, EDWIN M. Harper's Ferry and its lesson. A sermon for the times. 2d ed. Boston, The Fraternity. 1859. 22p. 2516

WHIPPLE, CHARLES K. The non-resistance principle; with particular application to the help of slaves by abolitionists. Boston. R. F. Wallcut. 1860. 24p. 2517

WILLIAMS, EDWARD W. The views and meditations of John Brown. Washington. The author. n.d. 16p. 2518

WRIGHT, HENRY C. The Natick resolution; or, Resistance to slaveholders the right and duty of southern slaves and northern freemen. Boston, The author. 1859. 36p. 2519

XXIX. The Civil War and Slavery, Negroes, Official records, documents, reports and other topics relating to the war and to persons connected therewith.

ABEL, ANNIE H. The American Indian as slave-holder and secessionist; an omitted chapter in the diplomatic history of the southern confederacy. Cleveland, A. H. Clark co. 1915. 394p. 2520

ABBOTT, A. O. Prison life in the South; at Richmond, Macon, Savannah, Charleston, Columbia, Charlotte, Raleigh, Goldsborough, and Andersonville, during the years 1864 and 1865. New York, Harper & bros. 1865. x, 374p. 2521

ADAMS, FRANCIS C. Siege of Washington, D. C. written expressly for little people. New York, Dick & Fitzgerald. 1867. 130p. 2522

ADAMS, JOHN G. The abolition of slavery the right of the government under war power. Boston, R. F. Wallcut. 1862. 24p. 2523

AGNEW, DANIEL. Our National Constitution; its adaptation to a state of war or insurrection. Philadelphia, C. Sherman, son & co. 1863. 39p. 2524

AIKMAN, WILLIAM. The future of the colored race in America . . . an article in the Presbyterian quarterly review, July, 1862. New York, Anson D. F. Randolph. 1862. 35p. 2525

THE ALARM BELL, no. 1. By a constitutionist. New York, Baker & Godwin. 1863. 16p. 2526

AMBROSE, PAUL. Slavery the mere pretext for the rebellion; not its cause. By a southern man. (Rpt. from the National Intelligencer, Mar. 1863.) Philadelphia, C. Sherman, son & co. 1863. 16p. 2527

AMERICAN SOCIETY for promoting national unity. Proceedings . . . New York, The society. 1861. 16p. 2528

AMES, CHARLES G. A discourse on morals in America. Albany, N. Y., J. Munsell. 1864. 16p. 2529

AMES, CHARLES G. Stand by the President. An address delivered before the National Union association of Cincinnati, March 6, 1863. Cincinnati. The association. 1863. 14p. 2530

ANDERSON, CHARLES C. Fighting by Southern federals. New York, Neale pub. co. 1912. 408p. 2531

ANTICIPATIONS OF THE FUTURE to serve as lessons for the present time; in the form of extracts from an English resident in the U.S., to the London Times, from 1864 to 1870; with an appendix on the causes and consequences of the independence of the South.

Richmond, Va., J. W. Randolph. 1860. 416p. 2532

APPLETON, NATHAN. Letter . . . to Hon. Wm. C. Rives, of Virginia; also two editorials from the Boston Courier. Boston, John Clark & co. 1860. 13p. 2533

APTHEKER, HERBERT. The Negro in the Civil War. New York, International pub. co. 1938. 48p. 2534

ARNOLD, ISAAC N. The history of Abraham Lincoln and the overthrow of slavery. Chicago, Clarke & co. 1866. xvi. 736p. 2535

ASHLEY, JAMES M. (OHIO) Speech. . . in the House of representatives, on the Constitutional amendment for the abolition of slavery, Jan. 6, 1865. New York, Wm. C. Bryant & co. 1865. 22p. 2536

AUGHEY, JOHN H. The iron furnace, or Slavery and secession. Phila., William S. & Alfred Martien. 1863. 296p. 2537

AUGHEY, JOHN H. Tupelo: Imprisonment of Union Sympathizers in the Confederate prison at Tupelo, Miss. Lincoln, Nebraska, The author. 1888. 595p. 2538

AYER, I. WINSLOW. The great treason plot in the North during the war . . . Chicago, U. S. Pub. co. 1895. 453p. 2539

BAKER, GENERAL L. C. History of the United States secret service during the Civil war. Philadelphia, The author. 1867. 704p. 2540

BARKER, JACOB. The ballot box, the palladium of our liberties. New Orleans. The author, 1863. 65p. (Reprinted from The National Advocate) 2541

BARROWS, WILLIAM. A discourse, delivered in the Old South Church, Reading, Mass., Dec. 28, 1862.

Boston, John M. Whittemore & co. 1863. 18p. 2542

BARTLETT, JOHN R. The literature of the rebellion. A catalogue of books and pamphlets relating to the Civil war in the United States, and on subjects growing out of that event, together with works on American slavery, and essays from reviews and magazines on the same subjects. Boston, Draper & Halliday. Providence. Rider & bros. 1866. 477p. 2543

BASSETT, GEORGE W. A Northern plea for the right of secession. Ottawa, Ill., Free trader. 1861. 24p. 2544

BASSETT, GEORGE W. The wickedness and folly of the present war. Discourse delivered in the courthouse at Ottawa, Ill., Aug. 11, 1861. Ottawa, Free trader. 1861. 24p. 2545

BEACH, LEWIS. A word or two about the war. New York, John F. Trow. 1862. 28p. 2546

BEECHER, HENRY W. American rebellion... Speeches... delivered at public meetings in Manchester, Glasgow, Edinburgh, Liverpool and London . . . (Union emancipation society). London, Sampson Low & co. 1864. 175p. New York, Frank F. Lovell & co. 1887. 368p. 2547

BEECHER, HENRY W. Freedom and war, discourses on topics suggested by the times. Boston, Ticknor & Fields. 1863. iv, 445p. 2548

BEECHER, HENRY W. War and emancipation; a Thanksgiving sermon. Philadelphia, T. B. Peterson bros. 1861. 31p. 2549

BERNARD, GEORGE S. (ed.) War talks of Confederate veterans and the battle of the crater. Petersburg, Va., Fenn & Owen. 1892. 8lp. 2550

BIGELOW, MAJOR JOHN. The campaign of Chancellorsville, April 27 – May 5, 1863. With a critical review by James H. Wilson. (Reprinted from the N. Y. Sun for Nov. 6, 13 and 20, 1910.) Wilmington, Del., Chas. L. Story. 1911. 77p. 2551

BINGHAM, JOHN (OHIO) Speech . . . on self-preservation the right and duty of the general government. The rebel states but organized conspiracies – not constitutional states, nor entitled to state rights. Delivered in the House of representatives, Mar. 12, 1862. Washington. 1862. 2552

BISHOP, JOEL P. Secession and slavery. . . considered as a question of constitutional law. Boston, A. Williams & co. 1864. iv, 112p. 2553

BLAINE, JAMES G. Twenty years of Congress; from Lincoln to Garfield. With a review of the events which lead to the political revolution of 1860. Norwich, Conn. Henry Bill pub. co. 1884. 2v. 2554

BLEDSOE, ALBERT T. Is Davis a traitor; or was secession a constitutional right previous to the war of 1861? Baltimore, The author. 1866. 263p. 2d ed. Richmond, Va. Hermitage press. 1907. 263p. 2555

BOARD OF EDUCATION FOR FREEDMEN. Report . . . Department of the Gulf, 1864. New Orleans, True Delta office. 1865. 25p. 2556

BOTUME, ELIZABETH H. First days amongst the contrabands. Boston, Lee & Shepard. 1893. 286p. 2557

BOUTWELL, GEORGE S. Emancipation, its justice, expediency and necessity, as the means of securing a speedy and permanent peace. Delivered in Tremont temple. Boston. (The Emancipation

League) Dec. 16, 1861. Boston, Emancipation league. 1861. 12p. 2558

BOUTWELL, GEORGE S. Speeches and papers relating to the rebellion and the overthrow of slavery. Boston, Little, Brown & co. 1867. vii, 628p. 2559

BOWEN, JAMES L. Massachusetts in the war, 1861-1865. Springfield, C. W. Bryan & co. 1889. 1029p. 2560

BOYNTON, H. V. Sherman's historical raid. The memoirs in the light of the record. A review based upon compilation from the files of the war office. Cincinnati, Wilstach, Baldwin & co. 1875. 276p. 2561

BRECKINRIDGE, ROBERT J. State of the country. (Reprinted from the Danville quarterly review, June 1861.) Cincinnati. Danville review. 1861. 318p. 2562

BROCKETT, L. P. The camp, the battlefield, and the hospital; or, lights and shadows of the great rebellion . . . Philadelphia, Chicago, St. Louis, National pub. co. Cincinnati, Junkin & co. Boston, New England pub. co. 1866. 512p. 2563

BROOKS, NOAH. Washington in Lincoln's time. New York, Century co. 1896. 328p. 2564

BROWN, BENJAMIN G. Address . . . slavery in its national aspects as related to peace and war. St. Louis, General emancipation society of Missouri. Sept. 17, 1862. 8p. 2565

BROWNE, JUNIUS. Four years in secessia; adventures within and beyond the Union lines . . . Hartford. O. D. Case & co. Chicago, Geo. & C. W. Sherwood. London, Stevens bros. 1865. 450p. 2566

BROWNLOW, WILLIAM. Sketches of the rise, progress and decline of secession; with a narrative of personal adventures among the rebels. Philadelphia, Geo. W. Childs. 1862. 458p. 2567

BUTLER, BENJAMIN F. Autobiography and personal reminiscences . . . A review of his legal, political and military career. Boston, A. M. Thayer & co. 1892. 1154p. 2568

CAIRNES, JOHN E. The revolution in America. A lecture delivered before the Dublin young men's christian association. Dublin, Hodges, Smith & co. 1862. 44p. 2569

CAIRNES, JOHN E. The slave power; its character, career and probable designs; being an attempt to explain the real issues involved in the American contest. New York, Carleton. 1862. xv, 171p. 2570

CAMPAIGNS OF THE CIVIL WAR. New York, Charles Scribner's sons. 1882. 15v. (Volume editors vary). 2571

CAMPBELL, RANDOLPH. God's dealings with the nation in the present Civil war . . . A discourse preached Nov. 24, 1864 at Newburyport, Mass. Newburyport, The author. 1864. 20p. 2572

CANNON, LEGRAND B. Personal reminiscences of the rebellion. New York, The author. 1895. 228p. 2573

CARPENTER, F. B. Six months at the White House with Abraham Lincoln; the story of a picture. New York, Hurd & Houghton. 1866. 359p. 2574

CARPENTER, HUGH S. The final triumph of equity; a sermon delivered at Brooklyn on November 26, 1863. New York, W. A. Townsend. 1864. 2575

CASTLEMAN, ALFRED L. The army of the Potomac, behind the scenes. Milwaukee, Strickland co. 1863. 288p. 2576

CHANNING, WILLIAM H. The Civil War in America; or, The slaveholder's conspiracy. An address. Liverpool, W. Vaughan. London, John & Abel Heywood. 1861. 100p. 2577

CHASE, CARLETON. Discourse . . . Jan. 4, 1861, the day appointed by the President of the United States, for general fasting and prayer, on account of the distracted state of the country. Claremont, N. H., G. G. & L. N. Ide. 1861. 16p. 2578

CHEEVER, GEORGE. The salvation of the country secured by immediate emancipation. New York, John A. Gray. 1861. 24p. 2579

CHILD, DAVID L. Rights and duties of the United States relative to slavery under the laws of war. No military power to return any slave. "Contraband of war" inapplicable between the United States and their insurgent enemies. (Republished with notes, from "The Liberator.") Boston, R. F. Wallcut. 1861. 48p. 2580

CHITTENDEN, LUCIUS E. A report of the debates and proceedings in the secret sessions of the conference convention, for prosposing amendments to the constitution, held at Washington in February, 1861. New York, D. Appleton & co. 1864. 626p. 2581

CHITTENDEN, LUCIUS E. Personal reminiscences, 1840-1890; including some not hitherto published of Lincoln and the war. New York. Richmond, Croscup co. 1893. 434p. 2582

CHITTENDEN, LUCIUS E. Abraham Lincoln's speeches. New York, Dodd, Mead & co. 1895. vi, 371p. 2583

CITIZEN OF NEW YORK. (pseud.)

Remarks upon a plan for the total abolition of slavery in the United States. New York. The author. n.d. 16p. 2584

CLARKE, JAMES F. Secession, concession, or self-possession: Which? By a citizen of Massachusetts. Boston, Walker, Wise & co. 1861. 48p. 2585

CLEMENS, SHERRARD (VA.) Speech . . . State of the Union. Delivered in the House of representatives, Jan. 22, 1861. Washington. 1861. 2586

COCHIN, AUGUSTIN. The results of emancipation. Tr. from the French by Mary L. Booth. Boston, Walker, Wise & co. 1863. xiv, 412p. 2587

COFFIN, CHARLES C. (pseud. "Carleton".) Following the flag from August 1861, to November, 1862, with the Army of the Potomac. Boston, Ticknor & Fields. 1865. 336p. 2588

A COLLECTION OF CIVIL WAR post cards, caricatures, envelopes, etc. 1861-65. (collected, pasted and bound in one volume). 2589

COLYER, VINCENT. Brief report of the services rendered by the freed people to the United States army in North Carolina in the spring of 1862, after the battle of New Bern. New York, author, 1864. 64p. 2590

CONGDON, CHARLES T. Tribune essays; articles contributed to the New York Tribune from 1857 to 1863 with an introduction by Horace Greeley. New York, Redfield. 1869. 406p. 2591

CONWAY, MONCURE. The rejected stone; or insurrection and resurrection in America. By a native of Virginia. 2d ed. Boston, Walker, Wise & co. 1862. 132p. 2592

CORDNER, JOHN. The American

conflict. An address before the New England society of Montreal . . . Dec. 22, 1864. Montreal, The author. 1864. 48p. 2593

COULTER, ELLIS M. The Civil war and readjustment in Kentucky. Chapel Hill, University of North Carolina press. 1926. 450p. 2594

COX, SAMUEL S. (OHIO) Speech. . . on the state of the freedmen. Delivered in the House of representatives, Feb. 17, 1864. Washington. Govt. print office. 11p. 2595

COX, SAMUEL S. (OHIO) Eight years in Congress from 1857-1865. Memoir and speeches. New York, D. Appleton & co. 1865. 442p. 2596

CRAVEN, JOHN J. Prison life of Jefferson Davis. New York, G. W. Dillingham co. 1866. 320p. 2597

CRAWFORD, SAMUEL W. The history of the fall of Fort Sumter; the Genesis of the Civil War. New York, The author. 1896. 486p. 2598

DARLING, HENRY. Slavery and the war; a historical essay. Philadelphia, J. B. Lippincott & co. 1863. 48p. 2599

DAVIS, HENRY W. The Southern rebellion, and the constitutional powers of the Republic for its suppression. An address delivered at Brooklyn, N. Y. December 26, 1861. (The Pulpit and Rostrum series, no. 24) New York, E. D. Barker, 1862. 31p. 2600

DAVIS, HENRY W. Speeches and addresses delivered in the Congress of the United States, etc. New York, Harper & bros. 1867. 596p. 2601

DOOLITTLE, JAMES R. (WIS.) Speech . . . on emancipation and colonization. Delivered in the U. S.

Senate, Mar. 19, 1862. 8p. 2602

DOUBLEDAY, ABNER. Reminiscences of Forts Sumter and Moultrie in 1860-61. New York, Harper & bros. 1876. 183p. 2603

DRAKE, CHARLES D. Union and anti-slavery speeches, delivered during the rebellion. Published for the benefit of the Ladies Union aid society of St. Louis. Cincinnati, Applegate & co. 1864. 431p. 2604

DRAKE, CHARLES D. The War of slavery upon the Constitution . . . Address . . . on the anniversary of the constitution, delivered in St. Louis, Sept. 17, 1862. 7p. 2605

DRAPER, JOHN W. History of the American civil war. New York, Harper & bros. 1867. 3v. 2606

DRESSER, HORACE E. The battle record of the American rebellion. New York, S. Torrey. 1863. 72p. 2607

DUNCAN, LOUIS C. The medical department of the United States army in the Civil War. n.d. n.p. 13, 16, 18p. 2608

DUNNING, WILLIAM A. Essays on the Civil War and reconstruction and related topics. New York, MacMillan Co. 1898. 376p. 2609

DWINELL, ISRAEL E. Hope for our country. A sermon preached in Salem, Mass. on Oct. 19, 1862. Salem, The author. 1862. 19p. 2610

EATON, JOHN and MASON, ETHEL O. Grant, Lincoln and the freedmen. Reminiscences of the Civil war. New York, London, Longmans, Green & co. 1907. 331p. 2611

EDMONDS, S. EMMA E. Nurse and spy in the Union army; comprising adventures and experiences of a woman in the hospitals, camps, and battlefields. Hartford, S. Williams & co. 1865. 384p. 2612

ELLIS, DANIEL. Thrilling adventures . . . during the great southern rebellion. New York, Harper & bros. 1867. 480p.　　　2613

ELLISON, THOMAS. Slavery and secession in America, historical and economical. London, Sampson Low, son & co. 1861. xxxv, 371p.　　　2614

THE EMANCIPATION LEAGUE of Boston. Facts concerning the freedmen; their capacity and their destiny. Boston, The League. 1863. 12p.　　　2615

EMILIO, LUIS F. History of the 54th regiment of Massachusetts volunteer infantry, 1863-1865. 2d ed. rev. enl. Boston. The author. 1894. 452p.　　　2616

EVERETT, DAVID. An oration on the great issues now before the country; delivered in New York, July 4, 1861. New York, James G. Gregory. 1861. 48p.　　　2617

FAULKNER, CHARLES J. History of the revolution in the southern states . . . New York, John F. Trow. 1861. 94p.　　　2618

FENTON, R. E. New York state legislative honors to the memory of President Lincoln; the message of Governor Fenton to the legislature. Albany, Weed, Parsons & co. 1865. 118p.　　　2619

FESSENDEN, WILLIAM P. (ME.) Speech . . . on the abolition of slavery in the District of Columbia. Delivered in the U. S. Senate, April 1, 1862 . . . Also the speech of Morton S. Wilkerson (Minn.) on the same subject, in the U. S. Senate, Mar. 26, 1862. Washington. 1862. 16p.　　　2620

FISHER, GEORGE P. (DEL.) Remarks . . . the olive branch. Delivered in the House of representatives, March 11, 1862. Washington. 1862. 9p.　　　2621

FORBES, EDWIN. Bullet and shell. War as the soldier saw it; camp, march, and picket; battlefield & bivouac, prison and hospital. New York, Fords, Howard & Hulbert. 1883. 454.　　　2622

FOWLER, WILLIAM C. The sectional controversy; or passages in the political history of the United States; including causes of the War between the sections. New York, C. Scribner. 1863. 269p.　　　2623

FREMAN, WARREN H. (ed.) Letters from two brothers serving in the war for the Union to their family, at home in West Cambridge, Mass., Cambridge, privately printed. 1871. 164p.　　　2624

FREESE, J. R. Secrets of the late rebellion, now revealed for the first time. Philadelphia, Crombarger & co. 1882. 351p.　　　2625

FREMONT, JESSIE B. The story of the guard; a chronicle of the war. Boston, Ticknor & Fields. 1863. 227p.　　　2626

FRENCH, MRS. A. M. Slavery in South Carolina and the ex-slaves; or, The Port Royal mission. New York, Winchell & French. 1862. xii, 312p.　　　2627

FRIENDS, SOCIETY OF. New York yearly meeting . . . upon the condition and wants of the colored refugees. Annual report . . . of a committee of representatives . . . Collection has: 1st, 2d, 3d. 1862. 1863, 1864. New York, The society. 1862-64.　　　2628

GARRISON, WILLIAM L. Southern hatred of the American government, the people of the north, and free institutions. Boston, R. F. Wallcut. 1862. 48p.　　　2629

GASPARIN, AGENOR E. Les Etats-Unis en 1861. Un grand peuple qui se releve. Paris. M. Levy. 1862. 415p. 2630

GASPARIN, AGENOR E. The uprising of a great people. The United States in 1861. Tr. from the French by Mary L. Booth. New York. Scribner. 1861, x, 263p. 2631

GASPARIN, AGENOR E. and LABOULAYNE, EDOUWARD, et al. Reply to the loyal national league of New York . . . (Tr. from the French by J. A. Stephens, jr.); together with the addresses of the league, adopted in New York, April 11, 1863. New York, Wm. C. Bryant & co. 1864. 30p. 2632

GILMORE, JAMES R. (pseud. Kirke, Edmund.) Among the guerillas. New York, Carleton. 1866. 286p. 2633

GILMORE, JAMES R. Down in Tennessee, and back by way of Richmond. New York, Carleton. 1864. 282p. 2634

GILMORE, JAMES R. Patriot boys and prison pictures. Boston, Ticknor & Fields. 1866. 306p. 2635

GLAZIER, WILLARD W. Battles for the Union . . . Hartford, Gilman & co. 1878. 407p. 2636

GLAZIER, WILLARD W. The capture, the prison pen, and the escape; giving a complete history of prison life in the south. 2d ed. enl. New York, The author. 1868. 422p. 2637

GLAZIER, WILLARD W. Three years in the Federal cavalry. New York, The author. 1870. 339p. 2638

GOODWIN, THOMAS S. The natural history of secession; or, Depotism and democracy at necessary, eternal, exterminating war. 2d ed. New York, Derby & Miller. 1865. 328p. 2639

GORDON, JOHN B. Reminiscences of the Civil War. Memorial ed. New York, Charles Scribner's sons. Atlanta, Martin & Hoyt co. 1904. 474p. 2640

GRANGER, MOSES M. Washington vs. Jefferson; the case tried by battle in 1861-65. Boston, New York, Houghton, Mifflin & co. 1898. 207p. 2641

GRANT, ULYSSES S. Personal memoirs . . . New York, Century co. 1895. 2v. 2642

GREELEY, HORACE. The American conflict; a history of the great rebellion in the United States of America, 1860-64; its causes, incidents, and results; intended to exhibit especially its moral and political phases, with the drift and progress of American opinion respecting human slavery from 1776 to the close of the war for the union. Hartford, O. D. Case & co. Chicago, G. & C. W. Sherwood. 1864-66. 2v. 2643

GUROWSKI, ADAM. Diary from March 4, 1861 to November 12, 1862. Boston, Lee & Shepard. 1862. 315p. 2644

HAGUE, WILLIAM & KIRK, EDWARD N. Addresses . . . at the annual meeting of the Educational commission for freedmen, Old South Church, Boston, May 28, 1863. Boston, David Clapp. 1863. 16p. 2645

HALE, EDWARD E. (comp.) The President's words; a selection of passages from the speeches, addresses, and letters of Abraham Lincoln. Boston, Walker, Fuller & co. 1865. viii, 11-186p. 2646

HALE, JOHN P. (N.H.) Speech . . . on the abolition of slavery in the District of Columbia. Delivered in the U. S. Senate, Mar. 18, 1862. Washington. 1862. 8p. 2647

HALPINE, CHARLES G. Life and

adventures, songs, services, and speeches of private Miles O'Reilley, 47th regiment New York volunteers. 2d ed. enl. New York, Carleton. 1866. 378p. 2648

HARPER'S PICTORIAL HISTORY of the great rebellion. New York, Harper & bros. 1866. 2v. 2649

HARRIS, J. MORRISON (MD.) State of the Union. Speech . . . in the House of representatives, Jan. 29, 1861. Washington, H. Polkinhorn, Seam. 1861. 8p. 2650

HARRISON, RICHARD A. (OHIO) Speech . . . The suppression of the rebellion. Delivered in the House of representatives, May 4, 1862. Washington. 1862. 8p. 2651

HARRISON, WALTER. Pickett's men; a fragment of war history. New York, D. Van Nostrand. 1870. 202p. 2652

HASKELL, T. N. Christian patriotism; a sermon delivered at East Boston, Mass., April 30, 1863. Boston, The author. 1863. 40p. 2653

HAWES, JOEL. North and South; or, Four questions considered . . . A sermon preached at Hartford, Sept. 26, 1861. Hartford, Case, Lockwood & co. 1861. 31p. 2654

HEACOCK, W. J. Speech, in the New York state assembly at Albany, April 16, 1863, in favor of a vigorous prosecution of the war-sustaining the administration in its emancipation policy, and advocating an extensive and general use of the Negro in the Army and Navy. Albany, Weed, Parsons & co. 1863. 15p. 2655

HEADLEY, P. C. Massachusetts in the rebellion. A record of the historical position of the commonwealth . . . in the civil war of 1861-65. Boston, Walker, Wise & co. 1866. 688p. 2656

HEADLEY, P. C. The life and campaigns of Lieut-Gen. U. S. Grant . . . New York, Derby & Miller pub. co. 1866. 720p. 2657

HENDRICK, BURTON J. Statesmen of the lost cause. Jefferson Davis and his cabinet. Boston, Little, Brown & co. 1939. 452p. 2658

HENRY, C. S. Patriotism and the slave-holder's rebellion. An oration. New York, D. Appleton & co. 1861. 34p. 2659

HEPWORTH, GEORGE H. The whip, hoe and sword; or, The Gulf department in '63. Boston, Walker, Wise & co. 1864. 298p. 2660

HITCHCOCK, ROSWELL D. Thanksgiving for victories. A discourse delivered . . . in Brooklyn, Sept. 11, 1864. New York, John A. Gray & Green. 1864. 7p. 2661

HOLLAND, JOSIAH G. The life of Abraham Lincoln, Springfield, Mass., Gurdon Bill, 1866. 544p. 2662

HOUGH, SABIN. A letter to the public . . . the Union; how shall it be reconstructed and saved? Cincinnati, 1861. 16p. 2663

HOWARD, OLIVER O. Autobiography . . . New York, Baker & Taylor. 1908. 2v. 2664

HOWE, SAMUEL G. The refugees from slavery in Canada West. (Report to the Freedmen's inquiry commission). Boston, Wright & Potter. 1864. iv, 110p. 2665

HUNNICUTT, JAMES W. The conspiracy unveiled. The South sacrificed; or, The horrors of secession. Philadelphia, J. B. Lippincott & co. 1863. 454p. 2666

HUNT, E. B. Union foundations; a study of American nationality as a fact of science. New York, D. Van Nostrand. 1863. 61p. 2667

HYDE, THOMAS W. Following the

Greek cross; or, Memories of the Sixth army corps. Boston. New York, 1897. 279p.   2668

INGERSOLL, L. D. (comp.) Speeches. The opinions of Lincoln, Arnold on Lincoln, Andrew Johnson, etc. New York, Privately bound. 1864. 584p.   2669

JAMES, HORACE. Annual report of the Superintendent of Negro affairs in North Carolina, 1864. With an appendix containing the history and management of the freedmen in this department up to June 1, 1865. Boston, W. F. Brown & co. 1865. 64p.   2670

JAY, JOHN. The great conspiracy. An address delivered in West Chester county, N. Y. July 4, 1861. New York, Ree, Lockwood & son. 1861. 50p.   2671

JOHNSON, ANDREW (TENN.) Speech . . . on the war for the Union. Delivered in the Senate of the United States, July 27, 1861. Washington, Congressional Globe. 1861. 12p.   2672

JOHNSON, CHARLES B. Muskets and medicine or army life in the sixties. Philadelphia, F. A. Davis co. London, Stanley Phillips. 1917. 276p.   2673

JOHNSON, REVERDY (MD.) Speech . . . in support of the resolution to amend the Constitution so as to abolish slavery. Delivered in the U. S. Senate, April 5, 1864. Washington. 1864. 22p.   2674

JOHNSON. REVERDY (MD.) Remarks on popular sovereignty as maintained and denied respectively by Judge Douglas and Attorney-General Black. Washington, L. Towers. 1863. 16p.   2675

JOHNSON, ROBERT U. and BUEL, CLARENCE C. (eds.) Battles and leaders of the Civil War. New York,

Century co. 1887. 4v.   2676

JOINVILLE, PRINCE DE. The army of the Potomac, its organization, its commander and its campaign. Tr. from the French with notes by Wm. H. Hurlbert. New York, Anson D. F. Randolph. 1862. 118p.   2677

JONES, ERNEST. The slaveholder's war; a lecture delivered at Asher, Eng., Nov. 16, 1863. Manchester, Ashton-under-Lyne union and emancipation society. 1863. 44p.   2678

JOYCE, JOHN A. Jewels of memory. Washington, Gibson bros. 1895. 245p.   2679

JUDKIN, GEORGE. Political fallacies. An examination of the false assumption, and refutation of the sophistical reasonings which have brought on this Civil War. New York, Chas. Scribner. 1863. 332p.   2680

KEIFER, JOSEPH W. Slavery and four years of war. A political history of slavery in the United States together with a narrative of the campaigns and battles of the Civil War in which the author took part; 1861-1865. New York. London, G. P. Putnam's sons. 1900. 2v.   2681

KELLEY, WILLIAM D. (PA.) Remarks . . . in opposition to the employment of slaves in navy-yards, arsenals, dockyards, etc. and in favor of the Pacific railroad. Delivered in the House of representatives, May 9, 1862. Washington, Seammell & co. 1862. 8p.   2682

KELLEY, WILLIAM D. (PA.) Speech . . . on the policy of the administration. Delivered in the House of representatives. Jan. 31, 1862. Washington. 1862. 7p.   2683

KELLEY, WILLIAM D. (PA.) Speech . . . on freedmen's affairs. Delivered

in the House of representatives, Feb. 23, 1864. (The House having under consideration a bill to establish a Bureau of freedmen's affairs). Washington. 1864. 8p.
2684

KELLEY, WILLIAM D. (PA.) Speech . . . in the Northrop-Kelley debate at Spring Garden institute, September 28, 1864. 12p. 2685

KELLEY, WILLIAM D. (PA.) DICKINSON, ANNA E., and DOUGLASS, FREDERICK. Addresses . . . at a mass meeting held at national hall, Philadelphia, July 6, 1863, for the promotion of colored enlistments. Philadelphia. 1863. 8p. 2686

KELLOGG, ROBERT H. Life and death in rebel prisons . . . Hartford, L. Stebbins. 1865. 398p. 2687

KENNEDY, ANTHONY (MD.) Speech . . . on the abolition of slavery in the District of Columbia. Delivered in the U. S. Senate, Mar. 25, 1862. Washington. 1862. 8p. 2688

KERBEY, J. O. The boy spy; a substantially true record of events during the war of the rebellion. Chicago. New York. San Francisco, Belford, Clarke & co. 1889. 556p.
2689

KETTELL, THOMAS P. History of the great rebellion, from its commencement to its close, giving an account of its origin, the secession of the southern states, and the formation of the Confederate government. . . from official sources. Hartford, L. Stebbins. 1865. 778p. 2690

KETTELL, THOMAS P. Southern wealth and Northern profits . . ; The necessity of Union to the future prosperity and welfare of the republic. New York, George W. & John A. Wood. 1860. 173p. 2691

KEYES, E. D. Fifty years' observation of men and events, civil and military. New York, Chas. Scribner's sons. 1884. 515p. 2692

KIRKLAND, CHARLES P. A letter to the Hon. Benjamin R. Curtis, late judge of the Supreme court of the United States, in review of his pamphlet on the "Emancipation Proclamation" of the president. 2d ed. New York, Anson D. F. Randolph. 1863. 20p. 2693

KIRKLAND, CHARLES P. A letter to Peter Cooper on "The treatment to be extended to the rebels individually," and "the mode of restoring the rebel states to the union." With a reprint of a review of Judge Curtis' paper . . . and a letter from President Lincoln. New York, Anson D. F. Randolph. 1865. 20p. 2694

KNOX, THOMAS P. Camp-fire and cotton-field; southern adventure in time of war. Life with the Union armies, and a residence on a Louisiana plantation. Philadelphia, Cincinnati, Jones bros. & co. 1865. 524p. 2695

KNOX, THOMAS P. Startling revelations from the department of South Carolina, and expose of the so-called National freedmen's relief association. Boston, Wm. M. Kendall. 1864. 16p. 2696

LAPSLEY, ARTHUR BROOKS (ed.) The writings of Abraham Lincoln. New York, G. P. Putnam's sons. 1903. 8v. Constitution ed. New York, G. P. Putnam's sons. 1905. 8v. 2697

LIBERTAS, (pseud.) The power of the commander-in-chief to declare martial law, and decree emancipation; as shown from B. R. Curtis. Boston, A. Williams & co. 1862. 24p. 2698

171

THE LIGHT & DARK of the rebellion. Philadelphia, Geo. W. Childs. 1863. 303p. 2699

LINCOLN, ABRAHAM. His book; a facsmile reproduction of the original explanatory note by J. McCan Davis. Extracts of newspaper clippings of Lincoln's statements about "Negro equality." New York, McClure, Phillips & co. 1901. 35p. 2700

LINCOLN, ABRAHAM. Opinions upon slavery. n.d. 16p. 2701

LOGAN, JOHN A. The great conspiracy; its origin and history. New York, A. R. Hart & co. 1886. 810p. 2702

LORING, CALEB W. Nullification, secession, Webster's argument and the Kentucky and Virginia resolutions considered in reference to the constitution and historically. New York, G. P. Putnam's sons. 1893. 171p. 2703

LOYAL PUBLICATION SOCIETY. New York. Loyal publication society, 1863-1865. 87 pamphlets. Collection has:

no. 1. The future of the northwest in connection with the scheme of reconstruction without New England. Robert Dale Owen. 1863. 15p.

no. 2. The venom and the antidote. (Reprints from newspapers and periodicals supporting the Union). 1863. 16p.

no. 6. Northern men and southern traitors. 1863. 7p.

no. 7. Character and results of war . . . Benj. F. Butler. 1863. 16p.

no. 8. Separation; war without end. Edward Laboulaye. 1864. 19p.

no. 9. The venom and the antidote. 1864. 4p.

no. 10. . . . Words in behalf of the loyal women of the U. S. . . . 1864. 23p.

no. 11. No failure for the North. (From the 'Atlantic Monthly'). 1864. 23p.

no. 12. How a free people conduct a long war. Charles J. Stille. 1864. 16p.

no. 13. An address to King Cotton. Eugene Pelletan. 1864. 19p.

no. 14. Preservation of the Union . . . (From 'German Commercial Gazette'). 1863. 12p.

no. 15. Elements of discord in secessia. 1863. 12p.

no. 16. No party now, but all for our country. Francis Lieber. 1863. 10p.

no. 17. The cause of the war . . . Chas. Anderson. 1863. 16p.

no. 18. Opinions of the early presidents and of the fathers of the republic upon slavery. 1863. 19p.

no. 20. Military despotism . . . 1863. 16p.

no. 21. Letter to Opera house meeting, Cincinnati. Chas. Anderson. 1863. 15p.

no. 22. Emancipation is peace. 1863. 7p.

no. 23. Letter . . . slave emancipation. Peter Cooper. 1863. 8p.

no. 24. Patriotism a Christian virtue Rev. Fransioli. 1863. 24p.

no. 25. Conditions of reconstruction. Robert D. Owen. 1863. 24p.

no. 28. The death of slavery. Peter Cooper. 1864. 12p.

no. 29. Plantation for slave labor . . . Francis Lieber. 1865. 8p.

no. 30. Rebel conditions of peace and the mechanics of the south. 1863. 4p.

no. 31. Loyal leagues of New York state to the people of New York. 1863. 4p.

no. 33. The two ways of treason. n. d. 12p.

no. 34. The Monroe Doctrine. . . Edward Everett. 1863. 17p.

no. 35. Arguments of secessionists. Francis Lieber. 1863. 7p.

no. 36. Prophecy and fulfillment . . . A. H. Stephens. 1863. 45p.

no. 37. How the south rejected compromise . . . in 1861. Salmon P. Chase. n.d. 11p.

no. 38. Letters on our national struggle. T. F. Meagher. 1863. 15p.

no. 39. Bible view of slavery, examined . . . reconsidered part I: H. Drisler. part II: L. Newman. 1863. 34p.

no. 40. The conscription act. Geo. B. Butler. n.d. 22p.

no. 46. How the war was commenced (From Cincinnati Daily Commercial). 1864. 16p. Results of serf emancipation in Russia. J. Laing. 1864. 8p.

no. 48. Resources of the U. S. S. B. Riggles. 1864. 12p.

no. 50. Constitution vindicated. J. Hamilton. 1864. 13p.

no. 51. No property in man. Chas. Sumner. 1864. 13p.

no. 52. Rebellion, slavery and peace. N. G. Uphan. 1864. 13p.

no. 54. Our burden and our struggle. David A. Wells. 1864. 39p.

no. 58. Mastership and its fruits. J. McKaye. 1864. 38p.

no. 60. Peace through victory. J. P. Thompson. 1864. 16p.

no. 62. The war for the Union. Wm. Swinton. 1863. 16p.

no. 77. Address on secession . . . Francis Lieber. 1865. 12p.

no. 79. Letter . . . on amendment to abolish slavery. Francis Lieber. 1865. 35p.

no. 83. Amendments of the Constitution. Francis Lieber. 1865. 39p.

no. 84. An Englishman thoughts on the crimes of the south. W. W. Brown. 1865. 24p.

no. 86. . . . A national system of education. C. Brooks. 1865. 22p.

no. 87. Gasparin's letter to president Johnson. 1865. 11p.
2704

MACON, T. J. Reminiscences of the first company of Richmond Howitzers. Richmond, Va., Whittet & Shepperson. n.d. 126p. 2705

MAGAUL, MICHAEL (pseud.) E. R. McCall. No history vs. no war; or, the great tootle rebellion exposed. New York, The author. 1885. 402p. 2706

MAHAN, A. T. The navy in the Civil war. New York, Chas. Scribner's sons. 1883. 3v. 2707

MAHONY, D. A. The prisoner of state. New York, Carleton. 1863. 414p. 2708

MARKS, J. J. The Peninsula campaign in Virginia; or, Incidents and scenes on battlefields and in Richmond. Philadelphia, J. B. Lippincott Co. 1864. 444p. 2709

MASSACHUSETTS ADJUTANT-GENERAL. Record of the Massachusetts volunteers. 1861-1865. Boston, Wright & Potter. 1868. 793p. 2710

MASSIE, JAMES W. America; the

173

origin of her present conflict; her prospect for the slave and her claim for anti-slavery sympathy; with incidents of travel during a tour in the summer of 1863 . . . London, John Snow. 1864. viii, 477p.   2711

MAYER, BRANTZ, (pseud.) Maryland. The emancipation problem in Maryland. (Enl. republished from the Baltimore American). Baltimore. 1862. 4p.   2712

M'KIM, J. MILLER. Address . . . the freedmen of South Carolina, delivered in Sauson hall, July 9, 1862. Together with a letter from the same to Stephen Colwell, chairman of the Port Royal relief committee. Philadelphia, Willis P. Hazard. 1862. 32p.   2713

McMASTER, JOHN B. History of the people of the United States during Lincoln's administration. New York, D. Appleton & co. 1927. xxxi, 693p.   2714

MESSAGE OF THE PRESIDENT of the United States and accompanying Documents to the two houses of Congress at the commencement of the first session of the thirty-eight Congress. Annual report of the war department. 38th Congress, 1st session, House of representatives, ex. doc. no. 1. Washington, Govt. print. office. 1863. 510p.   2715

MILLER, FRANCIS T. (ed.) The photographic history of the Civil war, 1861-65. New York, Review of reviews co. 1911. 10v. (Plates and photographs principally by Mathew Brady, official union photographer).   2716

MOORE, FRANK. Anecdotes, poetry and incidents of the war; North & South, 186- - 1865. New York, printed for subscribers. 1866. 560p.   2717

MOORE, FRANK. (ed.) The rebellion record; a diary of American events, with documents, narratives, illustrative incidents, poetry, etc. New York, G. P. Putnam. 1861-63. 5v.   2718

MOORE, FRANK. Speeches of John Bright, m.p. on the American question. Boston, Little, Brown & co. 1865. 278p.   2719

MORSE, SIDNEY E. A geographic, statistical and ethical view of the American slaveholders' rebellion. New York, Anson Randolph. 1863. 19p.   2720

MORTON, JOSEPH W. Jr. (ed.) Sparks from the camp fire; or, Tales of the old veterans . . . as retold today around the modern campfire. Philadelphia, Keystone publ. co. 1895. 688p.   2721

MOSBY, JOHN S. War reminiscences and Stuart's cavalry campaigns. Boston, Geo. A. Jones & co. 1887. 256p.   2722

MOTLEY, JOHN L. The causes of the American Civil War; a paper contributed to the London Times. 1861. (Pulpit & Rostrum series, no. 20) 20p. New York, James G. Gregory. 1861. 36p.   2723

MUNFORD, BEVERLY B. Virginia's attitude toward slavery and secession. New York, Longmans, Green & co. 1909. xiii, 329p. 2724

MUNFORD, MARY C. B. and others. Outline and questions based on 'Virginia's attitude toward slavery and secession,' by Beverly Bland Munford, Richmond, Va., The author. 1915. 36p.   2725

MUNICIPALIST. Addenda to the Municipalist. Letter xxiv. Separation of the United States, Confederate States of America, etc. . . . Secession no rebellion, etc. 303-348p.   2726

NASHVILLE (TENN.) PATRIOT. The conspiracy to break up the Union; the plot and its development . . . Washington, Buell & Blanchard. 1860. 16p.   2727

NATIONAL FREEMAN'S RELIEF ASSOCIATION of the District of Columbia. Annual report . . . 1st, 2d. 1863-1864. Washington, M'gill & Witherow. 1863. 1864.   2728

NEW ENGLAND FREEDMEN'S AID SOCIETY. Annual report of the Educational commission for freedmen . . . 1st, 2d, 3d, 1863-64-65. Boston, Prentiss & Deland. 1863. Boston, The society. 1864. 1865.   2729

NEW ENGLAND FREEDMEN'S AID SOCIETY. Extracts from letters of teachers and superintendents of the Educational commission for freedmen. 4th series, Jan. 1, 1864. Boston, David Clapp. 1864. 14p. 5th series, Oct. 15, 1864. Boston, John Wilson & co. 1864. 20p. 2730

"THE NEWSPAPER MAN" (pseud.) Fagots from the camp fire. Washington, L. J. DuPre. 1881. 199p.   2731

NEW YORK CITY COMMON COUNCIL. Obsequies of Abraham Lincoln. . . New York, Edmund Jones & co. 1866. 254p.   2732

NEW YORK MONUMENTS COMMISSION. Final report of the battlefield of Gettysburg. Albany, V. B. Lyon co. 1902. 3v.   2733

NICHOLS, GEORGE W. The story of the great march; from the diary of a staff officer. 2d ed. enl. New York, Harper bros. 1866. 456p.   2734

NICOLAY, JOHN G. Campaigns of the Civil war. New York, Chas. Scribner's sons. 1881. 14v.   2735

NORDHOFF, CHARLES. The freedmen of South Carolina; some account of their appearance, character, condition, and peculiar customs. New York, C. T. Evans. 1863. 27p.   2736

NORTON, OLIVER W. Army letters, 1861-1865; being extracts from private letters to relatives and friends from a soldier in the field during the late Civil War. Chicago, The author. 1903. 355p.   2737

NOTT, C. C. Sketches of the war, 2d ed. New York. 1875. 174p.   2738

OF THE BIRTH AND DEATH OF NATIONS. A thought for the crisis. New York, G. P. Putnam. 1862. 33p.   2739

OFFICIAL records of Union and Confederate Armies in the war of the Rebellion. (series 1, 2, 3, and 4 of army orders, reports, and correspondence, and civil correspondence). Washington, Govt. print. office. 1881-1901. 128v.
                                        2740

OFFICIAL records of Union and Confederate Navies in the War of the Rebellion. (Series 1 and 2). Washington, Govt. print. office. 1804-1914, 1927. 31v.   2741

OLDROYD, OSBORN H. (ed.) The Lincoln memorial; album — immortelles. Original life pictures, with autographs . . . from contemporaries of . . . Abraham Lincoln. Together with extracts from his speeches, letters, sayings. London, S. Low, son & co. 1882. 571p.   2742

ON THE RELATIONS OF SLAVERY to the war, and the treatment of it necessary to permanent peace. 1862. 8p.   2743

O'REILLY, HENRY (ed.) Origin and objects of the slaveholders' conspiracy against democratic principles, as well as against the national union . . . illustrated in the speeches of Andrew Jackson

Hamilton and the statements of Lorenzo Sherwood. New York, Baker & Godwin. 1862. 24p.　2744

ORTH, GODLOVE S. (IND.) Speech . . . Our duty and our destiny; delivered in the House of representatives, Jan. 6, 1865. Washington. 1865. 16p.　2745

OWEN, ROBERT D. The policy of emancipation; in three letters to the Secretary of war, the President of the United States, and the Secretary of the treasury. Philadelphia, J. B. Lippincott & co. 1863. 48p.　2746

OWEN, ROBERT D. The wrong of slavery. The right of emancipation and the future of the African race in the United States. Philadelphia, J. B. Lippincott & co. 1864. 246p.　2747

PALMER, SARAH L. Six months among the secessionists. A reliable and thrilling narrative of . . . sufferings and trials. Philadelphia, Barclay & co. 1862. 40p.　2748

PARKER, JOEL. Habeas corpus, and law. A review of the opinion of chief justice Tavey in the case of John Merryman. Cambridge, Welch, Bigelow & co. 1861. 58p.　2749

PARKER, JOEL. The war powers of Congress, and of the President. An address delivered before the National club of Salem. March 13, 1863. Cambridge, H. O. Houghton. 1863. 60p.　2750

PARSONS, THEOPHILUS. Slavery. Its origin, influence, and destiny. Boston, Wm. Carter & bro. 1863. 36p.　2751

PARTON, JOSEPH. The life of Horace Greeley. Boston, Fields, Osgood & co. 1869. 598p.　2752

PILLSBURY, ALBERT E. Lincoln and slavery. Boston. New York,

Houghton, Mifflin & co. 1913. 97p.　2753

PINKERTON, ALLAN. The spy of the rebellion; being a true history of the spy system of the U. S. army during the late rebellion, revealing many secrets hitherto not made public. Compiled from official reports. New York, G. W. Carleton & co. 1884. 688p.　2754

PITMAN, BENN (comp.) The assassination of President Lincoln and the trial of the conspirators. New York, Moore, Wilstach & Baldwin. 1865. 421p.　2755

PITMAN, BENN (ed.) The trials for treason at Indianapolis, disclosing plans for establishing a Northwestern confederacy. Cincinnati, Moore, Wilstach & Baldwin. 1865. 339p.　2756

PITTENGER, WILLIAM. Capturing a locomotive; a history of secret service in the late war. Philadelphia, J. B. Lippincott & co. 1894. 354p.　2757

PITTENGER, WILLIAM. Daring and suffering; a history of the great railroad adventure. Philadelphia, J. W. Daughaday. 1864. 288p.　2758

POLLARD, EDWARD A. Life of Jefferson Davis, with a secret history of the southern confederacy, gathered "behind the scenes in Richmond." Philadelphia, National pub. co. 1869. 536p. 2759

POLLARD, EDWARD A. Southern history of the war series. 1st, 2d, and 3d years of the war. 3v. V. 1. Richmond, West & Johnston. 1862. 368p. v. 2-3. New York, Chas. B. Richardson. 1865.　2760

PUTNAM, GEORGE H. A prisoner of war in Virginia, 1864-5. New York. London, G. P. Putnam's sons. 1912. 127p.　2761

THE QUESTION before us. Boston, John Wilson & son. 1862. 12p.2762

RAYMOND, HENRY J. Disunion and slavery. A series of letters to Hon. W. L. Yancey of Alabama. New York 1860. 36p.   2763

RAYMOND, HENRY J. History of the administration of President Lincoln, including his speeches, letters, etc. . . New York, J. C. Derby & Miller. 1864. 496p. 2764

REED, WILLIAM H. Hospital life in the army of the Potomac. Boston, Wm. V. Spencer. 1866. 199p. 2765

REYNOLDS, E. W. Relations of slavery to the war; and the position of the clergy at the present time. Three discourses preached at Watertown, N. Y. Watertown, The author. 1861. 48p.   2766

REYNOLDS, E. W. The true story of the barons of the South; or, The rationale of the American conflict. Boston, Walker, Wise & co. 1862. 240p.   2767

RICE, ALLEN T. (ed.) Reminiscences of Abraham Lincoln by distinguished men of his time. New York. North American review. 1888. 650p. Rev. ed. New York, Harper & bros. 1909. 428p.   2768

RICHARDSON, ALBERT D. The secret service, the field, the dungeon, and the escape. Hartford, American pub. co. 1865. 512p.
2769

RICHARDSON, JAMES D. A compilation of the messages and papers of the Confederacy. Nashville, U. S. pub. co. 1906. 2v.   2770

ROBINSON, WILLIAM S. A conspiracy to defame John Albion Andrew, being a review of the proceedings of Joel Parker, Limes Child and Leverett Saltonstall at the peoples convention, (so called,) held in Boston, Oct. 7, 1862.

Boston, Wright & Potter. 1862. 16p.   2771

RUGGLES, SAMUEL B. The past and the present. Semi-centennial address to the Yale college and graduates of 1814, at their annual meeting, July 27, 1864. New York, Wm. C. Byrant & co. 1864.   2772

RUSSELL, SIR WILLIAM. My diary North and south. Boston, The author. 1863. 116p.   2773

ST. BENJAMIN (pseud.) The new gospel of peace. New York. Sinclair Tousey. 1863-64. 3v.   2774

SARGENT, F. W. England, the United States and the Southern Confederacy. 2d ed. rev. London, Hamilton, Adams & co. 1864. 184p.   2775

A SAVOURY DISH for loyal men. Philadelphia. Berlin. 1863. 16p.2776

SCHARF, J. THOMAS. History of the Confederate States Navy from its organization to the surrender of its last vessel. New York, Rogers and Sherwood. 1887. 824p.   2777

SCHERER, JAMES A. B. Cotton as a world power; a study in the economic interpretation of history. New York, F. A. Stokes co. 1916. 452p.   2778

SCHURZ, HON. CARL. The life of slavery, or the life of the Nation? Speech . . . at the mass meeting, Cooper Institute, New York, Mar. 6, 1862. (Reprinted from the Rebellion Record) New York, G. P. Putnam. 1862. 11p.   2779

SCOTT, JOHN. Partisan life with Col. John S. Mosby. New York, Harper & bros. 1867. 492p.   2780

SEWARD, WILLIAM H. (N.Y.) Speech . . . on freedom and the union. Delivered in the U. S. Senate, Feb. 29, 1860. Albany, Weed, Parsons & co. 1860. 12p. New York, The Tribune. 1860.

14p. (Tribune tracts, no. 3).   2781
SEYMOUR, HORATIO. Annual message of the Governor of the state of New York, transmitted to the legislature on Jan. 7, 1863. Albany, Comstock and Cassidy. 1863. 44p.   2782
SHAFFNER, T. P. The war in America; a historical and political account of the southern and northern states. London. New York, London print. & pub. co. 1862. 418p.   2783
SHEA, JOHN G. (ed.) The Lincoln Memorial; a record of the life, assassination, and obsequies of the martyred President. New York, Bruce & Huntington.   2784
SHERMAN, JOHN (OHIO) Remarks . . . on slaves and· slavery; how affected by the war. Delivered in the U. S. Senate, April 2, 1862. Washington, Scammell & co. 1862. 15p.   2785
SHERWOOD, LORENZO. The great questions of the times, exemplified in the antagonistic principles involved in the slaveholder's rebellion against democratic institutions. . . New York, C. S. Westcott & co. 1862. 31p.   2786
SICKLES, DANIEL E. (N.Y.) Speech . . . on the state of the union, delivered in the House of representatives, Dec. 10, 1860. Washington. 1860. 12p.   2787
SIMMONS, JAMES F. (R.I.) Speech . . . on the state of the Union. Delivered in the Senate of the United States, Jan. 16, 1861. Washington, Buell & Blanchard. 1861. 16p.   2788
SIMONS, ERZA D. The 125th New York state volunteers. A regimental history. New York, The author. 1888. 352, xxxp.   2789
SIZER, THOMAS J. The Crisis; its

rationale. I. Our National force, The proper remedy. II. Restoration of legitimate authority, The end and object of the war. Buffalo, Reed, Butler & co. 1862. 100p.   2790
SMART, CHARLES S. (comp.) The medical and surgical history of the war of the rebellion. Washington, Govt. print. office. 1888. 3v.   2791
SMITH, CHARLES. What we have secured by the War, and what remains to be secured; a discourse delivered on December 7, 1865 at Andover, Mass. Andover, The author. 1866. 22p.   2792
SMITH, GERRIT. Speeches and letters . . . on the rebellion. New York, American News co. 1865. 2v.   2793
SMITH, GOLDWIN. The Civil war in America; an address read at the last meeting of the Manchester Eng. union and emancipation society. London, Simpkin, Marshall & co. 1866. 96p.   2794
SPENCER, CORNELIA P. The last ninety days of the war in North Carolina. New York, Watchman pub. co. 1866. 287p.   2795
STANTON, R. L. The Church and the Rebellion; a consideration of the rebellion against the government of the U. S. and the agency of the church, North and South, in relation thereto. New York, Derby & Miller. 1864. 562p.   2796
STEPHENS, A. H., DAVIS, JEFFERSON et al. Echoes from the South; comprising the most important speeches, proclamations, and public acts emanating from the south during the Civil war. New York, E. B. Treat & co. 1866. 211p.   2797
STILLE, CHARLES J. Northern interests and southern independence; a plea for united action. Phila-

178

delphia, W. & A. Martieu. 1863. 50p.   2798

STODDARD, A. F. Slavery of freedom in America or the issue of the war. A lecture delivered at Paisley (scot.) Jan. 28, 1863. Glasgow, Thos. Murray & son. 1863. 64p.   2799

STODDARD, WILLIAM O. Inside the White House in War times. New York, Charles L. Webster & co. 1892. 244p.   2800

STODDARD, WILLIAM O. A volunteer special. The volcano under the city; an account of the draft riot of 1863. New York, Fords, Howard & Hurlbert. 1887.   2801

SUMNER, CHARLES (MASS.) Speech . . . on the bill to establish a Bureau of freedmen. Delivered in the U. S. Senate, June 13 and 15, 1864. Washington. H. Polkinhorn. 1864. 15p.   2802

SUMNER, CHARLES (MASS.) Emancipation! It's policy and necessity as a war measure for the suppression of the rebellion. A speech . . . at Faneuil Hall, Boston, Oct. 6, 1862. Boston, 1862. 23p.   2803

SUMNER, CHARLES (MASS.) The rebellion − its origin and mainspring. An oration . . . under the auspices of the Young Men's republican union of New York, Nov. 27, 1861. New York, The Union. 1861. 14p.   2804

SUMNER, CHARLES (MASS.) Slavery and the rebellion, one and inseparable. Speech . . . before the New York Young Men's republican union, Cooper Institute, New York, Nov. 5, 1864. Boston, Wright & Potter. 1864. 30p.   2805

SUMNER, CHARLES (MASS.) The war and slavery; or, Victory only

through emancipation. Boston, R. F. Wallcut. 1863. 8p.   2806

TAYLOR, WALTER H. Four years with General Lee; being a summary of the more important events touching the career of General Robert E. Lee, in the war between the states . . . New York, D. Appleton & co. 1877. 199p.   2807

TAYLOR, WILLIAM. Cause and probable results of the Civil war in America, facts for the people of Great Britian. London, Simpkin, Marshall & co. 1862. 30p.   2808

THARIN, R. SEYMOUR. Arbitrary arrests in the south; or, scenes from the experience of an Alabama unionist. New York, John Brandburn. 1863. 245p.   2809

THOMAS, BENJAMIN F. (MASS.) Remarks . . . on the relation of the "seceded states" (so-called) to the union, and the confiscation of property and emancipation of slaves in such states. Delivered in the House of representatives, April 10, 1862. Boston, John Wilson & son. 1862. 37p.   2810

THOMAS, BENJAMIN F. (MASS.) A few suggestions upon the personal liberty law and "secession" (so-called) in a letter to a friend. Boston, John Wilson & son. 1861. 22p.   2811

THOMAS, BENJAMIN F. (MASS.) Revolution against free government not a right but a crime. An address . . . delivered before the Union league club. New York, The Club, 1864. 46p.   2812

TRAIN, GEORGE F. (. . . unionist on Thomas Colley Grattan, secessionist). England and the disrupted states of America, by T. O. Grattan; or the last speech and dying confession of the rebel commissioners, Yancey, Mann and Rost . . . Boston, Lee & Shepard. 1862. 48p. 2813

TREMAIN, HENRY E. Last hours of Sheridan's cavalry. A reprint of war memoranda. New York, Bonnell, Silver & Bowers. 1904. 563p. 2814

TOMES, ROBERT. The war with the South; a history of the great American rebellion. New York, Virtue & Yorkston. 1863. 3v. 2815

UNION CONGRESSIONAL COMMITTEE. A few plain words with the rank and file of the union armies. Washington, L. Towers. 1864. 7p. 2816

U. S. AMERICAN FREEDMEN'S INQUIRY COMMISSION. Preliminary report touching the condition and management of emancipated refugees; made to the secretary of war, June 30, 1863. New York, Pub. by authority of the secretary of war. J. F. Trow. 1863. 40p. 2817

U. S. ARMY. Department of the Gulf. Report on the condition of freedmen. T. W. Conway, superintendent, Bureau of free labor, U.S.A. to Major N.P. Banks, commanding. New Orleans, H. P. Lathrop. 1864. 11p. 2818

U. S. CONGRESS. Senate reports, 38th Congress, 2d session. Report of the Joint committee on the attack on Petersburg, July 30, 1864. Washington, Govt. print. office. 1865. 272p. 2819

U. S. CONGRESS. Supplemental Report of the Joint Committee on the Conduct of the War: being supplemental to the United States Senate report no. 142 (38th Congress, 2d session). Washington, Govt. print. office. 1866. 2v. 2820

U. S. HOUSE OF REPRESENTATIVES. Report of the Committee on the conduct of the war. Fort Pillow massacre. Returned prisoners. (H.R. report no. 65, 38th Congress, 1st session). Washington, Govt. print. office. 1864. 42p. 2821

U. S. HOUSE OF REPRESENTATIVES. Report of the Select committee on emancipation and colonization . . . (H.R. report no. 148, 37th Congress, 2d session). Washington, Govt. print. office. 1862. 83p. 2822

U. S. SANITARY COMMISSION. A sketch of its purposes and its work. Compiled from documents and private papers. Boston, Little Brown & co. 1863. 299p. 2823

U. S. SANITARY COMMISSION. Report of a commission of inquiry . . . Narrative of privatious and sufferings of United States officers and soldiers while prisoners of war. Philadelphia, The commission. 1864. 283p. 2824

U. S. TREASURY DEPARTMENT. Commercial intercourse with and in states declared in insurrection, and the collection of abandoned and captured property, embracing departmental circulars and regulations, etc. Sept. 11, 1863, Washington, Govt. print. office. 1863. 56p. 2825

U. S. TREASURY DEPARTMENT. Rules and regulations concerning commercial intercourse with and in states and parts of states declared in insurrection, the collection, receipt, and depositions of abandoned, captured, and confiscable property, and the employment and general welfare of freedmen. Washington. Govt. print. office. 1864. 76p. 2826

U. S. WAR DEPARTMENT. The mastership and its fruits; the

emancipated slave face to face with his old master. A supplemental report to Hon. Edwin M. Stanton, secretary of war, by James McKaye, special commissioner. New York, Wm. C. Byrant co. 1864. 38p. 2827

VAN BUREN, T. B. Speech . . . on the bill to ratify the amendment to the Constitution of the United States prohibiting slavery. Delivered in the New York House of Assembly, Mar. 15, 1865. Weed, Parsons & co. 1865. 24p. 2828

VERMONT GENERAL ASSEMBLY. Revised roster of Vermont volunteers and lists of Vermonters who served in the army and navy of the U. S. during the war of the rebellion, 1861-66. Montepelier. 1892. 863p. 2829

VICTOR, ORVILLE J. Incidents and anecdotes of the war; together with life sketches of eminent leaders and narratives of the most memorable battles for the union. New York, James D. Torrey. 1862. 400p. 2830

WALKER, ROBERT J. Jefferson Davis. Repudiation, recognition and slavery. A letter. 2d ed. London, Wm. Ridgeway. 1863. (From the Continental Monthly, Aug.-Sept. 1863. 2831

WILBUR, HENRY W. President Lincoln's attitude towards slavery and emancipation with a review of events before and after the Civil war. Philadelphia, Walter H. Jenkins. 1914. 220p. 2832

WILEY, BELL I. Southern Negroes, 1861-1865. New Haven, Yale University press. London, Oxford University press. 1938. viii, 24-366p. 2833

WILLS, CHARLES W. Army life of an Illinois soldier; including a day by day record of Sherman's march to the sea. Letters and diary . . .

Washington, Globe print. co. 1906. 383p. 2834

WILSON, HENRY (MASS.) The death of slavery is the life of the nation. Speech. . . on the proposed amendment to the Constitution prohibiting slavery within the United States. Delivered in the Senate of the United States, Mar. 28, 1864. Washington, B. Polkinhorn. 1864. 16p. 2835

WILSON, HENRY. History of the anti-slavery measures of the Thirty-seventh and Thirty-eighth United States Congresses, 1861-1864-1865. Boston, Walker, Wise & co. 1864. 384p. 2d ed. rev. enl. Boston, Walker, Fuller & co. 1865. 424p. 2836

WILSON, PETER M. Southern exposure. Chapel Hill, University of North Carolina press. 1927. 200p. 2837

WILSON, THOMAS. Sufferings endured for a free government; or, a history of the cruelities and atrocities of the rebellion. Philadelphia, Smith & Peters. 1864. 374p. 2838

WISE, JOHN S. End of an era. Boston. New York, Houghton, Mifflin co. 1902. 474p. 2839

WOOD, BENJAMIN (N.Y.) Speech . . . on the state of the Union. Delivered in the House of representatives, May 16, 1862. Washington, McGill. 1862. 12p. 2840

WOOD, ROBERT C. Confederate book; a compilaton of important data and other interesting and valuable matter relating to the War between the states, 1861-1865. New Orleans, Graham press. 1900. 127p. 2841

WOODBURN, JAMES A. The attitude of Thaddeus Stevens toward the conduct of the Civil war. (In

American historical assn. report for the year 1906). Reprinted. Washington. 1908. v1, p. 211-31.
2842

WORMERLEY, KATHERINE P. The other side of war with the army of the Potomac. Boston, Ticknor & co. 1889. 210p.
2843

WRIGHT, ELIZUR. The lesson of St. Domingo; how to make the war short and the peace righteous. (From the New York Tribune, May 27, 1861.) Boston, A. Williams & co. 1861. 24p.
2844

WRIGHT, MARCUS J. (comp.) General officers of the Confederate army. New York, Neale pub. co. 1911. 188p.
2845

XXX. The Negro as a Soldier.

APTHEKER, HERBERT. The Negro in the Civil War. New York, International Publishers, 1938. 46p.
2846

ATLANTA UNIVERSITY BULLETIN. Published quarterly. Atlanta. Atlanta University. Feb. 1918. Letters from training camps. Negroes in training for war.
2847

BOKER, GEORGE H. Washington and Jackson on Negro soldiers. Gen. Banks on the bravery of Negro troops. A poem — the Second Louisiana. Philadelphia, Henry C. Baird. 1863. 8p.
2848

BOSTON. GAZETTE AND COUNTRY JOURNAL. Monday, Mar. 12, 1770. Containing a contemporary account of the Boston massacre, Mar. 5, 1770.
2849

BROWN, WILLIAM W. The Negro in the American rebellion, his heroism and his fidelity. Boston, Lee & Shepard, 1867. xvi, 380p.
2850

CASHIN, HERSCHEL V. Under fire with the tenth U. S. cavalry; being a brief, comprehensive review of the Negro's participation in the wars of the United States . . . London. New York, Chicago, F. T. Neely. 1899. 361p. illus. 2d ed. Chicago. American pub. house. 1902. 361p. illus.
2851

COSTON, W. HILARY. The Spanish-American War volunteer. Ninth U. S. volunteer infantry roster and muster. Biographies. Cuban sketches, Middletown, Pa., The author. 1899. 224p.
2852

CURTIS, MARY. The black soldier or the colored boys of the United States army. Washington, Murray bros. 1918. 60p.
2853

DAVIS, ARTHUR K. (ed.) Virginians of distinguished service in the World War. Richmond. Executive committee. 1923. 243p. (Publications of the Va. War history commission, source v.1).
2854

FLEETWOOD, CHRISTIAN A. The Negro as a soldier written . . . for the Negro Congress, at the cotton states exposition, Atlanta, Ga., Nov. 11-23, 1895. Washington, G. F. Cook. 1895. 19p.
2855

FLIPPER, HENRY O. The colored cadet at West Point; autobiography (of the) first graduate of color from the U. S. Military academy. New York, Homer, Lee & co. 1878. 322p.
2856

FORAKER, JOSEPH B. (OHIO) The black battalion. They ask no favors because they are Negroes but only for justice because they are men. Speech . . . Senate of the United

States. April 14, 1908. Washington, Govt. print. office. 1908. 45p. 2857

GARRISON, WILLIAM L. The loyalty and devotion of colored Americans in the revolution and War of 1812. New York, Young's book exchange. 1918. 24p. (Rpt. from Boston ed. R. F. Wallcut, 1861). 2858

GUTHRIE, JAMES M. Campfires of the Afro-American; or the colored man as a patriot . . . Philadelphia, Afro-American pub. co. 1899. 710p. 2859

HEYWOOD, CHESTER D. Negro combat troops in the World war. The story of the 371st infantry. With maps, photographs and illustrations. Worcester, Commonwealth press. 1928. 310p. 2860

HIGGINSON, THOMAS W. Army life in a black regiment. Boston, Fields, Osgood & co. 1870. 296p. 2861

HUNTON, ADDIE D. and JOHNSON, KATHYN M. Two colored women with the American expeditionary forces. Brooklyn, Eagle press. 1920. 256p. 2862

JOHNSON, EDWARD A. History of Negro soldiers in the Spanish-American war, and other items of interest. Raleigh, N. C. Capital print. co. 1899. 147p. 2863

JOHNSON, WILLIAM H. History of the colored volunteer infantry of Virginia, 1871-99. Petersburg, Va., privately printed. 1923. 102p. 2864

KELLEY, WILLIAM D. Addresses . . . at a mass meeting. Philadelphia, July 6, 1863, for the promotion of colored enlistments. Philadelphia, 1863. 8p. (Also contains an address by Frederick Douglass). 2865

LITTLE, ARTHUR W. From Harlem to the Rhine, the story of New York's colored volunteers. New York, Covici-Friede. 1936. xviii, 382p. 2866

LIVERMORE, GEORGE. An historical research respecting opinions of the founders of the Republic on Negroes as slaves, as citizens, and as soldiers. Boston, John Wilson & son. 1862. xiv, 215p. 2d ed. Boston, John Wilson & son. 1863. xiv, 184p. 2867

LYNK, MILES V. The black troops, or the daring heroism of the Negro soldiers in the Spanish-American war. Jackson, Tenn., M. V. Lynk pub. house. 1899. 163p. 2868

MARCY, R. B. Thirty years of army life on the border. New York, Harper & bros. 1866. 442p. 2869

MASON, MONROE and FURR, ARTHUR. The American Negro soldier with the red hand of France. Boston, Cornhill co. 1920. 180p. 2870

MILLER, KELLY . . . history of the World war for human rights . . . and the important part taken by the Negroes . . . Washington. Chicago, Austin Jenkins co. 1919. xiii. 608p. 2871

MOORE, GEORGE H. Historical notes on the employment of Negroes in the American army of the revolution. New York, Charles T. Evans. 1862. 24p. 2872

MOORE, L. B. How the colored can help in the problems issuing from the war. New York, National security league. 1918. 24p. 2873

NANKIVELL, JOHN H. (comp.) History of the twenty-fifty regiment United States infantry, 1869-1926. Denver, Smith-Brooks print. co. 1927. xvii, 212p. 2874

NEGRO SOLDIERS. A collection of newspaper accounts of Negro soldiers and sailors in the service of the United States. 1896-1919. 72v. 2875

NELL, WILLIAM C. The colored patriots of the American revolution, with sketches of several distinguished colored persons; to which is added a brief survey of the condition and prospects of colored Americans. Boston, R. F. Wallcut. 1855. 396p. 2876

NELL, WILLIAM C. Services of colored Americans, in the wars of 1776 and 1812. 2d ed. Boston, Robert F. Wallcut. 1852. 40p. 2877

NEW YORK NATIONAL GUARD. Dedicated to the old 15th infantry . . . which served gloriously in France as the 369th infantry, U.S. army. New York, National guard. 1921. 10p. 2878

REMOND, SARAH P. The Negroes and Anglo-Americans as freedmen and soldiers. (Ladies' London emancipation society, tract no. 7). London, Emily Faithful. 1864. 31p. 2879

RIDER, SIDNEY S. An historical inquiry concerning the attempt to raise a regiment of slaves by Rhode Island during the War of the revolution. Providence, The author. 1880. 86p. 2880

SCOTT, EMMETT J. The American Negro in the World war . . . Illustrated with official photographs. Washington, The author. 1919. 608p. 2881

SMITH, BOLTON. The Negro in wartime with a rejoinder by James Weldon Johnson. (Published in The Public, Aug. 31 and Sept. 21, 1918). (Reprinted by the NAACP Nov. 1918.) 10p. 2882

STEWARD, THEOPHILUS G. The colored regulars in the United States army, with a sketch of the history of the colored America, and an account of his services in the wars of the country, from the period of the Revolutionary war to 1899. Philadelphia, A.M.E. book concern. 1904. 344p. 2883

STEWARD, THEOPHILUS G. How the black St. Domingo legion saved the patriot army in the siege of Savannah, 1779. Washington, The academy. 1899. 15p. (Occasional papers, no. 5. 2884

TAYLOR, MRS. SUSIE R. Reminiscences of my life in camp with the 33d, U. S. colored troops, late 1st South Carolina volunteers. Boston, The author. 1902. xii, 7, 82p. 2885

ULLMANN, DANIEL. Address . . . before the soldier's and sailor's union of the state of New York, on the organization of colored troops and the regeneration of the South. Albany, Feb. 5, 1868. Washington, Great republic office. 1868. 16p. 2886

U. S. SENATE. Summation of the Brownsville, Texas military investigation. (Senate documents, 59th Congress, 2d session, v. 11). Washington, Govt. print. office. 1910. 201p. 2887

U. S. SENATE. Report of the proceedings of the court of inquiry relative to the shooting affray at Brownsville, Texas, by Companies B, C, D, 25th U. S. infantry. Washington, Govt. print. office. 1911. 12v. 2888

U. S. WAR DEPARTMENT. Summary discharge or mustering out of regiments or companies. Washington, Govt. print. office. 1907. 2889

WATKINS, WILLIAM J. Our rights as men. An address delivered in Boston before the Legislative committee on the militia, Feb. 24, 1853, in behalf of sixty-five colored petitioners, praying for a charter to form an independent military company. Boston, B. F. Roberts. 1853. 21p. 2890

WHITING, WILLIAM. The war powers of the president and the legislative powers of Congress in relation to rebellion, treason and slavery. 2d ed. Boston, John L. Shorey. 1862. 143p. 2891

WILDER, BURT G. Fifty-fifth regiment of the Massachusetts volunteer infantry, colored, June 1863-Sept. 1865. 3rd ed. Chestnut Hill, Mass., The author. 1919. 8p. 2892

WILLIAMS, CHARLES H. Sidelights on Negro soldiers. Boston, B. J. Brummer co. 1923. 284p. 2893

WILLIAMS, GEORGE W. A history of the Negro troops in the war of the rebellion, 1861-1865. . . New York, Harper & bros. 1888. xvi, 353p. 2894

WILSON, JOSEPH T. The black phalanx. A history of the Negro soldiers of the United States in the Wars of 1775-1812-1861-65. Hartford. American pub. co. 1888. 528p. 2895

XXXI. The Negro in the Reconstruction Period.

ALLEN, JAMES S. Reconstruction, the battle for democracy, 1865-1878. New York, International publishers. 1937. 256p. 2896

ALLEN, WALTER. Governor Chamberlain's administration in South Carolina; a chapter of reconstruction in the southern states. New York. London, G. P. Putnam's sons. 1888. xv, 544p. 2897

ALVORD, J. W. Letters . . . from the South relating to the condition of the freedmen, addressed to Major Gen. O. O. Howard. Washington, Howard University press. 1870. 42p. 2898

AMERICAN ANNUAL CYCLOPAEDIA. and register of important events. New York, D. Appleton co. 1866-75; after 1875 continued as Appleton's annual cyclopaedia. 2899

THE AMERICAN FREEDMAN. A monthly journal devoted to the promotion of freedom, industry, education, and christian morality in the South. New York. American freedmen's & union commission. 1866-Collection has: v1. nos. 1, 2, 3. 2900

AMERICAN FREEDMEN'S AID COMMISSION. Woman's work for the lowly, as illustrated in the work . . . among the freedmen. Boston, American missionary assn. 1873. 16p. 2901

AMERICAN MISSIONARY ASSOCIATION. Woman's work for the lowly, as illustrated in the work . . . among the freedmen. Boston, American missionary assn. 1873. 16p. 2902

AMES, MARY. From a New England woman's diary in Dixie in 1865. Springfield, Mass., Plimpton press. 1906. 125p. 2903

ANDREW, SIDNEY. The South since the war, as shown by fourteen weeks of travel and observation in Georgia and the Carolinas. Boston, Ticknor & Fields. 1866. viii, 400p. 2904

AVARY, MYRTA L. Dixie after the war. An exposition of social conditions existing in the South during the twelve years succeeding the fall of Richmond. New York, Doubleday, Page & co. 1906. 435p. 2905

BASCOM, JOHN W. The three amendments. Annals Am. Acad. 27: 597-609. May, 1906. 2906

BEARD, JAMES M. K.K.K. Sketches, humorous and didatic, treating the more important events of the Ku-Klux Klan movement in the South with a discussion of the causes which gave rise to it and the social and political issues emanating from it. Philadelphia, Claxton, Remson, & Haffelfinger. 1877. 192p. 2907

BECK, JAMES B. (KY.) Speech . . . against the proposed amendment to the reconstruction bill. Delivered in the House of representatives, Jan. 15, 1868. Washington. Rives. 1868. 15p. 2908

BENTON, JACOB (N. H.) Speech. . . on the reconstruction and the record and policy of the Democratic party; in the House of representatives, Feb. 25, 1868. Washington, Congressional office. 1868. 8p. 2909

BINGHAM, JOHN A. (OHIO) Remarks . . . impeachment of the President; in the House of representatives, Feb. 22, 1868. Washington Congressional globe. 1868. 8p. 2910

BINGHAM, JOHN A. (OHIO) Speeches . . . in the House of representatives, Jan. 13-14, 1868 on the judiciary and reconstruction bills. Washington, Great republic. 1868. 16p. 2911

BOSTON CITY DOCUMENT NO. 126. Bronze group commemorating emancipation. A gift to the city of Boston from Hon. Moses Kimball, dedicated. Dec. 6, 1879. Boston, City council. 1879. 75p. 2912

BOSTON DAILY ADVERTISER. Boston, published daily . . . collection has: Jan. 27, 29; Feb. 1, 3, 13, 20, 21, 23, 24, 26, 28; Mar. 3, 7, 8, 9, 13, 14, 30, 1866. 2913

BOWERS, CLAUDE G. The tragic era, the revolution after Lincoln. Boston, Houghton Mifflin co. 1929. 2914

BRITISH and FOREIGN FREEDMEN'S AID SOCIETY. The Freedman. A monthly magazine devoted to the interests of the freed coloured people. London, British & foreign freedmen's aid society. 1866. Collection has: v. 2, no. 1(Sept. 1866). 2915

BROWN, WILLIAM G. The lower South in American history. New York, London, Macmillan co. 1902. xi, 271p. 2916

BRUCE, PHILIP A. The plantation Negro as a freedman, observations on his character, condition, and prospects in Virginia. New York, London, G. P. Putnam's sons. 1889. 262p. 2917

BUCKALEW, CHARLES R. (PA.) Speech . . . Reconstruction . . . delivered in the Senate of the United States, Jan. 29, 1868. Washington. 1868. Washington, Govt. print. office. 1868. 2918

BURGESS, JOHN W. Reconstruction and the Construction, 1866-1876. New York, Charles Scribner's sons. 1902. xii, 342p. 2919

BUTLER, BENJAMIN F. Personal vindication . . . in reply to attacks upon him in the United States Senate . . . Speech in the House of representatives, April 20, 1871. Washington, McGill & Witherow. 1871. 8p. 2920

CABLE, GEORGE W. The Creoles of Louisiana. New York, Chas. Scribner's sons. 1886. 320p. 2921

CALHOUN, ARTHUR W. A social history of the American family from colonial times to the present. Cleveland, A. S. Clark co. 1917-19. 3v. 2922

CAMPBELL, SIR GEORGE, White and black; the outcome of a visit to the United States. New York, R. Worthington. 1879. xviii, 420p. 2923

CLOWES, LAIRD W. Black America; a study of the ex-slave and his late master. (Rept. with additions from the (London) "Times." London, Paris, Melbourne. Cassell & co. 1891. 240p. 2924

THE COLORED PEOPLE OF MISSOURI. An address by the colored people of Missouri to the Friends of equal rights. St. Louis. Missouri democrat print. 1865. 4p. 2925

CROLY, HERBERT. The promise of American life. New York, Macmillan co. 1909. 468p. 2926

CURRY, JABEZ L. M. The Southern states of the American union. Considered in their relations to the constitution of the U. S. and to the resulting union. Richmond, Va., B. F. Johnson pub. co. 1895. 272p. 2927

DAVIS, WILLIAM W. The Civil war and reconstruction in Florida. New York. Columbia university press. 1913, xxvi, 769p. (Columbia studies, v. 53). 2928

DAWES, HENRY L. Speech . . . on the Kentucky election . . . delivered in the House of representatives, Feb. 13, 1868. Washington, Govt. print. office. 1868. 15p. 2929

DEFELICE, G. Appelen faveur des naires emancipes daus les Etats-Unis. Paris, Grassart. 1865. 32p. 2930

DELAWARE ASSOCIATION FOR

THE MORAL Improvement and Education of the Colored People. Report . . . 1868. Wilmington, 1868. 23p. 2931

DIXON, WILLIAM H. New America. Philadelphia, J. P. Lippincott co. 1867. 495p. 2932

DIXON, WILLIAM H. White conquest. London, Chatto & Winders. 1876. 2v. 2933

DU BOIS, W. E. BURGHARDT. Black reconstruction. An essay toward a history of the part which black folk played in the attempt to reconstruct democracy in America, 1860-1880. New York, Harcourt, Brace & co. 1935. 746p. 2934

DUNNING, WILLIAM A. Essays on the Civil war and reconstruction and related topics. Rev. ed. New York. London, Macmillan co. ix, 297p. 2935

DUNNING, WILLIAM A. Reconstruction, political and economic, 1865-77. New York, London, Harper & bros. 1907. xvi. 378p. 2936

ELDRIDGE, C. A. (WIS.) Speech. . . the Constitution against confiscation and outside reconstruction. Delivered in the House of representatives, Dec. 10, 1867. Washington. 1867. 11p. 2937

ELIOT, THOMAS D. (MASS.) Speech . . . on the continuation of the Freedman's bureau. In the House of representatives, March 11, 1868. Washington. 1868. 2938

FIELD, HENRY M. Blood is thicker than water, a few days among our southern brethern. New York, Geo. Munro. 1886. 151p. 2939

FIELD, HENRY M. Bright skies and dark shadows. New York, Chas. Scribner's sons. 1890. 316p. 2940

FISHER, SAMUEL J. Work among the freedmen. Address before the

Synod of Pennsylvania, Allegheny, Oct. 17, 1902. Allegheny, Pa., 1912. 10p. 2941

FLEMING, WALTER L. Documentary history of reconstruction, political, military, social, religious, educational and industrial, 1865 to. the present time. Cleveland, A. H. Clark co. 1906-07. 2v. 2942

FLEMING, WALTER L. I. Freedmen's bureau documents. II. The Freedmen's saving bank. Morgantown. University of West Va., 1904. 63p. 2943

FLEMING, WALTER L. The sequel of Appomattox, a chronicle of the reunion of the states. New Haven, Yale University press. 1921, ix. 322p. Chronicles of America series, v. 32. 2944

FREEDMEN'S AID SOCIETY OF THE METHODIST EPISCOPAL CHURCH. Annual report . . . 3d, 8th, 11th, 16th (1869, 1875, 1878, 1883); Cincinnati. The society. 1869-75-78-83. 2945

FRIEND'S ASSOCIATION of Philadelphia for the Aid and Elevation of the Freedmen. Annual report . . . 2d-8th (1866-1872). Philadelphia, Merrihew & son. 1866-1872. 2946

GARFIELD, JAMES A. (OHIO) Speech. . . in the House of representatives, Aug. 4, 1876. Can the Democratic party be safely trusted with the administration of government? Washington, 1876. 16p. 2947

HARTSHORN, W. N. (ed.) An era of progress and promise 1863-1910. The religious, moral, and educational development of the American Negro since his emancipation. Boston. Priscilla pub. co. 1910. 576p. 2948

HAYS. CHARLES (ALA.) Alleged outrages in the Southern states.

Delivered in the House of representatives, May 4, 1872. Washington, Gov. print. office. 1872. 2950

HENDERSON, JAMES H. D. (ORE.) Speech . . . on reconstruction. Delivered in the House of representatives, June 13, 1866. Washington, Congressional globe. 1866. 2951

HENDRICKS, THOMAS A. (IND.) Speech . . . on reconstruction. Delivered in the Senate of the United States, Jan. 30, 1868. Washington. Rives. 1868. 2952

HERBERT, HILARY A. (ed.) Why the solid South? or, Reconstruction and its results. Baltimore, R. H. Woodward & co. 1890. xvii, 452p. 2953

HOAR, GEORGE F. (MASS.) and TOWNSEND, W. (PA.) et al. General Howard and the freedmen's bureau. Remarks . . . in the House of representatives, Feb. 23, 1871. Washington, 1871. 8p. 2954

HOLBROOK, JOHN C. Recollections of a nonagenarian . . . including a mission to Great Britain in behalf of the southern freedmen. Boston. Pilgrim press. 1897. 351p. 2955

HOLMES, SIDNEY T. (N.Y.) Speech . . . on reconstruction. In the House of representatives, Mar. 10, 1866. Washington. 1866. 20p. 2956

HOWE, T. O. (WIS.) Speech . . . The authority of the nation, supreme and absolute; that of the state, subordinate and conditional. In the Senate of the United States, Jan. 10. 1866. Washington, Polkinhorn, 1866. 20p. 2957

HUNTER. OSBORNE, JR. The North, South and the Freedman, The relative position of each to that of the other. An address . . . Eighth annual exhibition of the North

Carolina Industrial Association. Washington, The author. 1886. 32p. 2958

KENDRICK, BENJAMIN B. The journal of the Joint committee of fifteen on reconstruction, 39th Congress, 1865-67. New York, Columbia Univ. press. London, Longmano, Green & co. 1914. 414p. 2959

LATHAM, HENRY. Black and white; a journal of a three months' tour in the United States. London, Macmillan co. 1867. xii, 304p. 2960

LEIGH, FRANCIS B. Ten years on a Georgia plantation since the war. London, R. Bentley & sons. 1883. xi, 347p. 2961

LELAND, JOHN A. A voice from South Carolina. Twelve chapters before Hampton. Two chapters after Hampton. With a journal of a reputed Ku Klux... Charleston, S. C., Walker, Evans & Cogswell. 1879. x, 231p. 2962

LESTER, J .C. and WILSON, D. L. Ku Klux Klan, its origin, growth and disbandment. Nashville, Tenn., Wheeler, Osborn & Duckworth co. 1884. 117p. 2963

LOWE, CHARLES. The condition and prospects of the South; a discourse delivered in Somerville, Mass. June 4, 1865. Boston, Walker, Fuller & co. 1865. 8p. 2964

LYNCH, JOHN R. The facts of reconstruction. New York, Neale pub. co. 1913. 325p. 2965

MACRAE, DAVID. Amongst the darkies, and other papers. Glasgow, John S. Marr & sons. 1880. 126p. 2966

MCCARTHY, CHARLES H. Lincoln's plan of reconstruction. New York, McClure, Phillips & co. 1901. xxiv, 531p. 2967

MCCONNELL, JOHN P. Negroes and their treatment in Virginia from 1865 to 1867. Pulaski, Va. Smith & bros. 1910. 126p. 2968

MCPHERSON, EDWARD. A political manual for 1866, including a summary of the important executive, legislative and politico-military facts of the period from President Johnson's accession to July 4, 1866; and containing a full record of the action of each branch of the government on reconstruction. Washington, Philip & Solomons. 1866. 128p. 2969

MILLER, GEORGE F. (PA.) Speech . . . on the true mode of reconstruction. In the House of representatives, April 21, 1866. Washington. 1866. Washington. 1866. 2970

MORGAN, A. T. Yazoo; or, on the picket line of freedom in the South. A personal narrative. Washington. The author. 1884. 512p. 2971

MORRILL, LOT M. (ME.) Speech . . . on reconstruction. Delivered in the Senate of the United States, Feb. 5,. 1868. Washington. Govt. print. office. 1868. 2972

MORTON, O. P. (Ind.) Speech . . . reconstruction. Delivered in the Senate of the United States, Jan. 24, 1868. Washington. 1868. 2973

NEWELL, WILLIAM A. (N.J.) Speech . . . Restoration of the rebellious states. In the House of representatives, Jan. 4, 1867. Washington. 1867. 2974

NEWELL, WILLIAM A. (N.J.) Speech . . . on reconstruction. In the House of representatives, Feb. 15, 1866. Washington. 1866. 12p. 2975

NYE, JAMES W. (NEV.) Speech . . . on reconstruction. In the Senate of the United States, Jan. 24, 1868. Washington. 1868. 2976

PARKER, JOEL. Revolution and reconstruction. Two lectures delivered in the Law school of Harvard college in January 1865 and January, 1866. New York, Hurd & Houghton. 1866. 89p.
2977

PATTERSON, JAMES W. (N.H.) Speech . . . on reconstruction. Delivered in the House of representatives, May 19, 1866. Washington, McGill. 1866. 2978

PETITION AND MEMORIAL of the citizens of the United States to the Senate and House of representatives in Congress assembled. (A plea for universal suffrage). New York. 1865. 2979

PROTESTANT EPISCOPAL FREEDMEN'S COMMISSION. Occasional papers . . . Jan., 1866. Boston, The commission. 1866. 28p. 2980

RAYMOND, HENRY J. (N.Y.) Speech . . . on reconstruction, delivered in the House of representatives on the bill to provide for establishing governments in the southern states, January 24, 1867. New York. Baker & Godwin. 1867. 14p. 2981

RAUM, GREEN B. The existing conflict between republican government and southern oligarchy. Washington, C. M. Green. 1884. 479p. 2982

ROY, JOSEPH E. Pilgrim's letters; bits of current history picked up in the west and the south, during the last thirty years . . . Boston. Chicago. Congregational pub. society. 1888. 310p. 2983

SCHURZ, CARL (MO.) Speech . . . on usurpation of the war powers. In the United States Senate, March 28, and 29, 1871. Washington, 1871.
2984

SCOTT, EBEN G. Reconstruction during the Civil war in the United States of America. Boston, New York, Houghton, Mifflin & co. 1895. x, 432p. 2985

SHELLABARGER, SAMUEL (OHIO) On the bill to provide for restoring to the states lately in rebellion their full political rights. Speech in the House of representatives, Jan. 24, 1867. Washington, Union Congressional committee. 1867. 8p. 2987

SINCLAIR, WILLIAM A. The aftermath of slavery. A study of the condition and environment of the American Negro. Boston, Small, Maynard & co. 1905. 358p. 2988

SOCIETY FOR THE DIFFUSION OF POLITICAL KNOWLEDGE. Emancipation and its results. No. 6. New York, The society. 32p. 2989

SPEAR, SAMUEL T. The citizens duty in the present crisis. A sermon delivered in Brooklyn, Oct. 7, 1866. New York, N. Tibbals. 1866. 31p. 2990

SPIRIT OF THE SOUTH: or Persecution in the name of the law, as administered in Virginia. Related by some of the victims thereof . . . Washington, Publ. for the trade and the people. 1869. 76p. 2991

SPRING, LINDLEY. The Negro at home; an inquiry after his capacity for self-government and the government of whites for controlling, leading, directing or cooperating in the civilization of the age. . . New York, The author. 1868. 237p.
2992

STEARNS, CHARLES. The Black man of the south, and the rebels; or the characteristics of the former, and the recent outrages of the latter. New York, The author. 1872. 562p. 2993

STEPHENSON, NATHANIEL W. The confederacy and reconstruction.

New York. Yale University press. 1926. ix, 214p., iii, 322p.　　2994

STONE, FREDERICK (MD.) Speech . . . admission of Virginia. Delivered in the House of representatives, Jan. 14, 1870. Washington. 1870.　　2995

SUMNER, CHARLES (MASS.) Speech . . . on the bill concerning the rights of American citizens. No reprisals on innocent persons. Delivered in the Senate of the United States, July 18, 1868. Washington, Rives. 1868.　　2996

SUMNER, CHARLES (MASS.) Speech . . . Validity and necessity of fundamental conditions on states. In the Senate of the United States, June 10, 1868.　　2997

SUMNER, CHARLES (MASS.) Security and reconciliation for the future; Propositions and arguments on the Re-organization of the Rebel States. Boston, Geo. C. Rand & Avery. 1865. 32p.　　2998

SUMNER, CHARLES (MASS.) The National security and the national faith. Guarantees for the national freedman and the national creditor. Speech. . . at the Republican State Convention in Worcester. Sept. 14, 1865. Boston, Wright & Pottery print. 1865. 21p.　　2999

SUMNER, CHARLES (MASS.) The one man power vs. Congress address . . . at the Music Hall, Boston, Oct. 2, 1866. Boston, Wright & Pottery print, 1866. 24p.　　3000

SWEENEY, WILLIAM N. (KY.) Speech . . . Admission of Virginia. Delivered in the House of representatives, Jan. 14, 1870. Washington, 1870.　　3001

TAYLOR, ALRUTHEUS A. The Negro in South Carolina during the reconstruction. Washington,

Association for the study of Negro life and history. 1924. iv, 341p.　　3002

TAYLOR, ALRUTHEUS A. The Negro in the reconstruction of Virginia. Washington, Association for the study of Negro life and history. 1926. iv, 300p.　　3003

TOWNE, LAURA M. Letters and diaries . . . written from the Sea Islands of South Carolina, 1862-1884. Cambridge, Privately issued. 1912. xviii, 310p.　　3004

TREMAIN, HENRY E. Sectionalism unmasked. New York. Bounell, Silver & co. 1907. xi, 322p.　　3005

TRUMBULL, LYMAN (ILL.) Speech. . . on the civil rights veto message. Delivered in the U.S. Senate, April 4, 1866. Washington, Congressional globe office. 1866. 16p.　　3006

ULLMAN, DANIEL. An address . . . on the organization of colored troops and the regeneration of the South, delivered at Albany, Feb. 5, 1868. Washington, Great republic print. 1868. 16p.　　3007

U. S. BUREAU OF REFUGEES, Freedmen, and Abandoned Lands. Annual report . . . 6th, 7th, 8th, 9th. (1867-70). Washington, Govt. print. office. 1867-1870.　　3008

U. S. BUREAU OF REFUGEES. Office Manual. Washington, Govt. print. office. 1866. 137p.　　3009

U. S. CONGRESS. Report of the joint select committee on the condition of affairs in the late insurrectionary states, (42d Congress, 2d session, H. R. report, no. 22). The Ku Klux Klan conspiracy. Washington, Govt. print. office. 1872. 13v.　　3010

U. S. CONGRESS. Trial of Andrew Johnson, president of the United States, before the Senate of the U. S. on representatives for high crimes and misdemeanors.

Washington. Govt. print. office. 1868. 3v. 3011

U. S. HOUSE OF REPRE-SENTATIVES. Riot at Norfolk. Letter from the secretary of war, in answer to a resolution of the House, Dec. 10, 1866, calling for information relative to the riot. Washington. Govt. print. office. 1867. 71p. 3012

VAUGHAN, WALTER R. "Freemen's pension bill." Being an appeal in behalf of men released from slavery. A plea for American freedmen and a rational proposition to grant pensions to persons of color emancipated from slavery. Omaha. 1890. 125p. 3013

WALWORTH, MRS. JEANETTE R. Southern silhouettes. New York, Henry Holt & co. 1887. 376p. 3014

WARNER, SAMUEL L. (CONN.) Speech. . . on reconstruction. Delivered in the House of representatives, Jan. 18, 1867. Washington, Congressional globe. 1867. 3015

WELLS, GIDEON. Diary . . . (of the) secretary of the Navy under Lincoln and Johnson. Boston. New York, Houghton, Mifflin co. 1911. 3v. 3016

WELLS, JAMES M. The Chisolm massacre: a picture of "home-rule" in Mississippi. Chicago. Chisolm monumental fund. 1877. 291p. 3d ed. Washington. Chisolm monumental assn. 1878. 329p. 3017

WHITE MAN bery unsartin, Nigger haint got no friends, no how. The blackest chapter in the history of the Republican party. The men who robbed and combined to rob the freedmen of their hard earnings. Washington. Joseph Shillington. 1867. 39p. 3018

WILLIAMS, THOMAS (PA.) Speech . .

. on reconstruction of the Union. Delivered in the House of representatives, Feb. 10, 1866. 31p. 3019

WILLIAMS, WILLIAM H. The Negro in the District of Columbia during reconstruction. Washington. 1924. 52p. (Howard University studies, no. 5). 3020

WILSON, HENRY (MASS.) Speech . . . on representation of rebel states. Delivered in the Senate of the United States, Mar. 2, 1866. Washington. Congressional globe. 1866. 3021

WILSON, JOSEPH T. Emancipation. Its course and progress, from 1481, B. C. to A.D. 1875, with a review of Lincoln's proclamations, the thirteenth amendment, and the progress of the freed people since emancipation; with a history of the emancipation movement. Hampton, Va. Normal school press. 1882. 242p. 3022

WILSON, PETER. Southern exposure. Chapel Hill, Univ. of North Carolina press. 1927. 200p. 3023

WINDOM, WILLIAM (MINN.) Speech . . . Rights of citizens. Delivered in the House of representatives, Mar. 2, 1866. Washington. 1866. 3024

WOOD, FERNANDO (N.Y.) Continuance of freedmen's bureau. Negro capacity for self-government. Speech . . . in the House of representatives, Mar. 19, 1868. Washington, F. & J. Rives & Geo. A. Bailey. 1868. 8p. 3025

WOOD, NORMAN B. The white side of a black subject, a vindication of the Negro race. Cincinnati, W. H. Ferguson. 1899. 408p. 3026

ZINCKE, FOSTER B. Last winter in the United States; being a table talk

collected during a tour through the
late southern confederacy, the far
west, the Rocky mountains, etc.
London, John Murray. 1868. 314p.
3027

XXXII. Negro Suffrage and Politics.

ARNETT, A. M. The populist movement in Georgia; a view of the
agrarian crusade in the light of
solid-south politics. New York,
Columbia University press. 1922.
239p.   3028

BEARD, CHARLES A. Contemporary
American history, 1877-1913. New
York. London, Macmillan co. 1914.
vii, 397p.   3029

BOLDING, B. J. What of the Negro
race? Bolding vs. Hasskarl.
Chambersburg, Pa., Democratic
news. 1898. 176p.   3030

BOWIE, S. J. Remarks . . . at
Tammany hall, July, 1904. Shall
southern representation in Congress
be reduced? New York, 1904. 16p.
3031

BREWER, JOHN M. Negro legislators
of Texas and their descendants . . .
Dallas, Tex., Mathis publ. co. 1935,
x, 134p.   3032

BUTLER, BENJAMIN F. The Negro
in politics. Review of recent legislation for his protection – Defense
of the colored man against all
accusers. Address of General Butler
in North Russell St. Church,
Boston, May 8, 1871. Lowell,
Marden & Rowell. 1871. 19p. 3033

CABLE, GEORGE W. The Southern
struggle for pure government. An
address . . . before the Massachusetts club on Washington's birth-
day, 1890. Boston, Press of Samuel
Usher. 1890. 29p.   3034

CAFFEY, FRANCIS G. Suffrage

limitations at the South. Boston,
Ginn & co. 1905. 15p.   3035

CHANDLER, JULIAN A. C. The
history of suffrage in Virginia.
Baltimore, Johns Hopkins press.
1901. 70p.   3036

COLORED CITIZENS OF
NORFOLK, VA. Address . . . on
equal suffrage to the people of the
United States. New Bedford, Mass.,
E. Anthony & sons. 1865. 26p.
3037

DEMOCRATIC NATIONAL
COMMITTEE. The campaign text
book of the Democratic party for
the Presidential election of 1892.
New York, Dem. Nat. Comm.
1892. 312p.   3038

DISFRANCHISEMENT. A collection
of newspaper accounts and editorial
opinion relating to disfranchisement of the Negro in the various
states. 1898-1915. 36v.   3039

DU BOIS, W. E. BURGHARDT.
Disfranchisement. New York,
National American woman suffrage
assn. 1912. 11p.   3040

ECKENRODE, HAMILTON J. The
political history of Virginia during
the reconstruction. Baltimore,
Johns Hopkins press. 1904. 128p.
3041

FORD, JAMES W. The Negro and the
democratic front. New York
International publishers. 1938. viii,
9, 222p.   3042

FORTUNE, T. THOMAS. Black and
white; land, labor, and politics in

the South. New York, Fords, Howard & Hulburt. 1884. iv, 310p. 3043

GOSNELL, HAROLD F. Negro politicans, the rise of Negro politics in Chicago. Chicago, University of Chicago press. 1935. xxxi, 404p. 3044

GRIMKE, ARCHIBALD H. The ballotless victim of one-party governments. Annual address. Washington, The academy. 1913. 18p. 3045

GRIMKE, ARCHIBALD H. Why disfranchisement is bad. Philadelphia, E. A. Wright. 1904. 12p. 3046

HALLOWELL, RICHARD P. Why the Negro was enfranchised. Negro suffrage justified. Boston, Published at the request of colored citizens of Boston. 2d ed. G. H. Ellis co. 1903. 35p. 3047

HAMILTON, JAMES A. Negro suffrage and congressional representation. New York, Winthrop press. 1910. 68p. 3048

INTER-RACIAL COMMITTEE OF PHILADELPHIA. A reply to Mr. Taft on "The Negro in Politics." Philadelphia. The committee. n.d. 4p. 3049

KELLEY, WILLIAM D. (PA.) Speech . . . on suffrage in the District of Columbia. Delivered in the House of representatives, January 10, 1866. Washington, Congressional globe. 1866. 8p. 3050

LEVINSON, PAUL. Race, Class & Party. A history of Negro suffrage and white politics in the south. New York, Oxford University press, 1932, 302p. 3051

LONG, JOHN D. (ed.) The Republican Party; its history, principles and policies, with contributions by leading republicans of the time.

New York, M. W. Hazen co. 1892. 423p. 3052

LOVE, JOHN L. The disfranchisement of the Negro. Washington, The academy. 1889. 27p. 3053

MAC CORKLE, WILLIAM A. The Negro and the intelligence and property franchise. Address . . . before the Southern conference on race problems, Montgomery, Ala., May 9, 1900. Cincinnati, Robert Clarke & co. 1900. 41p. 3054

MARTIN, ROBERT E. Negro disfranchisement in Virginia. Washington, Howard University press. 1938. (Howard University social studies, v.1, no. 1). 3055

MATHEWS, JOHN M. Legislative and judicial history of the fifteenth amendment. Baltimore, Johns Hopkins press. 1909. x, 115p. 3056

MCILWAINE, RICHARD. Suffrage . . . an address before the Virginia constitutional convention, Norfolk, Jan. 6, 1902. Richmond. 1902. 13p. 3057

MCPHERSON, EDWARD. A hand book of politics for 1880; being a record of important political action, national and state from July 1878 to July, 1880. Washington, Jas. J. Chapmen. 1880. 215p. 3058

MERRIAM, GEORGE S. The Negro and the nation. A history of American slavery and enfranchisement. New York, Henry Holt & co. 1906. 436p. 3059

MILLER, KELLY. The political capacity of the Negro. Washington, Murray bros. 1910. 17p. 3060

MILLER, KELLY. Roosevelt and the Negro. Washington, Hayworth pub. house, 1907. 21p. 3061

MONTGOMERY ADVERTISER. Montgomery, Ala., published daily. 1901. Official report of the proceedings of the Constitutional convention of Alabama. June 1, 1901-Aug. 13, 1901. 70 issues. 3062

MORRELL, EDWARD DE V. (PA.) Negro suffrage. Should the 14 and 15 amendments be repealed? Speech . . . on appropriations for the support of the Military Academy for the fiscal year June 30, 1905 . . . delivered in the House of representatives, April 4, 1904. Washington, Govt. print. office. 1904. 64p. 3063

MORTON, O. P. (LA.) Speech . . . on democratic violence, proscription, and intolerance — spirit of the White-line democracy — duty of the Republican party to maintain the rights of colored men — startling democratic defalcations — unparalleled corruption and maladministration. Delivered in the United States senate, January 19, 1876 on the Mississippi election. Washington. 1876. 23p. 3064

MORTON, O. P. (LA.) The South; the political situation. An address delivered in Indianapolis, September 18, 1878. 16p. 3065

MORTON, RICHARD L. The Negro in Virginia Politics, 1865-1902. Charlottesville, Va. Univ. of Va. press, 1919. (Publications of the Univ. of Va. Phelps-Stokes Fellowship Papers, Number Four) 3066

MURPHY, EDGAR G. An open letter against the proposed constitutional convention. Montgomery, Ala. Alabama print. co. 1901. 12p. 3067

NEGROES IN POLITICS. A collection of newspaper accounts and editorial opinion relating to Negro politicians and politics. 1888-1919. 16v. 3068

NOWLIN, WILLIAM F. The Negro in American national politics. Boston, Stratford co. 1931. 4p. 148p. 3069

PATTON, J. HARRIS. The Democratic party; its political history and influence. New York, Fords, Howard & Hulburt. 1884. 349p. 3070

PIKE, JAMES S. The prostrate state; South Carolina under Negro government. New York, D. Appleton & co. 1874. 279p. 2d ed. New York, Loring & Massey. 1935. 279p. 3071

PILLSBURY, ALBERT E. The disfranchisement of the Negro. Boston, The author. 1903. 10p. 3072

POLLARD, EDWARD A. The lost cause regained. New York, G. W. Carleton & co. 1868. 214p. 3073

PORTER, KIRK H. A history of suffrage in the United States. Chicago, University of Chicago press. 1918. ix, 260p. 3074

REPUBLICAN NATIONAL COMMITTEE. What had McKinley done for the colored man? Query: What would Bryan do for the colored man? Document no. 118. New York, Republican National committee. 4p. n.d. 3075

RILEY, JEROME R. Evolution or racial development. (The Bright series, no. 81., April, 1901.) New York, J. S. Ogilvie pub. co. 1901. 150p. 3076

RILEY, JEROME R. The philosophy of Negro suffrage. Hartford, American pub. co. 1895. 110p. 3077

RUFFIN, FRANCIS G. The Negro as a political and social factor. Richmond, J. W. Randolph & English, 1888. 32p. 3078

SCHURZ, CARL. An open letter . . . to the independent voter. New York, Parker independent clubs. 1904. 43p. 3079

SIMKINS, FRANCIS B. The Tillman movement in South Carolina.

Durham, Duke University press. 1926. ix, 274p. 3080

SMALLEY, E. V. The Republican Manual; history, principles, early leaders, and achievements of the Republican party, with sketches of James A. Garfield and Chester A. Arthur. New York, American Book Exchange, 1880. 431p. 3081

SMALLS, SARAH V. (comp.) Speeches at the South Carolina constitutional convention by Gen. Robert Smalls. With the right of suffrage resolution passed by the convention. Charleston, Enquirer print. 1896. 39p. 3082

SMITH, SAMUEL D. Negro in Congress, 1870-1901. Chapel Hill, Univ. of North Carolina press. 1940. 3083

STOREY, MOORFIELD. Negro suffrage is not a failure. Address before the New England Suffrage conference March 30, 1903. Boston, Geo. H. Ellis co. 1903. 19p. 3084

THOMAS, A. F. The Virginia constitutional convention and its possibilities. Lynchburg, Va., J. P. Bell co., 1901. 77p. 3085

U. S. LIBRARY OF CONGRESS, Division of bibliography . . . list of discussions of the fourteenth and fifteenth amendments, with special reference to Negro suffrage. Washington, Govt. print. office. 1906. 18p. 3086

VIRGINIA CONSTITUTIONAL CONVENTION. A collection of newspaper accounts and editorial opinion relating to the Virginia constitutional convention, 1900-1902. 8v. 3087

WHAT A COLORED MAN should do to vote. The committee of twelve for the advancement of the interests of the Negro people. Cheyney, Pa., 1914. 3088

WHITE, GEORGE H. (N.C.) Defence of the Negro. Race; charges answered. Speech . . . delivered in the House of representatives, Jan. 29, 1901. Washington, Govt. print. office. 1904. 14p. 3089

XXXIII. Negro Church and Religious Life.

AFRICAN METHODIST EPISCOPAL CHURCH. The doctrine and discipline of the A.M.E. church. Philadelphia, A.M.E. book concern. 1932. 540p. 3090

AMERICAN BOARD OF COMMISSIONERS FOR Foreign Missions. Memorial volume of the first fifty years . . . Boston, The board. 1861. 462p. 3091

AMERICAN CHURCH INSTITUTE FOR NEGROES. Annual report . . . 6th, 1911-1912; 1925, 1928. New York, The Institute. 1912-25-28. 3092

AMERICAN MISSIONARY ASSOCIATION. Annual report . . . 1st-93d, 1846-1939. New York, The association. 1846-1939. 3093

AMERICAN MISSIONARY ASSOCIATION. A collection of newspaper accounts of the American missionary association from 1900 to 1910. 2v. 3094

AMERICAN MISSIONARY ASSOCIATION. History . . . with illustrative facts and anecdotes. New York, The association. 1874. 72p. 3095

ANDERSON, MATHEW. Presbyterianism, its relation to the Negro. Philadelphia, John McGill White & co. 1897. 263p.   3096

ARNETT, BENJAMIN W. (ed.) The budget; containing annual reports of the general officers of the African Methodist Episcopal church of the United States; with facts and figures, historical data of the colored Methodist church in particular and universal Methodism in general. Religious, educational, political and general information pertaining to the colored race. Philadelphia, A.M.E. book concern. 1886. 343p.   3097

ARNETT, BENJAMIN W. (ed.) Contennial address on the mission of Methodism to the extremes of society. Xenia, Ohio, Torchlight co. 1884. 40p.   3098

ARNETT, BENJAMIN W. (ed.) The contennial budget containing an account of the celebration, Nov. 1887, in the different parts of the church and the principal addresses delivered . . . together with religious, educational, political and general information pertaining to the colored race. Philadelphia, A.M.E. book concern. 1888.   3099

ARTHUR, GEORGE R. Life on the Negro frontier; a study of the objectives and the success of the activities promoted in the Young Men's Christian Associations operating in "Rosenwald" buildings. New York, Assn. press. 1934. 259p.   3100

BAIRD, ROBERT. Religion in America, or, an account of . . . the Evangelical churches in the United States. New York, Harper & Bros. 1856. 696p.   3101

BAPTIST HOME MISSION SOCIETY. Baptist home missions in North America, including a full report of the proceedings and addresses . . . 1832-1882. New York, Baptist home mission rooms. 1883. 619p.   3102

BEBEE, JOSEPH A. and others. The doctrines and discipline of the colored Methodist episcopal church in America. Rev. ed. Jackson, Tenn., A.M.E. book concern. 1894. 310p.   3103

BEARD, AUGUSTUS F. A crusade of brotherhood. A history of the American missionary association. New York, Pilgrim press. 1909. xii, 334p.   3104

BENNETT, WILLIAM W. Memorials of Methodism in Virginia from its introduction into the state in the year 1772 to the year 1829. 2d ed. Richmond, The author. 1870. 741p.   3105

BLYDEN, EDWARD W. Christianity, Islam and the Negro race. 2d ed. London, W. B. Whittingham & co. 1888. 432p.   3106

BOWEN, TREVOR. Divine white right. A study of race segregation and interracial cooperation in religious institutions. New York. London, Harper & bros. 1934.   3107

BRAGG, GEORGE F. Jr. Afro-American church work and workers. Baltimore, Church advocate print. 1904. 40p.   3108

BRAGG, GEORGE F. Jr. The first Negro priest on southern soil. Baltimore, The author. 1909. 72p.   3109

BRUNNER, EDMUND D. Church life in the rural South; a study of the opportunity of Protestantism based upon data from seventy counties. New York, Geo. H. Doran co. 1923. 117p.   3110

CATTO, WILLIAM T. History of the Presbyterian movement. A semi-centenary discourse delivered in Philadelphia, May 1857. Philadelphia, J. M. Wilson. 1857. 111p. 3111

DANIEL, WILLIAM A. The education of Negro ministers. Based upon a survey of theological schools for Negroes in the United States. New York, Geo. H. Doran co. 1925. 187p. (Institute of social and religious research). 3112

DIFFENDORFER, RALPH E. (ed.) The world service of the Methodist Episcopal church. Chicago, Committee on conservation and advance. 1923. 704p. 3113

DOUGLASS, HARLAN P. Christian reconstruction in the South. Boston, New York, Pilgrim Press, 1909. v-xvi, 17-407p. 3114

DUBOIS, W. E. Burghardt. The Negro church, report of a social study made under the direction of Atlanta University; together with the proceedings of the Eighth Conference for the study of the Negro problems, held at Atlanta University, May 26, 1903. Atlanta, Atlanta Univ. press. 1903. 212p. 3115

EARNEST, JOSEPH B. The religious development of the Negro in Virginia. Charlottesville, Va., Michie co. 1914. 233p. 3116

FADUMA, ORISHATUKEH. The Defects of the Negro Church. Washington, American Negro Academy. 1904. 17p. Occasional reports, no. 10. 3117

FULLER, T. O. History of the Negro baptists of Tennessee. Memphis, Haskin print. co. 1936. 3118

GILLARD, JOHN T. The Catholic church and the American Negro. Baltimore, St. Joseph's society press. 1929. 3119

GAINES, WESLEY J. African

methodism in the south; or, twenty-five years of freedom. Atlanta, Franklin pub. house. 1890. 305p. 3120

GREENE, S. L. (comp.) The doctrine and discipline of the African methodist episcopal church. 30th ed. rev. Philadelphia, A.M.E. book concern. 1932. 539p. 3121

HAMILTON, C. HORACE and ELLISON, JOHN M. The Negro church in rural Virginia. Blacksburg, Va. Virginia Polytechnic Institute. 1930. 40p. (Bulletin no. 273). 3122

HARLAN, HOWARD H. John Jasper, a case history in leadership. Charlottesville, Va., University of Virginia press. 1936. (Phelps-Stokes papers). 3123

HOOD, J. W. One hundred years of the African Methodist Episcopal church. New York, A.M.E. Zion book concern. 1895. xii, 625p. 3124

HOOD, J. W. (bb.) The Negro in the Christian pulpit, or the two characters and two destinies . . . as delineated in twenty-one pratical sermons. Raleigh, Edward & co. 1884. 363p. 3124a

HOSHOR, JOHN. God in a rolls-royce. The rise of Father Divine, madman, menace, or messiah. New York, Hillmancurl. 1936. 272p. 3125

HUNTON, WILLIAM A. Colored young men. History, methods and relationships of association work among them. New York, International committee, Y.M.C.A. 44p. 3126

IMES, G. LAKE. Improving the county church among Negroes. An address delivered at the Negro christian student conference,

Atlanta, May, 1914. Atlanta, 1919. 18p. 3127

JONES, RAYMOND J. A comparative study of religious cult behavior among Negroes with special reference to emotional group conditioning factors. Washington, Howard University press. 1939. 125p. (Howard University social studies, v. a, no. 2). 3128

JORDAN, LEWIS G. Negro baptist history, U.S.A., 1750-1930. Nashville, Sunday school pub. board. 1930. 394p. 3129

JOURNAL OF RELIGIOUS EDUCATION. Chicago. Religious education association. 1906. Collection has. v. 4-15. 1910-1920. 3130

MAYS, BENJAMIN E. The Negro's God as reflected in his literature. Boston, Chapman & Grimes. 1938. 269p. 3131

MAYS, BENJAMIN E. The Negro's church. New York, Institute for social & religious research. 1933. xiii, 321p. 3132

MOORLAND, JESSE E. The demand and supply of increased efficiency in the Negro ministry. Hampton, Va., Institute press. 1907. 8p. 2d ed. Washington, The Academy. 1909. 14p. 3133

MORGAN, JOSEPH H. History of the New Jersey conference of the A.M.E. church. Philadelphia, A.M.E. church review press. 1887. 254p. 3134

MURPHY, EDGAR G. The church and the Negro episcopate. 16p. 3135

NEGRO CHRISTIAN STUDENT CONFERENCE. The new voice in race adjustments; addresses and reports. May 14-18, 1914. New York, Student volunteer movement, 1914. vi, 230p. 3136

NEGRO CHURCHES. A collection of newspaper accounts and editorial opinion relating to various religious denominations of Negroes, Negro churchmen, pastors, bishops, etc., Conferences, and association with white church groups. 1872-1920. 24v. 3137

PARKER, ROBERT A. The incredible messiah. The deification of Father Divine. Boston, Little Brown & co. 1937. xiii, 323p. 3138

PERRY, CALBRAITH B. Twelve years among the colored people. A record of the work of Mount Calvary Chapel of St. Mary, The Virgin, Baltimore. New York, James Pott & co. 1884. 174p. 3139

PRESBYTERIAN CHURCH. Board of missions for freedmen. Annual report . . . 1865-1909. 3140

RANSOM, BISHOP REVERDY C. The Negro; The hope, or the despair of christianity. Boston, Ruth Hill, 1935. 98p. 3141

REED, JOHN H. Racial adjustment in the Methodist Episcopal Church. New York, Neale pub. co. 1914. 193p. 3142

RUSH, CHRISTOPHER. A short account of the rise and progress of the American M.E. Church in America, also a concise view of church order of government, from scripture, and from some of the best authors on the subject of church government, relative to Episcopacy. New York, The author. 1843. 106p. 3143

SATOLLI, FRANCIS. Loyalty to church and state. Baltimore. John Murphy & co. 1895. 249p. 3144

SMALL, JOHN B. The human heart illustrated by nine figures of the heart, representing the different stages of life, and two death-bed scenes: The wicked and the righteous. York, Pa., Dispatch print. 1989. 257p.　　3145

SMALL, JOHN B. Practical and exegetical pulpiteer. A synopses of discourses. P. Anstadt & sons. 1895. 312p.　　3146

STEVENSON, JOHN W. How to get and keep churches out of debt, and also a lecture on the secret of success in the art of making money. Albany, Weed, Parsons and co. 1886. 283p.　　3147

TANNER, BENJAMIN T. An apology for African methodism, Baltimore, xxiii. n.p. 1867. A.M.E. Book. depository.　　3148

TANNER, BENJAMIN T. An apology for African methodism. Baltimore, A.M.E. book depository. 1869. xxiii, 468p.　　3149

TANNER, BENJAMIN T. An outline of our history and government for African Methodist churchmen, ministerial and lay. In catechetical form. Philadelphia, Grant, Faires & Rodgers, 1884. 206p.　　3150

TUCKER, JOHN L. The relation of the church to the colored race. Jackson, Miss., Charles Winkley. 1882. 91p.　　3151

TURNER, HENRY M. Methodist polity, or the genius and theory of Methodism. Philadelphia, A.M.E. book concern. 1885. 318p.　　3152

TURNER, HENRY M. The hymn book of the African Methodist episcopal church, being a collection of hymns, sacred songs and chants, designed to supersede all others hitherto made use of in that church. 26th ed. Philadelphia, A.M.E. church. 1876. 957p.　　3153

VELDE, LEWIS G. V. The Presbyterian churches and the Federal union, 1861-1869. Cambridge, Harvard University press. 1932.　　3154

WHEELER, B. F. The Varick family. Story of the founder of the A.M.E. Zion church. Mobile, The author. 1906.　　3155

WOODSON, CARTER G. The history of the Negro church. 2d ed. Washington, Associated publishers. 1921. x. 330p.　　3156

YOUNG MEN'S CHRISTIAN ASSOCIATION. Annual report . . . Chicago, New York, Philadelphia branches. 1916, 17-18-19.　　3157

XXXIV.　Negro Secret Societies.

CRAWFORD, GEORGE W. Prince Hall and his followers; being a monograph on the legitimacy of Negro masonry. New York. Crisis. 1914. 95p.　　3158

GRIMSHAW, WILLIAM H. Official history of freemasonry among the colored people in North America, tracing the growth of masonry from 1717 down to the present day. New York. London. Broadway pub. co. 1903. xi, 392p.　　3159

HOYLE, WILLIAM. The Negro exclusion; a reply to Joseph Malin .

. . on the exclusion . . . of the Negroes (from) the order of good Templars. 2d. ed. London, E. Curtice & co. 1877. 48p.　　3160

INDEPENDENT ORDER OF GOOD TEMPLARS. The Negro question and the Independent order of good templars. Report of a conference held in London, Oct. 19-21, 1876. London, J. Kempster & co. 1876. 105p.　　3161

NEGRO FRATERNALS, CLUBS AND ORDERS. A collection of newspaper accounts relating to

Negro fraternals, clubs, and orders and their activities, 1868-1925. 8v. 3162

ROY, JOSEPH E. Deacon Philo Carpenter. New York, American missionary assn. 1886. 3163

SEVERSON, WILLIAM H. History of Felix lodge, no. 3, F.A.A.M., or Freemasonary in the District of Columbia from 1825 to 1908. Washington, R. L. Pendleton. 1908. 33p. 3164

THOM, W. T. The true reformers. Washington, Govt. print. office. 1902. (Bulletin 41, bureau of labor). 3165

UPTON, WILLIAM H. Light on a dark subject, being a critical examination of objections to legitimacy of the Masonry existing among the Negroes of America. Seattle, Pacific mason. 1899. 137p. 3166

UPTON, WILLIAM H. Negro masonry; being a critical examination of objections to the legitimacy of the masonry existing among the Negroes of America. Cambridge, M. W. Prince Hall lodge. 1902. xii, 264p. 3167

WESLEY, CHARLES H. The history of Alpha Phi Alpha; a development in Negro college life. Washington, Howard Univ. press. 1929. xix, 21, 294p. 3168

WILLIAMS, E. A. and others. History and manual of the colored Knights of Pythias, N.A., S.A., E.A., A. & A. Nashville, National bapt. pub. board. 1917. 1019p. 3169

WILLIAMSON, HENRY ALBRO. (comp.) The Negro in Masonic literature. Brooklyn, The author. 1922. 30p. 3170

XXXV. Negro Education.

ALVORD, J. M. Semi-annual report on schools for freedom . . . 8th, July 1, 1869. Washington, Govt. print. office. 1869. 89p. 3171

AMERICAN CHURCH INSTITUTE FOR NEGROES. Acknowledge of an honest debt. Negro education. New York, The institute. 1925. 57p. 3172

AMERICAN MISSIONARY ASSOCIATION. Annual report . . . 1st - 93d, 1846-1939. New York, The association. 1846-1939. 3173

ANDREWS, CHARLES C. The history of the New York African free schools, from their establishment in 1787, to the present time; embracing a period of more than forty years: also a brief account of the successful labors, of the New York manumission society. New York, M. Day. 1830. 148p. 3174

ARMSTRONG, MRS. MARY F. Hampton and its students. By two of its teachers, with fifty cabin and plantation songs, arranged by Thomas P. Fenner. New York, G. P. Putnan's sons. 1874. 255p. 3175

ARMSTRONG, SAMUEL C. Twenty-two years' work of the Hampton normal and agricultural institute at Hampton, Virginia. Records of Indian and Negro graduates and ex-students, . . . Hampton, Va.: Normal school press. 1891. 530p. 3176

ARMSTRONG, SAMUEL C. Ideas on education expressed by S. C. Armstrong. Hampton, Va., Armstrong league. 1908. 37p. 3177

ASSOCIATION OF COLLEGES AND SECONDARY SCHOOLS FOR NEGROES. Proceedings . . . 1st - 6th, 1934-39. 3178

BECKNER, WILLIAM M. Speech . . . on the land grants for school purposes. Delivered in the House of representatives, Feb. 4, 1895. Washington, Govt. print. office. 1895. 8p.   3179

BIDE, MATHEW. A study of the development of Negro education under Catholic auspices in Maryland and District of Columbia. Baltimore, Johns Hopkins press. 1935. 125p.   3180

BLAIR, LEWIS A. The prosperity of the South dependent upon the education of the Negro. Richmond, Everett Waddey. 1889. 147p. 3181

BLASCOER, FRANCES. Colored school children in New York. New York, Columbia university press. 1915. 176p.   3182

BLOSE, DAVID T. AND CALIVER, AMBROSE. Statistics of the education of Negroes, 1933-34 and 1935-36. Bulletin 1938, no. 13, U. S. office of education. Washington, Govt. print. office. 1939. 67p.
3183

BOARD OF MISSIONS FOR FREEDMEN OF THE PRESBYTERIAN CHURCH IN THE UNITED STATES. Annual report . . . 1st-44th, 1862-1909. Pittsburgh, The board. 1865-1909.   3184

BOARDMAN, SAMUEL W. The injunction upon the faculty and teachers of Maryville college by the board of trustees, Aug. 23, 1882. Athens, Penn. 1882. 8p.   3185

BOARDMAN, SAMUEL W. Pledge and report concerning "agreements" made with the donors, made to the board of directors of Maryville college. (The case of barring Negroes from this Tennessee college). Athens, Tenn. 1901. 24p.   3186

BOND, HORACE M. The education of the Negro in the American social order. New York, Prentice-Hall. 1934. xx, 501p.   3187

BOND, HORACE M. Negro education in Alabama. A study in cotton and steel. Washington, associated pub. 1939. 358p.   3188

BOTUME, ELIZABETH H. First days among the contrabands. Boston, Lee & Shepard. 1893. 286p.   3189

BRAWLEY, BENJAMIN G. Doctor Dillard of the Jeanes fund. New York; Chicago, Fleming H. Revell co. 1930. 151p.   3190

BROUSSEAU, KATE. L'education des Negres aux Etats unis. Paris, F. Alcan. 1904. xvi, 396p.   3191

BROWN, H. E. Plea for industrial education among the colored people. New York, The auth. 1884. 30p.   3192

BROWN, WILLIAM H. The education and economic development of the Negro in Virginia. Charlottesville, Va., Surber-Arundale co. 1923. 150p.   3193

BRUCE, ROSCOE C. The work of Tuskegee. Boston. 1902. 15p. 3194

BULLETIN; organ of the National association of teachers in colored schools. A monthly.   3195

BUSH, GEORGE G. . . . History of education in Florida. Washington, Govt. print. office. 1889. 54p. 3196

CALIVER, AMBROSE. Availability of education to Negroes in rural communities. Bulletin 1935, no. 12, U.S. office of education. Washington, Govt. print. office. 1936. 86p.   3197

CALIVER, AMBROSE. A background study of Negro college students. Bulletin, 1933, no. 8, U.S. office of education. Washington, Govt. print. office. 1933. 132p.   3198

CALIVER, AMBROSE. Bibliography on the education of the Negro.

Bulletin, 1930, no. 17, U.S. office of education. Washington, Govt. print. office. 1931. 3199

CALIVER, AMBROSE. Education of Negro teachers. (v. 6, National survey of the education of teachers, bulletin, 1933, no. 10, U.S. office of education.) Washington, Govt. print. office. 1933. ix, 123p. 3200

CALIVER, AMBROSE. Fundamentals in the education of Negroes. Bulletin, 1935, no. 6, U.S. office of education. Washington, Govt. print. office. 1935. 90p. 3201

CALIVER, AMBROSE. A personal study of Negro college students; a study of the relative between certain background factors of Negro college students and their subsequent careers in college. New York, Columbia univ. press. 1931. 146p. 3202

CALIVER, AMBROSE. Rural elementary education among Negroes under Jeanes supervising teachers. Bulletin 1933, no. 5, U.S. office of education. Washington, Govt. print. office. 1933. 57p. 3203

CALIVER, AMBROSE. Secondary education for Negroes. Bulletin 1932, no. 17, U.S. office of education. (Monograph no. 7, National survey of secondary education.) Washington. Govt. print. office. 1933. 121p. 3204

CALIVER, AMBROSE. Vocational education and guidance of Negroes. Washington, Govt. print. office. 1937. 137p. (Dept. of interior, office of education, bulletin 38). 3205

CALVIN, MARTIN V. Recent progress of public education in the South . . . a paper read before the Georgia teacher's association at Savannah, May 5, 1870. Augusta,

Ga., The auth. 1870. 19p. 3206

CAMPBELL, THOMAS M. The movable school goes to the Negro farmer. (Extension service, United States department of agriculture) Tuskegee Institute, Ala., Inst. press. 1936. 170p. 3207

CARNEGIE, ANDREW. Education of the Negro a national interest. An address delivered on the 25th anniversary of the founding of Tuskegee institute, April 5, 1906. Tuskegee, Ala. Inst. press. 1906. 15p. 3208

CHRISTIAN EDUCATOR. Annual report number, 1903. The industrial and higher education of the Negro. Cincinnati, Freedmen's aid and southern education society. 1903. 56p. 3209

CHURCH, J. W. The Halifax plan for the practical education of the Negro. Hampton, Va., Hampton institute press. 1910. 15p. 3210

CIVIS, (pseud.) The public school in its relations to the Negro. (Republ. from the southern planter and farmer) Richmond, The auth. 1877. 39p. 3211

CLARK, FELTON A. The control of state-supported teacher-training program for Negroes. New York, Teachers college press. 1934. 113p. 3212

COLORED MEN OF FLORIDA. Proceedings of the state conference, an address by the president, James Dean. Gainsville, Ga., Feb. 5, 1884. 23p. 3213

CONFERENCE FOR EDUCATION IN THE SOUTH. Proceedings . . . 2d - 14th. 1899-1910. 3214

CONFERENCE ON EDUCATION FOR NEGROES IN TEXAS. Proceedings . . . Prairie View, Tex. 1930. 126p. 3215

CONFERENCE OF PRESIDENTS OF

NEGRO LAND GRANT COLLEGES. Proceedings . . . 1st - 16th, 1922-1938.   3216

CONFERENCE OF STATE SUPERVISORS AND COLORED TEACHER TRAINERS and digest of the second annual report of the new farmers of America. Washington, Govt. print. office. 1936.   3217

COOKE, DENNIS H. The white superintendent and the Negro schools in North Carolina. Nashville, Geo. Peabody college press. 1930. 176p.   3218

COOLEY, ROSSA B. Homes of the freed. New York, New republic. 1926. xiv, 199p.   3219

COOLEY, ROSSA B. School acres. An adventure in rural education. New York; New Haven, Yale University press; London; Oxford Univ. press. 1930. 166p.   3220

COON, CHARLES L. Public taxation and Negro schools; paper read before the 12th annual conference for education in the South. Atlanta, Ga., April 14, 15, 16, 1909. Cheyney, Pa. Committee of twelve for the advancement of the interests of the Negro race. 1909. 11p.   3221

COOPER, RICHARD W. Negro school attendance in Delaware. A report to the State board of education. Newark, Del., Univ. of Delaware press. 1923. 389p.   3222

COREY, CHARLES H. A history of the Richmond theological seminary with remininscences of thirty years' work among the colored people of the South. Richmond, Va., J. W. Randolph co. 1895. 240p.   3223

CRAWFORD, GEORGE W. The Talladega manual of vocational guidance. Talladega, Ala. Board of trustees. 1937. 146p.   3224

CURRY, JABEG L. A brief sketch of George Peabody, and a history of the Peabody education fund through thrity years. Cambridge, Harvard Univ. press. 1898. x, 161p.   3225

DABNEY, CHARLES W. Educational principles for the South. Knoxville, Univ. of Tennessee press. 1904. 16p.   3226

DABNEY, CHARLES W. Illiteracy of the voting population in the United States. (U.S. bureau of education report, 1902). Washington, Govt. print. office. 1903. 29p.   3227

DABNEY, CHARLES W. Man in the democracy; his educational rights . . . Knoxville, Univ. of Tennessee press. 1904. 5p.   3228

DABNEY, CHARLES W. The public school problem in the South. An address delivered at Winston-Salem, April 18, 1901, before the conference for education in the South. Richmond, The conference. 1901. 15p.   3229

DABNEY, CHARLES W. Universal education in the South. Chapel Hill, Univ. of North Carolina press. 1936. 2v.   3230

DABNEY, CHARLES W. Land grant and other colleges and the national defense. Washington. Govt. print. off. 1899. 15p.   3231

DABNEY, CHARLES W. The education of Negro ministers, based upon a survey of theological schools for Negroes in the United States. New York, Geo. H. Doran co. 1925. 187p.   3232

DAVIS, JACKSON. The Jeanes visiting teachers. An address given at the inter-territorial Jeanes conference, Salisbury, Southern Rhodesia, May 27, 1935. New York, Carnegie corp. 1936. 29p.   3233

DAVIS, JACKSON. The Negro in country life. Hampton, Va., Hampton Inst. press. 1911. 14p.
3234

DAVIS, JACKSON. Practical training in Negro rural schools. Hampton, Va., Hampton Inst. press. 1913. 13p.
3235

DAVIS, WILLIAM A. The development and present status of Negro education in East Texas. New York, Columbia Univ. press. 1934. 150p.
3236

A DECLARATION OF PRINCIPLES. By representative Negroes of North Carolina, Raleigh, Sept. 26, 1919. Raleigh, office of Sup't. of public instruction. 1919. 12p.
3237

DELAWARE NEGRO CIVIC LEAGUE. The new bright future for Delaware Negroes; what the school code means to the colored people; Mr. Dupont's gift will build the best schools in America. Wilmington, The league. 1919. 8p.
3238

DOUGLASS, MRS. MARGARET C. Educational laws of Virginia. The personal narrative of Mrs. Margaret Douglass, a southern woman, who was imprisoned for one month in the common jail of Norfolk, under the laws of Virginia, for the crime of teaching free colored children to read. Boston, J. P. Jewett & co. 1854. 65p.
3239

DREHER, JULIUS D. The education of the Negro in the South. An address before the Southern educational association, Richmond, Va., 1900. Richmond, The assn. 1900. 9p.
3240

DUBOIS, W. E. (ed.) The college-bred Negro. (Atlanta Univ. publications, no. 5) Atlanta, Atlanta Univ. press. 1900. 115p. Rpt. U.S. bureau of education, 1902. Washington, Govt. print. office. 38p.
3241

DUBOIS, W. E. (ed.) The Negro common school. Report of a social study made under the direction of Atlanta University. (Atlanta Univ. publications, no. 6). Atlanta, Atlanta Univ. press. 1901. 120p.
3242

DUBOIS, W. E. (ed.) From servitude to service; being the old South lectures on the history and work of southern institutions for the education of the Negro. Boston, American unitarian assn. 1905. 232p.
3243

EVANS, HENRY R. Educational boards and foundations, 1920-22. (Bureau of education bulletin, no. 38, 1922) Washington, Govt. print. office. 1922.
3244

EVERETT, FAYE P. The colored situation. A book of vocational and civic guidance for the Negro youth. Boston, Meador pub. co. 1936. 309p.
3245

FAVROT, LEO M. Securing an adequate supply of prepared teachers for Negro rural schools. 1920. 3p.
3246

FAVROT, LEO M. Some problems in the education of the Negro in the South and how we are trying to meet them in Louisiana. Baton Rouge, Ramires-Jones print. co. 1919. 16p.
3247

FRISSELL, HOLLIS B. The aim and the methods of Hampton. An address delivered in New York City. February 12, 1904. New York, Armstrong assn. 1904. 12p.   3248

FOREMAN, CLARK. Environment factors in Negro elementary education. New York, Julius Rosenwald Fund. Chicago, W. W. Norton & co. 1932. 88p.   3249

FREEDMEN'S AID AND SOCIAL

EDUCATION SOCIETY. A collection of newspaper reports on the activities... 1900-1916. 3250

FROST, WILLIAM G. Remarks . . . against House bill, no. 25, as an invasion of personal liberty and academic freedom. Delivered before the senate committee of the state of Kentucky in support of co-education of races at Berea college. 7p. 3251

GALLAGHER, BUELL G. American caste and the Negro college. New York, Columbia univ. press. 1938. 463p. 3252

GALLOWAY, CHARLES B. The South and the Negro. An address delivered at the seventh annual conference for education in the South at Birmingham, April 26, 1904. New York, Southern education board. 1904. 16p. 3253

GENERAL EDUCATION BOARD. Summary of reports of state agents for Negro rural schools. New York, The board. 1915-16. 3254

GORE, GEORGE W. JR. In-service professional improvement of Negro public school teachers. New York, Columbia Univ. press. 1940. 3255

GRABILL, STANTON B. VON. Letters from Tuskegee; being the confessions of a Yankee. Birmingham, Ala., Roberts & sons. 1905. 43p. 3256

GUGGISBERY, FREDERICK G. The justice of the Negro. London, Student Christian movement press. 1929. 152p. 3257

GUNBY, A. A. Two addresses on Negro education in the South. New Orleans, H. C. Thomason. 1890. 66p. 3258·

HAMPTON (VA.) INSTITUTE. Acts of incorporation, laws of the state of Virginia, by laws, etc. of Hampton normal and agricultural

institute. Hampton, Va., Inst. press. 1883. 14p. 3259

HAMPTON (VA.) INSTITUTE. Annual reports . . . 1868-1939. Hampton, Va., Inst. press. 1868-1939. 3260

HAMPTON (VA.) INSTITUTE. The Hampton normal and agricultural institute and its work for the Negro and Indian youth. Hampton, Va., Normal school press. 1896. 7p. 3261

HAMPTON (VA.) INSTITUTE. Hampton normal and agricultural institute. A brief history. Hampton, Va., Normal school press. 1883. 38p. 3262

HAMPTON (VA.) INSTITUTE. Hampton Institute. 1868-1885. Its work for the two races. Hampton, Va., Normal school press. 1885. 34p. 3263

HAMPTON (VA.) INSTITUTE. Proceedings of a meeting held in New York City, Feb. 12, 1904, under the direction of the Armstrong association. Addresses of Andrew Carnegie, Charles W. Eliot and others. New York, The association. 1904. 38p. 3264

HAWKINS, ELMER T. Sex problems and the preparation for parenthood in Negro county high schools, in Maryland. Baltimore. 1934. 37p. 3265

HAWKINS, J. R. The seventh quardrennial report of the department of education of the African Methodist episcopal church, submitted to the general conference at Kansas City, Mo. Kittrell, N. C., Commissioner and secretary of education. 64p. 3266

HAYGOOD, ATTICUS G. Address ... at Claflin University, Orangeburg, S.C., April 30, 1890. Washington, U.S. dept. of interior, arts and industry. 1898. p. 885-891. 3267

HAYGOOD, ATTICUS G. Pleas for progress. Cincinnati, Granston & Stowe; New York, Phillips & Hunt. 320p. 3268

HEATWOLE, CORNELIUS J. A history of education in Virginia. New York, MacMillan co. 1916. 382p. 3269

HINSDALE, BURKE A. President Garfield and education. Boston, J. R. Osgood & co. 1882. 433p. 3270

HOLMES, DWIGHT O. W. Evolution of the Negro college. New York Teachers college, Columbia Univ. press. 1934. 221p. 3271

HUBBARD, GEORGE W. A history of the colored schools of Nashville, Tenn. Nashville. 1874. 34p. 3272

JACKSON, LUTHER P. A history of the Virginia state teachers association. Norfolk, Guide pub. co. 1937. 112p. 3273

JOHN F. SLATER FUND. Occasional papers . . . Baltimore. Charlottesville, Va., The trustees. 1894-1935. Collection has:

1. Documents relating to the origin and work of the Slater trustees. 1894.
2. A brief memoir of the life of John F. Slater. S. H. Howe. 1894.
3. Education of the Negroes since 1860. J.L.M. Curry. 1894.
4. Statistics of the Negroes in the United States. Henry Gannett. 1894.
5. Difficulties, complications, and limitations connected with the education of the Negro. J.L.M. Curry. 1895.
6. Occupations of the Negroes. Henry Gannett. 1895.
7. The Negroes and the Atlanta exposition. Alice M. Bacon. 1896.
8. Report of the fifth Tuskegee Negro conference. John Quincy Johnson. 1896.
9. A report concerning the colored women of the South. Mrs. E. C. Hobson and Mrs. C. E. Hopkins. 1896.
10. A study in black and white. D. C. Gilman. 1897.
11. The South and the Negro. C.B. Galloway. 1904.
12. Report of the society of the southern industrial classes, Norfolk, Va. 1907.
13. Report on Negro universities in the south. W.T.B. Williams. 1913.
14. County teacher training schools for Negroes. 1913.
15. Duplications of schools for Negro youths. W.T.B. Williams. 1914.
16. Sketch of Bishop Atticus G. Haygood. G.B. Winton. 1915.
17. Memorial address in honor of Dr. Booker T. Washington. 1916.
18. Suggested course for county training schools. 1917.
19. Southern women and racial adjustments. Mrs. L. H. Hammond. 1917. 2d ed. 1920.
20. Reference list of southern colored schools. 1918. 2d ed. 1921. 3d ed. 1925.
21. Report on Negro universities and colleges. W.T.B. Williams. 1922.
22. Early effort for industrial education. Benjamin G. Brawley. 1923.
23. Study of county training schools. Leo M. Favrot. 1923.

24. Five letters of university commission. 1927.
25. Native African races and culture. James Weldon Johnson. 1927.
26. A decade of Negro self-expression. Alain Locke. 1928.
27. Selected writings of James Hardy Dillard. 1932. 2d ed. 1933.
28. The Slater and Jeanes funds, an educator's approach to a difficult social problem. W.W. Alexander. 1934.
29. Public secondary schools for Negroes in the southern states of the United States. 1935. 3274

JOHN F. SLATER FUND. Proceedings and reports of the trustees of the John F. Slater fund for the education of freedmen. 1882-1939. 92v. 3275

JOHN, WALTON C. Hampton normal and agricultural institute; its evolution and contribution to education as a federal land-grant college. Washington, Govt. print. office. 1923. v, 118p. (U.S. Bureau of education. Bulletin, 1923. no. 27). 3276

JOHNSON. CHARLES S. The Negro college graduate. Cahpel Hill, Univ. of North Carolina press. 1938. 399p. 3277

JOHNSON. M. K. School conditions in Clark County. Georgia, with special reference to Negroes. (Bulletin of the university of Georgia. V. xvi. no. 112. 1916). Athens, Ga.. University of Ga. press. 1916. 50p. 3278

JONES, LANCE G. The Jeanes teacher in the United States, 1908-1933. An account of twenty-five years experience in the supervision of Negro rural schools. Chapel Hill, Univ. of North Carolina press. 1937. 146p. 3279

JONES, LANCE G. Negro schools in the southern states. Oxford, Oxford Univ. press. 1928. 160p. 3280

JONES, LAURENCE C. The spirit of Piney Woods, New York, Fleming H. Revell co. 1931. 3281

JONES, THOMAS J. Recent progress in Negro education. Washington, Govt. print. office. 1920. 16p. 3282

JONES, THOMAS J. (ed.) Educational adaptations. Report of ten years work of the Phelps-Stokes fund; 1910-1920. New York, Phelps-Stokes fund. 1923. 92p. 3283

JONES, THOMAS J. Recent movements in Negro education. Washington, Govt. print. office. 1913. 256p. (Reprint from report of the Commission of Education, June 30, 1912. Chapt. VII, v. 1.) 3284

JOURNAL OF NEGRO EDUCATION. A quarterly review of problems incident to the education of Negroes. Washington, Bureau of educational research, Howard University. 1932-1940. v. 1-9 3285

KENDALL, J. S. Scholastic population and apportionment of the available school fund for school year 1900-01. Department of education, Austin, Texas. Austin, State print. 1900. 16p. 3286

KNIGHT, EDGAR W. Public school education in North Carolina. Boston, Houghton, Mifflin co. 1916. viii, 384p. 3287

LAMB. DANIEL S. (comp.) Howard University medical department, Washington, D. C. A historical, biographical and statistical

souvenir. Washington. 1900. 301p.
3288

LAMONT, HAMMOND. Negro self-help. (Rpt. from N. Y. Evening post.) Tuskegee, Ala. Tuskegee Inst. press. 28p. 3289

LESTER, ROBERT M. The corporation and the Jeanes teacher. New York, Carnegie corp. 1938. 22p.
3290

LONG, HOLLIS M. Public secondary education for Negroes in North Carolina . . . New York, Columbia University press. 1932. 115p. 3291

LOUISIANA STATE DEPARTMENT OF EDUCATION. Aims and needs in Negro public education in Louisiana. Baton Rouge. 1920. 12p. 3292

LOUISIANA STATE DEPARTMENT OF EDUCATION. Report on special activities in Negro schools in Louisiana, 1919-20. Bulletin 14, 1920. Baton Rouge, Department of education. 1920. 28p. 3293

LUDLOW, HELEN W. (ed.) Tuskegee normal and industrial school for training colored teachers. Its story and its songs. Hampton, Va., Institute press. 1884. 69p. 3294

MADDOX, WILLIAM A. The free school idea in Virginia before the Civil war. Charlottesville, Va. 1918.
3295

MASON, U. G. Appeal to white citizens for better Negro schools in Birmingham, Ala. Birmingham. 1909. 7p. 3296

MAY, SAMUEL J. The right of colored people to education vindicated. Letters to Andrew T. Judson, esq., and others in Canterbury remonstrating with them on their unjust and unjustifiable procedure relative to Miss Crandall and her school for colored females.

Brooklyn, Conn., Advertiser press. 1833. 24p. 3297

MAYO, AMORY D. The future of the colored race. (U.S. bureau of education report, 1898-99). Washington, Govt. print. office. 1900. 21p. 3298

MAYO, AMORY D. How shall the colored youth of the South be educated? (Reprinted from the New England magazine for October, 1897. 11p. 3299

MAYO, AMORY D. Industrial education in the South. (U.S. bureau of education, circular of information, no. 5, 1888) Washington, Govt. print. office. 1888. 86p. 3300

MAYO, AMORY D. The work of certain northern churches in the education of freedman, 1861-1900. (U.S. bureau of education report). Washington, Govt. print. office. 1903. 30p. 3301

MCALLISTER, JANE E. The training of Negro teachers in Louisiana. New York, Columbia Univ. press. 1929. v. 1, 95p. 3302

MCCUISTON, FRED. Higher education of Negroes. A summary. Nashville, Southern association of secondary schools and colleges. 1923. 40p. 3303

MCKENZIE, FAYETTE A. Ideals of Fisk. Nashville, Fisk Univ. press. 1915. 10p. 3304

MCKINNEY, THEOPHILUS E. Higher education among Negroes. . . Charlotte, N. C., J. C. Smith Univ. 145p. 3305

MILLER, KELLY. The education of the Negro. (Commissioner of education report, 1900. Chapt. 16). Washington, Govt. print. office. 1902. 128p. 3306

MOORE, C. H. Report before the North Carolina state teachers association, at Greensboro, June,

1910. Durham, N. C. 1916. 18p.
3307
MOORE, JOANNA P. Fireside school
manual. Minutes of the first
mother's conference. Little Rock,
Ark., Tunnah & Pittard. 1894.
102p.   3308
MYRTILLA MINER: A memoir.
Boston; New York, Houghton
Mifflin co. 1885. 129p.   3309
NATIONAL ASSOCIATION OF
COLLEGIATE DEANS AND
REGISTRARS IN NEGRO
SCHOOLS. Proceedings . . . 1931.
Nashville, A.M.E. Sunday school
union. 1931.   3310
NATIONAL ASSOCIATION OF
COLORED AGRICULTURAL
COLLEGES. A collection of news-
paper accounts relating to the
activities. . . 1904-1905.   3311
NATIONAL ASSOCIATION OF
PERSONNEL DEANS AND
ADVISERS OF MEN IN NEGRO
EDUCATIONAL INSTITUTIONS.
Proceedings . . . 1st - 5th,
1935-1939. Tuskegee Institute, Ala.
The assn. 1935-39.   3312
NATIONAL ASSOCIATION OF
TEACHERS IN COLORED
SCHOOLS. Proceedings . . . 1904,
1905, 1910, 1921, 1922.   3313
NATIONAL ASSOCIATION FOR
TEACHERS OF COLORED
SCHOOLS. ASSOCIATION OF
NEGRO INDUSTRIAL AND
SECONDARY SCHOOLS.
NATIONAL EDUCATIONAL
CONGRESS. A collection of news-
paper accounts relating to the
activities . . . 1900-1920. 2v. 3314
NATIONAL CAPITAL SEARCH-
LIGHT. A monthly journal devoted
to education among colored people.
Washington, M. Grant Lucas. 1901.
Collection has: v. 1, no. 2.
(February, 1901)   3315

NATIONAL CONGRESS OF
COLORED PARENTS AND
TEACHERS. Proceedings . . .
Atlanta. The Congress. 1937.
Contains proceedings of annual
convention, 1927-1936.   3316
NATIONAL RESPONSIBILITY FOR
EDUCATION OF THE COLORED
PEOPLE. (a) Kelly Miller. (b)
W.T.B. Williams. (c) Isaac Fisher.
1918. 12p.   3317
NEGRO EDUCATION. A Collection
of magazine and newspaper
accounts relating to Negro
education, educators, institutions,
and other topics connected there-
with. 1868-1925. 157p.   3318

NEGRO ILLITERACY. A collection
of newspaper accounts and editorial
opinion relating to the illiteracy
rate among Negroes. 1895-1912.
2v.   3319
NEWBOLD, N. C. Five North Carolina
Negro educators. Chapel Hill, Univ.
of North Carolina press. 1939.
142p.   3320
NORTHROP, HENRY D. and others.
The college of life or practical self-
educator. A manual of self-
improvement for the colored race .
. . The whole embracing business,
social, domestic historic and
religious education. Chicago,
Chicago & Litho. co. 1895. 720p.
3321
OGDEN, ROBERT C. Samuel Chapman Armstrong. A sketch. New
York, Fleming H. Revell co. 1894.
40p.   3322
ORR, GUSTAVUS J. Education of the
Negro. An address. Atlanta, J. P.
Harrison & co. 1880. 15p.   3323
ORR, WILLIAM. Educational work of
the Young Men's Christian
association, 1916-1918. (U.S.
bureau of education. bulletin. no.

53, 1919). Washington, Govt. print. office. 1919. 3324

PEABODY EDUCATION FUND. Memorial of the trustees of the Peabody education fund, with the report of their committee on the subject of the education of the colored population of the southern states. Feb. 1880. Cambridge, Mass., John Wilson sons. 1880. 34p. 3325

PEABODY, FRANCIS G. Education for life, the story of Hampton Institute told in connection with the fiftieth anniversary . . . New York, Doubleday, Page & co. 1918. xxiv, 393p. 3326

QUARTERLY REVIEW OF HIGHER EDUCATION. Among Negroes. Charlotte, N. C. J. C. Smith University. 1933-1937. 5v. 3327

REDCAY, EDWARD E. County training schools and public secondary education for Negroes in the South. (John F. Slater studies in Negro education.) Washington. Slater fund. 1935. x, 168p. 3328

REID, IRA DeA. Adult education among Negroes. Washington, Associates in Negro folk education. 1936. 73p. 3329

ROYCE, SAMUEL. Deterioration and race education with practical application to the conditions of the people and industry. New York, The author. 1878. 504p. 3330

RUFFNER, HENRY, and OTHERS. Some historical documents bearing upon common school education in Virginia and South Carolina previous to the Civil war. (U.S. bureau of education report, 1899-1900). Washington, Govt. print. office. 1901. 109p. 3331

SADLER, MICHAEL E. Education of the colored race. 1902. 49p. (Board of education in the United States.) 3332

SCARBOROUGH, WILLIAM S. The educated Negro and his mission. Washington, The academy. 1903. 3333

SCHUYLER, GEORGE S. A Negro critic appraises institute schools. New York, American church institute for Negroes. 12p. 3334

SCOTT, EMMETT J. and STOWE, LYMAN B. Booker T. Washington, builder of a civilization. New York. Doubleday, Page & co. 1916. xx, 331p. 3335

SMITH, HENRY C. (ed.) Bulletin of Negro education and industry . . . devoted to the Christian national mutual and industrial order. v. 1, April, 1899. New York, The order. 1899. 12p. 3336

SOUTHERN EDUCATION ASSOCIATION. Journal of proceedings and addresses . . . 1890-1928. 3337

STATE DEPARTMENTS OF EDUCATION. Annual reports . . . for each of the southern states, 1870-1939. 3338

STORRS, RICHARD S. Our nation's work for the colored people. A discourse delivered in Brooklyn in behalf of the American Missionary association. New York, The assn. 1890. 22p. 3339

STOWELL, JAY S. Methodist adventures in Negro education. New York. Cincinnati, Methodist book concern. 1922. 190p. 3340

SUTTON, WILLIAM S. The education of the southern Negro. Austin, Tex., Univ. of Texas. 1912. 24p. 3341

TALBOT, EDITH A. Samuel Chapman Armstrong, a biographical study. New York, Doubleday, Page & co. 1904. 301p. 3342

THRASHER, MAX B. Tuskegee; its story and its work, Boston. Small, Maynard & co. 1900. xvi, 251p. 3343

TOURGEE, ALBION W. The education of the Negro. 1890. 7p. 3344

U. S. BUREAU OF EDUCATION. Annual report, 1895. (Pt. II. p. 1360). Higher education and the Negro. Washington, Govt. print. office. 1996. 2v. 3345

U. S. BUREAU OF EDUCATION. Education in various states. Education of the colored race. Slater fund and education of the Negro. Washington, Govt. print. office. 1896. 148p. 3346

U. S. BUREAU OF EDUCATION. General laws relating to agricultural and mechanical land grant colleges. (Report, 1901-02, Chapt. I). Washington, Govt. print. office. 1902. 3347

U. S. BUREAU OF EDUCATION. Negro education. A study of the private and higher schools for colored people in the United States. Washington, Govt. print. office. 1917. 2v. (Bulletin, 1916, no. 33). 3348

U. S. BUREAU OF EDUCATION. Report of the U. S. Commissioner of education. 1895-1939. Washington, Govt. print. office. 1895-1938. 3349

U. S. BUREAU OF EDUCATION. Schools for colored people. Atlanta private schools. Washington, Govt. print. office. 1915. 27p. 3350

U. S. BUREAU OF EDUCATION. Survey of Negro colleges and universities. Washington, Govt. print. office. 1929. 964p. (Bulletin, 1928, no. 7). 3351

U. S. FEDERAL BOARD FOR VOCATIONAL EDUCATION . . . A study of home-economics edu-

cation in teacher training institutions for Negroes. Washington, Govt. print. office. 1923. 124p. 3352

U. S. FEDERAL BOARD FOR VOCATIONAL EDUCATION. Vocational education in agriculture for Negroes; recommendations for the establishment of agricultural schools and programs for Negroes. May, 1926. Washington, Govt. print. office. 1926. ix, 92p. (Bulletin no. 111, agricultural service.) 3353

VIRGINIA STATE TEACHERS ASSOCIATION. Bulletin. . . 1923-1939. 16v. 3354

WARNER, C. D. Education of the Negro, through his fashions in literature. 1902. 31p. 3355

WASHINGTON, BOOKER T. Character building; being addresses delivered Sunday evenings to students of Tuskegee institute. Garden City, N. Y., Doubleday, Page & co. 1902. 291p. 3356

WASHINGTON, BOOKER T. Education of the Negro. Albany, N. Y., J. B. Lyon & co. 1900. 44p. 2d ed. New Orleans, Louisiana purchase exposition co. 1904. 44p. 3357

WASHINGTON, BOOKER T. My larger education; being chapters from my experience. New York, Doubleday, Page & co. 1911. viii, 313p. 3358

WASHINGTON, BOOKER T. Putting the most into life. New York. T. Y. Crowell & co. 1906. 35p. 3359

WASHINGTON, BOOKER T. Some results of the Armstrong idea. Rpt. from the Southern Workman. Hampton, Va. Hampton Institute press. 1909. 13p. 3360

WASHINGTON, BOOKER T. Sowing and reaping. Boston, L. C. Page & co. 1900. 29p. 3361

WASHINGTON, BOOKER T. The

story of my life and work. Toronto. Naperville, Ill., J. L. Nichols & co. 1900. 423p. 3362

WASHINGTON, BOOKER T. Tuskegee and its people, their ideals and achievement. New York, London, D. Appleton & co. 1910. xiv, 354p. 3363

WASHINGTON, BOOKER T. Working with the hands; being a sequel to "Up from slavery," covering the author's experiences in industrial training at Tuskegee. New York, Doubleday, Page & co. 1904. x, 246p. 3364

WEEKS, STEPHEN B. History of public school education in Alabama. (U.S. bureau of education bulletin, 1915, no. 12). Washington, Govt. print. office. 1915. 209p. 3365

WILKERSON, DOXEY A. Special problems of Negro education. Staff study no. 12, prepared for the Advisory committee on education. Washington, Govt. print. office. 1939. 171p. 3366

WOODSON, CARTER G. The education of the Negro prior to 1861; a history of the education of the colored people of the United States from the beginning of slavery to the Civil War. New York, London, G. P. Putnam's sons. 1915. v, 454p. 3367

WOODSON, CARTER G. The miseducation of the Negro. Washington, Associated publishers. 1933. 207p. 3368

WRIGHT, ARTHUR D. The Negro rural school fund, inc. (Anna T. Jeanes foundation). 1907-1933. A record of the establishment of the fund, a sketch of its donor, the minutes of the proceedings of the Board of trustees from 1908 to 1932, and the policies developed under the directions of the Board of trustees. Washington, Negro rural school fund. 1933. 177p. 3369

WRIGHT, RICHARD R. A brief historical sketch of Negro education in Georgia. Savannah, Robinson print. house. 1894. 58p. 3370

WRIGHT, RICHARD R. Self-help in Negro education. Cheyney, Pa., Committee of twelve for the advancement of the interests of the Negro race. 1909. 29p. 3371

XAVIER UNIVERSITY, NEW ORLEANS. Occupational monographs. New Orleans, Xavier Univ. press. 1937-38. 25v. 3372

XXXVI. Negro Folklore.

ADAMS, EDWARD C. L. Congaree sketches; scenes from Negro life in the swamps of the Congaree and tales by Tad and Scip of heaven and hell with other miscellany. Chapel Hill, University of North Carolina press. 1927. 116p. 3373

BARZUN, JACQUES. Race, a study in modern superstition. New York, Harcourt, Brace & co. 1937. x, 353p. 3374

BONNER, MRS. SHERWOOD MCDOWELL. Dialect Tales. New York, Harper & bros. 1883. 187p. 3375

CHRISTENSON, A.M.H. Afro-American folklore told round cabin fires on the Sea islands of South Carolina. Boston, The author. 1898. 116p. 3376

CORROTHERS, JAMES. The black cat club. Negroes humor and

folklore. New York, London. Funk & Wagnalls co. 1902. 264p.   3377

CULBERTSON, ANNE V. Banjo talks. Indianapolis, Bobbs-Merril co. 1915. 171p.   3378

DOBIE, FRANK J. Texas and southwestern lore. Austin, Texas folklore society. 1927. 259p.   3379

FINCK, HENRY T. Primitive lore and love stories. New York, C. Scribner sons. 1899. xvii, 851p.   3380

HARMON, MARION F. Negro wit and humor, also containing folklore, folk songs, race peculiarities, race history . . .Louisville, Harmon pub co. 1914. 124p.   3381

HARRIS, JOEL C. Balaam and his master and other sketches and stories. Boston, New York, Houghton Mifflin co. 1891. 293p.   3382

HARRIS, JOEL C. Mingo and other sketches in black and white. Boston, New York. Houghton Mifflin co. 1884. 273p.   3383

HARRIS, JOEL C. Uncle Remus and his friends. Boston. New York, Houghton Mifflin co. 1892. 357p. New ed. rev. New York, D. Appleton & co. 1921. xxi, 3-265p.   3384

HARRIS, JOEL C. Witch wolf, and uncle Remus story. Cambridge. Bacon & Brown. 1921. 30p.   3385

HOBSON, ANNE. In old Alabama; being a chronicle of Miss Mouse, the little black merchant. New York, Doubleday. Pope & co. 1903. 237p.   3386

HURSTON, ZORA N. Johah's gourd vine. Philadelphia. J. B. Lippincott co. 1934. 316p.   3387

HURSTON, ZORA N. Mules and men. Philadelphia. J. B. Lippincott co. 1935. 342p.   3388

HURSTON, ZORA N. Tell my horse. Philadelphia, J. B. Lippincott & co. 1938.   3389

JOHNSON, GUY B. Folk culture on St. Helena island, S. C. Chapel Hill, University of North Carolina press. 1930. xi, 183p.   3390

JOHNSON, GUY B. John Henry; a Negro legend. Chapel Hill, University of North Carolina press. 1928.   3391

JONES, CHARLES C. Jr. Negro myths from the Georgia coast told in the vernacular. Boston. New York, Houghton Mifflin & co. 1888. x, 171p. 2d ed. 1925. 174p.   3392

JOURNAL OF AMERICAN FOLKLORE. New York, 1895-1912.   3393

KREY, MRS. LANNA L. And tell of time. Boston, Houghton Mifflin co. 1938. 712p.   3394

ODUM, HOWARD W. Rainbow round my shoulder; Blue trail of black Ulysses. Indianpolis, Bobbs-Merrill co. 1928.   3395

OWEN, MARY A. Voodoo tales as told among the Negroes of the southwest. Collected from original sources. New York, G.P. Putnam's sons. 1893. x, 310p.   3396

PICKENS, WILLIAM. American Aesop. Negro and other humor. Boston, The author. 1926. 183p.   3397

PICKETT, LASALLE C. In de miz series. Washington, Neale co. 1900-01. 4v.   3398

PUCKETT, NEWBELL N. Folk beliefs of the southern Negro. Chapel Hill. University of North Carolina press. Oxford University press. 1926. xvi, 644p.   3399

STONEY, SAMUEL G. and SHELBY, GERTRUDE M. Black genesis, a chronicle. New York, MacMillan co. 1930. 192p.   3400

TALLEY, THOMAS W. Negro folk

rhymes. New York, MacMillan co.
1922. xiii, 347p.   3401
YOUNG, MARTHA. Behind the dark
pines. London. New York, D.
Appleton & co. 1912. xiv, 287p.
                          3402

XXXVII. Negro Folk Music.

ALLEN, WILLIAM F. and others.
Slaves songs of the United States.
New York, A. Simpson & co. 1867.
liv, 115p.   3403
BALLANTA-(TAYLOR) NICHOLAS.
G. J. Saint Helena island spirituals.
Recorded and transcribed at the
Penn School, St. Helena island,
South Carolina. Penn School. 1925.
93p.   3405
BOLTON, D. G. (ed.) Old songs
hymnal; words and melodies from
the state of Georgia. Music arr. by
Harry T. Burleigh. New York,
Century co. 1929.   3406
BOTSFORD, FLORENCE H. Folk
songs of many peoples, with English
versions by American poets. New
York, Woman's press. 1921-23. 2v.
                          3407
BURLEIGH, HARRY T. Negro folk
songs. New York, G. R. Ricordi &
co. 1921. 4v.   3408
BURLEIGH, HARRY T. Negro
minstrel melodies; a collection of
twenty-one songs with piano
accompaniment . . . New York,
Schirmer. 1909. 52p.   3409
BURLIN, MRS. NATALIE C.
Hampton series. Negro folk-songs.
Books I, II, III, and IV. New York,
G. Schirmer. 1918-19.   3410
CABIN and plantation songs as sung
by Hampton students. Arranged by
Thomas Fenner, F. G. Rathburn
and Bessie Cleveland. To which are
added a few Indian songs, gathered
at Hampton Institute, Negroes'

battle hymn, and the grace as sung
at Hampton. New York, G. P.
Putnam's sons. 1901. vi, 166p.
                          3411
CAMPBELL, OLIVE D. and SHARP,
CECIL J. (comps.) English folk
songs from the southern
Appalachians. . . New York,
London, G. P. Putnam's sons. 1917.
xxviii, 341p.   3412
COHEN, LILY Y. Lost spirituals.
Forty-one compositions composed
by Negroes. New York, W. Neale.
1928. xix, 21-143p.   3413
COX, JOHN H. (ed.) Folk songs of the
South; collected under the auspices
of the West Virginia folklore
society. Cambridge, Howard
University press. 1925. xxxi, 545p.
                          3414
DETT, ROBERT N. The Dett
collection of Negro spirituals.
Chicago, Hall & McCreary co. 1936.
4v.   3415
DETT, ROBERT N. Religious folk-
songs of the Negro as sung at
Hampton Institute. Hampton, Va.,
Hampton Institute press. 1927.
xxvii, 236p.   3416
FENNER, THOMAS P. Religious
folk-songs of the Negro as sung on
the plantation. n.ed. Hampton, Va.,
Hampton Institute press. 1909.
178p.   3417
HALLOWELL, EMILY (ed.) Calhoun
plantation songs. Sung by the
students of Calhoun colored school.

Boston, C. W. Thompson & co. 1907. 74p.   3418

HANDY, WILLIAM C. Blues: an anthology tracing the development of the most spontaneous and appealing branch of Negro folk music from the folk blues to modern jazz. New York, Boui. 1926. 180p.   3419

HOWARD, JOHN T. Our American music. New York, Thomas Y. Crowell co. 1931.   3420

JAMES, U. P. The Negro melodist; containing a great variety of the most popular airs, songs, and melodies, comic, humorous, sentimental and patriotic. Cincinnati, The author. 66p.   3421

JAMES, U. P. The new Negro forget-me-not songster; containing all the new Negro songs ever published with a choice collection of ballads, now sung in concert. Cincinnati, The author. 41p.   3422

JENKS, F. H. and KIDSON, FRANK. Negro music of the United States. (In Grove's dictionary of music and musicians, v. 3). London. 1907.
3423

JESSE, EVA A. My spirituals. New York, Robbings-Engel. 1928.   3424

JOHNSON, JAMES W. (ed.) The book of American Negro spirituals. New York, Viking press. 1925. 187p.
3425

JOHNSON, JAMES W. (ed.) The second book of Negro spirituals. New York, Viking press. 1926. 189p.   3426

JOHNSON, JOHN R. Rolling along in song; a chronological survey of American Negro music. . . New York, Viking press. 1937. 224p.
3427

JUBILEE SONGS. As sung by the Jubilee singers of Fisk University. New York. Biglow & Main. 1872.

28p. enl. ed. Boston. O. Ditson & co. 1887. 80p.   3428

KENNEDY, ROBERT E. Black cameos. New York, Boni. 1924. xxv, 210p.   3429

KENNEDY, ROBERT E. Mellows, a chronicle of unknown singers. New York, Albert & Charles Boni. 1925. 183p.   3430

KENNEDY, ROBERT E. More mellows. New York, Dodd, Mead & co. 1931. vi, 179p.   3431

KREHBIEL, HENRY E. Afro-American folksongs; a study in racial and national music. New York, London, G. Schirmer. 1914. xii, 176p.   3432

LOMAX, JOHN A. and ALAN. American ballads and folk songs. New York, MacMillan co. 1934. xxxix, 625p.   3433

LOMAX, JOHN A. and ALAN. (ed.) Negro folk songs as sung by Lead Belly, "King of the twelve-string guitar players of the world". . . New York, MacMillan co. 1936. xiv, 242p.   3434

MARSH, J.B.T. The story of the Jubilee singers. London, Hodder & Stoughton. 1876. 232p.   3435

MARSH, J.B.T. The story of the Jubilee singers with their songs. Boston, Houghton, Osgood & co. 1880. 243p. rev. ed. Boston, New York, Houghton Mifflin co. 1880. viii, 265p. Cleveland, Cleveland print. & pub. co. 1892. 311p. 3436

MCILHENNY, EDWARD A. (comp.) Befo' de war spirituals; words and melodies. Boston, Christopher pub. house. 1933. 255p.   3437

METFESSEL, MILTON. Phonophotography in folk music; American Negro songs in a new notation. Chapel Hill. University of North Carolina press. 1928. 181p.
3438

MILLER, JAMES W. Sing with Africa. Negro spirituals taken from plantation melodies. Chicago, Rodeheaven co. 1906. 3p. 3439

ODUM, HOWARD W. and JOHNSON, GUY B. The Negro and his songs. A study of typical Negro songs in the South. Chapel Hill, University of North Carolina press. 1925. vii, 306p. 3440

ODUM, HOWARD W. and JOHNSON, GUY B. Negro workaday songs. Chapel Hill, University of North Carolina press. 1926. xii, 306p. 3441

PIKE, GUSTAVUS D. The Jubilee singers and their campaign for twenty thousand dollars. Boston, Lee & Shepard. 1873. 219p. 3442

PIKE, GUSTAVUS D. The singing campaign for ten thousand pounds; or the Jubilee singers in Great Britain. London, Hodder & Stoughton, Boston, Lee & Shepard. 1873. 202p. 3443

PROCTER, HENRY H. Theology of the songs of southern slaves. (Rpt. from the Southern Workman, Nov.-Dec. 1907). Hampton, Va. 59p. 3444

RODEHEAVER, HOMER A. . . Negro spirituals. Chicago, Rodeheaver co. 1923. 51p. 3445

RODEHEAVER, HOMER A. Plantation melodies. Chicago, The author. 1918. 48p. 3446

SAINT SIMONS MISSION. Selected spirituals for use in St. Simons mission. 1935. 38p. 3447

SCARBOROUGH, DOROTHY. On the trail of Negro folk songs. Cambridge, Harvard University press. 1925. 289p. 3448

SOCIETY FOR THE PRESERVATION OF SPIRITUALS. The Carolina low-country. New York, MacMillan co. 1931. 329p. 3449

STILL, WILLIAM G. Twelve Negro spirituals arranged. New York, Handy bros. Music co. 1937. 6p. 3450

TALBOT, EDITH A. True religion in Negro hymns. (Rpt. from Southern Workman). Hampton, Va., Hampton Institute press. 1922. 16p. 3451

TALLEY, THOMAS W. Negro folk-rhymes, wise and otherwise. New York, MacMillan co. 1922. xii, 347p. 3452

WEEDEN, HOWARD. Songs of the old South. New York, Doubleday, Page & co. 1900. 3453

WHITE, NEWMAN I. American Negro folk-songs. Cambridge, Harvard university press. 1928. x, 504p. 3454

WORK, FREDERICK J. (ed.) Folk songs of the American Negro. Nashville, Work bros. 1907. 48p. 3455

WORK, JOHN W. Folk songs of the American Negro. Nashville, Fisk University press. 1915. 131p. 3456

XXXVIII. The Negro and Modern Music, Painting, Sculpture, The Theatre and Sports.

ARMSTRONG, LOUIS. Swing that music. New York, Longmans, Green & co. 1936. 3458

ARVEY, VERNA. Studies of contemporary American composers. William Grant Still. New York, J. Fischer & co. 1939. 48p. 3459

BRAWLEY, BENJAMIN G. The Negro in literature and art in the United States. New York, Duffield & co. 1921. 197p. 3460

BURLEIGH, HARRY T. Arrangements for miscellaneous songs. New York, G. Ricord & co. 1917-25. 3461

COLERIDGE-TAYLOR, S. Twenty-four Negro melodies, transcribed for the piano. op. 59. Boston, O. Ditson co. New York, C. H. Ditson & co. 1905. ix, 127p. 3462

COLORED INTERCOLLEGIATE ATHLETIC ASSOCIATION. Hampton, Va., Hampton Institute press. 1914-1939. Proceedings . . . 1914-1939. 3463

DETT, ROBERT N. I'm a-goin' to see my friends ag'in. New York, J. Church co. 1924. 3464

DETT, ROBERT N. Listen to the lambs. Anthem. New York, G. Schirmer. 1923. 3465

EAKIN, FRANK and MILDRED. Junior teacher's guide on Negro Americans, based on "We sing America." New York, Friendship press. 47p. 3466

EAKIN, FRANK and MILDRED. Primary teacher's guide on Negro Americans, based on "We sing America." New York, Friendship press. 48p. 3467

FLEISCHER, NAT. Black dynamite. The story of the Negro in the prize ring from 1782 to 1938. New York, The author. 1938. 4v. 3468

GELLERT, LAWRENCE. Negro songs of protest. New York, American music league. 1936. 3469

GRISSOM, MARY A. The Negro sings a new heaven. Chapel Hill, University of North Carolina press. 1930. 3470

HANDY, WILLIAM C. Negro authors and composers of the United States. New York, Handy bros. music co. 1938. 24p. 3471

HARE, MAUDE C. Negro musicians and their music. Washington, The associated publishers. 1936. xii,

439p. plates, ports. facsim. 3472

HENDERSON, EDWIN B. The Negro in sports. Washington, Associated publishers. 1939. 371p. 3473

HUTTON, L. The Stage Negro (Rpts. "In his curiosities of the American state, 1891). pp. 87-144. 3474

JOHNSON, JAMES W. Lift every voice and sing. Quartette for mixed voices. New York, D. Marks music corp. 1932. 3475

KAUFMAN, MRS. HELEN (LOEB) From Jehovah to jazz. New York. 1937. 3476

LEE, GEORGE W. Beale street, where the blues began. New York, R. O. Ballou. 1934. 296p. 3477

LOCKE, ALAIN L. Negro art; past and present. Washington, Associates in Negro folk education. 1936. 125p. 3478

LOCKE, ALAIN L. The Negro and his music. Washington. The Associates in Negro folk education. 1936. 145p. (Bronze booklet no. 2). 3479

MURRAY, FREEMAN H. Emancipation and the freed American sculpture; a study in interpretation. Washington, The author. 1916. xxviii, 239p. 3480

NEGRO ATHLETES. A collection of newspaper accounts relating to Negro athletes and pugilists. 1900-1925. 8v. 3481

NEGRO ART. A collection of newspaper and magazine accounts of Negro art. 1851-1925. 22v. 3482

NEGRO MUSIC. A collection of newspaper accounts relating to Negro music and musicians. 1890-1925. 15v. 3483

NEGRO ON THE STAGE. A collection of newspaper accounts relating to the Negro and the theatre. 1900-1925. 10v. 3484

NILES. JOHN J. Singing soldiers. New

York. London, C. Scribner's sons. 1927. x, 171p.　　　3485

RAMSEY, FREDERIC and SMITH, CHARLES E. (eds.) Jazz men. New York, n.d. xv, 360p.　　　3486

RICE, EDWARD L. Monarchs of ministrelsy. From "Daddy" Rice to date. New York, Kenny pub. co. 1911. 366p.　　　3487

SAYERS, W. C. B. Samuel Coleridge Taylor, musician. His life and letters. London. New York, Cassell & co. 1915. xii, 328p.　　　3488

STOKES, ANSON P. Art and the color line. Washington, Marion Anderson committee. 1939. 26p.　　　3489

TANNER, HENRY O. A collection of newspaper accounts relating to Henry O. Tanner and his paintings. 1914-1919. 2v.　　　3490

TROTTER, JAMES M. Music and some highly musical people; containing brief chapters on description of music; the music of nature; history of music; the power of music and sketches of lives of remarkable musicians of the colored race. Boston, Lee & Shepard. 1885. 504p.　　　3491

WHITE, CLARENCE C. (comp.) Forty Negro spirituals . . . Philadelphia, T. Presser & co. 1927. 129p.　　　3492

WHITING, HELEN A. Negro art, music and rhyme, for young folks. Book II. Washington, Associated publishers. 1938. 38p.　　　3493

YOUNG, GEORGE. The marvelous musical prodigy, Blind Tom, the Negro boy pianist, whose performance at the great St. James and Egyptian halls, London and Salle Hertz, Paris, have created a profound sensation. (Anecdotes, songs, sketches of the life, testimonials of musicians and . . . opinions of the press of "Blind Tom.") New York, French & Wheat. 1870. 30p.　3494

XXXIX. Negro Population and Migration.

DUBLIN, LOUIS I. (ed.) Population problems in the United States and Canada. An authoritative and contemporary discussion of the most critical phases of the population problem, by twenty-five authors. New York, Houghton Mifflin co. 1926. xi, 318p.　　　3495

EPSTEIN, ABRAHAM. The Negro migrant in Pittsburgh. A study in social economics. Pittsburgh, University of Pittsburgh. 1918. 75p.　　　3496

THE EXODUS. Boston. Garrison & co. for the Boston exodus committee. Collection has: no. 2 (January, 1881.)　　　3497

FLETCHER, FRANK H. Negro exodus. Kansas city. 1881. 24p.　　　3498

JOHNSON, GERALD W. The wasted land. Chapel Hill, University of North Carolina press. 1937. vi, 21-3-110p.　　　3499

JONES, THOMAS J. Negroes and the census of 1910. (Rept. from Southern Workman, Aug. 1912). Hampton, Va., Hampton Institute press. 1912. 16p.　　　3500

KENNEDY, LOUIS V. The Negro peasant turns cityward; the effects of recent migrations to northern cities. New York, Columbia University press. 1930. 270p. 3501

KISER, CLYDE V. Sea island to city. A study of St. Helena islanders in

Harlem and other urban centers. New York, Columbia University press. 1932. 272p. 3502

LEWIS, EDWARD E. The mobility of the Negro. A study in the American labor supply. New York, Columbia University press. 1931. 144p. 3503

LORING, FRANCIS W. and ATKINSON, C. F. Cotton culture and the South, considered in reference to emigration. Boston, A. Williams & co. 1869. 183p. 3504

MARTIN, ASA E. Our Negro population. A sociological study of the Negroes of Kansas City, Missouri. Kansas City, Mo., Franklin Hudson pub. co. 1913. 189p. 3505

NEGRO MIGRATION. A collection of newspaper accounts and editorial opinions relating to Negro migration and migrants. 1900-1925. 14v. 3506

NEGRO POPULATION. A collection of newspaper accounts relating to the various trends, changes, shifts, etc. in the Negro population. 1900-1918. 3v. 3507

REID, IRA DE A. The Negro immigrant . . . 1899-1937. (Columbia University studies, no. 449). New York, Columbia University press. 1939. 261p.. 3508

REUTER, EDWARD B. Population problems. Philadelphia, J. B. Lippincott co. 1923. xviii, 338p. 3509

ROBINSON, CHARLES S. The Pharaohs of bondage and the exodus. New York, Century co. 1887. 199p. 3510

ROSS, FRANK A. and KENNEDY, LOUIS V. A bibliography of Negro migration. New York, Columbia University press. 1934. 6-3-251p. 3511

SCOTT, EMMETT J. Negro migration during the war. (Preliminary economic studies of the war, no. 16). New York, Oxford University press. 1920. 189p. 3512

U. S. BUREAU OF THE CENSUS. Negroes in the United States, 1900. Washington, Govt. print. office. 1904. 333p. 3513

U. S. BUREAU OF THE CENSUS. Negroes in the United States, 1910. Washington, Govt. print. office. 1915. 207p. 3514

U. S. BUREAU OF THE CENSUS. Negro population, 1790-1915. Washington, Govt. print. office. 1918. 844p. 3515

U. S. BUREAU OF THE CENSUS. Negroes in the United States, 1920-32. Washington, Govt. print. office. 1935. 845p. 3516

U. S. DEPARTMENT OF LABOR, Division of Negro economics. Negro migration in 1916-17. Reports by R.H. Leavell, T.R. Snavely, T.J. Woofter, Jr., W.T.B. Williams and F.D. Tyson. Washington, Govt. print. office. 1919. 158p. 3517

WOOD, JUNIUS B. The Negro in Chicago. How he and his race came to dwell in great numbers in a northern city . . . Chicago, Chicago daily news. 1916. 31p. 3518

WOODSON, CARTER G. A century of Negro migration. Washington, Assn. for the study of Negro life and history. 1918. vii, 221p. 3519

WOOFTER, THOMAS J. Jr. Negro migration. Changes in rural organization and population of the cotton belt. New York. W. D. Gray. 1920. 195p. 3520

220

ASSOCIATION FOR THE PROTECT-
ION OF NEGRO WOMEN. Reports
. . .1912-1916. Atlanta, The
Association. 1912-16.   3521

BROWN, HAILLE Q. (comp.) Homespun heroines and other women of
distinction. Xenia, Ohio, Adiline
pub. co. 1926. viii, 248p.   3522

CONSUMERS' LEAGUE OF
EASTERN PENNSYLVANIA.
Colored women as industrial
workers in Philadelphia; a study . . .
Philadelphia, The league. 1920.
47p.   3523

COOPER, ANNA J. A voice from the
South. By a black woman of the
south. Xenia, Ohio. Aldine pub. co.
1892. iii, 304p.   3524

CRUMMELL, ALEXANDER. The
black woman of the South. Her
neglects and her needs. Washington,
B. S. Adams. 1883. 16p.   3525

DANIEL, SADIE I. Women builders.
Sketches of Janie P. Barrett, Maggie
L. Walker and others. Washington,
Associated publishers. 1931. 187p.
                               3526

HACKLEY, E. AZALIA. The colored
girl beautiful. Kansas City, Mo.,
Burton pub. co. 1916. 206p. 3527

HAMMOND, MRS. L. H. Southern
women and race adjustment.
Lynchburg, Va., Bell & co. 1917.
32p.   3528

HOBSON, MRS. ELIZABETH C. A
report concerning the colored
women of the South. Baltimore, J.
Murphy & co. 1896. 15p.
(Slater papers, no. 9).   3529

LE BEAU, FAY BOWMAN. A study
of the incomes of two hundred
women graduated from the college
at Hampton Institute, Virginia,
1926-1933.   3530

MOORE, MRS. E. S. Negro woman-
hood – Its past. 8p.   3531

MOSSELL, MRS. N. F. The work of
the Afro-American woman. Philadelphia, George S. Ferguson co.
1894. 178p.   3532

NATIONAL ASSOCIATION OF
COLORED WOMEN. Biennial
report . . .1st-28th, 1912. 1939.
                               3533

NATIONAL ASSOCIATION OF
COLORED WOMEN. A collection
of newspaper accounts and editorial
opinion relating to the National
association of colored women.
1915-1925. 3v.   3534

NEGRO WOMEN. A collection of
newspaper accounts relating to
prominent American Negro women.
1900-1925. 5v.   3535

OLCOTT, JANE (comp.) The work of
colored women. New York,
Colored work committee, Y.W.C.A.
1919. 136p.   3536

OVINGTON, MARY W. Half a man;
the status of the Negro in New
York. New York, Longmans, Green
& co. 1911. 236p.   3537

REED, RUTH. The Negro women of
Gainesville, Georgia. Athens, Ga.,
University of Georgia press. 1921.
61p. (Phelps-Stokes papers, no. 6).
                               3538

XLI. Economic Conditions of the Negro. (Business, Industry, Agriculture, Organized Labor, etc.)

AFRO-AMERICAN NEWSPAPERS. A survey of the Negro market covered by the Afro-American newspapers. Baltimore, Washington, Philadelphia and Richmond. Baltimore, Afro-American. 1938. 3539

AMERICAN ACADEMY OF POLITICAL AND SOCIAL SCIENCE. Annals . . . 1900-1937. Philadelphia, The academy. 1900-37. 3540

AMERICAN ACADEMY OF POLITICAL AND SOCIAL SCIENCE. The improvements of labor conditions in the United States. Philadelphia, The Academy. 1906. iv, 221p. 3541

AMERICAN FEDERATION OF LABOR. Proceedings . . . annual convention. 1900-1939. 3542

ARMSTRONG ASSOCIATED OF PHILADELPHIA. A comparative study of occupations and wages of the children of working age in the Durham and Potter schools, Philadelphia. Philadelphia, The association. 1913. 3543

ARMSTRONG ASSOCIATED OF PHILADELPHIA. The Negro in business in Philadelphia. An investigation . . . Philadelphia, The association. 1917. 14p. 3544

BANKS, CHARLES. Negro banks of Mississippi; to which is added Negro progress in a Mississippi town; being a study of conditions in Jackson, Miss., by D. W. Woodward. Cheyney. Pa., Committee of twelve. 11p. 3545

BANKS, E. M. Economics of land tenure in Georgia, New York, Columbia University press. 1905. 142p. 3546

BARBADOES. F. G. Catalogue of the first industrial exposition by the colored citizens of the District of Columbia. Washington, Union bethel church. 1887. 31p. 3547

BITTING, SAMUEL T. Rural land ownership among Negroes in Virginia with special reference to Albemarle county. Charlottesville, Va., Michie co. 1915. 110p., (Phelps-Stokes papers, no. 2). 3548

BIZZELL, WILLIAM B. Rural Texas. New York, MacMillan co. 1924. xvi, 477p. 3549

BLACK, FORD S. (comp.) Blue book. Chicago colored business and professional people. Chicago, The compiler. 1919. 96p. 3550

BRANSON, E. C. Farm life conditions in the South. Athens, Ga., The author. 16p. 3551

BRANTLEY, WILLIAM G. Peonage; remarks in the House of representatives, Mar. 28, 1904. Washington, Govt. print. office. 1904. 24p. 3552

BROWN, THOMAS I. (ed.) Economic cooperation among the Negroes of Georgia. Report of a social study made by Atlanta University, with the proceedings of the 22d annual conference for the study of Negro problems, Atlanta, May 28, 1917. Atlanta, Atlanta University press. 1917. 56p. 3553

BROWN, W. H. The education and economic development of the Negro in Virginia. Charlottesville, Va., University of Virginia press. 1923. 150p. (Phelps-Stokes papers, no. 6). 3554

CAYTON, HORACE and MITCHELL, GEORGE S. Black workers and the new unions. Chapel Hill, University

of North Carolina press. 1939.
473p.   3555
COMAN, KATHARINE. The Negro as
a peasant farmer. Boston, American
statistical press. 1904. 15p.   3556
COMMONS, JOHN R. and others. A
documentary history of American
industrial society. Cleveland, A. H.
Clarke co. 1910. 2v.   3557
DAVIS, JACKSON. The Negro in
country life. Hampton, Va.,
Hampton Institute press. 1911.
14p.   3558
DILLINGHAM, PITT. Land tenure
among the Negroes. (Rpt. from the
Yale Review, Aug. 1896.) 1896.
17p.   3559
DU BOIS, W. E. BURGHARDT (ed.)
Economic cooperation among
Negro Americans. Report of a
survey made by Atlanta University .
. . together with the proceedings of
the 12th conference for the study
of the Negro problems. Atlanta,
University of Atlanta press. 1907.
184p.   3560
DU BOIS, W. E. BURGHARDT (ed.)
The Negro artisan. Report of a
social study made under the
direction of Atlanta University;
with the proceedings of the 7th
conference for the study of Negro
problems. Atlanta, Atlanta
University press. 1902. 192p. 3561
DU BOIS, W. E. BURGHARDT (ed.)
The Negro farmer. (Rpt. from
Negroes in the United States).
Washington, Govt. print. office.
1904. 19p.   3562
DU BOIS, W. E. BURGHARDT (ed.)
Negro in the black belt; some social
sketches. Washington, Govt. print.
office. 1899. 16p. (Bulletin of the
Department of Labor, no. 22, May,
1899.)   3563
DU BOIS, W. E. BURGHARDT (ed.)
The Negro in business. Report of a

social study made under the
direction of Atlanta University,
May 30-31, 1899. Atlanta, Atlanta
University press. 1899. 77p.   3564
DUTCHER, DEAN. The Negro in
modern industrial society; an
analysis of the changes in the
occupations of Negro workers.
1910-1920. Lancaster, Pa., The
author. 1930. 137p.   3565
EDWARDS, PAUL K. The southern
urban Negro as a consumer. New
York, Prentice-Hall. 1932. xix,
323p.   3566
FEDERAL REPORTER. A semi-
monthly news magazine. St. Paul,
Minn., West pub. co. 1883-.
Collection has issues, dealing with
Negro peonage; Dec. 17, 1904; Mar.
4, June 1, Aug. 17, 1905.   3567
FLEMING, WALTER L. The
freedmen's saving bank; a chapter
in the economic history of the
Negro race. Chapel Hill, University
of North Carolina press. London,
Oxford Univ. press. 1927. 170p.
                               3568
FRANKLIN, CHARLES L. The Negro
labor unionist of New York.
Problems and conditions among
Negroes in the labor unions in
Manhattan with special reference to
the NRA and the post NRA
situations. New York, Columbia
University press. London, P. S.
King & co. 1936. 415p.   3569
GARNETT, WILLIAM E. and
ELLISON, JOHN M. Negro life in
rural Virginia, 1865-1934. Blacksburg, Va., Virginia Polytechnic
institute. 1934. 59p. (Bulletin no.
295).   2470
GARRISON, W. C. The Negro in
manufacturing and mechanical
industries. Trenton, New Jersey
bureau of statistics. 1903. 103p.
                               3571

223

GREENE, LORENZO and WOOD-SON, CARTER G. The Negro wage-earner. Washington, Assn. for the study of Negro life and history. 1930. 388p. 3572

G. R. S. The southern Negro as he is. Boston, The author. 1877. 32p. 3573

HALL, EGERTON E. The Negro wage-earner of New Jersey. A study of occupational trends in New Jersey. New Brunswick, N.J. W.S. Rutgers University, 1935. 115p. tables, biblio. 3574

HAMILTON, C. HORACE and ELLISON, JOHN M. Negro organizations in rural Virginia Blacksburg, Va., Virginia Polytechnic Institute. 1934. 37p. (Bulletin no. 290. 3575

HAMMOND, M. B. The cotton industry; an essay in American economic history. New York, MacMillan co. 1897. 375p. 3576

HAMPTON NEGRO CONFERENCE. Papers on business enterprises conducted by the Negro. Hampton, Va.. Hampton Institute press. 1898. 144p. 3577

HARMON, J. H. Jr., ARNETT, LINDSAY and WOODSON, CARTER G. The Negro as a business man. Wash., The association for the study of Negro life and history. 1929. v., 111p. 3578

HARRIS, ABRAM L. The Negro as capitalist. Philadelphia, American academy of political and social science. 1936. 3579

HAYNES, GEORGE E. The Negro at work during the World war and during reconstruction. Statistics. problems, and policies relating to the greater inclusion of Negro wage earners in American industry and agriculture. Washington, Govt. print. office. 1921. 144p. (U. S.

dept. of labor, 2d study on Negro labor). 3580

HAYNES, GEORGE E. The Negro at work in New York City; a study in economic progress. New York, Columbia University press. 1912. 158p. 3581

HERBST, ALMA. The Negro in the slaughtering and meat-packing industry in Chicago, Boston and New York; Houghton Mifflin co., 1932. 182p. 3582

HILL, T. ARNOLD. The Negro and the economic reconstruction. Washington. Associates in Negro folk education. 1937. 78p. 3583

INTERNATIONAL CONFERENCE OF NEGRO WORKERS. Report of proceedings and decisions . . . 1st, 1930. Hamburg, Germany, International trade union committee. 1930. 3584

JACKSON, GILES B. and DAVIS D. WEBSTER. The industrial history of the Negro race in the United States. Richmond, Va., Virginia press. 1908. 400p. 3585

JOHNSON, CHARLES S. Shadow of the plantation. Chicago, University of Chicago press. 1934. xxiv, 214p. 3586

JOHNSON, CHARLES S., EMBREE, EDWIN R. and ALEXANDER, W. W. The collapse of cotton tenancy. Chapel Hill, University of North Carolina press. 1935. 3587

JORDAN, B. L. The Southern aid society of Virginia. Richmond, John Mitchell, Jr. 1909. 56p. 3588

KELSEY, CARL. The evolution of Negro labor. Philadelphia, American academy of political and social science. 1903. 21p. 3589

KELSEY. CARL. The Negro farmer. Chicago, Jenkins & Pye. 1903. 103p. 3590

KENNY. JOHN A. The Negro in

medicine. Tuskegee, Ala., Tuskegee Inst. press. 60p.   3591

MASSACHUSETTS BUREAU OF STATISTICS. Social and industrial condition of the Negro in Massachusetts. Boston, Wright & Potter co., 1904. 319p.   3592

NATIONAL NEGRO BUSINESS LEAGUE. Annual reports . . .1st-39th, 1900-1939.   3593

NATIONAL NEGRO BUSINESS LEAGUE. Report of the survey of Negro business. New York, The league. 1928.   3594

NATIONAL NEGRO INSURANCE ASSOCIATION. Proceedings of annual sessions . . . 1st-19th, 1920-1939.   3595

NATIONAL URBAN LEAGUE. The forgotten tenth. An analysis of unemployment among Negroes in the United States and its social costs, 1932-1933. New York, The league. 1933. 63p.   3596

NATIONAL URBAN LEAGUE. The Negro at work in the United States. New York, The league. 1933. 31p.   3597

NEGRO AGRICULTURE. A collection of newspaper and magazine accounts and editorial opinion relating to the Negro in agriculture, farmer's conferences, rural labor, peonage, etc. 1898-1925. 8v.   3598

NEGRO BUSINESS. A collection of newspaper accounts relating to Negro banks, businesses, business and professional men and women. 1900-1925. 10v.   3599

NEGRO ECONOMIC CONDITIONS. A collection of newspaper accounts and editorial opinion relating to the economic conditions of Negroes. 1899. 1925. 4v.   3600

NEGRO LABOR. A Collection of newspaper accounts relating to Negro labor and laborers in the United States. 1900-1925. 12v.3601

PADMORE, GEORGE. The life and struggles of Negro toilers. London, international trade union committee of Negro workers, 1931. 126p.   3602

PINCHBECK, RAYMOND B. The Virginia Negro artisan and tradesman. Richmond, Wm. Byrd press. 1926. 146p. (Phelps-Stokes papers, no. 7).   3603

RAPER, ARTHUR F. Preface to peasantry. Chapel Hill, University of North Carolina press. 1936. 3604

REDDIX, JACOB L. The Negro seeks economic security through cooperation. An address. . . on consumer's cooperation . . . Indianapolis, Jan. 1, 1936. Chicago,, Central states cooperative league. 1936. 24p.   3605

REID, IRA DE A. Negro membership in American labor unions. New York Alexander press. 1930. 179p. 3606

ROSENBERG, SAMUEL A. Negro managed building and loan associations in the United States. Hampton, Va., The author. 1940. 76p.   3607

SCARBOROUGH, DONALD D. An economic study of Negro farmers, as owners, tenants, and croppers. Athens, Ga., University of Georgia press. 1924. 37p. (Phelps-Stokes papers, no. 7.).   3608

SCHOMBERG, ARTHUR A. Economic contribution by the Negro to America. Washington. American Negro academy. 1915. (Papers of the Academy).   3609

SPERO, STERLING and HARRIS, ABRAM L. The black worker. The Negro and the labor movement. New York, Columbia University press. 1931. 509p.   3610

U. S. BUREAU OF FOREIGN AND DOMESTIC COMMERCE. Causes

of Negro insurance company failures. (Bulletin, no. 15). Washington, 1937. 22p. 3611

U.S. BUREAU OF FOREIGN AND DOMESTIC COMMERCE. Negro trade associations. Washington. 1936. 15p. 3612

U.S. BUREAU OF THE CENSUS. Farm tenancy in the United States; an analysis of the 1920 census relative to farms, classified by tenure, supplemented by pertinent data from other sources. . . Washington, Govt. print. office. 1924. (Census monographs, no. 4). 3613

U.S. BUREAU OF THE CENSUS. The Negro farmer in the United States. (Fifteenth census of the U.S., 1930). Washington, Govt. print. office. 1933. 84p. 3614

U.S. BUREAU OF THE CENSUS. Negro newspapers and periodicals in the United States, 1939. (Negro statistical bulletin, no. 1). Washington, 1940. 22p. 3615

U.S. BUREAU OF THE CENSUS. Negro retail business, 1920-32. Washington, Govt. print. office. 1934. 40p. 3616

U.S. BUREAU OF THE CENSUS. Special reports. Occupations at the twelfth census. Washington, Govt. print. office. 1904. cclxvi, 763p. 3617

U. S. DEPARTMENT OF THE INTERIOR. The urban Negro worker in the United States, 1925-1936. An analysis of the training, types, and conditions of employment and the earnings of 200,000 skilled and white-collar Negro workers. Washington, Govt. print. office. 1938. 2v. (Dept. of the interior, office of director of Negro affairs, WPA.). 3618

WASHINGTON, BOOKER T. The Negro and his relation to the economic progress of the south. An address . . . before the Southern industrial convention, Huntsville, Ala., Oct. 12, 1899. Tuskegee Institute, Ala., Tuskegee Institute press. 1900. 6p. 3619

WASHINGTON, BOOKER T. The Negro in business. (Rpt. from Gunton's magazine, Mar. 1901). New York, Gunton co. 1901. 12p. 3620

WASHINGTON, BOOKER T. The Negro in business. Boston, Chicago, Hertel, Jenkins & co. 1907. 379p. 3621

WASHINGTON, F. B. A study of Negro employees of apartment houses in New York City. New York, National urban league. 1931. 36p. 3622

WEATHERFORD, W. D. The Negro life in the South. Present conditions and needs with special chapter on the economic condition of the Negro by G. W. Dyer. New York, Y.M.C.A. press, 1910. 183p. 3623

WESLEY, CHARLES H. Negro labor in the United States, 1850-1925. A study in American economic history. New York, Vanguard press. 1927. 343p. 3624

WHITING, STUART L. The economic development of the Negro in Virginia. New York, New York University press. 1931. 95p. 3625

WOODSON, CARTER G. The Negro professional man and the community with special emphasis on the physician and the lawyer. Washington, Assn. for the study of Negro life and history. 1934. xviii, 365p. 3626

WOODSON, CARTER G.' The rural Negro. Washington, Association for the study of Negro life and history. 263p. 3627

WOOFTER, THOMAS J. JR. Landlord and tenant on the cotton

plantation. Washington, Division of social research, W.P.A. 1936. 3628

WRIGHT, CARROLL D. The Industrial progress of the South. Address before the 13th annual convention, the National assoc. of officials of Bureaus of labor statistics. Nashville, Tenn., May 21, 1897. Portland, Conn., The allocation. 1897. 25p. 3629

XLII. Negro Health, Housing, and Social Conditions.

AERY, WILLIAM A. Titustown; a community of Negro homes. Hampton, Va., Hampton Institute press. 1915. 16p. (Rpt. from the Southern Workman). 3630

ARMSTRONG ASSOCIATION OF PHILADELPHIA. A study of living conditions among colored people in towns in the outer part of Philadelphia and in other suburbs both in Pennsylvania and New Jersey. Philadelphia, The assn. 1915. 57p. 3631

ATWATER, W. O. and WOODS, CHARLES D. Dietary studies with reference to the good of the Negro in Alabama in 1895 and 1896. Washington, Govt. print. office. 1897. 69p. (Bulletin 38, U.S. dept. of agriculture). 3632

BENT, MICHAEL and GREENE, ELLEN F. Rural Negro health. A report on a five-year experiment in health education in Tennessee. (Joint health education committee). Nashville, Julius Rosenwald fund. 1937. 859p. 3633

CHARITY ORGANIZATION SOCIETY. The Negro in the cities of the North. Charities, v. 15. New York, The society. 1905. 96p. 3634

CHASE, THOMAS M. (ed.) Mortality among Negroes in cities. 2d ed. Proceedings of the Conference for investigation of city problems held at Atlanta, May 26-27, 1896. Atlanta, Atlanta University press. 1903. 24p. 3635

CHICAGO LEAGUE ON URBAN CONDITIONS AMONG NEGROES. Annual report . . . 1st-6th, 1917-1922. Chicago, The league. 1917-22. 3636

COBB, W. MONTAGUE. The first Negro medical society. A history of the medico-chirurgical society of the District of Columbia, 1849-1939. Washington, Associated publishers. 1939. 15p. 3637

COLCORD, JOANNA C. Your community. Health, education, safety, welfare. New York, Russell Sage foundation. 1939. 249p. 3638

DUBLIN, LOUIS I. The health of the Negro. New York, Metropolitan life insurance co. 1934. 12p. 3639

DUBLIN, LOUIS I. Recent changes in Negro mortality . . . address before the National Conference of Social Work. Toronto. July 2, 1924. New York, The National urban league. 1924. 10p. 3640

DUBLIN, LOUIS I. The reduction of mortality among colored policy holders. An address to the National urban league. New York, Metropolitan life insurance co. 1920. 7p. 3641

DU BOIS, W. E. BURGHARDT (ed.) Mortality among Negroes in cities. Proceedings of the conference for investigation of city problems, held at Atlanta, May 26-27, 1896. Atlanta, Atlanta University press. 1896. 51p. 3642

DU BOIS, W. E. BURGHARDT (ed.) The Negro American family. Report of a social study made principally by the college classes of 1909-10 of Atlanta University under the patronage of the John F. Slater fund, together with proceedings of the 13th annual conference for the study of Negro problems, Atlanta, May 26, 1908. Atlanta, Atlanta University press. 1908. 156p.   3642a

DU BOIS, W. E. BURGHARDT (ed.) The problem of housing the Negro. (Rpt. from Southern Workman). Hampton, Va., Hampton Institute press. 62p.   3643

DU BOIS, W. E. BURGHARDT (ed.) Social and physical condition of Negroes in cities. Report of an investigation under the direction of Atlanta University; with proceedings of the second annual conference for the study of Negro city problems, Atlanta, May 25-26, 1897. Atlanta, Atlanta University press. 1897. 72p.   3644

DU BOIS, W. E. BURGHARDT (ed.) Social betterment among Negro Americans. Report of a social study made by Atlanta University under the patronage of the John F. Slater fund; together with the proceedings of the 14th annual conference for the study of Negro problems, Atlanta, May 24, 1909. Atlanta, Atlanta University press. 1910.
                                          3645

DU BOIS, W. E. BURGHARDT (ed.) Some efforts of American Negroes for their own betterment. Report of an investigation under the direction of Atlanta University; together with the proceedings of the third annual conference for the study of Negro problems, Atlanta, May 25-26, 1898. Atlanta, Atlanta University press. 1898. 65p.   3646

FRAZIER, E. FRANKLIN. The Negro

family in Chicago. Chicago, University of Chicago press. 1932.
                                          3647

FRISSELL, HOLLIS and BEVIER, ISABEL. Dietary studies of Negroes in eastern Virginia in 1897-98. Washington, Govt. print. office. 1899. 45p. (Bulletin 71, U.S. Dept. of agriculture).   3648

GEE, WILSON and CORSON, JOHN J. A statistical study of Virginia. Charlottesville, Va., Institute for research in the social sciences. 1927. 201p.   3649

GILLIGAN, F. J. The morality of the color line. New York, 1928. 16p.
                                          3650

GUNTON'S MAGAZINE. Negroes under Northern conditions. (Rpt. from Gunton's, Jan. 1896). New York, Political science pub. co. 1896. 86p.   3651

JONES, THOMAS J. The sociology of a New York city block. New York. Columbia University press. 1904. 133p. (Studies in history, economics and public law, v. xxi, no. 2).   3652

JONES, WILLIAM H. The housing of Negroes in Washington, D. C. A study in human ecology. Washington, Howard University press. 1929. 191p.   3653

JONES, WILLIAM H. Recréation and amusement among Negroes in Washington, D.C. A sociological analysis of the Negro in an urban environment. Washington, Howard University press. 1927. 216p. 3654

JULIUS ROSENWALD FUND. Child health problems. National conference on fundamental problems in the education of Negroes. Nashville, The fund. 1934. 24p.   3655

JULIUS ROSENWALD FUND. Negro hospitals. A compilation of available statistics. Chicago, The fund. 1931. 57p. 3656

KENNY, JOHN A. The Negro in medicine. Tuskegee Institute, Ala., Tuskegee Institute press. 1912. 60p. 3657

KNIGHT, CHARLES L. Negro housing in certain Virginia cities. Charlottesville, Va., University of Virginia press. 1927. 158p. (Phelps-Stokes papers, no. 8). 3658

LATTIMORE, FLORENCE. A palace of delight. Hampton, Va., Hampton Institute press. 1915. 19p. 3659

LEE, G. C. Negroes in the United States. Negroes under northern conditions. (Rpt. from Gunton's magazine). 1896. 3660

MARCY, C. HOWARD. The race factor in the tuberculosis problem. Pittsburgh. The tuberculosis league. 1934. 7p. 3661

MARYLAND TUBERCULOSIS ASSOCIATION. Our tuberculous Negro. Where is he now? An appeal to the citizens and legislators of Maryland for the control of tuberculosis. Baltimore, The assn. 21p. 3662

MASSACHUSETTS BUREAU OF STATISTICS. Social and industrial condition of the Negro in Massachusetts. Boston, Wright & Potter co. 1904. 3663

MAYS, THOMAS J. The increase of insanity and consumption among the Negro population of the South since the war. Philadelphia, Polyclinic hospital. 1923. 13p. 3664

NATIONAL MEDICAL ASSOCIAT-ION. Proceedings. . . 1911-1939. 3665

NATIONAL TUBERCULOSIS ASSOCIATION. A five-year study of tuberculosis among Negroes. New York. The assn. 1937. 77p. 3665a

NATIONAL URBAN LEAGUE. Bulletin . . . on urban conditions among Negroes. Report . . . 1915-1920. New York, Nashville, etc. 1915-25. 3666

NATIONAL URBAN LEAGUE. A collection of newspaper accounts relating to the work of the National urban league. 1917-1925. 2v. 3667

NEGRO CHARITIES. A collection of newspaper accounts relating to schools for Negro blind and deaf, orphans, day nurseries, old folks' homes, reform schools, homes for Negro women and girls, social work and settlement, etc. 1918-1925. 3v. 3668

NEGRO IN CITIES AND TOWNS. A collection of newspaper accounts and editorial opinion relating to Negroes in cities and towns and resultant problems. 1912-1925. 3v. 3669

NEGRO HEALTH. A collection of newspaper accounts and editorial opinion relating to various aspects of Negro health. 1900-1920. 3v. 3670

NEGRO HOMES. A collection of newspaper accounts relating to Negro homes and home ownership. 1916-1925. 2v. 3671

NEGRO HOSPITALS. A collection of newspaper accounts relating to Negro hospitals and their work. What they need, the necessity of building new hospitals, where they are needed, etc. 1900-1920. 3672

NEGRO MORTALITY. A collection of newspaper accounts and editorial opinion relating to the mortality rates among Negroes. 1914-1925. 2v. 3673

NEGRO AND NARCOTICS. A collection of newspaper accounts and editorial opinion relating to the use of drugs by Negroes, taken chiefly from the New York Sun, the Mobile Register. 1901-1907. 2v. 3674

NEGRO TOWNS. A collection of newspaper accounts relating to Negro towns throughout the United States. 1900-1925. 2v. 3675

NEGRO URBAN CONDITIONS. A collection of newspaper accounts relating to conditions under which Negro live and work in urban centers. 1900-1925. 3v. 3676

NEW JERSEY CONFERENCE OF SOCIAL WORK. The Negro in New Jersey. Report of a survey by the Interracial committee of the New Jersey conference of social work . . . Newark, The conference. 1932. 116p. 3677

NORFOLK JOURNAL AND GUIDE. Norfolk's thirty-six per cent. 64,000 colored, their social and economic status. Norfolk, Va., The Journal & guide. 1929. 16p. 3678

O'KELLEY, H. S. Sanitary conditions among the Negroes of Athens, Georgia. Athens, Ga., University of Georgia press. 1918. 28p. (Phelps-Stokes papers, no. 4). 3679

PATTERSON, RAYMOND. The Negro and his needs. 1911. 3680

PRESIDENT'S CONFERENCE ON HOME BUILDING AND HOME OWNERSHIP. Negro housing. Report of the committee. . . Washington, The conference. 1932. xiv, 282p. 3681

REID, IRA DE A. Negro youth, their social and economic back grounds. A selected bibliography. Washington, American Youth commission of the American commission on education. 1939. 75p. 3682

RICHMOND COUNCIL OF SOCIAL AGENCIES. The Negro in

Richmond, Virginia. Report of the Negro welfare committee . . . Richmond, The council. 1929. viii, 136p. 3683

SANDERS, WILEY B. Negro child welfare in North Carolina. A Rosenwald study. Chapel Hill, University of North Carolina press. 1933. 326p. 3684

SIBLEY, ELBRIDGE. Differential mortality in Tennessee, 1917-1928. Nashville, Fisk University press. 1930. 152p. 3685

SOUTHERN SOCIOLOGICAL CONGRESS. Proceedings and addresses . . . 1st-9th, 1912-1921. 3686

STATE OF WEST VIRGINIA. Report of the bureau of Negro welfare. Charleston, State printer. 1921-22. 1937-38. 3687

THOMAS, ADAH B. (comp.) Pathfinders. A history of the progress of colored graduate nurses. New York, The author. 1929. 240p. 3688

U. S. DEPARTMENT OF LABOR. Condition of the Negro in various cities. Washington, Govt. print. office. 1897. 112p. (Bulletin of the Dept. of labor, no. 10, 1897). 3689

U. S. DEPARTMENT OF LABOR. Statistics of cities. Mortality rates by color. Washington, Govt. print. office. 1901. 155p. (U.S. dept. of labor, bulletin 36, 1901). 3690

VIRGINIA SCHOOL FOR COLORED DEAF AND BLIND CHILDREN. Biennial report . . . 1st-21st, 1909-1938. Richmond, State department of public welfare. 1909-1938. 3691

WILLIAMS, W. T. B. Local conditions among Negroes. Hampton, Va., Hampton Institute press. 1906. 30p. 3692

WITCHEN, ELSIE. Tuberculosis and

the Negro in Pittsburgh. Pittsburgh, Tuberculosis league. 1934. 120p. 3693

WOOD, JUNIUS B. The Negro in Chicago. A first hand study. (Rpt. from Chicago Daily News, Dec. 11-27, 1916). Chicago Daily news. 1916. 31p. 3694

WOOFTER, THOMAS J. Negro problems in cities. Garden City, N. Y., Doubleday, Doran & co. 1928. xiii, 17-284p. 3695

WOOFTER, THOMAS J. A study of Negro neighborhoods in cities. New York, Institute of social and religious research. 1927. 3696

XLIII. The Negro and crime.

CABLE, GEORGE W. The silent South; together with the freedman's case in equity and the convict lease system. New York, Chas. Scribner's sons, 1895. vl, 213p. 3697

CHAMBERLAIN, BERNARD P. The Negro and crime in Virginia. Charlottesville, Va., University of Virginia press. 1936. 132p. (Phelps-Stokes studies, no. 15). 3698

DANIEL, ROBERT P. A psychological study of delinquent and non-delinquent Negro boys. New York, Bureau of pub. Teacher's college, Columbia Univ. 1932. 59p. 3699

DUBOIS, W. E. BURGHARDT. Some notes on Negro crime, particularly in Georgia; report of a social study made under the direction of Atlanta University; together with the proceedings of the ninth conference for the study of Negro problems, Atlanta, May 24, 1904. Atlanta, Atlanta University press. 1904. viii, 68p. (Publication no. 9.) 3700

GEORGIA STATE DEPARTMENT OF WELFARE. Annual report . . . 1920-1939. Atlanta, state printer. 1920-39. 3701

HOWARD ASSOCIATION, LONDON. The coloured race in America. The convict camps and chain-gangs, a revival of slavery. London, The association. 1899. 4p. 3702

HOWARD ASSOCIATION, LONDON. Continuing cruelties in the convict chain-gangs and camps of the southern United States. London, The assn. 1901. 4p. 3703

LIGHTFOOT, ROBERT M. Negro crime in a small urban committee. Charlottesville, Va., University of Virginia press. 1934. 86p. (Phelps-Stokes studies, no. 12). 3704

MC CORD, CHARLES H. The American Negro as a dependent, defective and delinquent. Nashville, Benson print. co. 1914. 342p. 3705

NEGRO CRIME. A collection of newspaper accounts relating to Negro crime and findings of the courts. 1899-1920. 4v. 3706

NEGRO REFORMATORY ASSOCIATION OF VIRGINIA. Annual report . . . to the Governor and General Assembly. Richmond, 1901-03. 1903-05. 3707

RAMSEY, D. HIDEN. Negro criminality. Charlottesville, Va., University of Virginia press. 1915. 60p. (Phelps-Stokes studies). 3708

STOREY, MOORFIELD. The Negro question. An address delivered before the Wisconsin bar association, June 27, 1918. Rpt. by the N.A.A.C.P. New York. 1918. 30p. 3709

TANNENBAUM, FRANK. Darker phases of the South. New York, G.P. Putnam's sons. 1924. vii, 203p. 3710

THOMAS, WILLIAM H. The Negro and crime, an address before the Southern Sociological Congress in Nashville, May 7-10, 1912. Montgomery, Ala., Paragon press. 1912. 13p. 3711

VIRGINIA STATE DEPARTMENT OF PUBLIC WELFARE. Annual reports . . . 1908-09—1938-39. Richmond, Division of purchase and printing. 1909-1939. 3712

WILLCOX, WALTER F. Negro criminality. An address delivered before the American social science association, Saratoga, Sept. 6, 1899. Boston, G. H. Ellis. 1899. 25p. 3713

WILLIAMS, GEORGE C. The Negro offender, presented at the fifty-first congress of the American prison association, Jacksonville, 1921. New York, Russell Sage foundation. 1922. 11p. 3714

WORK, MONROE N. Negro criminality in the South. Annals of the American Academy. September, 1913. 3715

XLIV. The Negro and lynching and riots.

ANTI-LYNCHING LEGISLATION. A collection of newspaper accounts and editorial opinion relating to anti-lynching legislation in various states and in Congress. 1900-1925. 6v. 3716

BAKER, RAY S. What is a lynching? A study of mob justice, South and North. (Rpt. from McClure's, Feb. 1905.) 8p. 3717

BLECKLEY, L. E. Outrages by Negroes no excuse for lynching. (Rpt. from Forum, 1894.) 2p. 3718

BRUCE, JOHN E. The blood red record of the horrible lynchings and burnings of Negroes by civilized white men in the United States, as taken from the records. Albany. The auth. 1901. 27p. 3719

CHADBOURN, JAMES H. Lynching and the law. Chapel Hill, University of North Carolina press. 1933. 3720

CHICAGO COMMISSION ON RACE RELATIONS. The Negro in Chicago. A study of race relations and a race riot. Chicago, University of Chicago press. 1922. xxiv, 672p. 3721

CITIZENS' PROTECTIVE LEAGUE, N. Y. Story of the riot, published by the Citizens' protective league. New York. 1900. 79p. 3722

COLLINS, WINFIELD H. The truth about lynching and the Negro in the South, in which the author pleads that the South be made safe for the white race. New York, Neale pub. co. 1918. 163p. 3723

CUTLER, JAMES E. Lynch law; an investigation into the history of lynching in the United States. New York, Longmans, Green & co. 1905. xiv, 287p. 3724

DETROIT BUREAU OF GOVERNMENTAL RESEARCH. The Negro in Detroit. Detroit, Wayne University press. 1926. 12v. 3725

DUBOIS, W. E. B. AND GRUENING, MARTHA. The massacre of East St. Louis; an account of an investigation for the National association for the advancement of colored people. New York, The assn. 1917. 20p. (Rpt. from Crisis. Sept. 1917). 3726

GRAVES, JOHN T. AND OTHERS. The mob spirit in America. A series of addresses delivered at Chantauqua, N.Y. during the conference on the mob spirit. Chantauqua, Chantauqua press. 1903. 69p. 3727

GREGG, JAMES E. Lynching: a national menace. The white South's protest against lynching. (Rpt. from the Southern workman). Hampton Inst., Va. Institute press. 1920. 17p. 3728

GRIMKE, FRANCIS J. The lynching of Negroes in the South: its causes and remedy. Washington, The auth. 81p. 3729

GRIMKE, FRANCIS J. The Atlanta riot. A discourse. Atlanta, The auth. 1906. 14p. 3730

HEALEY, J. T. The great riots of New York, 1712 to 1873, including a full account of the four day's draft riot of 1863. New York, E.B. Treat. 1873. 359p. 3731

JOHNSON, ANDRES. Message for the president . . . Transmitting all papers relative to the New Orleans riots. Washington, Govt. print. office. 1867. 3732

JOHNSON, JAMES W. The burning of Eli Person at Memphis, Tenn., an investigation. . . for the National association for the advancement of colored people. (Rpt. from the Crisis, July, 1917). New York, N.A.A.C.P. 1917. 8p. 3733

JOHNSON, J.P. Lynchings in the United States; a national disgrace and a menace to higher civilization; or a consensus of opinions for and against lynchings, with comments. Washington, Age print. co. 1898. 64p. 3734

JOHNSON, JULIA E. Ku Klux Klan. New York, H.W. Wilson co. 1923. 105p. 3735

LYNCHING. A collection of newspaper accounts and editorial opinion relating to lynching, white cops, Ku Klux Klan, etc. 1898-1925. 10v. 3736

MERTINS, LEON E. "Has the United States government the power to prosecute 'lynching' as a federal crime without an amendment to the Constitution." New York, J.A. Quail. 1921. 24p. 3737

MISSISSIPPI (STATE) BAR ASSOCIATION. Mississippi and the mob. Jackson, Miss., Jackson print. co. 1924. 78p. 3738

MORGAN, A. T. Yazoo; or, on the picket line of freedom in the South. Washington, The auth. 1884. 3739

NATIONAL ASSOCIATION FOR THE ADVANCEMENT OF COLORED PEOPLE. An American lynching . . . the burning at the stake of Henry Lowry, Nodena, Ark., Jan. 26, 1921, as told in American newspapers. New York, The assn. 1921. 7p. 3740

NATIONAL ASSOCIATION FOR THE ADVANCEMENT OF COLORED PEOPLE. A ten year fight against lynching. New York, The assn. 1920. 7p. 3741

NATIONAL ASSOCIATION FOR THE ADVANCEMENT OF COLORED PEOPLE. Thirty years of lynching in the United States, 1889-1918. New York, The assn. 1919. 105p. 3742

NEGRO NEWSPAPERS. Accounts relating to the Chicago race riots, August, 1919. Collection has: Pittsburgh Courier, Richmond

Planet, Louisville American Baptist, Nashville Globe, Indianapolis Recorder, Savannah Tribune, Norfolk Journal and Guide, and Indianapolis Freeman. 3743

PAGE, WALTER H. Last hold of the southern bully. (Rpt. from Forum, 1894). 11p. 3744

PICKENS, WILLIAM. Lynching and debt-slavery. New York, American civil liberties union. 1921. 8p. 3745

RACE RIOTS IN CHICAGO, 1899-1919. A collection of newspaper accounts of Chicago race riots at various times between 1899 and 1919. 3746

RACE RIOTS IN EAST ST. LOUIS, ILL. A collection of newspaper accounts of the race riots in East St. Louis, Ill., resulting from labor strikes, etc. 1917. 3747

RACE RIOTS: General and by states, 1901-1905. A collection of newspaper accounts of race riots through the United States, 1901-1905. 3748

RACE RIOTS IN LOUISIANA, 1900-03. A collection of newspaper accounts and editorial opinion relating to race riots and mob rule in New Orleans, etc. 1900-1903. 3749

RACE RIOTS IN NEW YORK, 1899-1900. A collection of newspaper accounts of race riots in New York city, 1899-1900. 2v. 3750

RAPER, ARTHUR F. The tragedy of lynching. Chapel Hill, University of North Carolina press. 1933. 499p. 3751

SANDBURG, CARL. The Chicago race riots, July, 1919. New York, Harcourt, Brace & Howe. 1919. 71p. (Rpt. from Chicago Daily News). 3752

SCROGGS, WILLIAM O. Mob violence; an enemy of both races. An address before the Southern sociological congress in New Orleans, April 19, 1916. 8p. 3753

SHAY, FRANK. Judge Lynch, his first hundred years. New York, I. Washburn. 1938. 288p. 3754

SOUTHERN COMMISSION ON THE STUDY OF LYNCHING. Lynchings and what they mean. Atlanta, The commission. 1933. 73p. 3755

U. S. HOUSE OF REPRE-SENTATIVES. Report of the select committee, (39th Congress, 2d session, report no. 16). The New Orleans riots. Washingtion, Govt. print. office. 1867. 596p. 3756

U. S. SENATE. Report of the committee on the judiciary, 69th Congress, 1st session. Hearing on Senate bill, S 121, to prevent and punish the crime of lynching, Feb. 16, 1926. Washington, Govt. print. office. 1926. 44p. 3757

U. S. SENATE. Senate committee reports, 1883-84. 7v. v. 6, no. 597. 48th Congress, 1st session. Alleged outrages in Virginia; report of the Senate committee on privileges and elections . . . directed to inquire into the alleged massacre of colored men at Danville, Nov. 3, 1883. Washington, Govt. print. office. 1884. 3758

WASHINGTON, BOOKER T. An open letter . . . upon lynchings in the South. (Rpt. from The Montgomery Advertiser, The New Orleans Times-Democrat, etc.) Tuskegee Institute press. 1899. 7p. 3759

WHITE, WALTER F. Philadelphia race riots, July 26-31, 1918. An investigation. New York, Philadelphia, N.A.A.C.P. 1918. 7p. 3760

WHITE, WALTER F. Rope and

234

faggot; a biography of Judge Lynch. New York, London, A. Knopf. 1929. xiii, (3) 272p.   3761

WILSON, WOODROW. Mob violence. Statement of the President of the United States denouncing mob violence and appealing to his fellow countrymen to keep the nation's fame untarnished. Washington, Govt. print. office. 1918. 2p.   3762

WOOLEY, CELIA P. Lessons from the Atlanta riots. Atlanta. 1907.   3763

XLV. Race characteristics.

AMERICAN JOURNAL OF PHYSICAL ANTHROPOLOGY. Philadelphia, 1900-.   3764

ANTHROPOLOGICAL REVIEW. London, Truber & co. 1868. 665p. v. vi.   3765

ATKINSON, EDWARD. "The Negro a beast." (Rpt. from the North American review, Aug., 1905). New York. 1905. 14p.   3766

BAKER, HENRY E. The colored inventor: a record of fifty years. New York, Crisis pub. co. 1913. 12p.   3767

BERNARD, L.L. An introduction to social psychology. New York, Henry Holt & co. 1926. x, 651p.   3768

BOAS, FRANZ. The mind of primitive man. New York, Macmillan co. 1911. x, 249p.   3869

BOSTETTEN, CHARLES V. De. The man of the north, and the man in the south; or the influence of climate. New York, F. W. Christern. 1864. 200p.   3770

BRINTON, DANIEL G. Race and people. Lectures on the science of ethnography. New York, Hodges. 1890. 313p.   3771

BURMEISTER, HERMANN. The black man. The comparative anatomy and psychology of the African Negro. Tr. from the German by Julius Friedlander and Robert Tomes. New York, Byrant & co. 1853. 23p.   3772

CABELL, J. L. The testimony of modern science to the unity of mankind: being a summary of the conclusions announced by the highest authorities in the several departments of physiology, zoology, etc. New York, Robert Carter & bros. 1859. 344p.   3773

CADY, GEORGE L. Race values and race destinies. New York, American missionary assn. n.d. 16p.   3774

CARROLL, CHARLES. "The Negro a beast; or, in the image of God;" the reasoner of the age, the revelator of the century! The Bible as it is! The Negro and his relation to the human family . . . The Negro not the son of Ham. St. Louis, American book & Bible house. 1900. 382p.   3775

CAUCASIAN (pseud.) Anthropology for the people. A reputation of the theory of the Adamic origin of races. Richmond, Va., Everett Waddey co. 1891. 334p.   3776

CHASE, ARABELLA V. A peculiar people. Washington, William C. Chase, Jr. 1905. 79p.   3777

DAVENPORT, CHARLES B. Heredity of skin color in Negro-white crosses. Washington, The Carnegie Institution of Washington. 1913. 106p.   3778

DAY, CAROLINE B. A study of some Negro-white families in the United States. Notes on the anthropometric data by E.A. Hooten.

Cambridge, Harvard University. 1932. 126p. 3779

DENIKER, The races of man: an outline of anthropology and ethnography. New York, Charles Scribner's sons. 1901. xxiii, 611p. 3780

DIXON, RONALD B. The racial history of mankind. New York, Charles Scribner's sons. 1923. xvi, 583p. 3781

DOUGLASS, FREDERICK. The claims of the Negro ethnologically considered. An address before the literary societies of Western Reserve college, July 12, 1854. Rochester, Lee, Mann & co. 1854. 37p. 3782

ETHNOLOGY. A collection of newspaper accounts relating to enthnology, origin of Negroes, etc. 1900-1912. 3783

FIGUIER, LOUIS. The human race. New York, D. Appleton & co. 1872. 548p. 3784

FONTAINE, EDWARD. How the world was peopled. Ethnological lectures: New York, D. Appleton & co. 1872. 341p. 3785

GARTH, THOMAS R. Race psychology; a study of racial mental differences. New York, McGraw-Hill book co. 1931. 260p. 3786

GOBINEAU, JOSEPH A. The inequality of human races. Tr. from the French by Adrian Collins. New York, G.P. Putnam's sons. 1915. 217p. 3787

GOBINEAU, JOSEPH A. The moral and intellectual diversity of races, with particular reference to their respective influence in the civil and political history of mankind. Tr. from the French by H. Hotz. Philadelphia, J.B. Lippincott & co. 1856. 512p. 3788

GREGG, JAMES E. The comparison of races. (Rpt. from Scientific Monthly, Mar. 1925). Hampton, Va., Hampton Institute press. 1925. 6p. 3789

HANKINS, FRANK H. The racial basis of civilization; a critique of the Nordic doctrine. New York, A. A. Knopf. 1926. xii, 384p. 3790

HELPER, HINTON R. The Negroes in Negro-land; the Negroes in America; and Negroes generally. Also, the general races of white men, considered as the involuntary and pre-destined supplanters of the black races. New York, George W. Carleton. 1868. 254p. 3791

HELPER, HINTON R. No jo que; a question for a continent. New York, Carleton co. 1867. 479p. 3792

HERTZ, FRIEDRICH O. Von. Rasse und kultur, eine kritische untersuchung der rassentheorien. 3d ed. Leipzig, A. Kroner. 1925. xii, 426p. 3793

HOFFMAN, FREDERICK L. Race traits and tendencies of the American Negro. New York, American economic assn. 1896. x, 329p. 3794

HUNTINGTON, ELLSWORTH. Character of races as influenced by physical environment, natural selection and historical development. New York, Charles Scribner's sons. 1924. xvi, 393p. 3795

JOURNAL OF THE ANTHROPOLOGICAL INSTITUTE OF GREAT BRITAIN AND IRELAND. London, Truber & co. Collection has: 1873, 1879, 1880. 3796

KNOX, ROBERT. The races of man: a philosophical enquiry into the influence of race over the destinies of nations. 2d ed. London, Henry Renshaw. 1862. 600p. 3797

LAVATER, JOHN C. Essays on

physiognomy. Tr. from the German by Thomas Holcroft. London, Wm. Tegg. 1867. 507p. 3798

LAWRENCE, WILLIAM. Lectures on physiology and zoology and the natural history of man. London, John T. Cox & Edward Partwine. 1834. 374p. 3799

MAURY, ALFRED AND OTHERS. Indigenous races of the earth; or, new chapters of ethnological inquiry . . . with fresh investigations by J.C. Nott and George R. Gliddon. Philadelphia, J.B. Lippincott & co. 1868. 656p. 3800

MURPHY, EDGAR G. The basis of ascendency of public policy involved in the development of the Southern states. New York, Longmans, Green, & co. 1909. 250p. 3801

NOTT, JOSIAH C. AND GLIDDON, GEORGE R. Types of mankind: or ethnological researches based upon the ancient monuments, paintings, sculptures, and crania of races. . . Philadephia, Lippincott, Grambo & co. 1854. 738p. 3802

ODUM, HOWARD W. Social and mental traits of the Negro; research into the conditions of the Negro race in southern towns. New York, Longmans, Green & co. 1910. 302p. 3803

PAYNE, BUCKNER H. (pseud.) ARIEL. The Negro: what is his ethnological status? Is he the progeny of Ham? 2d ed. Cincinnati, The auth. 1867. 48p. 3d ed. Cincinnati, The auth. 1872. 171p. 3804

RANDLE, E.H. Characteristics of the southern Negro. New York, Neale pub. co. 1910. 129p. 3805

REID, MAYNE. Odd people: being a description of singular races of man. Boston, Ticknor & Fields. 1860. 461p. 3806

RICHARDSON, GEORGE H. A defence of the colored race. "A reply to "The Mulatto," which appeared in the Popular Science Monthly for June, 1913. Washington, Washington Bee. 1913. 34p. 3807

SMITH, SAMUEL S. An essay on the causes of the variety of complexion and figure in the human species. New Brunswick, N.J., J. Simpson & co. 1810. 411p. 3808

SNYDER, LOUIS L. Race, a history of modern ethnic theories. New York, Longmans, Green & co. 1939. x, 342p. 3809

TAYLOR, GRIFFITH. Environment and race. A study of the evolution, migration, settlement and status of the races of man. London, Oxford University press. 1927. 354p. 3810

VAN EVRIE, JOHN H. White supremacy and Negro subordination; or, Negroes a subordinate race, and (so-called) slavery its normal condition . . . New York, Van Evrie, Horton & co. 1867. 339p. 3811

VIRCHOW, RUDOLF. The cranial affinities of man and the ape. Boston, Lee & Shepard. 1872. 31p. 3812

WARWICK, EDEN. Nasology: or hints towards a classification of noses. London, R. Bentley. 1848. 263p. 3813

WELLS, H. G. "The tradegy of color." (Rpt. from Alexander's magazine, Oct. 1906). 1906. 8p. 3814

WILDER, BURT G. The brain of the American Negro and other addresses. (Rpt. from the proceedings of the first National Negro conference, New York, May 31-June 2, 1909). New York,

National Negro committee. 1909.
62p.   3815
WISSLER, CLARK. Man and culture.
New York, T. Y. Crowell co. 1923.
xi, 371p.   3816

XLVI. Race mixture.

CALHOUN, ARTHUR W. A social history of the American family from colonial times to the present. Cleveland, A. S. Clark co. 1917-19. 3v.   3817

COX, EARNEST S. Let my people go: a message from white men who wish to keep the white race white, to black men who wish to keep the black race black, including the terms of an alliance between these groups against the whites who wish to mix with the Negroes and the Negroes who wish to mix with the whites. Richmond, Va., White America society. 1925. 34p.   3818

COX, EARNEST S. White America. Richmond, Va., White America society. 1923. 389p.   3819

CROLY, DAVID G. Miscegenation: the theory of the blending the American white man and Negro. New York, H. Dexter, Hamilton & co. 1864. 72p.   3820

ESTABROOK, ARTHUR H. and MCDOUGLE, IVAN E. Mongrel Virginians. The Win tribe. Baltimore, Williams & Wilkins co. 1926. 205p.   3821

GRANT, MADISON. The passing of the great race or the racial basis of European history. 4th rev. ed. New York, Charles Scribner's sons. 1921. ix, 441p.   3822

GREGORY, JOHN W. The menace of color. A study of the difficulties due to the association of white and colored races, with . . . measures proposed for their solution . . .

Philadelphia, J. B. Lippincott co. 1925. 264p.   3823

GRIMKE, ARCHIBALD H. The sex question and race segregation. Washington, American Negro academy. 1915. (Papers of the Academy).   3824

HERSKOVITS, MELVILLE J. The American Negro; a study in racial crossing. New York, A. A. Knopf. 1928. 85p.   3825

MCKINNEY, T. T. All white America. A candid discussion of race mixture and race prejudice in the United States. Boston, Meador pub. co. 1937. 214p.   3826

RACE AMALGAMATION. A collection of newspaper accounts and editorial opinion relating to race mixtures, marriages, etc. 1900-1918. 2v.   3827

RACE INTEGRITY. A collection of newspaper accounts and editorial opinion relating to racial integrity and racial purity laws in various states. 1900-1927. 8v.   3828

REUTER, EDWARD B. The mulatto in the United States; including a study of the role of mixed-blood races throughout the world. Boston, R. G. Badger. 1918. 417p.
                                3829

SAMPSON, JOHN P. Mixed races: their environment, temperament, heredity and phrenology. Hampton, Va., Hampton Institute press. 1881. 147p.   3830

SCHULTZ, ALFRED P. Race or mongrel. A brief history of the rise and fall of the ancient races of earth. A theory that the fall of nations is due to intermarriage with alien stocks: a demonstration that a nation's strengh is due to racial purity: a prophecy that America will sink to early decay unless immigration is rigorously restricted. Boston, L. C. Page & co. 1908. 369p. 3831

SEAMAN, L. What miscegenation is. 1864. 12p. 3832

SHANNON, ALEXANDER H. The Negro in Washington. A study in race amalgamation. New York, W. Neale. 1930. 332p. 3833

SHANNON, ALEXANDER H. Racial integrity and other features of the Negro problem. Dallas, Gorham press. 1907. 305p. 3834

SCHUFELDT, ROBERT W. The Negro, a menace to American civilization. Boston, Gorham press. 1907. 281p. 3835

SMITH, WILLIAM B. The color line; a brief in behalf of the unborn. New York, McClure, Phillips & co. 1905. 261p. 3836

SUBGENATION: The theory of the normal relation of the races; an answer to "Miscegenation." New York, John Bradburn. 1864. 72p. 3837

WALKER, ALEXANDER. Intermarriage: or the mode in which and the causes why, beauty, health, and intellect, result from certain unions, and deformity, disease, and insanity from others demonstrated. New York, J. & H. G. Langley. 1839. 384p. 3838

WELLS, WILLIAM C. Two essays, and an account of a white female part of whose skin resembles that of a Negro and observations. London, Constable & co. 1818. 16p. 3839

U. S. HOUSE OF REPRESENTATIVES. Intermarriage of whites and Negroes in the District of Columbia . . . Hearing before the committee on the District of Columbia, 64th Congress, 1st session, Feb. 11, 1916. Washington, Govt. print. office. 1916. 3840

XLVII. Race problems and race relations.

ADLER, FELIX. The Negro problem in the United States, with special reference to Mr. DuBois' book, "The soul of black folk." An address . . . at Carnegie Hall, New York, Jan. 10, 1904. New York, Ethical addresses. 1904. (v. 11, no. 7). 3841

ALL COLORS. A study outline on woman's part in race relations. New York, The inquiry. 1926. iv, 153p. 3842

AMERICAN ACADEMY OF POLITICAL AND SOCIAL SCIENCE. America's race problems. Addresses at the 5th annual meeting . . . April 12, 13, 1901. Philadelphia, The academy. 1901. 187p. 3843

ARCHER, WILLIAM. Through Afro-America. An English reading of the race problem. London, Chapman & Hall. 1910. 295p. 3844

ATKINSON, EDWARD. The race problem: its possible solution. Brookline, Mass., The auth. 1901. 8p. 3845

PAILEY, THOMAS P. Race orthodoxy in the South and other aspects of the Negro question. New York, Neale pub. co. 1914. 386p. 3846

BAKER, PAUL E. Negro-white adjustment; an investigation and analysis of the methods in the interracial movement in the United States . . . New York Association press. 1934. 267p.   3847

BAKER, RAY S. Following the color line; an account of Negro citizenship in the American democracy. New York, Doubleday, Page & co. 1908. xii, 314p.   3848

BAKER, RAY S. The Negro in a democracy. (Rpt. from The Independent, Sept. 9, 1909). New York, The independent. 1909. 5p.
3849

BAKER-CROTHERS, HAYES. Problems of citizenship. New York, Henry Holt & co. 1924. xiv, 514p.
3850

BARROWS, ISABEL C. (ed.) First Mohonk conference on the Negro question, Lake Mohonk, N.Y., June 4-6, 1890. Boston, G. H. Ellis. 1890. 142p.   3851

BARROWS, WALTER M. The new South. A paper read at the national anniversary society, June, 1884. New York, American home missionary society. 1884. 16p.
3852

BINGHAM, JOHN A. (ed.) Select discussions of race problems; a collection of papers of especial use in study of Negro American problems; with the proceedings of the 20th annual conference for the study of Negro problems, Atlanta University, May 24, 1915. Atlanta, Atlanta University press. 1916. 108p.   3853

BINGHAM, ROBERT. An ex-slave holder's view of the Negro question in the South. (Rpt. from the European ed. of Harper's Monthly magazine, July, 1900). New York, Harper's. 1900. 16p.   3854

BOGARDUS, EMORY S. Immigration and race attitudes. Boston; New York, D. C. Heath & co. 1928. xi, 268p.   3855

BOWEN, TREVOR. Divine white right. A study of race segregation and interracial cooperation in religious organizations and institutions in the United States, with a section on "The Church and Education for Negroes" by Ira de A. Reid. New York, Harper & bros. 1934. 310p.   3856

BRAWLEY, BENJAMIN G. Your Negro neighbor. New York, MacMillan co. 1918. 100p.   3857

BROWN, THOMAS F. and ROUCEK, JOSEPH S. (eds.) Our racial and national minorities; their history, contributions, and present problems. New York, Prentice-Hall. 1937. 877p.   3858

BROWN, WILLIAM M. The crucial race question; or, where and how shall the color line be drawn. 2d ed. Little Rock, Ark., Arkansas churchman's pub. co. 1907. xxxvi, 323p.
3859

BRUCE, WILLIAM C. The Negro problem. Baltimore, J. Murphy & co. 1891. 33p.   3860

BUNCHE, RALPH J. A world view of race. Washington, Associates in Negro folk education. 1936. 98p. (Bronze booklet, no. 4).   3861

CABLE, GEORGE W. The Negro question. New York Association press. 1888. 32p.   3862

CAMPBELL, ROBERT F. Some aspects of the race problem in the South. 2d ed. Asheville, N. C., Citizen co. 1899. 24p.   3863

CARNEGIE, ANDREW. The Negro in America; an address delivered before the Philosophical institute of Edinburgh, Oct. 16, 1907.

Inverness. Scotland, R. Carruthers & sons. 1907. 44p. 3864

COMMONS, JOHN R. Races and immigrants in America. n.d. New York, MacMillan co. 1920. xxix, 242p. 3865

COSTON, WILLIAM H. A freeman and yet a slave. New Haven, Planet book print. 1888. 112p. 3866

COOPER, WILLIAM A. A portrayal of Negro life. Durham, N.C., Duke University press. 1936. 110p. 3867

COZART, WINFIELD F. The chosen people. Boston, Christopher pub. house. 1924. 153p. 3868

CURRY, E. W. B. The Negro defended; an address before the Chantauqua, Cadiz, Ohio, Aug. 12, 1909; being a reply to an address by Senator Ben R. Tillman . . . 1909. 15p. 3869

DABNEY, CHARLES W. The problem in the South. An address. 1904. 23p. 3870

DOLLARD, & DAVIS, ALLISON. Caste and class in a southern town. Yale University press. 1937. 502p. 3871

DOUGLASS, FREDERICK. Three addresses on the relations subsisting between white and colored people of the United States. Washington, Gibson bros. 1886. 16p. 3872

DOW, GROVE S. Society and its problems. An introduction to the principles of sociology. New York, T. Y. Crowell co. 1920. xiv, 594p. 3873

DOWD, JEROME. The Negro in American life. London, Century co. 1926. xx, 647p. 3874

DOWMAN, C. E., GRAVES, JOHN T. AND OTHERS. The possibilities of the Negro in symposium. A solution of the Negro problem psychologically considered. The Negro not a "beast." Atlanta, W. B. Parks. 1904. 165p. 3875

DOYLE, BERTRAM W. The etiquette of race relations in the South. Chicago, University of Chicago press. 1937. 3876

DUBOIS, W. E. B. The gift of black folk; the Negroes in the making of America. Boston, Stratford co. 1924. iv, 349p. 3877

DUBOIS, W. E. B. The Negro. New York, Henry Holt & co. 1915. 245p. 3878

DUBOIS, W. E. B. The study of the Negro problem. A paper submitted to the American academy of political and social science, together with a report of the discussion of this subject at the 44th Scientific session of the academy. London, P. S. King & son; Paris, L. Larose; Berlin, Mayer & Muller; Rome, Direzione del Giornale; Madrid, E. Capdeville. 1898. 29p. 3879

ELWANG, WILLIAM W. The Negroes of Columbia, Missouri. A concrete study of the race problem. Columbia, Mo., University of Missouri. 1904. 69p. 3880

EVANS, MAURICE S. Black and white in the southern states; a study of race problems in the United States from a South Africa point of view. London; New York, Longmans, Green & co. 1915. xii, 299p. 3881

FINOT, JEAN. Race prejudice. Tr. from the French by Florence Wade-Evans. New York, E. P. Dutton & co. 1926. xvi, 320p. 3882

FLEMING, WILLIAM H. Slavery and the race problem in the South, with special reference to the state of Georgia. An address before the alumni society of the University of Georgia, Athens, June 19, 1906. Boston, D. Estes & co. 1906. 66p. 3883

FULLER, T. O. Bridging the racial

chasms. A brief survey of interracial attitudes and relations. Memphis, The auth. 1937. 73p. 3884

GAINES, WESLEY J. The Negro and the white man. Philadelphia, A.M.E. pub. house. 1897. 218p.. 3885

GARDINER, CHARLES A. A constitutional and educational solution of the Negro problem; an address delivered at the University of the state of New York, Albany, June 29, 1903. Albany, The university. 1903. 224p. 3886

GEORGE, HENRY. Menace of privilege, a study of the dangers to the republic of the existence of a favored class. New York, MacMillan co. 1905. 421p. 3887

GOLD, HOWARD R. AND BYRON, K. ARMSTRONG. A preliminary study of interracial conditions in Chicago. (Survey division, industrial relations department, inter-church world movement). New York, Home missions council. 1920. 15p. 3888

GRADY. HENRY W. New South and other addresses. New York, The auth. 1890. 136p. 3889

GRIFFS. WILLIAM E. Does the Bible throw any light on the race question? (Rpt. from the Homiletic review. Aug. 1915) New York, Funk & Wagnalls co. 1915. 3890

GRIMKE. ARCHIBALD H. The shame of America; or the Negro's case against the republic. Washington. The academy. 1924. 18p. 3891

GRIMKE. FRANCIS J. Christianity and race prejudice. Washington. W. E. Cobb. 1910. 29p. 3892

GRIMKE. FRANCIS J. God and the race problem. A discourse delivered in Washington. May 3. 1903. on the day set apart as a day of fasting, prayer. and humiliation for the colored people throughout the United States. Washington. 1903. 12p. 3893

GRIMKE, FRANCIS J. The Negro; his rights and wrongs, the forces for and against him. Washington, 1898. 100p. 3894

GROW, OSCAR. The antagonism of races, or the functions of human institutions in the struggle for existence. 1912. 218p. 3895

HALLOWELL, RICHARD P. The southern question, past and present. An address delivered before the Harvard historical society, Cambridge, Mar. 12, 1890. Boston, Samuel Usher. 1890. 34p. 3896

HAMMOND, MRS. LILY H. In black and white; an interpretation of southern life. New York, Fleming H. Revell co. 1914. 244p. 3897

HAMMOND, MRS LILY H. In the vanguard of a race. New York, Council of women for home missions and missionary education movement. 1922. xiv, 176p. 3898

HAMPTON, WADE AND MORGAN, JOHN T. The race problem in the South. New York, Forum pub. co. 1890. 28p. 3899

HART, ALBERT B. The southern South. New York; London, D. Appleton & co. 1910. 444p. 3900

HAYGOOD, ATTICUS G. Our brother in black: his freedom and his future. New York, Phillips & Hunt; Cincinnati, Walden & Stone; Nashville. Southern methodist pub. house. 1881. 252p. 3901

HAYNES, GEORGE E. The trend of the race. New York. Council of women for home missions. 1922. 205p. 3902

HELM. MARY. From darkness to light. the story of Negro progress. New York; Chicago. F. H. Revell & co. 1909. 218p. 3903

HELM, MARY. The upward path, evolution of a race. Cincinnati, Jennings & Groham. 333p.   3904

HILL, JOHN L. Negro: national asset or liability? New York, Literary associates. 1930. 233p.   3905

HOLCOMBE, WILLIAM H. The mystery of New Orleans: solved by new methods. A symposium on the race problem. Philadelphia, J. B. Lippincott & co. 1890. 332p.   3906

HOME MISSION COUNCIL. Christian America: race relations. New York, The council. 1920. 16p.   3907

HUMPHREY, SETH K. Mankind; racial values and the racial prospect. New York, Charles Scribner's sons. 1917. xvi, 223p.   3908

HUMPHREY, SETH K. The racial prospect; a re-writing and expansion of "mankind." New York, Charles Scribner's sons. 1920. xxi, 261p.   3909

INTERRACIAL COMMITTEE. Nashville plan of interracial work. Atlanta, The committee. 1909. xxiv, 250p.   3910

INTER-RACIAL COMMISSION OF KENTUCKY. Report . . . 1921-22. Louisville, The commission. 1923. 14p.   3911

JACKSON, ALGERNON B. Jim and Mr. Eddy. A dixie motorlogue. Washington, Associated publishers. 1930. 199p.   3912

JOHNSEN, JULIA E. (comp.) Selected articles on the Negro problem. New York, H. W. Wilson co. London, Grafton & co. 1921. 370p.   3913

JOHNSON, CHARLES S. The Negro in American civilization. A study of Negro life and race relations in the light of social research. New York, Henry Holt & co. 1930. xiv, 538p.   3914

JOHNSON, CHARLES S. A preface to racial understanding. New York, Friendship press. 1936. ix, 206p.   3915

JOHNSON, EDWARD A. Light ahead for the Negro. New York, Grafton press. 1904. vi, 11-132p.   3916

JOHNSON, HARVEY. The question of race. A reply to W. Cabell Bruce. Baltimore, J. F. Weishampel. 1891. 31p.   3917

JOHNSON, JAMES W. Negro Americans, what now? New York, Viking press. 1934. viii, 103p. 3918

JONES, LAWRENCE C. The bottom rail. Papers on the Negro in Mississippi and interracial relations in the South for 25 years. New York, Fleming H. Revell co. 1935. 96p.   3919

JOSEY, CHARLES C. Race and national solidarity. New York, Chas. Scribner's sons. 1923. ix, 227p.   3920

KELLEY, WILLIAM D. The old South and the new. A series of letters. New York, London; G. P. Putnam's sons. 1888. 162p.   3921

KING, WILLIS J. The Negro in American life; an elective course for young people on Christian race relations. New York; Cincinnati, Methodist book concern. 1926. 154p.   3922

LaFARGE, JOHN S. T. Interricial justice. A study of the Catholic doctrine of race relations. New York, American press. 1937. xii, 226p.   3923

LASKER, BRUNO. Race attitudes in children. New York, Henry Holt & co. 1929.   3924

LEAP, WILLIAM L. Red Hill — neighborhood life and race relations in a rural section. Charlottesville, Va., University of Virginia press. 1933. 165p. (Phelps-Stokes papers).   3925

MAETERLINCK, MAURICE AND OTHERS. What is civilization? New York, Duffield & co. 1926. 217p. 3926

MATHEWS, BASIL J. The clash of color. New York, Missionary education movement. 1924. viii, 181p. 3927

MAYO, AMORY D. The duty of the white American towards his colored fellow-citizen. An address. 1892. 32p. 3928

MAYO, AMORY D. The third estate of the South. An address delivered before the American social science association, Saratoga, N. Y., Sept. 2, 1890. Boston, G. H. Ellis. 1890. 24p. 3929

MCDOUGALL, WILLIAM. The indestructible union; rudiments of political science for the American citizen. Boston, Little, Brown & co. 1925. ix, 249p. 3930

MCGUINN, ROBERT A. The race problem in the churches. Baltimore, J. F. Weishampel. 1890. 59p. 3931

MCKINLEY, CARLYLE. An appeal to Pharoah. The Negro problem, and its radical solution. New York, Fords, Howard & Hulbert. 1889. 205p. 3932

MEBANE, GEORGE A. The Negro problem as seen and discussed by southern white men. New York. Alliance pub. co. 1900. 40p. 3933

MILLER, KELLY. An appeal to conscience; America's code of caste a disgrace to democracy. New York, MacMillan co. 1918. 108p. 3934

MILLER, KELLY. An appeal to reason on the race problem. An open letter to John Temple Graves. Washington, The auth. 1906. 21p. 3935

MILLER, KELLY. As to the leopard's spots; an open letter to Thomas Dixon, Jr. Washington, The auth. 1905. 21p. 3936

MILLER, KELLY. The everlasting stain. Washington, Associated publishers. 1924. xiii, 352p. 3937

MILLER, KELLY. Out of the house of bondage. New York, Neale pub. co. 1914. 242p. 3938

MILLER, KELLY. Race adjustment; essays on the Negro in America. Washington, Neale pub. co. 1908. 306p. 3939

MIMS, EDWARD. The advancing South. Stories of progress and reaction. Garden City, N.Y., Doubleday, Page & co. 1926. xviii, 319p. 3940

MITCHELL, GEORGE W. The question before Congress, a consideration of the debates and final action by Congress upon various phases of the race question in the United States. Philadelphia, A.M.E. book concern. 1918. 247p. 3941

MONTGOMERY, HARRY E. Vital American problems. An attempt to solve the "trust," "labor," and the Negro" problems. New York; London, G.P. Putnam's sons. 1908. 384p. 3942

MORTON, JAMES F. The curse of race prejudice. New York, The auth. 1906. 78p. 3943

MORGAN, THOMAS J. The Negro in America and the ideal American republic. Philadelphia, American baptist pub. society. 1898. 203p. 3944

MOTON, ROBERT R. Racial goodwill. (Collected addresses reprinted from the Southern Workman.) Hampton Inst., Va., Institute press. 1916. 38p. 3945

MOTON, ROBERT R. Some elements necessary to race development. Hampton, Va., Hampton Institute press. 1913. 22p. 3946

MOTON, ROBERT R. What the Negro thinks. New York, Doran, Doubleday, Page & co. 1928. 225p.   3947

MURET, MAURICE. The twilight of the white races. New York, Charles Scribner's sons. 1926. 286p.   3948

MURPHY, EDGAR G. Problems of the present South. A discussion of certain of the educational, industrial and political issues in the southern states. New York; London, MacMillan & co 1904. 335p.   3949

MURPHY, EDGAR G. The white man and the Negro at the South. An address delivered before the American academy of political and social science. Philadelphia, 1904.   3950

MURRAY, GEORGE W. Race ideals; effects, causes and remedy for the Afro-American race troubles. Rev. ed. Newark, N. J., Rilograph press. 1914. 100p.   3951

NATIONAL CONFERENCE ON THE CHRISTIAN WAY OF LIFE, NEW YORK. And who is my neighbor? An outline for the study of race relations in America. New York, Association press. 1924. 231p. 3952

NATIONAL LEAGUE. The wrongs of the Negro; the remedy. Boston, The league. 1888. 14p.   3953

NATIONAL URBAN LEAGUE, Department of industrial relations. He crashed the color line. New York, The league. 1933. 32p. 3954

NEFF, LAWRENCE W. Race relations at close range; watching the Negro problem settle itself. Emory University, Ga., Banner press. 1931. 35p.   3955

NEGRO CHRISTIAN STUDY CONFERENCE. The new voice in race adjustments. Addresses and reports of the Negro Christian student conference, May 14-18, 1914. Atlanta. Ed. by A.M.

Trawick. New York, Student volunmovement. 1914. 230p.   3956

OLDHAM, JOSEPH H. Christianity and the race problem. New York, Geo. H. Doran co. 1924. xx, 280p. New York, Geo. H. Doran co. 1925. 75p.   3957

PAGE, THOMAS N. The Negro: The Southerner's problem. New York, Chas. Scribner's sons. 1904. 324p.   3958

PATTERSON, RAYMOND. The Negro and his needs. New York. Chicago, Fleming H. Revell co. 1911. 212p.   3959

PHELPS-STOKES FUND. Twenty year report . . . 1911-1931, with a series of studies of Negro progress and developments of race relations in the United States and Africa during the period, and a discussion of the present outlook. By J. H. Dillard, Thos. Jesse Jones, and others. New York, The fund. 1932. 127p.   3960

PICKETT, WILLIAM P. The Negro problem; Abraham Lincoln's solution. New York. London, G.P. Putnam's sons. 1909. x, 580p. 3961

PRESBYTERIAN GENERAL ASSEMBLY, Committee on colored evangelization. The church and the race problem. 1906. 91p.   3962

PRINGLE, ELIZABETH (Pseud.) Pennington, Patience. A woman rice planter. New York, MacMillan co. 1913. xiii, 450p.   3963

RACE RELATIONS – NEGRO PROBLEM. A collection of newspaper accounts and editorial opinion relating to the Negro problem and race relations. 1900-1925. 15v.   3964

REED, JOHN H. Racial adjustments in the Methodist Episcopal church. New York, Neale pub. co. 1914. 191p.   3965

245

REUTER, EDWARD B. The American race problem, a study of the Negro. New York, T. Y. Crowell co. 1927. xii, 448p.　　　　3966

RILEY, BENJAMIN F. The white man's burden; a discussion of the interracial question with special reference to the responsibility of the white race to the Negro problem. Birmingham, Ala., The auth. 1910. 239p.　　　　3967

ROGERS, J. A. From superman to man. Chicago, Godspeed press. 1917. 128p.; New York, Lenox pub. co. 1924. 128p.　　　　3968

ROYCE, JOSIAH. Race questions, provincialism and other American problems. New York, Mac Millan co. 1908. xiii, 287p.　　　　3969

RUIS, SUAREZ B. The color question in the United States. Tr. from the Spanish by J. G. Gordon New York, Hunt pub. co. 1922. 111p.
　　　　3970

SCHRIEKE, BERTRAM J. O. Alien Americans; a study of race relations. New York, Viking press. 1936. xi, 208p.　　　　3971

SELIGMANN, HERBERT J. The Negro faces America. New York. London. Harper & bros. 1920. 319p.　　　　3972

SHALER, NATHANIEL S. Neighbor: the natural history of human contacts. Boston. New York, Houghton. Mifflin co. 1904. 342p.
　　　　3973

SHUFELDT. ROBERT W. America's greatest problem: the Negro. Philadelphia. F. A. Davis & co. 1915. xii, 377p.　　　　3974

SIEGFRIED. ANDRE. America comes of age. Tr. from the French by H. H. Hemming. New York, Harcourt. Brace & co. 1927. x, 358p.　　3975

SIMMONS. ENOCH S. A solution of the race problem in the South. An essay. Raleigh, N. C., Edwards & Broughton. 1898. 150p.　　3976

SIMPSON, BERTRAM L. (pseud.) WEALE, B.L.P. The conflict of colour; the threatened upheaval throughout the world. New York, MacMillan co. 1910. ix, 341p. 3977

SOMERVILLE, H. M. Great sermon on the race question, with favorable comments by leading white and colored citizens. Norfolk, Va., Guide pub. co. 1921. 12p.　　3978

SOUTHERN SOCIETY FOR THE PROMOTION OF THE STUDY OF RACE CONDITIONS AND PROBLEMS IN THE SOUTH. A collection of newspaper accounts and editorial opinion relating to the first meeting . . . in Montgomery, Ala., May 8-10, 1900. 2v.　　3979

SOUTHERN SOCIETY FOR THE PROMOTION OF THE STUDY OF RACE CONDITIONS AND PROBLEMS IN THE SOUTH. Race problems in the South; report of the proceedings of the first annual conference, Montgomery, Ala., May 8-10, 1900. 240p.　　3980

SOUTHERN SOCIOLOGICAL CONGRESS. Proceedings and addresses. . . 1st-8th, 1912-1919.
　　　　3981

SPEER, ROBERT E. Of one blood, a short study of the race problem. New York, Council of women for home missions and missionary education movement. 1924. vi, 258-.　　　　3982

STEMMONS, JAMES S. The key; a tangible solution of the Negro problem. New York, Neale pub. co. 1916. 156p.　　　　3983

STEWART. ALEXANDER. The dogwatch meetings . . . London, Edinburgh; New York, Marshall bros. 1926. 240p.　　　　3984

STODDARD. THEODORE L.

Reforging America. The story of our nationhood. New York, Charles Scribner's sons. 1927. 387p. 3985

STODDARD, THEODORE L. The rising tide of color against white world supremacy. New York, Charles Scribner's sons. 1920. xxxii, 320p. 3986

STONE, ALFRED H. Studies in American race problems. New York, Doubleday, Page & co. 1908. xxii, 555p. 3987

STONE, ALFRED H., DILLARD, JAMES H. AND OTHERS. Lectures and addresses on the Negro in the South. Charlottesville, Va., University of Virginia press. 1915. 128p. (Phelps-Stokes papers). 3988

STOREY, MOORFIELD. The Negro question. An address. New York, N.A.A.C.P. 1918. 30p. 3989

STOWELL, JAY S. J.W. thinks black. v. 2 in the John Wesley, Jr. series. New York, Cincinnati, Methodist book concern. 1922. 190p. 3990

STREET, JAMES H. Look away. New York, Viking press. 1936. 3991

THE TASK OF THE LEADER. A discussion of some of the conditions of public leadership in our southern states. (Rpt. from the Sewanee review, Jan., 1907). 1907. 39p. 3992

TAYLOR, CAESAR A. P. The conflict and commingling of the races. A plea not for the heathens by a heathen to them that are not heathens. New York, Broadway pub. co. 1913. 119p. 3993

THOMAS, WILLIAM H. The American Negro. What he was, what he is, and what he may become. A critical and practical discussion. New York. London, MacMillan co. 1901. xxv, 440p. 3994

THOMAS, WILLIAM H. The new South; an inside view. Montgomery, Ala., Paragon press. 1908. 21p. 3995

TILLMAN, BENJAMIN R. (S.C.) The race problem. Speech . . . delivered in the U. S. Senate, Feb. 23-24, 1903. Washington, Govt. print. office. 1903. 32p. 3996

TILLMAN, BENJAMIN R. (S.C.) The race question. (Rpt. from Van Norden magazine, April, 1907). New York, 1907. 9p. 3997

TUFTS, JAMES H. American social morality. New York, Henry Holt & co. 1933. x, 376p. 3998

UNIVERSAL RACES CONGRESS, LONDON. Papers on interracial problems, communicated to the first Universal races congress, London, July 26-29, 1911. Ed. by G. Spiller. London, P. S. King & son; Boston, Ginn & co. 1911. xvi, 485p. 3999

UNIVERSITY COMMISSION ON SOUTHERN RACE QUESTIONS. Minutes of the organizational meeting, Nashville, Tenn., May 24, 1912. . . and of subsequent meetings, 1912-17. Lexington, Va., 1918. 75p. 4000

VERTREES, JOHN J. Negro problem: its solution, an explanation of the causes of increasing race antipathy and of the policy to be adopted with reference to the Negroes of the United States . . . Nashville, Marshall, Bruce co. 1905. 29p. 4001

WALKER, C. T. An appeal to Caesar, a sermon on the race question. Delivered at Carnegie Hall, New York, May 27, 1900. A review of the race conference, held in Montgomery, Ala., and a reply to the criticisms of Rev. Henry Frank upon the Negro race. New York, Pusey & Troxell. 1900. 32p.   4002

WASHINGTON, BOOKER T. Education will solve the race problem. (Rpt. from North American review, Aug., 1900). Tuskegee Inst., Ala., Tuskegee Institute press. 1903. 11p.   4003

WASHINGTON, BOOKER T., DUBOIS, W.E.B. AND OTHERS. The Negro problem; a series of articles by representative Negro Americans. New York, James Potts & co. 1903. 234p.   4004

WASHINGTON CONFERENCE ON THE RACE PROBLEM IN THE U.S. How to solve the race problem. Proceedings of the conference held under the auspices of the National sociological society, Washington, Nov. 9-12, 1903. Washington, Beresford. 1904. 286p.   4005

WEATHERFORD, WILLIS D. (comp.) Interracial cooperation. A study of the various agencies working in the field of racial welfare. Atlanta, Interracial committee of the war work council. 1918. 83p.   4006

WEATHERFORD, WILLS D. (comp.) Negro life in the South. Present conditions and needs. New York, Association press. 1910. 181p.   4007

WEATHERFORD, WILLIS D. AND JOHNSON, CHARLES S. Race relations; adjustment of whites and Negroes in the United States. New York, D. C. Heath & co. 1934. 590p.   4008

WHIPPLE, PHILA M. Negro neighbors bond and free. Lessons in history and humanity. Boston, Woman's American baptist home mission society. Pittsfield, Mass., Sun print. co. 1907. 143p.   4009

WHITE, JOHN E. The need of a southern program on the Negro problem. (Rpt. from South Atlantic quarterly, April, 1907). 1907. 14p.   4010

WILLIAMS, FLORA B. A unit – the Negro. A cooperative activity. Richmond, Va., Virginia commission on interracial cooperation. 1937. 12p.   4011

WILLIAMS, TALCOTT. The fallacy of the "selected group" in the discussion of the Negro question. (Rpt. from Southern Workman). Hampton, Va. Hampton Institute press. 1903. 7p.   4012

WILSON, PHILLIP W. An unofficial statesman, Robert C. Ogden. Garden City, N. Y., Doubleday, Page & co. 1925. xi, 275p.   4013

WOOFTER, THOMAS, JR. The basis of racial adjustment. Boston, Ginn & co. 1925. 258p.   4014

WOOFTER, THOMAS, JR., AND FISHER, ISAAC (eds.) Cooperation in southern communities. Suggested activities for county and city interracial committees. Atlanta, Commission on interracial cooperation. 1930. 66p.   4015

YOUNG, DONALD. American minority peoples. New York, Harper & bros. 1932.   4016

XLVIII. The Negro and Civil Rights and Law.

ARNETT, B. W. Speech . . . on the black laws, Delivered in the Ohio house of representatives. Mar. 10,
1886. Columbus, 1886. 17p.   4017

BALDWIN, JOHN D. Human rights and human races. In favor of the

civil rights of Negroes. Washington, Great Republic office. 1868. 4p.
4018

BEMIS, EDWARD W. Local government in the South and the southwest with an article on the popular election of the United States senators by John Haynes. Baltimore, Johns Hopkins press. 1893. 118p. (Johns Hopkins studies, 11th series, no. xi-xii).
4019

BURGESS, JOHN W. Reconstruction and the Constitution, 1866-1876. New York, Charles Scribner's sons. 1902. xii, 342p. (American history series, v. 7)
4020

BUTLER, CHARLES H. (comp.) Cases adjudged in the Supreme court of the United States, at the October term, 1902. U.S. reports, v. 189, pt. 3. New York, Banks law pub. co. 1903. 206p.
4021

COLORED NATIONAL LEAGUE. Open letter . . . to President William McKinley by the colored people of Massachusetts. Boston, The league. 1899. 11p.
4022

DOUGLASS, FREDERICK and INGERSOLL, ROBERT G. Proceedings of the Civil rights mass meeting, Washington, Oct. 22, 1883. Washington. 1883.
4023

FIFTEENTH AMENDMENT. Various newspaper accounts of the criticisms against the fifteenth amendment to the Constitution. 1866-1900.
4024

GRIMKE, FRANCIS J. A resemblance and a contrast between the American Negro and the children of Israel in Egypt, or the duty of the Negro to contend earnestly for his rights guaranteed under the Constitution. A discourse delivered in Washington, Oct. 12, 1902. Washington. 1902. 14p.
4025

GRIMKE, FRANCIS J. Equality of full rights for all citizens, black and white, alike. Washington. 1907. 19p.
4026

GUILD, JUNE P. Black Laws of Virginia. A summary of the legislative acts of Virginia concerning Negroes from earliest times to the present. Richmond, Whittet and Shepperson. 1936. 249p.
4027

HEWIN, F. THOMAS. Separate car law in Virginia. (Reprinted from the Colored American Magazine, May 1900). Boston, The author. 1900. 7p.
4028

INDIANOLA POST OFFICE CONTROVERSY. Various newspaper accounts of "Threats to close a postoffice, because the postmistress is colored" at Indianola, Miss. 1903-1904.
4029

LANGSTON, JOHN M. Civil rights law. 1884. 24p.
4030

LOU, HERBERT H. Juvenile courts in the United States. Chapel Hill, University of North Carolina press. London, Oxford University press. 1927. 300p.
4031

MOSS, FRANK. Persecution of Negroes. New York, 1900.
4032

MURPHY, EDGAR G. The peonage case in Alabama. Three letters . . . Montgomery, Ala., 1903. 17p. (Rpt. from N. Y. Post, June 15, 1903).
4033

NATIONAL ASSOCIATION FOR THE ADVANCEMENT OF COLORED PEOPLE. Proceedings and reports . . . 1st-40th, 1909-1917; 1918-1939. New York, The association. 1909-39.
4034

RIDDLE, ALBERT G. Law students and lawyers, the philosophy of political parties, and other subjects. Washington, Morrison. 1873. 275p.
4035

RURAL SEGREGATION. Various

newspaper accounts of a form segregation bill, strongly supported by Clarence Poe, editor of the "Progressive Farmer." 1v. 4036

SCARLETT, GEORGE C. Laws against liberty. New York, The author. 1937. 135p. 4037

SEGREGATION COURT CASES. Various newspaper accounts and editorials on Negroes winning cases against segregation, etc. 1913-1918. 2v. 4038

SEGREGATION IN SCHOOLS. Various newspaper accounts of measures prohibiting white teachers from teaching in Negro schools. Also Negroes barred from public schools. 1900-18. 1917-18. 2v.
4039

SEGREGATION, RESIDENTIAL. Various newspaper accounts of the Supreme court decision against the city of Louisville. 1914-1917. 4040

SEPARATE RAILWAY CAR LAWS. Various newspaper accounts. 2v. v. 1, Alabama – Texas. 1895-1905. v. 2, Virginia. 1900-1919. 4041

SKAGGS, WILLIAM H. The southern oligarchy. An appeal in behalf of the silent masses of our country against the despotic rule of the few. New York. Devin-Adair co. 1924. xi, 472p. 4042

SMITH, WILFORD H. Negro's right to jury representation. Cheyney, Pa., Committee of twelve for the advancement of the interests of the Negro race. 1914. 4p. 4043

STEPHENSON, GILBERT T. Race distinctions in American law. New York. London. D. Appleton & co. 1910. xiv, 388p. 4044

STEVENS, W. S. Duties of clerks of the Superior court toward the colored race. A speech delivered at Waynesville. N.C., July 6, 1922.

Raleigh, Edwards & Broughton. 1922. 5p. 4045

STYLES, FITZHUGH L. Negroes and the law in the race's battle for liberty, equality and justice under the Constitution of the United States. A manual of rights of the race under law. Boston, Christopher pub. house. 1937. 320p. 4046

U. S. HOUSE OF REPRESENTATIVES. Report . . . of a hearing on segregation of clerks and employees in the Civil service. Washington, Govt. print. office. 1914. 22p. 4047

U. S. HOUSE OF REPRESENTATIVES. (64th Congress, 1st session). Report of a hearing before the House committee on the District of Columbia, Feb. 11, 1916, on the intermarriage of whites and Negroes in the District of Columbia and separate accommodations in street cars for whites and Negroes. Washington, Govt. print. office. 1916. 30p.
4848

U. S. SUPREME COURT. Opinion in the case of Tarrance vs. Florida; Negroes excluded from jury which tried a Negro, Oct. term, 1902. Washington, 1902. 6p. 4049

U. S. SUPREME COURT. Opinion in the case of Buchanan vs. Warley. Washington. 1917. 11p. 4050

U. S. SUPREME COURT. Opinion relative to the court of appeals of the state of Kentucky in error, disallowing a Negro to occupy certain residence. No. 33, October term, 1917. Washington, 1917. 11p. 4051

WARMOTH, H. C. Annual message of the Governor to the General assembly of Louisiana, delivered at the opening of the session of 1872.

New Orleans, Republican office. 1872. 26p.   4052

WHITE, GEORGE C. (N.C.) Speech . . . on the defense of the Negro race – with charges answered. Delivered in the House of representatives, Jan. 29, 1901. Washington, Govt. print. office. 1901. 14p.   4053

WHY COLORED PEOPLE IN PHILA-DELPHIA are excluded from the street cars. Philadelphia, Merrihew & son. 1866. 27p.   4054

WILSON, WOODROW – TROTTER, WM. MUNROE. Various newspaper accounts of a conference between President Wilson and Wm. Munroe Trotter, chairman and spokesman for a delegation representing the "National independence equal rights league." 1912.   4055

XLIX. Histories, Historical, Sociological and Other Studies Relating to the Negro.

ALEXANDER, WILLIAM T. History of the colored race in America. Containing also their ancient and modern life in Africa, modes of living, employments, customs, habits, social life, etc. The origin and development of slavery in the old world and its introduction on the American continent; the slave trade; slavery and its abolition in Europe and America. The Civil war, emancipation education, and advancement of the colored race, their civil and political rights. 3d ed. rev. New Orleans. Palmatto pub. co. 1887. 600p.   4056

ALLEN, JAMES S. The Negro question in the United States. New York, International pub. 1936.   4057

AMERICAN ACADEMY OF POLITICAL AND SOCIAL SCIENCE, PHILADELPHIA. The annals. . . 1898 – Philadelphia, The academy. 1898- collection has: 1900-1928. 28v.   4058

AMERICAN NEGRO ACADEMY, WASHINGTON. Occasional papers . . . 1896-1919. Washington, The Academy. 1896-1919.   4059

ARNOLD, JOSEPH I. Problems in American life. Evanston. Ill. New York, Row, Peterson & co. 1934. xviii, 619p.   4060

ATLANTA UNIVERSITY. Leaflets . . . 1900 – Atlanta, Atlanta University press. 1900 – Collection has: 1st-20th.   4061

BEACH, WALTER G. American social problems. Palo Alto, Calif., Stanford University press. London, Oxford University press. 1934. ix, 391p.   4062

BLUMENTHAL, ALBERT. Small town stuff. Chicago, University of Chicago press. 1932. xvii, 416p.   4063

BLYDEN, EDWARD W. The Negro in ancient history. (Rpt. from Methodist quarterly review, Jan. 1869). Washington, M'Gill & Witherew. 1869. 28p.   4064

BOGARDUS, EMORY S. History of social thought. Los Angeles, J. R. Milles. 1928. 668p.   4065

BRAWLEY, BENJAMIN G. A short history of the American Negro. New York, MacMillan co. 1913. 247p. 2d ed. rev. New York, MacMillan co. 1929. xvii, 280p.   4066

BRAWLEY, BENJAMIN G. A social history of the American Negro; being a history of the Negro problem in the United States, including a history and study of the republic of Liberia. New York, Macmillan co. 1921. 420p.   4067

BROOKS, LEE M. Manual for southern regions. Chapel Hill, University of North Carolina press. 1937. 194p.   4068

BROWN, INA C. The story of the American Negro. New York, Friendship press. 1936. xiii, 208p.   4069

CALDWELL, ARTHUR B. History of the American Negro and his institutions. Atlanta, Caldwell pub. co. 1917. 2v.   4070

CALDWELL, ERSKINE and BOURKE-WHITE, MARGARET. You have seen their faces. New York, Viking press. 1937. 190p.   4071

CALVERTON, VICTOR F. The Negro. (In America now, 1938) New York. 1938. 11p.   4072

CASON, CLARENCE. 90° in the shade. Chapel Hill, University of North Carolina press. 1935. xiii, 3-186p.   4073

COHN, DAVIS L. God shakes creation. New York. London, Harper & bros. 1935. xvi, 299p.   4074

COLUMBIA UNIVERSITY. Studies in history, economics, and public law. v. 49. Ed. by the faculty of Columbia University. New York, Longmans, Green & co. London, P. S. King & son. 1912. 158p.   4075

COOPER, JAMES W. Historical paper. Sixty years and beyond. New York, American missionary association. 1900. 13p.   4076

CROMWELL, JOHN W. The early Negro convention movement. Washington, American Negro academy. 1904. 23p.   4077

CUTHBURT, MARION. We Sing

America. New York, Friendship press. 1936. 117p.   4078

DABNEY, WENDELL P. Cincinnati's colored citizens. Historical, sociological and biographical. Cincinnati, Dabney pub. co. 1926. 44p.   4079

DANIELS, JOHN. In Freedom's Birthplace: a study of the Boston Negroes. Boston. New York, Houghton, Mifflin co. 1914. 496p.   4080

DECORSE, HELEN C. The Negro in Charlottesville, Virginia. Charlottesville, Va., University of Virginia press. 1933. 102p. (Phelps-Stokes papers).   4081

DUBOIS, W. E. BURGHARDT. The Philadelphia Negro. A social study, together with a report on domestic service by Isabel Eaton. Philadelphia, University of Pennsylvania. 1899. 520p.   4082

DUBOIS, W. E. BURGHARDT. Black folk, then and now; an essay in the history and sociology of the Negro race. New York, H. Holt & co. 1939. ix, 401p.   4083

DUBOIS, W. E. BURGHARDT. The black north; a social study. (Rpt. from the "New York Times" for Nov. 17, 24 and Dec. 1, 8, 15, 1901.)   4084

DUBOIS, W. E. BURGHARDT. The Negro, New York, Henry Holt & co. London, Williams & Norgate. 1915. 254p.   4085

DUBOIS, W. E. BURGHARDT. The Negro in the black belt; some social sketches. (Bulletin of the Dept. of labor, no. 22, 1899.) Washington, Govt. print. office. 16p.   4086

DUBOIS, W. E. BURGHARDT. Negroes of Farmville, Virginia; A social study. Washington, Govt. print. off. 1898. 38p. (Bulletin of the Dept. of labor, no. 14).   4087

DURHAM, JOHN S. To teach the

Negro History, a suggestion. Philadelphia, David McKay. 1897. 48p.
4088

ELDRIDGE, SELA. Major problems of democracy; social conditions in the United States. New York, D. Appleton & co. 1938. 585p. 4089

EMBREE, EDWIN R. Brown America, the story of a new race. New York, Viking Press. 1931. 311p. 4090

EPPSE, MERL R. A guide to the study of the Negro in American history. Nashville, National educational pub. co. 1939. 4091

EPPSE, MERL R. The Negro, too, in American history. Chicago, New York, National educational pub. co. 1938. xxii, 544p. 4092

FEDERAL WRITERS' PROJECT. (North Carolina, Tennessee, Georgia) These are our lives. Chapel Hill, University of North Carolina press. 1939. xx, 421p. 4093

FERRIS, WILLIAM H. The African Abroad, or His evolution in Western civilization tracing his development under Caucasian Milieu. New Haven, Tuttle, Morehouse & Taylor. 1913. 2v. 4094

FORD, THEODORE P. God wills the Negro; an anthropological and geographical restoration of the lost history of the American Negro people . . . Chicago, Geographical Institute press. 1939. 159p. 4095

FRAZIER, E. FRANKLIN. The Negro family in the United States. Chicago, University of Chicago press. 1939. 686p. 4096

FULLER, THOMAS O. Pictorial history of the American Negro. Memphis, Tenn. Pictorial history, inc. 1933. 375p. 4097

GILLETTE, JOHN M. Current social problems. New York. Cincinnati, American book co. 1933. x, 819p. 4098

GONZALES, AMBROSE E. The captain: stories of the black border. Columbia, S.C., State co. 1924. xvi, 384p. 4099

GRADY, HENRY W. The New South, with a character sketch of Henry W. Grady by Oliver Dyer. New York, Robert Bonner's sons. 1890. 273p.
4100

HALL, SAMUEL W. Tangier island. A study of an isolated group. Philadelphia, University of Pennsylvania press. London, Oxford University press. 1929. x, 122p. 4101

HAMPTON NEGRO CONFERENCE. Proceedings . . . 1897-1911. Hampton, Va., Hampton Institute press. 1897-1911. 11v. 4102

HARLAN, HOWARD H. Ziontown, a study in human ecology. Charlottesville, Va., University of Virginia press. 1935. 65p. (Phelps-Stokes papers). 4103

HARRIS, JOHN. A century of emancipation. London, J. M. Dent & sons. 1933. 4104

HEYWOOD, JANE S. Brown jackets. Columbia, S.C., State co. 1923. 64p. 4105

HILYER, ANDREW F. (comp.) A historical, biographical and statistical study of colored Washington. A compilation of the efforts of the colored people. . . for social betterment. Washington. Union league. 1901. 174p. 4106

HOLMES, SAMUEL J. The Negro's struggle for survival, a study in human ecology. Berkeley, Calif., University of California press. 1937. xv, 296p. 4107

INGLE, EDWARD. The Negro in the District of Columbia. Baltimore, Johns Hopkins press. 1893. 110p. (Johns Hopkins studies, 11th series, no. III.-IV.) 4108

IRVIN, MAJORIE F. The Negro in

Charlottesville and Albemarle county, Virginia. Charlottesville, Va., University of Virginia press. 1929. 94p. (Phelps-Stokes papers). 4109

JACKSON, GILES B. and DAVIS, D. WEBSTER. The industrial history of the Negro race in the United States. Richmond, Va., The authors. 1908. 400p. 4110

JARVIS, J. Brief history of the Virgin islands. St. Thomas, V. I., Art shop. 1938. 4111

JOHNSON, EDWARD A. A school history of the Negro race in America, from 1619 to 1890, with a short introduction as to the origin of the race; also a short sketch of Liberia. Philadelphia, The author. 1891. 447p. Rev. ed. Philadelphia, Sherman & co. 1892. 447p. 3d ed. Chicago, W. B. Conkey co. 1894. 4112

JOHNSON, GUION GRIFFIS. A social history of the Sea islands with special references to St. Helena island, S. C. Chapel Hill, University of North Carolina press. 1930. x, 245p. 4113

JOHNSON, JAMES W. Black Manhattan. A historical survey of the Negro in New York City. New York, Alfred A. Knopf. 1930. 284p. 4114

JOHNSON, JAMES W. Negro Americans, What now? New York, Viking press. 1934. 4115

JOURNAL OF NEGRO EDUCATION. A quarterly review of problems incident to the education of Negroes. Washington, Bureau of educational research, Howard University. 1932-40. v. 1-8. 4116

JOURNAL OF NEGRO HISTORY. A quarterly journal of historical and sociological research pertaining to

Negro life and history. Washington, Assn. for the study of Negro life and history. 1916-1940. v. 1-25. 4117

KLINEBERG, OTTO. Negro intelligence and selective migration. New York, Columbia Univ. press. 1935. 64p. 4118

LAWSON, ELIZABETH. Study outline history of the American Negro people. New York, Workers book shop. 1939. 105p. 4119

LEE, GEORGE W. Beale street — where the blues began. New York, R. O. Ballou. 1934. 4120

LEWIS, R. B. Light and Truth; collected from the Bible and ancient and modern history, containing the universal history of the colored and the Indian race, from the creation of the world to the present time. Boston, A committee of colored gentlemen. 1844. 400p. 4121

LICHTENBERGER, J. P. (ed.) The Negro's progress in fifty years. Philadelphia. American academy of political and social science. 1913. 244p. 4122

LOCKE, ALAIN. The Negro in America. Chicago. American library association. 1933. 64p. 4123

LOCKE, ALAIN. (ed.) The new Negro; an interpretation. New York, A. & C. Boni. 1925. 446p. 4124

MILLER, NORA. Girl in a rural family. Chapel Hill, University of North Carolina press. 1935. ix, 108p. 4125

MORRISEY, R. A. Colored people in Bible history. Hammond, Ind., The author. 1925. 133p. 4126

MOTON, ROBERT R. What the Negro thinks. Garden City, N.Y., Doubleday, Page & co. 1929. 4127

MUNROE, DAY. Chicago families, a

study of unpublished data. Chicago, University of Chicago press. 1932. xxi, 344p.   4128

NEARING, SCOTT. Black America. New York, Vanguard press. 1929. 275p.   4129

NEGRO IN DETROIT, prepared for the mayor's interracial committee by a special survey staff. Detroit, Bureau of governmental research. 1926. 12v.   4130

NEW JERSEY CONFERENCE OF SOCIAL WORK. The Negro in New Jersey. A survey by the interracial commission, conference of social work, in cooperation with the state. Newark, The conference. 1932. 116p.   4131

ODUM, HOWARD W. American social problems. New York, Henry Holt & co. 1939. vii, 549p.   4132

ODUM, HOWARD W. Southern regions of the United States. Chapel Hill, University of North Carolina press. 1936. xi, 664p.   4133

OTKEN, CHARLES H. The ills of the South; or, related causes hostile to the general prosperity of the Southern people. New York, G. P Putnam's sons. 1894. 277p.   4134

PENDLETON, MRS. LELIA A. A narrative of the Negro. Washington, R. L. Pendleton press. 1912. 217p.   4135

PENN, I. GARLAND (ed.) The United Negro: his problems and his progress; containing the addresses and proceedings of the Negro Young People's Christian & Educational Congress, August 6-11, 1902 with letters by W. J. Gaines, B. T. Washington and others. Atlanta, Ga., Luther Pub. co. 1902. 600p.   4136

PENNINGTON, JAMES W. Text book of the origin and history . . . of the colored people. Hartford, L.

Skinner. 1841. 96p.   4137

PERRY, RUFUS L. The Cushite of the Descendants of Ham as found in the sacred scriptures and in the writings of ancient historians and poets from Noah to the Christian Era. Springfield, Mass., Willey & co., 1893. 175p.   4138

PETERKIN, JULIA. Roll Jordon, Roll, with photographic studies by Doris Ullman. New York, R. O. Ballou. 1933. 251p.   4139

PORCH, MARVIN E. The Philadelphia main line Negro. A social, economic, and educational survey. Philadelphia, The author. 1938. 125p.   4140

POWDERHOUSE, HORTENSE. After freedom; a cultural study in the deep South. New York, Viking press. 1939. xx, 408p.   4141

PRESIDENT'S RESEARCH COMMITTEE ON SOCIAL TRENDS. Recent trends in the United States. New York, London, McGraw-Hill co. 1933. 2v.   4142

REID, IRA DeA. In a minor key. Negro youth in story and fact. Prepared for the American Youth Commission. Washington, American Council on Education. 1940. 134p.   4143

ROMAN, CHARLES V. American Civilization and the Negro; the Afro-American in relation to National Progress. Philadelphia, Davis Co., 1921. 434p.   4144

ROUSSEVE, CHARLES B. The Negro in Louisiana. New Orleans, Xavier University press. 1937. xvii, 212p.   4145

SCHOMBURG, ARTHUR A. Racial integrity; a plea for a chair of Negro history in our schools. New York, Negro society for historical research. 1913. 19p.   4146

SHACKLEFORD, JANE D. The

child's story of the Negro. Washington, Associated publishers. 1938. 219p. 4147

SIMPSON, GEORGE E. The Negro in the Philadelphia press. Philadelphia, University of Pennsylvania. 1936. 158p. 4148

SNAVELY, TIPTON R. The taxation of Negroes in Virginia. Charlottesville, Va., University of Virginia press. 1917. 97p. (Phelps-Stokes papers). 4149

SPIVAK, JOHN L. Georgia nigger. New York, Brewer Warren & Putnam. 1932. 241p. 4150

STANFORD, PETER T. The tragedy of the Negro in America, a condensed history of the enslavement, sufferings, emancipation, present condition and progress of the Negro race in the United States. Boston, Ca. A. Wasto. 1897. 230p. 4151

STRAKER, DAVID A. The new South investigated. Detroit, The author. 1888. viii, 241p. 4152

TANSER, H. A. Settlement of Negro in Kent county, Ontario, and a study of the mental capacity of their descendents. Chatham, Ont. The author. 1939. 4153

THOM, WILLIAM T. Negroes of Sandy Spring, Maryland: a social study. Washington, Govt. print. off. 1901. 59p. (Bulletin of the Department of labor, no. 32, Jan. 1901.) 4154

THOM, WILLIAM T. Negroes of Lit walton, Virginia; a social study of the "Oyster Negro." Washington, Govt. print. office. 1901. 55p. (Bulletin of the Dept. of labor, no. 37, 1901.) 4155

TILLINGHAST, JOSEPH A. The Negro in Africa and America. New York, Macmillan co. 1902. vi,

232p. (American economic assn.) 4156

VAN DEUSEN, JOHN G. The black man in white America. Washington, Associated pub. 1938. v, 338p. 4157

VERIDIER, EVA L. Some experiences while taking the census among the low country Negroes of South Carolina. Beaufort, S.C., 1932. 13p. 4158

VIRGINIA WRITERS' PROJECT. The Negro in Negro; the rise of a race from slavery. New York, Doubleday, Page & co. 1909. 2v. 4159

WASHINGTON, BOOKER T. The story of the Negro; the rise of a race from slavery. New York, Doubleday, Page & co. 1909. 2v. 4160

WATTERSON, HENRY (ed.) Oddities in southern life and character. Boston, Houghton Mifflin co. 1883. 485p. 4161

WEATHERFORD, WILLIS D. The Negro from Africa to America. New York, Geo. H. Doran co. 1924. vi, 487p. 4162

WEATHERFORD, WILLIS D. A survey of the Negro boy in Nashville, Tenn. New York, Associated pub. 1932. 4163

WILLIAMS, GEORGE W. History of the Negro race in America, from 1619 to 1880, Negroes as slaves, as soldiers, and as citizens. New York, G. P. Putnam's sons. 1883. 2v. 4164

WOODSON, CARTER G. The Negro in our history. Washington, Associated publishers. 1922. xv, 393p. 4th ed. Washington, Associated publishers. 1927. xxx, 616p. 6th ed. Washington, Associated publishers. 1931. xxx, 673p. 4165

WOODSON, CARTER G. The story of the Negro retold. Washington,

Associated publishers. 1935. 369p.
4166
WOOFTER, THOMAS J. Jr. Black
yeomanry, life on St. Helena island.
New York, Henry Holt & co. 1930.
291p.   4167
WOOFTER, THOMAS J. Jr. The
Negroes of Athens, Georgia.
Athens, University of Georgia.
1913. 62p. (Phelps-Stokes papers).
4168

WRIGHT, RICHARD R. Jr. The Negro
in Pennsylvania; a study in
economic history. Philadelphia,
A.M.E. book concern. 1912. 250p.
4169
WRIGHT, RICHARD R. Jr. Negroes
of Xenia, Ohio; a social study.
Washington, Govt. print. office.
1903. 38p. (Bulletin of the Department of Labor. no. 48, Sept. 1903).
4170

L. Bibliographies and General Reference Works on the Negro.

ALLEN, EATON. A bibliography of
social surveys, fact finding studies
made as a basis for social action.
New York, Russell Sage foundation. 1930. xlviii, 467p.   4171
AMERICAN LIBRARY
ASSOCIATION. Booklist: a guide
to new books. Chicago, The
association. 1905.   4172
BARTLETT, JOHN R. The literature
of the rebellion. A catalogue of
books and pamphlets relating to the
Civil war in the United States, and
on subjects growing out of that
event, together with works on
American slavery, and essays from
reviews and magazines on the same
subjects. Boston, Draper &
Holliday. 1866. iv. 477p.   4173
CALIVER, AMBROSE & GREEN,
ETHEL G. Education of Negroes. A
selected bibliography, 1931-1935.
Washington, Govt. print. office.
1937. Bureau of education bulletin
no. 8).   4174
CROMWELL, JOHN. American Negro
bibliography of the year. Washington. American Negro academy.
1915.(Papers of the Academy).4175
DUBOIS, W. E. BURGHARDT. (ed.)
A select bibliography of the Negro
American for general readers.
Atlanta, Atlanta University press.
1901. 11p.   4176

DUBOIS, W. E. BURGHARDT.
(comp.) A select bibliography of
the Negro American. A compilation
made under the direction of
Atlanta University; together with
proceedings of the 10th conference
for the study of Negro problems,
May 30, 1905. Atlanta, Atlanta
University press. 1905. 71p. 4177
DUBOIS, W. E. BURGHARDT.
(comp.) A suggested list of subjects
which an encyclopaedia of the
Negro should treat. 1936. 2v. 4178
FISK UNIVERSITY. Literature
pertaining to the Negro . . .
Nashville, Fisk University press.
1935. 24p.   4179
GRIFFIN, APPLETON P. C. (comp.)
List of discussions of the 14th and
15th amendments with special
reference to Negro suffrage. U.S.
Library of Congress, Division of
bibliography. Washington, Govt.
print. office. 1906. 18p.   4180
GRINSTEAD, S. E. (comp.) A select,
classified, and briefly annotated list
of two hundred fifty books by or
about the Negro, published during
the past ten years. The Negro.
collection. Fisk University library.
Nashville, Fisk University. 1939.
4181
HAMPTON INSTITUTE. Historical
books about the Negro race in the

Hampton Institute library. Hampton, Va., The library. 1928. 7p. 4182

HUBBARD, G. H. and FOWLER. J.S. A classified catalogue of the collection of anti-slavery propaganda in the Oberlin College library. Oberlin, O., Oberlin library bulletin. v. 2, no. 3. 1932. 4183

JOHNSON, JULIA E. (comp.) Selected articles on the Negro problem. New York, H. W. Wilson Co. 1921. xxvi, 370p. 4184

LOCKE, ALAIN L. The Negro in America. Chicago, American library association. 64p. 1933. 4185

NATIONAL URBAN LEAGUE. Department of research. Selected bibliography on the Negro. Rev. ed. New York. The league. 1939. 47p. 4186

NEGRO YEAR BOOK. An encyclopedia of the Negro. Published separately for 1912 and 1913; every two years from 1915 to 1938 except 1920-21, 1923-24, 1927-28, 1933-34, and 1935-26. Monroe N. Work, ed. Tuskegee, Ala., Negro yearbook pub. co. V. 1-9. 4187

NEW YORK PUBLIC LIBRARY, 135th St. Branch. The Negro, a selected bibliography. New York, The library. 1935. 21p. 4188

REID, IRA D. Negro youth; a selected bibliography on their social and economic backgrounds. Unpublished studies 1900-1938. Washington, American youth Commission. 1939. 71p. 4189

RICHARDSON. C. (ed.) The national cyclopedia of the colored race. Montgomery, Ala., National pub. co. 1919. 622p. 4190

ROSS, FRANK A. and KENNEDY, LOUIS V. A bibliography of Negro migration. New York, Columbia University press. 1934. 251p. 4191

STONE, A. H. Some recent race problem literature. (Rpt. from Southern Historical Society publications. Nov. 1904, v. 8, no. 6).. 10p. 4192

U. S. EMPLOYMENT SERVICE. A bibliography of Negro labor. Washington, office of Negro field service. 1938. 4193

U. S. LIBRARY OF CONGRESS. Select list of references on the Negro question; comp. under the direction of A.P.C. Griffin. Washington, Govt. print. office. 1903. 28p. 4194

WORK, MONROE N. (comp.) A. bibliography of the Negro in Africa and America. New York, H. W. Wilson & co. 1928. xxi. 698p. 4195

WORKS PROGRESS ADMINISTRATION. Catalogue of books in the Moorland foundation, Howard University. Washington, Howard University press. 1939. 4196

LI. Negro and Literature.

1.General discussions of the Negro and literature.

BRAITHWAITE, WILLIAM S. B. (ed.) Anthology of magazine verse and year book of American poetry. Collection has: Years 1913-14-15-16-17. 1918-21. 1922-23-24-25. Boston. New York. 1913-25. 12v. 4197

BRAWLEY, BENJAMIN G. A new survey of English literature. A text book for colleges. New York, F. S. Crofts & co. 1936. 388p. 4198

BRAWLEY, BENJAMIN G. Early Negro American writers. Selections with biographical and critical introductions. Chapel Hill, University of North Carolina press. 1935. ix, 305p. 4199

BRAWLEY, BENJAMIN G. The Negro genius: a new appraisal of the achievement of the American Negro in literature and the fine arts. New York, Dodd, Mead & co. 1937. 366p. 4200

BRAWLEY, BENJAMIN G. The Negro in literature and art in the United States. Atlanta, Ga., The auth. 1910. 60p. 2d ed. New York, Duffield co. 1918. 180p. Rev. ed. New York, Duffield co. 1921. 197p. 4th ed. New York, Duffield co. 1929. 210p. 5th ed. New York, Duffield co. 1934. 257p. 4201

BROWN, STERLING A. The Negro in American fiction. Washington, Associates in Negro folk education. 1937. 209p. (Bronze booklet no. 6) 4202

BROWN, STERLING A. Negro poetry and drama. Washington, Associates in Negro folk education. 1937. 142p. (Bronze booklet, no. 7) 4203

CALVERTON, VICTOR F. (ed.) Anthology of American Negro literature. New York, Modern library. 1929. 535p. 4204

COOK, MERCER. Le noir; morceaux choicis de vingt-neuf Francais celebre. New York. Cincinnati, American book co. 1934. x, 173p. 4205

CROMWELL, OTELIA and others. (eds.) Readings from Negro authors . . . with a bibliography of Negro literature. New York, Harcourt, Brace & co. 1931. xii, 388p. 4206

CULLEN, COUNTEE (ed.) Caroling dusk. An anthology of verse by Negro poets. New York, Harper & bros. 1927. 237p. 4207

CULP, DANIEL W. (ed.) Twentieth century Negro literature, or a cyclopedia of thought on the vital topics relating to the Negro. Naperville, Ill., J. L. Nichols & co. 1902. 472p. 4208

CUNARD, NANCY (comp.) Negro, an anthology, 1931-1933. London, Wishart & co. 1934. viii, 854p. 4209

ELEAZER, ROBERT B. Singers in dawn — supplement to a study of American literature. Atlanta, Conference on education and race relations. 1934. 23p. 4210

FEDERAL WRITERS' PROJECT, (N.Y.) American stuff. An anthology of prose and verse. New York, Viking press. 1937. 301p. 4211

FORD, NICK A. The contemporary Negro novel, a study in race relations. Boston, Meador pub. co. 1936. 108p. 4212

GAINES, FRANCIS P. The southern plantation. A study in the development and the accuracy of a tradition. New York, Columbia University press. 1925. viii, 243p. 4213

GREEN, ELIZABETH L. The Negro in contemporary American literature. Chapel Hill, University of North Carolina press. 1928. 94p. 4214

GREGOIRE, HENRI. An enquiry concerning the intellectual and moral faculties, and literature of Negroes. . . An account of the life and works of fifteen Negroes and mulattoes distinguished in science, literature, and the arts. Tr. from the French by D.B. Warden. Brooklyn, Thomas Kirk. 1810. 240p. 4215

GREGOIRE, HENRI. De la literature des Negroes, etc. Paris, Chez Maradan. 1808. 287p. 4216

HAZARD, LUCY L. The frontier in American literature. New York, T. Y. Crowell co. 1927. xx, 308p. 4217

HIBBARD, CLARENCE A. The South in contemporary literature. Chapel Hill, University of North Carolina press. 1925. 45p. 4218

JOHNSON, CHARLES S. (ed.) Ebony and topez. A collectanea. New York, National urban league. 1927. 164p. 4219

JOHNSON, JAMES W. (ed.) The book of American Negro poetry . . . with an essay on the Negro's creative genius. New York, Harcourt, Brace & co. 1922. xlviii, 217p. 2d ed. New York, Harcourt, Brace & co. 1931. xlviii, 217p. 4220

KERLIN, ROBERT T. Negro poets and their poems. Washington, Associated pub. 1923. xv, 285p. 2d ed. Washington, Associated publishers. 1935. 300p. 4221

KRAPP, GEORGE P. English language in America. Oxford, Oxford University press. 1925. 2v. 4222

KREYMBORG, ALFRED. Lyric America. New York, Tudor pub. co. 1935. 4223

LOCKE, ALAIN L. (comp.) A decade of Negro self-expression, . . . foreword by Howard W. Odum. Charlottesville, Va., Occasional papers no. 26, John F. Slater Fund. 1928. 20p. 4224

LOCKE, ALAIN L. The new Negro. New York, Boni. 1925. xviii, 446p. 4225

LOGGINS, VERNON. The Negro author: his development in America. New York, Columbia University press. 1931. ix, 480p. 4226

MANLY, LOUISE. Southern literature from 1579 to 1895. Richmond, Va., 1900. 4227

MAYS, BENJAMIN E. The Negro's God as reflected in his literature. Boston, Chapman & Grimes. 1938. viii, 269p. 4228

MIRSKY, D. S. Pushkin. (Republic of letters). New York, E. P. Dutton & co. 1926. v, 266p. 4229

MORTON, BEATRICE L. Negro poetry in America. Boston, Stratford co. 1926.. 71p. 4230

MURPHY, BEATRICE M. (ed.) Negro voices. An anthology of contemporary verse. New York, Henry Harrison. 1938. 173p. 4231

NEGRO AND LITERATURE. A collection of newspaper accounts and magazine articles relating to Negro authors and their works. 1890-1918. 8v. 4232

NEGRO AUTHORS AND POETS. A collection of newspaper accounts relating to Negro literature and Negro authors and poets. 1900-1925. 10v. 4233

NEGRO DIALECTS. A collection of newspaper accounts and editorial opinions relating to Negro dialects. 1901-15. 2v. 4234

NELSON, JOHN H. The Negro character in American literature. Lawrence, Kan., Dept. of journalism press. 1926. 146p. (University of Kansas humanistic studies, v. 4, no. 1). 4235

NEWSON, JOHN T. C. The composer's friend and compendium of useful information. New York, P. Anstadt & sons. 1896. 305p. 4236

O'BRIEN, HELEN M. and others. The brown thrush. Anthology of verse by Negro students. Memphis, Malcolm-Roberts co. 1935. 65p. 4237

REDDING, JAY S. To make a poet

black. Chapel Hill, University of North Carolina press. 1939. x, 3-142p. 4238

REVIEWS OF BOOKS ON THE NEGRO. A collection of newspaper and magazine reviews of books relating to the Negro. 1893-1917. 4v. 4239

SCHOMBERG, ARTHUR A. (comp.) A bibliographical check list of American Negro poetry. New York, C. F. Heartman. 1916. 57p. 4240

TOOMER, JEAN. Essentials. Definitions and aphorisms. Chicago, privately printed. 1931. 54p. 4241

TRENT, W. P. Southern writers; selections in prose and verse. New York, MacMillan co. 1905. 544p. 4242

TRENT, W. P. and others (eds.) Cambridge history of American literature. New York, G. P. Putnam's sons. 1917-21. 2v. 4243

TURNER, LORENZO D. Anti-slavery sentiment in American literature prior to 1865. Washington, Assn. for the study of Negro life and history. 1929. 188p. 4244

UNTERMEYER, LOUIS. American poetry since 1900. New York, Harcourt, Brace & co. 1923. 4245

WOODSON, CARTER G. (ed.) Negro orators and their orations. Washington, Associated pub. 1925. 4246

2. Poetry by and about Negroes.

BAXTER, J. HARVEY. Sonnets for the Ethiopians. Roanoke, Va., Magic city press. 1936. 4247

BELL, JAMES M. Poetical works . . . Lansing, Mich., Wynkoop Hallenbeck Crawford co. 1901. 221p. 4248

BRAITHWAITE, WILLIAM S. B. The house of falling leaves with other poems. Boston, John W. Luce & co. 1908. xi, 112p. 4249

BRAITHWAITE, WILLIAM S. B. Lyrics of life and love. Boston, Herbert B. Turner & co. 1904. 80p. 4250

BREWER, J. MASON. Negrito, Negro dialect poems of the southwest. San Antonio, Naylor print. co. 1933. 97p. 4251

BROWN, SOLOMON G. Dedication poem. Masonic lodge; dedication grand lodge of the District of Columbia. Oct. 30, 1893. Washington, The lodge. 1893. 3p. 4252

BROWN, STERLING A. Southern road. New York, Harcourt, Brace & co. 1932. 135p. 4253

BURLEIGH, WILLIAM H. Poems . . . Philadelphia, J. Miller; Pittsburgh, Ingram & M'Candless; New York, Wiley & Putnam. 1841. 248p. 4254

BUTLER, H. L. Adventures of a colored lady. Push and pluck. Poems. 12p. 4255

CAMPBELL, LOOMIS J. and ROOT, OREN, Jr. (comps.) The Columbian speaker. Boston, Lee & Shepard. 1874. 240p. 4256

CANNON, DAVID W., Jr. Black labor chant and other poems. New York, National council on religion in higher education. 1939. 55p. 4257

CARMICHAEL, WAVERLY T. From the heart of a folk. A book of songs. Boston, Cornhill co. 1918. 60p. 4258

CHILD, MARIA L. The coronal. A collection of miscellaneous pieces, written at various times. Boston, Carter & Hendee. 1882. 285p. 4259

CHILDS, MARY F. De namin ob de

twins and other sketches from the cotton land. New York, Dodge & co. 1908. 139p.   4260

COFFIN, F. B. Poems. . . with Ajax ordeals. Little Rock, Ark., The auth. 1897. 248p.   4261

COOK, JOSEPHINE M. Bandana days. New York, Broadway pub. co. 1908. 21p.   4262

CORBETT, MAURICE N. The harp of Ethiopia. Nashville, National baptist pub. board. 1914. 27p. 4263

COTTER, JOSEPH S. Jr. The band of Gideon and other lyrics. Boston, Cornhill co. 1918. 29p.   4264

COTTER, JOSEPH S. Jr. A white song and a black one. Louisville, Bradley & Gilbert co. 1909. 64p.   4265

COX, JOHN T. News from dreamland. Lynchburg, Va., The auth. 1921. 32p.   4266

CULLEN, COUNTEE. The ballard of the brown girl. An old ballard retold. New York. London, Harper & bros. 1927. 11p.   4267

CULLEN, COUNTEE. The black Christ and other poems. New York, Harper & bros. 1929. 110p.   4268

CULLEN, COUNTEE. Color, a collection of poems. New York, Harper & bros. 1925. xvii, 108p.   4269

CULLEN, COUNTEE. Copper sun. New York, London, Harper & bros. 1927. 89p.   4270

CULLEN, COUNTEE. The Medea and some poems. New York. London, Harper & bros. 1935. 97p.   4271

CURRIE, JAMES. The wrongs of Africa. A poem. London, R. Faulder. 1787. 43p.   4272

DAVIS, DANIEL W. 'Weh down Souf and other poems. Cleveland, Helman-Taylor co. 1897. 136p.   4273

DAVIS, FRANK M. Black man's verse. Chicago, Black cat press. 1935. 83p.   4274

DAVIS, FRANK M. I am the American Negro. Chicago, Black cat press. 1937. 69p.   4275

DETT, R. NATHANIEL. The album of a heart . . . poetic sketches. Jackson, Miss., The auth. 1911. 69p.   4276

DRAKE, W. ALLEN. Selection from Drake's poems, vol. II dedicated to Selma University. 24p.   4277

DUNBAR, PAUL L. Candle-lightin' time. New York, Dodd, Mead & co. 1901. 127p.   4278

DUNBAR, PAUL L. Christmas is a' comin' and other poems. New York, Dodd, Mead & co. 1907. 19p.   4279

DUNBAR, PAUL L. Complete poems. . . New York, Dodd, Mead & co. 1913. xxxii, 289p. 2d ed. 1929. 3d ed. 1935. 4th ed. 1940.   4280

DUNBAR, PAUL L. Howdy, honey, howdy. New York, Dodd, Mead & co. 1905. 125p.   4281

DUNBAR, PAUL L. In old plantation days. New York, Dodd, Mead and co. 1903. 307p.   4282

DUNBAR, PAUL L. Joggin' erlong. New York, Dodd, Mead and co. 1906. 119p.   4283

DUNBAR, PAUL L. Life and works . . . containing his complete poetical works; his best short stories, numerous anecdotes, and a complete biography of the famous poet, by Mrs. Lida Keck Wiggins. Naperville, Ill., J. L. Nichols & co. 1907. 430p.   4284

DUNBAR, PAUL L. Little brown baby. Poems for young people. Selections, with biographical sketch, by Bertha Rodgers. New York, Dodd, Mead & co. 1940. 106p.   4285

DUNBAR, PAUL L. Li'l gal. New

York, Dodd, Mead & co. 1904.
123p. 4286

DUNBAR, PAUL L. Lyrics of love and laughter. New York, Dodd, Mead & co. 1903. 180p. 4287

DUNBAR, PAUL L. Lyrics of lowly life. New York, Dodd, Mead and co. 1897. 208p. 4288

DUNBAR, PAUL L. Lyrics of sunshine and shadow. New York, Dodd, Mead & co. 1909. 109p.
4289

DUNBAR, PAUL L. Lyrics of the hearthside. New York, Dodd, Mead & co. 1899. 227p. 4290

DUNBAR, PAUL L. Majors and minors. Toledo, Ohio, Hadley & Hadley. 1896. 148p. 4291

DUNBAR, PAUL L. Oak and ivy. Dayton, United brethern pub. house. 1893. 4292

DUNBAR, PAUL L. Poems of cabin and field. New York, Dodd, Mead & co. 1899. 125p. 4293

DUNBAR, PAUL L. Speakin' o' Christmas and other Christmas and special poems. New York, Dodd, Mead & co. 1914. 96p. 4294

DUNBAR, PAUL L. When Malindy sings. New York, Dodd, Mead and co. 1903. 144p. 4295

FORTUNE, TIMOTHY T. Dreams of life. New York, Fortune & Peterson co. 1905. 192p. 4296

FULTON, DAVIS B. Mother of mine; ode to the Negro woman. New York City, August Valentine Bernier. 1923. 12p. 4297

GARDNER, BENJAMIN F. Black. Poems of a dining car porter. Caldwell, Ohio, Caxton print. 1933. 79p. 4298

GORDON, ARMISTEAD C. and PAGE, THOMAS NELSON. Befo' de war. Echoes in Negro dialect. New York, Chas. Scribner's sons. 1888. 131p. 4299

GRAVES, LINWOOD D. Its the same old story – a tribute to Joe Louis. Big Stone Gap, Va., The auth. 1939. 4p. 4300

GRAVES, LINWOOD D. Poems of simplicity and the living dead – a short true story. Kingsport, Tenn., The auth. 1938. 116p. 4301

HAINES, ELWOOD L. Poems of the African trail. Milwaukee, Morehouse pub. co. London, A. R. Mowbray & co. 1928. 62p. 4302

HALE, EDWARD E. For Christmas and New York. n.p. n.d. 59p. 4303

HAMPTON, ARLAND C. Sonnets for the weaker sex as well as certain other poems. Hampton, Va., Laboratory press. 1939. 25p. 4304

HARPER, MRS. FRANCIS E. W. Moses, a story of the Nile. 2d ed. Philadelphia, The auth. 1869. 47p.
4305

HARPER, MRS. FRANCIS E. W. Poems . . . Philadelphia, The auth. 1871. 48p. 2d ed. Philadelphia, The auth. 1900. vi, 90p. 4306

HAYSON, MAXWELL N. Samuel Coleridge-Taylor. An ode of welcome. Washington, The auth. 1906. 10p. 4307

HEYWARD, DUBOSE. Jasha Brown and selected poems. New York, Farrar & Rhinehart. 1924. 96p. 2d ed. New York, Farrar & Rhinehart. 1931. 96p. 4308

HILL, LESLIE P. Toussaint L'Ouverture. A dramatic history. Boston, Christopher pub. co. 1921. 138p. 4309

HILL, LESLIE P. The wings of oppression and other poems. Boston, Stratford co. 1921. 124p.
4310

HOLDER, JAMES E. The colored man's appeal to white Americans. Atlantic City, N.J., The auth. n.d. 6p. 4311

HOWE, JULIA W. Later lyrics. Boston, J. E. Tilton & co. 1865. 326p. 4312

HUGHES, LANGSTON. The dream keeper and other poems. New York, A. A. Knopf. 1932. 77p.4313

HUGHES, LANGSTON. Fine clothes to the Jew. New York, A. A. Knopf. 1929. 4314

HUGHES, LANGSTON. The Negro mother. New York, Golden stair press. 1931. 20p. 4315

HUGHES, LANGSTON. Scottsboro limited. Four poems and a play in verse. New York, Golden stair press. 1932. 9p. 4316

HUGHES, LANGSTON. The weary blues. New York, Alfred A. Knopf. 1927. 109p. 4317

JAMISON, ROSCOE C. Negro soldiers ("These truly are the brave.") and other poems. St. Joseph, Mo., Neil & co. 1918. 16p. 4318

JOHNSON, FENTON. A little dreaming. Chicago, The auth. 1913. 80p. 2d ed. Chicago, Peterson co. 1914. 80p. 4319

JOHNSON, FENTON. Songs of the soil. New York, The auth. 1915. 39p. 4320

JOHNSON, JAMES W. Fifty years and other poems. Boston, Cornhill co. 1918. xiv, 93p. 4322

JOHNSON, JAMES W. God's trombones; seven sermons in verse. New York, Viking. 1927. 56p.4323

JOHNSON, JAMES W. Saint Peter relates an incident. 3d ed. New York, Viking press. 1935. 105p. 4342

JOHNSON, GEORGIA D. Bronze: a book of verse. Boston, Brimmer & co. 1922. 101p. 4325

JOHNSON, GEORGIA D. The heart of a woman and other peoms. Boston. Cornsill co. 1918. 62p. 4326

JONES, CHARLES P. An appeal to the sons of Africa. A number of poems, readings, operations and lectures designed especially to inspire youth of African blood with sentiments of hope and true nobility as well as to entertain and instruct all classes of readers and lovers of redeemed humanity. Jackson, Miss., Truth pub. co. n.d. 131p. 4327

JONES, EDWARD S. The sylvan cabin; a centenary ode on the birth of Lincoln, and other verse. Boston, Sherman, French & co. 1911. 96p. 2d ed. San Francisco, The auth. 1915. 14p. 4328

KERLIN, ROBERT T. (ed.) Contemporary poetry of the Negro. Hampton, Va., Hampton Institute press. 1921. 23p. 4329

LINDSAY, VACHEL. The Congo and other poems. New York, MacMillan co. 1918. 159p. 4330

LOCKE, ALAIN L. (ed.) Four Negro poets. New York, Simon & Schuster. 1927. 31p. 4331

MALONE, WALTER. Songs of north and south. Louisville, J. P. Morton & co. 1900. 103p. 4332

MCCLELLAN, GEORGE M. The path of dreams. Louisville, J. P. Morton & co. 1916. 76p. 4333

MCCORKLE, GEORGE W. Poems of perpetual memory. n.d. n.p. 35p. 4334

MCGIRT, JAMES E. Avenging the Maine, a drunken A. B. and other poems. Philadelphia, G. F. Lasher. 1899. 119p. 4335

MCGIRT, JAMES E. For your sweet sake. Philadelphia, J. C. Winston & co. 1906. 79p. 4336

MCGIRT, JAMES E. Some simple poems and a few ambitious attempts. Philadelphia, G. F. Lasher. 1901. 72p. 4337

MCKAY, CLAUDE. Harlem shadows. New York, Harcourt, Brace & co. 1922. 95p.   4338

PUSHKIN, ALEXANDER. Works, lyrics, narrative poems, folk tales, plays, provs. Selected & edited by Avrahm Yarmolinsky. New York, Random house.. 1936. 896p.   4339

REYNOLDS, JAMES R. The wolf brothers and poems. New York, The auth. 63p. n.d.   4340

RODGERS, RICHARD C. Day-dreams from dixie. Hampton, Va., Hampton Institute press. 1902. 28p.   4341

SHACKLEFORD, THEODORE H. My country and other poems. Philadelphia, The auth. 1918. 216p.   4342

THOMAS, CHARLES C. A black lark caroling. Dallas, Tex., Kaleidograph press. 1936.   4343

THORNTON, GEORGE B. Best poems. Orangeburg, S. C., The auth. 1937. 27p.   4344

TILTON, THEODORE. Sonnets to the memory of Frederick Douglas. Paris, Brentano's. 1895. 12p.   4345

TODD, WALTER E. Gathered treasures. Washington, Murray bros. 1912. 39p.   4346

TOOMEY, RICHARD E. S. Thoughts for true Americans; a book of poems, dedicated to the lovers of American ideals. Washington, Neale pub. co. 1901. 80p.   4347

TYNES, BERYL E. Penpoint drippings. Lynchburg, Va. 1935. 16p.   4348

WALKER, JAMES R. Poetical diets. n.d. n.p. 146p.   4349

WATKINS, LUCIAN B. Voices of solitude. Chicago, The auth. 1903. 21p.   4350

WEEDEN, HOWARD. Bandana ballards. New York, Doubleday & McClure co. 1901. 90p.   4351

WEEDEN, HOWARD. Old voices. New York, Doubleday, Page & co. 1904. 94p.   4352

WEEDEN, HOWARD. Songs of the old South. New York, Doubleday, Page & co. 1900. 94p.   4353

WEST INDIAN ECLOGUES. London, J. Philips & W. Lowndes. 1787. 32p.   4354

WHEATLEY, PHILLIS. Memoir and poems. . . Dedicated to the friends of the Africans. 2d ed. Boston, Light & Horton. 1835. 110p. 3d ed. Boston, I. Knapp. 1838. 155p.   4355

WHEATLEY, PHILLIS. Poems . . . Ed. by Charlotte R. Wright. Philadelphia, The Wrights. 1930. 104p.   4356

WHEATLEY, PHILLIS. Poems and letters. First collected edition. Charles Fred Heartman, ed. With an appreciation by Arthur A. Schomburg. New York, Printed for ed. 1924. 111p.   4357

WHEATLEY, PHILLIS. Poems on various subjects, religious and moral. Boston, A. Bell. 1773. 124p. 2d ed. Philadelphia, W. Woodward. 1801. 244p. 3d ed. Cleveland, Revell pub. co. 1886. 149p.   4358

WHEATLEY, PHILLIS. Six broadsides relating to . . . New York, Twenty-five copies printed for C. F. Heartman. 1915. 6p.   4359

WILKERSON, HENRY B. Idle hours. New York, F. H. Hitchcock. 1927. 86p. 5259   4360

WILKERSON, HENRY B. Shady-rest. New York, F. H. Hitchcock. 1928. 67p.   4361

WILLIAMS, FRANK B. Fifty years of freedom. Washington, The auth. 1913. 7p.   4362

3. Fiction relating to the Negro or with Negro characters prior to 1865.

ADAMS, F. C. Manuel Pereira; or, The sovereign rule of South Carolina, with views of southern laws, life, and hospitality. Washington, Buell & Blanchard. 1853. 302p.   4363

ADAMS, W. T. (pseud.) OLIVER OPTIC. Hatchie, The guardian slave. 1853.   4364

ARMSTRONG, ORLAND K. Old massa's people; the old slaves tell their story. Indianapolis, Bobbs-Merrill co. 1931. 5-13-357p.   4365

BANKS, MARY R. Bright days in the old plantation time. Boston, Lee & Shepard; New York, Chas. T. Dillingham. 1882. 266p.   4366

BELOT, ADOLPHE. Article 47. A romance. Tr. from the French by James Furbish. Philadelphia, J. P. Lippincott & co. 1873. 161p.   4367

BENNETT, JOHN. Madame Margot; a grotesque legend of old Charleston. New York, Century co. 1921. 110p.   4368

BESANT, WALTER. For faith and freedom. A novel. New York, Harper & bros. 1889. 383p.   4369

BONTEMPS, ARNA. Black thunder. New York, MacMillan co. 1936. 298p.   4370

BONTEMPS, ARNA. Drums at dusk. New York, MacMillan co. 1939. 226p.   4371

BOSHER, MRS. K. L. (pseud.) CAIRNS, KATIE. Bobbie. Richmond, Va., B. F. Johnson. 1899. 134p.   4372

BOUVE, PAULINE C. Their shadows before. A story of the Southampton insurrection. Boston, Small, Maynard & co. 1899. 202p.   4373

BOYKIN, VIRGINIA F. Uncle Abe's Miss Ca'line. Boston, Roxbourgh pub. co. 1923. 142p.   4374

BRADFORD, ROARK. Kingdom coming. New York, Harper & bros. 1933. 319p.   4375

BROWN, WILLIAM G. Gentlemen of the South. A memory of the black belt from the manuscript memoirs of the late Col. Staunton Elmore. New York, London, MacMillan co. 1903. 232p.   4376

BROWN, WILLIAM W. Clotel; or, The president's daughter; a tale of the southern states. London. 1853. 238p.   4377

BRUCE, JEROME. Studies in black and white. A novel in which are exemplified the lights and shades in the friendship and trust between black and white — master and slave — in their intercourse with each other in ante bellum days. New York. Washington, Neale pub. co. 1906. 472p.   4378

BRUCE, WILLIAM C. Below the James; a plantation sketch. New York, Neale pub. co. 1918. 157p.   4380

CABLE, GEORGE W. Bonaventure, a prose pastoral of Arcadian Louisiana. New York, International association of newspapers and authors. 1901. vii, 314p.   4381

CABLE, GEORGE W. Grandissimes, a story of Creole life. New York, Charles Scribner sons. 1883. 9-448p.   4382

CABLE, GEORGE W. John March, southerner. New York, Charles Scribner's sons. 1894. viii, 513p.   4383

CABLE, GEORGE W. Old Creole

days. New York, Charles Scribner's sons. 1883. 4, 303p.　　　4384

CHASE, LUCIEN B. English serfdom and American slavery; or, Ourselves as others see us. London. 1854.
　　　4385

CHOPIN, MRS. KATE (O'FLAHERTY). Bayou folk. Boston. New York, Houghton, Mifflin & co. 1894. 2, 313p.　　4386

CLEMENS, SAMUEL (pseud.) MARK TWAIN. The adventures of Tom Sawyer. New York. London, Harper & bros. 1903. 321p.　　4387

CLEMENS, SAMUEL (pseud.) MARK TWAIN. Pudd'n head Wilson and those extraordinary twins. New York, Harper & bros. 1903. 324p.
　　　4388

CLEMENS, SAMUEL (pseud.) MARK TWAIN. Tom Sawyer abroad, and other stories, etc. New York, Harper & bros. 1917. 452p.　　4389

COCKRAN, JOHN S. Bonnie Belmont, a historical romance of the days of slavery and the Civil war. Wheeling, W. Va., Wheeling news. 1907. 291p.　　　4390

COLLINGWOOD, HARRY. Congo covers; a story of Joseph Rosens of the slave squadron. New York, Worthington co. 382p.　　　4391

COLLINGWOOD, HERBERT W. Andersonville violets; a story of northern and southern life. Boston, Lee & Shepard; New York, Chas. T. Dillingham. 1889. vii, 270p.　4392

CONNELLY, EMMA M. Tilting at windmills; a story of the blue grass country. Boston, D. Lothrop & co. 1888. 439p.　　　4393

COOKE, JOHN E. Canolles; the fortunes of a partisan of '61. Detroit, E. B. Smith & co. 1877. 313p.　　　4394

COOKE, JOHN E. Stories of the old

dominion, from the settlement to the end of the revolution. New York, Harper & bros. 1879. 337p.
　　　4395

COOPER, JAMES F. The last of the Mohicans. 1826. The pioneers. 1823. The red rover. 1828. 1873. 193p. The spy. 1821.　　4396

CREECY, JAMES R. Scenes in the South, and other miscellaneous pieces. Washington, Thomas McGill. 1860. 294p.　　　4397

DAVIS, MARY E. M. In war times at LaRose Blanche. Boston, D. Lothrop co. 1888. 257-.　　4398

DICKINSON, ANNA E. What answer? Boston, Ticknor and Fields. 1868. 301p.　　　4399

DIXON, THOMAS, Jr. The southerner; a romance of the real Lincoln. New York, Grosset & Dunlap. 1913. 543p.　　4400

EASTMAN, MARY. Aunt Phillis's cabin; or, Southern life as it is. Philadelphia, Lippincott, Grambo & co. 1852. 11-280p.　　4401

EDWARDS, HARRY S. Eneas Africanus. Macon, Ga., J. W. Burke & co. 1920. 44p.　　4402

EDWARDS, HARRY S. Two runaways, and other stories. New York, Century co. 1889. 246p.
　　　4403

EMORY, FREDERIC. A Maryland manor, a novel of plantation aristocracy and its fall. New York, Frederick A. Stokes co. 1901. 449p.　　　4404

FITZHUGH, GEORGE. Cannibals all. or slaves without masters. 1857.
　　　4405

FLANDERS, MRS. G. M. Ebony idol. New York, D. Appleton & co. 1860. 2843p.　　　4406

FLOYD, NICHOLAS J. Thorns in the flesh. A romance of the war and Ku

Klux periods. A voice of vindication from the South in answer to "A fool's errand" and other slanders . . . Philadelphia. New York, Hubbard bros. 1884. 607p.
4407

FRANCES, MARY (pseud.) Daddy Dave. New York, Funk & Wagnalls. 1887. 7, 116p.
4408

FRESNEAU, MADAME A. Theresa at San Domingo; a tale of the Negro insurrection of 1791. Tr. from the French by E. G. Magrath. Chicago, A. C. McClurg & co. 1889. 213p.
4409

GIELOW, MARTHA S. Manny's reminiscences, and other sketches. New York, A. S. Barnes & co. 1898. 109p.
4410

GIELOW, MARTHA S. Old plantation days. New York, R. H. Russell. 1902. 183p.
4411

GILLIAM, EDWARD W. 1791: a tale of San Domingo. Baltimore, John Murphy & co. 1890. 308p.
4412

GILMAN, MRS. CAROLINE H. Recollections of a southern matron. New York, Harper & bros. 1838. vii, 272p.
4413

GILMAN, MRS. CAROLINE H. Recollections of a southern matron and a New England bride. Philadelphia, G. G. Evans. 1859. 403p.
4414

GILMORE, JAMES R. (pseud.) KIRKE, EDMUND. Among the pines; or the South in secession time. New York, The auth. 1862. 310p.
4415

GILMORE, JAMES R. (pseud.) KIRKE, EDMUND. My southern friends. New York, Carleton. 1864. 308p.
4416

GILMORE, JAMES R. (pseud.) KIRKE, EDMUND. On the border. Boston, Lee & Shepard. 1867. 333p.
4417

GLASGOW, ELLEN A. G. The battle-ground. New York, Doubleday, Page & co. 1905. viii, 512p.
4418

HALE, MRS. SARAH J. Liberia; or Mr. Peyton's experiments. 1853.
4419

HALL, BAYNARD R. Frank Freeman's barber shop. 1852.
4420

HARRIS, JOEL C. Balaam and his master and other sketches. New York, Houghton, Mifflin co. 1891. 293p.
4421

HARRIS, JOEL C. The chronicles of Aunt Minervy Ann. New York, Chas. Scribner's sons. 1899. ix, 145p.
4422

HARRIS, JOEL C. Daddy Jake the runaway. New York, The century co. 1896. 198p.
4423

HARRIS, JOEL C. Free Joe and other Georgian sketches. New York, Chas. Scribner's sons. 1887. 236p.
4424

HARRIS, JOEL C. Mingo and other sketches in black and white. Boston. New York, Houghton Mifflin co. 1884. 273p.
4425

HARRIS, JOEL C. Tales of home folks in peace and war. Boston, Houghton, Mifflin co. 1898. 417p.
4426

HARRISON, MRS. BURTON. Flower de hundred; the story of a Virginia plantation. New York, Cassell pub. co. 1890. 301p.
4427

HAWTHORNE, NATHANIEL. The house of the seven gables. 1851.
4428

HILDRETH, RICHARD. L'esclave blanc. Paris, G. Barba. 1853. 332p.
4429

HILDRETH, RICHARD. The slave; or memoirs of Archy Moore. 6th ed. Boston, 1846. 2v.
4430

HOBSON, ANNE. In old Alabama; being the chronicles of Miss Mouse, the little black merchant. New

York, Doubleday, Page & co. 1903. 237p. 4431

HUGO, VICTOR M. The slave king. (From the Bug-Journal; also St. Domingo). Philadelphia, Carey, Lee & Blanchard. 1833. 259p. (From the library of romance, ed. by Leitch Ritchie. v. 6). 4432

HUNGERFORD, JAMES. The old plantation, and what I gathered there in an autumn month. New York, Harper & bros. 1859. 369p. 4433

JOHNSTON, MARY. Slave ship. Boston, Little, Brown, co. 1924. 330p. 4434

JOHNSTON, RICHARD M. Ogechee crossfirings; a novel. New York, Harper & bros. 1889. 149p. 4435

JOHNSTON, RICHARD M. Old Mark Langston; a tale of Duke's Creek. New York, Harper & bros. 1883. 338p. 4436

JOHNSTON, RICHARD M. The Primes and their neighbors; ten tales of middle Georgia. New York, D. Appleton & co. 1891. 310p. 4437

JONES, MAJOR JOSEPH. John's alive; or, the bride of a ghost, and other sketches. Philadelphia, David McKay. 1883. 264p. 4438

KENNEDY, JOHN P. Swallow barn, or, A sojourn in the old dominion. Rev. ed. New York, G. P. Putnam. 1851. 506p. 4439

LEWIS, BESSIE. To save their souls. Boston, Christopher pub. house. 1939. 303p. 4440

LEIGHTON, WILLIAM R. Sons of strength; a romance of the Kansas border wars. New York, Doubleday & McClure co. 1899 242p. 4441

LIVERMORE, MRS. ELIZABETH D. Zoe; or the quadroon's triumph. A tale for the times. Cincinnati, Truman & Spofford. 1855. 2v. 4442

LOWERY, I. E. Life on the old plantation in ante bellum days, or, A story based on facts. Columbia, S. C. State co. 1911. 185p. 4443

MARTINEAU, HARRIETT. The hour and the man. Boston. 1840. 170p.; New York, Harper & bros. 1873. 176p. 4444

McDOUGALL, MRS. FRANCES H.W.G. Shahmah in pursuit of freedom; or, The branded hand. New York, Thatcher & Hutchinson. 1858. xxxviii, 599p. 4445

MEADE, WILLIAM. Sketches of old Virginia family servants. Philadelphia, I. Ashmead. 1847. 126p. 4446

MELVILLE, HERMAN. White jacket. 1850. 4447

MERRICK, CAROLINE E. Old times in dixieland, a southern matron's memories. New York, Grafton press. 1901. 241p. 4448

MITCHELL, MARGARET. Gone with the wind. New York, MacMillan co. 1835. 732p. 4449

MURFREE, MARY N. (pseud.) CHAS. EGBERT CRADDOCK. Bushwhackers & other stories. Chicago: New York, Herbert S. Stone & co. 1899. 312p. 4450

OLD PINE FARM: or, The southern side. Comprising loose sketches from the experiences of a southern country minister. Nashville, Southwestern pub. house, New York, Sheldon & co. 1859. 202p. 4451

OUTALISSI: A tale of Dutch Guiana. London, J. Hatchard & son. 1826. 324p. 4452

PAGE, J. W. Uncle Robin, in his cabin in Virginia, and Tom without one in Boston. Richmond, Va., J. W. Randolph. 1853. 4453

PAGE, THOMAS N. The burial of the guns. New York, Charles Scribner's sons. 1894. 258p. 4454

PAGE, THOMAS N. A captured Santa Claus. New York, Charles Scribner's sons. 1904. 81p.　　　4455

PAGE, THOMAS N. Elsket, and other stories. New York, Chas. Scribner's sons. 1891. 208p.　　　4456

PAGE, THOMAS N. In old Virginia. New York, Chas. Scribner's sons. 1887. xi, 275p.　　　4457

PAGE, THOMAS N. Polly; a Christmas recollection. New York, Charles Scribner's sons. 1894. 49p.　　　4458

PAGE, THOMAS N. Unc' Edinburg; a plantation echo. New York, Chas. Scribner's sons. 1895. 53p.　　　4459

PAGE, WALTER H. (pseud.) NICHOLAS WORTH. The southerner, a novel; being autobiographical. New York, Doubleday, Page & co. 1909. vi, 424p.
　　　4460

PATTESON, CAMM. Young bachelor. Lynchburg, Va., The auth. 1900. 119p.　　　4461

PAYNTER, JOHN H. Fugitives of the pearl. Washington, Associated pub. 1930. 209p.　　　4462

PIERSON, MRS. EMILY C. Jamie Parker the fugitive. Hartford. 1851.
　　　4463

PIERSON, MRS. EMILY C. Ruth's sacrifice; or, Life on the Rappahannock. Boston, The auth. 1864. 259p.　　　4464

PLANTATION JIM and the freedom which he obtained . . . also right and about right. New York. n.d. 96p.　　　4465

POE, EDGAR A. The gold-bug. 1843.
　　　4466

PYRNELLE, LOUISE C. Diddie, Dumps, and Tot: or plantation child-life. New York. Harper & bros. 1882. 217p.　　　4467

RANDOLPH, J. THORNTON. The cabin and the parlor: or, Slaves and masters. Philadelphia, T. B. Peterson. 1852.　　　4468

RICHMOND, LEIGH. Annals of the poor. London, J. Nisbet. 1826. 231p.　　　4469

ROBERTS, OCTAVIA. Perilous isle: a story of the San Domingo uprising based on an old family journal. New York. London, Harper & bros. 1926. 281p.　　　4470

ROBINSON, NINA H. Aunt Dice: the story of a faithful slave. Nashville, M. E. Church, South. 1897. 144p.
　　　4471

ROBINSON, ROWLAND E. Out of bondage and other stories. Ed. by Llewellyn R. Perkins. Rutland, Vt., Chas. E. Tuttle co. 1936.　　　4472

SCHOOLCRAFT, MRS. MARY H. The black gauntlet, a tale of plantation life in South Carolina. Philadelphia, J. B. Lippincott co. 1860.　　　4473

SCOTT, EVELYN. Migration. An arabesque in histories. New York, Boni. 1927. 337p.　　　4474

SHERWOOD, JOHN D. The comic history of the United States, from a period prior to the discovery of America to times long subsequent to the present. Boston, Fields, Osgood & co. 1870. 549p.　　　4475

SIMMS, WILLIAM G. Complete works. Chicago, M. A. Donahue & co. 17v.　　　4476

SMITH, FRANCIS H. Colonel Carter's Christmas, and romance of an old-fashioned gentleman. New York, Chas. Scribner's sons. 1903. 1907. 206p.　　　4477

SMITH, W. L. G. Life at the South, or, "Uncle Tom's cabin" as it is. Philadelphia. 1852.　　　4478

STOWE, MRS. HARRIET B. Dred: a tale of the Dismal swamp. Boston, Phillips, Sampson & co. 1856. 2v.
　　　4479

STOWE, MRS. HARRIET B. The story of "Uncle Tom's cabin." Boston, Old South work. 1897. 28p. 4480

STOWE, MRS. HARRIET B. Uncle Tom's cabin; or, Life among the lowly. Boston, J. P. Jewett & co. 1853. 560p. 4481

STROTHER, D. H. Virginia illustrated. 1857. 4482

SWIFT, MRS. HILDEGARDE H. Railroad to freedom; a story of the Civil War. New York, Harcourt, Brace & co. xix, 364p. 4483

TOURGEE, ALBION W. Figs and thistles; a romance. New York, Fords, Howard, & Hulbert. 1879. 538p. 4484

TOURGEE, ALBION W. A royal gentleman and 'Zouri's Christmas. New York, Fords, Howard & Hulbert. 1881. 529p. 4485

TOURGEE, ALBION W. The veteran and his pipe. Chicago. New York, Belford, Clarke & co. 1888. 269p. 4486

TUCKER, NATHANIEL B. The partisan leader; a novel, and an apocalypse of the origin and struggles of the southern confederacy. Richmond, West & Johnson. 1862. 4487

4.Fiction relating to the Negro or with Negro characters since 1865.

ADAMS, EDWARD C. L. Congaree sketches. Scenes from Negro life in the swamps of the Congaree and tales by Tad and Scip of Heaven and hell with other miscellany. Chapel Hill, University of North Carolina press. 1927. 133p. 4488

ALEXANDER, MRS. LILLIE M. Candy. New York, Dodd, Mead & co. 1934. 310p. 4489

ALLEE, MAJORIE H. Susanna and Tristram. Boston, Houghton Mifflin co. 1929. 4490

ARTHUR, JOHN. Dark metropolis. Boston, Meador pub. co. 1936. 4491

ASHBY, WILLIAM M. Redder blood; a novel. New York, Cosmopolitan press. 1915. 188p. 4492

AYRES, KATHARINE S. Charcoal sketches. Stories of the present-day southern Negro. Macon. Ga., J. W. Burke & co. 1927. 150p. 4493

BAILEY. CAROLYN S. Lil' Hannibal. New York. Platt & Munk co. 1938. 4494

BAPTIST, R. HERNEKIN (pseud.) Four handsome negresses, the record of a voyage. New York, J. Cape & H. Smith. 1931. vii, 235p. 4495

BAPTIST, R. HERNEKIN (pseud.) Wild Deer. New York, Day & co. 1934. 347p. 4496

BARKER, ROLAND and WM. DOERFLINGER. The middle passage. New York, MacMillan co. 1939. 410p. 4497

BLUMBERG, MRS. FANNIE B. Rowena, Teena, Tot and the runaway turkey. Chicago, Whitman. 1936. 32p. 4498

BONTEMPS, ARNA. God sends Sunday. New York, Harcourt, Brace & co. 1931. 199p. 4499

BONTEMPS, ARNA. Sad faced boy. Boston, Houghton Mifflin co. 1937. 122p. 4500

BONTEMPS, ARNA. You can't pet a possum. New York. Wm. Morrow & co. 1934. 130p. 4501

BONTEMPS, ARNA. Popo and Fifina, children of Hayti. New York, MacMillan co. 1932. 105p. 4502

BOOTHBY. GUY N. Dr. Nikola's

experiment. New York, 1899. 308p. 4503

BOYD, JAMES. Marching on. New York, Chas. Scribner's sons. 1927. 426p. 4504

BOYLE, MRS. VIRGINIA F. Devil tales. New York, Harper & bros. 1900. xi, 210p. 4505

BRADFORD, ROARK. John Henry. New York. London, Harper & bros. 1931. 255p. 4506

BRADFORD, ROARK. Let the band play Dixie, and other stories. New York, Harper & bros. 1934. 320p. 4507

BRADFORD, ROARK. Ol' King David and the Philistine boys. New York, Harper & bros. 1930. 227p. 4508

BRADFORD, ROARK. Ol' man Adam an' his chillun. New York. London, Harper & bros. 1928. xxiv, 264p. 4509

BRADFORD, ROARK. This side of Jordan. New York, Harper & bros. 1929. 255p. 4510

BRADY, CYRUS T. Doctor of philosophy; a novel. New York, Chas. Scribner's sons. 1903. 302p. 4511

BRAWLEY, BENJAMIN (ed.) The best short stores of Paul Lawrence Dunbar. New York, Dodd, Mead & co. 1938. 4512

BRUSH, CHRISTINE C. The colonel's opera clock. Boston, Little, Brown & co. 1904. 252p. 4513

BRYK, FELIX. Dark rapture. 4514

CABLE, GEORGE W. Madame Delphine. New York, Chas. Scribner's sons. 1881. iv, 125p. 4515

CALDWELL, ERSKINE. Kneel to the rising sun, and other stories. New York, Viking press. 1935. 246p. 4516

CALDWELL, ERSKINE. Southways.

New York, Viking press. 1938. 206p. 4517

CALDWELL, ERSKINE. Trouble in July. New York, Duell, Sloan & Pearce. 1940. 4518

CAMPBELL, THOMAS B. Black Sadie, a novel. Boston. New York. Houghton Mifflin co. 1928. 303p. 4519

CANNON, MRS. ELIZABETH P. and WHITING, ADELE H. Country life stories. New York, E.P. Dutton & co. 1938. xiii, 17-95p. 4520

CARMER, CARL. Stars fell on Alabama. New York, Farrar & Rinehart. 1934. 4521

CARTER, MARY N. North Carolina sketches. Phases of life where the galax grows. Chicago, A.C. McClurg & co. 1900. 313p. 4522

CHESTNUTT, CHARLES W. The colonel's dream. New York, Doubleday, Page & co. 1905. vii, 249p. 4523

CHESTNUTT, CHARLES W. The conjure woman. New York, Houghton Mifflin co. 1899. 229p. 4524

CHESTNUTT, CHARLES W. The house behind the cedars. New York, Houghton, Mifflin co. 1900. 294p. 4525

CHESTNUTT, CHARLES W. The narrow of tradition. Boston, Houghton, Mifflin co. 1901. 329p. 4526

CHESTNUTT, CHARLES W. Wife of his youth, and other stories of the color line. Boston. New York, Houghton, Mifflin co. 1901. 323p. 4527

CHILDERS, JAMES S. In the deep South. New York, Farrar & Rhinehart. 1936. 276p. 4528

CHOPIN, MRS. KATE O'FLAHERTY. Bayou folk. Boston. New York, Houghton,

Mifflin co. 1894. 313p. 4529

CLARK, EMILY. Stuffed peacocks. New York. London, A. A. Knopf. 1927. 228p. 4530

COBB, IRVIN S. J. Poindexter, colored. New York, Geo. H. Doran co. 1922. vii, 270p. 4531

COCHRAN, LOUIS. Bossman. Caldwell, Idaho. Caxton print. 1939. 270p. 4532

COHEN, OCTAVUS R. Assorted chocolates. New York, Dodd, Mead & co. 1922. 330p. 4533

COHEN, OCTAVUS R. Highly colored. New York, Dodd, Mead & co. 1921. 331p. 4534

COHEN, OCTAVUS R. Sun clouds. New York, Dodd, Mead & co. 1924. 303p. 4535

COLEMAN, ALBERT E. Romantic adventures of Rosy, the Octoroon, with some account of the persecution of the southern Negroes during the reconstruction period. Boston, Meador pub. co. 1929. 121p. 4536

COLEMAN, RICHARD. Don't you weep . . . don't you moan. New York, MacMillan co. 1935. 288p. 4537

COLLINS, MRS. JANE S. Free at last. Pittsburgh, Murdoch, Kerr & co. 1896. 208p. 4538

CONRAD, JOSEPH. The nigger of the narcissus. Garden City, N. Y., Doubleday, Page & co. 1914. xiii, 217p. 4539

CULLEN, COUNTEE. One way to heaven. New York, Harper & bros. 1932. 280p. 4540

CULPEPPER, GEORGE B. King Solomon's son, or, The old coffin-maker of Pleasant Ridge. Nashville. Parthenon press. 1938. 40p. 4541

CURTIS, CLARA K. Fighters for freedom. Rochester, The auth. 1933. 4542

DAINGERFIELD, MRS. HENRIETTA G. Our mammy and other stories. Hampton, Va., Hampton Institute press. 1906. 143p. 2d ed. Lexington Ky., The auth. 1906. 143p. 4543

DANA, KATHERINE F. Our Phil and other stories. Boston, Houghton, Mifflin co. 1889. 147p. 4544

DAVENPORT, BENJAMIN R. Blood will tell; the strange story of a son of Ham. Cleveland, Caxton book co. 1902. 8-340p. 4545

DAVIS, REUBEN. Butcher bird. Boston, Little, Brown & co. 1936. 298p. 4546

DELEON, THOMAS C. a novelette trilogy. London. New York, F. T. Neely. 1897. 234p. 4547

DELEON, THOMAS C. John Holden, unionist, a romance of the days of destruction and reconstruction. St. Paul, Price-McGill co. 1893. ix, 338p. 4548

DEMING, PHILANDER. Tompkins and other folks; stories of the Hudson and the Adirondacks. Boston. New York, Houghton, Mifflin co. 1884. 223p. 4549

DINESEN, ISAK. Out of Africa. New York, Random house. 1938. 389p. 4550

DIX, DOROTHY (pseud.) Mirandy exhorts. Philadelphia, Penn pub. co. 1922. 300p. 4551

DIXON, ROYAL. Half dark moon. Dallas, Tex., Manfred, Van Nort & co. 1939. 3-179p. 4552

DIXON, ROYAL. Signs is signs. Philadelphia. Geo. W. Jacobs & co. 1915. 209p. 4553

DIXON, THOMAS, Jr. The clansman; an historical romance of the Ku Klux Klan. New York, Doubleday, Page & co. 1905. 11-374p. 4554

DIXON, THOMAS, Jr. The leopard's spots, a romance of the white man's burden, 1865-1900. New York, Doubleday, Page & co. 1902. 465p. 2d ed. New York, A wessels co. 1902. 469p.   4555

DIXON, THOMAS, Jr. The traitor, a story of the fall of the invisible empire. New York, Doubleday, Page & co. 1907. 331p.   4556

DONNELLY, IGNATIUS (pseud.) Doctor Huguet; a novel. Chicago, Schulte & co. 1891. 309p.   4557

DUBOIS, W. E. BURGHARDT. Dark princess. New York, Harcourt, Brace & co. 1928.   4558

DUBOIS, W. E. BURGHARDT. The quest of the silver fleece. Chicago, A. C. McClurg & co. 1911. 434p.   4559

DUNBAR, MRS. ALICE R. M. The goodness of Saint Rocque and other stories. New York, Dodd, Mead & co. 1899. 224p.   4560

DUNBAR, PAUL L. Fanatics. New York, Dodd, Mead & co. 1901. vi, 312p.   4561

DUNBAR, PAUL L. Folks from Dixie. New York, Dodd, Mead & co. 1898. 263p.   4562

DUNBAR, PAUL L. Heart of Happy Hollow. New York, Dodd, Mead & co. 1904. 309p.   4563

DUNBAR, PAUL L. In old plantation days. New York, Dodd, Mead & co. 1903. 307p.   4564

DUNBAR, PAUL L. Love of Landry. New York, Dodd, Mead & co. 1900. 200p.   4565

DUNBAR, PAUL L. The sport of the gods. Philadelphia, J. B. Lippincott co. 1901. (Rpt. from Lippincott's magazine. May. 1901). New York, Dodd. Mead & co. 1902. 255p.   4566

DUNBAR, PAUL L. Strength of Gideon and other stories. New York, Dodd. Mead & co. 1900. 362p.   4567

DUNBAR. PAUL L. The Uncalled; a novel. New York, Dodd. Mead & co. 1898. 255p. 2d ed. New York, International assn. of newspapers & authors. 1898. 255p.   4568

DURHAM, JOHN S. Diane, priestess of Haiti. Philadelphia, J. B. Lippincott & co. 1902. 79p.   4569

EARL, VICTORIA. Aunt Lindy; a story founded on real life. New York, The auth. 1893. 16p.   4570

EARLE, MARY T. The man who worked for Collister. Boston, Copeland & Day. 1898. 284p.   4571

EHRLICH, LEONARD. God's angry man. New York, Simon & Schuster. 1932.   4572

ENDORE, GUY. Babouk. New York, Vanguard press. 1934. 297p.   4573

EVANS, EVA K. Araminta. New York, Minton. 1935. 84p.   4574

EVANS, EVA K. Emma Belle and her kinfolks. New York, G. P. Putnam's sons. 1940. 174p.   4575

EVANS, EVA K. Jerome Anthony. New York, G. P. Putnam's sons. 1936. 88p.   4576

EVANS, EVA K. Key corner. New York, G. P. Putnam's sons. 1938. 206p.   4577

FAUSET, ARTHUR H. Symphonesque. (In the O. Henry Memorial award.) Garden City, N. Y., Doubleday, Page & co. 1927. 308p.   4578

FAUSET, JESSIE R. Comedy, American style. New York, Frederick A. Stokes co. 1933. 330p.   4579

FAUSET, JESSIE R. The Chinaberry tree. New York, Frederick A. Stokes co. 1932. 341p.   4580

FAUSET, JESSIE R. Plum bun; a novel without a moral. New York, Frederick A. Stokes & co. 1929. 379p.   4581

FAUSET. JESSIE R. There is

confusion. New York, Boni & Liveright. 1924. 297p. 4582

FIRBANK, A. A. RONALD. Prancing nigger. New York, Brentano's. 1924. xi, 126p. 4583

FISHER, DOROTHY CANFIELD. Bent twig. New York, Grosset & Dunlap. 1918. vi, 480p. 4584

FISHER, DOROTHY CANFIELD. Brimming cup. New York, Grossett & Dunlap. 1922. 409p. 4585

FISHER, RUDOLPH. The conjure-man dies; a mystery tale of dark Harlem. New York, Covici-Friede. 1932. 316p. 4586

FISHER, RUDOLPH. The walls of Jericho. New York, A. A. Knopf. 1928. 307p. 4587

GARNETT, DAVID. The sailor's return. New York, A. A. Knopf. 1925. 189p. 4588

GILBERT, MERCEDES. Aunt Sara's Wooden god. Boston, Christopher pub. co. 1938. 4589

GILHOOLEY, LORD. Son; or, The wisdom of "Uncle Eph," the modern Yutzo. New York, Frederick A. Stokes & co. 1902. 457p. 4590

GILLIAM, EDWARD W. Uncle Sam and the Negro in 1920. Lynchburg, Va., J.P. Bell & co. 1926. 469p. 4591

HAIGH, RICHMOND. An Ethiopian saga. New York, Henry Holt & co. 1919. x, 207p. 4592

HARBEN, WILL N. Northern Georgia sketches. Chicago, A. C. McClurg & co. 1900. 305p. 4593

HARPER, MRS. FRANCES E. W. Iola Leroy; or, Shadows uplifted. Philadelphia, J. H. Earle. 1893. 282p. 4594

HENDERSON, GEORGE W. Ollie Miss; a novel. New York, Frederick A. Stokes & co. 1935. 276p. 4595

HEYWARD, DUBOSE. Mamba's daughters. Garden City, N. Y., Doubleday. 1929. 311p. 4596

HEYWARD, DUBOSE. Porgy: a novel of Negro life in old Charleston. New York, Geo. H. Doran co. 1925. 196p. 4597

HEYWARD, DUBOSE. The half-pint flask. New York, Farrar & Rinehart. 1929. 4598

HEYWARD, JANE S. Brown jackets. Columbia, S. C., State co. 1923. 64p. 4599

HILL, JOHN H. Princess Malah. Washington, Associated pub. 1933. 4600

HOGAN, INEZ. Nicodemus and his gran' pappy. New York, E. P. Dutton. 1938. 4601

HOGAN, INEZ. Nicodemus and his new shoes. New York, E. P. Dutton & sons. 1937. 4602

HOGAN, INEZ. Nicodemus and Petunia. New York, E. P. Dutton. 1937. 4603

HOGAN, INEZ. Twin kids. New York, E. P. Dutton. 1937. 4604

HOPKINS, PAULINE E. Contending forces: a romance illustrative of Negro life. North and South. Boston, Colored cooperative pub. co. 1. 402p. 4605

HOWARD, JAMES H. Bond and free; a true tale of slave times. Harrisburg, Pa., Edwin K. Meyers. 1886. 280p. 4606

HOWELLS, WILLIAM D. An imperative duty. New York, Harper & bros. 1892. 4607

HUGHES, LANGSTON. Not without laughter. New York, A. A. Knopf. 1934. viii, 324p. 4608

HUGHES, LANGSTON. The ways of white folks. New York, Alfred A. Knopf. 1934. 248p. 4609

HURSTON, ZORA N. Jonah's gourd vine. Philadelphia, J. B. Lippincott co. 1924. 17-316p. 4610

HURSTON, ZORA N. Moses; man of the mountain. Philadelphia, J. B. Lippincott co. 1934. 351p.　　4611

HURSTON, ZORA N. Their eyes were watching God. Philadelphia, J. B. Lippincott co. 1937. 286p.　　4612

IN DIXIELAND: stories of the reconstruction era, New York, Purdy press. 1926. 266p.　　4613

INGLE, EDWARD. Southern sidelights. New York, Thos. Y. Crowell & co. 1896. 393p.　　4614

JEROME, THOMAS J. Ku Kux Klan, no. 40. Raleigh, N.C., Edwards & Broughton. 1895. 259p.　　4615

JOHNSON, FENTON. Tales of darkest America. Chicago, Favorite magazine pub. 1920. 34p.　　4616

JOHNSON, JAMES W. The autobiography of an ex-colored man. Boston, Sherman, French & co. 1912. 207p. 2d ed. New York, A. A. Knopf. 1927. xii, 211p.　　4617

JOHNSTON, RICHARD M. Mr. Absalom Billingslea and other Georgia folk. New York, Harper & bros. 1887. 414p.　　4618

JOHNSTON, RICHARD M. Widow Guthrie; a novel. New York, D. Appleton & co. 1890. 309p.　4619

JONES, JOSHUA H., Jr. By sanction of law. Boston, B. J. Brimmer co. 1924. 366p.　　4620

JONES, MAJOR JOSEPH. Georgia scenes. New York, J. S. Ogilvie. 1893. 198p.　　4621

KELLY, WELBOURN. Inchin' along. New York, William Morrow & co. 1932. 277p.　　4622

KENNEDY, ROBERT E. Black cameos. New York, Boni. 1924. xxv, 210p.　　4623

KENNEDY, ROBERT E. Gritny people. New York, Dodd, Mead & co. 1927. 250.p.　　4624

KESTER, PAUL. His own country.

Indianapolis, Bobbs-Merrill co. 1917. 692p.　　4625

KIRKBRIDE, RONALD D. Dark surrender. New York, Sears pub. co. 1931. 283p.　　4626

KREY, LAURA. And tell of time. Boston, Houghton, Mifflin co. 1938.　　4627

LARSEN, NELLA. Passing. New York, A. A. Knopf. 1929. 216p.　　4628

LARSEN, NELLA. Quicksand. New York, A. A. Knopf. 1928. 302p.　　4629

LEE, GEORGE W. River George. New York, Macauley co. 1937. 275p.　　4630

LEE, JOHN M. Counter-clockwise. New York, Wendell Malliet & co. 1940. 103p.　　4631

LLOYD, JESSIE. Gastonia. New York. 1930.　　4632

LOCKE, DAVID R. (pseud.) PETROLEUM V. NASBY. Ekkoes from Kentucky; Bein a perfect record ov the ups, downs, and experiences uv the dimocrisy, doorin the eventful year, 1867, ez seen by a naturalized Kentuckian. Boston, Lee & Shepard. 1868. 324p.　　4633

MARTIN, MRS. ATTWOOD R. Children of the mist. New York. London, D. Appleton & co. 1920. ix, 285p.　　4634

McGIRT, JAMES E. The triumph of Ephraim. Philadelphia, The auth. 1907. 131p.　　4635

MCKAY, CLAUDE. Banana bottom. New York, Harper & bros. 1933. 321p.　　4636

MCKAY, CLAUDE. Banjo; a story without a plot. New York. London, Harper & bros. 1929. 326p.　4637

MCKAY, CLAUDE. Gingertown. New York. London, Harper & bros. 1932. 274p.　　4638

MCKAY, CLAUDE. Home to Harlem. New York, Harper & bros. 1928. 340p. 4639

MCKAY, CLAUDE. Songs of Jamaica. Kingston, B. W. I., Aston W. Gardener & co. 1912. 140p. 4640

MEADE, JULIAN R. The back door. New York, Longmans, Green & co. 1938. 310p. 4641

MEREDITH, WILLIAM T. Not of her father's race. New York, Cassell pub. co. 1890. 291p. 4642

MERRICK, LEONARD. Quaint companions. New York, E. P. Dutton & co. 1924. 299p. 4643

MERRICK, LEONARD. Violet Moses. New York, E. P. Dutton & co. 1924. 299p. 4644

MILLIN, MRS. SARAH G. God's stepchildren. New York, Boni & Liveright. 1924. 319p. 4645

MOODY, MINNIE H. Death is a little man. New York, Messner. 1936. 4646

MOORE, JOANNA P. Little sunshines and their mamma sunshine . . . Nashville, The auth. 1901. 127p. 4647

MORRIS, CLARA. Little "Jim Crow," and other stories of children. New York, Century co. 1899. 226p. 4648

MORRISON, MARY G. Sea-farers; a romance of a New England coast town. New York, Doubleday, Page & co. 1900. 326p. 4649

MOTT, EDWARD. The black Homer of Jimtown. New York. Grosset & Dunlap. 1900. 5-9-286p. 4650

ODUM. HOWARD W. Wings on my feet; Black Ulysses at the wars. Indianapolis. Bobbs-Merrill co. 1929. 308p. 4651

OVINGTON, MARY W. Hazel. New York. Crisis pub. co. 1913. 162p. 4652

OVINGTON. MARY W. The shadow. New York, Harcourt, Brace & Howe. 1920. 352p. 4653

OVINGTON, MARY W. Zeke. New York, Harcourt, Brace & co. 1931. 205p. 4654

PAGE, THOMAS N. Marse Chan. New York, Chas. Scribner's sons. 1896. 4655

PAGE, THOMAS N. Meh lady. New York, Chas. Scribner's sons. 1896. 4656

PAGE, THOMAS N. Red rock: a chronicle of reconstruction. New York, Chas. Scribner's sons. 1899. 584p. 4657

PAGE, THOMAS N. and others. Stories of the South from Scribner's. New York, Chas. Scirbner's sons. 1893. 222p. 4658

PAGE, THOMAS N. Two prisoners. New York, R. H. Russell. 1898. 82p. 4659

PEMBERTON, CAROLINE H. Stephen, the black. Philadelphia, George W. Jacobs & co. 1899. 282p. 4660

PENDLETON, LOUIS B. In the wire grass, a novel. New York. D. Appleton & co. 1889. 245p. 4661

PENDLETON, LOUIS B. Sons of Ham; a tale of the new South. Boston, Roberts bros. 1895. 328p. 4662

PETERKIN, JULIA M. Black April. Indianapolis, Bobbs-Merrill co. 1927. 316p. 4663

PETERKIN, JULIA M. Bright skin. Indiapapolis, Bobbs-Merrill co. 1932. 4664

PETERKIN, JULIA M. Green Thursday. New York, Bobbs-Merrill & co. 1931. 188p. 4665

PETERKIN, JULIA M. Roll, Jordan, roll. New York, Robert O. Ballou. 1933. 251p. 4666

PETERKIN. JULIA M. Scarlet sister

Mary. New York, Bobbs-Merrill & co. 1928. 4667

PHILIPS, F. A. A question of color. New York, Frederick A. Stokes co. 1895. 147p. 4668

PRATT, LUCY. Ezekiel. New York, Doubleday, Page & co. 1909. 254p. 4669

PRATT, LUCY. Ezekiel expands. Boston. New York, Houghton, Mifflin co. 1914. 228p. 4670

PRATT, LUCY. Felix tells it. New York. London, D. Appleton & co. 1915. 355p. 4671

PRYOR, G. LANGHORNE. Neither bond nor free: a plea . . . New York, J. S. Ogilvie pub. co. 1902. 239p. 4672

RAYNER, EMMA. Handicapped among the free. New York, Dodd, Mead & co. 1903. 376p. 4673

ROBINSON, ROWLAND E. Out of bondage and other stories. Rutland, Vt., Tuttle co. 1936. 4674

ROCHE, FRANCOIS dela. Mississippi mood. Chicago, Howard A. Burke & co. 1937. 273p. 4675

ROYALL, WILLIAM L. A reply to "A fool's errand by one of the fools." 3d ed. New York, Hale & son. 1881. 160p. 4676

RUTLEDGE, ARCHIBALD H. It will be daybreak soon. New York, Fleming H. Revell co. 1938. 129p. 4677

RYLEE, ROBERT. Deep dark river. New York, Farrar & Rinehart. 1935. 308p. 4678

SANBORN, GERTRUDE. Veiled aristocrats. Washington, Associated publishers. 1923. 241p. 4679

SATTERWAIT, ELISABETH C. A son of the Carolinas, a story of the hurricane upon the Sea Islands. Philadelphia, Henry Altemus. 1898. 273p. 4680

SAXON, LYLE. Children of strangers.

Boston, Houghton Mifflin co. 1937. 294p. 4681

SCARBOROUGH, DOROTHY. In the land of cotton. New York, Harcourt, Brace & co. 1923. x, 370p. 4682

SCHUYLER, GEORGE. Black no more. New York, Macauley co. 1931. 4683

SCOTT, ANNE. George Sampson Brite. Boston, Meador pub. co. 1939. 154p. 4684

SCOTT, EVELYN and SOUZZ, ERNEST. Migrations; an arabesque in histories. New York, Boni. 1927. 337p. 4685

SHANDS, HULBERT A. White and black. New York, Harcourt, Brace & co. 1922. 304p. 4686

SHARPE, STELIA G. Tobe. Chapel Hill, University of North Carolina press. 1939. 121p. 4687

SHAW, GEORGE B. The adventures of a black girl in her search for God. New York, Dodd, Mead & co. 1933. 75p. 4688

SHELBY, GERTRUDE M. and STONEY, SAMUEL G. Po' buckra. New York, MacMillan co. 1930. 426p. 4689

SMITH, F. HOPKINSON. Colonel Carter of Cartersville. Boston, Houghton Mifflin co. 1891. 208p. 4690

SPIVAK, JOHN. Georgia nigger. New York, Warren & Putnam. 1932. 4691

STRIBLING, T. S. Birthright; a novel. New York, Century co. 1922. 309p. 4692

STUART, MRS. RUTH McE. A golden weeding, and other tales. New York, Harper & bros. 1893. 366p. 4693

STUART, MRS. RUTH McE. George Washington Jones, a Christmas that went a-begging. Philadelphia, H.

Altemus co. 1903. ix, 160p.   4694

STUART, MRS. RUTH McE. Holly
and pizen and other stories. New
York, Century co. 1899. 216p.
4695

STUART, MRS. RUTH McE. Moriah's
mourning, and other half-hour
sketches. New York, London,
Harper & bros. 1898. 3-218p.   4696

STUART, MRS. RUTH McE.
Napoleon Jackson, the gentleman
of the plush rocker. New York,
Century co. 1902. 132p.   4697

STUART, MRS. RUTH McE. The
second wooing of Salina Sue, and
other stories. New York, Harper &
bros. 1905. 236p.   4698

STUART, MRS. RUTH McE. Solomon
Crow's Christmas pockets and other
tales. New York, Harper & bros.
1896. 201p.   4699

TARKINGTON, BOOTH. Penrod.
Garden City, N. Y., Doubleday,
Page & co. 1920. vi, 348p.   4700

TARKINGTON, BOOTH. Penrod and
Sam. Garden City, N. Y., Doubleday, Page & co. 1916. ix, 356p.
4701

TENSAS, MADISON. Louisiana
swamp doctor and other southern
sketches. Philadelphia, Peterson &
bros. 1881. 203p.   4702

THURMAN, WALLACE. Infants of
the spring. New York, Macauley co.
1932. 284p.   4703

THURMAN, WALLACE. The blacker
the berry; a novel of Negro life.
New York, Macauley co. 1929.
9-262p.   4704

TOMMER, JEAN. Cane. New York,
Boni & Liveright. 1923. xi. 239p.
4705

TOURGEE, ALBION W. An appeal to
Caesar. New York, Fords, Howard
& Hulbert. 1884. 422p.   4706

TOURGEE, ALBION W. A fool's
errand, by one of the fools. New

York, Fords, Howard & Hulbert.
1879. 361p.   4707

TOURGEE, ALBION W. Bricks without straw. New York, Fords,
Howard & Hulbert. 1880. 521p.
4708

TOURGEE, ALBION W. Figs and
thistles, a novel. New York, Fords,
Howard & Hulbert. 1879p.   4709

TOURGEE, ALBION W. Hot plow-
shares. New York, Fords, Howard
& Hulbert. 1883. 610p.   4710

TOURGEE, ALBION W. The invisible
empire: Part I. A new, illustrated,
and enlarged ed. of A fool's errand .
. .; the famous historical romance
of life in the South since the war.
Part II. A concise review of recent
events, showing the elements on
which the tale is based. New York,
Fords, Howard & Hulbert. 1880.
viii. 521p.   4711

TOURGEE, ALBION W. John Eax
and Mamelon; or, The south without the shadow. New York, Fords,
Howard & Hulbert. 1882. ix, 300p.
4712

TOURGEE, ALBION W. Man who
outlived himself. New York, Fords,
Howard & Hulbert. 1898. 215p.
4713

TOURGEE, ALBION W. With Gauge
& Swallow, attorneys. Philadelphia,
J. B. Lippincott co. 1889. 271p.
4714

TUPPER, FREDERIC A. Moonshine; a
story of the reconstruction period.
New York, John W. Lovell co.
1884. 233p.   4715

TURPIN, WATERS E. O'Canaan! New
York, Doubleday, Doran & co.
1939. 3-311p.   4716

TURPIN, WATERS E. These low
grounds. New York, London,
Harper & bros. 1937. 344p.   4717

VAN VECHTEN, CARL. Nigger

heaven. New York, A. A. Knopf. 1926. 286p.   4718

WALROND, ERIC D. Topic death. New York, Boni & Liveright. 1926. 283p.   4719

WARD, ELIZABETH S. P. Lost hero. Boston, Little, Brown & co. 1891. 62p.   4720

WARING, ROBERT. As we see it. Washington, C. F. Sudwarth. 1910. 233p.   4721

WELSH, JAMES. White baby. New York. London, Frederick A. Stokes co. 1895. 190p.   4722

WESTMORELAND, MARIA J. Clifford Troup: a Georgia story. New York, G. W. Carleton & co; London, S. Low, son & co. 1873. 338p.   4723

WHITE, WALTER F. Flight. New York, A. A. Knopf. 1926. 300p.   4724

WHITE, WALTER F. Rope and faggot. New York, A. A. Knopf. 1929.   4725

WHITE, WATER F. The fire in the flint. New York, A. A. Knopf. 1924. 300p.   4726

WISE, JOHN S. Lion's skin; a historical novel and a novel history. New York. Doubleday. Page & co. 1905. 404p.   4727

WOOD, CLEMENT. Nigger; a novel. New York. E. P. Dutton co. 1922. vii, 232p.   4728

WORTH, NICHOLAS. The southerner; a novel, being autobiographical. New York. Doubleday. Page & co. 1909. vi, 424p.   4729

WRIGHT, RICHARD. Native son. New York. London, Harper & bros. 1939.   4730

WRIGHT, RICHARD. Uncle Tom's children. New York, Harper & bros. 1938. 317p.   4731

YOUNG, FRANCIS B. Sea horses. New York, A. A. Knopf. 1925. 321p.   4732

YOUNG, FRANCIS B. Woodsmoke. New York, E. P. Dutton & co. 1924. 372p.   4733

5. Plays by or about the Negro or with Negro characters.

BIRTH OF A NATION. A collection of newspaper accounts and editorial opinions relating to the photoplay "Birth of a nation" as adapted from Thomas Dixon's "The Klansman," 1915-1921. 3v.   4734

BOUCICAULT, DIONYSIUS L. The octoroon; or, Life in Louisiana, a play in five acts. New York. 1867. 40p.   4735

CONNELLY, MARC C. The green pastures; a fable suggested by Roark Bradford's southern sketches, "Ol' man Adam and his chillun." New York, Farrar & Rinehart. 1929. 173p.   4736

COTTER, JOSEPH S. Caleb, the degenerate: a play in four acts. A study of the types, customs, and needs of the American Negro. Louisville, Bradley & Gilbert co. 1901. 57p.   4737

CULBERTSON, ERNEST H. Color in court, a play of Negro life in one act. New York, Samuel French. 1933. 37p.   4738

CULBERTSON, ERNEST H. Goat alley, a tragedy of Negro life. Cincinnati, Stewart Kidd co. 1922. 155p.   4739

CUMBERLAND, R. The West Indian, a comedy as it is performed at the Theater Royal in Drury Lane.

London, W. Griffin. 1771. 102p.
4740

DODD, NELLIE C. Broken chains. New York, Missionary education movement of the U. S. and Canada. 1915.
4741

DRINKWATER, JOHN. Abraham Lincoln; a play. New York, Houghton Mifflin co. 1919. xii, 112p.
4742

EASTON, WILLIAM E. Dessalines; a dramatic tale. A single chapter from Haiti's history. Galveston, Tex., J. W. Burson. 1893. 138p.
4743

EDMONDS, RANDOLPH. Shades and shadows. Boston, Meador pub. co. 1930. 171p.
4744

EDMONDS, RANDOLPH. Six plays for a Negro theatre. Boston, Walter H. Baker co. 1934. 155p.
4745

FITCH, CLYDE. Barbara Frietchie, the Frederick girl; a play in four acts. New York, Life co. 1900. 128p.
4746

GALSWORTHY, JOHN. The forest, a drama in four acts. New York, Chas. Scribner's sons. 1924. 115p.
4747

GREEN, PAUL. The field god and In Abraham's bosom. New York, Robert M. McBride & co. 1927. 317p.
4748

GREEN, PAUL. In Aunt Mahaly's cabin, a Negro melodrama in one act. New York, Samuel French. 1925. 35p.
4749

GREEN, PAUL. Lonesome road; six plays for the Negro theatre. New York, R. M. McBride & co. 1926. xx, 217p.
4750

GRIMKE, ANGELINA W. Rachel; a play in three acts. Boston, Cornhill co. 1920. 96p.
4751

GRINNELL PLAYS. Four one act plays. Two gifts for Negro actors. Aaron Stevens, abolitionist.

Chicago, Dramatic pub. co. 1935. 104p.
· 4752

HEYWARD, DUBOSE. Brass ankle; a play in three acts. New York, Farrar & Rinehart. 1931. 133p.
4753

HEYWARD, DUBOSE. Mamba's daughters, dramatized from the novel. New York. Toronto, Farrar & Rinehart. 1939. 5-182p.
4754

JOHNSON, GEORGIA D. Plumes; a play in one act. New York, Samuel French. 1927. 15p.
4755

KOCH, FREDERICK H. (ed.) American folk plays. New York, D. Appleton-Century co. 1939. 592p.
4756

KOCH, FREDERICK H. (ed.) Carolina folk comedies. New York, Samuel French. 1931. 311p.
4757

LOCKE, ALAIN L. and GREGORY, MONTGOMERY (eds) Plays of Negro life: a source book of native American drama. New York. London, Harper & bros. 1927. 430p.
4758

MEYER, ANNIE N. Black souls; a play in six scenes. New Bedford, Mass., Reynolds press. 1932. 99p.
4759

MOODY, WILLIAM V. The faith healer, a play in three acts. New York, MacMillan co. 1910. 164p.
4760

O'NEILL, EUGENE G. All God's chillun got wings . . . New York, Boni & Liveright. 1924. 170p. 4761

O'NEILL, EUGENE G. The Emperor Jones, a study of the psychology of fear and of race superstition. Cincinnati, Stewart, Kidd co. 1921. 54p. 2d ed. New York, Boni & Liveright. 1921. 54p. Student ed. New York, D. Appleton-Century co. 1934. 60p.
4762

PETERS, PAUL and SKLAR, GEORGE. Stevedore; a play in

three acts. New York, Covici-Friede. 1934. 123p.   4763

RICHARDSON, WILLIS (comp.) Plays and pageants from the life of the Negro. Washington, Associated publishers. 1930. x, 373p.   4764

RICHARDSON, WILLIS and MILLER, MAY (eds.) Negro history in thriteen plays. Washington, Associated publishers. 1935. vii, 333p.   4765

SHAKESPEARE, WILLIAM. Othello, the moor of Venice.   4766

SHAW, GEORGE B. Back to Methuselah; a metabiological pentateuch. New York, Brentano's. 1921. 330p.   4767

SHELDON, EDWARD. The nigger; an American play in three acts. New York, MacMillan co. 1910. 269p.   4768

STEINBECK, JOHN. Of mice and men; a play in three acts. New York, Covici-Friede. 1937. 172p.   4769

STEPHENS, ANN B. Roseanne. New York, Greenwich Village theatre. 1924.   4770

SUTHERLAND, EVELYN G. Po' white trash and other one act plays. Chicago, Herbert S. Stone & co. 1900. 232p.   4771

TORRENCE, HEDERIC R. Granny Maumee; the rider of dreams; Simon, the Cyrenian. Plays for a Negro theater. New York, MacMillan & co. 1917. 111p.   4772

WEXLEY, JOHN. They shall not die. New York, A. A. Knopf. 1934. 191p.   4773

6. Miscellaneous essays, orations, addresses and other works by or about the Negro.

ABBOTT, LYMAN. Sermon . . . delivered at the fiftieth annual meeting of the American missionary society, Oct. 1896. New York, American missionary society. 1896. 14p.   4774

AKIN, EMMA E. Ideals and adventures. Oklahoma City, Harlow pub. co. 1938. 251p.   4775

AMERICAN NEGRO ACADEMY. Occasional papers . . . Washington, The academy. 1897-1920. Collection has: nos. 1-16.   4776

ATKINSON, GEORGE W. The great republic; whither is it drifting? An address before the Chautauqua assembly, July 6, 1907. Moundsville, W. Va. 1907. 20p.   4777

BAKER, HENRY E. The colored inventor, a record of fifty years. New York, Crisis pub. co. 1913. 12p.   4778

BARRINGER, P. B. The American Negro, his past and his future. An address before the tri-state medical society. 3d ed. Raleigh, N.C., The society. 1900. 23p.   4779

BLYDEN, EDWARD W. Liberia's offering: being addresses, sermons, etc. New York, John A. Gay. 1862. 167p.   4780

BLYDEN, EDWARD W. The elements of permanent influence. A discourse. Washington, The auth. 1890. 18p.   4781

BOWEN, J. W. E. What shall the harvest be? A series of plain talks to the colored people of America, on their problems. Washington, The auth. 87p.   4782

BRACKETT, JEFFREY R. Notes on the progress of the colored people of Maryland since the war. (A supplement to the Negro in Maryland, a study of the institution of slavery). Baltimore, Johns Hopkins press. 1890. 96p. (Johns Hopkins Univ. Studies Eighth series VII-VIII-IX). 4783

BRAITHWAITE, WILLIAM S. B. "The Reserves of Peace;" a commencement address delivered at Atlanta University in June, 1918. "The Negro Franchise," topic for discussion selected by the Twenty Third annual conference for the study of Negro problems. Atlanta University bulletin: (Quarterly) Series 2-No. 32. July, 1918. 24p. 4784

BROWN, WILLIAM W. My southern home: or, The South and its people. Boston, A. G. Brown & co. 1882. 253p. 4785

BROWN, WILLIAM W. Sketches of places and people abroad with a memoir of the author. Boston, John P. Jewett & co. 1855. 320p. 4786

BROWN, WILLIAM W. Three years in Europe; or, Places I have seen and people I have met. London, Chas. Gilpin. 1852. 312p. 4787

BRUCE, ROSCOE C. Service by the educated Negro. An address . . . at the commencement exercises of the M Street high school, Washington, D. C. June 16, 1903. 17p. 4788

BURROWS, FREDERICK M. Not as a colored man, but as a man. A speech delivered at the celebration of the Emancipation Proclamation. Eastville, Va., Jan. 1, 1891. Hampton, Va., Hampton Institute press. 1891. 12p. 4789

CARNEGIE, ANDREW. The Negro in America. An address delivered

before the Philosophical institution of Edinburgh, Oct. 16, 1907. Inverness, Scotland, R. Carruthers & sons. 1907. 44p. 4790

CARTER, E. R. The black side, a partial history of the business, religious, and educational side of the Negro in Atlanta, Ga. Atlanta, The auth. 1894. 323p. 4791

CARTER, RANDALL A. Gathered fragments. Collected sermons and addresses. Chicago, The auth. 1939. 278p. 4792

COUNCILL, WILLIAM H. Bright side of the southern question. A speech at Carona, Ala. Aug. 25, 1903. 17p. 4793

COUNCILL, WILLIAM H. Negro development in the South. An address before the southern industrial convention. Normal, Ala. 1901. 11p. 4794

COUNCILL, WILLIAM H. The young Negro of 1864; The young Negro of 1904; The problem then; the problem now. Speech delivered before the students' lecture bureau George R. Smith College, Sedalia, Mo., March 25, 1904; and before the Intercollegiate lecture bureau, Nashville, April 8, 1904. Boston, Charles Alexander. 1904. 20p. 4795

COZART, W. F. The chosen people. New York, Christopher press. 1924. 153p. 4796

COZART, A. B. The Negro from a to z. Washington, 1897. 12p. 4797

CROGMAN, WILLIAM H. Talks for the times. Atlanta, Ga., Franklin print. & pub. co. 1896. xxiii, 330p. 4798

CROSS, SAMUEL C. The Negro and the sunny South. A lecture. Martinsburg, W. Va., The auth. 1899. 136p. 4799

CRUMMELL, ALEX. A defence of the

Negro race in America from the assaults and charges of Rev. J. L. Tucker, D. D. of Jackson, Miss., in his paper before the "Church Congress" of 1882, on "The relations of the Church to the colored race." Washington, J. Detweiler. 1883. 35p. 4800

CRUMMELL, ALEX. Incidents of hope for the Negro race in America. A Thanksgiving sermon. Washington. 1895. 15p. 4801

CRUMMELL, ALEX. The greatness of Christ and other sermons. New York, Thomas Whittaker. 1882. 352p. 4802

CRUMMELL, ALEX. Tracts for the Negro race. Washington. 1898. 32p. (Collection has nos. 1, 2, 3, 4). 4803

DAVIS, WALKER M. Pushing forward; a history of Alcorn A. & M. College. Ikolona, Miss., Okolona industrial school. 1938. 124p. 4804

DORR, D. F. A colored man round the world. Cleveland, The auth. 1858. 192p. 4805

DOUGLASS, FREDERICK. Address . . . delivered on the twenty-first anniversary of emancipation in the District of Columbia, April 16, 1883. Washington, 1883. 16p. 4806

DOUGLASS, FREDERICK. Address . . . on the lessons of the hour, Jan. 9, 1894. Washington. 1894. 36p. 4807

DOUGLASS, WILLIAM. Sermons preached in the African Protestant Episcopal Church. Philadelphia, King & Baird. 1854. 251p. 4808

DUBOIS, W. E. BURGHARDT. The soul of black folk. Essays and sketches. Chicago, A. C. McClurg & co. 1903. 265p. 4809

DUNBAR, MRS. ALICE R. The Dunbar speaker and entertainer, containing the best prose and poetic selections by and about the Negro race with programs arranged for special entertainments. Naperville, Ill., J. L. Nichols & co. 1920. 288p. 4810

DUNBAR, MRS. ALICE R. Masterpieces of Negro eloquence: the best speeches delivered by the Negro from the days of slavery to the present time. New York, Bookery pub. co. 1914. 512p. 4811

ECOB, JAMES. America's problem; the dehumanized citizen. Philadelphia, Unitarian book-room. n.d. 13p. 4812

ESSAYS on miscellaneous subjects by a self-educated colored youth. Cleveland, Nevin's steam print. house. 1866. 48p. 4813

FULTON, DAVID F. (pseud.) THORNE, JACK. Recollections of a sleeping car porter. Jersey City, The auth. n.d. 45p. 4814

GARNET, HENRY H. A memorial discourse delivered in the House of representatives, Feb. 12, 1865. Philadelphia, Joseph M. Wilson. 1865. 91p. 4815

GIBSON, JOHN W. The colored American from slavery to honorable citizenship. Atlanta. Naperville, Ill. Toronto, J. L. Nichols & co. 1903. 732p. 4816

GIBSON, JOHN W. Progress of a race . . . Naperville, Ill., J. L. Nichols. 1912. 732p. Rev. ed. 1920. 480p. 4817

GRIMKE, FRANCIS J. Equality of rights for all citizens, black and white, alike. A discourse delivered in Washington, Mar. 7, 1909. Washington. 1909. 19p. 4818

GRIMKE, FRANCIS J. Gideon bands for work within the race and for work without the race; a message to the colored people of the United

States. Washington. The auth. 4819

GRIMKE, FRANCIS J. The Negro;his rights and wrongs, the forces for him and against him. Washington, The auth. 1898. 102p.   4820

GRIMKE, FRANCIS J. The things of paramount importance in the development of the Negro race. Washington. 1903. 13p.   4821

HAWKINS, JOHN R. Fourteen specific articles as a basis of democracy at home. Washington. 1918. 61p.   4822

HAYGOOD, ATTICUS G. Our brother in black: his freedom and his future. New York, Phillips & Hunt. 1881. 252p.   4823

HAYGOOD, ATTICUS G. Pleas for progress. Nashville, The auth. 1889. 320p.   4824

HELM, MARY. From darkness to light. The story of Negro progress. New York, Felming H. Revell co. 1909. 218p.   4825

HELM, MARY. The upward path: the evolution of a race. Cincinnati, Jennings & Graham. 1913. xix, 357p.   4826

ILLINOIS COMMISSION. Commission appointed by the governor of Illinois, July 1, 1913, to arrange half-century anniversary of Negro freedom under act passed by 48th General Assembly. First annual report, 1913-14. Springfield, Ill. 1914. 39p.   4827

INBORDEN, THOMAS S. An estimate of Negro life and character. Enfield, N. C., The auth. n.d. 6p.   4828

JEFFERSON, T. LeROY. The old Negro and the new Negro. Boston, Meador pub. co. 1937. 118p.   4829

JOHNSON, EDWARD A. Light ahead for the Negro. New York, Grafton press. 1904. 132p.   4830

JOHNSON, EMORY R. (ed.) The Negro's progress in fifty years. (The annals, vol. xlix September, 1913). Philadelphia, American Academy of Political and Social Science. 1913. 266p.   4831

JOHNSON, W. D. Past and future of the Negro race in America. Boston, C. A. Wasto. 1897. 44p.   4832

JOHNSON, WILLIAM E. The scourge of the Negro. A sermon delivered in Washington, April 10, 1904. Washington, Oscar D. Morris. 1904. 14p.   4833

JOHNSON, WILLIAM E. The scourging of a race, and other sermons and addresses. Washington, Beresford. 1904. 228p.   4834

JONES, GILBERT H. Education in theory and practice. Library of educational methods. Boston, R. R. Badger. 1919. 396p.   4836

JOSEY, CHARLES C. Race and national solidarity. New York, Chas. Scribner's sons. 1923. ix, 227p.   4836

KLETZING, A. M. and CROGMAN, W. H. Progress of a race; or, The remarkable advancement of the Afro-American Negro. Atlanta. Naperville, Ill. Toronto, J. L. Nichols & co. 1898. 664p.   4837

LANGSTON, JOHN M. Freedom and citizenship. Selected lectures and addresses. Washington, R. H. Darby. 1883. 286p.   4838

LEUPP, FRANCES E. Negro self-uplifting. Tuskegee Institute, Ala. 1902. 190. (Rpt. from New York Evening Post.)   4839

MACBRADY, J. E. (ed.) A new Negro for a new century. An accurate and up-to-date record of the upward struggles of the Negro race. Essays by Booker T. Washington, N. B. Wood and others. Chicago,

American pub. house. n.d. 428p.
4840
MAYO, A. D. The colored American;
. working man of the new time. An
address. Hampton, Va., Hampton
Institute press. 1898. 33p.   4841
MILLER, KELLY. As to the
Leopard's spots: an open letter to
Thomas Dixon, Jr. Washington, The
auth. 1905. 21p. 20th thousand,
Washington, Hayworth pub. house.
1905. 21p.   4842
MILLER, KELLY. The everlasting
stain. Essays on issues growing out
of the post-world war period and
the Negro. Washington, Associated
publishers. 1924. 352p.   4843
MILLER, KELLY. The primary needs
of the Negro race. An address
delivered before the alumni
association of Hampton Institute,
June 14, 1899. Washington,
Howard University press. 1899.
18p.   4844
MOTON, ROBERT R. What the Negro
thinks. Garden City, N. Y., Doubleday Doran & co. 1929. 267p. 4845
NEGRO ADDRESSES AND
SPEECHES. A collection of newspaper accounts, reviews, and
editorial opinions relating to
addresses and speeches made by
various Negroes. 1898-1920. 12v.
4846
OVINGTON, MARY WHITE and
PRITCHARD, THOMAS M. The
upward path; a reader for colored
children. New York, Harcourt,
Brace & co. xi, 255p.   4847
PAYNTER, JOHN H. Joining the
navy; or, Abroad with Uncle Sam.
Hartford, Conn., American pub. co.
1895. 298p.   4848
PENDLETON, MRS. LELIA A. A
narrative of the Negro. Washington,
R. L. Pendleton. 1912. 217p. 4849
PENN, I. GARLAND (ed.) The united

Negro: his problems and his
progress, containing the addresses
and proceedings of the Negro
young people's Christian and
educational congress, Aug. 6-11,
1902. Atlanta, D. E. Luther pub.
co. 1902. xxx, 600p.   4850
PICKENS, WILLIAM. The new Negro,
his political, civil and mental status,
and related essays. New York,
Neale pub. co. 1916. 239p.   4851
PIPKIN, JOSEPH P. The Negro in
revelation, in history, and in
citizenship. What the race has done
and is doing. St. Louis. New York,
N. D. Thompson. 1902. xix, 524p.
4852
POWELL, A. CLAYTON. Palestine
and saints in Caesar's household.
New York, Richard R. Smith.
1939. 217p.   4853
POWELL, WILLIAM J. Black wings.
Los Angeles, Ivan Deach, Jr. 1934.
218p.   4854
RICE, WILLARD. The Negro around
the world. New York, Geo. H.
Doran and co. 1925. 75p.   4855
RICHINGS, G.F. Evidences of progress among colored people. Philadelphia, Geo. S. Ferguson co. 1896.
432p.   4856
SHERWOOD, W. H. Solid shot: a few
of the sermons of the Negro
evangelist. (Reported by George F.
Thompson) Boston, The auth.
1891. 112p.   4857
STORRS, R. S. Our nation's work for
the colored people. A discourse
delivered in behalf of the American
missionary association. New York,
Holt bros. 1890. 22p.   4858
WALKER, CHARLES T. A colored
man abroad; what he saw and heard
in the Holy Land and Europe.
Augusta, Ga., The auth. 1892.
148p.   4859
WASHINGTON, BOOKER T. Address

delivered at the cotton states and international exposition, Atlanta, Sept. 1895. Atlanta. 1895. 11p. 4860

WASHINGTON, BOOKER T. Character building; being addresses delivered on Sunday evenings to the students of Tuskegee Institute. New York, Doubleday, Page & co. 1902. 290p. 4861

WASHINGTON, BOOKER T. Educational and industrial emancipation of the Negro; an address before the Brooklyn Institute of arts and science. Tuskegee Ala. Inst. Print. 1903. 16p. 4862

WASHINGTON, BOOKER T. The man farthest down. A record of observation and study in Europe. Garden City, N. Y., Doubleday, Page & co. 1912. 390p. 4863

WASHINGTON, BOOKER T. My larger education; being chapters from my experience. Garden City, N.Y., Doubleday, Page & co. 1911. 313p. 4864

WASHINGTON, BOOKER T. The Negro and the signs of civilization and the Negro's part in the up-building of the South. Tuskegee, Ala., Tuskegee Institute press. 1899. 8p. 4865

WASHINGTON, BOOKER T. Putting the most into life; talks to Tuskegee students. New York, Thos. Y. Crowell & co. 1906. 36p. 4866

WASHINGTON, BOOKER T. Selected speeches. Ed. by E. Davidson Washington. New York, Doubleday, Doran & co. 1932. 283p. 4867

WASHINGTON, BOOKER T. Sowing and reaping. Boston, L. C. Page & co. 1900. 29p. 4868

WASHINGTON, BOOKER T. The story of the Negro. The rise of the race from slavery. New York, Doubleday, Page & co. 1909. 2v. 4869

WASHINGTON, BOOKER T. and DuBOIS, W. E. BURGHARDT. The Negro in the South, his economic progress in relation to his moral and religious development. Philadelphia, Geo. W. Jacobs co. 1907. 312p. 4870

WASHINGTON, E. DAVIDSON (comp.) Quotations of Booker T. Washington. Tuskegee, Ala., Tuskegee Inst. press. 1938. 37p. 4871

WILLIAMS, DANIEL B. Freedom and progress and other choice addresses. Introduction by John Mitchell, Jr. Petersburg, Va., The auth. 1890. 148p. 4872

7. Biographies and autobiographies of Negroes.

ANDREWS, ROBERT McC. John Merrick, a biographical sketch. Durham, N.C., Seamon press. 1920. 200p. 4873

ARMSTRONG, LOUIS. Swing that music. An autobiography. . . New York, Longmans, Green & co. 1936. 4874

ASHER, JEREMIAH. An auto-biography with details of a visit to England and some account of the history of the Meeting street Baptist church, Providence, R.I., and of the Shiloh Baptist Church, Philadelphia. Philadelphia, The auth. 1862. x, 227p. 4875

BAKER, HENRY E. Benjamin Banneker, the Negro mathematician

and astronomer. (Rpt. from Journal of Negro history, April, 1918). Washington. 1918. pp. 99-118.4876

BENJAMIN, R.C.O. Life of Toussaint L'Ouverture, warrior and statesman, with a historical survey of the island of San Domingo from 1492 to 1803. Los Angeles, The auth. 1888. 109p. 4877

BORRESEN, PETER. Nungme, sinerissap kujatdliup nakiteriviane. (A life of Booker T. Washington in Eskimo). 1930. 168p. 4878

BRADFORD, SARAH E. Scenes in the life of Harriet Tubman. Auburn, N.Y., W.J. Moses. 1869. 132p. 4879

BRADFORD, SARAH E. Harriet, the Moses of her people. New York, Lockwood & son. 1886. 149p. 4880

BRAGG, GEORGE T. Men of Maryland. Baltimore, Church advocate press. 1914. Rev. ed. 1925. 135p. 4881

BRAWLEY, BENJAMIN G. Negro builders and heroes. Chapel Hill, University of North Carolina press. 1937. 315p. 4882

BRAWLEY, BENJAMIN G. The Negro genius. A new appraisal of the achievement of the American Negro in literature and the fine arts. New York, Dodd, Mead & co. 1937. 366p. 4883

BRAWLEY, BENJAMIN G. Paul Laurence Dunbar, poet of his people. Chapel Hill, University of North Carolina press. 1936. 159p. 4884

BROWN, HALLIE Q. Homespun heroines and other women of distinction. Xenia, O., Aldine pub. co. 1926. 248p. 4885

BROWN, HALLIE Q. (comp.) Pen pictures of pioneers of Wilberforce. Xenia, O., The auth. 1937. 96p. 4886

BROWN, WILLIAM W. The black man, his antecedents, his genius, and his achievements. 4th ed. Boston, R. F. Wallcut. 1865. 312p. 4887

BROWN, WILLIAM W. The rising son; or, The antecedents and advancement of the colored race. Boston, Brown & co. 1874. ix. 552p. 4888

BRUCE, JOHN E. (comp.) Short biographical sketches of eminent Negro men and women in Europe and the United States, with brief extracts from their writings and public utterances. Yonkers, N.Y., Gazette press. 1910. 103p. 4889

BULLOCK, RALPH W. In spite of handicaps; brief biographical sketches with discussion outlines of outstanding Negroes now living who are achieving distinction . . . New York, Association press. 1927. 140p. . 4890

CANSLER, CHARLES W. Three generations. The story of a colored family of eastern Tennessee. Kingsport, Tenn., Kingsport press. 1939. viii, 173p. 4891

CHAMBERS, E. K. Samuel Taylor Coleridge; a biographical study. New York, Oxford University press. 1939. 4892

CHILD, MRS. LYDIA M. The freedman's book. Biographical sketches of Negroes. Boston, Ticknor & Fields. 1865. 276p. 2d ed. Boston, Fields, Osgood & co. 1869. 276p. 4893

CLARK, DAVIS W. Life and times of Rev. Elijah Hedding, D. D. New York, Carleton & Phillips. 1855. 686p. 4894

COAN, JOSEPHUS R. Daniel Alexander Payne; Christian educator. Philadelphia, A.M.E. book concern. 1935. 139p. 4895

CONWAY, M. D. Benjamin Banneker, the Negro astronomer. (Rpt. from Atlantic monthly) London. n.d. 15p. 4896

COOLEY, TIMOTHY M. Sketches of the life and character of the Rev. Lemuel Haynes. . . New York, J.S. Taylor. 1837. xxv, 345p. 4897

COOPER, WILLIAM M. (ed.) Virginia's contribution to Negro leadership. Biographies of outstanding Negroes born in Virginia. Hampton, Va., Hampton Institute press. 1936. 77p. 4898

COPPIN, LEVI J. Unwritten history, an autobiography. Philadelphia, A.M.E. book concern. 1919. 375p. 4899

CORROTHERS, JAMES D. In spite of handicap; an autobiography. New York, Geo. H. Doran & co. 1916. 238p. 4900

CROMWELL, JOHN W. The Negro in American history; men and women eminent in the evolution of the American of African descent. Washington, American Negro academy. 1914. xiii, 284p. 4901

CUTHBERT, MARION. Juliette Derricotte. New York, Woman's press. 1933. 55p. 4902

DABNEY, WENDELL P. Maggie L. Walker and the I.O. of Saint Luke. Cincinnati, Dabney pub. co. 1927. 135p. 4903

DANIEL, SADIE I. Women builders. Washington, Associated pub. 1931. 181p. 4904

DAVIS, D. WEBSTER. The life and public service of the Rev. William Washington Brown. Philadelphia, A.M.E. pub. house. 1911. 4905

DAVIS, WILLIAM R. (comp.) Annual missionary album of the African M.E. church V.I. New York, The auth. 1895. 148p. (Biographies of the ministers of the church.) 4906

DAWSON, E. C. James Hannington, first bishop of eastern equatorial Africa. A history of his life and work. New York, Anson D.F. Randolph. 1887. 471p. 4907

DEANE, CHARLES (ed.) Letters of Phillis Wheatley, the Negro-slave poet of Boston. Boston, privately printed. 1864. 19p. 4908

DISTINGUISHED NEGROES. A collection of newspaper accounts and editorial opinions relating to the lives and works of various distinguished Negroes. 1890-1925. 58v. 4909

DOUGLASS, FREDERICK. Narrative of the life of Frederick Douglass, an American slave. Written by himself. Boston, Anti-slavery office. 1845. Hartford, Park pub. co. 1881. 516p. xvi, 125p. New rev. ed. Boston, De Wolfe, Fiske & co. 1893. 752p. 4910

DRINKER, FREDERICK E. Booker T. Washington: the master-mind of a child of slavery . . . Philadelphia, National pub. co. Washington, Geo. W. Bertron. 1915. viii, 320p. 4911

DuBOIS, W. E. BURGHARDT. Dark water; voices from within the veil. An autobiography. 2d ed. Chicago, A.G. McClurg & co. 1905. 264p. 17th ed. New York, Harcourt, Brace & co. 1920. 276p. 4912

EDWARDS, WILLIAM J. Twenty-five years in the black belt. Boston, Cornhill co. 1918. xvii, 143p. 4913

ELLIOTT, WILLIAM G. The story of Archer Alexander: from slavery to freedom, March 30, 1863. Boston, Cupples, Upham & co. 1885. 123p. 4914

EQUIANO, OLAUDAH. The interesting narrative of Olaudah Equiano or Gustavus Vassa, the African.

Written by himself. London. 1814. 2v. 4915

FAUSET, ARTHUR H. For freedom. A biographical story of the American Negro. Philadelphia, Franklin pub. co. 1927. 200p. 4916

FAUSET, ARTHUR H. Sojourner Truth, God's faithful Pilgrim. Chapel Hill, University of North Carolina press. 1938. 4917

FISHER, MILES M. The master's slaves, Elijah John Fisher. Philadelphia, Judson press. 1922. 195p. 4918

FLIPPER, HENRY O. The colored cadet at West Point; an autobiography of the first graduate of color from the U.S. Military Academy. New York, Homer Lee & co. 1878. 328p. 4919

FLOYD, SILAS X. The life of Charles T. Walker. . . Nashville, National Baptist pub. board. 1902. 4920

GIBBS, MIFFLIN W. Shadow and light; an autobiography. Washington, the auth. 1902. xv, 372p. 4921

GOLLOCK, GEORGINA A. Lives of eminent Africans. London, Longmans, Green & co. 1922. 152p. 4922

GOLLOCK, GEORGINA A. Sons of Africa. New York, Friendship press. 1928. 239p. 4923

GORDON, TAYLOR. Born to be. New York, Covici-Friede. 1929. 235p. 4924

GRAHAM, STEPHEN. Children of slaves. London, MacMillan & co. 1920. 315p. 4925

GREEN, A. R. The life of the Rev. Dandridge F. Davis, of the African Methodist Episcopal church; also, a brief sketch of the Rev. Daniel Conyou. Pittsburgh, Ohio

conference. A.M.E. church. 1853. 130p. 4926

HAMMOND, L. H. In the vanguard of a race. New York, Council of women for home missions. 1922. 176p. 4927

HARE, MAUD C. Norris Wright Cuney. A tribute of the black people. New York, Crisis pub. co. 1913. xv, 230p. 4928

HARLAN, HOWARD H. John Jasper; a case history in leadership. Charlottesville, Va., University of Virginia press. 1936. 29p. (Phelps-Stokes papers, no. 14). 4929

HASKIN, SARA E. The handicapped winners. Nashville. Dallas. M.E. church, south pub. house. 1922. 116p. 4930

HATCHER, WILLIAM E. John Jasper; the unmatched Negro philosopher and preacher. New York. Chicago, Toronto, Fleming H. Revell & co. 1908. 183p. 4931

HAYNE, COE. Race grit; adventures on the border-land of liberty. Philadelphia, Judson press. 1922. 210-p. 4932

HAYNES, MRS. ELIZABETH R. Unsung heroes. Sketches of Douglass, Dunbar and others. New York, Dubois & Dill. 1921. 279p. 4933

HEARD, WILLIAM H. From slavery to bishopric. Philadelphia, A.M.E. pub. house. 1924. 4934

HENSON, MATTHEW A. A Negro explorer at the North pole. New York, F. A. Stokes co. 1912. 200p. 4935

HERNDON, ANGELO. Let me live. New York, Random house. 1937. 409p. 4936

HOLLAND, FREDERIC M. Frederick Douglass, the colored orator. New York. 1891. Rev. ed. New York,

Funk & Wagnalls. 1891. vi, 431p. 4937

HOLTZCLAW, WILLIAM H. The black man's burden. New York, Neale pub. co. 1915. 232p. 4938

HORSHOR, JOHN. God in a Rolls Royce. The rise of Father Divine. New York, Hillman-Curl. 1936. 4939

HOWE, M.A. DeWOLFE. Causes and their champions. Boston, Little, Brown & co. 1926. 331p. 4940

HOWE, M.A. DeWOLFE. Frederick Douglass. 4th ed. Boston, Small, Maynard co. 1899. 141p. (Beacon Biographies). 4941

HUBBARD, ELBERT. Little journeys to the homes of great teachers, vol. xxiii. Biographical sketches of Booker T. Washington and others. New York, Roy Crofters. 1908. 176p. 4942

HUNTON, MRS. ADDIE W. William A. Hunton, a pioneer prophet of young men. New York, Association press. 1938. 176p. 4943

JACKSON, W. C. A boys' life of Booker T. Washington. New York, Macmillan co. 1922. 147p. 4944

JENNESS, MARY. Twelve Negro Americans. New York, Friendship press. 1936. 180p. 4945

JOHNSON, JAMES W. Along this way. An autobiography. New York, Viking press. 1933. 9-418p. 4946

JOHNSON, WILLIAM H. A sketch of the life of Rev. Henry Williams, D.D. Petersburg, Va., The auth. 1901. 86p. 4947

LANGSTON, JOHN M. From the Virginia plantation to the national capital; or, The first and only Negro representative in Congress from the Old dominion. Hartford, Conn., American pub. co. 1894. x, 534p. 4948

LATROBE, JOHN H. B. Memoir of Benjamin Benneker; read before the Maryland historical society, May 1, 1845. Baltimore, John D. Toy. 1845. 16p. 4949

LEWIS, JOHN W. The life, labors and travels of Elder Charles Bowles, of the free will baptist denomination, together with essays on the character and composition of the African race and on the Fugitive Slave Law. Watertown, Mass., Ingalls & Stowell. 1852. 285p. 4950

LOCKWOOD, LEWIS C. Mary S. Peake; The colored teacher at Fortress Monroe. Boston, American tract society. 1870. 64p. 4951

McKAY, CLAUDE. A long way from home. New York, Lee-Furman. 1937. 354p. 4952

MERRITT, RALEIGH H. From captivity to fame or the life of George Washington Carver. Boston, Meador pub. co. 1938. 196p. 4953

MITCHELL, JOSEPH. The missionary pioneer; or, A brief memoir of the life, labors, and death of John Stewart (man of colour) founder . . . of the mission among the Wyandotts. New York, The auth. 1827. 96p. 4954

MOORMAN, JOSEPH H. (ed.) Leaders of the colored race in Alabama. Mobile, News pub. co. 1928. 107p. 4955

MOTON, ROBERT R. Finding a way out; an autobiography. Garden City, N.Y., Doubleday, Page & co. 1920. 295p. 4956

MOTT, MRS. ABIGAIL. Biographical sketches and interesting anecdotes of persons of colour. New York, M. Day. 1826. 192p. 4957

MOTT, MRS. ABIGAIL. Narratives of coloured Americans. New York, W. Wood & co. 1877. 276p. 4958

NATIONAL CYCLOPEDIA of the

colored race. Ed. by Clement Richardson. Montgomery, Ala., National pub. co. 1919. 630p. 4959

OVINGTON, MARY W. Portraits in color. New York, Viking press. 1927. 241p. 4960

PARKER, ROBERT A. the incredible Messiah: The deification of Father Divine. Boston, Little, Brown & co. 1937. xiii. 323p. 4961

PETERSON, DANIEL H. The looking glass: being a true report and narratives of the life, travels, and labors of a colored clergyman from 1812 to 1854 and including his visit to western Africa. New York, The auth. 1854. 150p. 4962

PEYTON, FOUNTAIN. A glance at the life of Ira Frederick Aldridge. New York, The auth. 1917. 24p. 4963

PHILLIPS, CHARLES H. From the farm to the bishopric, an autobiography. Nashville, The auth. 1932. 308p. 4964

PICKENS, WILLIAM. The heir of slaves, an autobiography. Boston, Pilgrim press. 1911. 138p. Rev. enl. and pub. as Bursting bonds. Boston, Jordan & More. 1923. 222p. 4965

PIKE, GODFREY H. From slave to college president; being the life story of Booker Taliaferro Washington. London, T. Fisher Unwin. 1902. 111p. 4966

PLUMMER, NELLIWA. Out of the depths; or, The triumph of the cross. Hyattsville, Md., The auth. 1927. 412p. 4967

PONTON, M. M. Life and times of Henry M. Turner. Atlanta, A. B. Caldwell pub. co. 1917. 173p. 4968

POWELL, A. CLAYTON. Against the tide: an autobiography. New York, Richard R. Smith. 1939. xxxi, 327p. 4969

PROCTER, C. H. The life of James Williams, better known as Professor Jim, for half a century janitor of Trinity College. Hartford, Case, Lockwood & Brainard. 1875. 79p. 4970

PROCTER, HENRY H. Between black and white. Autobiographical sketches. Boston, Chicago, Pilgrim press. 1925. ix, 189p. 4971

QUICK, W. H. Negro stars in all ages of the world. Richmond, Va., S. D. Adkins & co. 1898. 447p. 4972

RANDOLPH, PETER. From slave cabin to pulpit, an autobiography. Boston, Jas. H. Earle. 1893. 220p. 4973

RILEY, B. F. The life and times of Booker T. Washington. New York, Fleming H. Revell co. 1916. 301p. 4974

ROBESON, ESLANDA G. Paul Robeson, Negro. New York, Harper & bros. 1930. 178p. 4975

ROLLIN, FRANK A. Life and public services of Martin R. Delany, sub-assistant commissioner, Bureau of relief of refugees, freedmen and abandoned lands, and late major 104th U.S. colored troops. Boston, Lee & Shepard. 1868. 367p. 4976

ROWLAND, REGINALD. An ambitious slave, a biography of Rufus Walton. Buffalo, Peter Paul book co. 1897. 91p. 4977

SANCHO, IGNATIUS. The life of Ignatius Sancho, an African. London, J. Nicholson & co. 172. 2v. 4978

SCOTT, EMMETT J. and STOWE, LYMAN B. Booker T. Washington; builder of a civilization. New York, Doubleday, Page & co. 1916. 331p. 4979

SHAW, G. C. John Chavis, 1763-1838, a remarkable Negro who conducted a school in North Carolina for white boys and girls. Binghampton,

N.Y., The auth. 1931. 60p.   4980

SHERWOOD, HENRY N. Paul Cuffee. Washington, Association for the ✓ study of Negro life and history. 1923.   4981

SIMMONS, WILLIAM J. Men of mark: eminent, progressive, and rising. Cleveland. Baltimore, Revell pub. co. 1891. 736p. 2d ed. 1896. 2v.   4982

SMITH, MRS. AMANDA BERRY. An autobiography . . . Chicago, Christian witness co. 1893. xvi, 506p.   4983

SPRATLIN, V. B. Juan Latino, slave and humanist. New York, The auth. 1938. 216p.   4984

STOKES, ANSON P. A brief biography of Booker T. Washington. Hampton, Va., Hampton Institute press. 1936. 42p.   4985

THOMPSON, JOHN W. An authentic history of the Douglass monument. Biographical facts and incidents in the life of Frederick Douglass. Rochester, N.Y., The auth. 1903. 204p.   4986

THOMS, MRS. ADAH B. Pathfinders; a history of the progress of colored graduate nurses . . . wih biographies of many prominent nurses. New York, Kay print. house. 1929. 240p.   4987

VAIERIO, EUSEBIO A. Sieges and fortunes of a Trinidadian in search of a doctor's diploma. Philadelphia, Dewey & Eakins. 1909. 48p.   4988

VAN EVERY, EDWARD. Joe Louis, man and super-fighter. New York, Frederick A. Stokes and co. 1936. 183p.   4989

WASHINGTON, BOOKER T. An autobiography. The story of my life and work. Naperville, Ill. Toronto, J.L. Nichols co. 1901. 455p.   4990

WASHINGTON, BOOKER T. Frederick Douglass, a biography. Philadelphia, Geo. W. Jacobs co. 1906. 365p. (American crisis biographies.)   4991

WASHINGTON, BOOKER T. Up from slavery, an autobiography. New York, Doubleday, Page co. 1900. xxiii, 330p. (Collection has: Danish, French, German, Turkish, and Hindustandi translations.)   4992

WASHINGTON, BOOKER T. Working with the hands, being a sequel to "Up from slavery." New York, Doubleday, Page co. 1904. 246p.   4993

WAXMAN, PERCY. The black Napoleon. New York, Harcourt, Brace co. 1931.   4994

WESLEY, CHARLES H. Richard Allen, apostle of freedom. Washington, Associated pub. 1935. 300p.   4995

WHO'S WHO OF THE COLORED RACE IN AMERICA: A general biographical dictionary of notable persons of African descent in America. Ed. by Joseph J. Boris co. Chicago. 1915. New York, Who's Who in colored America corp. 1927-1940. 6v.   4996

WIGGINS, LIDE K. The life and works of Paul Lawrence Dunbar. Memphis, J. L. Nicholas co. 1896. 430p.   4997

WOODSON, CARTER G. Negro makers of history. Washington, Associated pub. 1928. 362p.   4998

WOODSON, CARTER G. Ten years of collecting and publishing the records of the Negro. Washington, Association for the study of Negro life and history. (Rpt. from the Journal of Negro history, Oct. 1925.) pp. 598-606.   4999

9. The Negro Press and Periodicals.

AFRICA. Journal of the International institute of African languages and cultures. London, Oxford University press. 1927-1940. v. 1-13. 5000

AFRICAN. A journal of African affairs. New York, African magazine co. 1937-1938. 5001

AFRICAN METHODIST EPISCOPAL CHURCH REVIEW. A quarterly devoted to the advancement of humanity and the A.M.E. church. Philadelphia, board of publication, A.M.E. 1883-1940. v. 1-56. 5002

AFRICAN REPOSITORY AND COLONIAL JOURNAL. A monthly magazine devoted to African colonization for American Negroes. Washington. American colonization society. 1826-1892. 66v. 5003

AFRICAN'S FRIEND. A monthly newspaper published by Quakers for Negroes in the North and South. Philadelphia, Religious society of friends. Collection has: editions from August, 1886 to December, 1898. 5004

AFRO-AMERICAN. a weekly. Baltimore, Richmond, Washington, Philadelphia, Afro-American newspapers. v. 47-48, 1939-1940. 5005

AGRICULTURE NEWS. devoted to the interests of agricultural education among Negroes. Hampton Institute, Va., School of agriculture. 1912-1940. v. 1-13. 5006

ALEXANDER'S MAGAZINE. Boston, Chas. Alexander. 1905-1909. Collection has: v. 1, nos. 5, 7, 9, 10. (Sept., Nov., 1905; Jan., Feb., 1906): v. 5, nos. 4, 6. (Feb., April, 1908). 5007

AMERICAN BAPTIST. a weekly.

Louisville, General ass'n of Negro Baptists in Ky. v. 59-60. 1938-1940. 5008

AMERICAN MISSIONARY. a monthly devoted to missions and schools among the freedmen at home and abroad. New York, American Missionary association. 1856 — Collection has: v. 14-15. 1870-1871. 5009

ANGLO-AMERICAN MAGAZINE. New York. Thomas Hamilton. 1859-1860. Collection has: v. 1, nos. 8-12. (Aug.-Dec., 1859). v. 2, nos. 1-3. (Jan.-Mar., 1860). 5010

ATLANTA WORLD. a daily. Atlanta, Scott newspaper syndicate. v. 10-11, 1938-1939. 5011

BLACK DISPATCH. a weekly. Oklahoma City, Okla., Black Dispatch pub. co. v.24-25, 1939-1940. 5012

BROWN AMERICAN. a monthly. Philadelphia, Research institute on Negro affairs. 1936-1940. v.1-4. 5013

BROWNIE'S BOOK. a monthly magazine for colored boys and girls. New York, DuBois and Dill. 1920-21. 2v. 5014

CAPPON, LESTER J. Virginia Newspapers, 1821-1935. a bibliography with historical introduction and notes. Charlottesville, Va. University of Virginia press. 1936. 5015

CHICAGO DEFENDER. a weekly. Chicago, R. S. Abbott pub. co. v. 34-35, 1938-1940. 5016

CHRISTIAN RECORDER. Philadelphia, A.M.E. book concern. Collection has: 1938-1940. v. 90-92. 5017

CHURCH-SCHOOL HERALD-JOURNAL. Charlotte,

N.C., A.M.E.Z. pub. house. Collection has: v. 20-22. 1938-1940. 5018

CINCINNATI UNION. a weekly. Cincinnati, W.P. Dabney pub. co. v.32-33. 1938-1940. 5019

COLORED AMERICAN MAGAZINE. an illustrated monthly devoted to literature, science, music, art, religion, facts, fiction, and traditions of the Negro race . . . Boston, Colored cooperative pub. co. 1900-1909. 17v. 5020

CONGO MISSION NEWS. a quarterly journal of the congo protestant church. Leopoldville, Congo Belge. 1912-1939. 5021

CRISIS. a record of the darker races. New York, National association for the advancement of colored people. 1910-1940. 30v. 5022

DETMEILER, FREDERICK C. The Negro press in the United States. Chicago, University of Chicago press. 1922. 274p. 5023

FOUNDATION. Atlanta, Gammon Theological seminary. Collection has: 1938-1939. v. 28-29. 5024

HAMPTON SCRIPT. student publication of Hampton institute, Va., 1927-1940. 13v. 5025

HARLEM. a forum of Negro life. New York, H. K. Parker pub. co. 1928. Only issue. v. 1, no. 1 (Nov. 1928.) 5026

HARLEM DIGEST. organ of the colonel Young memorial foundation. New York, The Foundation. 1938-1939. 2v. 5027

HOME MISSION COLLEGE REVIEW. organ of the colleges for Negro youth mainly supported by the American Baptist home mission society . . . Raleigh, N.C., Home missions college review. 1926-1930. v. 1-4. 5028

HOPE. a monthly. Nashville, Tenn. National Baptist pub. board. Collection has: v. 42-44. 1938-1940. 5029

HORIZON. a journal of the color line . . . Washington, Niagra movement. 1906-1910. 6v. 5030

HOWARD'S NEGRO AMERICAN MAGAZINE. devoted to the educational, religious, industrial, social, and political progress of the colored race. Harrisburg, Pa., J.H.W. Howard. 1895-1902. Collection has: v. 4, nos. 3-4 (Oct., Nov., 1899). v. 6, nos. 8-9. (Mar., April, 1901) 5031

INDIANAPOLIS RECORDER. Indianapolis, Fannie C. Stewart. v. 42-44, 1938-1940. 5032

INTERNATIONAL REVIEW OF MISSIONS. a quarterly. London. International Missionary council. 1911-1940. v. 1-29. 5033

INTERRACIAL REVIEW. a journal for Christian democracy. New York. Interracial review. 1927-1940. 5034

JOURNAL OF NEGRO EDUCATION. a quarterly review of problems incident to the education of Negroes. Washington, Bureau of educational research, Howard University. 1932-1940. v. 1-8. 5035

JOURNAL OF NEGRO HISTORY. a quarterly journal of historical and sociological research pertaining to Negro life and history. Washington, Association for the study of Negro life and history. 1916-1940. v. 1-25. 5036

KERLIN, ROBERT T. The voice of the Negro. New York, E. P. Dutton co. 1919. 188p. 5037

LOUISIANA COLORED TEACHERS JOURNAL. a journal devoted to the problems of education as they relate to the . . . welfare of the Negroes of Louisiana. Baton Rouge,

Louisiana colored teachers ass'n. 1928-1940. v. 1-13.　　5038

METROPOLITAN. a monthly review. New York, Meeks pub. co. 1935. Only issue. v. 1, no. 1.　　5039

MISSISSIPPI EDUCATIONAL JOURNAL. a monthly magazine for teachers in colored schools. Jackson, Miss., Miss. ass'n of teachers in colored schools. 1924-1940.　　5040

MOON ILLUSTRATED WEEKLY. Memphis, E. L. Simon co. 1905-1906. Collection has: v. 1, nos. 30-32. (June 24, 31; July 7, 1906).　　5041

MOREHOUSE JOURNAL OF SCIENCE. organ of the Alabama association of science teachers and the Georgia association of teachers of science in Negro schools. Atlanta. Morehouse college. 1940-.　　5042

NATIONAL EDUCATIONAL OUTLOOK among Negroes. a monthly devoted to the advancement of education among Negroes. Washington, National education press. 1937-1940. v. 1-4.　　5043

NATIONAL NEGRO HEALTH NEWS. Washington, U. S. public health service. 1932-1940. v. 1-8.　　5044

NEGRO BUSINESS. Journal of the National business league. Tuskegee institute, Ala., The league, 1939-1940.　　5045

NEGRO DIGEST. a mirror of Negro life, thought and achievement. New York, Negro world digest. 1940. v. 1, nos. 1-4.　　5046

NEGRO HISTORY BULLETIN. Washington, Assn. for the study of Negro life and history. 1936-1940. v. 1-4.　　5047

NEGRO PRESS. a collection of News-paper accounts and magazine articles relating to the Negro press in the United States. 1903-1922. 4v.　　5048

NEGRO PROGRESS RECORD. a monthly. Hampton, Va., Richmond., Va., Virginia organization society. 1922-1940.　　5049

NEGRO STUDENT. . . New York, Readers and writers club. May 1937, v. 1, no. 1. Only issue.　　5050

NEGRO WORKER. organ of the international trade union committee of Negro workers. London, The committee. 1930-1937. v. 1-7.　　5051

NEGRO YEAR BOOK. an encyclopedia of the Negro. Tuskegee Institute, Ala., Negro year book pub. co., 1912-1936. v. 1-9.　　5052

NEWPORT NEWS STAR. a weekly. Newport News, Va., Star pub. co. 1935-1940. v. 39-44.　　5053

NEW YORK AGE. a weekly. New York, F. R. Moore corp. 1938-1940.　　5054

NEW YORK AMSTERDAM NEWS. New York, Powell-Savery corp. v. 29-30, 1939-1940.　　5055

NORFOLK JOURNAL AND GUIDE. a weekly Norfolk, Va., Guide pub. co. v. 38-40. 1938-1940.　　5056

OPPORTUNITY. a journal of Negro life. New York, National Urban league. 1923-1940. v. 1-18.　　5057

PENN, I. GORLAND. The Afro-American press and its editors. Springfield, Mass., The author. 1891-. 565p.　　5058

PHYLON. Atlanta university review of race and culture. Atlanta. Atlanta university. a quarterly. 1939-1940. 4 quarterly issues.　　5059

PITTSBURGH COURIER. a weekly. Pittsburgh, Courier pub. co. v. 19-31. 1938-1940.　　5060

QUARTERLY REVIEW OF HIGHER

EDUCATION AMONG NEGROES. Charlotte, N.C., Johnson C. Smith University. 1932-1940. v.1-8. 5061

RACE. a quarterly devoted to social, political and economic equality. New York, conference on social and economic aspects of the race problem. 1936. v. 1, no. 1, winter, 1936. 5062

SAINT LOUIS AMERICAN. a weekly. St. Louis, Greater St. Louis American print. co. v. 11-13, 1938-1940. 5063

SAINT LOUIS CALL. a weekly. St. Louis, Call pub. co. v. 5, 1939-1940. 5064

SAVANNAH TRIBUNE. a weekly. Savannah, Ga., S.C. Johnson. v. 55-56, 1938-1940. 5065

SILVER CROSS. organ of the International order of the Kings daughters and sons. Plainfield, N.J. Collection has: 1938-1940. v. 51-52. 5066

SOUTH AFRICA MISSIONARY ADVOCATE. a quarterly. Cleveland, Transcaal central mission press. Collection has: v. 19, 1938. 5067

SOUTH AFRICAN OUTLOOK. a journal dealing with missionary and racial affairs. London, James Clarke co. Collection has: 1937-1939. v. 67-69. 5068

SOUTHERN WORKMAN. a monthly devoted to the interests of the undeveloped races. Hampton, Va., Hampton institute press. 1872-1939. 68v. (ceased publication, July, 1939). 5069

STAR OF ZION. Charlotte, N.C. A.M.E.Z. pub. house. 1938-1940. 5070

SUNDAY SCHOOL INFORMER. a monthly. Nashville, Tenn., National Baptist convention. Collection has: 1938-1940. v. 5-7. 5071

TOPEKA PLAINDEALER. a weekly. Kansas City, Kan., Plaindealer pub. corp. v. 41-4-. 1939-1940. 5072

VIRGINIA TEACHERS BULLETIN. organ of the Virginia state teachers association. Newport News, Va., The association. 1923-1940. v. 1-17. 5073

VOICE OF ETHIOPIA. New York, Voice of Ethiopia, Inc. 1936-1940. v. 1-4. 5074

VOICE OF THE NEGRO. a monthly. Atlanta. 1904-1906. 3v. 5075

□

INDEX

A

Abbott, A. O., 2521
Abbott, John S. C., 1222
Abbott, Lyman, 4774
Abbott, William L., 308
Abel, Annie H., 1891, 2520
Abolitionist attack, 1853
Account of shooting in Jamaica, 1946
Adams, Charles Francis, 1407, 1408, 2152, 2224
Adams, Edward C. L., 3373, 4488
Adams, Francis C., 1574, 1575, 2522, 4363
Adams, John Calvin, 1608
Adams, John G., 2523
Adams, John Q., 1681, 1740, 2023
Adams, Nehemiah, 1769, 1833
Adams, William T., 4364 (See also Ashton, Warren T.)
Adler, Felix, 3841
Adventures of Congo, 1834
Aery , William A., 3630
Africa, 5000
African, 5001
African Educational Commission, 733, 734
African's Friend, 5004
African Methodist Episcopal Church, 3090
African Methodist Episcopal Church Review, 5002
African Repository and Colonial Journal. 991, 5003
African Slave Trade, 901
Afro-American Newspapers, 3539, 5005
Agitation of Slavery, 2153
Agnew. Daniel. 2524
Agriculture News. 5006

Aiken, John F., 821
Aikman, William, 2525
Akley, Carl E., 133, 134
Akley, Delia J., 135
Akley, Mary L., 133, 136
Akin, Emma E., 4775
Alarm, Bell, no. 1, 2526
Alexander, J. E., 1223
Alexander, Lillie M., 4489
Alexander's Magazine, 5007
Alexander, William T., 4056
Alexander, W. W., 3274 (28), 3587
All Colors, 3842
Allee, Majorie H., 4490
Allen, Eaton, 4171
Allen, George, 1409, 1410
Allen, James L., 1835
Allen, James S., 2896, 4057
Allen, Richard, 961
Allen, Walter, 2887
Allen, William F., 3403
Allison, John, 2225
Alvord, J. W., 2898, 3171
Ambrose, Paul, 2527
American Abolition Society, 1344
American Academy of Political and Social Science, 3540, 3541, 3843, 4058
American Annual Cyclopaedia, 2899
American Baptist, 5008
American Board of Commissioners for Foreign Missions. 3091
American and Foreign Anti-slavery Society, 2025, 1356, 1357, 1358, 1359
American Anti-slavery Society, 902, 1345, 1346, 1347, 1348, 1349, 1350, 1351, 1452, 1353. 1354, 1355
American Anti-slavery Almanac, 1394

299

Arthur, Henry, 149
Arthur, John, 4491
Arthur T. S., 822
Arvey, Verna, 3459
Arvine, K., 2026
Ashby, William M., 4492
Asher, Jeremiah, 4875
Ashley, James M., 2536
Ashley-Montagu, M. F., 360
Ashton, Warrent, 1576
Association for the Protection of Negro Women, 3521
Association of Colleges and Secondary Schools for Negroes, 3178
Association of Negro Industrial and Secondary Schools, 3314
Atkinson, C. F., 3504
Atkinson, Edward, 1194, 3766, 3845
Atkinson, George W., 4777
Atlee, Edwin P., 1415
Atlanta University Leaflets, 4061
Atlanta University Bulletin, 2747
Atlanta World, 5011
Atwater, W. O., 3632
Aughey, John H., 2537, 2538
Austin, George L., 1649
Austin, James T., 1416
Avary, Myrta L., 2905
Avey, Elijah, 2488
Avery, William T., 2226
Ayres, Katharine S., 4493
Ayer, I. Winslow, 2539
Azikiwe, Nnamdi, 234

B

Babington, Churchill, 1893
Backhouse, James, 3
Bacon, Alice M., 3274 (7)
Bacon, Leonard, 1417, 1855
Bacon's Political Guide, 2409
Badger, George E., 2227
Bailey, Carolyn S., 4494
Bailey, Thomas P., 3846
Baird, James B., 236
Baird, Robert, 1143, 3101
Baker, Henry E., 3767, 4778, 4876

Baker, L. C., 2540
Baker, Paul E., 3847
Baker, Ray S., 3717, 3848, 3849
Baker, Richard St. B., 235
Baker, Samuel W., 4, 5, 6, 626, 772
Baker-Crothers, Hayes, 3850
Baldridge, Cyrus L., 539
Baldwin, Ebenezer, 1000
Baldwin, John B., 2154
Baldwin, John D., 4018
Baldwin, Roger S., 2027
Balfour, H., 309
Ball, Charles, 1270, 1271
Ballagh, James C., 823, 824
Ballanta, Nicholas, G. J., 3404
Ballou, Adin, 1418, 1419
Balls, W. Lawrence, 137
Balme, J. M., 1894
Bancroft, George, 825
Bancroft, Hubert H., 826
Bandinel, J., 904
Banks, Charles, 3545
Banks, E. M., 3546
Banks, Mary R., 4366
Banneker, Benjamin, 4876, 4896, 4949
Baptist Home Mission Society, 3102
Baptist, R. Hernekin, 403, 4495, 4496
Barbadoes, F. G., 3547
Barber, John W., 2028
Barclay, Alexander, 1949
Barker, E. L., 1397 (9)
Barker, Jacob, 2541
Barker, J. Ellis, 546
Barker, Roland, 4497
Barker, William H., 361
Barlow, Joel, 1609
Barnard, Lady Anne, 7
Barnes, Albert, 1074, 1144
Barnes, Gilbert, 1420
Barnes, James, 138
Barns, Thomas A., 547
Barringer, P. B., 4779
Barrow, John, 8
Barrow, John H., 1650
Barrows, David P., 237, 512
Barrows, Elijah P., Jr., 1856
Barrows, Harlad H., 139

301

Bissell, William H., 2233
Bitting, Samuel T., 3548
Bizzell, William B., 3549
Black Dispatch, 5012
Black, Ford S., 3550
Blagden, G. W., 1770
Blair, Lewis A., 3181
Blair, Montgomery, 1858
Blair, William, 833
Blaine, James G., 2554
Blake, John W., 553
Blake, William O., 834
Blanchard, Jonathan, 1423, 1806
Blascoer, Frances, 3182
Bledsoe, Albert T., 1771, 1781, 2555
Bleby, Henry, 1954
Bleek, Wilhelm, 363
Blyden, Edward W., 141, 240, 364,
    515, 659, 3106, 4064, 4780, 4781
Blose, David T., 3183
Blumberg, Fannie B., 4498
Blumenthal, Albert, 4063
Board of Education for freedmen,
    2556
Board of Missions for Freedom of the
    Presbyterian in the U.S., 3184
Boardman, Samuel W., 3185, 3186
Boas, Franz, 3769
Bodley, R.V.C., 142
Bogardus, Emory S., 3855, 4065
Boker, George H., 2848
Bolding, B. J., 3030
Bolton, D. G., 3406
Bond, Horace M., 3187, 3188
Bonner, Sherwood McD., 3375
Bontemps, Arna, 4370, 4371, 4499,
    4500, 4501, 4502
Bonynge, Francis, 1424
Boothby, Guy Newell, 406, 407, 4503
Border Ruffian Code, 2034
Borreson, Peter, 4878
Borton, Elizabeth, 452
Bosher, K. L., 4372
Bostetten, Chas. V. de., 3770
Boston Citizens Committee, 2035
Boston City Document. no. 126, 2912
Boston Courier, 1425, 1859, 2413
Boston Daily Advertiser. 2913

Boston Female Anti-slavery Society,
    1373
Boston, Gazette and Country Journal,
    2849
Boston Slave Riot, 2036
Botsford, Florence H., 3407
Botume, Elizabeth H., 2557, 3189
Boucicault, D. L., 4735
Bourke-White, Margaret, 4071
Boutwell, George S., 2558, 2559
Bouve, Pauline C., 4373
Bow in the Cloud, 1895
Bowditch, William I., 1397 (1) (2),
    2037
Bowers, Claude G., 2914
Bowen, James L., 2560
Bowen, J.W.E., 751, 4782
Bowen, T. J., 660
Bowen, Trevor, 3107, 3856
Bowie, S.J., 3031
Bowles, Charles, 1426, 1711
Bourne, Edward G., 835
Bourne, George, 1076, 1077, 1078,
    1148, 1149
Boyce, William D., 143
Boyd, James, 4504
Boykin, Virginia F., 4374
Boyle, Virginia F., 4505
Boynton, H.V., 2561
Brackenbridge, Hugh H., 1577
Brackett, Jeffrey R., 836, 4783
Bradford, Gamaliel, 1427
Bradford, Roark, 4375, 4506, 4507,
    4508, 4509, 4510
Bragg, George F., 3108, 3109, 4881
Braithwaite, Joseph B., 1657
Braithwaite, William S. B., 4197,
    4249, 4250, 4784
Bradley, Mrs. Eliza, 13
Bradley, Mary H., 144
Bradwell, James B., 2038
Brady, Cyrus T., 4511
Branagan, Thomas, 1428, 1429, 1611
Branson, E. C., 3551
Brantley, William G., 3552
Brawley, B.G., 3190, 3274(22), 3460,
    3857, 4066, 4067, 4198, 4199,
    4200, 4201, 4512, 4882, 4883, 4884

303

Castleman, Alfred L., 2576
Caswell, Henry, 1152
Catterall, Helen T., 2042
Catto, William T., 3111
Caucasian, 3776
Cayton, Horace, 3555
Cecil (see Fisher, Sidney G.)
Cendrars, Blaise, 244, 367
Chadbourn, James H., 3720
Chadwick, John W., 1662
Chaille-Long, Charles, 22
Chamberlain, Bernard P., 3698
Chamberlain, James F., 149
Chamberlain, Joseph E., 2491
Chambers, E. K., 4892
Chambers, William, 1901
Chandler, Elizabeth M., 1616
Chandler, John A., 2245
Chandler, Julian A. C., 3036
Chandler, Peleg W., 1661
Chanler, William A., 23
Channing, Edward, 2433
Channing, William E., 1398 (16),
    1416, 1663, 1664, 1687, 1861, 1862,
    1863, 1864, 1865, 1960, 2414, 2492
Channing, William H., 1663, 1664, 2577
Chapman, James, 24
Chapman, Marie W., 1329, 1397 (14),
    1580, 1626, 1628, 1717
Charity Organization Society, 3634
Charlton, Dimmock, 1277
Chase, Arabella V., 3777
Chase, Charleton, 2578
Chase, Ezra B., 2415
Chase, Henry, 1197
Chase, Lucien B., 1836, 4385
Chase, Salmon P., 1442, 2246, 2274,
    2704 (37)
Chase, Thomas M., 3635
Chatelain, Heli, 368, 632
Chavis, John, 4980
Chauvet, Stephen, 369
Cheever, George B., 1080, 1081, 1082,
    · 1153, 2579
Cheever, Henry T., 1154
Chestnut, Charles W., 4523, 4524,
    4525, 4526, 4527
Chevalier, Michael, 1227

Chicago Commission on Race Relations,
    3721
Chicago Defender, 5016
Chicago League on Urban Conditions,
    3636
Child, David L., 1432, 2416, 2580
Child, Lydia Maria, 1228, 1278, 1394,
    1398 (1), (6), (9), (12), 1433, 1434,
    1435, 1581, 1617, 1665, 1666, 4259,
    4893
Child, Mary F., 4260
Childers, James S., 4528
Chiswell, Archdeacon, 410
Chittenden, Lucius E., 2581, 2582, 2583
Choate, Joseph H., 1668
Chopin, Kate O., 4386, 4529
Christian Educator, 3209
Christian Recorder, 5017
Christenson, A. M. H., 3376
Christy, David, 454, 1774, 1781
Church Anti-slavery Society, 1374
Church, J. W., 3210
Church-School Herald-Journal, 5018
Cincinnati Union, 5019
Citizen of New York, 2584
Citizens' Protective League (N.Y.), 3722
Civis, 3211
Clapperton, Hugh, 25
Claridge, G. C., 245
Clark, B. C., 786, 1961
Clark, Davis, 4894
Clark, Emily, 4530
Clark, Felton A., 3212
Clark, George W., 1618, 1619
Clark, John, 1962
Clark, Lewis G., 1279, 1280
Clark, Milton, 1280
Clark, Rufus W. 1436
Clarke, James F., 1330, 1437, 2043,
    2585
Clarke, Richard F., 909
Clarke, Walter, 1438
Clarkson, Thomas, 776, 1155, 1680,
    1693, 1902, 1903, 1904, 1905
Claver, Peter, 663
Clay, Cassius M., 1439, 1440, 1441
Clay, Henry, 1004, 1543, 1670, 1729,
    1752, 2247, 2248, 2249

Clemens, Butler, 2250
Clemens, Samuel, 4387, 4388, 4389
Clemens, Sherrard, 2586
Clericus, 1063
Clergyman, 2417
Cleveland, Bessie, 3411
Cleveland, Charles D., 1442
Cleveland, Chanucey F., 2251
Cleveland, John F., 2177
Clough, Ethlyn T., 737
Clowes, Laird W., 2924
Cluskey, M. W., 2164
Coan, Joseph R., 4895
Coates, Benjamin, 1005

Cobb, Joseph B., 1776
Cobb, Irvin S., 4531
Cobb, Thomas R. R., 842, 2044
Cobb, W. Montague, 3637
Cochen, Augustin, 1963, 2587
Cochran, Hamilton, 787
Cochran, John S., 4390
Cochran, Louis, 4532

Coffin, Charles C., 2588
Coffin, F. B., 4261
Coffin, Joshua, 950, 1398 (3)
Coffin, Levi, 1669
Cohen, Lily Y., 3413
Cohen, Octavus R., 4533, 4534, 4535
Cohn, Davis, 4074

Colcord, Joanna C., 3638
Coleman, Albert E., 4536
Coleman, Richard, 4537
Colenso, John W., 1808
Coleridge-Taylor, Samuel, 3462, 3488, 4892
Colfax, R. H., 1866
Colfax, Schuyler, 2252

Collamer, Jacob, 2253, 2254, 2255, 2256, 2257
Collection of Civil Souvenirs, 2589
Collie, 1906
Collin, John F., 2418
Collins, Jane S., 4538
Collins, Robert, 1777
Collins, Winfield H., 910, 3723
Collingwood, Harry, 4391 (see also Lancaster, W. J. R.)

Colonization Society of the City of New York, 1006
Colonization Society (Conn.), 1007
Colored American Magazine, 5050
Colored Citizens of Norfolk, Va., 3037
Colored Intercollegiate Athletic Assn., 3463
Colored Men in Florida, 3213
Colored National League, 4022
Colored People of Missouri, 2925
Colquhoun, Ethel M., 738
Colton, Calvin, 1009, 1229, 1670, 1867, 1868, 2165
Columb, Capt., 911
Columbia University Studies, 4075
Colville, Zelie, 246
Colvin, Ian D., 556
Colwell, Stephen, 1198, 1778
Colyer, Vincent, 2590
Coman, Katharine, 3556
Commissioners of Alms (N.Y.), 2045
Commons, John R., 3557, 3865
Commonwealth of Massachusetts, 2261, 2262
Concessions and Compromises, 2474
Condenhoue, Hans, 247
Congdon, Charles T., 1671, 2591
Conference of Presidents of Negro Land Grant Colleges, 3216
Conference of State Supervisors and Colored Teacher Trainers, 3217
Conference on Education for Negroes in Texas, 3215
Congo, 557
Congo Mission News, 5021
Congo Protestant Council, 752
Congregational Union of Scotland, 1907
Congregationalist Director, 1156
Connelly, Emma M., 4393
Connelly, Marc C., 3736
Conrad, Joseph, 4539
Constitutional Meetings, 2166
Convention for the Improvement of the Free People of Colour in these United States, 962, 979
Convention of Congregational Ministers, 1157
Conventions of Ministers, 1158

307

Converse, J. K., 843
Conway, T. W., 2818
Conway, Moncure D., 1444, 1672, 2592, 4896
Consumers League of Eastern Pennsylvania, 3523
Cook, Josephine M., 4262
Cooke, Mercer, 4205
Cooke, Dennis H., 3218
Cooke, John E., 844, 4394, 4395
Cooley, Henry S., 845
Cooley, Rossa B., 3219, 3220
Cooley, Timothy, 4897
Cooley, William D., 26
Coon, Charleton S., 455
Coon, Charles L., 3221
Cooper, Anna J., 3524
Cooper, James F., 4396
Cooper, James W., 4076
Cooper, Joseph, 633
Cooper, Peter, 2704 (23), (28)
Cooper, Richard W., 3222
Cooper, Thomas, 1908
Cooper, William A., 3867
Cooper, William M., 4898
Copley, Esther, 846
Coppin, Levi J., 4899
Corbett, Maurice N., 4263
Cordner, John, 2593
Corey, Charles H., 3223
Corporation of Charleston, S.C., 951
Corrothers, James D., 3377, 4900
Corson, John J., 3649
Coston, William H., 2852, 3866
Cotter, Joseph S., Jr., 4264, 4265, 4737
Cutler, Ellis M., 2594
Council of the Anti-slavery League, 2046
Councill, William H., 4793, 4794, 4795
Country Gentleman, 1909
Coupland, Reginald, 558, 1673
Couto, Jose F. de, 2475
Cox, Earnest S., 3816, 3819
Cox, John H., 3414
Cox, John T., 4266
Cox, Samuel S., 2476, 2595, 2596
Cozart, Winfield F., 3868, 4796
Cozey, A. B., 4797

Craddock, Charles E. (see Murfree, Mary N.)
Cragin, Aaron H., 2258
Craige, John H., 788
Crandall, Reuben, 2047
Crapsey, Algernon S., 1445
Craven, John J., 2597
Crawford, Arthur, 1768
Crawford, Daniel, 664
Crawford, George W., 3158, 3224
Crawford, Samuel W., 2598
Creecy, James R., 4397
Crisfield, John W., 2259
Crisis Magazine, 5022
Crisis, no. 1, 2419
Cripps, Arthur S., 519
Crittenden, Joan J., 2260
Criswell, Robert, 1837
Crogman, William H., 4798, 4837
Croly, David G., 3820
Croly, Herbert, 2926
Cromwell, John W., 963, 4077, 4175, 4901
Cromwell, Otelia, 4206
Cronise, Florence M., 370
Crooper, James, 1910, 1911
Cross, Samuel C., 4799
Crow, Capt. Hugh, 27
Crow, Robert, 1674
Crowther, Samuel A., 665
Crummell, Alexander, 483, 486, 520, 964, 1010, 3525, 4800, 4801, 4802, 4803
Cudahy, John, 150
Cuffee, Paul, 4981
Culbertson, Anne V., 3378
Culbertson, Ernest H., 4738, 4739
Culvin, Stewart, 319
Cullen, Countee, 4207, 4267, 4268, 4269, 4270, 4271, 4540
Cullom, William, 2263
Culp, Daniel W., 4208
Culpepper, George B., 4541
Cumberland, R., 4740
Cummins, George D., 666
Cunard, Nancy, 4209
Cunningham, James F., 320
Currie, James, 4272

Curry, E. W. B., 3869
Curry, Jabez M., 2264, 2420, 2927, 3225, 3274 (3), (5)
Curti, Merle, 1675
Curtis, Clara K., 1676, 4542
Curtis, Charles P., 151
Curtis, George W., 28
Curtis, H., 1447
Curtis, Mary, 2853
Cuthbert, Marion, 4078, 4902
Cutler, James E., 3724

D

Dabney, Charles W., 3226, 3227, 3228, 3229, 3230, 3231, 3232, 3870
Dabney, Wendell P., 4079
Daingerfield, Henrietta G., 4543
Dallas, A. T., 2048, 2049
Dallas, Robert C., 1964
Daly, J. Fairley, 667
Dana, Daniel, 1011
Dana, James, 912
Dana, Katharine F., 4544
Daniel, Robert P., 3699
Daniel, Sadie I., 3526, 4904
Daniel, William A., 3112
Daniels, John, 965, 4080
Danvers Historical Society, 1331
Darley, Henry A., 634
Darling, Henry, 2599
Darlow, David J., 411
Davenport, Benjamin R., 4545
Davenport, Charles B., 3778
Davis, Allison, 3871
Davis, Arthur K., 2854
Davis, D. Webster, 3585, 4110, 4273, 4905
Davis, Frank M., 4274, 4275
Davis, Henry W., 2265, 2600, 2601
Davis, J. Merle, 635
Davis, Jackson, 3233, 3234, 3235, 3558
Davis, Jefferson, 2250, 2266, 2267, 2597, 2797, 2831
Davis, John, 2268
Davis, Mary E. M., 4398

Davis, Noah, 1281
Davis, Richard H., 559
Davis, Reuben, 4546
Davis, Walker M., 4804
Davis, William A., 3236
Davis, William F., 1678
Davis, William R., 4906
Davis, William W., 2928
Dawes, Anna L., 1677
Dawes, Henry L., 2929
Dawson, Alec J., 412
Dawson, E. C., 4907
Dawson, William H., 248, 521
Day, Caroline B., 3779
Day, Thomas, 1448, 1620
Dayton,H., 1838
Dean, Harry, 152
Dean, Henry C., 1159
Deane, Charles, 4908
DeCharms, Richard, 1160
DeCorse, Helen C., 4081
Declaration of Principles, 3237
Defelice, G., 2930
Defensor (see Thomas, William)
Delafosse, Maurice, 249
Delaney, Martin R., 966, 4976
Delaware Association for the Moral improvement and education of colored people, 2931
De La Rue, Sidney, 487
Delaware Negro Civil League, 3238
DeLeon, Thomas C., 4547, 4548
DeMay, R., 29
Deming, Philander, 4549
Democratic Association, 2167
Democratic National Committee, 2168, 2169, 2170, 3038
Democratic National Union Club, 2171
Denham, Dixon, 30
Deniker, J., 3780
Dennett, Richard E., 250, 371, 372
Deputies of St. Domingo, 1965
Derricotte, Juliette, 4902
Detroit Bureau of Governmental Research, 3725, 4130
Dett, Robert N., 3415, 3416, 3464, 4276
Detweiler, Frederick C., 5023
Dew, Thomas R., 1779

Dewet, Christian R., 560
Dewey, D. M., 2050
Dewey, Orville, 2421
Dewees, Jacob, 1012
Dickerson, Anne E., 2686, 4399
Dickerson, James T., 1449
Dicky, Sam, 913
Diffendorfer, R. E., 753, 3113
Dilke, Charles W., 561
Dillard, James H., 3274 (27), 3960, 3988
Dillingham, Pitt, 3559
Dimmock, Milo M., 2269
Dinesen, Isak, 4550
Disfranchisement, 3039
Distinguished Negroes, 4909
Divine, Father, 4939, 4961
Dix, Dorothy, 4551
Dixon, James (Sen.), 2270
Dixon, James, 1230
Dixon, Ronald B., 3781
Dixon, Royal, 4552, 4553
Dixon, Thomas, Jr., 4400, 4554, 4555, 4556
Dixon, William H., 2932, 2933
Dobie, Frank J., 3379
Document for Canvass, 2051
Dodd, Nellie C., 4741
Dodd, William E., 2422
Dodge, David, 967
Doerflinger, William, 4497
Doke, Clement M., 251
Dollard, John, 3871
Donnan, Elizabeth, 914
Donnell, E. J., 2423
Donnelly, Ignatius, 4557
Donnithorne, Fred A., 153
Doolittle, James R., 2602
Dorr, D. F., 4805
Dorr, James A., 1780, 2052
Doubleday, Abner, 2603
Douglas, Robert D., 154
Douglass, Frederick, 1282, 1283, 1332, 1400, 1690, 1701, 2076, 2177, 2493, 2686, 2865, 3782, 3872, 4023, 4806, 4807, 4910, 4933, 4937, 4941, 4986, 4991

Douglass, Harlan P., 3114
Douglass, Margaret C., 3239
Douglass, Stephen, 2187, 2271, 2272, 2273, 2274, 2339
Douglass, William, 968, 4809
Dow, George F., 915
Dow, Grove S., 3873
Dowd, Jerome, 252, 253, 3874
Dowman, C. E., 3875
Doyle, Arthur C., 562, 563
Doyle, Bertram W., 3876
Drake-Brockman, Ralph E., 564
Drake, Charles D., 2604, 2605
Drake, W. Allen, 4277
Draper, Charlotte, 668
Draper, John W., 2606
Drayson, Alfred W., 155
Drayton, Daniel, 2046, 2142
Dreher, Julius D., 323
Dresser, Amos, 1450
Dresser, Horace E., 2607
Drew, Benjamin, 1284
Drew, Thomas, 2494
Driberg, Jack H., 254, 321, 565
Drinkwater, John, 4742
Drinker, Frederick E., 4911
Drummond, Henry, 31
DuBois, W. E. B., 3560, 3561, 3562, 3563, 3564, 3642, 3643, 3644, 3645, 3646, 3700, 3726, 3841, 3877, 3878, 3879, 4004, 4082, 4083, 4084, 4085, 4086, 4087, 4176, 4177, 4178, 4558, 4559, 4809, 4870, 4912, 916, 917, 2495, 2934, 3040, 3115, 3241, 3242, 3243
Dublin, Louis I., 3495, 3639, 3640, 3641
DuChaillu, Paul B., 32, 33, 156, 413
Dugmore, Arthur R., 157, 158, 255
Dunbar, Alice R. M., 4560, 4810, 4811
Dunbar, Paul L., 4278, 4279, 4280, 4281, 4282, 4283, 4284, 4285, 4286, 4287, 4288, 4289, 4290, 4291, 4292, 4293, 4294, 4295, 4561, 4562, 4563, 4564, 4565, 4566, 4567, 4568, 4884, 4933, 4997
Dumas, Alexander, 34, 414

Dumond, Dwight L., 1420
Duncan, David, 256
Duncan, James, 1083
Duncan, Louis C., 2608
Dunlop, John, 1375, 1451
Dunn, Ballard S., 1966
Dunning, William A., 2609, 2935, 2936
DuPuis, Joseph, 35
Durham, John S., 4088, 4569
Durkheim, Emile, 373
Dutcher, Dean, 3565
Dwinell, Israel E., 2610
Dwight, Theodore, 1452

E

Eagan, H. W. A., 426
Eakin, Frank, 3466, 3467
Eakin, Mildred, 3466, 3467
Eakin, Mildred, 3466, 3467
Earl, Victoria, 4570
Earle, Mary T., 4571
Earle, Thomas, 1679
Earnest, Joseph B., 3116
Earthy, E. Dora, 257
Easton, Hosea, 969
Easton, William E., 4743
Eastman, George, 159
Eastman, Mary H., 1839, 4401
Eaton, John, 2611
Ecob, James, 4812
Eckenrode, Hamilton J., 3041
Eddy, A. B., 669
Edgar, Cornelius H., 1453
Edmonds, J. Wiley, 2275
Edmonds, Randolph, 4744, 4745
Edmonds, S. Emma E., 2612
Edwards, Amelia B., 160
Edwards, Bryan, 1967
Edwards, Harry S., 4402, 4403
Edwards, Jonathan, 777, 918, 1024
Edwards, Paul K., 3566
Edwards, William J., 4913
Egerton, F. Clement, 161, 258
Ehrlich, Leonard, 2496, 4572
Eicher, Lillian, 259
Einstein, Carl, 322, 374

Elder, William, 1454
Eldridge, C. A., 2937
Eldridge, Elleanor, 1286, 1287
Eldridge, Sela, 4089
Eleazer, Robert B., 4210
Eliot, Thomas D., 2172, 2938
Eliot, William G., 1285
Elliott, Charles, 1084
Elliott, C. W., 1968
Elliott, E. N., 1781
Elliott, William G., 4914
Ellis, Alfred B., 36
Ellis, Edward S., 597
Ellis, Daniel, 2613
Ellis, George W., 323, 415
Ellis, William, 37
Ellison, John M., 3122, 3570, 3575
Ellison, Thomas, 2614
Elmes, James, 1680

Erskine, Mrs. Stewart, 324
Elmore, F. H., 1395 (8)
Elton, James F., 38
Elwang, William W., 3880
Emancipation League, 2615
Emancipator, 1399
Embree, Elihu, 1399
Embree, Edwin R., 3587, 4090
Emerson, Ralph W., 1969
Emilio, Luis F., 2616
Emory, Frederic, 4404
Endore, Guy, 4573
England, Bishop, 919
Enormity of the Slave Trade, 1130
Ephraim, Joseph (see Hayford, Casely)
Epstein, Abraham, 3496
Eppse, Merl R., 4091, 4092
Equiano, Olaudah, 1288, 4915
Erwing, Elbert W. R., 2053

Estabrook, Arthur H., 3821
Estes, Matthew, 1782, 1840
Estimates of the Value of Slaves, 1199
Estlin, J. B., 1333
Ethnology, 3783
Evans, Eva K., 4574, 4575, 4576, 4577
Evans, Henry R., 3244
Evans, Maurice S., 522, 3881
Everett, David, 2617

311

Everett, Edward, 1013, 1681, 2177, 2276
Everett, Faye P., 3245
Exodus, 3497
Ewart, David, 1111
Extracts from American Slave Code, 2054

F

Fabens, Joseph H., 789
Faduma, Orishatukeh, 3117
Fairbank, Calvin, 2143
Falconbridge, Alexander, 778
Farago, Ladislas, 456
Farnam, Henry W., 2424
Farnsworth, John F., 2277
Faulkner, Charles J., 2278, 2618
Fauset, Arthur H., 1682, 4578, 4916, 4917
Fauset, Jessie R., 4579, 4580, 4581, 4582
Favrot, Leo M., 3246, 3247, 3274 (23)
Featherstonehaugh, G. W., 1231
Federal Reporter, 3567
Federal Writers' Project (N.C., Tenn., Ga.), 4093
Federal Writers' Project (N.Y.), 4211
Fell, J. R. 375
Felton, Mrs., 1232
Fenner, Thomas P., 3411, 3417
Fenton, Reuben E., 2279, 2619
Ferris, William H., 523, 4094
Fessenden, William P., 2620
Field, Henry M., 39, 2939, 2940
Fields, Annie, 1683
Fife, C. W., 260
Fifteenth Amendment, 4024
Figuier, 3784
Finck, Henry T., 261, 3380
Finlason, W. F., 1970
Finlay, A. A. C., 790
Finot, Jean, 3882
Firbank, A. A. R., 4583
Fisher, Charles E., 2425
Fisher, Dorothy C., 4584, 4585
Fisher, Isaac. 3317, 4015

Fisher, Miles M., 4918
Fisher, Rudolph, 4586, 4587
Fisher, R. B., 376
Fisher, Ruth A., 920
Fisher, Samuel J., 2941
Fisher, Sidney G., 2425
Fisher, Thomas, 1913
Fisk University Library, 4179
Fitch, Charles, 1455
Fitch, Clyde, 4746
Fitch, James D., 970
Fitzgerald, Walter, 162
Fitzgerald, W. P. N., 1085
Fitzhugh, George, 1841, 4405
Fitzpatrick, J. P., 566
Flanders, G. M., 4406
Flanders, Ralph B., 847
Flandrall, Grace, 163
Flaubert, Gustave, 416
Fleetwood, Christian A., 2855
Fleischer, Nat., 3468
Fletcher, C., 2173
Fletcher, Frank H., 3498
Fletcher, J. C., 1983
Fletcher, John, 1783
Fletcher, Roland S., 377
Fleming, Francis, 40
Fleming, Walter L., 2942, 2943, 2944, 3568
Fleming, William H., 3883
Flippen, Percy S., 848
Flipper, Henry O., 2856, 4919
Floyd, Nicholas J., 4407
Floyd, Silas X., 4920
Follen, E. L., 1397 (8) (12), 1627
Fontaine, Edward, 3785
Foot, Samuel A., 2055
Foote, Andrew H., 1014
Foote, Julia A., 1684
Foraker, Joseph B., 2857
Forbes, Edgar A., 164
Forbes, Edwin, 2622
Forbes, Rosita, 457
Ford, James W., 458, 3042
Ford, Joseph C., 790
Ford, Nick A., 4212
Ford, Theodore P., 4095
Ford, Thomas, 2056

312

Foreign Missions Conference of North America, 754
Foreman, Clark, 3249
Forman, J. G., 2057
Forrest, A. S., 165, 791
Fortune, T. Thomas, 3034, 4296
Foster, Eden B., 1456, 2426
Foster, Stephen C., 1716
Foster, Stephen S., 1161, 1397 (7)
Foster, William, 1233
Foundation, 5024
Fowler, J. S., 4183
Fowler, Orwin, 2280
Fowler, William C., 1015, 2623
Fox, George T., 670
Frances, Mary, 4408
Frank, Louis, 567
Franklin, Charles L., 3569
Franklin, James, 1971
Fraser, Donald, 671, 672, 673
Frazer, John F., 166, 325
Frazer, James G., 378
Frazier, E. Franklin, 971, 3647, 4096
Freedley, Edwin T., 1457
Free Churchman, 1162
Freedmen's Aid and Social Education Society, 3250
Freedmen's Aid Society of the Methodist Episcopal Church, 2945
Freedom's Gift, 972
Freeman, Frederick, 674, 1016
Freeman, O. S., (see Rogers, Edward C.)
Freese, J. R., 2625
Freman, Warren H., 2624
Fremont, Jessie B., 2626
French, A. M., 2627
French, Richard, 2281
Fresneau, Madame A., 4409
Friendly Remonstrance, 1914
Friends, Association of, 1163
Friends Association of Philadelphia, 2946
Friends' Library, 1164
Friends of New England, 1165
Friends, Religious Society of, 1166, 1167, 1168, 1169, 1200, 1685, 1882, 1934 2628,
Friend's Review, 1401

Friends, Society of Philadelphia, 923
Friends Society in London, 921
Friends, (Society) in Pennsylvania, 922
Friends, Yearly Meeting of, 1170
Frissell, Hollis B., 3248, 3648
Frobenius, Leo, 326, 327, 328, 329
Frost, William G., 3251
Frothingham, Octavius B., 1397 (3), 1686, 1784
Frothingham, Paul R., 1681
Froude, James A., 568
Fugitt, James P., 1785
Fuller, Richard, 1086
Fuller, Robert H., 167, 569
Fuller, T. O., 3118, 3884, 4097
Fulton, Davis B., 4297
Fulton, David F., 4814
Furlong, Charles W., 168
Furness, William H., 1458, 1459, 1460, 2058
Furr, Arthur, 2870

G

Gaines, Francis P., 849, 4213
Gaines, Wesley J., 3120, 3885, 4136
Gallagher, Buell G., 3252
Gallatin, Albert, 1201
Galloway, Charles B., 3253, 3274 (11)
Galsworthy, John, 4747
Galton, Francis, 675
Gannes, Harry, 458
Gannett, David, 4588
Gannett, Ezra S., 2174
Gannett, Henry, 3274 (4) (6)
Gannett, William E., 3570
Ganse, Hervey D., 1087
Gardiner, Charles A., 3886
Gardiner, Oliver C., 2175
Gardner, Benjamin F., 4296
Garfield, James A., 2947
Garnet, Henry H., 4815
Garrison, Francis J., 1689
Garrison, Wendell P., 1689
Garrison, W. C., 3571
Garrison, William L., 1065, 1066, 1371, 1398 (2) (4) (10) (14), 1402, 1461,

Green, A. R., 4926
Green, Beriah, 1395 (7a), 1691, 1692
Green, Elizabeth L., 4214
Green, James, 572
Green, Lawrence G., 172
Green, Paul, 4748, 4749, 4750
Greene, S. L., 3121
Greene, Ellen F., 3633
Greene, Ethel G., 4174
Greene, Graham, 173, 488
Greene, Lorenzo, 3572
Gregg, James E., 3728, 3789, 3892, 3893, 3894
Gregory, James M., 1690
Gregory, John W., 524, 3823
Greville, Robert K., 1174
Griffin, Appleton P. C., 4180
Griffin, Edward D., 677, 740
Griffith, Francis L., 174
Griffiths, Julia,1622
Griffiths, Mattie, 1290
Griffs, William E., 3890
Grimke, Angelina E., 1395 (2), 1466, 1467, 1654
Grimke, Angelina W., 4751
Grimke, Archibald H., 1694, 1695, 3045, 3046, 3824
Grimke, Francis J., 3729, 3730, 4025, 4026, 4818, 4819, 4820, 4821
Grimke, Sarah, 1654
Grimshaw, William H., 3159
Grinnell Plays, 4752
Grinstead, S. E., 4181
Griggs, Earl L., 1693
Grissom, Mary A., 3470
Grogan, Ewart S., 175
Grout, Lewis, 678
G. R. S., 3573
Grosvenor, Cyrus P., 1468
Grover, Martin, 2286
Grow, Oscar, 3895
Guggisbury, Frederick G., 573, 3257
Guild, Jane P., 4027
Guillaume, Paul, 330
Gunby, A. A., 3258
Guenbault, J. H., 1787
Gunton's Magazine, 3651

Gurley, Ralph R., 1017, 1018, 1019, 1020
Gurney, Joseph J., 1657, 1915, 1975
Gurowski, Adam, 851, 1235, 1975
Guthrie, James M., 2859

H

Hace, Gertrude R., 679
Hackley, E. A., 3527
Haggard, H. Rider, 418, 419, 574
Haggard, John, 1916
Hague, William, 2645
Hahn, Emily, 176, 461
Haigh, Richmond, 421, 463, 4592
Haines, Elwood L., 420, 4302
Hale, Edward E., 1291, 2646, 4303
Hale, John P., 2287, 2288, 2289, 2647
Hale, Sarah J., 1021, 422, 4419
Hailey, William M., 525
Hall, Arthur V., 177
Hall, Bayard R., 1583, 4420
Hall, Egerton E., 3574
Hall, Marshall, 2477
Hall, Nathaniel, 1471, 2497
Hall, Samuel W., 4101

Hallowell, Anna D., 1696
Hallowell, Emily, 3418
Hallowell, Richard P., 3047, 3896
Halpine, Charles G., 2648
Halsey, Luther, 1697

Hambly, W. D., 331

Hamilton, C. Horace, 3122, 3575
Hamlin, Hannibal, 2290
Hammond, J. H., 1775, 1781, 2291
Hammond, Lily H., 3274 (19), 3528
Hammond, Mathew B., 1202, 3576
Hampton, Arland C., 4304
Hampton Institute, 3259, 3260, 3261, 3262, 3263, 3264
Hampton Institute Library, 4182
Hampton Negro Conference, 3577, 4102
Hampton Script, 5025

Hampton, Wade, 3899
Hancock, William J., 2066
Hand Books on the Missions of the
    Episcopal, 755
Handy, William C., 3419, 3471
Harben, Will N., 4593
Hardy, Georges, 332
Hardy, John, 1203
Hare-Cuney, Maude, 3472, 4928
Hargrave, Francis, 1976
Harland, Howard H., 4103, 4929
Harland, James, 2292, 2293
Harlem, 5026
Hankins, Frank H., 3790
Harmsworth, Geoffrey, 464
Hannibal, Julius, 1844
Hanno, 47
Harmon, J. H., 3578
Harmon, Marion F., 3381
Harper, Frances E.W., 4305, 4306,
    4594
Harper, Robert G., 1022
Harper's Ferry, 24
Harper's Pictorial History, 2649
Harris, Abram L., 3579, 3610
Harris, Joel C., 3382, 3383, 3384,
    3385, 4421, 4422, 4423, 4424,
    4425, 4426
Harris, John, 4104
Harris, John H., 636, 637, 638,
    639, 640, 681
Harris, J. Morrison, 2650
Harris, Lawrence, 576
Harris, Norman D., 575
Harris, William, 455
Harris, William L., 1175
Harrison, Alexina, 682, 683
Harrison, Mrs. Burton, 4427
Harrison, C. W., 1292
Harrison, Jesse B., 1204
Harrison, Richard A., 2651
Harrison, Walter, 2652
Harrison, W. P., 1132
Harsha, David A., 1698
Hart, Albert B., 2432, 2433, 3900
Hartford-Batterysby, Charles F., 680

Hartsford Fourth Congregational,
    1397 (16)
Hartsford, W. N., 2948
Hartzell, Charles, 793
Harvard African Expedition, 489
Harvey, Peter, 1699
Harvey, Thomas, 2010
Haskell, T. N., 2653
Haskin, Sara E., 4930
Hatcher, William E., 4931
Hatfield, Edwin F., 1623
Haven, Gilbert, 1754, 2434
Haviland, Laura S., 2144
Hawes, Joel, 2654
Hawkins, Elmer, 3265
Hawkins, J. R., 3266
Hawkins, William G., 974
Hawks, Francis L., 48
Hawthorne, Nathaniel, 4428
Hayden, James J., 2042
Hayden, William, 1293
Hayford, Casely, 466
Haygood, Atticus G., 3267, 3268, 3274
    (16), 3901, 4823, 4824, 4825, 4826
Hayne, Robert Y., 956
Hayne, Coe, 4932
Haynes, Elizabeth R., 4933
Haynes, George, 3580, 3581, 3902
Haynes, Lemuel, 4897
Hays, Charles, 2950
Hayson, Maxwell N., 4307
Haywood, Austin, 178
Hazard, Lucy L., 4217
Hazard, Samuel, 1977
Heacock, W. J., 2655
Head, Major F. B., 49
Headley, P. C., 2656, 2657
Healey, J. T., 3731
Heard, William H., 4934, 684
Heatwole, Cornelius J., 3269
Hedding, Elijah, 4894
Helm, Mary, 3903, 3904
Helps, Arthur, 852, 853
Helsre, Albert D., 423
Helper, Hinton R., 1205, 1206
Helper, Hinton R., 3791, 3792
Henderson, Edwin B., 3473

Henderson, George W., 4595
Henderson, James H., 2951
Henderson, John, 791
Hendrick, Burton, 2658
Hendricks, Thomas A., 2952
Hening, William W., 2067, 2068
Henry, C. S., 2659
Henry, Howell M., 854
Henson, John, 791
Henson, Josiah, 1294, 1295, 1296
Hepworth, George H., 2660
Herald of Peace for the Year 1825, 1917
Herbert, Hilary A., 2953
Herbert, Lady, 685
Herbst, Alma, 3582
Herndon, Angelo, 4936
Hershaw, Lafayette M., 975
Herskovits, Melville J., 333, 794, 795, 796, 3825
Hertslet, Edward, 577
Hertz, Friedrich O., 3793
Hesse-Wartegg, Ernest, 267
Hewin, F. Thomas, 4028
Heyrick, Elizabeth C., 1918
Heywood, DuBose, 4308, 4596, 4597, 4598, 4753, 4754
Heywood, Chester D., 2860
Heywood, Jane S., 4105, 4599
Hiatt, J. M., 2179
Hibbard, Clarence A., 4218
Hicks, Elias, 1207
Hickman, John, 2294
Hiester, Isaac E., 2295
Higginson, Thomas W., 1397 (4) (20) 2861, 2069, 952
Hildreth, Richard, 1397 (6), 1472, 1584, 1585, 1586
Hildreth, Richard, 4429, 4430
Hill, John H., 4600
Hill, John H., 3905
Hill, Leslie P., 4309, 4310
Hill, Pascoe G., 925
Hill, T. Arnold, 3583
Hillegas, Howard C., 268
Hiller, Oliver P., 855
Hiller, Richard, 1208
Hilliard, George S., 1700

Hilliard, Henry W., 2435
Hilyer, Andrew F., 4106
Hinsdale, Burke A., 3270
Hinton, Richard J., 2499
History of Prince Lee Boo, 976
Hitchcock, Roswell D., 2661
Hoar, George F., 2954
Hoard, Charles B., 2296
Hobson, Annie, 3386, 4431
Hobson, Elizabeth C., 3529
Hodge, F. W., 856
Hodges, C. E., 1397 (11)
Hodgson, Adam, 1209
Hoefler, Paul L., 179
Hoffman, Carl Von, 379
Hoffman, Frederick L., 3794
Hoffman, Malvina, 334
Hogan, Inex, 4601, 4602, 4603, 4604
Holbrook, John C., 2955
Holcombe, William H., 1112, 1176, 1789, 3906
Holden Anti-Slavery Society, 1376
Holder, James E., 4311
Holland, Frederic M., 1701, 4937
Holland, Josiah G., 2662
Holley, James T., 1978
Holley, Sallie, 1662
Holloway, J. E., 269
Holmes, Arthur, 2180
Holmes, Daniel, 1624
Holmes, Dwight O. W., 3271
Holmes, Elias B., 2297
Holmes, John, 686
Holmes, Prescott, 50
Holmes, Samuel J., 4107
Holmes, Sidney T., 2956
Holst, Hermann V., 2500
Holtclaw, William H., 4938
Holub, Emil, 51
Home Mission College Review, 5028
Home Mission Council, 3907
Hood, J. W., 3124, 3124a
Hooper, Isaac T., 1665
Hopkins, C. E., 3274 (9)
Hopkins, John H., 1113, 1114
Hopkins, Pauline E., 4605
Hopkins, Samuel, 1473, 1474, 1587
Horizon, 5030

317

Horn, A. A., 180
Hornbostel, Eric M., 380
Horne, C. Silvester, 52
Horne, Melville, 687
Horne, Samuel G., 797
Horsmanden, Daniel, 953, 954
Hoshor, John, 3125, 4939
Hosmer, William, 1177, 2070
Hossack, John, 1398 (11)
Hotten, John C., 467
Hough, John, 1023
Hough, Sabbin, 2663
Hough, Walter, 468
Houghton, Louise S., 689
House of Commons, 1943, 1944, 2012
House of Lords, 1945
Hovey, Sylvester, 1919
Howard Association, London, 3702,
    3703
Howard, Benjamin, 2071
Howard, James H., 4606
Howard, John T., 3420
Howard, Oliver O., 2664
Howard, William A., 2298
Howard's Negro American Magazine,
    5031
Howe, Daniel, 2436
Howe, Julia W., 1979, 4312
Howe, Henry, 857
Howe, M.A. DeWolfe, 1475, 4940,
    4951
Howe, Samuel B., 1115
Howe, Samuel G., 2145, 2665
Howe, S. H., 3274 (2)
Howe, T. O., 2957
Howell's,William D., 4607
Hoyle, William, 3160
Hoyningen-Huene. G.. 181
Hoyt, Gould, 2048
Hubbard, Elbert, 4942
Hubbard, G. H., 4183, 1339
Hubbard, George W., 3272
Hubbard, Jonathan H., 2297
Hubbard, Wynant D., 469
Hudson, Charles, 2300
Hueston, Samuel, 1980
Huffman, Ray, 381

Hughes, Langston, 4313, 4314, 4315,
    4316, 4317, 4608, 4609
Hughes, Louis, 1297
Hughson, Shirley, 490
Hugo, Victor M., 4432, 424
Hume, John F., 1702
Humphrey, Herman, 2437
Humphrey, Seth K., 3908, 3909
Hundley, Daniel R., 1790
Hungerford, James, 4433
Hunnicutt, James W., 2666, 3126
Hunt, E. B., 2667
Hunt, Theodore G., 2301
Hunter, Monica, 526
Hunter, Osborne, 2958
Hunter, Robert M. T., 2302
Huntington, Ellsworth, 3795
Hunton, Addie D., 2862
Hunton, Addie W., 4943
Hunton, William A., 4943
Hurd, John C., 977, 2072, 2073
Hurlburt, William H., 1981
Hurston, Zora N., 3387, 3388, 3389,
    4610, 4611, 4612
Huss, Bernard, 739
Hutton, L., 3474
Huxley, Julian S., 182
Hyde, Thomas W., 2668

I

Imes, G. Lake, 3127
Inborden, Thomas S., 4828
Illinois Anniversary Commission, 4827
Inconsistency. . . of Van Buren, 2181
Incorporated Society for the
    Conversion and Religious Instruction
    and Education of Negro Slaves, 1133
Independent Order of Good Templars,
    3161
Indianola Postòffice controversy, 4029
Indianapolis Recorder, 5032
In Dixie Land, 4613
Infidelity and Abolitionism, 1869
Ingersoll, Colin M., 2303
Ingersoll, L. D., 2669

Ingersoll, Robert G., 4023
Ingle, Edward, 2438, 4108, 4614
Ireland, William, 688
Iron Gray, 1476

J

Jack, James W., 690
Jackson, Algernon B., 3912
Jackson, Giles, 3585, 4110
Jacobs, Harriet B., 1298
Jackson, Henry R., 1791
Jackson, James G., 53
Jackson, John, 2014
Jackson, Luther, P., 3273
Jackson, W. C., 4944
Jackson, William, 1210
Jagger, William, 1792
James, Cyril L. R., 798, 955, 1982
James, F. L., 270
James, George P., 1588
James, Horace, 1482, 2670
James, U. P., 3421, 3422
Jameson, Professor, 54
Jamieson, Annie S., 1703, 2146
Jamison, Roscoe C., 4318
Japp, Alexander H., 691
Jardine, Douglas, 578
Jarvis, J., 4111
Jasper, John, 4929, 4931
Jay, John, 2185, 2671
Jay, William, 1067, 1089, 1477, 1478,
    1479, 1480, 1481, 1704, 1751,
    2074, 2176, 2439, 2440
Jeanes Fund, 3369
Jefferson, Thomas, 858
Jefferson, T. LeRoy, 4829
Jenks, F. H., 3423
Jenner, Alice, 271
Jenness, Mary, 4945
Jernegan, Marcus W., 1134
Jerome, Thomas J., 4615
Jervey, Theodore D., 926, 956
Jesse, Eva A., 3424
Joannes, Leo Africanus, 55
John, Walton C., 3276
Johnson, Andrew, 2304, 2672, 3732

Johnson, Alexander, 2441
Johnson, Charles B., 2673
Johnson, Charles S., 3277, 3586, 3587,
    3914, 3915, 4008, 4219
Johnson, Edward A., 491, 2863, 3916,
    4112, 4830
Johnson, Emory R., 4831
Johnson, Fenton, 4319, 4320, 4321,
    4616
Johnson, Frank, 183
Johnson, Georgia D., 4325, 4326, 4755
Johnson, Gerald W., 3499
Johnson, Guion G., 4113
Johnson, Guy B., 3390, 3391, 3440
Johnson, Harvey, 3917
Johnson, James Weldon, 335, 2882,
    3274 (25), 3425, 3426, 3475, 3733,
    3918, 4114, 4115, 4220, 4322,
    4323, 4324, 4617, 4946,
Johnson, John Q., 3274 (8)
Johnson, John K., 3427
Johnson, J. P., 3734
Johnson, Julia E., 3735, 3913, 4184
Johnson, Kathryn M., 579, 2862
Johnson, M. K., 3278
Johnson, Oliver, 1705
Johnson, Reverdy, 2674, 2675
Johnson, Robert U., 2676
Johnson, S. M., 2442
Johnson, William, 2075
Johnson, William B., 4833, 4834
Johnson, William C., 2305
Johnson, William H., 2864, 4947
Johnson, W. D., 4832
Johnston, Harry, 56, 188, 189, 492,
    493, 580, 581, 779, 860
Johnston, James, 57
Johnston, Keith, 58
Johnston, Mary, 4434
Johnston, Richard M., 4435, 4436,
    4437, 4618, 4619
Johnston, William D., 859
Joinville, Prince de, 2677
Jones, A. M., 382
Jones, Charles C., 3392
Jones, Charles H., 59, 60
Jones, Charles J., 1483
Jones, Charles P., 4327

Knight, Edgar W., 3287
Knight, Charles L., 3658
Knight, Helen, 495
Knight, H. C., 1026, 1708
Knospler, Marie C., 693
Knox, Robert, 3797
Knox, Thomas P., 2695, 2696
Koch, Frederick H., 4756, 4757
Krapf, J. Lewis, 692
Krapp, George P., 4222
Krebs, John M., 2079
Krehbiel, Henry E., 3432
Kremble, Frances Ann, 1237, 1484
Krey, Lanna L., 3394
Krey, Laura, 4627
Kreymborg, Alfred, 4223
Kumm, Herfnann K., 192

L

Laboulaye, Edward, 2704 (8)
Lacerda, Francisco J. M., 66
Ladd, Durant F., 641
Ladies' Society for Relief of Slaves,
  1884
Lafarge, John S. T., 3923
Laird, Macgregor, 68
Laing, Alexander G., 67
Laing, J., 2704 (46)
Lamar, L. Q. C., 2309
Lambert, J. C., 695
Lamont, Hammond, 3289
Lancaster, William J. R., 425
Lander, John, 69
Lander, Richard, 69
Lane, Daniel S., 3288
Lane, Edward W., 274
Lane, Lunsford, 978
Langston, John M., 4030, 4838, 4948
Lanning, John F., 193
Lapsley, Arthur B., 2697
La Ronciere, Charles G. M. B., 862
Larned, Edwin C., 2080
Larrymore, Constance B., 583
Larsen, Nella, 4628, 4629
Lascelles, E. C. P., 863

Lasker, Bruno, 3924
Latham, Henry, 2960
Latimer, Elizabeth W., 584
Latino, Juan, 4984
Latrobe, Christian I., 70, 694
Latrobe, John H. B., 1027, 1028, 1029,
  1030, 4949
Lattimore, Florence, 3659
Lauber, Almen W., 864
Lauigerie, Cardinal, 642
Laurens, Henry, 1486
Lavater, John C., 3798
Lawrence, William, 3799
Laws of Race and Slavery, 1793
Lawson, Elizabeth, 4119
Leap, William L., 3925
League of Nations, 643
Leakey, L. S. B., 339
Learned, Joseph D., 2444
Leavitt, A. J., 426
Le Beau, Fay B., 3530
Lee, G. C., 3660
Lee, George W., 3477, 4120, 4630
Lee, Hannah F., 1985
Lee, John M., 4631
Lee, Luther, 1090
Lee, Sarah R., 427
Leech, Samuel V., 2502
Legal Review of the Dred Scott
  decision, 2081
Legendre, Sidney J., 194
Leicester Auxiliary Anti-slavery
  Society, 1885
Leigh, Benjamin W., 2310
Leigh, Francis B., 2961
Leighton, William R., 4441
Leland, John A., 2962
Leo XIII, 1178
Lester, Charles E., 1710
Lester, J. C., 2963
Lester, Robert M., 3290
Leupp, Frances E., 4839
Letters to a Member of the Congress,
  United States of America, 1922
Levinson, Paul, 3051
Lewin, Evans, 760
Lewis, Bessie, 4440

321

Miller, Kelly, 2871, 3060, 3061, 3306, 3317, 3934, 3935, 3936, 3937, 3938, 4842, 4843, 4844
Miller, Nora, 4125
Miller, Seaver A., 2505
Milligan, Harold V., 1716
Milligan, Robert H., 279
Millin, Sarah G., 280, 433, 528, 4645
Mills, Dorothy R. M., 502
Milum, John, 701
Mims, Edward, 3940
Miner, Charles, 2324
Miner, Myrtilla, 3309
Minutoli, Baroness von, 76
Mirsky, D. S., 4229
Missionary Museum, 702
Mississippi Bar Association, 3738
Mississippi Educational Journal, 5040
Mitchell, George W., 3941
Mitchell, James, 1034
Mitchell, Joseph, 4954
Mitchell, Margaret, 4449
Mitchell, William M., 2148
Moffat, J. S., 591
Moffatt, Robert, 703
Mofolo, Thomas, 434
Moister, W., 77
Mollien, Gaspar, 78
Monteiro, Joachim J., 79
Montgomery Advertiser, 3062
Montgomery, Harry E., 3942
Montgomery, James, 1630
Moody, Loring, 2449
Moody, Minnie H., 4646
Moody, William V., 4760
Moon Illustrated Weekly, 5041
Moore, Bartholmew F., 2089
Moore, C. H., 3307
Moore, E. S., 3531
Moore, Ernest D., 645
Moore, Francis, 80
Moore, Frank, 2717, 2718, 2719
Moore, George H., 869, 870, 2872
Moore, Joanna P., 3308, 4647
Moore, L. B., 2873
Moore, Sydenham, 2506
Moorland, Jesse E., 3133
Moorman, Joseph H., 4955

Moral, etc. Condition of Our Colored Population, 1501
Morand, Paul, 435
Mordecai, Samuel, 1247
More, Hannah, 1593
Morehouse Journal of Science, 5042
Morel, Edmund D., 592, 593, 594, 646, 647, 648
Morell, John R., 81
Morgan, A. T., 2971, 3739
Morgan, John T., 3899
Morgan, Joseph H., 3134
Morgan, Thomas J., 3944
Morrell, Edward de V., 3063
Morrill Justin S., 2325, 2326
Morrill, Lot M., 2972
Morrill, Madge H., 744
Morris, Clara, 4648
Morrisey, R. A., 4126
Morrison, George W., 2327
Morrison, Mary G., 4649
Morse, Jedidiah, 929
Morse, Samuel F. B., 1502
Morse, Sidney E., 1503, 2720
Mortimer, M., 82
Morton, Beatrice L., 4230
Morton, James F., 3943
Morton, Joseph W., 2721
Morton, O. P., 2973, 3064, 3065
Morton, Richard L., 3066
Mosby, John S., 2722
Moss, Frank, 4032
Mossell, Charles W., 1994
Mossell, N. F., 3532
Motley, John L., 2723
Moton, Robert R., 3945, 3946, 3947, 4127, 4845, 4956
Mott, Abigail F., 1631, 4957, 4958
Mott, Alexander, 1305
Mott, Edward, 4650
Mott, James, 1696
Mott, Lucretia, 1696
Municipalist, 2726
Munford, Beverly B., 2724
Munford, Mary C. B., 2725
Munro, Thomas, 330
Munroe, Day, 4128
Murdock, William D. C., 2450

Muret, Maurice, 3948
Murfree, Mary N., 4450
Murphy, Beatrice M., 4231
Murphy, Edgar G., 3067, 3135, 3801, 3949, 3950, 4033
Murray, Charles A., 1249
Murray, Freeman H., 3480
Murray, George W., 3951
Murray, Henry A., 1995
Murray, Hugh, 54
Murray, John, 83
Musson, John P., 1996
Myers, John B., 704
Myths of the Zulus, 387

N

Nankivell, John H., 2874
Nashville Banner, 2727
Nason, Elias, 1719, 1720
Nassau, Robert H., 209, 388, 389
National Association for the Advancement of Colored People, 3740, 3741, 3742, 4034
National Association of Collegiate Deans and Registrars in Negro Schools, 3310
National Association of Colored Agricultural Colleges, 3311
National Association of Colored Women, 3533, 3534
National Association of Personnel Deans and Advisors of Men in Negro Educational Institutions, 3312
National Association of Teachers in Colored Schools, 3195, 3314
National Capital Searchlight, 3315
National Colored Cyclopedia, 4959
National Conference on the Christian Way of Life, 3952
National Congress of Colored Parents and Teachers, 3316
National Freedman's Relief Association, 2728
National Educational Congress, 331
National Educational Outlook, 504

National League, 3953
National Medical Association, 3665
National Negro Business League, 3593, 3594
National Negro Health News, 5044
National Negro Insurance Association, 3595
National Tuberculosis Association, 3665a
National Responsibility for Education of Colored People, 3317
National Urban League, 3596, 3597, 3666, 3667, 3954, 4186
Naville, Edouard H., 343
Naylor, Wilson S., 706
Nearing, Scott, 4129
Nebraska Question, 2329
Neff, Lawrence W., 3955
Negro Addresses and Speeches, 4846
Negro Agriculture, 3598
Negro and Literature, 4232
Negro and Narcotics, 3674
Negro Art, 3482
Negro Athletes, 3481
Negro Authors and Poets, 4233
Negro Business, 3599
Negro Business Journal, 5045
Negro Charities, 3668
Negro Christian Student Conference, 3135, 3956
Negro Churches, 3137
Negro Crime, 3706
Negro Dialects, 4234
Negro Digest, 5046
Negro Economic Conditions, 3600
Negro Education, 3318
Negro Fraternals, Clubs and Orders, 3162
Negro Health, 3670
Negro History Bulletin, 5047
Negro Homes, 3671
Negro Hospitals, 3672
Negro Illiteracy, 3319
Negro in Cities and Towns, 3669
Negro in Detroit, 4130
Negro Labor, 3601

Paxton, John D., 1096
Payne, Daniel A., 4895
Paynter, John H., 4462, 4848
Peabody, Andrew P., 1518
Peabody Education Fund, 3325
Peabody, Francis G., 3326
Peabody, Selim H., 2453
Peake, Mary S., 4951
Pearce, James A., 1801, 2196
Pearl, Cyril, 1045
Peaslee, Charles H., 2194
Peck, Lucius B., 2336
Peel, Capt. W., 89
Peissner, Elias, 2482
Pelletan, Eugene, 2704(13)
Pemberton, Caroline H., 4660
Pendleton, Lelia A., 4135, 4849
Pendleton, Louis B., 4661, 4662
Penn, I. Garland, 4136, 4850, 5058
Pennington, James W., 980, 4137
Pennington, Patience, (see Pringle,
    Elizabeth)
Pennsylvania Anti-slavery Society,
    1386, 1387, 1406
Pennsylvania Protestant Episcopal
    Church, 1184
Pennsylvania Society for Promoting the
    Abolition of Slavery, 981, 1388,
    1389, 1390
Peoples Club of Philadelphia, 2195
Perkins, George W., 1519, 2095
Perry, Calbraith B., 3139
Perry, Rufus L., 4138
Peterkin, Julia, 4139, 4663, 4664,
    4665, 4666, 4667, 4668, 4669,
    4670, 4671
Peters, Paul, 4763
Peterson, D. H., 1308, 4962
Peterson, Henry, 1520
Peyton, Fountain, 4963
Phelps, Amos A., 1521, 2483
Phelps-Stokes Fund, 3960
Philadelphia Anti-slavery Society,
    1391
Philip, John, 344, 712
Philippo, James M., 1999
Phillips, Charles H., 4964
Phillips, Francis C., 437

Phillips, Philip L., 215
Phillips, Ray E., 536
Phillips, Stephen C., 2454
Phillips, Ulrich B., 877, 878
Phillips, Wendell, 1069, 1395(11), 1398
    (8),(13), 1522, 1523, 1524, 1525,
    1526, 1628, 1649, 1718, 1724, 1725,
    1743, 2076, 2096, 2097, 2098, 2099,
    2100
Phillips, William, 2455
Phylon, 5059
Pickard, Kate E.R., 1309
Pickens, Francis W., 2337
Pickens, William, 982, 3397, 3745, 4965
Pickett, Albert J., 879
Pickett, LaSalle C., 3398
Pickett, William P., 3961
Pickstone, H.E.V., 537
Picture of Slavery, 2101
Pierre, J.H.G., 1255
Pierson, Emily C., 1310, 1594, 1595,
    1596, 4463, 4464
Pike, Godfrey H., 4966
Pike, Gustavus D., 3442, 3443
Pike, James S., 3071
Pike, Mary H., 1597, 1598
Pillsbury, Albert E., 2753, 3072
Pillsbury, Parker, 1185, 1726
Pimblett, W., 90
Pinchbeck, Raymond B., 3603
Pinckney, H.L., 2338
Pinkerton, Allan, 2754
Pinn, Bedford, 2000
Pipkin, Joseph P., 4852
Pitman, Benn, 2755, 2756
Pitman, Emma R., 713
Pittenger, William, 2757, 2758
Pittsburgh Courier, 5060
Planter, 1802
Planter's Victim, 1599

Plantation Jim, 4465
Platt, Smith H., 1311
Plomer, William C.F., 438
Plumer, William, 1136
Plummer, Nelliwa, 4967
Plea for the Slave, 1403
Poe, Edgar A., 4466

Political Constitution of the
  Dominican Republic, 805
Pollard, Edward A., 1803, 2757,
  2760, 3073
Pollock, A.D., 1046
Ponton, M.M., 4968
Popular Sovereignty, 2339
Porch, Marvin E., 4140
Porter, A. Toomer, 1727
Porter, Kirk H., 3074
Porter, William D., 2456
Portuguese Delegation to the VI
  Assembly of the League of
  Nations, 653
Powderhouse, Hortense, 4141
Powell, Aaron M., 1728
Powell, A. Clayton, 4853, 4969
Powell, Edward A., 216, 217, 476, 595
Powell, William J., 4854
Powers, H.H., 218
Powys, Llewlyn, 439
Pratt, Samuel J., 1632
Pratt, Thomas G., 2196
Prentice, G.D., 1729
Prentiss, George L., 1730
Prentiss, Samuel, 2340
Presbyterian Church, 3140
Presbyterian General Assembly, 3962
Prescott, William H., 880
President's Conference on Home
  Building, 3681
President's Research Committee on
  Social Trends, 4142
Price, Nancy, 1732
Price, Thomas, 881, 1731
Prichard, Hesketh, 806
Priest, Josiah, 1119, 1120
Princeton Review, 1186
Pringle, Elizabeth, 3963
Pritchard, Thomas M., 4847
Procter, Henry H., 3444, 4971
Procter, C. H., 4970
Pro-slavery Argument, 1809
Protection to West India Sugar, 1925
Protestant Episcopal Freedmen's
  Commission, 2980
Pryor, G. Langhorne, 4672

Pryne, Abraham, 1430
Puckett, Newbell N., 3399
Puleston, Fred., 392
Purviance, Samuel A., 2341
Purvis, John B., 285
Pushkin, Alexander, 4229, 4339
Putnam, George H., 2761
Pyrnelle, Louise C., 4467

Q

Quarles, James M., 2342
Quarterly Anti-slavery Magazine, 1404
Quarterly Review of Higher Education
  Among Negroes, 3327, 5061
Quarterly Review, 596
Quatrefages de Breau, A., 286
Quesne, J. S., 782
Quick, W. H., 4972
Quincy, Edmund, 1733
Quincy, Josiah, 1527, 1733, 2197, 2198
Quinn, David, 1804

R

Race, 5062
Race Amalgamation, 3827
Race Integrity, 3828
Race Relations – Negro Problem, 3964
Race Riots, General and by States, 3748
Race Riots in Chicago, 3743, 3746
Race Riots in East St. Louis, 3747
Race Riots in Louisiana, 3749
Race Riots in New York, 3750
Radical Political Abolitionists, 2199
Rainsford, Marcus, 2001
Ralph Iron (see Schreiner, Olive)
Ramsey, D. Hiden, 3708
Ramsey, Frederic, 3486
Ramos, Arthur, 807
Ramsey, James, 1137, 1805, 1926
Rand, Asa, 2102
Randolph, J. Thornton, 1845, 4468
Randolph, Peter, 1312, 4973
Randole, E. H., 3805

Randtoul, Robert, 2103
Rankin, F. H., 91
Rankin, John, 1528
Rankin, Thomas, 1528
Ranson, Reverdy C., 3141
Rapelje, George, 92
Raper, Arthur F., 3604, 3751
Raphall, Morris J., 1121
Rathburn, F. G., 3411
Rattray, Robert S., 287, 345
Raum, Green B., 2982
Raumer, Frederick Von, 1529
Ravenstein, E. G., 93
Rawlinson, George, 94
Raymond, Henry J., 2763, 2764, 2981
Rayner, Emma, 4673
Rayual, Abbe, 2002
Read, Hollis, 538
Reade, T. C., 714
Reade, Winwood, 95
Reading, Joseph, 96
Redcay, Edward E., 3328
Redding, Jay S., 4238
Reddix, Jacob L., 3605
Redmond, Sarah P., 2879
Redpath, James, 1600, 2508, 2003
Reed, Henry, 1217
Reed, John H., 3142, 3965
Reed, Ruth, 3538
Reed, William H., 2765
Reese, David M., 1047, 1392, 1492
Reeves, Henry; 2216
Register of Trades, 983
Reid, C. L., 219
Reid, H., 1256
Reid, Ira De A., 3329, 3508, 3606, 3682, 3856, 4143, 4189
Reid, Mayne, 3806
Religious Tracts, 1313
Remarks on Slavery and Emancipation, 1530
Remarks to Illinois Citizens, 2457
Remsburg, John E., 1187
Report of the Arguments (Mass. vs. Aves), 2104
Republican Committee of Seventy-Six, 2200

Republican Convention, 2201, 2202
Republican Imperialism, 2203
Republican National Committee, 3075
Resolutions Against Colonization, 1070
Responsibility of the North...to Slavery, 1531
Reuter, Edward B., 3509, 3829, 3966
Revere, Paul N., 715
Reviews of Books on the Negro, 4239
Review of Pamphlets on Slavery, 1048
Review of Some of the Arguments which are Commonly Advanced, 1927
Rey, Charles F., 477
Reynolds, E. W. 2766, 2767
Reynolds, James R., 4340
Rhoads, Samuel, 1401
Rhode Island Legislature, 2343
Rice, Allen T., 2768
Rice, David, 1533
Rice, Edward L., 3487
Rice, Nathan L., 1049, 1423, 1806, 2484
Rice, Willard, 4855
Richard, C., 151
Richardson, Albert D., 2769
Richardson, C., 4190
Richardson, George H., 3807
Richardson, James D., 2770
Richardson, Willis, 4764, 4765
Richings, G. F., 4856
Richmond Council of Social Agencies, 3683
Richmond, Leigh, 1138, 4469
Riddle, Albert G., 4035
Rider, Sidney S., 2880
Ridpath, John C., 597
Riggles, S. B., 2704(48)
Riley, Benjamin F., 3967, 4974
Riley, James, 97
Riley, Jerome R., 3076, 3077
Riley, W. W., 98
Ritchie, David, 2344
Ritchie, J. Ewing, 99
Rivers, Fox P., 346
Robbins, Archibald, 100
Roberts, J. J., 503, 1050
Roberts, John S., 101

Roberts, Octavia, 4470
Robeson, Eslanda G., 4975
Robeson, Paul, 4975
Robinson, Charles S., 3510
Robinson, John B., 1807
Robinson, Nina H., 4471
Robinson, Rowland E., 4472, 4674
Robinson, William S., 2771
Robson, William, 716, 1257
Roche, Francis, 4675
Rodgers, Richard C., 4341
Rodheaver, Homer A., 3445, 3446
Roe, Alfred S., 2509
Rogers, Edward C., 2105
Rollin, Frank A., 4976
Roman, Charles V., 4144
Romer, Jonathan, 102
Roosevelt, Theodore, 1734
Root, David, 1735
Root, Oren, Jr., 4256
Ropes, H.A.C., 2458
Rosario, John, 347, 348
Rosenberg, Samuel A., 3607
Rosenthal, Eric, 220
Ross, Alexander, 1532, 1736
Ross, Edward A., 654
Ross, Frank A., 3511
Ross, Frederick A., 1122, 1808
Roucek, Joseph S., 3858
Rousseve, Charles B., 4145
Rowley, Henry, 717
Rowland, Reginald, 4977
Roy, Joseph E., 2983, 3163
Royal African Company, 933
Royal Institute of International
    Affairs, 478
Royall, William L., 4676
Royce, Josiah, 3969
Royce, Samuel, 3330
Rubek, Sennoi (see Burke, John)
Rudin, Harry R., 598
Ruffin, Francis G., 3078
Ruffner, Henry, 1534, 3331
Ruggles, Samuel B., 2772
Ruis, Suarez B., 3970
Rural Segregation, 4036
Rush, Benjamin, 1535
Rush, Christopher, 3143

Russell, John H., 984
Russell, Michael, 103
Russell, Thomas, 1719
Russell, William H., 1259, 1260
Russell, William, 2773
Rutledge, Archibald H., 4677
Rylee, Robert, 4678

S

Sackett, William A., 2345
Sadler, Michael E., 3332
Sadler, Michael, 349
Saint-Benjamin, 2774
Saint-John, Spencer, 809
Saint John, J. A., 104
Saint Louis American, 5063
Saint Louis Call, 5064
Saint Simons Mission, 3447
Salmon, C. S., 2005
Salt, Henry, 479
Sampson, John P., 3830
Sanborn, Charles W., 1197
Sanborn, Franklin B., 1737, 2006,
    2510
Sanborn, Gertrude, 4679
Sancho, Ignatius, 288, 4978
Sandburg, Carl, 3752
Sanders, Wiley B., 3684
Sands, Alexander, H., 1810
Sanford, H. S., 1218
Santo Domingo Commission, 2004
Sargent, F. W., 2775
Sargent, Lucius M., 1847
Satolli, Francis, 3144
Satterwait, Elizabeth C., 4680
Savage, William S., 2459
Savannah Tribune, 5065
Savory, Isabel, 221
Sawtell, E. N., 1536
Sawyer, George S., 882
Sawyer, Leicester A., 1188
Sawyer, William, 2346
Saxon, Lyle, 4681
Sayers, W.C.B., 3488
Scarborough, Donald D., 3608
Scarborough, William S., 3333

Scarborough, Dorothy, 3448, 4682
Scarlett, George C., 4037
Schapera, Isaac, 289, 350, 599
Scharf, J. Thomas, 2777
Scheinfurth, Georg A., 105, 351
Schenck, Robert C., 2347
Scherer, James A.B., 2778
Schillings, Carl G., 222
Schoelcher, V., 1928
Schomburg, Arthur A., 3609, 4146, 4240
Schoolcraft, Mary H., 1601, 4473
Schreiner, Olive, 440, 441
Schrieke, Bertram J.O., 3971
Schultz, Alfred P., 3831
Schurz, Carl, 1668, 1738, 2204, 2779, 2984, 3079
Schuyler, George S., 442, 3334, 4683
Schweitzer, Albert, 223, 393
Scott, Anna M., 718
Scott, Anne, 4684
Scott, Eben G., 2985
Scott, Emmett J., 2881, 3335, 3512, 4979
Scott, Evelyn, 4474, 4685
Scott, John, 2780
Scott, O., 1537
Scroggs, William O., 3753
Seabrook, William B., 224, 290
Seabury, Samuel, 1811
Seamon L., 2205, 3832
Searle, Amorancy, 1678
Sedgwick, C. B., 2206
Sedgwick, Theodore, 2460
Seeber, Edward D., 1929
Segregation Court Cases, 4038
Segregation in Schools, 4039
Segregation, Residential, 4040
Seligman, Charles G., 291
Selous, Frederick C., 225, 107
Separate Railway Car Laws, 4041
Severson, William, H., 3164
Seward, William H., 1139, 1739, 1740, 2177, 2207, 2208, 2209, 2348, 2349, 2350, 2351, 2352, 2781
Sewell, William G., 8101, 2007
Seymour, Horatio, 2782
Shackleford, Jane D., 4147

Shackleford, Theodore H., 4342
Shaffner, T.P., 2783
Shakespeare, William, 4766
Shaler, Nathaniel S., 3973
Shands, Hulbert A., 4686
Shannon, Alexander H., 3833, 3834
Sharp, Arthur H., 175
Sharp, Cecil J., 3412
Sharp, Granville, 1746, 1930, 1931
Sharpe, Stella G., 4687
Shaw, George B., 443, 4688, 4767
Shaw, G. C., 4980
Shay, Frank, 3754
Shea, John G., 2784
Sheean, Vincent, 226
Shelby, Gertrude M., 3400
Sheldon, Edward, 4768
Shellabarger, Samuel, 2987
Shepard, R.H.W., 444
Shepherd, Samuel, 2068
Sheppard, Moses, 934
Sheppard, William H., 719
Sherman, Henry, 883
Sherman, John, 2210, 2785
Sherwood, Henry N., 4981
Sherwood, John D., 4475
Sherwood, Lorenzo, 2876
Sherwood, W. H., 4857
Shipherd, Jacob R., 2106
Shirreff, Emily, 1932
Shoberl, Frederic, 106
Shoemaker, Michael M., 227
Shooter, Joseph, 292
Shufeldt, Robert W., 3835, 3974
Sibley, Elbridge, 3685
Sickles, Daniel E., 2353, 2787
Siebert, Wilbur H., 2149
Siegfried, Andre, 3975
Sierra Leone Company, 600, 935
Silbey, J. L., 504
Silver, Cross, 5066
Simkins, Francis B., 3080
Simmons, Enoch S., 3976
Simmons, George A., 2354
Simmons, James F., 2788
Simmons, William J., 4982
Simmons, Ezra D., 2789
Simms, William G., 4476
Simpson, Bertram L., 3977
Simpson, George E., 4148

Spencer, Charles S., 2361
Spencer, Cornelia P., 2795
Spencer, Ichabod S., 2108
Spero, Sterling, 3610
Spinner, Alice, 811
Spirit of the South, 2991
Spivak, John L., 4150, 4691
Spooner, Lysander, 2099, 2109, 2110
Spring, Gardiner, 1051
Spring, Laverett W., 2461
Spring, Lindley, 2992
Sprague, William B., 1742
Spratlin, V. B., 4984
Stafford, Wendell P., 1743
Stanfield, James F., 1635
Stanford, Peter T., 4151
Stanley, Henry M., 113, 114, 115, 116, 293, 294, 609, 655
Stanton, Benjamin, 2362
Stanton, E. Cody, 1545
Stanton, R. L., 2796
Star of Emancipation, 1634
Star of Zion, 5070
Stark, James H., 812
Starksborough H. and Lincoln Anti-slavery Society, 1393
Starr, Frederick, 353, 505, 610
State Departments of Education,3338
State of West Virginia, 3687
Statistics of Cities, 813
Statues of North Carolina, 2111
Stearns, Charles, 2993
Stearns, Edward J., 1815
Stearns, Frank P., 2500
Stearns, Oliver, 2112
Stebbins, Giles B., 1071
Steedman, Andrew, 117
Steer, George, 481
Steevens, G. W., 611
Steinbeck, John, 4769
Steiner, Bernard O., 885
Stemmons, James S.. 3983
Stephens, Alexander H., 1775, 2215, 2363, 2364, 2704(36), 2797
Stephens, Ann B., 4770
Stephens, James, 2008
Stephens, J. L., 118
Stephenson, Gilbert T., 4044

Stephenson, Nathaniel W., 2994
Stephenson, Wendell H., 886
Stetson, Caleb, 2462
Stevens, Charles E., 2113
Stevens, Thaddeus, 2842
Stevens, W. S., 4045
Stevenson, John W., 3147
Steward, Theophilus G., 2011, 2883, 2884
Stewart, Alexander, 3984
Steward, Austin, 1316
Stewart, Alvan, 1546, 2114
Stewart, Charles, 1547
Stewart, James, 722
Stewart, James A., 2365
Stewart Missionary Foundation for Africa, 767
Stewart, T. M., 506
Stigand, Chauncy H., 229
Stiles, Joseph C., 1816, 1817, 1818
Still, William G., 3450
Still, William, 2151
Stille, Charles J., 2704(12), 2798
Stirling, James, 1261
Swift, Hildegarde H., 4483
Swinton, William, 2704(62)
Sweeney, William N., 3001
Stockton, Robert F., 2366
Stockton, R.F., 1819
Stone, Alfred H., 3987, 3988, 4192
Stoddard, A. F., 2799
Stoddard, Theodore L., 3985, 3986
Stoddard, William O., 2800, 2801
Stokes, Anson P., 748, 3489, 4985
Stone, Frederick, 2995
Stone, Thomas T., 1548
Stoney, Samuel G., 4689
Stoney, Samuel G., 3400
Storey, Moorfield, 3084, 3709, 3989
Storrs, Richard S., 3339
Storrs, R. S., 4858
Stoughton, John, 1744
Stow, George W., 354
Stowe, Harriet B., 1317, 1602, 1603, 1604, 1605, 1606, 1607, 1636, 1637, 1638, 1683, 1715, 1745, 1835, 4479, 4480, 4481
Stowe, Lyman B., 3335, 4979

Thompson, John W., 4986
Thompson, John, 1319
Thompson, J.P., 2704(60)
Thompson, Joseph, 123, 124
Thompson, Joseph P., 1101, 1102
Thompson, William T., 1851
Thoms, Adah B., 4987
Thomson, M., 2123
Thornhill, J. B., 613
Thornton, George B., 4344
Thornton, John W., 1052
Thornton, Thomas C., 889
Thornwell, James H., 1140, 1822, 2465
Thorpe, Thomas B., 1852
Thoughts on Slavery, 1127, 1823
Thrasher, Max B., 3343
Thurman, Wallace, 4703, 4704
Thurnwold, Richard C., 541
Tilden, Samuel, 2466
Tilmon, Levin, 1320
Tilton, Theodore, 4345
Tillinghast, Joseph A., 231, 4156
Tillman, Benjamin R., 3996, 3997
Tissot, V., 125
Todd, Walter F., 4346
Tolman, George, 1321
Tomes, Robert, 2815
Toombs, Robert, 2378
Toomer, Jean, 4241, 4705
Toomey, Richard, E.S., 4347
Tompkins, C.B., 2377
Topeka Plain Dealer, 5072
Toqueville, Alexis de, 2216

Torday, Emile, 297
Torrence, Hederic R., 4772
Torrey, Charles T., 1712
Torrey, Jesse, 941, 1054
Tourgee, Albion W., 3344, 4484, 4485,
    4486, 4706, 4707, 4708, 4709,
    4710, 4711, 4712, 4713, 4714
Tower, Philo, 1265
Towne, Laura M., 3004
Townsend, John, 1824, 1825
Townsend, Lucy, 1103
Townsend, W., 2954
Tragedy of Errors, 1640
Tragedy of Success, 1641

Transvaal Indigency Commission, 612
Tracy, Joseph, 725, 783, 1053
Train, George F., 1936, 2813
Treadwell, Seymour B., 2124
Tremain, Henry E., 2814, 3005
Tremearue, Arthur J.N., 298
Trent, W. P., 4242, 4243
Trexler, Harrison A., 890
Trollope, Anthony, 815
Trotter, James M., 3491
Trotter, W. Munroe, 4055
Truman, George, 2014
Trumbull, Lyman, 3006
Trustees of Donations for Education
    in Liberia, 507
Truth, Sojourner, 1322, 1682, 4917
Tubman, Harriet, 1655, 1656, 1750,
    4879, 4880
Tucker, A. N., 397
Tucker, Charlotte, 726
Tucker, George, 1560
Tucker, John L. , 3151
Tucker, Nathaniel B., 1873, 4487
Tuckerman, Bayard, 1751
Tufts, James H., 3998
Tupper, Frederic A., 4715
Turner, Edward R., 891, 892
Turner, Henry M., 3152, 3153
Turner, Lorenzo D., 1341
Turner, Lorenzo D., 4244
Turner, Nat, 957, 958
Turner, Walter L., 508
Turpin, Walter E., 4716, 4717
Twain, Mark, 614
Twenty Millions Thrown Away, 1937
Tyler, Edward R., 1104
Tyler, Josiah, 727
Tynes, Beryl E., 4348
Tyson, Bryan, 1826
Tyson, Job R., 1055

U

Ullmann, Daniel, 2886, 3007
Uncle Tom in England, 1939
Uncle Tom's Cabin Almanac, 1938

Union Congressional Committee, 2816
Union Safety Committee, 2217, 4051
Union of South Africa, 543
United Free Church of Scotland, 769
United Presbyterian Board of
    Publication, 1105
University Commission on Southern
    Race Questions, 4000
Universal Races Congress, 3999
Unkulunkulu, 398
Untermeyer, Louis, 4223
Upham, Charles W., 2379, 2380, 2381
Upham, N. G., 2704(52)
Upton, William H., 3166, 3167
U.S. American Freedmen's Inquiry
    Commission, 2817
U.S. Army, 2818
U.S. Bureau of Education, 3345, 3346,
    3347, 3348, 3349, 3350, 3351
U.S. Bureau of the Census, 3513, 3514,
    3515, 3516, 3613, 3614, 3615,
    3616, 3617
U.S. Bureau of Foreign and Domestic
    Commerce, 3611, 3612
U.S. Bureau of Refugees, 3008, 3009
U.S. Congress, 816, 942, 943, 944, 985,
    1752, 2125, 2382, 2383, 2384,.
    2715, 2819, 2820, 3010, 3011
U.S. Department of Labor, 3517, 3689,
    3690
U.S. Department of the Interior, 3618
U.S. Department of State, 945, 2015
U.S. Employment Service, 4193
U.S. Federal Board for Vocational
    Education, 3352, 3353
U.S. House of Representatives, 1056,
    1220, 2126, 2127, 2128, 2385,
    2386, 2821, 2822, 3012, 3756,
    3840, 4047, 4048
U.S. Library of Congress, 3086, 4194
U.S. Sanitary Commission, 2823, 2824
U.S. Senate, 657, 2129, 2387, 2388, 2389
    2390, 2512, 2887, 2888, 2979, 3757,
    3758
·U.S. Supreme Court, 2130, 4049,
    4050, 4051
U.S. Treasury Department, 2825, 2826
U.S. War Department, 2827, 2889

V

Vaierio, Eusebio A., 4988
Vail, Eugene A., 1266
· Vail, Stephen M., 1106
Vallandigham, C. L., 2218
Van Buren, T. B., 2828
Vandercook, John W., 817, 818
Van Dousen, John G., 4157
Van Dyke, Henry J., 1827
Van Every, Edward, 4989
Van Evrie, John H., 1828, 1829, 3811
Van Vetchen, Carl, 4718
Van Wych, Charles H., 2392
Vance, Zebulon B., 2391
Vassa, Gustavus, (see Equiano, Olaudah)
Vaughan, Walter R., 3013
Vaux, Roberts, 1753
Vedder, Heinrich, 126, 615
Velde, Lewis G.V., 3154
Veridier, Eva L., 4158
Verrill, Alpheus H., 819
Vermont Colonization Society, 1057
Vermont General Assembly, 2829
Vermonter, 1191
Verner, Samuel P., 728
Vertrees, John J., 4001
Victor, Orville J., 959, 2830
Views of American Slavery, 1107
Villard, Oswald G., 2513
Vinton, Alexander H., 2219
Virchow, Rudolf, 3812
Virginia Constitutional Convention,
    3087
Virginia State Department of Public
    Welfare, 3712
Virginia State Association, 3354
Virginia School for Colored Deaf
    and Blind, 3691
Virginia State Teachers' Bulletin,
    5073
Virginia Writers' Project, 4159
Voice of Ethiopia, 770, 5074
Voice of the Negro, 5075

W

Wack, Henry W., 616
Wade, Benjamin F., 2393, 2394, 2514
Wade, Deborah B.L., 893
Wakefield, David G., 1561
Waldron, Henry, 2395
Walker, Alexander, 3838
Walker, David, 986
Walker, Charles T., 4002, 4859
Walker, F., 299
Walker, F. Deauville, 729
Walker, H. De R., 820
Walker, Horace, 730
Walker, James R., 4349
Walker, Jonathan, 1562, 2131
Walker, Maggie L., 4903
Walker, Robert J., 2230, 2831
Walley, Samuel H., 2396
Walrond, Eric D., 4719
Walsh, Robert, 1830, 2016, 2132
Walton, E.P., 2397
Walworth, Jeanette R., 3014
Wamsley, James E., 2467
Wanters, Alphonse J., 127
Ward, Elizabeth S.P., 4720
Ward, Henry W., 370
Ward, Herbert, 300, 301
Ward, Samuel R., 1323
Waring, Robert, 4721
Warmouth, H.C., 4052
Warner, C. D., 3355
Warner, Samuel L., 3015
Warren, Robert P., 2515
Warren, William F., 1754
Warwick, Eden, 3813
Washburn, Cadwallader C., 2398
Washburn, Emory, 894
Washburn, Israel, 2133, 2399
Washburne, Elihu B., 2468
Washington, Booker T., 1668,
    3274(17), 3335, 3356, 3357,
    3358. 3359, 3360, 3361, 3362,
    3363, 3364, 3619, 3620, 3621,
    3759, 4003, 4004, 4136, 4160,
    4840, 4860, 4861, 4862, 4863,
    4864, 4865, 4866, 4867, 4868,
    4869, 4870, 4871, 4878, 4911,
    4942, 4944, 4966, 4974, 4985,
    4990, 4991, 4992, 4993
Washington, Bushrod, 2134
Washington, E. Davidson, 4871
Washington, Emory, 2017
Washington, F.B., 3622
Washington Tribune, 5076
Watkins, Lucien B., 4350
Watkins, William J., 2890
Watson, Henry, 1324
Watterson, Henry, 4161
Waugh, Evelyn, 302
Waxman, Percy, 4994
Wayland, Francis, 1086
Weale, B.L.P., (see Simpson,
    Bertram L.)
Weatherford, Willis D., 3623, 4006,
    4007, 4008, 4162, 4163
Weaver, Emily, 1642
Webb, Richard D., 1342
Webster, Daniel, 1446, 1563, 1699,
    1755, 1756, 1757, 1758, 1759,
    1761, 1791, 1819, 2116, 2400,
    2401, 2469
Webster, Fletcher, 1759
Weeden, Howard, 3453, 4351, 4352,
    4353
Weeks, John H., 303
Weeks, Stephen B., 1141, 1192, 3365
Weiss, John, 1760, 2135
Weld, Theodore D., 1108, 1395(4,5,6),
    (10), 1564, 1565
Welsh, James, 4722
Wells, Alfred, 2402
Wells, David A., 2704(54)
Wells, Gideon, 3016
Wells, H.G., 3814
Wells, James M., 3017
Wells, John G., 2470
Wells, William C., 3839
Werner, Alice, 304, 356, 399
Wertenbaker, Thomas J., 895
Wesley, Charles H., 3168, 3624, 4995
Wesley, John, 1109
West African Pilot, 771

Westermann, Diedrich, 305, 357, 749
West Indian, 2018
West Indian Emancipation, 2019
West Indies, 1643
West Indies Eclogues, 4354
Westmoreland, Maria J., 4723
Weston, George M., 896, 1221
Weule, Karl, 358
Wexley, John, 4773
Wharton, Edith, 230
Wheat, Marvin T., 1128
Wheatley, Phillis, 4355, 4356, 4357,
    4358, 4359, 4908
Wheeler, B.F., 3155
Wheeler, Jacob D., 2136
Wheelock, Edwin M., 2516
Whig Almanac, 2221
Whipple, Charles K., 960, 1193, 1397
    (19), 1405(40), 1566, 1567, 2517
Whipple, Edwin P., 1761
Whipple, Phila M., 4009
Whitby, William, 897
Whitcomb, William C., 2137
White, Clarence C., 3492
White, George C., 4053
White, George H., 3089
White, John E., 4010
White, Newman I., 3454
White, Stewart E., 231
White, Walter F., 3760, 3761,
    4724, 4725, 4726
Whitfield, Theodore M., 2471
Whiting, Adele H., 4520
Whiting, Helen A., 3493
Whiting, Stuart L., 3625
Whiting, William, 2891
Whitson, Samuel J., 731
Whittier, John G., 1395(6a), 1644,
    1645, 1646, 1705, 1706
Who's Who in Colored America, 4996
Wide-Awake Tracts, 2222
Wiggins, Lide K., 4997
Wigham, Hannah M., 1762
Wikoff, Henry, 1568
Wilberforce, Robert I., 1763
Wilberforce, Samuel, 1763
Wilberforce, William, 1659, 1673,
    1731, 1744, 1763, 1940, 1991

Wilbur, Henry W., 2832
Wilder, Burt C., 2892, 3815
Wiley, Bell I., 2833
Wilkerson, Gardner, 128
Wilkerson, Henry B., 4360, 4360a
Wilkerson, James J.G., 400, 732
Wilkerson, Morton S., 2403
Willard, Joseph, 2472
Wilkeson, Samuel, 509, 1059
Willcox, Walter F., 3713
Willey, Austin, 1343
Williams, Charles H., 2893
Williams, Daniel B., 4872
Williams, E.A., 3169
Williams, Edward W., 2518
Williams, Flora B., 4011
Williams, Frank B., 4361
Williams, George C., 3714
Williams, George W., 510, 2894, 4164
Williams, J., 2020
Williams, James, 1325, 1395(6a)
Williams, Joseph J., 232
Williams, Passamore, 1326, 2138
Williams, Talcott, 4012
Williams, Thomas, 3019
Williams, William H., 3020
Williams, W.T.B., 3274(12), (15), (21),
    3317, 3692
Williamson, Henry A., 3170
Willoughby, William C., 401, 544
Wills, Charles W., 2834
Willson, Beckles, 447
Willson, E.B., 2139
Wilson, Daniel, 1941
Wilson, D.L., 2963
Wilson, Henry, 898, 1719, 2140, 2223,
    2404, 2405, 2406, 2835, 3021
Wilson, James, 55, 129
Wilson, John L., 130, 946
Wilson, Joseph R., 1129
Wilson, Joseph T., 2895, 3022
Wilson, Peter M., 2837, 3023
Wilson, Phillip W., 4013
Wilson, Thomas, 2838
Wilson, Woodrow, 3762, 4055
Windom, William, 3024

Winn, T.S., 2021
Winsor, Justin, 899
Winthrop, Robert C., 1764
Winton, G.P., 3274(16)
Wise, John S., 2839, 4227
Wissler, Clark, 3816
Witchen, Elsie, 3693
Wolfe, Samuel M., 1831
Wollaston, A. F., 233
Wood, Benjamin, 2840
Wood, Clement, 4728
Wood, Fernando, 3025
Wood, Junius B., 3518, 3694
Wood, Norman B., 3026, 4840
Wood, Robert C., 2841
Woodburn, James A., 2842
Woods, Charles D., 3632
Woodson, Carter G., 131, 306, 402, 987,
    988, 989, 3156, 3367, 3368, 3519,
    3572, 3578, 3626, 3627, 4165,
    4166, 4226, 4998, 4999
Woodward, A., 1832
Woofter, Thomas J., 3520, 3628, 3695,
    3696, 4014, 4015, 4167, 4168
Wooley, Celia P., 3763
Woolman, John, 1569, 1765
Worcester, Leonard, 1766
Work, Ernest, 483
Work, Frederick J., 3455
Work, John W., 3456
Work, Monroe N., 3715, 4187, 4195
Works Progress Administration (D.C.)
    4196
Wormerley, Katherine P., 2843
Worsfold, William B., 132, 617, 618,
    619, 620
Worth, Nicholas, 4729, also Page,
    Walter H.
Wortley, Emmeline S., 1267
Wright, Arthur D., 3369
Wright, Carroll D., 3629
Wright, Elizur, 1570, 1767, 2844
Wright, Henry C., 1571, 1572, 1942,
    2519
Wright, James M., 990
Wright, Marcus J., 2845
Wright, R. R. Jr., 4169, 4170

Wright, Richard, 4730, 4731
Wright, Richard R., 3370, 3371
Wurdemann, J.G.F., 2022
Wylde, Augustus B., 484
Wyman, Lillie B., 1768
Wyndham, Richard, 307

X

Xavier University, 3372

Y

Yates, Edward, 1268, 1573
Yates, Richard, 2407
Yelliott, Coloman, 2485
Yonge, Samuel H., 900
Young, Donald, 4016
Young, Francis B., 448, 4732, 4733
Young, George, 3494
Young, James C., 511
Young, Martha, 3402
Young, S., 359
Young Men's Christian Association,
    3157
Youth's Poetical Instructor, 1647

Z

Zacharian, O., 621
Ziervogel, C., 545
Zimmermann, Emil, 622
Zincke, Foster B., 3027
Zook, George F., 947